Harold Arlen

Music advisor to Northeastern University Press
GUNTHER SCHULLER

Harold Arlen
RHYTHM, RAINBOWS, AND BLUES

EDWARD JABLONSKI

NORTHEASTERN UNIVERSITY PRESS
BOSTON

Northeastern University Press

Library of Congress Cataloging-in-Publication Data
Jablonski, Edward.
Harold Arlen : rhythm, rainbows, and blues / Edward Jablonski.
p.   cm.
Includes bibliographical references and index.
ISBN 1-55553-263-2 (cloth : alk. paper)
1. Arlen, Harold, 1905–1986.   2. Composers—United States—
Biography.   I. Title.
ML410.A76J33   1996
782.42164′092—dc20
[B]   95-44708
MN

Designed by Virginia Evans

Composed in Simoncini Garamond by Coghill Composition, Richmond, Virginia.
Printed and bound by Edwards Brothers, Inc., Ann Arbor, Michigan. The paper is
Glatfelter Offset, an acid-free stock.

MANUFACTURED IN THE UNITED STATES OF AMERICA
00   99   98   97   96   5   4   3   2   1

For
MATTHEW RICHARD AHLBERG

CONTENTS

ILLUSTRATIONS

ACKNOWLEDGMENTS

—

Research on this study began many years ago; in the time since, many who so graciously lent a hand, an insight, a suggestion, or a recollection are gone: Jerry Arlen, Irving Berlin, Robert Breen, Ira Gershwin, Stanley Green, Yip Harburg, Bill Sweigert, and Kay Swift. All contributed to a greater appreciation of the man and his music.

I am also indebted to several friends and relatives, Arlen's and mine, who unselfishly contributed to the writing of this book—many over a number of years. Gratifying was their enthusiasm, devotion, and love for the man and his music: Rita Arlen, New York; Samuel A. Arlen, New York; Ken Bloom, New York; Julianne Boyd, Berkshire Theater Festival; Wilva Breen, New York; Gary Chapman, Hartford (Connecticut) Conservatory; Robert Elliott Cohen, "Sweet 'n' Hot in Harlem" and Corte Madera, California; Kevin Cole, Bay City, Michigan; Dick DeBenedictis, Monticeto, California; Shelly and Dr. Norman Dinhofer, Brooklyn, New York; Bill Dyer, Hollywood; Michael Emmers, Brooklyn; Michael Feinstein, Hollywood and all points; Michael Kerker, ASCAP; Chester Kopaz, an indefatigable researcher, Bayonne, New Jersey; Richard Lalli, Yale, Vassar, and Madison, Connecticut; Lynn and Burton Lane, dear friends, New York; Maurice Levine, Lyrics and Lyricists, Ninety-second Street Y, New York; Jeanne Matalon, the Arlen Estate, Queens, New York; Walter Rappeport, creator of The Eponymous and consultant, New York; Ann Ronell, a lovely melodist, New York; Bill Rudman, Great Lakes Theater Festival and "Broadway Melody," Cleveland; Robin Rupli, Voice of America, Washington, D.C., whose encouragement, suggestions, and "wanderings" contributed so much to this work and others in a trying time; Berthe Schuchat, MPL Communications, New York, mother of all Arlen lovers; Lawrence D. Stewart, Beverly Hills, without whom, etc.; Robert Tartaglia, somewhere in Virginia at the keyboard; Joseph Weiss, MPL Communications, New York, living proof that even a music publisher can be a scholar as well as gentleman.

And finally, our children (now no longer children) Emily, Carla, and David, who knew Harold Arlen from childhood; Carla and Emily were there at the end. Their recollections throughout rekindled memories about a most pleasant, gentle, and kindly man whom they grew up to call simply Harold. They also grew up on the songs of Harold Arlen and listened to the praise from the long line of Arlen fans and devotees who came to listen, borrow sheet music, or interrogate. They were always delighted themselves when some asked, "*You* know Harold Arlen?"

Yes, they did, and I hope that some of that is evident in this book. I might add they were most helpful on some of the technical aspects of this study. To round this out, I should like to thank editor William A. Frohlich for his dedication and patience (to a point); also, Erica Bobone for her charming editorial assistance in assembling so many pieces and, gratitude too, to copy editor Larry Hamberlin for his meticulous work on a very untidy manuscript. Bless you all.

INTRODUCTION

Harold Arlen, in the words of Irving Berlin, "wasn't as well known as some of us, but he was a better songwriter than most of us and will be missed by all of us."

The occasion was a tribute to Arlen by the American Society of Composers, Authors, and Publishers (ASCAP) in November 1986. Berlin, then in his ninety-eighth year, had been one of Arlen's closest friends during the final wretched years of Arlen's life, phoning him frequently, cheering him with jokes, reminding him of an Arlen song he had heard on radio or television. Berlin was the patriarch of the "some" he referred to (George Gershwin, Richard Rodgers, Jerome Kern, Cole Porter)—a group to which Arlen belonged, though few, even those who sang and performed his music, were aware of his name.

Like so many gifted artists who have contributed to our culture and popular arts, Harold Arlen needs an introduction. That can be provided by a short list of only his more familiar songs:

>"Over the Rainbow"
>"Stormy Weather"
>"Blues in the Night"
>"I Love a Parade"
>"Between the Devil and the Deep Blue Sea"
>"Let's Fall in Love"
>"Happiness Is a Thing Called Joe"
>"The Man That Got Away"
>"Come Rain or Come Shine"
>"One for My Baby (And One More for the Road)"
>"My Shining Hour"
>"I've Got the World on a String"
>"That Old Black Magic"
>"Get Happy"

But Arlen would insist that he contributed only half of the song. The words, he said, even the title, were just as important as the melody—despite his tunes' wide popularity on their own as instrumentals, ranging from the lush sounds of Andre Kostelanetz to the jazzy permutations of André Previn. He often said, "A good lyric writer is the composer's best friend," and Arlen's friends included Ira Gershwin, Ted Koehler, Johnny Mercer, and E. Y. Harburg. In the exacting craft of songwriting, one could not hope for better friends.

"Songwriting is an art," he claimed in an article, "From Harlem to the Land of Oz and Beyond," written for the columnist Dorothy Kilgallen. His artistry often proved challenging to his "friends." "Arlen is no thirty-two bar man," Ira Gershwin once noted.

As one of the most individual of American show composers he is distinctive in melodic line and unusual construction ("Black Magic," seventy-two bars; "One for My Baby," forty-eight bars; "The Man That Got Away," sixty-two bars). "Gotta [Have Me Go with You]" [from the film *A Star Is Born*] is unusual not only in its twenty-four bar verse and forty-eight bar refrain but also in that the first eight bars of the verse music are introduced twice in the refrain.

When inspiration or something else worth-while hits Arlen, it is rarely a complete tune. It may be a fragment of only two bars or twelve—but it is the beginning of something worth mulling over, and onto an envelope or into a notebook it goes. These snatches or possible themes he calls "jots." Frequently with him the lyricist—whether Koehler or Mercer or Harburg or myself—finds himself wondering if a resultant song isn't too long or too difficult or too mannered for popular consumption. But there's no cause to worry. Many Arlen songs do take time to catch on, but when they do they join his impressive and lasting catalog.

Truman Capote, though no lyricist in the Gershwin league, also collaborated with Harold Arlen. "I had no true understanding of song writing (and Lord knows I still do not)," he told William K. Zinsser.

But Arlen, who I suppose never worked with an amateur before, was tolerant and infinitely encouraging and, well, a gent about the whole thing. . . .

For him, the music is the entire story. There, inside a world of sound, he is always courageous, intelligent, incapable of cliché. His songs invariably contain some melodic surprise, some *difficulty*—which is one of the reasons he has not had the recognition he deserves. He is too versatile and inventive to have created a large single image, an Arlen *sound,* in the sense that Porter and Gershwin have a sound. Of course, for those who really know his music, Arlen has a sound, a style, that is immediately recognizable, one more haunting than any of his contemporaries.

To the many who do not take their "light" music lightly, Harold Arlen belongs in a special place in our popular music. Some song enthusiasts go so far as to regard him as the successor to Stephen Foster; to others he is the one composer who helped fill the void left by the early death of George Gershwin. Arlen found such praise to be, while flattering, perplexing: if anyone followed in Foster's musical tracks it was Irving Berlin, and as for Gershwin, he was irreplaceable.

Still, there's some evidence to support the Foster analogy: When the producer-director Robert Breen was touring most of the world with *Porgy and Bess* in 1955, he attended a concert in Cairo. The final selection on the program, after the usual classical fare, was a section entitled "American Folk Music." To Breen's delight, it consisted of five "folk songs": "Stormy Weather," "Blues in the Night," "I Gotta Right to Sing the Blues," "Ac-cent-tchu-ate the Positive," and "Ill Wind." He sought out the conductor after the concert and was informed that no one had written the songs: "They are just old American ballads that we made into a folk medley." Breen noted that the medley was credited to one "H. Arlene." When informed that the arranger was not only alive but had in fact composed those "old American ballads," Breen later told William K. Zinsser, the conductor "just couldn't believe it."

Both Berlin and Capote touch on Arlen's lack of recognition by the general public, whose affections and currency are usually showered on the performer, not the creator (unless they are the same person). It was Al Jolson's "Swanee," not Gershwin's; it was Judy Garland's "Over the Rainbow," not Harold Arlen's—let alone lyricists Irving Caesar's and E. Y. Harburg's. The neglected songwriters hardly minded, for they shared profitably in the currency.

Gershwin was most active in a time when American society was going through a period of what Edmund Wilson (quoting Herman Melville) called "the shock of recognition." The 1920s blossomed with American literature, plays, poetry, and music. Even the lowbrow musical comedy took on a new sheen with the literate lyrics of Ira Gershwin, Lorenz Hart, Oscar Hammerstein II, and Cole Porter and the intelligently formed melodies of Porter, Jerome Kern, Richard Rodgers, Vincent Youmans, and George Gershwin.

New York was then the center of American culture and commerce. With the devastation of the Great Depression, the entertainment centers, even music publishing, moved west. When Arlen came on the scene a half generation later (as a performer, no less), he was influenced by his Broadway elders (a slippery term, for Gershwin was a mere seven years older—but Arlen belonged to the new generation of songwriters that would include Arthur Schwartz, Vernon Duke, and Burton Lane). Arlen also moved west.

Hollywood has never been noted for its kindness to writers, whether of script or song. Writers were situated near the bottom of the community's social structure, below the producer, the director, the star, even the agent. In Hollywood, the songwriter was just another technician, a notch above other near-anonymous contributors to the "property"—the cameramen (they were all men then), electricians, script "girls," et al.

Harold Arlen, temperamentally retiring, self-effacing, and peace-loving, eased comfortably into the lush, mostly relaxed West Coast environment. Scoring films was not as demanding as working in the musical theater. Fewer songs were required, there were no out-of-town headaches and heartaches (there were sneak previews, however, usually out of town). And there were frustrations, generated usually by what was known as the front office (often as not located in New York). The accountants, the relatives of studio heads, the singers with small voices and enlarged egos, all may have know little about songs, but they did know what they liked.

Arlen soon learned how to work within the strictures, devising an approach and attitude that would accomplish the job with the least friction. One of the better features of film work was that the writers worked at home, dropping into the studio to deliver a few songs and hoping for the best. It was a good idea not to inquire too deeply into the fate of your work.

The writing community was separated from the celebrity and executive communities. Songwriters, especially, banded together for parties, tennis, swims in the ubiquitous pools, poker parties, golf. Home movies (Arlen took his camera with him everywhere, including film sets) attest to the happy gatherings of songwriters, authors, and musicians. Absent from these lively events were the stars. Only the actors Lionel Stander and Luise Rainer—married to the playwright Clifford Odets—and the comedian Bert Lahr appear in the home movies. Under the shadow of the stars, Harold Arlen spent two decades in California, all but conspicuously incognito.

He broke out of this luxurious trap from time to time, going east to work on a Broadway show. Discounting his nightclub revues, Harold Arlen scored only eight musicals between 1931 and 1959 (during the same period, Richard Rodgers wrote twenty). Of these, only two achieved runs of more than five hundred performances. Of his failures, at least two became cult musicals by virtue of their extraordinary scores.

Of his thirty films, just two provided scripts worthy of the artistry he and his collaborators put into them: *The Wizard of Oz* and *A Star Is Born*. Both starred Judy Garland; one was at the beginning and the other at the end of her star-crossed career.

The films disappeared and the shows were forgotten, but the songs took on a life of their own. They lived in interpretations by some of the most gifted and widely popular musicians of our time: Judy Garland, Frank Sinatra, Ella Fitzgerald, Fred Astaire, Lena Horne, Bobby Short, Dinah Shore, Tony Bennett, Eileen Farrell, Bing Crosby, Anita Ellis.

Critics, Arlen believed, too often judged a song by its "orchestration or the artist singing the song. They should judge a song by the way it is written, how it is resolved, how fresh it is and what the composer did with the theme." This defines the artistic credo of Harold Arlen. A song, he stated another time, "moves mysteriously and manages to wait around patiently—sometimes for years—always being embraced by the few who care, and then by the many who belatedly become aware of its own true values." To Arlen the creation of a song was almost a mystical experience, "finding the unsought phrase," resolving it in an original manner, and then patiently waiting for its true values to be recognized by the many.

How does one respond to the frequent query: Why isn't Harold Arlen, considering the high level of his output, more widely known to the public? The answer lies in his choice of well-paid obscurity in Hollywood over a more public but less certain Broadway career. The weak books for his Broadway musicals don't help either. The untimely death of his wife and his own illness also closed his creative career; in his final fifteen years he produced no new music.

During those last years, however, his songs were taken up by vocalists; there were revues inspired by his songs, new recordings, and the publication, in 1985 (a year before his death), of a fine collection of his songs. This renewed interest initiated an ordering of his music and papers to simplify finding songs requested for a vocalist or recording; among these songs were many long out of print and others never published as sheet music. Materials that had been in storage in California since the early 1950s were shipped to New York, filling an entire room in his apartment on Central Park West.

The sorting of these large wooden crates was supervised by his sister-in-law, Rita, the wife of his brother, Jerry. These boxes contained a cornucopia of songs (many unknown), home recordings of Arlen working on a song, and recordings of Ira Gershwin, E. Y. Harburg, and Johnny Mercer playfully testing their work on one another. There were dozens of unopened letters dating from a bad period of his later years in Hollywood; one envelope contained a stale check for more than two thousand dollars. One of the initial finds was his Oscar for "Over the Rainbow," which had been thought lost. Rita immediately took it to the composer, who was sitting in his favorite chair in the den. He was delighted and had been wondering what all the hammering was about.

The boxes also yielded scrapbooks, clippings, film soundtrack recordings, and radio broadcasts, including two sample programs of a Harold Arlen radio show that never materialized. There were hundreds of photographs; letters (opened) from his father, his brother, and his many colleagues (the most amusing from Ira Gershwin); books, including signed copies from George Gershwin, William Faulkner, Noel Coward, Somerset Maugham, and others; and requests for autographs. There were documents and memorabilia from his life that Arlen had forgotten.

In 1961 my book *Harold Arlen: Happy with the Blues* was published. While not an "authorized" biographer (no one told me what to include or omit), I enjoyed good-humored, gentle cooperation from Anya and Harold Arlen, as well as his collaborators, family, and friends. Two decades later, the contents of the crates, some dating to his boyhood in Buffalo, revealed much that I had not known when writing *Happy with the Blues.* The wealth of new sources, even the unopened letters, revealed a man of amazing courage who created, often under difficult professional and personal circumstances, a world of lovely sounds beloved by the multitudes that did not even know his name. I don't believe he withheld this information three decades ago; he merely subconsciously suppressed it. He knew that I knew that at one unhappy point in his life he had had a serious drinking problem; only later did I learn the reason. Nor did I touch upon Anya Arlen's emotional problems, Arlen's relationship with his father and brother, or his friendship with Marlene Dietrich. In the years since the first book, I learned a great deal more about the man as well as his art.

When he reached the age of seventy-five, Harold Arlen was pleasantly surprised by ASCAP's birthday announcement in the *New York Times*. Ill and housebound, he was both beguiled by and wary of so venerable an anniversary. A friend of several decades, Robert Wachsman, visited at times. They sat side by side, Arlen with a walker and Wachsman with a cane, and recalled the years, almost a half century, back at the Cotton Club. Irving Berlin was mentioned, and Wachsman mused, half to himself, "What does a guy who's ninety do all day?"

"He sits and waits," Arlen told him.

Arlen was depressed by the state of American popular music and theater. His world and Berlin's and Gershwin's was in ashes. A friend, hoping to cheer him up, reminded him of the work he had done, so much of it still vital. His songs, at least many, were immortal.

"Immortality," he replied, "is for fools who don't believe in death."

But to the end he did not sit and wait; he fought his illness, including the one that proved fatal. His immortality is unquestioned and assured.

THE
CANTOR'S SON

*A*t the stroke of midnight on January 16, 1920, when Hyman Arluck of Buffalo, New York, was not quite fifteen, the Volstead Act, passed over the veto of President Woodrow Wilson, became the law of the land as the Eighteenth Amendment to the Constitution of the United States. It was an incipient social disaster.

The new law had no immediate effect on young Hyman's life, but it ushered in the Prohibition Era, proscribing, to the temporary dismay of the nation's drinkers, the intake of alcoholic beverages. This, in turn, sparked the concurrent growth of the speakeasy, bootlegging, and the nightclub, phenomena that, in time, would figure prominently in the professional life of Hyman Arluck.

Across the state from Buffalo, on the stage of New York City's Majestic Theatre, the popular vaudevillian Danny Healy marked the transition from a wet to a dry America with a grotesque, inebriated dance in the funereal costume of the cartoon figure "Mr. Prohibition," created by Rollin Kirby for the editorial page of the *New York World*.

Most New Yorkers acclaimed Healy's boozy parody and loathed the amendment, but it was the law, and the Volstead Act provided the enforcement machinery for it. One prescient future New York mayor, Fiorello LaGuardia, scrutinized that apparatus skeptically. He asserted that it would probably require 250,000 police to enforce the law in New York alone, and as many more to supervise the enforcers. Governor Al Smith publicly opposed the amendment, inspiring the

Texas senator Morris Shepard to denounce New York as "a revolutionary and anarchistic state." All were right. Within a month federal agents closed down their first speakeasy, a Chicago basement bar called the Red Lantern, Alphonse Capone, proprietor. In Manhattan, Prohibition opened up a new business world to another gangster: tough, deadly Owney Madden, a future employer of Danny Healy and Hyman Arluck.

Hyman was born in Buffalo on February 15, 1905, to Celia Orlin and Samuel Arluck. Theirs was a cross-country marriage of convenience that had its beginning in Louisville, Kentucky. Samuel, about five years old, had been brought there with a sister and brother from Vilna, then in Russian Poland. In 1885 or so Moses and Ida Danishewsky Arluck, fleeing the wars of their country, joined their relatives, friends, and neighbors who had preceded them. Louisville's major industry was the production of tobacco products; its second, until erased by the Eighteenth Amendment, was the distilling industry.

Moses Arluck was an Orthodox Jew whose wife kept a kosher household; he worked as the secretary of the B'nai Jacob congregation as well as for other Jewish organizations in Louisville. Samuel followed his father into these social-sectarian activities. Like his siblings, he was a lover of music and by his teens was a popular cantor. Visitors were greatly impressed not only with his voice but also with his assured presence, fine head of black hair, unobtrusive mustache, and stylish dress. Members of an enthusiastic group from Buffalo whose synagogue was seeking a cantor urged him to travel there—a trip of more than five hundred miles—and apply for the position.

He did, and he impressed the synagogue's board, only to learn that, along with his other attributes—which no one questioned—he was also supposed to bring a wife. Samuel Arluck had no wife. But he assured the board that, upon his return to Louisville, he would fetch a wife. Doing so required a stopover in Cincinnati, Ohio.

There, on Barr Street, lived Celia Orlin, the twenty-two-year-old daughter of Mottl and Mollie Orlin, also immigrants from the Vilna section of Poland. They had probably met at the Orlins' synagogue during one of Samuel's tours as a cantor (the family histories say nothing on this point). The unexpected haste of the marriage is evident: though they were married by a rabbi with a proper marriage license, the ceremony took place in the Orlin home on Friday, April 15, 1904. Celia quit her job in a local shop and with Samuel set off for Buffalo, where they were soon settled into a house near the Clinton Street Synagogue. It was in this house, less than a year after the wedding, that she gave birth to twins. The firstborn died the next day; the second, weighing only four pounds, survived and was named Hyman (Chaim, in Hebrew, meaning "life").

Seven years later a second son, Julius, was born on November 11, 1912. By this time the ambitious and popular Samuel had moved to a new address and a more substantial position at the Pine Street Synagogue. It was there that Hyman began his musical education, singing in his father's choir. At seven he was the choir's youngest, smallest, and shyest member, gifted with a clear soprano voice. In time he was permitted his first solo, which, as he frequently recalled, he nearly spoiled by choking up in midsong. Arluck, with stern aplomb, cued him in by stepping on his toe. Later, when he was moved to the back of the choir, Hyman was placed on a chair in order to be seen as well as heard. Hyman eventually overcame his shyness. He loved to sing and he loved the adulation he received from other members of the choir and the congregation.

Samuel Arluck's love of vocal music encompassed secular music, particularly opera and the recordings of Enrico Caruso and John McCormack. He also collected recordings of synagogue music and of the celebrated Cantor Rosenblatt, who became a friend of Samuel's. Neither Hyman nor Julius was permitted to use the phonograph, however, or to handle the fragile records. The Arluck household was run strictly, with Samuel as the often absent patriarch, who spent a great deal of time at the synagogue, and Celia as his equal as disciplinarian. She kept an Orthodox house, and all Shabbats and Jewish holidays were properly observed. As a youngster Hyman studied Hebrew, as would Julius.

When Hyman was nine, a piano was added to the phonograph as a source of music. It was Celia's idea; the boy was musical, and if he became a well-trained pianist, he could go on to become a teacher. As his own master, she explained, he could choose his own working hours and observe the Jewish holy days in an Orthodox observance. The instrument fascinated him, and he was an obedient son. He began lessons with a neighbor, a Miss Faller, using the standard musical primers, which he mastered easily. His talent was so evident that his father, who lacked formal musical education, recognized his son's budding musical proficiency.

As soon as Hyman had exhausted Miss Faller and her texts, Samuel enrolled him in classes with the city's best-known musician, Arnold Cornelissen. An all-around maestro, Cornelissen had mastered not only the piano but also the organ. Ambitious, he tried his hand at composition and was conductor of the Buffalo String Orchestral Society. To commemorate the graduation from Miss Faller to Maestro Cornelissen, Samuel presented his son with an expensive leather briefcase for his music books. Study with Cornelissen required an adventurous trip across Buffalo by streetcar, then bus. This was to continue for about two years as Hyman traversed a great deal of Chopin.

He enjoyed the Chopin but detested practice. He was facile enough to convince his teacher that he had applied himself, but Celia Arluck was not easily fooled. With Samuel spending most of the day at the shul, Celia oversaw Hyman's attention to his studies. He managed to get around her when she left the house to shop. Once she was out of earshot, he stopped practice, or read, or tried some musical ideas of his own; he delighted in improvisation.

Meanwhile, he glanced from time to time at one pane in the front room window. When his mother returned he could spot her approaching the porch in time to go back to Chopin.

Keyboard practice, the weekly trolley and bus ride to Cornelissen's studio, and attendance at P.S. 32 left little time for boyish play. And on Saturday, the Shabbat, activity was restricted, although there were small stirrings of revolt. Later in life, during interviews, he looked back on his years as a boy in Buffalo as a period of loving family warmth, remembering his mother as a sweet, poetic homemaker and his father as a stern but fair disciplinarian who was the major musical influence in his life. The passage of time painted that glowing picture of that family life. His father preferred the shul to their home; his mother, who was frustrated by Samuel's domination of her, dominated her sons. Julius, her baby, was the object of her special attention and devotion.

The first sign of resistance to family authority surfaced in Hyman's twelfth year. As a struggling student in P.S. 32, he found some relief from the perils of mathematics as a member of the school orchestra and as a vocalist in the regular school presentations of music and song. He soon realized there was more to music than Chopin and the liturgical chants of the synagogue.

One day in 1917 he came across a piano piece entitled "Indianola," a quasi-ragtime number by the pseudonymous "S. R. Henry and D. Onivas" (actually Domenico Savino, an Italian-born, conservatory-trained composer who specialized in concert pieces). Tin Pan Alley rags, which followed in the wake of the real thing, exquisitely represented in the works of Scott Joplin, were exploitive parodies of classic ragtime, which had run its course in the first decade of the twentieth century. In its later, commercial form, ragtime's characteristic syncopations, harmonies, and counterpoint were distorted into complex rhythmic showpieces, always crowd pleasers, despite Joplin's admonition: "It is never right to play Ragtime fast." But the new crop of ragtime publications were favorites with pianists capable of playing for audiences enthralled by histrionic pianistics.

To a twelve-year-old boy this was not as much a challenge as an opportunity. The unexpected skips and jumps of "Indianola" produced an instant shock in the Arluck home, where up to that time his father had made the musical choices; it was tolerated, but it did not please. His lessons with Cornelissen suffered as he began searching in the local music shop for similar piano "novelty pieces," as they were advertised. In the shop he also discovered the recordings of the Original Dixieland Jazz Band's "Tiger Rag." That same year, 1917, a young George Gershwin had succeeded in publishing his first solo piano piece, a rag entitled "Rialto Ripples," but it had not yet arrived in Buffalo.

There were other, more puzzling stirrings, as he approached his teens. All that P.S. 32 truly offered was an opportunity to perform and to see Lily Levine. He was certain he was in love; he waited for her at lunchtime, took walks till onerous classes resumed. And after they were freed, he would walk her home, carrying her books. Apparently Lily reciprocated, for he recalled a stolen kiss or two (on the cheek) and being "happy." He treasured their class graduation photo, which he framed and kept on a table in his workroom years later.

That graduation resulted in aggravated scholastic problems when, at fifteen, he entered Hutchinson Central High School. By this time he and Lily had gone their separate ways, and he was forced to walk the long distance to Hutchinson High alone or with the boys. He continued studying with Cornelissen, but to the dismay of his parents, his fascination with jazz had grown. He began bringing home recordings of bands producing sounds completely foreign and irritating to the Arlucks. Among his early heroes were the pianists Arthur Schutt and Frank Signorelli, whose bravura styles he tried to emulate, adding further to his parents' annoyance.

Schutt and Signorelli were not jazz or blues pianists in the mold of Jelly Roll Morton or Jimmy Yancey. They were trained musicians with a flair for showmanship and admirable technique. They fascinated Hyman, as did the Original Dixieland Jazz Band, whose improvisations approached the real thing. Even more true were the blues records of Bessie Smith, accompanied by such pianists as Clarence Williams, Fletcher Henderson, and James P. Johnson. They were also virtuosos, but with a deeper sense of the earthy message of the blues.

Hyman studied these cacophonies (to the ears of the senior Arlucks) more assiduously than he did the textbooks from Hutchinson High. He did better in the courses that required no reading, such as physical education, excelling especially in swimming and the high jump.

He struggled through his first semester, with Latin his formidable bête noire, and by the second was prepared to throw in the scholastic towel. When he announced this decision there was an outcry and wrath among the Arlucks. Neither parent had gone beyond high school, but they were ambitious for their first son. Samuel visualized an attorney or a physician in the family. Celia would have settled for a music teacher, except that the music Hyman brought home was not music to her. Worse, he had even begun to play in local bands in some of Buffalo's unsavory districts.

A fellow sufferer at Hutchinson High was Hymie (later Harold) Sandler, then about fourteen. They became best friends, sharing as they did an aversion to classes and a love of music. They also skipped classes, often aimlessly wending their way to the Iroquois Brewery (still in business) for a contest of tossing bottle corks. Sandler recalled that it was the other Hyman who won "a pile of them."

When both agreed to drop out of school, their parents resorted to bribery: a dollar each if they attended night classes at Hutchinson. As Sandler told Neil Graves of the *Buffalo News*, "instead we went to the Maple Leaf Café on Eagle and Oak Street." Bottled beer then, near the advent of Prohibition, cost a quarter, and a glass went for ten cents. An additional attraction was a nondescript little band playing the latest Tin Pan Alley tunes.

Sandler's ambition was to become a drummer, and in the Arluck parlor he provided the percussion accompaniment while his new friend flashed his hands over the keyboard with impressive dexterity. Sandler's instrument was provisional: knives and forks from Celia's kitchen. Before long, he acquired a real drum and sticks, and both musicians began to dream.

Funds for the drum were raised by the formation of the comedy team of Arluck and Sandler (or vice versa). Where the material for their act came from remains a mystery, as does the identity of the top banana and the straight man. But an act they were, and Sandler remembered their entering amateur night competitions at such theaters as the Emblem, the Broadway, and the Temple. Their clowning brought them several first prizes and the money for the drum. Then they gave up comedy for music.

A piano and a drum, they realized, did not constitute a band. Another teenager, Teddy Myers, more or less played the violin and was eager to break into the music business. Thus was formed Hyman Arluck's Snappy Trio, in recognition of seniority and experience. Before the Arluck-Sandler comedy act, Hyman had worked as a butcher boy in a burlesque theater (a probable source of quips), later playing piano in bands in local theaters. In a vaudeville house he developed a boyish crush on the band's vocalist, whom he found beautiful, "a little above burlesque," and who "reeked of the most glorious perfume." To go with this emerging show-business personality, he began dressing snappily—silk shirts and bell-bottomed trousers such as were sported in the Jazz Age drawings of John Held Jr.

With Teddy Myers rounding out the Snappy Trio, they were ready for work. A waiter from the Maple Leaf Café informed them that the regular band, in the words of Sandler, "got hopelessly drunk each night and was finally booted out of the joint." The waiter asked if they had "jobbed around." Of course they had, they informed him, but not that the jobbing had been done primarily in synagogues, not beer joints.

"That was all the house needed to hear," Sandler recalled, and it was the beginning of thirty-five dollars a week, plus the tips they shared with the singing waiters and waitresses. The glory lasted six weeks.

Then, in January 1920, the Volstead Act closed the Maple Leaf Café. Such shutdowns proved temporary, not only in Buffalo but across the country. Soon the more inventive and enterprising saloon owners found ways of circumventing the law by giving birth to the speakeasy and "blind pigs." And they provided illegal spirits as well as lively music.

The Maple Leaf experience, as brief as it was, was a harbinger; could fame and fortune be far behind?

Hyman Arluck, Sandler remembered, not only played piano and sang but also brought the sound of jazz to these boozy settings: "He played right off the riff when a lot of them [other musicians] didn't know how to. He played the melody but he mixed in a lot of stuff, and he was very terrific, very talented at it."

The Snappy Trio prospered, playing in several of the city's vaudeville houses, four shows a day, seven days a week, for which they split the sixty-dollar salary. The word spread to nearby Gowanda, whose Grange sought them out for an afternoon dance, provided they could expand the trio into a quartet; the added instrument should be a saxophone. At the moment there was no saxophonist in their circle, but the artful leader contrived the solution that got them the job. He borrowed a clarinet, which he could not play, then placed a kazoo into the mouthpiece. As Sandler saw it, they would "take the chance. They [the Grange] don't know [the difference]; they're all farmers. So we went down there, and sure enough they said, 'Oh, what wonderful musicians. Who's this guy, that clarinet player?' " For the afternoon's work, and a small deception, each received five dollars.

A larger group then seemed an excellent idea. With the addition of a real sax player, Harold Bernstein, the group now called itself the Se-Mor Jazz Band. It did not flourish. Their work at the Pine Ridge Inn ended when Prohibition agents closed it for selling alcoholic beverages. They landed another out-of-town engagement in Williamsville at a large dance hall called the Glen. Their renown had not preceded them; the vast hall was humiliatingly deserted; this the management attributed to the band. Worse, each member of the quartet was coerced into paying the owner a dollar and a half—"for expenses," he claimed—because they had failed to bring in the customers.

While not always profitable, or steady, leading his own band was a promising, glamorous way of life. Hyman reveled in the attention given his playing and singing and in the excitement of the racy night life. Only sixteen, in 1921 Hyman dropped out of Hutchinson High before the end of the second term. Cantor Arluck and his wife were shocked and distressed; this failure reflected poorly on them among the congregation. In desperation, Samuel appealed to a friend and member of the synagogue to convince the wayward son to remain in school.

The friend was Jack Yellen, then in his late twenties and a local celebrity. An ex-newspaperman covering sports for the *Buffalo Courier*, Yellen had branched out as a lyricist to collaborate with the composer Milton Ager, who was based in Manhattan. Eventually they would write the hit songs "I Wonder What's Become of Sally?" and "Happy Days Are Here Again." At the time of Samuel Arluck's appeal, the Yellen-Ager song "A Young Man's Fancy" was popular, and Yellen, back in Buffalo, basked in its success. If anyone, Samuel reasoned, this veteran of Tin Pan Alley and the ways of the music world could talk some sense to his music-crazy son.

That he should have chosen a surrogate father is curious. Samuel took his position as the head of the family seriously, as he did his religious practices. He may have been too stern at times, for his older son, peace-loving as he was, rebelled. The year before, Hyman and a friend met in a poolroom (another indiscretion) and complained about parental inequity to the point of running away from home. Compounding their offense, they timed their break for a Shabbat night.

Buffalo being a major port on Lake Erie, a few queries on the docks found them work in a ship's galley. Theirs was a choppy voyage, and before their ship had gone far, Hyman's friend suffered a severe attack of seasickness, leaving all the galley work to him. As soon as their ship docked in Detroit, the two boys deserted. In a strange city, cold and hungry, they were at a loss until Hyman remembered that one of his cousins lived in Cleveland.

The problem was getting there. They had left their jobs before they were paid and were completely broke. They found their way to the railroad station and boarded a train destined for Cleveland. They talked a sympathetic trainman into letting them stay in a sleeping car—no riding the rods for them. Hyman could not recall later whether this good Samaritan was the conductor, but never forgot that he provided them with sleeping space on the floor under a lower berth. Not once, between Detroit and Cleveland, did they disturb the woman asleep in the berth above.

They eventually found Hyman's cousin, who promptly phoned the heartsick Arlucks to inform them that their son had materialized in Cleveland. The boys had been mysteriously missing by then for two days, causing much distress in two Buffalo households. After the sighs of relief came justifiable anger. The next day two chastened runaways boarded the train for a gloomy return to Buffalo.

That failed dash for Detroit had been Hyman's most drastic form of rebellion, more upsetting than skipping classes at school. So was playing piano in disreputable dives in the town's tenderloin, and now he informed his father that he would drop out of school and make a life as a pianist-bandleader. This was no occupation for the cantor's son. There seemed to be no reasoning with a determined and stubborn sixteen-year-old boy.

Jack Yellen was a bit surprised when the cantor asked him to talk Hyman out of taking a wrong step, but he accepted the task. True, he was a graduate of the University of Michigan, a seasoned newsman, and a part-time New Yorker with music experience, if none in the band business.

In recalling the encounter with Hyman, Yellen (then twice the boy's age) found him playing at Minnie's, "a roadhouse of no good reputation." Both were nervous, and Yellen, lacking an original approach, began by asking Hyman what he wanted to be.

Hyman laughed, still uneasy, and replied, "A musician."

"Then play something for me," Yellen ordered.

The young Arluck sat at the piano and proceeded to dazzle his father's stand-in with a medley of popular songs, a little ragtime, and a little piece or two of his own. Yellen recognized a born musician, "his father's son." Later he called Samuel Arluck and told him, "It's all your fault. He's going to be a musician."

The cantor was stubborn, too. Jack Yellen's appraisal notwithstanding, he was still the father and Hyman the son. Though Hyman could continue with his band, he was forced to agree to attend classes at Technical High School to prepare him for a real job, if not one of the professions his parents had hoped for. His most loathed class at Tech High was shop, in which mostly thumbs, he built chairs. Working with wood and, in great peril, with tools was worse than Hutchinson.

He rebelled again, quit school, and concentrated on his band and its bookings. Resigned, Samuel Arluck agreed to let the band use the living room as a rehearsal hall. This was no problem for Samuel, since he spent so much time at the synagogue. Celia suffered through these sessions, however. Young Julius, now nine, was a fascinated spectator and listener. He was especially drawn to Teddy Myer's fiddle—or was it, as he recalled years later, Teddy's maestrolike long hair?

Prosperity encouraged growth, and as some of the Snappy Trio went on to other jobs, new members joined the band to form the six-piece Southbound Shufflers. The bigger group introduced the curious Julius to another instrument, the saxophone, which intrigued him for a while. During breaks, Hyman often tried his hand at playing it and was doing quite well. But when time came for his music lessons, Julius selected the more sedate violin as his instrument. Another Arluck was destined for a musical career.

In the summer of 1923 the Southbound Shufflers worked on the *Canadiana,* a lake boat that transported picnickers and serious drinkers from Buffalo to Crystal Beach, Ontario, where there were no Prohibition laws. As the boat crossed Lake Erie, the Shufflers accompanied the dancers with Jazz Age sounds that, in part, the leader had borrowed from recordings of the Original Memphis Five, an all-white band featuring jazzman Miff Mole on trombone and Hyman's mentor-hero Frank Signorelli on piano. Like the more exciting, more inventive black jazz bands of the period, such as King Oliver's or Jelly Roll Morton's, the Memphis Five, and in their train, the Southbound Shufflers, played free-and-easy arrangements of popular songs, as well as blues and jazzlike "novelties," with provision for solos by the group's musical stars. For dancing, the Shufflers had to curb their proclivity for improvisation, especially Hyman, whose playing could stop the dancers in their tracks. His playing was as fascinating to watch and hear as it was impossible to dance to.

In looking back, he realized that at the time, his youthful ambition, which he did not understand, was driving him somewhere. But where? His pyrotechnical keyboard style, his defiance of his parents, even his mode of dress and his ego (as he admitted)—all branded him as different.

He quickly rejected the self-analysis and devoted all his energies to music. He stopped lessons with Cornelissen and spent more time on orchestrations for the Shufflers. That Hyman had never studied the techniques did not stop him. Emulating the Memphis Five, he occasionally wrote an original number for his band. If he could invent arrangements, he reasoned, why not original compositions? Around 1924 he began dabbling in songwriting.

"Scratch a musician," was a favorite observation, "and you'll find a songwriter." A friend, Hyman Cheiffetz, was an embryo lyricist with whom Arluck attempted his first songs. The first, with the name of Hyman Arluck on it as composer, was "My Gal, Won't You Please Come Back to Me?" (later shortened to "My Gal, My Pal"). They were on their way.

They arranged for the publication of "My Gal, My Pal" in the spring of 1924, in time for promotion on the summer excursion boats and for the band's booking at the respectable Lake Shore Manor. For these appearances Hyman prepared miniature piano rolls on which the song's lyrics were printed. Dancers approaching the bandstand were presented with these rolls. The band would play their leader's first "published" song, plugging it in the traditional Tin Pan Alley manner. They sold no copies of that song.

There was an additional plug, thanks to the manager of the Lafayette Theatre, where Hyman had appeared with his Se-Mor Jazz Band. He remembered Hyman warmly and decided to advance Arluck's songwriting career. A saxophonist and friend of Hyman's, Stanley Meyers, would play the melody as the words were projected on the screen and the mystified audience was invited to sing along and, implicitly, to purchase the sheet music in the lobby. But even the composer's face, also on the screen, did not help.

Still there was no rush to buy. In later years the composer dismissed these early efforts as amateurish, like the songs that publishers receive in every mail delivery. Invariably the practice was to return these often inept endeavors unopened to avoid future plagiarism lawsuits. (A few unsuccessful songwriters virtually made a profession of this; Irving Berlin, also a publisher, was frequently annoyed by such false claims and litigation.)

"My Gal, My Pal" and especially the second Cheiffetz song, "I Never Knew What Love Could Do," are notable only as firsts and for a change in their composer's name, from Hyman to Harold, another subtle sign of defiance.

Having failed at songwriting, which did not appear to be particularly rewarding, he also became disenchanted with running the band. Working in vaudeville, roadhouses, and speakeasies during a hard Buffalo winter, in addition to finding bookings and keeping track of expenses, canceled the joy of being a local celebrity. Then, too, there was the shifting personnel. Sandler, for example, had left to become a member of the New England Six. As young Arluck admitted, running the Shufflers entailed "too many headaches." After their final summer on Lake Erie in 1925, he decided to disband the Southbound Shufflers. He was now twenty; he would give up the band, but not the business.

His skills, well known around the Buffalo band community, soon made him a member of the popular Yankee Six as pianist, vocalist, and arranger. The Six traveled in more prestigious circles than had his bands—college dances, proms, country clubs, and society weddings, with public appearances at the grand Geyer's Restaurant and Ballroom, in the center of Buffalo's theater district. Their success and prosperity could have been attributed to the band's makeup: four owner-founders and two employees.

During the band's stay at Geyer's, Harold became friendly with a twenty-one-year-old "eccentric dancer," Ray Bolger, who was then bringing record-breaking crowds into the Hippodrome.

Bolger frequently dropped by Geyer's after his show to listen to the band, now grown to eleven members and called the Buffalodians. It was the only band in town with a two-piano team. Dick George, one of the original founders, was also a pianist, and he and Harold frequently entertained the dancers with snappy piano duets. Bolger was impressed with the sophisticated, jazzy, bravura arrangements and learned that one of the pianists, the one who sang, Harold Arluck, had created them. They became fast friends, and Bolger spent most of his free time listening to the Buffalodians, which was good for Geyer's, since Bolger had become a Buffalo celebrity on his way to New York. He and Harold Arluck would soon meet again.

The band continued to prosper—Harold often earned as much as a hundred dollars a week, a considerable sum in the Buffalo of 1925. With their prosperity came prestige and with that, through an agency, bookings that would take them to the big cities, maybe Chicago, possibly even New York. The band's consensus was that it was the season to hit the road and head for the big time.

The inevitable parental confrontation ensued, although Samuel had all but given up in his attempts to guide his son onto a less secular pathway. This was not the work for the senior son of a distinguished cantor. Celia feared that in those sinful cities Harold could fall into the wrong female hands.

Harold stood up to them, respectfully, but made it clear that his mind was set. How much further could he go in Buffalo? He was, he reminded them, twenty, and the time had come for him to be on his own. Like Jack Yellen, he could come home now and then. If the tour did not pan out, he would return.

Samuel, resigned, had nothing to say. The Buffalodians had won the argument. But he could be stubborn, too. He would never accept his son's anglicizing of his given name; throughout his life, Samuel would call his firstborn Chaim.

2

THE BUFFALODIANS
AND THE BIG TIME

*D*ance bands flourished in the Jazz Age, more so than during the Swing Era
that followed. It was a rare high school or college without its student band
that played for the Friday night dances in the gym. The members of the band
were often refugees from the established school orchestra or marching band.
Their own groups gave them the chance to break away from the standard stuff
and to jazz up current popular songs.

A good example was Chicago's Austin High School band, consisting of a
quintet of students. They were Jim Lannigan, Jimmy and Dick McPartland, Lawrence Freeman (better known as "Bud"), and Frank Teschemacher, who began
playing for school dances or for parties in the homes of fellow students. Each
member went on to become celebrated jazz or dance band musicians in the
1930s.

Like the Austin High Gang, other student bands evolved into professional,
even successful, groups. As they became known, they booked into neighboring
cities. But the major goal of the most ambitious was New York City.

From barroom to ballroom, dancing had become a craze. Roadhouses mush-
roomed, abetted by the rising sales of the motor car. These halls provided a
dance floor and illicit alcohol. So did the more enterprising, risk-taking cabarets,
cafés, and hotels in town. Initially the owners hired such local bands as the
Buffalodians. There was plenty of work for smart, up-to-date, jazzy bands. *Variety*, the keeper of the records of the period, reported that in 1925 there were no

fewer than sixty thousand bands, amateur as well as professional, competing with the Buffalodians when they set out on their musical journey to Manhattan, with its dancing (and drinking) "flaming youth," flappers, and cake eaters.

Leaving Buffalo and environs meant that the Buffalodians had begun its rise from the status of a "territory band," as they were called. These were the hometown groups that, having prospered in the cities and towns within driving distance, often branched out, thanks to the broadcasts from local radio stations, which also had begun to burgeon. Popular dance bands filled in a lot of empty airtime.

When the Buffalodians set out on their quest for fame and fortune, the most celebrated and profitable band of the period was led by a former symphony violinist, Paul Whiteman. Its territory, in the west, had ranged from San Francisco to Los Angeles. Thanks in part to the quasi-jazzy arrangements by the pianist Ferde Grofé, the band was solidly lodged in the New York City scene in 1925. Others followed: Jean Goldkette from Detroit via Chicago (and recordings, which had spread the name); the Coon-Sanders Original Nighthawks, whose broadcasts from Kansas City brought them to New York. Ben Pollack moved in from Chicago. There were others, but many of those foundered and were never heard from again.

The most popular bands featured carefully prepared jazz-inspired arrangements, demanding disciplined musicianship, with "breaks" for a celebrity soloist to stand out from the ensemble. This was not the genuine jazz heard in black neighborhoods or on "race" records made for and sold in those parts of town. In the period when Paul Whiteman was hailed as the King of Jazz, the real royalty of this folk art were McKinney's Cotton Pickers; Bennie Moten; Luis Russell; "King" Oliver and his protégé, probably the true king, Louis Armstrong; and Jelly Roll Morton, who claimed he had invented jazz in New Orleans before the 1920s.

The arrangers for the white dance bands were familiar, through recordings primarily, with the work of these black bands and borrowed from them freely. Musical elements such as muted trumpets, syncopation, and blue notes gave Whiteman and his rivals the characteristic sound and "pep" that young dancers expected and that appalled their elders. This was the time of flaming youth.

By 1925, when Harold Arluck and his colleagues arrived in New York City, dancing had become pandemic, even more pervasive than during the craze inspired by the pre–World War I team of Vernon and Irene Castle. Their maxixe, tango, Castle walk, and turkey trot were supplanted by the provocative Charleston (a revived, more wicked shimmy) and the black bottom. Meanwhile, the waltz and fox trot survived, the latter readily jazzed up by hiking the tempo, appropriating from the blues (flatted thirds and sevenths), muting a trumpet with a bowler hat, and adding a saxophone.

The Buffalodians were ready for this challenge, especially with original arrangements by Harold Arluck. Their booking agency initiated their eastward journey in Cleveland, in a first-class restaurant in the heart of the city. They did so well with their jazzy renditions of current popular songs that their booking was extended. Coincidentally, at the nearby Lake Road Inn, in a Cleveland suburb, another newborn band, Guy Lombardo's Royal Canadians, had begun its run for the big time. With its "Sweetest Music This Side of Heaven," the Royal Canadians were musical opposites to the Buffalodians. The Buffalodians had never heard of them, and vice versa.

From Cleveland the Buffalodians moved on to Pittsburgh and finally, in the spring of 1926, arrived in New York City for an appearance at the shrine and last bastion of vaudeville, the Palace in Times Square, whose operators refused to permit the showing of films in their theater. Vaudeville, unbeknownst to everyone but the Palace management, was suffering through its final days because of the inroads of the motion picture (with sound just around the corner) and the newest nemesis, radio.

This was evident at the box office, and consequently the Buffalodians were not overpaid for their two-week stint. Happy finally to be in New York, they adapted to its rhythms and bustle as if they belonged, especially Harold Arluck. The town rocked with music in the clubs, theaters, hot spots, dance halls, and cabarets such as the Durante, Club Richman, and the House of Morgan (where you could hear Helen Morgan singing atop a piano). There was also the Casa Lopez, featuring the "jazz" band and piano of Vincent Lopez. Even the opulent Silver Slipper was drawing customers away from vaudeville.

Harold was drawn to the famous, capacious Roseland Ballroom, also on Broadway, four blocks north of the Palace. It was Times Square's major source of what eventually would be called hot jazz. New Yorkers and tourists who shunned Harlem were introduced to such dances as the collegiate, the lindy, and the shag at Roseland. It was here that Harold met and was befriended by the black bandleader, arranger, and pianist Fletcher Henderson. Young Arluck's affinity for the Henderson band's music, his sense of humor, his unaffected, quiet, easy manner, and his musicianship won over "the boys," as band members were called. Race was immaterial among equals.

Henderson, impressed with the twenty-one-year-old white kid's orchestrations, asked Harold to create some arrangements for the Henderson band. One was the perky "Dynamite," which Henderson's Dixie Stompers recorded in mid-April 1926. In tribute to his new friend and sometime employer, Arluck wrote a piece for the Buffalodians entitled "Deep Henderson," recorded by the band for the Columbia Phonograph Company on May 24, 1926. That was the Buffalodians first recording session, assuring them that they were really on their way.

The Buffalodians cavorted onstage and off in either plus fours (favored by golfing heroes of the time and college "men") or the double-breasted blazers and bell-bottomed white slacks so favored by representatives of the pleasure-seeking flaming youth who danced to their music with rouge-kneed flappers. New York was exhilirating, a city devoted to song, dance, and other pleasures that could be found in the new Prohibition-motivated speakeasies, where, if Joe sent you, you were permitted in to hear the band and drink real beer or real liquor smuggled in from Canada.

Compared with Harlem, Times Square was as sedate as a cotillion. After the theaters and the late clubs closed, the Harlem hot spots pulsated to the new sounds of Duke Ellington, Louis Armstrong, Luis Russell, and such remarkable pianists as James P. Johnson, master of the stride piano, and his pupil, Thomas Waller, best known simply as "Fats." After the final act in vaudeville, the musicians, bored with playing the same trite tunes, flocked north to Harlem to after-hours clubs such as Connie's Inn, Small's Paradise, and the Cotton Club. Likewise, after a show's curtain dropped, Broadway singers and dancers headed uptown to absorb jazzy pointers in vocal styling and the newest dance steps. They were followed by their audiences, often, in the words of Lorenz Hart, "in ermine and pearls." When the more legitimate clubs closed for the night, the "speaks" were open, as business picked up around three in the morning.

Musicians congregated to the "lap joints" (Harlemese for liquor clubs) to hear other musicians, black and white, and to join in jam sessions (where everyone jammed in counterpoint) and "cutting" sessions in which two musicians, playing the same instrument, performed alternately and together, to discover who pleased the crowd most. To a cantor's son, fresh out of Buffalo, it was heaven, and Arluck learned a lot. It was a musical education unavailable in any conservatory.

He recalled traveling to Brooklyn's branch of Roseland to hear the heroes of his youth, the Memphis Five. "When they came off the stand," he said, "I stood there with as much awe as if the president of the United States had just finished speaking."

Unlike many of the great songwriters of his generation—Burton Lane, Arthur Schwartz—he was initially drawn to and influenced by the music of jazzmen, white and black, before he seriously studied the show music of Irving Berlin, Jerome Kern, and especially George Gershwin. He was aware of them. He never forgot the effect of hearing "Swanee" for the first time. And in the beginning of his Buffalodian stint, he and Dick George prepared a two-piano arrangement of *Rhapsody in Blue* that was popular with their audiences. When the band had started on its rise in New York, one of his first arrangements was of Berlin's "Too Many Times." He also wrote a more elaborate arrangement for a larger orchestra (possibly the popular Arnold Johnson band) of Gershwin's "The Man I Love."

He knew and admired the songs of these masters, but it was the improvised music of the jazzmen that most affected him. All his energies were devoted to music, with little time for a private life. When he wasn't performing, or working on arrangements, he haunted the clubs where the music was an attraction. There was the night that, carried away by the song "I'm Comin', Virginia," whose recording by the Frank Trumbauer orchestra was notable for the trumpet solo by Bix Beiderbecke, that he hopped onto the bandstand and sang a chorus.

Arluck finished this impulsive act, and while he was basking in the applause of the dancers, Beiderbecke himself materialized from the crowd. His partner was, Harold recognized, the lovely Bee Palmer, the notorious "Shimmy Queen" of vaudeville. As they danced by, Beiderbecke exclaimed, "Great, kid!" Years later Harold was uncertain whether it was the jazzman's accolade that thrilled him, or the sight, up close, of the Shimmy Queen.

He loved to perform; when he did his innate shyness faded as he lost himself in the music. His affinity for jazz was, he believed, congenital. He frequently recalled an incident from his youth after he had begun collecting "race" records and put a new Louis Armstrong and His Hot Five recording on the turntable of the family phonograph. Samuel Arluck listened reluctantly, then sat up. Startled, he demanded to know where Armstrong had gotten a phrase he was playing.

Hyman explained that it was known as a "hot lick." In the Swing Era it would be called a "riff," a brief repeated musical phrase, a rhythmic variation on the tune.

That hot lick, Samuel maintained, was one of his own improvisations he had sung during a service at the synagogue. Harold later told Max Wilk that he heard a lot of Armstrong in his father's cantillation and vice versa. Since Samuel Arluck had grown up in Louisville, it is possible that he had heard gospel songs, spirituals, even the blues. There are harmonic and melodic correspondences between the music of the African American and the Jew; it is the rhythmic drive of the former that made the difference and contributed to the evolution of American jazz music.

His New York experience intensified his aspirations to become a performer. He maintained that he never dreamed of songwriting at the time. The greater glamour of the stage, whether in vaudeville or nightclub, attracted him, not the music business. He was tiring of the grind of playing in a band and writing arrangements for others.

This was the frequent subject of discussion Harold had with his roommate, Ray Bolger. The Buffalodians had moved from the Palace into the Monte Carlo, a prospering cabaret. To his delight, his eccentric dancer-friend was also on the bill. After some talk they decided to share the expenses of an apartment on the far western end of Fifty-seventh Street.

They were an unlikely pair. Bolger, then twenty-two (a year older than his roommate), was tall, wiry, and from another world, New England. He had left Dorchester, Massachusetts, determined to make a name for himself in show business. He and Harold, as different as they were—the outgoing dancer and the reserved musician—shared a flair for and love of the unconventional. Bolger's took the form of a unique dancing style (invariably described as "rubbery legged"), and Harold's in introducing distinctive, fresh musical ideas in performance and instrumentation.

Bolger remembered later that he was most impressed with Harold's wistfulness, gentleness, and refreshing sense of humor. He sensed not Harold's ambition but his devotion to music. (Bolger's aspirations were made of sterner stuff.) Later, Bolger, while starring in a one-man show at the Waldorf, remembered with affection losing sleep while his roommate worked at their battered upright piano, searching for the right musical phrase.

When Manhattan's steamy summer season began, the more affluent cabaret frequenters escaped to breezier parts. In July 1926 the Buffalodians followed with a booking at Gallagher's in Far Rockaway, Long Island. Though not as fashionable as Scott Fitzgerald's "Gold Coast" to the north, Far Rockaway was cooled by the gentle winds of the Atlantic and within easy reach of Manhattan.

It was in Far Rockaway that Harold Arluck's band career came to an abrupt end. For reasons he could never recall, he became the object of the wrath of the band's leader, Jack McLoughlin. Harold may have unwittingly triggered the flare-up by capering on the bandstand while singing a song whose lyric he judged silly, or by taking an extra bar or two during his solo, or by contributing an unexpected hot lick during the leader's violin solo. Or, as Harold later speculated, it being after hours, possibly McLoughlin had consumed too much of the Canadian imports that all but flooded Long Island during Prohibition.

All attempts to pacify the steaming McLoughlin failed. Harold's funny quips only incensed "Mac" further until the time came when Arluck realized it was time to run. With the cursing McLoughlin in pursuit, he sprinted through the usually serene streets of Far Rockaway. He also ran out of breath. Gasping and resigned, the born pacifist turned to face his pursuer. He put up his hands to protect his face. Caught off guard by the unexpected tack, McLoughlin obligingly charged into the upraised fists.

When the rest of the band caught up, they were amazed to find the reluctant runner peering down at the grounded McLoughlin, out cold. This was the second, and last, Arluck exercise of the manly art. The first occurred at P.S. 32 when he and one of his classmates squared off over some imagined insult. Hyman threw the first punch, with a resultant bloody nose and tears for his opponent. Remorsefully, Hyman escorted his teary former challenger home to the boy's mother. She forgave the kindhearted pugilist, but he never developed a taste for scrapping. Later, many colleagues criticized him for being too peaceable and too often willing to compromise. He was wiser than they thought; he found it less distressing and time consuming to shun the behind-the-scenes warring among the nest of vipers he encountered in the alleged magic world of show business, on Broadway and in Hollywood.

Late in August 1926 the Buffalodians returned to Manhattan to make their final recordings for Columbia Records. McLoughlin, for his own reasons, had already left. Harold Arluck was elected the leader of the band, a job for which he was neither ready nor equipped. He too left the band. He had sustained his dream of setting out on his own in show business, and as the band disintegrated, in a small exodus Buffalo-ward, he was free. The Buffalodians, despite the early promise, had proved to be just another lost hopeful in *Variety*'s sixty thousand.

As Harold embarked on his "at liberty" phase, his name began to take its final form, which it reached by the end of 1928. He attributed this to the telephone, next to the piano the most important instrument of his career. Communicating with producers, agents, and bandleaders face to face was difficult for him, so the telephone served him well. But one frequent hindrance was the name Arluck. Tired of hearing, "What's that name again?," he softened the final syllable by blending the names of his parents. Thus Arluck and Orlin combined to form Arlen. It worked, solved his problem, and would read well on posters, or even a marquee, should one ever come along.

He was not at liberty for long. Steady work came with the bandleader Arnold Johnson's return to New York from Florida. Classically trained, Johnson preferred popular music, provided it was well arranged and performed. By way of Chicago vaudeville, in which he alternated between accompanist and piano soloist, he formed the Frisco Jazz Band, featuring the saxophone virtuoso Rudy Wiedoeft. Next he organized the larger Arnold Johnson band, with which he toured the major vaudeville circuits, then abandoned the band business in the mid-1920s for a disastrous fling in real estate during the Florida land boom (as did many of his gullible fellow Americans). In September and October 1926 a couple of hurricanes blew most of that land into the ocean or submerged it under salt water.

Back in New York, Johnson reformed his band and became successful again, performing in clubs, cabarets, and, in time, the theater. The band began its theater work in the pit of the 1928 *Greenwich Village Follies*, which opened in April for a very brief stay. Johnson and band then moved into the Apollo Theatre on Forty-second Street for the ninth edition of *George White's Scandals* on July 2. It starred the dimple-kneed dancer Ann Pennington (who had introduced the naughty black bottom in the *Scandals* of 1926), the comedians Willie and Eugene Howard, and Harry Richman, an Al Jolson protégé whose imitation of his master's voice and style often led to Jolson's being accused of pirating from Richman. Also in the cast were Tom Patricola (who had introduced Gershwin's "Somebody Loves Me" in the *Scandals* of 1924), and the Arnold Johnson Orchestra, with principal vocalist Harold Arlen.

Johnson had heard Arlen when the Buffalodians were playing at the Monte Carlo. At the time, Harold had no inclination to give up his stellar position in the band to become perhaps a lesser star in the larger, more renowned Johnson orchestra. But when the Buffalodians broke up in 1926, Harold was free to join Johnson, especially since no work in vaudeville was forthcoming.

Johnson was then leading his band on the popular radio show "The Majestic Hour," broadcasting weekly from the fashionable Park Central Hotel, newly opened on Seventh Avenue and Fifty-fifth Street, "Where One Can Live Like a King."

The radio hour was sponsored by the manufacturers of the newly developed Majestic radio. Radio was still in its infancy in 1926. Hobbyists had taken it up after World War I, and commercial broadcasting had begun in 1922. By the close of the decade sales of radios and parts would have increased by 1,400 percent; there would be more radios in the country than bathtubs. A new technology had captivated the American people and, like its impending rival the talking picture, would play a major role in the entertainment business—and in the life of Harold Arlen.

Singing weekly over the air from the Park Central was heady, partly because his parents in Syracuse could tune in on him. (The Arlucks had recently moved to Syracuse, where Samuel was cantor at Temple Adath Yeshuron.) Still, his big Broadway moments occurred during the six-month run of the 1928 *Scandals*. Every night, and twice weekly on matinee days, he raised his voice during the entr'acte, following intermission. The spotlight fell on him in the orchestra pit as he stood to sing "I'm on the Crest of a Wave," music by the Buffalo-born composer Ray Henderson and lyrics by B. G. DeSylva and Lew Brown. As spotlights go, this was a dim one. He was merely reprising a song that had already been sung by the show's star male vocalist, Harry Richman. Reprising a show's hit song was considered a good way to assure popularity, but it did Harold little good. Late returnees from the lobby were distracting, even vocal. Nor did the band's recording of the song do much for Harold, whose vocal was submerged in a trio.

The experience was frustrating, certainly not the vocal stardom that he had dreamed of and spoke of with Ray Bolger. This was no great improvement over the Buffalodians.

The show's star female vocalist was the glamorous, platinum blonde Frances Williams, second in the billing only to the headliner, Ann Pennington. Williams not only had a fine, distinctive voice, but was also an impressive pianist. She and Harold soon became more than colleagues and much more than friends—he fell in love.

Born Frances Jellineck in St. Paul, Minnesota, she began singing in a San Francisco cabaret around 1922. She took the vaudeville route to New York and made her Broadway debut in the chorus of Sigmund Romberg's *Innocent Eyes*. The next year, 1925, she appeared in a successful musical, *Artists and Models,* which she abandoned for the Marx Brothers caper *The Cocoanuts*, in which she was billed as herself. This was a recognition of stature on Broadway.

In 1926 she starred in her first of three *Scandals*. The second was the 1928 edition. During rehearsals she was introduced to the pianist and one of the vocalists with the Arnold Johnson band. He was (still) Harold Arluck, a shy, good-looking young man two years younger than she who sang bewitchingly and was a marvelous pianist. He was obviously smitten, and they soon became the talk of Tin Pan Alley.

The hopeful swain was absent when the 1929 *Follies* premiered in the summer. Frances Williams was back with the resident comics, Willie and Eugene Howard, and even White himself, who had been a dancer in the *Ziegfeld Follies* before setting out on his own as a rival of his old boss. But the Arnold Johnson band and Harold Arlen had moved into the Paramount Hotel for a stay of several months, during which Frances and Harold were seen together regularly.

In July he left the Johnson band to begin that career he had hoped for. He made a recording of "I Can't Give You Anything But Love, Baby" accompanying himself, but Victor rejected it. In August he recorded another reject, this time with the Henry Busse Orchestra, the trumpeter-leader having left the Paul Whiteman band. This was not a promising beginning of his new life.

Things brightened a little when, during the run of the *Scandals*, Frances Williams appeared at the Palace, "courtesy of George White," according to the program. For this musical outing, Williams selected Harold as one of her accompanists. When her contract was up, he was determined to strike out in vaudeville.

He auditioned for a singing spot in a revue, *Maytime Follies*. The single big name on the program was the comedian Ted Healy in his pre–Hollywood–Three Stooges phase. In his spot Harold sang and played current popular songs, among them Richard Whiting and Neil Moret's "She's Funny That Way." He managed to break one of the unwritten rules of show business by including "Making Whoopee," from a current Eddie Cantor musical, *Whoopee,* produced by Florenz Ziegfeld. Producers, and especially Ziegfeld, did not take kindly to having songs from their shows appropriated for the productions of others. Young Arlen, who liked the mildly suggestive song, ignored the decree with impunity. No one, not even Ziegfeld, noticed—nor had the new single act, Harold Arlen and his songs, achieved much attention.

He kept trying, and regularly he suffered through an ordeal endemic to the trade: the audition. Harold found it "demeaning" to "sing in front of those potential hirers, with all those glaring, staring faces." One audition that he never forgot was for J. J. Shubert, familiarly, and unaffectionately, known as Jake. One of the most powerful men in show business, he was one half of the irascible, tough "Messrs. Shubert"; the other was his brother, the infamous Lee.

Hoping to get a job in a Shubert revue or show, Arlen demonstrated his routine while Shubert, at his desk, shuffled through papers, apparently indifferent to the nervous singing pianist. After ten unattended-to songs, Arlen gave up.

Shubert did notice the abrupt quiet.

"What happened?" he shouted.

"I ran out of throat," Arlen hoarsely explained, then left, thinking, "What a callous man." Thanks to a friend who had arranged for the audition, his schooling in the crudities of show business had at least begun at the top. Or was it the bottom? The lyricist E. Y. Harburg claimed that he had been fortunate to have been born in a period in history that would provide him with such rich grist for his socially conscious song mill. It was a time, he said, "of Mussolini, Hitler, Stalin—and the Shuberts."

Harold may have walked out on Jake Shubert, but the vagaries of chance would bring them together again—and with the Shubert-loathing Yip Harburg. In several interviews later in his career, Arlen stated with a mystical intensity that it was the hand of providence or simply luck that shaped his destiny after his arrival in New York City. It was luck, not his own determination, that converted the hopeful, not very successful performer into a creator. No Jolson, or Richman or Vallee, he had not impressed audiences as much as he did the professionals—musicians, singers, songwriters.

In May 1929, with his plan to become a vaudeville headliner leading nowhere, he answered a casting call for *Louisiana Lou,* a musical with a Southern setting. The show's composer, Vincent Youmans, had heard Arlen and liked his singing. Harold passed the audition, and Youmans hired him for a singing role in the musical, then in its early formative stage.

The willful Youmans was about to set out on a classic misadventure. Just thirty, Youmans already had several Broadway successes to his credit, most notably *No, No, Nanette* (1925) and *Hit the Deck* (1927), with such enduring songs as "I Want to Be Happy," "Tea for Two," "I Know That You Know" and "Hallelujah." His gift as a composer was never questioned; his character was the problem.

Smarting from the abject failure of his recent *Rainbow,* which he characteristically blamed on others, Youmans was determined to be in total command of *Louisiana Lou.* He would not only write but also publish the score (to lyrics by Edward Eliscu and Billy Rose). He would furnish the "characters and locale of the play," leaving the plot and dialogue to others. And he would be the producer, the master of all. In a convenient cliché, he was all things to all men and his own worst enemy. He compounded his difficulties by leasing a theater and renaming it "Youmans' Cosmopolitan." As the Cosmopolitan Theatre it was a well-known theatrical white elephant, hopelessly situated uptown from Times Square in Columbus Circle.

Harold Arlen went happily into this time bomb. He was actually cast in a real musical with a real part, as Cokey Joe, a singer-pianist. South of Columbus Circle, Frances Williams was also rehearsing for what was to be her final *Scandals,* and the two managed to see a great deal of each other for a time.

But Harold had not reckoned with his new employer. Neurotically competitive, driven by envy, Youmans regarded George Gershwin, born one day before him, as his major rival, even in the concert hall. Frequently in poor health and often drinking too much, Youmans trusted few.

Louisville Lou, "A Musical Play of the Southland," was his challenge to Jerome Kern's triumphant *Show Boat,* produced two years before and still running somewhere in the country on tour. Like *Show Boat,* the Youmans musical was set in the south, replete with plantations, levees, gamblers, and, as the program noted, "pickaninnies."

Arlen had joined the cast of the show in May. Youmans was impatient and eager to hurry the show on its way. Retitled *Great Day!,* the underrehearsed, unpolished, and uncompleted musical opened in Philadelphia on June 4, 1929. During the brief preparation period all the songs were completed and changes were made. One of the most peculiar was that of the name of one of the lyricists. The well-known Billy Rose was billed as William Rose. Youmans believed that, in consideration for the gravity of their work, Billy was too undignified.

The show was pilloried by the Philadelphia reviewers. The plot was "slipshod," "tedious," and "cumbersome." The show's big-name lead, a name acquired primarily through recordings and minimal stage experience, was Marion Harris, whose performance was dismissed by one critic with a simple "listless." The leading man, Don Lanning, was spared by omission, as was the lightly blackfaced piano player in act 2, scene 3, described with semantic precision as "a third-class dance hall." In this scene Arlen accompanied and joined in a duet with Frances Stevens (as Panzy) in "Doo, Dah, Dey," an obvious allusion to Stephen Foster's "Camptown Races."

Oblivious to the behind-the-scenes distress, Harold enjoyed his brief stint onstage and looked forward to his Broadway debut. Meanwhile, he got to know his employer better and would soon become entangled in the downhill ordeal of what became known along Broadway as "The Great Delay."

The morning-after Philadelphia press critiques initiated drastic changes. Youmans fired the principals, junked sets, postponed the Broadway premiere, and began reworking the book and songs. Youmans learned that his Piano Player was a trained musician who could actually read and write music. Youmans, who detested the chore of putting songs on paper and was burdened with the pressures of repairing an ailing show, drafted Harold Arlen as his musical secretary. Arlen now had two jobs.

Working with the harried Youmans was not easy. He was short-tempered under ordinary circumstances. (In an earlier collaboration, he had thrown Billy Rose out of his office because he thought the lyricist had spoken disparagingly about a Youmans tune.) Nor was the work without interruption. Young Arlen was as amazed as he was impressed by Youmans' prodigious alcoholic intake. And work stopped regularly for a time with the appearances of attractive young women at the Youmans suite, leaving the quite naïve musical secretary puzzled as his boss repaired to an adjacent room with the nubile visitor.

It was a time of desperation and frenzy, and Youmans momentarily considered closing down *Great Day!* and paying off its debts from the earnings from his recent successful shows. But somehow he managed to talk Florenz Ziegfeld into lending him ten thousand dollars; his original backers had already fled.

Youmans was faced with a dilemma: they could not remain in Philadelphia, nor were they ready to open in New York. He decided on the next best thing: he slipped into the New York area by booking his show into Werba's Jamaica Theater in Queens, across the East River from Manhattan. It was here that Harold Arlen's name appeared in the *Great Day!* playbill for the last time.

The troubled musical opened in early July, technically out of reach of the critics, but accessible to Manhattan's play doctors who might come around to suggest improvements. The rest of July and all of August and September were devoted to preparing for the opening in New York on October 17, 1929. Two weeks later Wall Street collapsed, and the show closed after thirty-six painful performances. In the five months of its extended gestation, *Great Day!* left a great deal of debris in its wake: the backers, designers, directors, actors, songs, and Ziegfeld.

But not the Piano Player. Harold Arlen left during the period of July revisions and rehearsals at the Cosmopolitan. A "lucky accident," as he called it, had occurred, one that would spare him the final paroxysms of *Great Day!* and even the adversities of the Great Depression.

3

PICKUP
AND JOTS

*I*t was fascinating, even exciting, to experience the creation of a big Broadway musical. "Construction" might be a more apt word, for *Great Day!* was literally pieced together from (often changing) parts. In one section of the theater the cast rehearsed their lines and songs, in another the chorus learned their music, and to add to the cacophony, the dancers worked out their routines onstage. The problem with this musical, it soon became evident, was that there were too many pieces and few jelled. In time, rehearsals became a tiresome bore.

A reunion with Fletcher Henderson in the early phase of the venture seemed promising to the neophyte Arlen. With his band temporarily disbanded, Henderson had been signed to do some of the orchestrations and to double as the dancers' rehearsal pianist. The choral director was Will Marion Cook. Then sixty, Cook was a musical veteran who not only composed (he penned the classic "I'm Comin', Virginia") but also taught voice, conducted, and was a respected violinist. Also a scholar, he had published his *Collection of Negro Songs*. Impressed with the young Buffalodian's affinity for black music, he took Arlen under his wing.

After the show left the Jamaica Theater for a pretour shakedown at the Cosmopolitan Theater in Manhattan, the composer and songplugger Harry Warren came on the scene—the third member of the quartet that would profoundly affect the life of Harold Arlen.

Warren had collaborated with Billy Rose the year before on a few songs and was known and respected in Tin Pan Alley for such moneymakers as "Rose of the Rio Grande" and the jazz musician's perennial "Nagasaki." A strong and steady popular song output since 1922 had earned him a contract as staff composer with the Remick Music Corporation, one of the biggest publishing firms in Tin Pan Alley. Warren had been born Salvatore Guaragna into an opera-loving Italian family and was a lifetime lover of opera; a self-taught musician, he had mastered no fewer than ten instruments. Initially he performed on one instrument or other in carnivals and vaudeville and was employed by the Vitagraph motion picture company as an onsite pianist to set the mood for performers in silent films.

Warren was in the Cosmopolitan one day in July 1929 and found Harold Arlen at the piano onstage. Fletcher Henderson had become ill and Harold was sitting in as dance accompanist. His small role in *Great Day!* as Cokey Joe left him plenty of time for other things, and he welcomed any relief from the monotony of playing the same music repeatedly.

Harold was familiar with the routine, having watched many dance rehearsals, and he knew the music very well. He sat through many tedious pauses as the choreographer corrected the dancers or demonstrated new steps; then, at a sign from the choreographer, Harold would signal the dancers with the "pickup," a two-bar vamp leading into the dance music. During the countless interruptions he amused himself by, as he put it, "fooling around" with the pickup— extending it, changing a note here and there, producing his own variation on a theme. When he was ready he would cue in the dancers with two emphatic chords. As the rehearsal progressed so did the variation. Arlen remembered that he continued "working away, fiddling with the chords, and . . . one of the people there says to me, 'What *is* that you're playing?'

"I didn't know; I wasn't composing anything. I was just improvising, naturally."

Will Marion Cook was the first of the professionals to sense a potential song in the mutating vamp. Noting its effect on the cast, he encouraged Arlen to develop it into a full-length song. It seemed like sage advice from a former composition student of Antonín Dvořák.

Enter Harry Warren. It was a hot day near the end of July and slightly cooler inside the Cosmopolitan; members of the company were clustered around the piano as the provisional rehearsal pianist amused them with a catchy, jazzy tune. He listened through a few bars, then asked Arlen what it was.

"Nothing," he was told, "just playing around with the pickup."

Warren convinced him that he had the makings of a song in his improvisation. When Warren learned that the song had no words, he said, "I know the guy to write it up."

Though not totally convinced, Arlen agreed to meet "the guy," who turned out to be an affable, unassuming veteran writer named Ted Koehler. About a decade older than Arlen, he was the perfect collaborator for an inexperienced songwriter who was then not particularly drawn to composition. "I didn't seek it out, or ask for it—it just happened," he told the writer Max Wilk years later.

Koehler, born in Washington, D.C., in 1894, was educated in New York and Newark, New Jersey. Because the family was musical, but not musically ambitious, he worked in his father's Manhattan photoengraving shop days; nights were spent playing in Newark's hot spots.

Koehler's moonlighting aggravated his father, who asserted that the late hours affected his son's work in the plant. He issued an ultimatum: Ted would be in his bed by midnight during the week (the weekends were his) or he could seek other employment and lodgings.

He did. He left home, walked over to the Sea Shell Theater, applied for the job of house pianist, and got it. In his midtwenties, Koehler began a career in music as a pianist, accompanist, and creator of songs, called "special material," for contemporary vaudeville stars, among them Sophie Tucker, Ruth Etting, even the film heartthrob Rudolph Valentino, whose career was in a temporary slump and who was compelled to freshen it up with appearances in vaudeville houses. This phase of Koehler's career took him as far west as Chicago, where he gave it up, then settled in New York. He joined the publishing firm of Piantadosi, then a subsidiary of Harry Warren's employer, Remick's, as a staff writer. By 1926 he had enough published songs to his credit to become a member of the American Society of Composers, Authors, and Publishers (ASCAP). Thus established, he married Elvira Hagen and the two settled in Brooklyn, where they lived when he was introduced to Harold Arlen.

Warren had arranged for them to meet at the Remick office in midtown Manhattan, the new site of Tin Pan Alley (the old office, once situated on East Twenty-eighth Street, had closed down and the publishers moved uptown to the West Forties). Koehler met a slender young man, well dressed, quiet, a bit diffident, ill at ease—until he sat at the piano and played his composition. Koehler knew immediately that he was not encountering just another "young fellow trying to be a writer." This fellow was a born musician, a superb pianist with a gift for composition.

Listening over and over to the piece (his habit, as Arlen would learn), Koehler began formulating an idea for a lyric. It was a rhythm number with the feel of a spiritual. His interest perked up when the second eight bars were repeated, a fourth higher than the first. The B section, the "release" or middle, as the composer generally called it, consisted of two statements of a striking four-bar sequence of descending seventh chords. Koehler realized he was not hearing a typical Tin Pan Alley effusion. Arlen's tune deviated from the standard A-A'-B-A song form by transposing the second section—possibly an echo of the blues, in which a phrase on the tonic chord is followed by a phrase on the subdominant, a fourth higher.

Koehler's attention was drawn to the emphatic three-note tag that rounded out the bugle call opening phrase. This pattern occurred throughout the three A sections.

"Get happy," he said.

They now had a tentative title, a three-syllable phrase repeated six times in the course of thirty-two bars of music. It remained for Koehler to fill in the lyrical blanks with words rooted in Negro spirituals, which had become a part of the American musical consciousness since the late nineteenth century with the debut of the Fisk Jubilee Singers. Koehler was a master of the vernacular, the language of the street, of folk expressions. His finished lyric employs references to "judgment day," "troubles," "the Lord," "the River" (patently the Jordan), and "sins" and "sinners." All they now required was the introductory verse; after some careful work, they had one, an unusual twenty-five bars instead of the conventional eight or sixteen, a recitativelike call to the sinners to come to a land "where the weary forever are free." The key word in the verse is "Hallelujah."

They had their song, and after playing and singing it for the Piantadosis, Harold Arlen was signed to a contract designating him a staff composer. The date was July 31, 1929. To his amazement he was to collect fifty dollars a week plus royalties, if any, simply to write songs. According to the twenty-one-year-old manager of Piantadosi, Edwin H. "Buddy" Morris, Arlen was not even required to work in their offices, except to show up with a tune now and then. Arlen immediately liked Morris; the two became lifelong friends and years later would become partners in their own publishing firm.

Encouraged by what he considered a generous financial arrangement, Arlen began to work with Koehler on other songs that summer. By the winter of 1929 that fifty dollars a week would seem like a veritable fortune. His next step was to leave the cast of the floundering *Great Day!*, and in time, with the assurance of affluence, he found himself new living quarters in the penthouse atop the Croydon Hotel on Madison Avenue at East Eighty-sixth Street.

Despite these symbols of success and his surface self-assurance, he suffered from anxiety. "Get Happy," he was certain, had been a felicitous accident, a gift out of the blue. He doubted that he could count on such providence again. As a precaution, Harold picked up a small, oblong book of manuscript paper from Carl Fischer's music shop, which he carried with him constantly in the event that another tune should drop from heaven. Whenever inspiration struck, he whipped out the book and wrote down anything from five or six notes to a bar or two. Out of these "jots," as he called them, he was able to develop an entire song when required.

Later, during a period when he was frequently interviewed, he referred to "Get Happy" as his "first song." Not quite true, although in his own mind, as he explained when questioned about this little misrepresentation, he amended the claim to "my first *professional* song." In the five years between 1924 and

1929 he had collaborated on an additional song with his first lyricist, Hyman Cheiffetz; in 1925 he had teamed up with another local aspirant for a couple of never-published songs; and during his tenure with the Buffalodians he had written a few songs and instrumentals. Among these were "Minor Gaff," a "blues fantasy" written with the band's second pianist, Dick George, and published in 1926, and his own piano solo, "Rhythmic Moments," published by Robbins in 1928, when he was still Harold Arluck.

"Rhythmic Moments" is a sprightly study in ragtime, complete with the traditional trio. More than a half century after its composition a young pianist, Kevin Cole, a specialist in American music, played it for him. Arlen was charmed by the piece and Cole's idiomatic interpretation. He then asked, "Who wrote that?" and was told, "You did." He chuckled and asked for the music, which he had not seen in fifty years and had forgotten. The subtitle, he read, was "A Modern Piano Solo." He laughed and suggested that it be revised to "A Minor Piano Solo."

When he and Koehler completed "Get Happy," Harold Arlen had already collaborated on ten compositions. Not counting the vanity publication, "My Gal, My Pal," only five were published, and none contributed to the fame of their composer. It would not be stretching too much to accept "Get Happy" as Harold Arlen's first song. His published pre-Koehler efforts did not amount to much, artistically or financially. The first, "The Album of My Dreams," grew out of an encounter at a party in February 1929. His playing attracted a proposal from Lou Davis, who was devoted to popular song and had ambitions of becoming a lyric writer. In his ASCAP biographical entry, Davis lists his occupations as "author" (i.e., lyricist) and "businessman." In short, his primary vocation was as a salesman dealing in meat for hotels and restaurants.

A not very distinguished ballad, "The Album of My Dreams" was recorded in August 1929 and did reasonably well. Arlen attributed the record's success to the song on the reverse side, but that song, "Perhaps," was in fact even less distinguished. A more likely reason was the performance, by the popular Rudy Vallee and His Connecticut Yankees. As for the not-prolific Davis, he did better financially with his 1922 collaboration with Henry Lange and the trumpeter Henry Busse, "Hot Lips."

Another 1929 publication was the attractive ballad "Rising Moon," with a lyric by Jack Ellis. It exhibits distinctive touches of the Arlen to come in its bluish harmonies and melodic turns. But neither "The Album of My Dreams" nor "Rising Moon" was preparation for the rhythmic logic and drive of "Get Happy."

In Ted Koehler, Arlen had found the ideal collaborator. While their song was being prepared for publication and the Piantadosi pluggers, Koehler and Arlen worked up additional numbers. They met regularly at an office in the Strand Theatre Building, then advertised as "the first deluxe moving picture palace in

New York." While they worked and waited there was no word from the Pian-tadosis about the progress of their work. For Arlen, the most memorable event of that summer was the August arrival over the city of the majestic Graf zeppelin. They quit work to observe the giant German airship soar overhead, then returned to a new song, "You Wanted Me, I Wanted You."

Sometime in autumn word spread that a producer named Ruth Selwyn was planning a musical revue to star a popular nightclub performer, Ruth Etting. A graduate of the Chicago Academy of Fine Arts, Etting had begun her career as a costume designer in a nightclub. Looking for more active participation, she found work in the chorus of the Marigold Gardens Theatre in 1925, when she met Ted Koehler. It was he who fully appreciated her distinctive vocal talents— she was a natural singer, but not much of a dancer. Koehler talked the manage-ment of the Gardens into giving her solo spots in their revue. Two years later she made her Broadway debut singing her zesty rendition of "Shaking the Blues Away" in the *Ziegfeld Follies of 1927,* following that with her torchy signature "Love Me or Leave Me" in the 1928 Eddie Cantor musical *Whoopee.* Ruth Etting was a star who could sing rhythm as well as blues. Her casting in the proposed Selwyn revue and her reunion with Ted Koehler had everything to do with the interpolation of "Get Happy" into the score of the show.

Ruth Selwyn, the wife of a major stage and film producer, Edgar Selwyn, was familiar with the revue form. As Ruth Wilcox she had appeared as a vocalist and dancer in some of the early *George White's Scandals* before she married Selwyn. Now, at age twenty-four, she was to earn the distinction of being Broadway's first female producer. Her show, to be called *Ruth Selwyn's Nine-Fifteen Revue,* would prove to be a hodgepodge, consisting of sketches by writers ranging from Ring Lardner to Anita Loos and Eddie Cantor. Most of the score was written by Kay Swift with lyrics by her banker-husband, James Paul Warburg, using the pen name "Paul James." (The diminutive Swift was classically trained and began writing songs under the influence of George Gershwin. The year before, she and Warburg had written the popular "Can't We Be Friends" for *The First Little Show.*)

Swift's further contribution to the show was the acquisition of a Gershwin song, "The World Is Mine," a reject from the 1927 Fred Astaire success *Funny Face.* With a few revisions in the lyric the song became "Toddling Along" in Selwyn's revue. The score, too, was a bit of a mélange, with assorted songs by the lyricist Edward Eliscu writing with the composers Manning Sherwin, Rudolf Friml, and (posthumously) Victor Herbert.

Except for his own songs, Harold Arlen later recalled only one that he ad-mired, the Swift-James "Up among the Chimney Pots," a stylish ballad sung by Ruth Etting. Of the three Arlen-Koehler songs Selwyn had selected, "Get Happy" was placed in the prime first-act finale spot. That, too, would be sung by the show's one star, Etting. Arlen was elated—his first time out as a professional songwriter and in a Broadway show! Koehler, the veteran, was a bit more subdued. Neither had reckoned with Busby Berkeley and his staging.

Before Christmas the company moved on to Boston. By coincidence, the Gershwins' *Strike Up the Band* was there, also in its tryout phase. Arlen's greatest thrill was meeting the Gershwin brothers and hearing George compliment him on the musical structure of "Get Happy."

If Gershwin found the song "exciting," it could not have been thanks to the song's setting in the show, which in Arlen's words, "made no sense." The curtain opened on a sunny, sandy beach. Etting, in a bathing suit, steps forth to begin her message to the sun-drenched "sinners" attired for an afternoon dip. When the lyric exhorted them to "wash your sins 'way in the tide," they were certainly dressed for it.

Despite Berkeley's incongruous staging, "Get Happy" was the most memorable, energetic number of the show, the sole musical survivor of a theatrical misconception. The graceful, literate "Up among the Chimney Pots" became a cult favorite among song aficionados, however.

In Boston, the *Nine-Fifteen Revue* was quickly perceived by the professional New York group as a pretty hopeless endeavor. Edgar Selwyn tried to help by dispatching the director of his hit *Strike Up the Band,* Alexander Leftwich, to try his magic on Mrs. Selwyn's show. Leftwich, on viewing the shambles, did the best he could; he also made certain that his name would not appear anywhere in the revue's credits.

The Selwyn name made history in 1930 by being associated with the year's first hit (Edgar and *Strike Up the Band*) and first flop (Ruth and her *Nine-Fifteen Revue*). Ruth's endeavor opened at the George M. Cohan Theatre in February 1930; the opening proved to be an inglorious event. As Arlen and Koehler watched, they saw two inadvertent pratfalls by two members of the chorus. Ruth Selwyn slipped out of the theater before the curtain fell on the second act. After six additional blundering performances the show was humanely shut down. Harold Arlen added another chapter to his study of the musical theater.

A curious, perhaps trivial but telling footnote: the *Nine-Fifteen Revue* premiered on the eleventh, a Tuesday. One week later, on the eighteenth, Ziegfeld's *Simple Simon* (with songs by Rodgers and Hart) opened at the Majestic. The star, who introduced the classic "Ten Cents a Dance," was none other than Ruth Etting. Having sensed the fate of a sinking vessel while dancing on its heaving deck, she jumped ship with remarkable alacrity. She had also, within a week, introduced two American song classics in two different theaters. For some unknown reason she never recorded "Get Happy."

The two happy beneficiaries of the brief life of the *Nine-Fifteen Revue* were Arlen and Koehler, for it had initiated the long life of their first song. "Get Happy" quickly became what at the time was called a "noisy song." Remick's (not their subsidiary Piantadosi) rushed it into print, with Ruth Etting's winsome face on the cover. Soon bands were playing "the hallelujah song" all over town. Recordings, predominantly jazz instrumentals, began to appear. At the time the song became, in Arlen's phrase, "a rhythm standard" rather than a pop tune, fascinating to play but difficult for singers. "Get Happy," he believed, did not blossom until two decades later, when Judy Garland revived it in 1950 in *Summer Stock*, her last picture at Metro-Goldwyn-Mayer. The song sequence, filmed weeks after the picture was practically completed, having been delayed by Garland's physical and emotional problems, is itself a classic in styling, vocal power, and movement.

The failed revue had a further benefit. The ambitious producer Earl Carroll had been one of the dissatisfied travelers who had seen the show in Boston; he, too, admired the song by two writers he had never heard of. Carroll aspired to surpass the great showman Florenz Ziegfeld as a producer of opulent musical revues. He did not succeed, lacking as he did Ziegfeld's flair for gorgeous sets and costumes, his canny choice of a smart production staff, and his ballyhooed "glorification of the American girl." Ziegfeld had been challenged earlier by an alumnus, George White with his *Scandals of 1919*. Carroll began his challenge when the *Vanities* were unveiled, so to speak, in 1923. White and Carroll were determined to go a step further in disrobing that Ziegfeldian "American girl."

Carroll was one up on his rivals: he had done time in a federal penitentiary, a decided asset in a law-flouting era. Carroll had earned his stripes because of a party he had given to celebrate the victory of Countess Vera Cathcart over the U.S. Bureau of Immigration. Because of the international sensation caused by her divorce in London from the earl of Cathcart, the Bureau barred her from the United States on the grounds of "moral turpitude." Upon her entry into the country, early in 1926, Carroll honored the fighting countess with an after-hours celebration in his theater to which he had invited hundreds of guests.

With consummate élan, Carroll placed a bathtub center stage and filled it with contraband champagne. As he curtained her with an opera cape, a seventeen-year-old artist's model, Joyce Hawley, shed her clothes and stepped into the tub. With a flourish Carroll dropped the cape and invited his guests to take a glass and imbibe or, if they wished, merely ogle the tall, blue-eyed beauty. The exhibition was cut short when Hawley suddenly burst into tears, and she, the tub, and champagne were whisked into the wings. Soon after, she began a brief career in the theater as "The Queen of the Bath."

This newsworthy event was reported in the press and excited the interest of the Federal Prohibition Bureau, which summoned Carroll before a grand jury. He swore that the tub on his stage had contained nothing but a nude woman and ginger ale. He was not believed and was found guilty of perjury and violation of the Volstead Act. Fined two thousand dollars, he was sentenced to a year and a day in the federal prison in Atlanta. After four months he was released and, with his notoriety enhanced by his short stay in jail, was ready for the next

Vanities. That edition, thanks to the Federal Prohibition Bureau, ran for more than four hundred performances. Carroll's *Sketch Book* of 1929 did an excellent even four hundred.

When Carroll offered Arlen and Koehler musical spots in his next show, the *Vanities of 1930,* they happily signed the contract. Their song "One Love," a beautifully fashioned waltz, would lead to another skirmish with the law. The transgressor this time was named Faith Bacon. Following the vocal by John Hale, she entered to dance to the suggestive choreography of LeRoy Prinz. The costumes that year were designed by Charles LeMaire and a twenty-one-year-old Vincente Minnelli. Bacon, however, was unencumbered by any of their designs, for her working ensemble consisted of her own skin and two large fans, artfully positioned most of the time.

After the show premiered in July, word of the "One Love" fan dance spread rapidly, which brought the morals squad into the New Amsterdam Theatre. An additional objection was filed against a skit in which a comic, Jimmy Savo, playing a window dresser, changed the outfits of the alleged mannequins. More brief nudity.

Having achieved good press coverage, Carroll promised, with a straight face, to sanitize the offending moments, and the show went on, still with Faith Bacon and the mannequins, well into the next year. Arlen and Koehler did well financially with their weekly royalties from Carroll, while their names now drew attention on Broadway and in the business.

While the *Vanities* proved to be a superb springboard for a beginning songwriting team, it was, like all revues, the usual mix of song, dance, and comedy, with sometimes peculiar motifs not always depending on undraped young women. The first-act finale, titled "Let Freedom Ring," was an attack on Prohibition, which the writers declared had been foisted on the American people against their will. Carroll's sojourn in Atlanta had not been for nothing. But it was a curious form of editorializing in what the theater historian Stanley Green describes, and rightly, as a "witless entertainment for wilted theatregoers" that "proudly claimed to be 'Meeting America's Demand for Sophisticated Entertainment,' a euphemistic assurance that the girls would be bare and the jokes raw."

So, instead of a lively musical number, act 1 closed with Jack Benny as George Washington (in a powdered wig) reading from the Declaration of Independence, then as Lincoln (beardless) intoning from the Gettysburg Address, and finally as a congressman extolling the virtues of spirits. "Preceding this final peroration," Green noted, "a platoon of doughboys were seen bravely going over the top to the strains of 'Over There,' while throughout the entire spectacle decorous young ladies, strategically sashed in red and blue satin (the girls provided the white), wearing Swiss Guard plumage, paraded about piping their determined objections to the oppressive law." One critic, Robert Benchley, viewed this sketch as Carroll's bid for a presidential nomination.

As always, other writers contributed to that year's *Vanities,* among them Jay Gorney and Edgar Y. Harburg. Arlen and Harburg, a short, trim, dynamic lyricist with a radical social conscience, would meet again.

Ironically, the major musical hit of the show was an import by the English writers Ray Nobel, James Campbell, and Reginald Connelly. "Goodnight, Sweetheart" was interpolated into the *Vanities* sometime after the show had opened (and was sung into extensive popularity by Rudy Vallee). It was a surprisingly innocuous song in light of the generally scandalous character of the *Vanities of 1930.* Harold Arlen's inventive little waltz deserved more than its fanned-up notoriety. It was his favorite among the songs he had written up to that time. There are few Arlen waltzes; "Get Happy" revealed him as a master of rhythm, "One Love" as a master of melody.

After the premiere, Celia and Samuel Arluck came from Syracuse to see, but primarily to hear, the frequently risqué *Vanities.* The Arlucks' reaction to the show was not recorded, but according to the *Buffalo Times,* which kept an eye on local celebrities, they had attended the show "because their son had written the music. They were very proud of their Hyman."

They, especially the cantor, were less pleased with Hyman's companion, a very blonde young woman named Frances Williams. She was also in the theater and appeared, earlier that year, in the *International Revue* (as a replacement for Gertrude Lawrence) and was preparing for a leading role in Cole Porter's forthcoming show *The New Yorkers.* She and their son appeared to be very friendly, even affectionate, but Samuel shrugged that off, since his son said nothing about marriage. Samuel doubted too that Hyman would marry out of his faith.

Another opportunity that came to Arlen and Koehler from the popularity of "Get Happy" was an invitation from the proprietors of the Silver Slipper, a club on Broadway at Forty-eighth Street. Regarded as one of the smartest clubs in Times Square, it was noted for its clientele: Broadway stars and less than stars, the Park Avenue rich and well-born, and criminals. Jimmy Durante, who had played the club, explained the welcomed presence of the last: "The stick-up man," he observed, "or the book-maker makes a bigger flash with his coin than the swankiest member of the four hundred." The Silver Slipper, like several nightclubs in the city, was in fact operated by the mob. It was considered punctilious not to bar rival underworld club owners from your establishment, provided the rivalry did not rise to a critical, even fatal pitch, as it did on occasion. Billy Rose, a sometime club operator, pointed out that the only locality in which to find a well-dressed bootlegger was Broadway, often as an investor in shows, especially musicals, and clubs.

The Silver Slipper provided not only expensive entertainment but also the contraband that had sent Earl Carroll to Atlanta. It was a major outlet for the alcoholic products of the local Phoenix Cereal Beverage Company.

Harold Arlen was innocent of these enterprises. He remembered an earlier experience at the club, when the great jazz musician Bix Beiderbecke had complimented him on his style. The show at the Silver Slipper was elegant and well produced, and it employed "name" performers; Arlen and Koehler thought it was an excellent setting for their songs. It would quickly move them up to Harlem.

No sooner had the Carroll revue opened than their new effort, inexplicably entitled *Biff-Boom-Bang* (and one Arlen forgot he had ever written) premiered at the Silver Slipper. Significantly, it featured a couple of numbers that were more germane to Harlem than Times Square, "Shakin' the African" and "I Was Born with the Blues in My Heart."

There was also the shamelessly conventional "I'll Call It Love," which, considering the glittering and hard-boiled mise-en-scène, was burdened with a lyric that the adept Koehler could only have written with tongue in both cheeks. The verse is satirically (one hopes) mawkish, portraying a dreamer who "Lives for fame / Not for the sake of gold / Or such worldly gain," but to leave behind "a mem'ry worthwhile." The chorus, too, is decidely un-Koehleresque:

> *I'll paint a heavenly masterpiece*
> *Wond'rous, for it will be fashioned after you dear*
> *With love to guide my hand dear*
> *'Twill bring me fame.*

Arlen chose to forget this song, although he saved a copy of the lyric. None of the *Biff-Boom-Bang* songs were published, though the Arlen-Koehler contribution to the show had made an impression on the management. As soon as they completed that little score, they were assigned to write the songs for another, more ambitious revue entitled *Brown Sugar,* starring, according to the program, the "Black Berries of 1931." The show would feature the Duke Ellington Orchestra and was scheduled to open in the fall of 1930 at another outlet owned by the Phoenix Cereal Beverage Company. The major stockholder, if that's the word, was Owen "Owney" Madden. They had never heard of him, but they were familiar—who wasn't?—with his establishment, the Cotton Club in Harlem.

COTTON
CLUB

*A*s an economically grim 1930 ended, the fortunes of Harold Arlen and Ted Koehler rose while the nation's declined dramatically. The cause was specified by a prescient investment advisor who told his clients in the late summer of 1929, "Sooner or later a crash is coming and it may be terrific." His prediction upset everyone on Wall Street, but he was right. The crash came on "Black Tuesday," October 29, 1929, inspiring *Variety*'s headline the next day: "WALL ST. LAYS AN EGG." What followed was not so amusing.

A Stock Exchange guard who had witnessed the upheaval on the floor described the scene: "They roared like a lot of lions and tigers. They hollered and screamed, they clawed at one another's collars. It was like a bunch of crazy men. Every once in a while, when Radio or Steel or Auburn would take another tumble, you'd see some poor devil collapse and fall to the floor." The wild ride in the market, which even less-affluent Americans had taken, ground to a sudden stop and collapsed.

Unemployment in 1929 stood at 3.2 percent; in 1930 it more than doubled, throwing over 4 million Americans out of work. But new job opportunities, thanks to the Eighteenth Amendment's outlawing of alcohol, were in the offing.

By January 1930 the amendment had been in force for about a decade and was obviously not working. In those ten years, the records of the Metropolitan Insurance Company revealed, deaths attributed to alcoholism among its policyholders alone was six times higher than it had been in 1920. Prohibition had, in fact, inaugurated a new mode of employment with its own occupational hazards and high mortality rate. One of the pioneers in this highly risky but highly profitable industry was Chicago's Al Capone, aptly described by the historian Carl H. Giles as the man who had been elected "President of Prohibition."

His was a solid platform: "Prohibition," he believed, "looked like a good opening for a lot of smart young men." He then assumed the leadership in the organization of the rackets in Chicago. The most lucrative was the distribution, often forcible, of liquor and beer to the bars, speakeasies, clubs, and hotels in that wide-open city.

His New York counterpart was Owney Madden, the behind-the-scenes proprietor of the Cotton Club, as well as the distributor of spirits to all of Manhattan's West Side. Unlike Capone, he shunned publicity, explaining that it was bad for business.

Madden's family had moved to Manhattan from Liverpool in 1903, when Madden was eleven, and settled in the predominantly Irish section of the West Side known as Hell's Kitchen. Most of Madden's education was picked up in the streets as a member of the murderous Gopher gang, which specialized in break-ins, raids on the New York Central freight yards, and an occasional killing. By age seventeen Madden had five murders to his credit and had earned the title of "Owney the Killer"; a local policeman called him "that little banty rooster from hell."

A slender, compact man, he was quiet, elusive, and deadly. With a record of forty-four arrests, he was found guilty of murder and sentenced to serve ten to twenty years "up the river," in the expression of the period, in Sing Sing, the state prison in Ossining, on the Hudson River in upstate New York. Despite Madden's protestations of innocence, there was no doubt that he and Little Patsy Doyle were rivals in the rackets and that Doyle was dead with six bullets in him, undoubtedly delivered at Madden's instigation.

When Harold Arlen met Owney Madden in 1930, free on parole for seven years, Madden was no longer "Owney the Killer." He had returned to his old haunts in Hell's Kitchen from Ossining to discover a changed world. The police had dealt harshly with his old gang, the Gophers, and put them out of business. Staked by his friend, the gangster Larry Fay, he began his new life in such modern enterprises as boxing and the "protection" of laundries and taxis. Fay introduced him to rum-running, hijacking, and assorted arts associated with Prohibition.

Madden was about thirty when he decided to take Al Capone's advice to the "smart young man." He announced that he was bored with "these legitimate rackets" and that he sought "an investment where you can put your money in this week and pull it out double next week, or the next." Encouraged by Fay, he founded the Phoenix Cereal Beverage Company, situated near his penthouse apartment on West Twenty-sixth Street. From this source flowed the cereal beverage known as "Madden's No. 1": real, full-strength beer. It could be consumed in virtually every bar, speakeasy, or club whose proprietor wished to stay in business on the West Side as far north as Harlem.

Arlen found Madden, whom he saw rarely in the Cotton Club, an unassuming, soft-spoken man with steel blue eyes and rarely a smile. The journalist Stanley Walker wrote that Madden had a profile "like a falcon's. . . . The nose was a fierce beak. He had the first requisite of leadership, 'a bone in the face.' " Madden dressed well and expensively, though his speech bore traces of his Hell's Kitchen upbringing.

A skilled chief executive officer, Madden left the day-to-day operation of the Cotton Club to his trusted lieutenants, Harry Block and George "Big Frenchy" DeMange. Madden remained deep in the background because consorting with known criminals and dealing in illegal spirits would have merited him a return trip to Ossining.

The putative "manager" of the Cotton Club was Herman Stark, an experienced nightclub operator with no known police record. Beefy Big Frenchy DeMange, Madden's inside man, was always around to oversee the functioning of the club. Harry Block, however, had been eliminated from the club's management before Arlen and Koehler had come on the scene. Shortly before they were hired by the Cotton Club, a misunderstanding occurred that resulted in the virtual demolition of its competitor in Harlem, the Plantation Club. In retaliation, Harry Block was found some weeks later, shot to death in the elevator of his apartment house.

It was no secret, though not noised about, that Madden was the major owner of the Cotton Club, as well as the Silver Slipper downtown and the West Side Winona Club. He was on good monetary terms with Tammany Hall leader James J. "Jimmy" Hines, who managed to secure case dismissals in magistrate's court and to arrange for the transfers of overzealous police officers. As a result, the Cotton Club was rarely troubled by the law.

Of greater significance than the shadowy proprietorship at the Cotton Club was Dan Healy, who had greeted Prohibition with his taunting impersonation of its dour-faced symbol. Danny had begun as a dancer, singer, and comic. He had appeared in Irving Berlin's army musical, *Yip-Yip-Yaphank* in 1918, after which he returned to vaudeville. He reunited with Berlin to appear in the *Ziegfeld Follies of 1927* after a brief stay in the short-lived Rodgers and Hart musical *Betsy*.

Like Harold Arlen, Healy had found the performer's life unsatisfactory; he preferred producing. Endowed with the gift of gab and a sharp, quick wit, he enjoyed serving as a waggish master of ceremonies, keeping the shows moving fast in nightclubs. Before joining the Madden group at the Cotton Club he had worked in a club show backed by a Madden rival, the trigger-happy Jack "Legs"

Diamond. While working on the Silver Slipper production of *Biff-Boom-Bang,* Healy met Harold and Ted, liked them, and loved their songs.

When he joined the staff of the Cotton Club, Healy put in a number of good words for Arlen and Koehler. He demonstrated for Herman Stark and Big Frenchy DeMange some of the Cotton Club–like numbers from the Silver Slipper revue—a blues and the peppy "Shakin' the African." And "Get Happy" was still making noise.

Healy's predecessor had been Lew Leslie, a specialist in all-black revues; when he left the Cotton Club for Broadway, he took its resident songwriters, Dorothy Fields and Jimmy McHugh, with him. Their Cotton Club songs have been forgotten, but once on Broadway they turned out such memorable songs as "I Can't Give You Anything But Love," "On the Sunny Side of the Street," and "Exactly Like You." After Broadway they moved on to Hollywood with equal success. Dorothy Fields, one of the outstanding lyricists of the time, would work also with Arthur Schwartz, Jerome Kern, and Harold Arlen.

Healy was a character out of Damon Runyon; his conversations crackled with Broadwayese. He described a well-known homosexual Broadway star as "tender," without a note of malice or judgment. DeMange was "The Big Frog" (but not to his forbidding face). Healy's formula for nightclub shows was "Pace, pace, pace!" They should be uptempo, particularly in the dances and the rhythm numbers. In between there were comic sketches with blackout lines of salacious intent. After all, the rich and well-born who went to Harlem in tuxedos, ermines, and pearls expected as much in a locale where song and dance were notoriously uninhibited and its residents flashed broad grins and had rhythm.

Arlen's first Cotton Club show was entitled *Brown Sugar,* with the added parenthetical "Sweet but Unrefined," lest anyone miss the intent of its entertainment. It would be, according to its flyer, a production "with the Proportions of a Broadway Revue." And it was. The basic ingredient was the band (Arlen was fortunate; during his time at the club, his songs were introduced by the bands of Cab Calloway, Jimmie Lunceford, and Duke Ellington). The club's own proportions encompassed a sizable dance floor, with dining areas surrounding it, and a stage large enough to hold the band and the show's headliners, vocalists, comedians, and star dancers. The chorus used the dance floor.

There were two shows, the first at midnight and the second at around two in the morning. Between acts and between the two shows, the band provided music for the dancers. The Cotton Club was advertised as "The Aristocrat of Harlem," a cachet that fell from the scarlet lips of Edwina, the Lady Mountbatten. At the same time she promised to tell all her friends in London about the Cotton Club. Maurice Chevalier, in from Paris, declared it "the most sophisticated café in New York."

When the Columbia Broadcasting System sent its sports announcer Ted Husing to introduce the club to a wider American public, its fame spread nationally as well as internationally. The opening-night broadcasts from the Cotton Club became an annual event. Initially, the manager, Herman Stark, resisted the broadcasts—he was not about to give anything away. But the broadcasts proved to be good for business. The tables were crowded with expectant (white) faces: show-business personalities and tourists, as well as "aristocrats" from Park Avenue, even London and Paris. It was the club's aristocratic policy, however, to bar Harlem residents from the club, unless they worked there.

Danny Healy kept the performers as active as the waiters in a lively show that ran for about two hours, with one intermission. Like a Broadway musical, *Brown Sugar* opened with the traditional "ice breaker," an energetic song-and-dance number ("Harlem's Hot As Hades") featuring the club's "bronze beauties" and a specialty dance by Maude Russell, blessed with the "best pair of legs in Harlem," according to Healy's program annotation.

If a new popular dance was making the rounds, it was duly noted. The recently imported dance from Cuba known as "La Rhumba" was introduced by a vocal solo, backed by a singing group and demonstrated by the dancers. Healy's program commentary exhorted the audience to reward the hardworking group with applause from "You and You and You."

The audience, having been primed, was now treated to a "specialty" by one of the club's resident stars, Cora La Redd. Her specialty was the mandatory bawdy song. Arlen detested these songs, but they did not faze Koehler. Once he had written the lyric, Arlen would apply the music with the proviso that the song would never be published. Harold was happy his parents did not come in for the Cotton Club shows; nightclubs were not for them.

Another parent, Lew Fields, the father of the lyricist Dorothy Fields and a major vaudeville star and producer, was infuriated by one of the specialties in the 1927 edition. It was his daughter's first Cotton Club show, and he attended opening night. Then an interpolated song, not by Fields and McHugh, was introduced. "It was so dirty," Dorothy Fields recalled, "I blushed." Lew Fields went further. He insisted that Stark announce to the audience that his daughter was not responsible for that lyric. Stark complied, amused at such indignation from a former burlesque comic.

For Arlen there was yet another embarrassing specialty in *Brown Sugar*'s second scene. Healy introduced Leitha Hill to sing a blues that she had learned "when she was a farmer's daughter or something." The audience was prepared, having enjoyed her rendition in the previous scene of a most salacious song about a pussy cat. The setting was a dentist's office, second only to a doctor's office for burlesque skits, replete with innuendo and double entendre. The scene involved "The Patient," "The Impatient Husband," and "That Certain Dentist." Leitha Hill was the patient who sang "Toothache Blues."

Harold Arlen went along with the management and Koehler in setting such lyrics as "Chase the Cat," insisting that he would not be credited for the music.

Since songs by Ellington and Calloway were interpolated into the shows, there was some question as to who wrote which song; besides, the audience was indifferent to authorship. Should anyone wish to acquire a copy of one of the specialties, however (sheet music was on sale in the lobby and checkroom), they would not be found there because of Arlen's objection to their publication.

Harold could understand that the Mink Set, as he called it, was "escaping Park Avenue for the earthier realities of Harlem" and expected spicy titillation. But the taxis and limousines that brought the Mink Set to the corner of Lenox Avenue and 142nd Street easily avoided the less glamorous addresses of Harlem. It did not concern their passengers, if they noticed at all, that the club's audiences were white. The performers (except on Sunday nights, when guest performers arrived from Broadway), the band, and the waiters were all black. At the tables a sea of white faces, attached to well-fed bodies and clothed in the best, reveled in Koehler's lyrical "realities."

As for the costumes of the dancers, "scanty" was the operative adjective. Billed as the Blackberries Crop of the Year, they were genetically black but boasted remarkably light complexions. "The cream of sepia talent," proclaimed the club's brochure, "bronze beauties" all. An excess of ethnicity, dark skin, or "Negroid" features would keep you out of the Cotton Club's dance troupe.

Koehler was more at ease at the club than Arlen; both got along well with the cast and musicians. Harold was a special favorite because of his music as well as his singing and playing, which were singularly compatible with the Harlem setting. Of the three white composers most admired by black jazz musicians—Gershwin, Hoagy Carmichael, and Harold Arlen—the compositions of Arlen are closest to black roots. Gershwin's jazz-age rhythmic drive and harmonies inspired many jazz improvisations and original pieces, such as Sidney Bechet's "Shag." Countless "originals" by jazzers from Charlie Parker to Woody Herman are based on the chord sequence of "I Got Rhythm." Arlen was accepted in Harlem, too, for his warmth and utter lack of bigotry.

Working with Koehler was remarkably free of friction, although at times it could be exasperating. Arlen's genial, soft-spoken collaborator could be frustratingly noncommittal about his tunes. Arlen liked this "quiet, philosophic" partner, who was decidedly non–show business and Tin Pan Alley—no cigar clenched in teeth and his eye out for the next hit.

It was Koehler's habit to stretch out on Arlen's sofa, eyes closed, while the composer played a new song idea over and over. Arlen suspected that his lyricist had drifted off to sleep.

"Ted!" he would snap. Koehler would sit up, explaining that he was "saving my cells," and that the melody was safely in his head and the lyric was in the works.

Arlen told Max Wilk in 1972 that he never understood Koehler's work habits. "You had to sit at the piano and play for days and days. Sometimes all night. . . .

I had the feeling sometimes that he couldn't stand being alone, and desperately wanted company." (A curious statement, for Koehler was married and had a home in Brooklyn; his marriage lasted a lifetime.)

For the younger Arlen it was, as he realized later, an exceptional experience in the art of songwriting. Koehler's unhurried, workmanlike routine initiated Arlen into a strife-free collaboration. More than one songwriting team evidenced fits of distrust, envy, even outright hostility. Consider the on-and-off association of Lerner and Loewe, Vernon Duke's not speaking to his lyricists, or Carolyn Leigh's hurling an ashtray at the composer Cy Coleman.

When Harold Arlen improvised himself out of a performance career, he believed he was leaving rivalry, petty skirmishing, and ignorance behind; he was mistaken. His relaxed apprenticeship with Koehler did not prepare him for what would come.

At the Cotton Club Ted Koehler contributed more than the lyrics to the show. He offered good production suggestions to Danny Healy, and he helped with the sets, from design to construction (one of his hobbies was carpentry). More introspective, Harold Arlen now began to compensate for the schooling he had avoided. He became an omnivorous reader, mostly nonfiction and often several books at a time. He carried small volumes of philosophy or poetry with him to dip into during his free moments. He was especially devoted to the stoic humanism and beauty (in translation) of Marcus Aurelius's *Meditations*. He was drawn to the poetry of Rainer Maria Rilke for its musicality and mysticism. Montaigne's studies of man and nature fascinated him. His lighter reading he found in several newspapers, especially the *New York Times, Tribune,* and the literate *Sun.*

In the club, while Koehler was busy with a hammer and saw, Arlen spent much time with the musicians and cast. He learned the latest local dance steps, "truckin'," the shim-sham-shimmy, variations on the old lindy hop. He delighted the performers with his parody of Broadway's racist paternalism; he picked up their speech and singing styles and, at the piano, captivated the musicians with a innate mastery of melody, rhythm, and improvisation.

A new musical friend, the ex-Texan Roger Edens, whom Arlen had met on one of his customary rounds of the music publishing houses, found this warm acceptance by the youngsters (most chorus members and dancers were in their teens) rather puzzling. Arlen was virtually a member of the tough, intolerant management. He could dine at the Cotton Club; they could not. He could use the patrons' rest room; they were forced to find other facilities. He could bring his friends; they could not. And still, Edens believed, Arlen's relationship with the Cotton Club's performers, from star to chorus member, was unusual. Harold was one of them, with his gentle sense of fun and his unaffected, deep, and hearty laugh.

Edens found it exhilarating and educational to accompany Arlen to rehearsals in those "happy, carefree, naïve days." The Great Depression seemed to pass them by. Arlen had his staff composer's income, which in time was doubled to a hundred dollars a week; in addition, he received fifty dollars a week during the run of the Cotton Club shows, and royalties from sheet music sales and recordings had begun to flow. He spent the extra money on stylish clothes and books.

Edens, soon after his arrival in New York and after being introduced to some of the right people by Arlen, began his theatrical (and later, film) rise as Ethel Merman's pianist in the Gershwin smash *Girl Crazy* in 1930. Three years later he accompanied Merman to Hollywood, where he stayed after she returned to Broadway. In Hollywood Edens became a powerful behind-the-scenes musical figure, particularly at Metro-Goldwyn-Mayer as a member of the Arthur Freed unit. He and Harold Arlen remained lifelong friends from the Cotton Club days on through Hollywood.

Cotton Club rehearsals were a good deal more relaxed and informal than those of *Girl Crazy* at the Alvin Theatre. Looking back years later, Edens, though aware of the club performers' "fierce insularity and dignity within themselves that resented so-called 'professional Southernism' that was rampant in New York in those days," noted that the resentment seemed not to apply to Harold Arlen.

Edens was no bigot, but as an outsider, he was only partially aware of the bitterness seething among members of the cast. Howard "Stretch" Johnson, a dancer at the Cotton Club (as was his fifteen-year-old sister, Winnie), conceded that the shows were

> very sophisticated, but they were cloaked in primitive and exotic garb. They were top-flight performances designed to appease the appetite for a certain type of black performance, the smiling black, the shuffling black, the blackfaced black, the minstrel coon-show atmosphere which existed. It was almost mandatory to have a jungle number with shake-dancers, with a lot of flesh exposed. And while it wasn't stated as such, certainly the light color of the flesh gave it a kind of exoticism and forbidden-fruit quality . . . that added to the excitement and exhilaration of the audience.

It was healthier to keep your bitterness to yourself. Johnson, after the Cotton Club was gone, may have overlooked some positive aspects of the Cotton Club productions. There were star vocalists known on Broadway as well as in Harlem: Leitha Hill, Adelaide Hall, and Ethel Waters. There were such dancers as Bill "Bojangles" Robinson, the Nicholas Brothers, Avon Long, and the eccentric dancers Earl "Snakehips" Johnson and "Dynamite" Hooker. There were comic skits with raunchier blackout curtain lines than those of Minsky's downtown burlesque.

The popular bands featured at the Cotton Club brought in the customers. The Sunday broadcasts spread the sounds and renown of Ellington, Calloway, and Lunceford across the nation and drew a celebrity audience of such popular musicians as Irving Berlin, Paul Whiteman, George Gershwin, and Cole Porter, as well as classical artists such as Jascha Heifetz and Maurice Ravel.

Though not especially noted for its cuisine, the Cotton Club offered a menu of American and Chinese dishes. There was also a "drink list" and a cover charge. Black stars were always welcome and were expected to provide a little free entertainment. As employees, Arlen and Koehler were entitled to free meals. Arlen particularly recalled the steak "frivolity sandwiches," which cost $1.50. In contrast, at the Croydon Hotel's dining room Arlen could order a complete dinner for $1.20: "Broiled Half Spring Chicken, Peas in Butter, Fried Sweet Potatoes." At the Cotton Club the same chicken went for $1.75; à la carte potatoes and peas added fifty cents each to the bill. A dinner, without alcoholic drinks, could amount to over five Depression dollars.

Barney Josephson, who later opened the first interracial nightclub, Café Society in Greenwich Village, recalled the Cotton Club's drink list: "The booze was all bootleg. In those days you could bring your own bottle. You brought your own pint on your hip, and they would serve you a glass bucket of ice cubes and splits of ginger ale or soda water, just one little bottle, enough to make one highball, and they would charge a good price for it." "Splits" were half bottles that cost a dollar—the corner grocery charged a nickel for a full bottle.

A bottle of Madden's No. 1 also went for a dollar; a glass of milk, an unlikely item on the Cotton Club menu, was fifty cents. The bootleg booze that Josephson remembered was the real McCoy, in Dan Healy's recollection. No stinting there.

The Cotton Club was like a peculiar island. Despite its gangland management, it was remarkably free of mobster incidents. Arlen remembered only two: the killing of Harry Block, before Arlen's time, and the kidnapping of Big Frenchy DeMange by an upstart gunman, Vincent Coll, who challenged Madden in Manhattan and Dutch Schultz in the Bronx over the distribution of beverages. Big Frenchy was returned unharmed, after Madden paid Coll thirty-five thousand dollars in ransom money, which Coll needed to pay his expensive attorney, Samuel Leibowitz. In a disagreement with Schultz, his former boss, Coll machine-gunned a street in Harlem, killing one five-year-old boy and leaving four other children, ranging in age from two to four, screaming in pain on the sidewalk. His target, one of Schultz's thugs, escaped unscathed, as did two bodyguards.

The shooting earned Coll the nickname "Mad Dog," and the imprudent kidnapping of Big Frenchy placed his name on some deadly lists, a unique coalition of the police and gangdom. Leibowitz got him off, but both the police and the mobsters put a price on "Mad Dog" Coll's head, "dead or alive."

He succeeded in eluding the law, but not Madden and Schultz. Newly married and needing money, Leibowitz having separated him from the bulk of his Big Frenchy ransom money, Coll decided to shake down Madden again. Rumor had it that he was on the phone with Madden when, by no coincidence, some of Schultz's men traced him to a booth in a West Twenty-third Street drugstore. The machine gunner sprayed the booth, and the twenty-three-year-old Mad Dog Coll slumped to the floor with fifteen steel-jacketed bullets in him.

Big Frenchy's kidnapping did not affect the smooth running of the Cotton Club. Harold Arlen did not associate his bosses with the headline coverage of Coll. As had Dorothy Fields before him, Arlen had found Big Frenchy and his associates at all times civil, despite some Hell's Kitchen roughage in their speech. When Fields was present the rule was "no profanity," and in retrospect, she remembered them to be "such gentlemen."

One late night after a show, Madden offered to drive Arlen home to the Croydon on Manhattan's Upper East Side, only slightly out of the way downtown to Madden's home on the West Side. It was the only time Arlen had ridden in a genuine Dusenburg, and bulletproof at that. He remembered, too, attending one of Madden's parties in his Hell's Kitchen penthouse with Frances Williams and Roger Edens, who was impressed with the mobster's luxurious way of life. Arlen knew very little until much later about Madden's source of income and saw him rarely. Once a Cotton Club show opened and was running, Arlen preferred to visit the downtown offices of Remick's or, later, Mills Music, which took over the publication of the songs written for the Cotton Club. Irving Mills was a manager, publisher, and collaborator of Duke Ellington's, who specialized in publishing the music of black songwriters.

When he wasn't socializing with the boys or strolling around Manhattan, Arlen worked with Koehler at the Croydon. During his first year at the club, Arlen, with several published songs to his credit and a sizable hit in "Get Happy," was eligible for membership in ASCAP, the prestigious organization devoted to the protection of professional songwriters and publishers from exploitation by the users of their works. It was initiated in 1914 by the composer Victor Herbert, who, while dining in a favorite restaurant, noticed that the diners were being treated to a performance of one of his songs by a small orchestra. Since the music was being used to entertain the patrons—"public performance for profit"—he felt that he, and any other composer whose works were played, was entitled to compensation. The restaurant owner and others, including hoteliers and cabaret proprietors, objected; they were not charging admission to hear the music. But when the case reached the Supreme Court, Justice Oliver Wendell Holmes and the court's members favored ASCAP, stating, in part, that "if the music did not pay, it would be given up." From that moment on, ASCAP has monitored the use of its members' works in various establishments and, later, in radio, television, films, and so on.

So it was that in September 1930 Harold Arlen joined the esteemed company of Jerome Kern, Irving Berlin, George Gershwin, Cole Porter, and Richard Rodgers, even though he did not have a single Broadway show to his credit.

Broadway in 1930 was financially less healthy than the Harlem of the Cotton Club. Some of its most successful producers, including Ziegfeld and the Shuberts, went bankrupt. Vaudeville was all but dead, and even movies, the least expensive form of entertainment, suffered, a victim of the conversion to sound and the demise of the careers of some of the most illustrious stars of silent films. Scrambling to catch up with the switch to sound, Hollywood produced a string of early talkies so ineptly directed, filmed, and written that even at the ten-cent admission price, audiences stayed away.

Of all forms of entertainment, however, Broadway was hardest hit by the Great Depression. Musicals continued to be produced, but in fewer numbers, as the trend switched to the musical revue, which cost less to produce and whose topicality proved to be more entertaining than poorly written "book" musicals. During the run of *Brown Sugar*, few musicals opened on Broadway to stay, but two revues were successful, Kay Swift's *Fine and Dandy* and the Arthur Schwartz–Howard Dietz gem *Three's a Crowd.* In October 1930 the Gershwins' *Girl Crazy*, with one of the year's most hapless books, became the hit of the year, thanks to its popular score and the debut of the unknown Ethel Merman. That same month Lew Leslie, formerly of the Cotton Club, presented *Blackbirds,* starring Ethel Waters; it closed after a poor showing of twenty-six performances.

Early in December, Arlen attended the first night of a Cole Porter musical, *The New Yorkers,* starring his very good friend Frances Williams and the aging juvenile Charles King. Despite a sparkling cast that included Jimmy Durante and Fred Waring's Pennsylvanians, and despite a good critical reception, Frances was out of work within twenty weeks, another Depression casualty. Arlen's early sponsor, Vincent Youmans, continued his Broadway losing streak with *Smiles*, which premiered a few weeks before *The New Yorkers* with an equally luminous cast, headlined by Fred and Adele Astaire and Marilyn Miller.

In the fall and spring season of 1929–30, thirty-two musicals opened, most for brief, unprofitable runs; by 1935 the number had dwindled to ten and Harold Arlen had fled the scene for sunnier and healthier parts.

As the Depression deepened, Arlen fared better than Cole Porter, Richard Rodgers, or Vincent Youmans. Of the nine songs written for *Brown Sugar*, only two were published, the self-pitying, misogynous "Song of the Gigolo" ("If I hate women / Who can blame this lonely gigolo?") and the plaintive but playful "Linda." The latter is a quintessential instrumental and typically Arlen in form. The release has nine, rather than the conventional eight, bars. Its characteristic Arlen touch is an octave drop. "Linda" is not bluesy, but the melodic twists attracted two of the period's incipient swing bands. Red Nichols and His Five Pennies recorded it on November 6, 1930, and Benny Goodman and his orchestra recorded it the next day. The vocalist on both recordings was Harold Arlen. Unfortunately, this unique double-disc exposure was as far as "Linda" got.

Arlen and Koehler hit their Cotton Club stride in the next show, the self-conscious, trickily titled *Rhyth-Mania,* the spring production of 1931. Besides some fine songs of lasting popularity, they produced one at the time that furnished the title for all future Cotton Club revues—a song not intended for the show at all.

One afternoon in the winter of 1930, they decided to take a break from writing the songs for *Rhyth-Mania.* Arlen, who loved to walk, suggested they take a stroll downtown to the Mills office and "schmooze with the boys." Koehler was aghast—a trek from East Eighty-sixth Street to West Forty-sixth—that was a two-mile traverse! It was out of the question to the congenitally sedentary, cell-saving Koehler. After some argument he conceded, and they set out on their journey across town, Koehler complaining about the cold, muttering disparagingly about his companion, and otherwise voicing his displeasure.

To warm his collaborator, Arlen accelerated their pace, ad-libbing a tune in march tempo. Koehler fell in and kept up; true, he was warmer, as were his comments. One was, "Why don't you join the army if you like to walk so much?" Arlen let that pass and continued humming. As they neared the office, Koehler began fitting words to the tune. When they arrived, as Koehler later recalled, "I Love a Parade" was virtually a completed song.

Dan Healy insisted that the march be interpolated into *Rhyth-Mania,* which he staged, after the vocal, for dancers dressed as drum majorettes twirling batons. With "Between the Devil and the Deep Blue Sea," introduced by Aida Ward, it was one of the major song hits of the year. And all subsequent Cotton Club shows were titled *Parades.*

Cab Calloway's orchestra had replaced Ellington's that year, and while he was not the bandleader that Ellingon was, Calloway brought his high energy and dynamic vocal style to his performances. He did not merely conduct, he danced across the bandstand as he delivered the lyrics. His Arlen-Koehler songs in the show were "Trickeration" and "Kickin' the Gong Around," which also went into the fall show. The biggest hit of the spring show, however, was Calloway's own "Minnie the Moocher" (written with his publisher-manager, Irving Mills), which introduced Calloway's trademark "hi-de-ho" scat singing. Calloway would improvise two bars, then the band would sing it back, in an updated version of the old call-and-response form that can be traced back to Africa by way of southern black "field hollers."

Koehler paid tribute to Calloway's hit song in "Kickin' the Gong Around" with a call and response in which Calloway shouted "Where is Minnie?" The chorus provided Calloway with several spots to voice his variations on the now-famous "hi-de-hos." The phrase "kicking the gong around" is Harlemese for taking drugs. In the *Parade* that followed the next year, the Arlen-Koehler sequel "Minnie the Moocher's Wedding Day" uses more drug terminology: "a million cokies" (cocaine users) and "a hundred thousand hoppies [for hophead, a heroin addict] . . . pickin' poppies"; the chorus again refers to kicking the gong around.

The same show included the ominous street cry "Wail of the Reefer Man," written for Calloway: "Happiness for sale, / Dreams, who'll buy them, / Dreams, who'll try them?"

The celebration of narcotics during the 1930s was not unique to the Cotton Club. Drugs were commonplace in hip society and more or less acceptable, unless one became seriously addicted—a "dope fiend," in the terminology of the time. Minnie, according to Koehler, acquired her supply in Chinatown, implying heroin. The drug of choice in Harlem was a Mexican import, marijuana, called "reefer" after the Spanish slang for addict, *grifa.*

Although Koehler's vernacular must have been incomprehensible to the general public, even the sophisticates that came to the Cotton Club, it was no mystery to Harlemites and musicians, black or white. The title of Louis Armstrong's admired "Muggles," for example, is a synonym for marijuana. One of Fats Waller's popular records was "The Viper's Drag," a viper being a marijuana smoker (after the hissing intake of smoke). It might be noted here that neither Harold Arlen nor Ted Koehler was a viper. Arlen, in fact, was only a light drinker at the time.

Arlen and Koehler worked on five shows for the Cotton Club, from *Brown Sugar* in 1930 to the *Parade of 1934,* with time off for other projects, including a film project that required skipping the winter edition of the 1933 *Parade.* Each of their Cotton Club shows, beginning with *Rhyth-Mania,* produced at least one outstanding song that has become part of the fabric of musical Americana: "Between the Devil and the Deep Blue Sea," "I Love a Parade," "I've Got the World on a String," "Stormy Weather," "As Long As I Live," "Ill Wind." These songs were conceived for specific entertainers, whose presence also determined the general form of the production. Dan Healy was important in the kinetic flow of the evening and structure. Once the spots were set—a comic skit, a song, a dance, a comic duo, a song, and so on—the placement and type of song would be decided in conferences, often at Arlen's penthouse at the Croydon. Final decisions were made during rehearsals. Though these shows were plotless revues, the thought that went into their creation was similar to that which resulted in a Broadway show.

Not every production, or every show, generated a great anecdote, so dear to the show-business or musical theater aficionado. Arlen and Koehler were making songs, not history. Koehler, especially, would not have been taken for a romantic's conception of a man who composed a kind of idiomatic poetry. His dress was casual, befitting his stocky physique; his younger collaborator was more fashionable. Slender, taller, he wore well-made suits, fine shirts, and proper neckties (a habit he had copied from his older cousin, Eddie Orlin, during his Buffalo years when he shyly courted Lily Levine). There was his own added touch: the "bluie," the flower in his lapel. This was a generic term; no matter what the color of the blossom, he called it a bluie. He favored tiny pink roses.

When Arlen and Koehler were seen together, there was no doubting that one definitely filled the role of the composer; Koehler could have been a bus driver or a carpenter.

One of their most memorable shows was their penultimate *Cotton Club Parade,* the twenty-second edition, in 1933. It brought Duke Ellington back to the club, since Calloway had found work elsewhere. Koehler and Arlen began working on the songs once the general outline of the show was more or less set. After an orchestral overture, the first scene, a ribald blackout skit, was set in a Harlem hospital. Scene 2, in the show's final form, presented George Dewey Washington setting the scene, "Somewhere in Mississippi," for scene 3, the song "Calico Days," for chorus and dancers. Washington, incidentally, was simultaneously appearing downtown at the Majestic in the Jimmy Durante musical *Strike Me Pink.* This loan was duly noted in the Cotton Club's program; one of the backers of that musical was the mobster Waxey Gordon, a friend of Madden's.

Following a specialty dance, a comedy routine, and a "plantation song," the Harlem spirit was represented by the Arlen-Koehler rhythm number "Happy As the Day Is Long," leading into an ensemble dance. The next song was Arlen's bête noire, a specialty for Sally Goodings, "I'm Lookin' for Another Handy Man."

Arlen found the lyric less objectionable than that of the "pussycat" song of *Brown Sugar.* As is customary with Arlen, its form is unconventional: a verse, a chorus, and a patter section, with wordless musical breaks. In the verse Goodings warned the women ("you Harlem queens") that she was on a manhunt because she had just given her "handy man the air." The chorus is her invitation to the "Harlem Romeoes / You Lovey Joe's and gigolos," informing them:

> *I'm mighty hard to satisfy*
> *So only experts need apply*
> *Cause I've gotta have a first-class handy man*
> *He's gotta grind my coffee—bake my cake*
> *Haul my ashes and broil my steak*
> *He must be handy all around*
> *And know just how to turn my damper down.*

The audience had little difficulty in understanding Koehler's use of the local patois. The vocal was followed by a dance by the Handy Men.

The next spot, scene 10, required a less frivolous song, a blues or a torch, a change in tempo. In the planning stages, Arlen decided to structure the song around Cab Calloway's distinctive "hi-de-ho." Arlen called it "Cab's front shout." He tried out the opening phrase at a party, then spent an afternoon with Koehler at the Croydon penthouse. The front shout occurs in the first three notes, a bluesy ascent through a half step and a minor third. Arlen worked the jot over two additional bars, all in the same narrow range, closing with an unexpected drop of an octave. The work went well, for within a half hour they had the music and lyric and took time out to go to the Croydon's coffeeshop for a sandwich.

Later, at the club, Healy presented them with a jolt. Calloway had left and Duke Ellington had replaced him. Ellington was no vocalist. They had what they considered, in Arlen's phrase, "a strong song," and no one to sing it. George Dewey Washington, on loan from *Strike Me Pink,* was not right for it.

Healy, who was on top of all show-business affairs, informed them that Ethel Waters, who had been absent from the Manhattan scene and fading, was reportedly back in town and at liberty. Emboldened by the good news, they arranged to see her.

They found her moody. Her marriage to her second husband, Edward Matthews (who would portray Jake in Gershwin's *Porgy and Bess*), had ended badly. Waters had not worked in New York since 1931, when she had appeared in the short-lived *Rhapsody in Black.* She moved on to Chicago, where for over a year she worked on the Al Capone nightclub circuit between that city and its corporate headquarters, in Cicero, Illinois. She was frozen into that limited dominion because working for Capone discouraged other club owners from hiring her, lest that somehow offend the boss. Early in 1933 she got out of Chicago. "I'm a child of the underworld," she said, but "I must say that I prefer working for people who never laid eyes on an Italian pineapple [hand grenade] or a sawed-off shotgun. I went back to New York glad to be alive."

Stark arranged for Arlen and Koehler to meet with her; it was a first meeting, though she was aware of "Get Happy," "Between the Devil and the Deep Blue Sea," "I Love a Parade," and "I've Got the World on a String." After Arlen's demonstration, she was impressed with the song, which required only slight editing to make it suitable for a female vocalist. It matched her current blue mood, and, she realized, it had great potential—so great that, once she agreed to sing it, she began making demands. Arlen and Koehler left that up to Healy and Stark—her high salary, her one song only per show, and that one to be dramatically showcased.

Arlen and Koehler were happy; they had their star (who could do more justice to the song than Calloway), and she had her song: "Stormy Weather."

Its reception at the club further convinced Arlen that "Stormy Weather," so casually and easily written, was not just another "torch." The blend of music and words—the "wedding," he called it—expressed a genuine emotion. Waters said it best: "When I got out there in the middle of the Cotton Club floor, I was telling things I couldn't frame in words. I was singing the story of my misery and confusion, of the misunderstandings in my life I couldn't straighten out, the story of wrongs and outrages done to me by people I had loved and trusted. . . . If there's anything I owe Eddie Matthews, it's that he enabled me to do one hell of a job on the song 'Stormy Weather.' "

And she did; on opening night, Sunday, April 6, 1933, the audience demanded twelve encores. Arlen and Koehler had another noisy song.

By a curious turn in the history of a song, the composer himself had prepared the way for her reception. Happy with the excitement the song had stirred up within the music business well before opening night, Arlen showed it to his friend, the society bandleader Leo Reisman. Educated at Harvard and the New England Conservatory, the Boston-born Reisman was a talented violinist who had played for a time with the Baltimore Symphony. By the age of twenty he had formed his own salon group specializing in genteel performances of popular songs. In 1921 his band was featured in Jerome Kern's *Good Morning, Dearie.* The perceptive Kern encouraged him to leave Boston, where the Reisman Orchestra was a favorite with the tea-dance crowds, and remain in New York. During the run of *Good Morning, Dearie* Reisman began recording and found his métier in well-arranged and -performed show tunes and the better popular songs. He found an ideal spot at the Central Park Casino, from which he broadcast weekly for Fleischmann's yeast and Pond's cold cream. Among his guest vocalists were the jazz-inspired Lee Wiley and Harold Arlen.

The Reisman Orchestra recorded an Arlen-Koehler song for the first time in January 1932, a number not associated with any show, "Stepping into Love." For his vocalist Reisman chose the composer. The following year he recorded a *Cotton Club Parade of 1932* song, "You Gave Me Ev'rything but Love," with his regular vocalist, Frank Luther. Reisman was not only an astute judge of songs but also a smart showman in the selection of vocalists—Fred Astaire, Clifton Webb, Dinah Shore. His band, at one time or another, included such musicians as Eddy Duchin, the trumpeter Bubber Miley (of the Ellington orchestra), and Benny Goodman.

One look at "Stormy Weather" galvanized Reisman into preparing an arrangement for his band before his next Victor recording session, scheduled for February 28, 1933—the *Cotton Club Parade of 1933* was set to premiere on April 6. The band recorded six sides, the fifth being "Stormy Weather" with Harold Arlen as vocalist; the final take, and the record's reverse side, was an Irving Berlin song, "Maybe It's Because I Love You Too Much," sung by Fred Astaire. (This happy accident brought in more in royalties than Berlin had expected from the little-known ballad.)

Victor rushed the pressings into record shops before the Cotton Club first night; within weeks, the "Stormy Weather" recording was a best-seller and was soon widely broadcast on radio and blaring from speakers of those music shops with sidewalk Victrolas.

In a rare display of vanity, Harold Arlen felt entitled to the credit for the line that formed on the stairs—the club was on the second floor, over the Douglas

Theater—and into the street long before the midnight curtain on that Sunday, April 6. Word had gotten around that the great Ethel Waters would sing the hit song "Stormy Weather."

Late in the first act, in that historic tenth scene, she finally made her entrance. She began softly, in what Arlen had marked "slow lament," the Calloway front shout: "Don't know why, there's no sun up in the sky, stormy weather / Since my man and I ain't together, keeps rainin' all the time." It was obvious to the audience, sitting in an almost breathless silence and undoubtedly unaware of her broken marriage, that she meant the words of that song.

As a dramatic interlude (not included on the composer's recording), Arlen worked in a rhythmically agitated twelve bars, beginning, "I walk around, heavy hearted and sad. / Night comes around and I'm still feelin' bad," leading into a touch of tone painting with groups of triplets on the words "pitterin' patterin' beatin' an' splatterin'." (When she recorded the song a month later, Waters included the interlude; it was omitted from the original publication, to be restored years later when published in the *Harold Arlen Songbook*.)

With or without the interlude, "Stormy Weather" stands out for the unusual phrasing of the chorus. Although cast in the typical A-A'-B-A format, it spans thirty-six bars, rather than the standard thirty-two. The first A section subdivides not into the expected series of four symmetrical two-bar phrases, but into an opening three-bar phrase (through the word "weather"), followed by a pair of two-bar phrases and a measure of rest: the expected eight bars, arrived at in a unorthodox way. The second A section repeats the melody with an extension, for a total of ten bars, grouped 3-2-3-2. The chorus then relaxes into a more conventional, symmetrical release, with simple, blues-inflected harmonies just where most songs get more chromatic. The song closes with a slightly altered return of the second, ten-bar, A section.

When the author and composer Alec Wilder questioned Arlen about the untraditional structure of "Stormy Weather," Arlen told him that he had not planned it that way. "I didn't count the measures till it was all over. That was all I had to say and the way I had to say it. George Gershwin brought it up and I didn't know it. . . . He said, 'You know you didn't repeat a phrase in the first eight bars?' And I never gave it a thought."

Gershwin was more analytical than Arlen and would have noticed this deviance from the common practice. Harold Arlen, like Gershwin, composed as he felt and kept what pleased him. He was often bemused by the fate of his songs in the hands of some musicians, saying ruefully, "At least they could do it straight once, before they go off."

"Going off" was characteristic of his own performances, and he could understand the instinct in others, but he wished for a clear statement of the theme before the variations (or distortions) were introduced. As for a close technical analysis of a popular song (invariably ex post facto and from printed sheet music and not the composer's possibly different original), he invoked the comment of the English philosopher and mathematician Alfred North Whitehead: "It requires a very unusual mind to undertake the analysis of the obvious." But then, many an Arlen creation is not obvious. He was, as his friend Robert Wachsman observed, "a feeler, not a thinker" when he was composing. He became absorbed, even lost, in the emotion; the technique was secondary.

"Stormy Weather" proved to be profitable not only to the Cotton Club but also to Arlen, Koehler, and Ethel Waters. His curiosity aroused by the hit song on the reverse of Astaire's recording, Irving Berlin attended a performance of the 1933 *Parade,* which resulted in Waters's leaving the Cotton Club in September to appear in Berlin's revue *As Thousands Cheer.* For her Berlin wrote two fine songs, the rhythm number "Heat Wave" and the poignantly bitter "Suppertime." Ethel Waters's career, thanks to one song, was revived, and she went on to further success, musical as well as dramatic, on Broadway, in Hollywood, and on television.

"Stormy Weather," salubriously, won Harold Arlen and Ted Koehler a ticket to Hollywood. While they were temporarily on the West Coast, drastic changes occurred at the Cotton Club, changes that had been foreshadowed the year before, in 1932, when Owney Madden chose to return to prison. He was as prudent as he was prescient.

Madden was having problems with the State Parole Board and with FBI investigations into his connections with the laundry rackets. He could also hear a more parlous knelling: "Mad Dog" Coll was dead, "Legs" Diamond was dead, even inoffensive Larry Fay was dead, shot by a disgruntled doorman of his Casa Blanca Club. But what sounded the death knell to Madden was that many, including the soon-to-be-victorious Franklin D. Roosevelt, were calling for a repeal of the hopeless Eighteenth Amendment. Thus, Madden chose to miss the gala premiere of the *Cotton Club Parade of 1932.* In the summer, sensing his own need for a change—a holiday from the racket wars, investigations he could not buy off, and with the word "repeal" ringing in his ears—he presented himself at the iron doors of Sing Sing wishing to pay his debt to society in full after admitting to a slight parole violation.

He arrived in style, driven to the prison in his Dusenburg and welcomed by Warden Lewis E. Lawes, who found Madden a good influence on other prisoners and an aid in keeping them on best behavior. He was "inside" when the most successful of the Cotton Club shows, the one that was called "The Stormy Weather Show," opened. A couple of months later, in 1933, he was released, but he never returned to the club and went into quiet retirement in the more healthful climate of Hot Springs, Arkansas.

Madden was proved right—at the end of the year Prohibition ended, late in October 1935, he would read in the local newspaper that "Dutch" Schultz had joined Diamond, Cole, and Fay after a bloody shooting in a Newark bar.

The era that had spawned the Cotton Club was over by December 1933; soon the "McCoy" was available all over town. There was hardly any point to making the trip to the club if it was no longer wicked. Even its star performers, Ellington and Calloway included, began migrating downtown.

Early in 1934 Arlen and Koehler returned from Hollywood (an uneasy experience, to be related in the next chapter) to their final *Cotton Club Parade,* the "entire production conceived and supervised by Ted Koehler," as the program noted. The star was Adelaide Hall, a Brooklyn-born soprano with a flair for jazz who had begun on Broadway in the chorus of the historic all-black musical *Shuffle Along* (1921) and achieved stardom in *Blackbirds of 1928,* in which she sang the hits of Fields and McHugh, "Diga, Diga, Doo" and "I Can't Give You Anything but Love." She toured with this hugely successful show in Europe, then returned to appear in the lackluster *Brown Buddies* in 1930. She then began singing in clubs in a distinctive soprano tinctured by a low, bluesy growl. She had recorded with the Duke Ellington band, and with Art Tatum as her accompanist.

Jimmie Lunceford's orchestra would accompany her in the twenty-fourth edition of the Cotton Club revue. Lunceford had only recently arrived in New York from the south, where he had taught music in a Memphis high school. His students formed the nucleus of his dance band, which in 1927 began touring the south, then moved northward. When the Lunceford band arrived in Manhattan in the fall of 1933, it was known for its swinging style (although "swing" as a form of music was not yet current), thanks to its gifted arranger and trumpeter, Sy Oliver. Lunceford arrangements were not in the "jungle" style that the club had advertised in its promotion of Ellington; nor was Lunceford the showman that Calloway was. Nevertheless, he established himself and his band at the Cotton Club. The Jimmie Lunceford Orchestra proved to be one of the finest swing bands of the 1930s and 1940s.

Hall's major song (aside from her own "specialty") was another in the Arlen series of weather songs, "Ill Wind." There is no verse to this forty-bar masterwork, which grew out of two jots, the opening four bars and three additional bars. In the published version, the marking is "slowly with expression," with the B section, the release, marked "rhythmic," eight bars in octaves of alternating crescendos and diminuendos. It dramatically contrasts with the more resigned cast of the main strain: "You're only misleadin' / The sunshine I'm needin'." In the next bar there is a simple, but marvelous, characteristic touch from both composer and lyricist: "Ain't that a shame?" Arlen's contribution here is the octave interval between "needin'" and "ain't"; it is like a defiant wail, but Koehler's lyric is a borrowing from the self-mockery and dark humor of the blues. The concluding twelve bars, a slight variation of the first ten, is a kind of peroration, repeating the words "no good" three times in a quiet, plaintive coda.

"Ill Wind" was originally published in two versions. In the second Arlen devised a complex "optional piano accompaniment" based on syncopated triplets.

It is the same song as in the more-familiar, simpler version, but it hardly fits into the popular mode. There is a truism often verified by many a song by Arlen (or Gershwin, Kern, or Youmans, to skim the top): "Some of the finest popular songs never become popular."

The relaxed, light-hearted collaboration of Ted Koehler and Harold Arlen is evident in the comments on the "Ill Wind" jots. Below the music, Arlen scrawled, "Havin' the time of my life." Under that Koehler wrote, "Says you."

Their final Cotton Club score assigned to that dependable purveyor of blatant innuendo, Leitha Hill, was the obligatory risqué number, "You Sure Don't Know How to Shake That Thing." But an even better, and lasting, number was the swingy, rhythmic "As Long As I Live." It followed the Hill specialty and was a song and dance choreographed by the Broadway dance director Bobby Connolly (that same year he designed the dances for the *Ziegfeld Follies*). It was to be a rather elaborate production piece, opening with a vocal by a male-female duo, then leading into a dance by the vocalists and the ballroom dance team of Mears and Mears. The male vocalist was Avon Long, in his Cotton Club debut. He had a fine voice, but his style of dance was traditional, tap primarily, unlike the favored contortions of the "snakehips" variety.

Before the show opened, Long's vocal partner, unhappy with her lot at the club, vanished into another part of town. Healy found a substitute in the chorus with a captivating voice, the beautiful teenager Lena Horne. In her second year at the Cotton Club, she was no happier there than her predecessor. She detested the racism and the minimal weekly stipend of twenty-five dollars (minus deductions for lateness or missing a rehearsal). Because of its dining policies, she had no meals at the club. She did recall one free meal on the Cotton Club, and that she was served in prison when she and members of the cast journeyed upstate to entertain Owney Madden and his fellow inmates at Sing Sing.

The production number was titled "Spring Breaks Through," and her singing and dancing of "As Long As I Live" earned her billing on the program and brought her to the attention of the producer Laurence Schwab, who offered her a small part in his new musical, *Dance with Your Gods*, on Broadway. She was then sixteen and cast as "The Quadroon Girl." With the intercession of the downtown mobsters, Schwab was able to arrange for Lena Horne to skip the early show at the Cotton Club, appear briefly on Broadway, then rush uptown to do her "As Long As I Live" routine with Long.

This arrangement was exhausting. She found she liked Broadway (even though *Dance with Your Gods* was a failure) and expressed her desire to quit the Cotton Club. As the Cotton Club chronicler Jim Hoskins recorded, the club's bosses maintained that "they could fire anyone they wanted, but no one was supposed to quit." Her leaving would spoil the popular "As Long As I Live," and they did not like that at all. When her stepfather objected at the club one night, he was dragged into the men's room—deplorably, the only way he could have gained entrance into the club's facility—where he was beaten and his head forced into the toilet bowl while it was flushed. Lena Horne left that night, never to return.

That twenty-fourth edition of the *Cotton Club Parade,* too, was Harold Arlen's final show at the club. Occasionally, during their Cotton Club tenure, he and Koehler took outside work together, including a film project and another *Earl Carroll's Vanities*; this last would be a pivotal experience for Arlen. On his own, also, he had written with other lyricists and taken three final flings in vaudeville as an accompanist and vocalist.

One of the collaborations away from Koehler in this period—a single song for an uninspired Shubert revue, *New Americana*—would completely change his professional life. The *Vanities* would profoundly affect his personal life.

The *Vanities* opened at the end of September 1932, *New Americana* in early October, and the *Cotton Club Parade* a couple of weeks later, on the twenty-third. Arlen's sole contribution to the Shubert show was the pulsating "Satan's Li'l Lamb," a powerful production number sung by Francetta Malloy and danced by an extraordinary trio of modern dancers, Doris Humphrey, Charles Weidman, and José Limón.

Its drive, in a slow blues tempo, is effected by repeated eighth notes on the repeated words in the lyric:

> *When the wind goes a-whip whip whip whip whippin' 'round my floor,*
> *And the rain comes a-rap rap rap rap rappin' at my door,*
> *Gimme gin to forget the sin sin sinner that I am,*
> *'Cause I'm only Satan's li'l lamb.*

The lyric, with music to match, is a hedonistic paean to evil in its summons to "thrills that'll break the Ten Commandments with a wham." The release is more lyrical, invoking a spiritual:

> *For it's glory, glory,*
> *While I'm livin';*
> *Purgatory*
> *When I'm gone.*

The conclusion repeats the pulse for a cynical final declaration:

> *Hi-de-ho*
> *While I'm waitin' for that fatal telegram,*
> *When I go, little daisies won't be caring who I am,*
> *'Cause it's heads he wins*
> *And it's tails you lose*
> *When you're Satan's little coal-black lamb.*

The last two bars dramatically end the song with a sequence of seven heavily accented chords (on the seven syllables of "Sat-an's lit-tle coal-black lamb"), hammering in the accompaniment as the piece becomes deliberately slower. Needless to say, the lyrics to "Satan's Li'l Lamb" assured its banning from the airwaves (as were such "suggestive" songs as Porter's "Love for Sale" and the Gershwins' "Nice Work If You Can Get It," both because of their obvious allusions—at least in the minds of the network censors).

This did not faze Ethel Merman, who recorded "Satan's Li'l Lamb" a week before *New Americana* opened: on the reverse, she sang "I Gotta Right to Sing the Blues," the major Arlen-Koehler contribution to the score of the *Vanities,* only two days after that had opened. Her rendition of the Satan song, accompanied by an orchestra conducted by Nat Shilkret, is kinetic. It is also the only recording of the song.

Of greater significance to Harold Arlen is that "Satan's Li'l Lamb" united him for the first time with two of his most gifted lyricists, E. Y. Harburg and John H. Mercer, who would soon be better known as Johnny Mercer. They had no hit in this song, but there was compatibility and mutual respect. (Harburg, in fact, had a major success in the show, "Brother, Can You Spare a Dime?," written with the show's musical director, Jay Gorney.)

Harburg was the catalyst in Arlen's leaving both the Cotton Club and Ted Koehler. They had met in 1930, when both wrote songs, with others, for the *Vanities.* Harburg had an affinity and "affection" for Arlen's "typically American approach. It was away from the Viennese derivation of the Kerns and other writers, and I took a shine to that gutsy, earthy [quality]. It was a combination of Hebrew and black music." Harburg, too, was impressed with one of the hits of that show, "Hittin' the Bottle," with a Koehler lyric. After *New Americana* opened, and before Arlen began working on the 1934 *Parade,* Harburg came to him with a small job. Billy Rose was producing a play by Ben Hecht and Gene Fowler, not a musical but a drama with a backstage setting entitled *The Great Magoo.* Hecht and Fowler took a jaundiced view of life in the theater, and Harburg thought it might be an idea to provide the show with a kind of theme song with a similar point of view. In no time they had a song entitled "If You Believed in Me," which Rose accepted, along with top billing as co-lyricist. (Later, Harburg laughed over that attribution, saying, "The only thing Billy contributed was the use of the Selwyn Theatre for eleven performances.")

The next year it was interpolated into the score of a film musical, *Take a Chance,* starring Buddy Rogers and June Knight. Harburg retitled the piece "It's Only a Paper Moon"; it became their first major hit, though to Harburg's chagrin, Rose shared the lyric credit. "It's Only a Paper Moon" expresses a more realistic view of show business than Irving Berlin's romantic "There's No Business Like Show Business."

This newly formed but temporary collaboration came to full fruition a couple of years later. Arlen and Koehler had returned from Hollywood and were at work on what would prove to be their last Cotton Club show together. Early the next year Harburg, during a period of peace with the Shuberts, approached his former Lower East Side schoolmate Ira Gershwin with an idea for a revue that the Shuberts were willing to produce. Harburg had just completed work on a *Ziegfeld Follies* that had opened in January 1934, and though rather wrung out, he did not want to let the opportunity slip away. If Gershwin could work with him as co-lyricist, he was certain he could handle the job.

Gershwin was feeling the effects of the Great Depression, thanks to Wall Street; he had recently written the words for two flop shows, and he was unemployed. His brother, George, was occupied at the time with an opera he was writing with the poet DuBose Heyward; Ira would eventually join the enterprise, after the completion of act 1.

But who, Ira Gershwin asked, would write the music? Harburg offered the name of Harold Arlen. Gershwin admired Arlen's work and agreed.

For Arlen, it was a challenge and a dream come true to write a full score for a major Broadway production for the Shuberts, with Yip Harburg and with, especially, Ira Gershwin. There was just one difficulty.

If he took the assignment—the show was scheduled the open in late August—there would be no Cotton Club songs from him in the fall. How could he tell Ted? He believed he owed a lot to Koehler, who had guided a green young songwriter through the maze of Tin Pan Alley and publishing. It was virtually a betrayal to abandon this kind, gentle man. Arlen was upset enough to avoid Koehler; he simply could not face him. He spoke of his misery with his friend Robert Wachsman, then in advertising and a great Arlen devotee.

Wachsman inquired about Ted, asking, "Did you tell him?"

Arlen admitted that he hadn't, that he couldn't.

"You have to let him know," Wachsman counseled him. "What are you going to do?"

"I wrote him a letter," was the morose answer.

Koehler had been busy during a rehearsal. When it was over he read Arlen's note. He came to the table where a distraught Arlen sat with Wachsman and said, "You'd be a fool if you didn't do it." He then returned to the rehearsal.

"You feel any better?" Wachsman asked.

"Not much," Arlen replied.

That night, Wachsman recalled, "Harold got loaded" and spent the evening and early morning extolling the virtues of Ted Koehler as a friend, lyricist, and even carpenter. Happily, there was no breach in their friendship; Koehler went on to write with others, among them Duke Ellington, Burton Lane, Jay Gorney, Jimmy McHugh, and again with Harold Arlen. Koehler even returned to the Cotton Club for its 1939 "World's Fair Edition." His collaborator was Rube Bloom, with whom he wrote the fine "Don't Worry 'bout Me." After that *Parade*

Ted Koehler decided to return to Hollywood, where he had been living since the mid-1930s.

Having been kindly reassured by Ted Koehler, Harold Arlen was free to work with Harburg and Gershwin on his first big Broadway musical.

EXCURSIONS
AND ANYA

*A*rlen had, in fact, written a Broadway score before he joined Gershwin and Harburg for the Shubert musical. He did not recall his first attempt with nostalgic pride. He was bullied into the job around the time he and Koehler were finishing up *Brown Sugar* for the Cotton Club.

This curious saga began in the summer of 1930 under the inexorable prodding of his father's friend Jack Yellen. In the shower one morning, Yellen had heard a snatch of a song he deemed "catchy" coming from the radio's speaker. He had missed the title, but remembered the tune.

When he arrived at the offices of Agar, Yellen, and Bornstein, still haunted by the song, Yellen canvassed the staff until he found someone who told him the song's title was "Get Happy."

A secretary was immediately sent to the nearby Schirmer's music shop for a copy of the sheet music. He readily linked something in the music, a characteristic sound, and the name of the boy pianist-singer he had known as Hyman Arluck in Buffalo. Soon after, Yellen encountered young Chaim, as he paternistically called him, and informed him on the spot that they were going to write a score for a Broadway show. Yellen was known in Tin Pan Alley as "Napoleon"; he invariably commanded and rarely requested. He ran his company and his collaborations like a martinet.

Harold Arlen was intimidated by the dynamic little man. He respected Yellen as an old friend of the family, his senior by more than a decade, and as the lyricist of several hit songs: "I Wonder What Became of Sally?," "My Yiddisha Momme" (for Sophie Tucker), "Ain't She Sweet?," and the currently popular "Happy Days Are Here Again." Arlen was aware, too, of Yellen's status as an important publisher. His awe and respect for the older man, however, were tempered by apprehension.

Harold Arlen's total output up to that chance meeting in Lindy's (a favorite haunt on Broadway near Times Square for gossip columnists, show people, and songwriters) consisted of a few interpolated songs and the skimpy score for *Brown Sugar.* A Broadway musical would require a dozen or more songs, which would have to be tailored for specific voices and characters and to have some relationship to the book's plot. As Yellen talked, Arlen's doubts grew and he fled, promising to meet at Yellen's office in the very near future.

Arlen did not show, feeling that he was not yet prepared to compose the songs for a show.

Weeks later, Yellen encountered Arlen again at Lindy's. The composer was forgiven for missing their appointment, but Yellen, taking command, escorted him to the offices of Agar, Yellen, and Bornstein around the corner on Seventh Avenue. He would not take no for an answer, and a slightly befuddled Harold Arlen found himself signing his name to a contract for a musical entitled *You Said It,* to star the comedian Lou Holtz. By coincidence, Holtz was also co-producer of the show with Yellen; further, Yellen was co-author of the book with a former comedian turned actor, lyricist, and writer, Sid Silvers. Yellen was the unquestioned Napoleon of *You Said It.*

When Yellen informed Holtz about his choice of composer for their production, the reaction was "Who the hell is Harold Arlen?" Silvers echoed Holtz, adding, "Do you think the kid [Silvers was all of two years older than Arlen] can do it?"

Yellen, inevitably, prevailed. Working with him, Arlen soon learned, would prove to be more strenuous than playing for Koehler night and day. They would meet mostly at Yellen's New York City apartment (he kept a house in Buffalo all his life) where the lyricist threw song ideas at Arlen: titles, maybe something about the popular new style of singing called crooning, a title song, and, since the setting of the show was a college, a song about Alma Mater. Yellen's quick, nervous mind never seemed to let up. "Even in the john," Arlen later recalled, when he would reflect with affectionate amusement on an experience that had perplexed him at the time. "I'd be at the piano and he'd be in there with the door ajar, sitting, working, and at times yelling out a line as I played."

After the opening of *Brown Sugar* in September 1930, Arlen devoted the rest of the year to work on *You Said It.* The score blossomed under his fingers, but he was a most insecure songwriter; he was still in his jot phase, and Yellen consumed them quickly. Yellen, too, looked back with jocular exaggeration. "Harold," he said, "would write a tune, then stand in the corner and pray for the next one."

The Arlen supplications were clearly answered, for by the end of the year he had provided Yellen with close to twice as many tunes as had been written for *Brown Sugar*.

The Yellen-Silvers book had cast the thirty-one-year-old Lou Holtz as "Pinkie Pincus," a freshman in mythical Kenton College. Instead of majoring in English (Holtz was a celebrated dialect comic), he organized the campus rackets, the laundry and the commissary. To spice up the plot, the dean's daughter, Helen Holloway (Mary Lawlor), had decided that her extracurricular activity would be bootlegging.

You Said It will not be remembered for its originality. It was merely another in the college musical series, undoubtedly inspired by the very successful *Good News!*, with songs by DeSylva, Brown, and Henderson, of three years before. Coincidentally, Mary Lawlor had starred in that musical as a coed singing "The Best Things in Life Are Free."

The one distinctive contribution by Yellen and Silvers was to take the setting out of the conventional form of the genre. There were no classrooms, no hero failing in geometry and thus unable to play in the critical football game. There were no gymnasiums or playing fields. The show would not have been out of place at the Cotton Club, except that its wily campus racketeer, Pinkie, proves to have a heart of gold. He saves the novice bootlegger, Helen, from the federal agents closing in on her by stealing the evidence.

You Said It was advertised as a "Musicollegiate Comedy" but was in fact a burlesque show hanging from a slender libretto. One critic advised his readers that it "is not the show for you if you like your fun clean and your dirt funny." It opened at the Forty-sixth Street Theatre on January 19, 1931, to generally unfavorable reviews, yet ran for a surprising 192 performances. Yellen, years later, called it "probably the worst show to run on Broadway" and remembered the music as being not much better than his bad lyrics. Still, as he also liked to emphasize, "it became one of the biggest laugh hits on Broadway." He believed that he deserved some credit for that, not because of his clever dialogue, but because of his discovery of someone who became known during the run of the show as "Broadway's Preferred Polish Blonde, Lyda Roberti."

Yellen had seen her during an early stay in Hollywood. He and his collaborator, Milton Ager, were writing songs for the film musical *Honky Tonk,* and Lyda Roberti was appearing at the time in vaudeville. She captivated Yellen with a natural comic flair, a good voice, and a striking physical presence. Roberti exuded an unconscious sensuality with her platinum blonde hair (not necessarily her natural color), a round Slavic face, lush lips, and a voluptuous figure. She was also called, and frequently, a bundle of energy. Much of her appeal to audiences of the time was attributed to a charming Polish accent (she was born in

Warsaw). Her pronunciation of words with the letter *h* was a guttural *ch*, as in the Yiddish expression *chutzpa*. For some reason this stirred audiences to gales of laughter.

The truth is that her voice was rather thin, but her untrammeled, jiggling vivacity and her way with dialogue made her a favorite in vaudeville and clubs. When Yellen saw her for the first time she was unknown on Broadway and in Hollywood.

The next year Yellen decided to take a weekend off work on *You Said It,* giving Harold Arlen a few days of welcome respite. Yellen went home to Buffalo to see his family; one evening when he and his wife, Lucille, were on the town, he spotted the name Lyda Roberti on a marquee. After the show finished, Yellen sought her out backstage. He had an idea. At twenty-one the curvaceous blonde could be readily acceptable as a sexy coed.

"I want no show," she told him when he suggested she come to New York for a Broadway show. "I want no New York," she expanded. "On Broadway is actors selling apples."

Yellen left her in Buffalo, but back in New York he went into his Napoleon routine. Through Roberti's agent at the William Morris Agency, he applied pressure on her, and to her surprise, she found herself on Broadway not selling apples but learning Arlen-Yellen songs. The fact that all parts in the show were filled and that there was no part in it for her did not disconcert Yellen. He simply wrote her into the script.

When he handed her the revised book, she glanced at it and giggled in her enchanting manner.

"It can't be that funny," Yellen said, and who would know better than he?

It was amusing to Lyda Roberti because she could not read English. Another member of the cast, the young comic Benny Baker, was assigned to work with her over the weekend to teach her her part and to work through the entire script to give her some idea of what the show was about. According to Yellen, she came to Monday morning's rehearsal with not only her part memorized but everyone else's as well.

In Philadelphia, during the tryout, Yellen began sensing that he had created a loser, a dog. During one performance, standing at the back of the theater with Lee Shubert, a backer, he felt obliged to offer his regrets for an atrocious book, a not very distinguished score, and poorly conceived dance numbers. Shubert listened noncommittally.

Hughie Clark and Peggy Bernier, the second leads, were singing a rhythm number that Arlen had based on a jazz riff he had heard played by a trumpeter in a club. Then Lyda Roberti strode onstage to join them. The song, written especially for her, was "Sweet and Hot." Yellen provided her with plenty of *h*s, from verse ("I don't like high brows / Who arch their eyebrows / When a jazz tune is played") through the chorus, in which he repeats "hot" seven times.

When the wild applause faded, Shubert turned to Yellen and predicted, accurately, "This'll clean up in New York." Though encores were demanded, there was none because Arlen and Yellen had not expected any. There was a further irony. Star and co-producer had objected to Yellen's giving Roberti the number (Holtz liked the song) because she was an unknown on the Broadway stage.

"That girl," Yellen always believed, "saved the show." After the New York premiere, he also recalled, she got "more free publicity than we could have possibly bought. . . . We didn't need a press agent after that." The disagreeable reviews were blithely disregarded by audiences who clamored to see, and hear, Broadway's Preferred Polish Blonde.

Lyda Roberti unquestionably contributed to the unexpected long run of *You Said It*: word of mouth (which saved many critically mauled shows) brought in the theatergoers to hear her mangle "Sweet and Hot," as they came to other shows to hear another unknown, Ethel Merman, belt out "I Got Rhythm," or Ethel Waters agonize through "Stormy Weather."

If Roberti saved the musical, Yellen could be credited with rescuing her from the expiring vaudeville and starting her on a new career, onstage and in Hollywood. She was typed as the vivacious, funny blonde (in *College Rhythm,* a 1934 film, she was seen again as a scatterbrained coed). On Broadway she sang "My Cousin in Milwaukee," a song from a Gershwin failure, *Pardon My English,* then moved to the successful Kern musical *Roberta.* One song, "I'll Be Hard to Handle," was clearly fashioned for her.

She returned to Hollywood to appear in some undistinguished films, including the 1935 *George White's Scandals,* with songs by Yellen. *Nobody's Baby,* released two years later, was mediocre to a fault, leaving her film career in limbo.

Yellen retained a paternal affection for the bright young woman he believed had saved *You Said It.* But playing in poor films with small, stereotyped roles—the sensual blonde with a cute accent—led nowhere. More tragic, Yellen revealed, was the cause of her death at the age of thirty-two. The official finding was a heart attack, but Yellen was certain it was suicide after an unhappy romance with a film director.

Were the *You Said It* songs as inferior as Yellen remembered them three decades later? Not really. While they are not among Arlen's most memorable, they are pleasant, revealing his versatility and capability to compose a sustained score—even integrated songs, long before Rodgers and Hammerstein.

The score is full of better-than-average songs, words as well as music. The integrated, or plot, songs include the obvious "Alma Mater" and the college cheer:

> We're raccooned—Rah!
> We're cartooned—Rah!
> We're lampooned—Rah!
> But what do we care?

There was also an interpolated medley of traditional college songs, including "The Victors," a salute to Yellen's alma mater, the University of Michigan. Such undergrad zeal was counterbalanced by the cynical plot song, "What'd We Come to College For?"

"Learn to Croon," alluding to the popular Russ Columbo and the rising Rudy Vallee, extols the advantages of "a singing voice and looks" over grinding "away at books":

> *You need no lecture by Dean or Prexy,*
> *If you perfect your voice to be sexy.*
> > *So*
> *Learn to moan into a megaphone,*
> *And it may be the making of you.*
> *You'll be repaid*
> *With rich reward;*
> *By ev'ry maid*
> *You'll be adored;*
> *If you can croon a sentimental tune,*
> *And end it with the words "I love you!"*

Two years later a song with the same title, but with a less suggestive message, was introduced by the soon-to-be-master crooner, Bing Crosby, in the film *College Humor.* Written by Sam Coslow and Arthur Johnston, it was the more popular of the two songs. The score also featured its own "Alma Mater."

There are two affecting Arlen ballads in *You Said It.* One is "While You Are Young," in which Yellen laments that "All too soon tomorrow turns to long ago." So, the lyric continues, with a bit of appropriation here and there, while you are young you'd best "Gather your rosebuds with the one who loves you" because "Too soon the song is gone, / The echo lingers on." The sentiments of Robert Herrick and Irving Berlin blend fittingly into the song.

The second ballad is the hopeful and poignantly worded "If He Really Loves Me." There is a charming, amusing duet, "You'll Do," and an elaborate confrontation number for solo voices, chorus, and dancers, "They Learn about Women from Me." The women have the last word. This is clearly a number fashioned to the libretto. Like it, too many of the songs from the show remain little known. Harold Arlen recorded, plaintively crooning, the title song and a jazzy "Sweet and Hot" with the Red Nichols band three days before the opening. The recording was reasonably successful, but no hit. And as time went by Arlen tended to dismiss his first Broadway show score. He had proved to himself that he could write plot songs and manage the musical variety required by a show:

rhythm numbers, dance numbers, ballads, comedy songs. That was enough for him.

Arlen had survived, with his muse, psyche, and sense of humor intact. He had created, however flawed, a full-scale Broadway musical; he had worked with a seasoned, demanding, taskmaster. He had watched the chaos of Youmans's *Great Day!* from the sidelines; *You Said It* forced him into the role of participant. Under pressure he was capable of rewriting, discarding, or producing an instant song to fill a "hole" in the show where Yellen, Silvers, or Holtz thought it was required. The experience was exhausting as well as exhilarating.

Curiously, Arlen and Yellen never collaborated again except for a couple of songs written for Yellen's own publishing house in 1932: the maudlin "I Forgive You" and "The Song That Makes Me Blue," both devoted to the theme of unrequited love. The latter, while bluesy, is a waltz. Both songs may have been leftovers from *You Said It.*

After these final efforts, Arlen and Yellen went their separate ways. Artistically, they were not compatible. Yellen was from the old Tin Pan Alley school, Arlen from the new. Arlen said he regarded Yellen as one of the great lyric writers, but in fact he was a journeyman wordsmith with an enviable early record. His considerable gifts were overshadowed by other lyricists from the new school: Lorenz Hart, Ira Gershwin, E. Y. Harburg, Cole Porter, even the allegedly un-schooled Irving Berlin.

Arlen was better attuned to the working man's poetry of Ted Koehler, Harburg's deft, often political wordplay, and Johnny Mercer's sophisticated folksi-ness. Yellen had an assured niche in the hierarchy of popular songwriting, but he was not, and he was aware of it, in their class. He was happy to have made his mark in the Alley, on Broadway, and in Hollywood. He worked, by the mid-1930s, primarily in Hollywood with Ray Henderson, Sammy Fain, and his early Tin Pan Alley collaborator Milton Ager. He was also proud of having hectored a young, reluctant Harold Arlen into writing his first Broadway musical—and a hit at that.

But it proved not to be a hit on the road. Neither the humor nor Lyda Rober-ti's pulchritude and accent saved *You Said It* in the hinterland. The show expired during the tour and forced the company to return to Manhattan and the tempo-rary refuge of a rapidly expiring vaudeville. Lou Holtz, still a "name" in New York—his portrayal of an upper-crust Englishman with a Yiddish accent un-doubtedly confounded the hinterlanders—managed to get himself and others from the show, among them Lyda Roberti, a booking at the Palace. Her recep-tion in *You Said It* and subsequent celebrity had convinced Holtz that she was a near equal; she was by then billed as "The Sweet and Hot Girl."

Holtz worked up some comic routines for himself and Roberti and talked Harold Arlen into becoming a part of the show. Arlen was introduced to perform a medley of his best-known songs at the time, among them "Get Happy" and

"Hittin' the Bottle." He then accompanied Lyda Roberti singing "Sweet and Hot" and a couple of her own specialties. Also on the program were Ethel Merman, accompanied by Roger Edens, the musical comedy star William Gaxton, and Roberti's script coach, Benny Baker.

Concurrent with rehearsals and the two shows a day, Arlen sometimes worked with Ted Koehler on *Rhyth-Mania* between shows on the Palace stage.

The show did so well during its Palace run that it moved to its rival, Warner's Hollywood, titled *Lou Holtz's Vaudeville Revue.* For the new edition, Harold Arlen had two additional songs for his medley, "I Love a Parade" and "Between the Devil and the Deep Blue Sea."

After her Palace stint, Merman went into a Nacio Herb Brown and Richard Whiting musical, *Humpty Dumpty,* co-starring Lou Holtz. A revue, its sketches and songs lampooned characters and incidents in American history. It closed after five performances in Pittsburgh. Revised, recast (Holtz was eliminated), with a real book and added songs by Vincent Youmans, it reopened as *Take a Chance.* It was one of the year's big hits and provided Merman with another signature song in "Edie Was a Lady," one of the few Whiting songs that remained in the score. Notably, the program credited Roger Edens with Miss Merman's vocal arrangement; more importantly, with B. G. DeSylva, he is credited with the lyric to the Edie song.

This relationship, valuable to Edens as well as Merman, began at the Palace before *Humpty Dumpty/Take a Chance.* Having been catapulted to stardom in *Girl Crazy* two years before, she was booked into the Palace with top billing. Edens created an act including her then-big numbers, "I Got Rhythm" and "Life Is Just a Bowl of Cherries," along with other current popular songs. He would, as he had during the run of the Gershwin musical, also be her accompanist. Edens felt, however, that a single piano would not do. With Harold Arlen in mind as lead pianist, he wrote for two pianos to accompany Merman and to fill in with a duo-piano spot while she changed for the second half of her act.

"Harold was the ideal choice," Edens reasoned. "He had a couple of very popular songs to his credit; he was attractive to look at; he could play the piano better than I; and he could sing like an angel."

As neophytes, Arlen and Edens ingenuously placed themselves into the experienced hands of William Gaxton and Lou Holtz for their initiation to the vaudeville stage. On the advice of the two veterans, they, as Edens later wrote, "bought enough [makeup] to last for years," then proceeded to slather it on. The stage manager, himself a veteran, pointed out to the greased and powdered pianists that they would be upstaged by Ethel Merman, for the pianos were behind her and the spot would be on her, not them.

Chagrined, they took no further advice from vaudeville comics. They did share a raffish sense of frolic themselves, however.

Ethel Merman was already a Broadway legend for, besides her big vocal equipment, her gift for plain speaking laced with the vocabulary of a sailor. With this in mind Arlen and Edens decided to spice up the act one matinee. Merman added her own flourishes upon her entrances, a bit of business to pique the interest of the audience.

She would come onstage wearing a tight gown with a matching cape or jacket. After a brief musical flourish, she sang her current hit, "Life Is Just a Bowl of Cherries." As the applause faded, she strutted to Arlen's piano and removed the cape or jacket. As she did, she noticed a note on the piano. Curious, she read the message: "Your left tit is hanging out." She read it again, her cape routine forgotten, then burst into an auditorium-pervading roar of laughter, undoubtedly mystifying the audience.

Soon in control, she moved into the rest of her songs to complete the first portion of her act. When the set finished, she left the stage to change while Arlen and Edens went into an Arlen medley. Even as they played, Edens recalled, "We could still hear her screaming with laughter."

Their indelicate little joke so delighted Merman that it became a daily ritual, a covert onstage comedy routine to which the audience was not privy. Merman and the stagehands expectantly waited to learn what the next jape would be. Merman, too, fell into the spirit of the thing. One day Arlen took his place at the piano and found a red rose on the keyboard—inside a jockstrap. On another, he and Edens arrived just in time for the curtain and did not have the time to prepare another ribald message. Merman was hurt by the omission, fearing that she had done something to alienate her playful pianists. Once she was reassured, the daily routine continued.

Ethel Merman finally brought their raillery to the audience. Before leaving the stage for her change, she introduced the Arlen segment of the act. He and Edens began their medley with "You Said It," segued into "Get Happy" and "I Love a Parade," and then Arlen sang "Kickin' the Gong Around" and "Between the Devil and the Deep Blue Sea." They finished with "Hittin' the Bottle" as the orchestra joined in on the final chorus.

As their run at the Palace was extended, Merman's introduction waxed more flowery to the point of fulsomeness. While it was all in fun, Edens found that in time it "rankled Harold's most modest soul for a week or two." They conspired "to put Madam in her place."

In her next florid introduction—she employed the word "immortal"— Merman went even further, but Arlen and Edens were ready. She moved into the wings and the thunderous overture rang out leading into the immortal "Arlen Medley," which on this occasion began with "Ol' Man River" (music by Kern). Merman caught on immediately, shouting from backstage, "And then he wrote": "Tea for Two" (Vincent Youmans), "The Man I Love" (Gershwin), "Hallelujah" (Youmans), and "My Heart Stood Still" (Rodgers). "I Got Rhythm" (Gershwin) served as the finale, leaving the orchestra absolutely in the dark waiting for their "Hittin' the Bottle" cue, which never came at that performance.

Between these downtown excursions, Arlen completed the Cotton Club songs and wrote some interpolations and single songs with Koehler and Yellen. *Earl Carroll's Vanities of 1932* was the single excursion that would prove to be everlastingly memorable and decisive. The major Arlen-Koehler contribution to this tenth in Carroll's series (and the one with the shortest run) was "I Gotta Right to Sing the Blues." It became an instant classic. But of even more importance to the composer was the presence in the cast of a young model, Anya Taranda. Carroll's advertising for the show promised "The Most Beautiful Girls in the World." In Anya Taranda the promise was kept.

The daughter of Russian emigrant parents, with minimal schooling, she had almost matured (she was about seventeen the year of that *Vanities*) into a beautiful, slender, blonde model. When Carroll chose her as one of his most beautiful girls, her golden profile was widely circulated in magazine advertisements and on the containers of Breck shampoo. She was, and would remain for a few years, the Breck Girl.

Her face, along with eleven other Carroll beauties, appears on the back cover of the show's sheet music. The accompanying text preserves for all time the producer's classic philosophy of pulchritude, along with a full-length portrait of the man. True to form, he is not fully clothed. He wears a dressing gown, shoes and spats, formal trousers with suspenders, and a white undershirt. He looks directly at the viewer.

The essay printed above his balding head, entitled "Earl Carroll Vanities: A Mecca of Beauty," is an unlikely literary effort to appear on a sheet music cover. In part, it reads: "Immediately after his first Vanities Mr. Carroll came to a full realization that in a revue feminine beauty and charm is [*sic*] paramount. He set for himself the highest standard and proceeded to adhere strictly to it in the selection of girls. The 'picking' of beauties is a ceremony almost as elaborate as the coronation of a foreign potentate—much more exacting than any other beauty pageant in the world," and so on at length about how seriously Carroll views this selection of the "girls"; how his "eyes sparkle and his enthusiasm warms when he sees a new specimen nearer to perfection just as does the lapidary or precious stone collector when he discovers a new gem." The reader is informed that Carroll "views nearly ten thousand applicants prior to every revue production" and that, despite this (inflated) number, "he exercises the same care with each individual."

A publicity shot for the *Vanities* depicts Carroll peering into an oversized suitcase into which his choices out of those ten thousand applicants—a dozen—are packed. All are smiling, wearing the latest in snappy hats (one beauty sports a fur collar). Carroll, hand on lid, stands over a grinning Anya Taranda.

Harold Arlen was truly smitten. Frances Williams and he had "palled around," as Richard Hanser had reported in the *Buffalo Times* early in 1931, but their romance had hardly evolved beyond that. Over about two years they were seen at Lindy's, the Cotton Club, the Silver Slipper, and other clubs, as well as the theater. Despite the Broadway and Tin Pan Alley gossip overheard by the young aspiring songwriter Ann Ronell (she would later write "Willow Weep for Me" and "Who's Afraid of the Big, Bad Wolf?"), their romance quite early became a convenient friendship. He relished being seen with the glamorous star, as Hanser described her, but her ambitions drove her to the point of restlessness. Though a striver who occasionally had little time for him, she never truly became a bona fide star and would eventually close her Broadway career as a replacement for Ethel Merman in touring companies and stock. In 1932, while the *Vanities* was in production, Frances Williams had just come out of a short-running *Everybody's Welcome,* in which she had starred (and introduced Herman Hupfeld's "As Time Goes By") and was at liberty again and uneasily desperate. She had to find something and had no time for romance; she was, of the two, the realist and Harold Arlen the romantic.

Anya represented Romance—beautiful, young (almost a decade younger than he), fun, simple but not unintelligent, and definitely interested. Still, perhaps because of her ineffable beauty or her renown as the Breck Girl (hers was a more readily recognized face than his), he found it difficult to make the usual overtures. His solution was simple: he invited two of Earl Carroll's beauties (despite the producer's "no fraternization" decree) to his Croydon penthouse for dinner. One of his guests was Anya Taranda. After this innocent rendezvous, the hypothetical chaperone was no longer required.

Although she lived with her parents, Anya spent much of her free time away from the theater at the Croydon, and there was a great deal of free time, for her major job at the Broadway was to stand around onstage. She was a quiet presence as Koehler and Arlen worked. Frances Williams, though not forgotten, was no longer a factor in Arlen's personal life. Anya was everything.

The extraordinary popularity of "Stormy Weather" from the *Parade* that succeeded the *Vanities* led to two additional jaunts away from Harlem. The first was a bright idea that originated with his friend Robert Wachsman, only recently arrived from Chicago. Wachsman was a forty-dollar-a-week advertising executive, endowed with a quick, lively mind and a love for the theater and for popular songs of quality. Arlen remembered him as a man with "imagination and ambition. Someone had to prod me; Bob did."

When they met, both were in their midtwenties, though Wachsman was more dynamically bubbling with ideas. Once in New York he cultivated songwriters, and at a party given by the composer Dana Suesse he met Yip Harburg. Wachsman was familiar with Suesse's "Jazz Nocturne" for piano, which had been transformed into the popular "My Silent Love," with a lyric by Edward Heyman.

With Harburg she had collaborated on an extraordinary and unusually structured "Moon about Town" for a future *Ziegfeld Follies*.

Harburg's name rang a bell. Wachsman knew him as one of the songwriters responsible for his current favorite song, "It's Only a Paper Moon." Actually, it was the tune that had captivated him. He learned from Harburg that Harold Arlen had written the melody; he learned too that the composer lived at the Croydon Hotel.

Soon after, in mid-April 1933, when "Stormy Weather" was the most popular song in town, Wachsman boldly presented himself at Arlen's door. He made an impressive entrance, complete with a businesslike briefcase. Even more splendid to the dress-conscious composer was Wachsman's natty derby.

Wachsman found himself in the presence of a slender, quiet young man "with an almost ascetic look." Arlen was not the Manhattan songwriter he had expected; there was something near-mystical about him. "When he sang, it was as if he were praying or in a spell."

Arlen listened attentively as Wachsman outlined his plan. Exploit the popularity of "Stormy Weather" by working up an act around it, with the composer singing, backed by a Negro chorus. Wachsman then proposed staging this at the recently opened Radio City Music Hall, advertised as the world's largest indoor theater, with a capacity of sixty-two hundred. Situated in Rockefeller Center, it was the center's most elaborate "variety house"—no films was the policy. The movies were booked into the smaller Center Theater.

The Music Hall was managed by S. L. Rothafel, known by everyone in the business as "Roxy," a name he brought with him from the Roxy Theater, which had failed as a variety house and sent Rothafel to the more resplendent Music Hall. It was one of the last of the vaudeville theaters holding out against Hollywood.

Thinking big, Wachsman arranged for a meeting with Roxy and his musical director, Leon Leonidoff. To his surprise, Wachsman learned that they had already conceived their own plan for an elaborate presentation of "Stormy Weather," and had already arranged for a wind machine. What they had not taken into consideration was that the song, newly minted for the Cotton Club and drawing customers in great numbers, was held dear by the club's shadowy management. Roxy realized that using "Stormy Weather" without permission could prove to be detrimental to him and, possibly, the Music Hall.

As he listened to Wachsman, Roxy said nothing about the wind machine, but with Harold Arlen involved, he could use the song without fear. Arlen demonstrated the song; Roxy and Leonidoff were convinced. Wachsman's idea of the chorus, they later admitted, was superior to their conception. Besides, they could still use the wind machine for some effect or other. A contract was agreed on. It then devolved on Wachsman to acquire permission from the Cotton Club bosses. The club's manager, Herman Stark, was adamantly negative; if people wanted to hear "Stormy Weather," let them come to the Cotton Club. A Radio City Music Hall act would hurt the show. Arlen and Wachsman pleaded and reasoned with Stark; they even hinted that it might be good for the club by piquing public curiosity.

Without conceding, Stark softened slightly and suggested that they take their proposition to "the other fellow," Big Frenchy DeMange. Arlen and Wachsman arrived in time for the midnight show, but the other fellow skipped it that night. They sat through to the early morning—still no Big Frenchy. Dispirited and bleary eyed, they finally saw him come in around seven for his usual breakfast, ham and eggs.

Arlen and Wachsman moved to his table and outlined their idea as DeMange sat quietly awaiting his breakfast. He said nothing. Wachsman started over again. It was unsettling: Big Frenchy's attention seemed to be drawn elsewhere; he barely looked at him and seemed not to listen. Resigned and exasperated, Wachsman stopped talking.

"What do you think?" he asked after a moment.

"I t'ink it's de nuts," DeMange replied. "Where's my ham and eggs?"

With DeMange's blessing, Bob Wachsman and Rothafel arranged for Harold Arlen's initiation into the meaning of "vaudeville grind." The contract would run for ten to twelve weeks, depending on the houses the group would attract. After a couple of weeks at the Music Hall, the "Stormy Weather" show would tour the Loew's circuit beginning in Baltimore and moving to Washington, D.C., where Celia and Samuel Arluck would see their son and the sights. A return to the New York area would take them to the Loew's theaters in Jamaica, on Long Island, and in the Bronx. The routine was simple, featuring Harold Arlen at the piano singing solo and with a chorus, one of whose members was Katherine Handy, daughter of "The Father of the Blues," W. C. Handy.

In addition to the tiring two-a-day grind, Arlen missed Anya and phoned her as often as he could while on the road. The show's reception was good and it ran the full term. Abel Green, in *Variety,* was enthusiastic about Arlen's solo spot, which Green called a "pianolog specialty," and liked " 'n' how!"

The "Stormy Weather" show had been a success, but for the Radio City Music Hall it was one of vaudeville's terminal gasps. It, too, was forced to put in a silver screen. Soon after, following a disagreement with the Rockefellers, Roxy Rothafel left for other parts.

The second bonus Harold Arlen received from "Stormy Weather" came soon after he returned to New York and had begun contemplating the next *Cotton Club Parade.* On an afternoon off from work with Koehler, he made the rounds of the music publishers and agencies to schmooze with colleagues and friends. While in the William Morris Agency he saw a teletype just in from Hollywood. He joined a group gathered around the machine and was stunned to read that

Columbia Pictures wanted to commission the team of Arlen and Koehler to write the songs for a film tentatively titled *Let's Fall in Love.*

His stomach churned and he fled to the men's room—just in case. Away from the boys, he calmed down, and breathing easier, he reached into his pocket for some jot paper. Basing the melody on the film's title, he sketched ten measures of music (half of which ultimately would be used). He then returned to the office. Koehler agreed that a trip to Hollywood would be a nice change, and a contract with Columbia was signed. This meant they would be forced to forgo the *Parade* that year. The problem was solved when Arlen persuaded Herman Stark to hire his brother, Jerry, to write the score with a friend from Syracuse University, Jimmy Van Heusen. (One song from their score survived, "There's a House in Harlem for Sale." Van Heusen went on to a successful career in Hollywood, primarily with the lyricist Johnny Burke. Jerry was not so fortunate and paid the frustrating price for being the kid brother of Harold Arlen.)

At the time neither Arlen nor Koehler was attracted to air travel, so they took the classic route to Hollywood, boarding the celebrated *Twentieth Century* at Grand Central Station, then changing to the *Chief* in Chicago. Their contract had stipulated that they arrive in Los Angeles by October 1, 1933, for a five-week stay.

They virtually had the *Chief* to themselves. Only the conductor and the porter, the latter to announce mealtimes with chimes, materialized from time to time. They also had the observation car to themselves, causing Arlen to fret. With all that privacy, they could do some work on songs for *Let's Fall in Love* en route during the eighteen hours it would take to get to California.

"Could have brought a portable organ," Arlen complained to Koehler, who was quite happy viewing the scenery and saving his cells.

One lunchtime, when the porter came to summon them with his chimes, Arlen commandeered the instrument to play around with the jot he had written at the Morris office. At that moment, it was all they had, for without a script they had no idea of the musical content of the film, or even if Columbia would want a song entitled "Let's Fall in Love." Nonetheless, when they arrived in California, on time, they had an almost finished title song.

Their train pulled into the Los Angeles station on a Sunday, a day when not much happens in Hollywood. For Arlen it was his first experience with palm trees, lush man-made landscaping, and eclectic Beverly Hills architecture.

"Sunday," F. Scott Fitzgerald had written about Hollywood, was "not a day, but rather a gap between two other days." The new arrivals took advantage of the gap to visit their benefactor, Harry Warren. At the time, he was the virtual king of the Hollywood musical. In 1933 alone, before their arrival, he had composed the music for *42nd Street,* with lyrics by Al Dubin ("Shuffle Off to Buffalo" and the title song), *Gold Diggers of 1933* (Dubin again and "We're in the Money" and "Shadow Waltz"), and *Honeymoon Hotel,* to which he and Dubin contributed the title song and "Shanghai Lil." Warren was on the verge of becoming the most successful of all film songwriters of the 1930s—and, to his bitter chagrin, one of the least known outside the boundaries of Hollywood.

Arlen and Koehler had come at the beginning of Hollywood's second musical film cycle. The first was initiated by Al Jolson's quasi-talkie *The Jazz Singer* in 1927. It was not quite a musical, though the few songs, including Berlin's "Blue Skies" and a Jolson specialty, "My Mammy," were recorded. But a few bits of dialogue, including Jolson's famed "Wait a minute! Wait a minute! You ain't heard nothin' yet," marked *The Jazz Singer* as the first film musical and first talkie. Whatever its label, it made the sound film Hollywood's next major development and the musical film inevitable.

In *The Jazz Singer*'s wake came a raft of attempts at the hopefully designated "All Talking–All Singing–All Dancing" musicals. The most successful, ignoring Jolson's next, *The Singing Fool,* which was neither all-talking nor -singing, was *The Broadway Melody,* released early in 1929. With a backstage plus onstage setting, it was a natural for the singing and dancing its advertising promised, and the first of a genre. In its immediate train the inevitable duplicates followed, either with a Broadway background (*On with the Show,* 1929) or a glorified vaudeville or variety-show setting, into which a studio poured everyone on the lot, whether or not they sang or danced. Among these were *The Hollywood Revue of 1929* (which gave us the evergreen "Singin' in the Rain"), *The Show of Shows* (featuring the Warner Brothers roster from John Barrymore to Rin Tin Tin), and *The King of Jazz* (1930), which featured the Paul Whiteman Orchestra performing Gershwin's *Rhapsody in Blue* from inside a forty-foot piano and introduced the newcomer Bing Crosby.

When *The King of Jazz* opened at the Roxy in New York it was a failure, even with Gershwin onstage to play the *Rhapsody in Blue* on a conventional piano, accompanied by Whiteman. Rothafel withdrew the film and canceled the stage show a week before its full run. The writing was on the box-office wall. The musical cycle was quickly running its course, prodded by the Depression and the popularity of radio, which provided the same revue songs and comedy, unseen, but with admission free. When the Gershwins' first original film, *Delicious,* opened in December 1931, it was another failure. The filmgoing public had tired of formula revues and inane plots that films such as *Delicious* offered.

During this phase of the musical's cycle, a few films were produced that intimated the promise of filming an original, made-in-Hollywood musical. These, directed by outsiders, one German and the other of Russian birth, taught the resident filmmakers how to use the camera and sound with ingenuity and artistry. The German was Ernst Lubitsch, whose *Love Parade* (1929) and *Monte Carlo* (1930) introduced a moving camera technique and filmic storytelling that revolutionized the industry. The Russian was Rouben Mamoulian, whose *Love Me To-*

night (1932) remains a classic of the cinematic musical in which songs, scoring, and plot are imaginatively woven by brilliant camerawork and editing.

A distinctive American touch would soon be added to the musical by Los Angeles–born Busby Berkeley. His contribution, seen in *42nd Street, Gold Diggers of 1933,* and the next year's *Dames*, was extensive use of the overhead camera and human figures forming geometric designs—something then impossible on Broadway. The Lubitsch and Mamoulian films, for all their sophistication and wit, were redolent of the operetta. Berkeley, though more choreographer than director, gave the musical film a twentieth-century American touch.

Harold Arlen and Ted Koehler arrived in Hollywood after a slump in musical film production. So many musicals, more than sixty in 1930, was too much for the country's box offices. Theater owners booked fewer musical films in favor of the new cycle of grittier gangster movies, dramas, and westerns. In 1932 the production of musical films dropped even lower; 1933 brought a renewed golden cycle, culminating in the sparkling films of Fred Astaire and Ginger Rogers.

Harold Arlen and Ted Koehler were there at the right time, but in the wrong place. Compared with other studios, especially RKO, Warner Brothers, Paramount, and MGM, Columbia had scanty experience with musicals. Before the release of *Let's Fall in Love,* a mere three musical films had been produced at Columbia—the second, *Rain or Shine* (1930), was directed by Frank Capra. In 1934, when the Arlen-Koehler film appeared, it was Columbia's only musical. The one other Columbia film using even one song was *Beyond the Law,* starring Tim McCoy, their leading cowboy hero.

On Monday morning, when Arlen and Koehler appeared at the Columbia studios, they learned that their producer would be Felix Young. This was encouraging. Young came from a musical family; he was the brother of Victor Young, a conductor and songwriter who later became celebrated for his film scoring. Felix came to their hotel early that morning to find "the boys," habitual late risers, still in pajamas. The script, they learned, had been written by Herbert Fields, Dorothy's brother. This impressed Arlen, though Fields's reputation intimidated him a little. Koehler took it with his customary imperturbability.

Fields had had good, solid Broadway experience before Hollywood. He had written librettos for Rodgers and Hart, Youmans, Cole Porter, and the Gershwins. Just beginning in Hollywood, Fields proved early that he was more at home on Broadway.

While Arlen admitted that he was in awe of Herbert Fields, there was nothing awesome about his screenplay for *Let's Fall in Love.* The premise of his plot was inspired by the then highly celebrated, beautiful, and aloof Swedish star Greta Garbo. She had first "talked" in the film version of Eugene O'Neill's *Anna Christie* in 1930. After several additional films, she achieved another peak in *Grand Hotel* in 1932. By 1933, when Fields conceived his story, Garbo was a major star.

His idea was simple: what if Garbo walked off a film in the initial stage of production? What would the studio do to protect its investment and cover itself after the publicity department had widely heralded the first film by a mysterious, new Swedish film star? The plot twisted around finding a convincing replacement. Since the public had never seen the original Garbo-like star, anyone who looked Swedish, that is, blonde, and spoke with a Swedish accent would do. For the further purposes of the film she should also be able to sing.

Selected to portray the part of the imposter was a petite Broadway soprano, Harriette Lake. In 1931 she had appeared in Rodgers and Hart's *America's Sweetheart,* with a book by Herbert Fields. His patent inspiration for this Hollywood tale was Mary Pickford. That same year, after the short-lived show closed, Lake moved into the cast of *Everybody's Welcome,* which starred Harold Arlen's friend Frances Williams. That, too, quickly failed, and Harriette Lake joined the touring company of the Gershwins' *Of Thee I Sing.* Once that musical ran its Depression-depleted course, she entrained for Hollywood as the lead in *Let's Fall in Love.*

To fit the part Harriette Lake underwent a couple of alterations; her brown hair was dyed blonde and she was renamed Ann Sothern, which, it was reasoned, looked better on marquees.

Cast opposite her, as a film producer, was Edmund Lowe, a dependable and popular leading man since his debut in *What Price Glory?,* a silent film. He made the transition to sound gracefully but appeared in a series of not very important films. No singer, he at least looked like a producer. Also cast as a studio head (in a broad takeoff on Samuel Goldwyn) was Gregory Ratoff, who delivered heavily Russian-accented malapropisms. The bandleader-vocalist Art Jarrett appeared as a composer.

Arlen and Koehler went through the script with Fields and Young, spotting songs for their vocalists. The hastily jotted title song was retained (to become one of the next year's popular songs and a standard); it was sung by Jarrett, as the composer, with piano accompaniment and by Sothern with full orchestra. Arlen, with a little study, managed to write a convincing quasi–folk song for Sothern, "Love Is Love Anywhere." He and Koehler rounded out their ballads in the film with the wistful, bluesy "This Is Only the Beginning." For lively rhythmic contrast they wrote a dance, "Breakfast Ball."

Considering the primordial state of the film musical in 1933, the two extended, integrated plot sequences they wrote were quite advanced for the time. One was a quartet in which Ratoff rejects Sothern as the substitute Swedish star, "She's Not the Type"; the other is the climactic "The Swede Is Not a Swede," when she is revealed by a jealous fiancée as an imposter.

But Columbia was not ready for such invention, and both numbers were dropped, along with "Breakfast Ball." The remaining songs belong with Arlen's best; Alec Wilder in *American Popular Song* pronounces them all remarkable.

Pleased with their efforts, Arlen and Koehler were not pleased to learn that, once they had presented their work to the studio, their work was finished. Even the mobsters at the Cotton Club gave them a freer hand. To Arlen's consternation, he had nothing to say about orchestration, a song's function in the film, even whether it stayed or went. He sensed an uneasy frustration. Everyone was affable but noncommittal. Nor did *Let's Fall in Love* lack cooks. One Los Angeles newspaper reported that the film employed no fewer than six directors—an exaggeration, for all movies required several technicians for such elements as lighting, sound, cameras, and costumes. The nominal director was David Burton; the musical director was Russian-born Constantin Bakaleinikoff, who may have done the orchestration, though uncredited. There was an art director, common to every film, and likewise a costume designer.

Among the film's credits were a "Swedish technical director," J. Henry Kruse; a director of "Swedish dance numbers," H. K. Hansen; and a Mr. G. G. Berglund, who oversaw the authenticity of the Swedish folk songs. Anyone aware of this promotional outpouring upon seeing the film's premiere at the Rialto in January 1934 would have wondered about the absence of folk songs and dances (though "Love Is Love Anywhere" qualified to a degree).

The consensus among critics was that *Let's Fall in Love* was just another variation on the worn backstage (sound stage, in this case) musical, with an interesting plot twist or two. In the *New York Tribune,* Richard Watts Jr., a fine judge of popular song, found it "fortunately lacking in elaborate chorus numbers" and employing "only two [sic] songs in its plot manipulations. It happens, however, that both of them are agreeable melodies and one of them, the air that gives the title to the photoplay, is particularly good."

The *World-Telegram* reviewer found reasons for the film's "slight distinction" in its "acting, its sane treatment and its pleasant tunes." He did not elaborate on what he meant by sane treatment, but, like many of his colleagues, he believed that Ratoff stole the show. Again like many of his colleagues, he did not mention the songwriters, an early lesson for Arlen in the fate of the Hollywood composer. Still, Arlen was happy to be unmentioned in P. K. Scheur's *Los Angeles Times* judgment of their score: "charming but irrelevant."

So much for six weeks in Hollywood.

Still, Arlen was happy to be back in friendlier Harlem and especially to be reunited with "Annie." His cross-country phone bills during those Hollywood days and nights were staggering. Hollywood was not for him. With little time out, he and Koehler began work on the *Cotton Club Parade of 1934,* their last, as fate would have it.

LIFE
BEGINS . . .

*A*s soon as he and Ted Koehler completed the songs for the Cotton Club *Parade* in early March 1934, Harold Arlen joined his new collaborators at Ira Gershwin's apartment on East Seventy-second Street, directly across the street from his brother George's duplex, in which George was then at work on his opera *Porgy,* later *Porgy and Bess.*

Because Ira Gershwin preferred working at home and late, they assembled at his place around eight or nine in the evening and worked until four or so in the morning. Arlen was invariably on time; Yip Harburg was invariably an hour or two late, which did not sit well with the prompt and meticulous Gershwin.

At their first meeting Arlen learned from Harburg that their project was to be a revue, still untitled. John Murray Anderson, who had been associated with several successful revues since the 1920s, was director. He had, in fact, "de-vised" the show, as the program put it, and was the producer, with the Shuberts the backers. Plotless, it would consist of satiric sketches by a veteran of the form, David Freedman, as well as Gershwin and Harburg.

The stars would be Bert Lahr, Luella Gear, and Arlen's former roommate, Ray Bolger. Frances Williams appeared in an important singing part as well as in some of the sketches. The final program also lists The (Charles) Weidman Danc-ers and "The Singers: Sally Gibbs, Grena Stone, Ethel Thorsen and Anya Ta-randa."

To Arlen, the Shubert revue was another challenge. It would be less earthy and more sophisticated than the Cotton Club shows; it was to be, in a current expression, smart. Its sketches would be satirical, topical, and comic. The songs would follow the same pattern; some of them would underscore miniature musical playlets, in addition to the traditional ballads and rhythm numbers. Even though several comic routines were without music, the show as a whole was filled with song, one of Arlen's most abundant and versatile scores.

They were a curious trio: Arlen, the virtual tyro, and veterans Gershwin and Harburg, both his senior by almost a decade. For Arlen, it was hardly an ordeal to make the transition; the quiet, methodical Gershwin was in many ways not unlike Ted Koehler, and Harburg, with his effervescent stream of ideas, was Yellen-like. But there the comparisons end, for Gershwin and Harburg were the authors of some of the most enduring lyrics written for the American stage and, to a lesser degree, films.

The lyricists had been friends since the early years when the Gershwins and the Hochbergs (the name was later changed to Harburg) lived on the Lower East Side. Ira introduced Yip to the songs of Gilbert and Sullivan; W. S. Gilbert's way with words was a major influence on both.

As Arlen would later say, "Yipper is a Gilbert and Sullivan lover. This means a torrent of lyrics. I had to adapt myself to his kind of thinking and find a way to please myself. Working with him didn't limit me—that is, I didn't have to set lyrics. . . . Ira is very much like Yip [as he did with his brother, Gershwin preferred working from a more or less finished melody]. . . . They sure gave me an interesting time!"

Gershwin later remembered Harold Arlen as youthful, a marvelous demonstrator of his songs (and everyone else's), with a refreshing sense of fun but "an almost supernatural belief in inspiration." After more than a decade of disciplined work with his brother, Gershwin's notion of inspiration was more down to earth. Often, when asked the inevitable question, "Which comes first, the words or the music?" his retort was almost invariably, "The contract."

Harburg found Arlen hard on himself. "He threw everything out. He was frightened of everything sounding like something else. . . . He works with discipline and passion. He will labor on one phrase sometimes for weeks, exploring every musical possibility with the patience of a chess champion."

Arlen and Harburg remembered a bonus diversion of their collaboration. They would take a break from their work, cross the street, and barge in on George Gershwin. He would play them music from his opera in progress. By April 1934, when he had finally begun the composition after some delays, Gershwin enthralled them with the first song, "Summertime," with words by DuBose Heyward. Arlen and his collaborators would then reciprocate by amusing Gershwin with their work in progress. "They were glorious days," Harburg remembered.

During this period Arlen had had a curious musical encounter that he never forgot and that always perplexed him. One early evening he dropped in on George Gershwin before going to Ira's. He had developed a jot that had been haunting him for some time and hoped to get Gershwin's opinion. Though it was in the standard thirty-two-bar form and was not "rangy" (the compass was only a ninth), the melody was definitely not one that sounded like something else.

Pleased with the still-unlyricized song, Arlen expectantly played it for Gershwin. Gershwin was not impressed and felt that such a song would never be popular (he was right). In fact, it made little sense to him; he found it complicated. "People can't sing these songs," he told Arlen. This, too, was true to a degree, for the underlying melancholy of the melody was accomplished with unexpected shifts of harmony and, in the release, octave jumps in the melody. According to Harburg, who finally wrote the lyric, Jerome Kern had also found this unique creation too esoteric. Unconvinced by these opinions, Arlen set the song aside and concentrated on the show at hand; besides, he did not think it was a show song. A year would elapse before Harburg wrote the apposite lyric, "Last Night When We Were Young."

Harburg, unlike Arlen and the Gershwins, was a child of the impoverished Lower East Side. He recalled his boyhood for the interviewer Max Wilk as "a desperate struggle against poverty and squalor." Had there been an East Side railroad, Yip Harburg would have been born on the wrong side of the tracks. He and Ira Gershwin became close friends while students at Townsend Harris Hall, a preparatory school for gifted students who hoped to go to the prestigious City College of New York.

Alphabetically seated, Harburg sat directly behind Gershwin in their classes. Both in time wrote for the school paper and shared a love for, and a gift for writing, light verse. "I remember," Harburg told Wilk, "once going up to hear the Victrola—that was a very new thing, Victrola records [at the Gershwins']. That was the first time I heard W. S. Gilbert's lyrics to Sullivan's music. Up to that time I thought he was simply a poet! Ira played *Pinafore* for me, and I had my eyes opened. I was starry-eyed for days."

In City College Gershwin and Harburg continued their writing. They authored a joint column entitled "Much Ado" for the school paper. It was signed Yip and Gersh. They submitted examples of their verse and quips to Franklin P. Adams, who printed some of their efforts in his *New York World* column, "The Conning Tower." This was a supreme honor, sharing space in FPA's column with Dorothy Parker or Marc Connelly and other literary luminaries.

Gershwin dropped out of college in his sophomore year ("when I heard that calculus was in the offing, I decided to call it an education"). Harburg, undaunted, continued and was graduated with a degree in science. Gershwin went on to work in his father's St. Nicholas Baths, and Harburg, through a recommendation of an alumnus, found a job in Uruguay, where he spent the years of the

First World War. It was a war in which he did not believe; Ira Gershwin, who was drafted, believed Harburg had gone to South America to avoid the draft. George Gershwin in 1917 was preparing for his call by learning the saxophone so he could play in the army band, but was never drafted. Ira was called— fortuitously, one day before the Armistice was declared.

Harburg returned to the United States in 1920 and formed an electrical appliance business with a friend, only to be wiped out by the Depression.

Harburg was often puzzling to Arlen with his extreme social attitudes, his political activism, his dramatic, often volatile, reaction to what he felt was social injustice. Of his two collaborators, Gershwin and Harburg, Yip was the more complex. But neither Arlen nor Gershwin had suffered through Harburg's privation as a child, which fueled his opposition to war and to the human devastation of the Great Depression. Politically, Harold Arlen was more conservative than either Gershwin or Harburg, but this did not affect their happy collaboration.

There was another aspect to Harburg's talent, besides a gift for light verse and parody: he loved acting. He was the bright student who loved school, with its class plays and the chance to recite such dramatic poems as "The Wreck of the Hesperus" and "Gunga Din." Even in his rough neighborhood he was, he recalled, respected as "the best goddamned little actor on the East Side." In City College he and Gershwin joined the literary Finley Club, which sponsored entertainment and readings at local settlement houses for their friends, family, and interested neighbors.

Gershwin preserved the program from one of those evenings, for which he served on the club's committee; it was presented at the Christadora House on Avenue B in March 1914. The program of music, song, recitations, and "a dialogue" concluded with a one-act play, *Lend Me Five Dollars.* The top billing, as "Mr. Golightly," was given to Isidore Hochberg, the East Side's best little actor. On the same program was a piano solo played by a fifteen-year-old George Gershvin, brother of Committeeman Isidore Gershvin. Characteristically, Ira chose to stay out of the limelight, leaving the performances to his brother and his friend.

All three eventually Americanized their names, a common practice among immigrants wishing to blend into the melting pot. Hochberg's transition was the most drastic; the Isidore was discarded and his last name became Harburg. His entry in the *ASCAP Biographical Dictionary* lists him simply as E. Y. Harburg. The *E*, he once conjectured, may have stood for Edgar; the *Y* could have stood for a variant spelling of his actual name, Yisrael. He, however, preferred "Yip," short for his boyhood nickname Yipsel (*yipsl* being Yiddish for "squirrel"). When asked about his unusual name metamorphosis (the Christadora House program had been discovered by a researcher), he preferred that Isidore Hochberg not be identified as Yip Harburg, adding with a twinkle, "What's in a name?"

He often signed photographs and informal letters "Yipper," which Harold

Arlen found most appropriate. He was short, stocky, energetic, and on the move. Frequently during their long collaboration, Arlen felt that this dynamic man, seething with ideas, was constantly at his heels.

If the Depression drove Harburg out of the appliance business, it was Ira Gershwin who got him into songwriting. After the stock market crash, he called Gershwin to tell him he was through with business and wanted to take up writing lyrics. Gershwin told him he should have done that long before, wrote him a check to keep him going for a while, and brought him together with the composer Jay Gorney, who needed a lyricist. Gorney had read some verses in FPA's column signed "Yip," liked them, and on Gershwin's recommendation, teamed up with Harburg for the 1929 *Earl Carroll's Sketch Book,* beginning a collaboration that culminated in their "Brother, Can You Spare a Dime?" three years later.

By 1934 Harburg and Arlen were almost as well established as Ira Gershwin in the musical theater. As far as Gershwin was concerned, it was a collaboration of equals. Arlen was, for a time, a little intimidated by the amount of work required for a revue, as opposed to a book musical. Gershwin was familiar with Harburg's fervor but found Arlen's approach unusual. This high-spirited young man, as Gershwin viewed him, would never "approach the simplest musical requirement, or idea, without first calling upon 'the fellow up there' "—jabbing his finger at the ceiling. Ira Gershwin was a practical adherent to his brother George's dictum: "When we most want it, it does not come. Therefore the composer does not sit around and wait for an inspiration to walk up and introduce itself."

They were an unusual trio: Arlen the mystic, Gershwin the methodical craftsman—"The Jeweler," as he was called by the composer Kay Swift because of his dedication to polishing his work interminably (often a source of annoyance to his faster-moving brother)—and Yipper, the peripatetic, skittering *yipsl.* Their unique collaboration resulted in one of the outstanding musical revues of the time.

Their contribution depended on the demands of John Murray Anderson's conception, David Freedman's sketches (some with songs, others without), and the cast. There were two star vocalists, Frances Williams and Ray Bolger, who tripled as singer, comedian, and dancer. Bert Lahr was no vocalist but stopped the show every night with his zany patter song, an example of Arlen's ability to sublimate the tune to the lyric. Lahr dominated the direction of the wit, satire, and irreverence that characterized the revue. Harburg later said that he and Gershwin had decided that, there being no plot, they would "write a satiric show and more or less cover the field. We weren't focusing on one thing. . . . We started off by kidding the theater."

The final word, however, belonged to Anderson, a veteran of revues since 1919, when he produced the first of his six *Greenwich Village Follies.* He set out on his own a decade later with *John Murray Anderson's Almanac*; earlier, he had worked on Irving Berlin's *Music Box Revue* and Rodgers and Hart's *Dearest Enemy*. Before taking on the Shubert revue with Arlen, Gershwin, and Harburg, he had worked for the Shuberts on the first *Ziegfeld Follies* produced after the producer's death (the advertised producer had been Ziegfeld's widow, Billie Burke). Harburg had collaborated on that score with Vernon Duke. It had been a strenuous job, one of the reasons he had asked Ira Gershwin to assist on the lyrics for the new revue.

Harburg, who rarely had a good word for producers and directors, waxed enthusiastically about Anderson. "I loved Murray," he told Max Wilk. "He was a very smart man. He had such class, style, taste, sophistication—everything. Always put on such beautiful sets and decor." By 1934 Anderson was renowned for his innovative staging, employing revolving stages, treadmills, and complicated sets. He was clever with names, devising descriptive sobriquets for his favorites. Harburg was called Zipper, Gershwin was the Rock of Gibraltar, Arlen was Ol' Man River ("He must know sumpin, but don't say nothin' "), and Anya was known as Schmanda Fair around the Winter Garden that spring of 1934.

Work on the show spread over nearly half a year; the songwriters began in early March with Gershwin and Harburg suggesting a possible song. Once agreed, Arlen would write the music. This method contradicted his customary dependence on jots, but it worked. By July practically the entire score was complete. Rehearsals then began in preparation for a Boston opening in the first week of August.

Anderson had his sketches, whose targets included the Roosevelt New Deal, Mayor Fiorello LaGuardia, Wall Street, the stiff-upper-lipped Briton, Eleanor Roosevelt, and such topical matters as the Depression, a little sex, even the theater itself. He had close to two dozen musical numbers. What he lacked was a title.

That problem was solved by Ira Gershwin following a luncheon at Anderson's at which he had hoped to find a title for their revue. All present had made suggestions, but nothing sounded right. Stymied, they gave up to leave for the rehearsals at the Winter Garden.

As they reached Anderson's foyer, Gershwin spotted a book on a table near the door, a popular best-seller, Walter B. Pitkin's inspirational *Life Begins at Forty*.

Modestly brightening, Gershwin said, "How about 'Life Begins at Eight-Forty'?" This was fitting, since the advertised curtain time for a show was 8:40, although it rarely went up on time. The suggested title was thus itself a satirical reference in tune with the show.

Co-producer Lee Shubert did not like the title, and the search began again. Gershwin suggested another, *Calling All Stars,* a nod in the direction of Lahr, Bolger, Gear, and Williams, and trite. That was rejected, too, during a conference onstage after the rehearsal was over. When the arc light was turned off and the dozen thinkers left the stage, the consensus was that their revue would be entitled *Life Begins at 8:40*. Gershwin had given them not only their title but also an idea for their opening number, a song kidding the theater, in Harburg's phrase. This song, further, set the bright tone of the show:

> *At exactly eight-forty, or thereabouts*
> *This little play world*
> *Not of this day world*
> *Comes to life.*

The Gershwin-Harburg conception is as much a scene as a song; they, not the credited authors of the sketches, fashioned the initial scene. "Our idea," Harburg explained to Max Wilk, "was that life begins when the curtain of the show goes up. We had this big Munich [a tall round] clock onstage, and out of the clock came all the characters that would appear in the revue. The husband, the lover, the wife, the blues singer, the comedian, the dancers and so on." The four-line refrain introduced each of the show types, including the Juvenile (an important figure in musical comedy); his female counterpart, the Ingenue; and the Sister Act. Each sang a verse about his or her specialty.

Once the lyricists had blocked out this elaborate and effective opening, it remained for Harold Arlen to set it to music. He conceived a production number for soloist (the Juvenile) and chorus, which provided commentary on show people and their habits:

> *They've been sleeping all day*
> *Theater folk are funny that way*
> *Art is art you mustn't forget*
> *Actors are a privileged set.*

This section was sung by a chorus of ten "Young Ladies," one of whom was Anya Taranda. Her presence made Arlen's work on the show an even happier event. There were some bad moments when he and Koehler had returned from Hollywood and he learned that Anya was scheduled to leave for the West Coast herself to appear in Earl Carroll's *Murder at the Vanities*. It was not a revue, but a film with a script that set the plot (no surprise) backstage at the *Vanities*. It was not well received. Anya and Arlen saw it and found Burns Mantle's appraisal amusing. "I know who did the murder," he wrote. "So far as I'm concerned his name is Carroll."

In *Life Begins*, Anya had more to do than merely stand around looking beautiful. In another song, "It Was Long Ago," Arlen wrote her a small obbligato to Josephine Houston's vocal.

Arlen wrote additional production numbers for extended musical scenes, "C'est la Vie," "What Can You Say in a Love Song?," and the finale, "Life Begins at City Hall," for which Gershwin and Harburg received program credit. Subtitled "Beautifying the City," the sequence reprises several songs, ingeniously arranged by Arlen, to fit into the Gershwin-Harburg scheme of a miniature operetta, not unlike what Gershwin had done with his brother in their political operettas, especially *Of Thee I Sing.*

In that vein, they have the chorus introduce Lahr as "The Dictator" who "gave the city class-o / There's dancing on the mall / He introduced Picasso / To the boys at City Hall."

The Dictator agrees:

> *I'm Dictator Fiorello*
> *I'm a many-sided fellow*
> *When you look at me you almost see Napoleon*
> *I love music, I'm artistic*
> *I'm a statesman pugilistic*
> *As a brain I'd even take Professor Moley on.*

(Raymond Moley, a political economist who had taught at Columbia University, was a leading member of Franklin Roosevelt's advisory "brain trust" in the White House.)

Mrs. Roosevelt, then noted for her peripateticism, and here impersonated by Luella Gear, describes a few of the stops of her day:

> *At seven o'clock this morning at Poughkeepsie*
> *I spoke at the opening of a bridal path*
> *Had breakfast in Savannah, then flew to Indiana*
> *To dedicate a woman's Turkish bath.*

Arlen managed to match the Gershwin-Harburg patter with fitting Sullivan-like tunes. His versatility excited Harburg. Arlen, he said, "had the facility to go to that long range from fun to high misery or comedy or whatever . . . and make the tune fit the idea."

That range encompassed the waltz ("C'est la Vie"), the madrigal touches in "Life Begins at 8:40" or the recently imported rhumba "Shoein' the Mare." Among the songs for which he composed long scenes were the wildly ribald "Quartet Erotica," the bitter "My Paramount-Publix-Roxy Rose," and "All the Elks and the Masons," a march. There was no consideration given to writing for the wider public in these songs; they were designed for the show.

By July, with the score complete and a final title, *Life Begins at 8:40* was ready for a tryout in Boston. The show was booked for a single week at the Shubert and scheduled to open on August 21 in New York at the Winter Garden. The short out-of-town run boded well; the Shubert management was confident that they had a winner.

In early August the company arrived in Boston. To Harold Arlen's surprise, and thanks to the Gershwins, he found himself the subject of his first major interview. George Gershwin's first biographer, Isaac Goldberg, who taught philology at Harvard, was also a student of popular song and wrote music criticism for the *American Mercury*. Besides the Gershwin biography, Goldberg had also produced *The Story of Gilbert and Sullivan,* as well as scholarly works on language. Goldberg found Arlen to be

a well-set youth . . . fair, blue-eyed . . . easy of action and manner. The picture of the Tin Pan Alley composer as a somewhat civilized thug who chisels out tunes on a piano with one finger, or whistles them at an arranger, became anachronistic some time ago.

Arlen is decidedly of the new generation. He is a fine pianist and not at all a bad singer. When he lets his voice out—for he is apt to begin his songs in a soft, even introspective, legato that may be an influence of his cantor-father—he makes an excellent propagandist for his wares. These songs, often as not, have a true melodic feeling for wide, yet smooth skips, and I suspect that the marked quality of what I have called ingratiation comes from the frequent employment of these half-glissando leaps. As he sits at the piano, playing and singing, his face tilted upward and his eyes half-closed, you seem to detect a relationship between his manner and matter.

He plays, by the way, as unostentatiously as he sings—as unselfconsciously as most people write, in privacy, a letter. His music, too, has this—shall we call it epistolary?—character. Arlen (and this is one of the reasons why I am inclined to herald him as one of the new hopes for our better popular music) has a rare combination of tenderness and humor. In other words, he has both the necessary sensuousness and the wise-crackiness of the Broadway wit.

I speak of his sensuousness in a purely esthetic way, regarding it as a musical generative source. For I have heard him object to words in a song ["Quartet Erotica"] that seemed to go off-color, and his objection was based, not on puritanical fussiness, but exclusively upon canons of good taste. . . . Arlen is no esthete of the parlors, nor is he a goody-goody; but he has intense artistic perceptions, even for the genre in which he is working at present.

Goldberg devoted several hundred words to a chronicle of the Arlen career up to 1934, from the Snappy Trio through the recent "Let's Fall in Love." As he had in his comprehensive volume *Tin Pan Alley,* Goldberg noted that the "affinity between the music of the Negro and that of the Jew, especially as blended in the American popular song, is one that has been especially noticed in the history of rag-time and jazz."

He observed, perceptively, that in Arlen's case "the man and his music are one; well-bred, soft, quietly confident, ingratiating. I believe, indeed, that 'ingratiating' is the key-word. About Arlen and his music there seems to be nothing raucous." He concluded the lengthy appreciation by writing that the music for *Life Begins at 8:40* reaffirmed Arlen's already distinctive style. If the performers sing them half as well as does Arlen himself, we shall soon be whistling some new hits. And, if prehearings count for anything, I should not at all be surprised to find, well in the lead, a typically Arlenesque tune called 'It's Fun to Be Fooled.' "

Goldberg's was an encouraging prelude to the show's indisputable "gala" premiere. The *New York Post* sent a reporter to cover the event. "Among the Broadway notables who attended," the column concluded, "were Harry Richman, Harpo Marx, George White . . . Victor Minelli [Vincente Minnelli]," and, among others, "Abe Berman, George Gershwin, Ray Henderson, Lew Brown and Mme. [Margaret] Matzenauer." The last, a celebrated Metropolitan opera and concert stage recitalist, had come from New York to see her daughter, Adrienne, sing "Shoein' the Mare." Abe Berman was the attorney A. L. Berman, who had become Arlen's legal advisor and friend. Among Berman's other clients were Ethel Merman, Lew Brown, Vincent Youmans, and Irving Berlin.

George Gershwin had recently returned from several weeks on Folly Island, off the coast of South Carolina, near Charleston, where he had worked on his opera, still titled *Porgy.* Tanned, excited, and enthusiastic over his brother's new show, Gershwin reassured an anxious Arlen. He also told a slightly distracted composer that during his researches in black churches and white gospel singers he was delighted to hear "Stormy Weather" sung as a folk song.

Reassured by Gershwin, Arlen slipped into his seat; Ira Gershwin preferred standing in the back of the theater, and Arlen had no idea where Harburg was. The curtain rose, the Juvenile (John McCauley) began "At exactly eight-forty, or thereabouts . . ." Anya, looking gorgeous, came onstage with all the Young Ladies, and the evening began.

The next morning's *Boston Globe* pronounced *Life Begins at 8:40* "a swiftly changing kaleidoscope of satirical skits and sketches, songs and dances, all in settings of astonishing beauty and amazing mechanical intricacy." This wonder, designed by Albert Johnson, was advertised by the Shuberts as the Rhythmic Stage.

Anderson described some of the sets' intricacies. "Our revolving stage," he explained, "includes an inner and an outer rim so that two groups of dancers, interpreting, say, sentimental and satirical themes, can be poised against each other for contrasting effect. Sort of a contrapuntal effect."

That effect would leave the *New York Post* reviewer John Mason Brown with, he claimed, an attack of vertigo caused by Johnson's scene 1 "lazy susan." It also gave the Shuberts a headache, because perfecting it postponed the show's New York opening for a week.

The delay made Arlen's opening-night jitters worse than he had suffered in Boston. Monday, August 27, finally dawned, and the night proved to be even more gala than in Boston. Arlen stood unobtrusively in a corner of the lobby of the Winter Garden with his friend and neighbor Dr. Miguel Elias. They watched a star-studded stream flow into the theater. Arlen recognized the conductor Walter Damrosch, Irving Berlin, George Gershwin (who waved a friendly hand across the clamorous lobby), and two people associated with Gershwin, the pianist Oscar Levant and the bandleader Paul Whiteman.

Nervously he saw Fanny Brice, then the formidable Brooks Atkinson of the *New York Times,* John Mason Brown (the *Post*), Gilbert W. Gabriel (the *American*), Percy Hammond (the *Tribune*), and Burns Mantle (the *News*)—the whole critical force. He caught a glimpse of his most faithful critic, his father, accompanied by his mother and the former Julius Arluck, now Jerry Arlen and his roommate at the Croydon Hotel. Jerry, after a short fling with songwriting, returned to the saxophone and singing and was doing well in the Whiteman orchestra.

The crowd, the chatter, and the thought of a Broadway opening night proved too much for Arlen. He took Elias's arm, said, "Wait a minute," and pulled the mystified doctor through the throng out to Broadway, where he could breathe. As a result, Harold Arlen and Miguel Elias missed the premiere of *Life Begins at 8:40.*

They spent the warm evening wandering around Times Square, not talking a great deal. Elias did not prod and Arlen could not explain precisely why he did not want to see the show that critical night. He later recalled that on the opening night in Boston he had sat beside Gershwin's friend, the composer Charles Martin Loeffler. Then over seventy years of age, Loeffler whispered to the anxious composer that he was tired, which to Arlen meant that Loeffler did not care for the show. Now, in New York, it was worse.

When Arlen and Elias returned to the Winter Garden a couple of hours later, the show was over and the audience was flocking out as they entered the theater. When Damrosch moved past them, Arlen heard him say, "Ah, such pulse, such rhythm!" That sounded complimentary but did not soothe his anxieties.

Later, when the family and Anya gathered at the Croydon, Arlen claimed that he had read every word of every review and believed he had come off badly. "I was literally sick to my stomach."

He may have read word for word, but he missed some of the good words. His vertigo induced by Johnson's lazy susan, John Mason Brown overlooked the music in his review. Percy Hammond concentrated on Anderson's production, finding *Life Begins at 8:40* to be superior in every way to previous Shubert revues. It was, he wrote, "brighter and richer than its predecessors and almost as unblushing."

Gilbert W. Gabriel, one of New York's most musically astute critics, found the show "chockful of happy Harold Arlen music" and praised the "good songs," among them especially "What Can You Say in a Love Song?," which, he was certain, would linger on the nation's lips along with what he called "a neighborly coo," "Let's Take a Walk around the Block." "After a summer of poison ivy," Gabriel concluded, "*Life Begins at 8:40* is all orchids and laurel. It seemed last night like the top-drawer of tunefulness, jollity and charm." This was, in fact, the consensus.

Samuel Arluck realized that his son was not enjoying the first-night celebration. Except for Chaim, everybody was elated over the morning-paper reviews. When his son explained the reason for his gloom, Samuel scolded him. He pointed out that some reviews may be good, some bad. In some you may be ignored, but if you did your job, you did your job.

Harold considered these words of wisdom. If he was to continue working in the little play world of the musical theater, he would have to expect its knocks. Newspapermen didn't review the Cotton Club shows; they wrote columns about them, praising the stars and songs, some of them overnight hits. Broadway would be different.

After the fatherly lecture, Harold Arlen decided "then and there never to be troubled by reviews. It's worked ever since." Brave words, at the time, but this philosophy would not always work; he would endure troubles in the future.

Samuel Arluck, for his part, was troubled by his son's affectionate friend named Anya Taranda. The young woman, a girl to Samuel, he had seen onstage in the show in those skimpy costumes. He noticed she had sung too, in a small voice. He asked his son about her background. Jerry told him she was a model, that her parents had come from Russia and belonged to the Russian Orthodox Church. She was not Jewish and therefore to Cantor Arluck she was also not for his son. He did not approve, though for the moment he said nothing. Later, when they had returned to Syracuse, he would voice his objections to Celia, who agreed with him. Since no one had mentioned marriage, it was best to ignore the situation. Cantor Arluck's thinly disguised feelings toward Anya Taranda would prove a tragic element in his son's and her future life.

Arlen sensed his father's disapproval but also thought it best to avoid confrontation. Once his parents left, happily without incident, he could relax when he realized he had written the music for a major hit. The songs were played on the radio; numerous recordings were made, including several he himself had recorded with Leo Reisman a week before the show opened. In September, after the show had been running a month, he was a guest on radio's "Music by Gershwin," during which he and George Gershwin talked about the show and its songs.

Those songs, Arlen soon realized, were coming into their own. The show's program carried an advertisement from G. Schirmer offering the sheet music for sale (at forty cents a copy) and six new recordings. Among the latter, the revue's most popular song was the novelty love song "You're a Builder Upper," with its lyric based on the self-conscious portmanteau trickery in the lyric: "breaker downer," "holder outer," "giver in-er," and so on (which sound more like Harburgisms than Gershwinisms). The words may sound contrived, as Alec Wilder finds them in *American Popular Song,* but their rhythmic dexterity (characterized by short lines of five or six syllables) presented Arlen with the opportunity to compose a typical light Arlen rhythm tune. "You're a Builder Upper" was heard early in act 1 and in the reprise of several of the songs in the finale, "Life Begins at City Hall." Ethel Merman recorded the song with Johnny Green's band.

Both "Fun to Be Fooled" and "What Can You Say in a Love Song?" were recorded by Harold Arlen, with Reisman's orchestra (though the composer is not mentioned in the ad) and Richard Himber's Ritz-Carlton Orchestra. Inexplicably, Wilder finds "Fun to Be Fooled," the show's major ballad, to be Kern-ish, that is, rather conventional. Arlen's unconventional touches are there, however; a forty-four-measure chorus, Wilder's esteemed octave leaps in the release, and the unexpected dip into the minor in the twelfth measure (on the words "Being fooled again").

"Fun to Be Fooled" is a rueful love song in which Arlen reflects the resigned humor of the lyric, a quasi-torch song. The lyricists borrowed their title, incidentally, from a cigarette advertising campaign. Weekly, under the rubric "It's Fun to Be Fooled, but It's More Fun to Know," the newspaper ad exposed the secret of elaborate magic tricks. By 1934 it had become a popular phrase, though not among magicians, and was grist for the Gershwin-Harburg mill.

"What Can You Say in a Love Song?" is another typical Gershwin-Harburg skewering of a popular convention. It is in fact a reworking of the same type of satiric parody as the Gershwins' "Blah, Blah, Blah" from their film *Delicious* of three years before. In the Arlen song, the chorus consists of humming followed by a cliché:

> *Mmm!—surrender,*
> *Mmm!—so tender,*
> *Mmm!—forevermore—*
> *What can you say in a love song that*
> *hasn't been said before?*

In *Life Begins at 8:40* this song was developed into an elaborate finale to the first act, tracing the course of love through history in three settings: 1780, 1880, and 1934. No songwriter could ask for better plugging than this.

Act 2 opened with a gentle musical-social commentary, "Let's Take a Walk around the Block," in which a young couple who "are flat in old Manhattan," plan for a Depression-free future that includes travels to the Grand Canyon, London, Venice,

> To Paris in time for a frock;
> To Boston in bean-time,
> Darling, meantime,
> Let's take a walk around the block.

This is a Depression song, but not in the bitter vein of Harburg's "Brother, Can You Spare a Dime?," which would have spoiled the mood of quasi-escapist good humor in which musical comedy reigned. Even the treatment of the time's realities in some of the nonmusical sketches, "New Deal Ladies' Circle" and "A Day at the Broker's," were satirical but light-hearted enough not to depress the audience.

When Harold Arlen read the reviews with miserable frustration, he failed to realize that the high, and low, comedy of *Life Begins at 8:40* practically swamped the music. The critics (and no doubt the majority of the audience) left the theater remembering Bert Lahr rather than Harold Arlen. And Arlen himself contributed to this reaction by setting lyrics to special songs that by definition could not have been expected to have a life out of the theater. He sublimated his flair for musical invention to the spirit of the show.

Bert Lahr's most memorable moment, a showstopper, came early in the second act. Few critics overlooked this part of the evening; it was Lahr's personal song, simply called "Things," a satirical puncturing of cloying art songs, mediocre poets, and, in Lahr's performance, the overweening baritone of the recital stage. The song had been inspired by Lahr's rendition (rending would be more apt) of Joyce Kilmer's "Trees," a staple of countless recitalists. Lahr had appeared of solemn mien, in black tie and surrounded by interested canines, as he made a shambles of "Trees" in the 1932 *George White's Music Hall Varieties.* Harold Arlen remembered the effect of Lahr's performance, as did Yip Harburg. Gershwin agreed; they would fashion a similar song for the comedian.

In the biography *Notes on a Cowardly Lion,* Lahr's son, John, described the scene:

Lahr came on stage in a tuxedo and sporting a brown hairpiece that brought his hairline, like a dorsal fin, to an abrupt point on his forehead. A piano player sat beside him, elegantly poised for the recital. Lahr turned graciously to the small audience on stage and began [the Gershwin-Harburg introduction]:

"Ladies and gentlemen, the first number of the second group was written while the composer was living in a little garret on the left bank of the Gowanus Canal. It is a little thing of moods and fancies, a little thing written entirely under astrological influences, though the song itself has no specific relationship with the signs of the Zodiac.

"The music lover will find especially impressive the polychromatic undulations, its rhythmic reverberation and purely American chi-chi based on legendary folk-lore.

"The title, I'm sure, will fill you with rapture! The title is called Things—T, H, I, N, G, S

"T for toast, H for horange ice, I for India relish, N for new pickles and so forth.

"Things!"

This explanatory analysis parodied the introductions spoken by Milton Cross on the Saturday afternoon broadcasts from the Metropolitan Opera and the program notes provided for the music lover at recitals for an exciting rendition of, say, "There Are Fairies in the Bottom of Our Garden" or "On the Road to Mandalay." Having delivered his musicological dissertation, Lahr proceeded to sing, to Arlen's bouncy and at times florid melody, the wonders of "The utter, utter Loveliness of things."

> Let others sing of Mandalay
> Let others sing of trees,
> Let others sing of mothers
> And the busy, busy bees—

Bits of stage business punctuated the performance. The pianist, goaded by the vocalist's trilling of "Things," adds his trills from the piano. He receives scowls from the singer, who goes on, as his toupee slides over his face. He recovers to sing, "Lickity split and to beddy for things / Fit as a fiddle and ready [winks at a woman in the front row] for things." He is then swamped by the orchestra led by a saxophone, gives up, and, as he is about to leave the stage in defeat, makes one more appeal for "things!" and gets a pie in the face from a well-dressed, obviously society lady from his onstage audience.

"He fussed and fumed to get gimmicks into 'Things,'" Arlen recalled for John Lahr. "It was an endless game for him, until he finally got as many laughs out of it as possible."

Life Begins at 8:40, despite his doubts, confirmed Harold Arlen to be an adroit, flexible, resourceful composer for the theater. If the New York critics did not hail him as warmly as had Isaac Goldberg in Boston, the growing popularity of some of the songs was proof positive. The year 1935 opened festively with a broadcast over WABC on which some of the principals appeared to sing a few of the popular songs.

A month later, on February 13, to celebrate the show's two-hundredth performance, the Shuberts prolonged the intermission, during which several bandleaders appeared to conduct some of the songs in their characteristic stylings. These included Rudy Vallee, Abe Lyman, and Al Goodman. More impressive, to Arlen, was the appearance of George Gershwin at the piano. He was especially touched because he knew that Gershwin was then occupied with the orchestration of what would become *Porgy and Bess.*

A month and forty-seven performances later, with receipts dwindling, the Shuberts sent *Life Begins at 8:40* on the road. It opened in Pittsburgh for a week on March 18, 1935, then moved to Philadelphia, Washington, D.C., Detroit, and Chicago, where it closed in May. It had proved to be most profitable for the Shuberts and all concerned in one of the worst years of the Depression. Happily, for Arlen, Anya skipped the tour to remain in Manhattan with him.

He was not happy, however, to be unemployed, despite the cushion provided by his royalties. Harburg, after two successive tough Shubert shows, decided to relax for a change. Gershwin, after completing his contribution to *Porgy,* returned to the Shuberts to collaborate with the composer Vernon Duke on a *Ziegfeld Follies.*

Ironically, Harold Arlen, having dramatically proved himself on Broadway, had arrived at the wrong time. A great change had come to Broadway and the music business (Tin Pan Alley was passé), a change that had been initiated in 1933 with the release of such film musicals as *Flying Down to Rio* and *42nd Street.* Film musicals were back, bolstered the next year with the release of *The Gay Divorcee, Roberta,* and *Top Hat.*

Something was happening in Depression Hollywood, whose cannier moguls had begun buying up the music publishers and thus obtaining the rights to their music. With the Broadway musical stage production withering, New York–based songwriters looked westward, to the Coast. A mass exodus began, the "Second California Gold Rush," to Hollywood. Abe Berman, Arlen's agent, astutely arranged for a journey to the legendary "land of silk and money." Harold Arlen and Anya Taranda were heading west, unmarried but a long way from Syracuse.

HOORAY FOR
HOLLYWOOD?

*T*he closing of *Life Begins at 8:40* in May 1935 brought to its end an exciting period in Harold Arlen's life. Before the New York run was over, he had been approached by Frank Black, the music director of the National Broadcasting Company and conductor of the popular General Motors Symphony Hour. Black, a composer, pianist (debut at the age of ten), and conductor, had been a pioneer in radio since the early 1920s. The Sunday Symphony Hour brought not only good popular song to the American public but also works by the great classical composers and contemporary composers of what was called "light music."

Black asked Arlen to write a short orchestral piece, a flattering but daunting proposition. Arlen had no intention of attempting to move into Gershwin's domain. Black had noted that Arlen's melodies were far afield from Tin Pan Alley, and as a musician himself, he admired Arlen's skill in developing a theme with extraordinary originality.

Arlen was most concerned about orchestrating for Black's symphony orchestra. The conductor was assuring—he would assign the orchestration to the indefatigable, and busy, Robert Russell Bennett, himself a composer, conductor, and orchestrator for Kern (*Show Boat*) and Gershwin (*Of Thee I Sing*).

Arlen agreed and promised to have a little composition ready for performance, as Black hoped, in mid-April 1935. With Anya in mind as a dancer, Arlen was determined to write a miniature ballet. He composed at the piano, often with her in the room; they were frequently joined by Robert Wachsman.

Arlen began the ballet with a stark melody (not unlike the open fifths that would begin Copland's *Billy the Kid* three years later). Not Gershwin, but it evokes a lonely, big-city sound. The spare theme is developed, thickening harmonically and agitating rhythmically. This leads into a gentle melody characterized by typical Arlenesque turns, building to a swinging big-band section (thanks to Bennett's orchestration), then quietly closes.

Once the piano copy was complete, Arlen played and Wachsman timed the piece with a stopwatch in hand. It came to five minutes fifty-nine seconds. This gave Arlen the idea for a title, "Six Minute Ballet."

Wachsman disagreed, feeling it was too conventional. He thought a moment, then said, "Mood in Six Minutes." Anya and Harold concurred, and the composition was delivered to Bennett. During the second week of April Wachsman recalled seeing his friend, having left a rehearsal in Radio City, dashing along Madison Avenue in a state of happy exhilaration.

The broadcast occurred on Sunday night, April 14, 1935. (The week before, Gershwin had appeared on the program playing his Concerto in F.) Unfortunately, that was the first and last performance of "Mood in Six Minutes." Arlen, however, would salvage pieces of his first "serious" composition—the opening section for an antiwar ballet in a forthcoming musical and the slow theme as a song, "Night after Night," written years later with the lyricist Dory Langdon Previn.

Once his adventure into a strange, new musical world was over, Arlen found himself with little to do but accumulate jots. Anya continued in her modeling career. During the *Life Begins* rehearsals Bob Wachsman came up with the idea of basing a radio show on the revue, with a script by Gershwin and Harburg and music by Arlen. It did not work out once Gershwin joined his brother on *Porgy* and Harburg, late in 1934, went off to Hollywood. Yip had been invited by Universal to produce a film centered around a popular song he had written with Vernon Duke, "April in Paris," from the 1932 revue *Walk a Little Faster*.

Harburg settled into a large, roomy Beverly Hills mansion he sublet from the baritone Lawrence Tibbett, who was under contract to the Metropolitan Opera for the season. Because of Universal's financial problems, the "April in Paris" project was abandoned and Harburg moved over to Warner Brothers to write a musical for their reigning juvenile, Dick Powell.

A. L. Berman came up with a happy idea about this time. He had been negotiating with United Artists for the film rights to *Strike Me Pink*, a revue of small distinction that had been written, in part, by one of his clients, the lyricist Lew Brown. Starring Jimmy Durante, the show disintegrated during its tryout in Washington, D.C., under the title *Forward March*. Rewritten, recast, and retitled, it opened in New York as *Strike Me Pink* for a lukewarm run. It was Brown's idea to retain the title, eject the music (by Ray Henderson) and fashion what remained into a film for Eddie Cantor. At United Artists, Samuel Goldwyn expressed an interest in producing it. In the recent past he had had good luck turning out Cantor musicals; the last, *Kid Millions* (1934) had been successful and had co-starred Ethel Merman (aged twenty-five) as Cantor's mother, the comedian then being over forty.

Merman, it happened, was also represented by Berman, who reasoned that, since Henderson's score had been eliminated, Brown would need a composer. He offered Harold Arlen, who was acceptable to Goldwyn and to Brown.

Lew Brown (né Louis Brownstein), with his parents, immigrated from Odessa, Russia, when he was five years old. They settled initially in New Haven, Connecticut, where he attended grammar school. Though Brown claimed he came from a musical family, there is no record of his own musical training. He did exhibit a flair for writing parodies of popular songs after his family had settled in New York's Lower East Side and he was enrolled in DeWitt Clinton High School. Short, stocky, and muscular, Brown worked during his summer vacations as a lifeguard at Rockaway Beach. During lulls he amused himself writing lyrics.

In high school he was less successful, and upon the advice of his Latin teacher he left school. Intrigued with songs, Lew Brown wandered into Tin Pan Alley, a mile or so uptown.

Brown fit into the rough and tumble of early Tin Pan Alley, home of the one-, at most two-, finger pianist, the aggressive plugger, the lyricist with a limited vocabulary, and the cutthroat publisher who could not read a note of music. He was fortunate at the start to write lyrics for an established composer and publisher, Albert Von Tilzer. He took Brown's lyric "I'm the Lonesomest Gal in Town," set it to music, and published it in 1912; the lyricist was then nineteen.

Wandering around the Alley, he met another aspiring songwriter, Ray Henderson, who, like Harold Arlen, came from Buffalo. They collaborated on several not very popular songs in the early 1920s and then, in 1925, teamed with another, more successful songwriter (who had written with Herbert, Kern, and Gershwin), George Gard DeSylva. A graduate of the University of Southern California, and also a former lifeguard, he earned the nickname of "Buddy" and preferred to be known as B. G. DeSylva.

The executive type, DeSylva took charge and formed one of the most successful and prolific songwriting teams of the 1920s, DeSylva, Brown, and Henderson. In 1925 one of their first songs, "It All Depends on You," was interpolated into *Big Boy*, starring Al Jolson. They produced their first full score for that year's *George White Scandals*. For the 1926 *Scandals* they initiated their hit output with "The Birth of the Blues" and "Black Bottom."

Their first major success for the theater was a college musical, *Good News!*, out of which came "The Varsity Drag," "The Best Things in Life Are Free," and "Lucky in Love." "You're the Cream in My Coffee" followed (*Hold Everything*, 1928) as did "Button Up Your Overcoat," from *Follow Through* in 1929, which ended their Broadway collaboration. Their Hollywood experience was even shorter, and by the 1930s, owing to personal friction—Brown believed that De-Sylva claimed more credit for their songs than he deserved—Brown quit the team. Since all three could write music, who did what in a DeSylva, Brown, and Henderson song was moot, although Henderson was recognized as the musician of the threesome.

Following the breakup, Brown and Henderson returned to New York, and DeSylva, though he moved between the coasts, settled in Hollywood as a producer rather than songwriter.

The *Strike Me Pink* troubles also closed the Henderson-Brown collaboration, and each went his separate way, the former to work with Ted Koehler and Jack Yellen, and Brown to work with Louis Alter, Harry Warren, Sammy Fain, and, with A. L. Berman's intervention, Harold Arlen.

Berman recalled some of the troubles with *Strike Me Pink*. Lew Brown, like so many talented people who came out of the Lower East Side, was acquainted with a number of questionable "businessmen," who were attracted to the glamour of Broadway, especially musicals and their "girls."

Although Henderson and Brown were billed as the producers of *Forward March*, then *Strike Me Pink*, the uncredited producer and major backer was the millionaire Irving Wexler. When the show ran into serious financial difficulties, Berman conveyed this to the unknown "angel." He received word soon after to go to the Majestic Theatre and find a seat on the aisle in the back row. At the appointed time, someone wearing a slouch hat and a long, dark overcoat approached him and asked, "You Abe Berman?"

"Yes," he was assured. The stranger dropped a brown paper bag in Berman's lap and slipped out of the theater. The mundane bag contained, in cash, additional funding for *Strike Me Pink*. The money kept the show going but did not assure its success, despite Jimmy Durante and Lupe Velez, the "Mexican Spitfire," who would fare better in Hollywood.

Strike Me Pink closed after 105 performances; the silent backer, Wexler, had put $150,000 into the production, most of which was lost. In nontheatrical circles Wexler was notoriously known as Waxey Gordon, former bootlegger, gangster, and property owner. He longed to be an impresario but failed. Also in 1933, when *Strike Me Pink* flopped, Wexler-Gordon was being pursued by the United States Attorney General for tax evasion. At the time, too, Berman believed it would be a good moment for Lew Brown to leave town.

Once it was certain that Goldwyn would take on the Cantor musical and Brown was signed as lyricist, Harold Arlen agreed to write the music. But there was more. Harburg, on his part, had gotten nowhere in his writing-producing career at Universal and Warner Brothers. It was time, he knew, to return to songwriting. Even before he began working on the Cantor picture, the *Hollywood Reporter* announced in September 1935, Harold Arlen had been signed to a three-picture agreement with Warner Brothers. His lyricist would be E. Y.

Harburg. Their first film would star a fading Al Jolson. Berman had been at work again, for he also represented Yip Harburg.

Harold Arlen's immediate future was settled for a year. So was his and Anya's housing; they moved in with Harburg. Possibly inspired by their surroundings, before taking on the Jolson script, Arlen and Harburg completed the song Arlen had begun in New York, "Last Night When We Were Young." Their landlord, Lawrence Tibbett, did not share George Gershwin's objection to the song and liked it so much that he tried to interpolate it into the score of his current film, *Metropolitan*, nearing completion at Twentieth Century–Fox. The song was rejected. Still its champion, Tibbett recorded "Last Night When We Were Young" for Victor Records after he arrived in New York to appear at the Metropolitan Opera.

On October 9, 1935, in an unprecedented recording—a twelve-inch disc, rather than the customary ten-inch "pops"—Tibbett recorded the Arlen-Harburg song. On the reverse was, inevitably perhaps, the Tibbett chestnut "On the Road to Mandalay," which had remained in the film. A couple of years later sixteen-year-old Frances Ethel Gumm, the youngest member of a vaudeville trio, the Gumm Sisters, found a copy of the recording in a pile of secondhand records. Because of the Arlen name, she bought the record, and "Last Night When We Were Young" immediately became her most beloved song. Years later, after acquiring a new name suggested by the vaudevillian George Jessel, she recorded it as Judy Garland.

Though she was no more successful than Tibbett in getting the song into her films—and she tried—she recorded it twice and sang it frequently on stage and on television. Garland regarded "Last Night When We Were Young," lyrically and melodically, one of the great love songs of all time. Harburg had no idea where he got the title, which is also the song's first line. "The juxtaposition of those two phrases is almost a whole world of philosophy," he once told the writer Deena Rosenberg. "I don't know where it comes from. . . . But I suppose the tune opened it up . . . the whole pathos of the human situation, of the human race, is in that musical phrase. Old Harold gave it to me. I rode in on the coattails of his genius."

Harold Arlen had no idea either where the resigned, melancholy melody came from. At the piano, he began with the six-syllable jot, developed it another eight, and he was on his way. Harburg caught the mood of the music and set it with one of his most poetic lyrics:

> *Last night when we were young,*
> *Love was a star, a song unsung.*
> *Life was so new, so real, so bright,*
> *Ages ago, last night.*

Neither as analytic as Harburg or Alec Wilder, Harold Arlen accepted the song as another gift from above. He was pleased to read in Wilder's book: "This is a most remarkable and beautiful song. It is one which goes far beyond the boundaries of popular music. For me, it is a concert song without a trace of trying to be. It hasn't any artiness about it or pretense." Wilder goes on to point out the ingenious chromatic writing, the suspensions in the harmonies, all those technical qualities that are recognized after the fact. Arlen merely wrote as he felt; the whole pathos of the human situation that Yip Harburg found in the melody did not reflect Arlen's personal life. He was in love and very happy. Still, in the years to come, whenever an interviewer asked him to name his personal favorite among his songs, he chose "Last Night When We Were Young," adding, "but no one's ever heard of it."

Once settled into Beverly Hills, he worked concurrently on *Strike Me Pink* and the Jolson film, to be called *The Singing Kid*. He found working with Lew Brown a problem. With rehearsals under way, they had a good sense of what songs were needed. Because Cantor and Merman were cast as entertainers who sang in clubs or onstage, their songs were written for definite spots and for the stars.

There would be a big dance number, a torch song for Merman, a novelty duet for Merman and Cantor, and a rhythm number for Merman. Arlen's problem with Brown was that, upon completing the lyric, he would come to the Tibbett house and proceed to sing the song, words as well as music, to Arlen. Apparently it had worked for DeSylva, Brown, and Henderson, but was not Harold Arlen's conception of a collaboration. He listened patiently and noncommittally a couple of times, then provided his own music. He solved the problem by suggesting that, instead of wasting time on travel, Brown read the lyric over the phone. Brown agreed and, unlike his collaborations with Koehler, Gershwin, and Harburg, Harold worked on these songs alone, without his collaborator present.

For Merman's torch, Arlen took his melodic cue from Brown's lyric, the refrain of which begins with "First you have me high / Then you have me low." He indulged in a little musical punning by making the note on the word "high" high (and held for five beats, a Merman vocal specialty). On the word "low" the melody drops a full octave. The release is ingeniously shaped in short melodic phrases, echoing the vocalist's emotional disorientation. The song closes, typically, with a brief variation on the opening four measures, then abruptly ends with "Do I want to live or want to die? / I don't know."

Merman's big rhythm number was "Shake It Off (With Rhythm)" which also served as the underscoring for a dance choreographed by Robert Alton. Another was Cantor's "The Lady Dances," set in a circus. The song is Cantor's spiel, the verse promising to show the yokels what the lady does provided they "Dig down in your pockets, / Come up with two bits." Inside the tent they learn that the lady dances.

The chorus is a wonderfully sinuous Arlen melody punctuated with triplets. That led into another big production number in which the lady who dances was the perky Rita Rio, a Mexican-born singer and dancer. Originally, her name was Rita Novello; later in her career she became better known as Dona Drake.

The songs were exceptionally well done and choreographed, but Harold Arlen's greater thrill came from the film he himself shot during rehearsals and the actual filming. One of his first acquisitions on arrival in California was a small sixteen-millimeter motion picture camera. During October 1935 he was on the set to film Anya in the "Shake It Off" and "The Lady Dances" sequences as one of the beautifully gowned "Gorgeous Goldwyn Girls."

Around the same time Arlen took his camera to a location shoot of *The Singing Kid* in nearby Franklin Canyon on a misty, coolish morning. Anya, not in this film, wore a heavy coat with a stylish fluffy white fur collar. Her companion was equally modish in an overcoat and scarf, no hat. He carried a pipe and sported a neat mustache. The proletarian Harburg came simply in slacks, sweater, and sport jacket. They waited for the filming, under the director William Keighley, to begin, comfortably seated on a pier near a small lake; there was a small upright piano on the pier.

In the scene to be filmed that morning, Al Jolson was to sing to six-year-old Sybil Jason, Warner's challenge to Fox's Shirley Temple. Like Temple, young Jason was a good little fixer and had solved Jolson's personal and professional problems in the course of the plot. He serenaded her with "You're the Cure for What Ails Me," one of Arlen's favorites among Harburg's lyrics. It is one of the earliest of what Arlen classified as Yip's "ish" songs. In the release he had written, "You're my pink of condish' / You're my Arrowhead Springs, and my Battle Creek, Mich." It is a good, bouncy tune, set to the lyric, though hardly one of Arlen's most inventive. He called it a lyric number, one in which the words take precedence over the music.

Another typical Harburg lyric number is the satiric "I Love to Sing-a," a variation on the theme of "What Can You Say in a Love Song?" It is also a subtle parody of Al Jolson's by 1935 familiar, eminently imitable style. Jolson, probably unconscious of his exaggerated diction, would often tack an additional syllable—usually "ah"—to the end of many of the words in a song.

In their small private joke, Arlen created a simple tune fitting Harburg's lyric (the first sound in the verse is "Ah!" sustained for two measures). The tacked-on "a" is associated with clichés:

> I love to sing-a
> About the moon-a and the June-a
> And the spring-a,
> I love to sing-a
> 'Bout a sky of blue-a

Or a tea for two-a

This Jolson self-parody is staged as the film's most elaborate production number, choreographed without credit or subtlety by Busby Berkeley. Jolson's declaration spills into the street, as he gets carried away with references to his earlier hits, Gershwin's "Swanee" ("with the South-a in my mouth-a") and "Mammy."

He is joined in the street by Cab Calloway and the Yacht Club Boys, a vocal quartet, who repeatedly attempt to stop him from breaking into "Mammy." The scene closes with "a cheer for Uncle Sammy and another one for my mammy." Traffic is at a standstill, the drivers draped on their vehicles or prostrated on the street, along with overcome pedestrians. So are the Yacht Club Boys, with Jolson, a foot planted on them, singing triumphantly with arms outstretched. Probably one of the most ludicrous musical sequences ever filmed, it added nothing to Al Jolson's diminishing stature.

Arlen remembered Jolson as being uncharacteristically self-effacing and moodily quiet during the filming of *The Singing Kid*. His infamous ego rarely came to the surface, and as seen on the Arlen film, he joked with the cast, particularly the comedian Allen Jenkins. He postured and mugged for Arlen's camera and affectionately cuddled Sybil Jason. At the time Arlen was unaware of Jolson's slippage in Hollywood. After completing *The Singing Kid*, he was ignored by the film industry, and when called back a few years later, he appeared in secondary roles. *The Singing Kid* was his last starring part.

Arlen and Harburg wrote the obligatory Jolson blackface number in the spiritual "Save Me Sister." The composer filmed the scene, in which Jolson is joined by Cab Calloway and a most unconvincing blackfaced Winifred Shaw, who had done better as the ill-fated singer, or "Broadway baby," of "The Lullaby of Broadway," sung by Dick Powell in *Gold Diggers of 1935*.

Powell, then Warner Brothers' leading musical performer and frequently teamed with Ruby Keeler, was the star of both films Arlen and Harburg worked on beginning early in 1936. Like the Jolson musical, the Powell pictures were "programmers," the musical equivalent of the low-budget western or comedy, the so-called B picture that constituted half of a double feature.

Arlen and Harburg were unaware or unconcerned that the films were second-rate. Besides, Berman had secured them lucrative contracts, and working conditions were excellent. As Harburg put it, "Life was luxurious. I had never lived in a house with a garden around me. Sunshine, sunshine, everyday, everywhere. Shorts, tennis, golf, swimming, kumquats . . ." Arlen agreed, it was a good, unhurried, life, as some of his home movies attest. He filmed Harburg in their garden working on a lyric, then he was filmed working on his music. There are scenes of tennis, swimming, and just sitting around the pool, usually at the Gershwins' on North Roxbury Drive.

By this time Arlen and Harburg had completed the first Dick Powell musical,

Stage Struck, and turned to the next and final one of their Warner contract, *Gold Diggers of 1937*, which they hoped to finish by December.

There was gold indeed in Beverly Hills, but at a price: damage to your artistry, your work, and your ego. Gershwin was among the first to sense this. Initially, he enjoyed the less frenzied pace of Hollywood and the pliant, undemanding work habits. Then he learned that once you had completed your work, others took over—arrangers, directors, producers, the stars (especially)—and you were expected to go away.

Arlen and Harburg were sorely indoctrinated on the *Gold Diggers* film, the penultimate in what had once been a popular series. In this, the fourth, Warner, hoping to improve its box-office chances, cast Joan Blondell opposite Dick Powell, with whom she was romantically linked. She was good at comedy, the ultimate wise-cracking blonde, and more charismatic than the rather stiff Ruby Keeler. In addition, the studio hired the highly successful director and choreographer Busby Berkeley to direct the musical sequences. Worse: Warner brought in Harry Warren and Al Dubin to write additional songs. This was the reason for Harburg's disaffection.

It had been exasperating to see so much of their score for *Stage Struck* jettisoned: the long sequence he had devised, full of typical wordplay, "Four Fugitives from a Bolero Chain Gang"; the affecting waltz "Why Can't I Remember Your Name?"; and another typical Harburg exercise, "You'd Be Kinda Grandish" (many of whose "ish" rhymes would be heard twelve years later in *Finian's Rainbow*'s "Something Sort of Grandish"). Arlen took this treatment with his usual equanimity. Two of their best songs remained in the film, "In Your Own Quiet Way" and especially "Fancy Meeting You," a romantic, lyrical, anthropological ballad staged in a museum of natural history.

In April 1936, still at work on *Gold Diggers*, the incensed Harburg contemplated returning to New York. He and Arlen received a telegram from Vincente Minnelli, who was working up another Shubert revue featuring Beatrice Lillie and Bert Lahr and hoped that Harburg and Arlen could come east to help with the score. Harburg, especially, was tempted, but was dissuaded by Abe Berman; there was little steady work on Broadway for songwriters.

In no time, Arlen and Harburg produced another Lahr classic, "The Song of the Woodman." From his friends the Gershwins, also mired in Hollywood, Minnelli got the waltz parody "By Strauss." When the revue finally opened in December 1936 as *The Show Is On*, Minnelli had succeeded in acquiring songs from several composers, ranging from Rodgers and Hart through Arthur Schwartz and Howard Dietz. Ironically, the show's one song hit was the sweetly maudlin "Little Old Lady" by Hoagy Carmichael and Stanley Adams.

Thanks to Lahr, the Arlen-Harburg song did better in *The Show Is On* than the delightful Gershwin waltz, which lingered among the rarities for fifteen years before being rediscovered in the film *An American in Paris*. "The Song of the

Woodman" was hailed as the show's most successful comic number (the second was Beatrice Lillie's "Rhythm" by Rodgers and Hart). Lahr kept his song alive over the years, performing it on television and, on stage, in an Arlen tribute years later. The song was specially conceived for Lahr, since it was unlikely that anyone else could do it. Harburg, for example, said that rhyming "Chaliapin" with "choppin' " was pure Lahr, and that he could not have written it for anyone else.

With the Bert Lahr song in the mail, Arlen and Harburg returned to Dick Powell, *Gold Diggers of 1937*, and, alas, Busby Berkeley. His assignment was not only the direction of the musical sequences but also their creation. Lloyd Bacon, a veteran of Warner Brothers musicals, directed only the dramatic scenes. Berkeley was riding high in Hollywood at the time. His forte was complex, geometric, lavish production numbers, which he shot from different angles with a single camera. He was especially fond of overhead shots of young women patterned as if seen in a kaleidoscope. The effect, though striking, was more mathematics than music.

When he began working on the film, Berkeley complained to Jack Warner that the Arlen-Harburg songs did not inspire him, that he wanted Harry Warren's kind of music. Warren and the lyricist Al Dubin formed the most formidable songwriting team on the Warner lot. Beginning in 1933, when they wrote the songs for the first *Gold Diggers* film, they had consistently turned out songs for no fewer than twenty musicals. Many of their songs became some of the most popular of the period: "We're in the Money (The Gold Digger's Song)," "Shadow Waltz," "Forty-second Street," "I'll String Along with You," "I Only Have Eyes for You," "Lullaby of Broadway," and on and on. Warren-Dubin songs dominated "Your Hit Parade," and the two men were regarded as royalty at Warner Brothers.

Warren, who hated interpolations himself, was not happy about adding songs to a score by his good friend Harold Arlen. Nor was he a great admirer of Busby Berkeley, who, Warren believed, was totally unmusical. "Arlen and Harburg were top-notch talents," he said, "really gifted men, and we had been friends for years. It was good to be appreciated by Berkeley, but it was tough trying to convince Harold and Yip that the whole thing hadn't been our idea."

As Berkeley planned, the film opened and closed with Warren-Dubin songs, the first another "money song," "With Plenty of Money and You," and the finale "All's Fair in Love and War." Squeezed in between were the surviving Arlen-Harburg songs. For the charmingly simple ballad "Let's Put Our Heads Together," Berkeley was inspired to the degree that he devised a flamboyant garden party that ends with an inexplicable sequence in which the cast cavorts on giant white rocking chairs, with one large enough to accommodate the dancer Lee Dixon in a tap routine. It seemed interminable, exemplifying Harry Warren's contention that Berkeley's handling of a musical number went on for so long that even the composer became bored with the song.

The sprightly ballad "Speaking of the Weather" was better staged, in an office, with vocals by Powell and Blondell. But Berkeley could not resist bits of business such as the wind blowing papers about the office as the stars rush around closing windows. The lyric is typical of Harburg's (or Ira Gershwin's) handling of the popular love song:

> *Speaking of the weather*
> *It isn't the humidity, it's you*
> *Come donner, come blitzen,*
> *Come pitter or pat,*
> *What in thunder is thunder,*
> *Compared to my heart when it beats like that.*

In the film Powell portrays an insurance salesman who longs to get into show business; Blondell plays a former stage performer turned secretary. The original twist to the plot is that Powell innocently sells a million-dollar policy to a hypochondriac, a theatrical producer played by a befogged Victor Moore. Powell has been tricked into selling Moore the insurance by Moore's partners, who hope the producer's death will assure the future financing of their show. When Powell realizes this trick, he watches over his client's health and gets his wish by taking over and starring in the production. Joan Blondell, too, returns to her former profession for a happy ending.

In the "Life Insurance Song," sung by Powell and other agents in their office, Harburg made some acute points:

> *You'll get pie in the sky*
> *When you die, die, die,*
> *If you buy, buy, buy*
> *Life insurance.*

The song closes with the observation, "You'll be in gravy when you're in the grave."

For the finish, Berkeley came up with an ingenious money-saving set, at the request of the Warner front office, for Harry Warren and Al Dubin's "All's Fair in Love and War," another of the battle-of-the-sexes numbers popular at the time. Berkeley used a stark black backdrop behind a polished, mirrorlike ebony floor. On this stage Joan Blondell, as a drum major, led a corps of seventy short-skirted women wearing white steel helmets of World War I vintage. All the costumes were white, as were the dancers' bugles, drums, and flags. Blondell sang the song, reminiscent of the more bitter "Remember My Forgotten Man," which she had introduced in *Gold Diggers of 1933*, also by Warren and Dubin and staged by Berkeley.

Drawing upon his military experience, Berkeley choreographed Warren's march in a precise close-order drill, geometric patterns, even a cannon firing women's faces at the audience. Drums beat, bugles blew, and flags waved for much longer than Harry Warren would have wished before the scene closed with a Blondell-Powell kiss in front of a wildly cheering audience. The film's "J. J. Hobart Revue" was a smash hit.

But *Gold Diggers of 1937* was not; ironically, its one song hit was the interpolated "With Plenty of Money and You," which was heard on "Your Hit Parade" for eight weeks early in 1937. None of Harold Arlen's film musicals written in his first Hollywood year was successful or well received by the film critics. Arlen believed that he and Brown, and especially Harburg, had done their work; the rest depended on writers, directors, and stars. The songs, if not outstanding, were good, but when the films were released the songs were handicapped by a disagreement between Music Publishers Holding Corporation and ASCAP, which licensed the songs of its members for radio broadcast. The networks, in an unusual move, sided with ASCAP, for ordinarily they were natural adversaries (a situation that led to the establishment in 1940 of Broadcast Music, Incorporated [BMI], as the networks' own licensing firm).

The effect of the feud surfaced early. When Al Jolson made a radio guest appearance he found that he could not perform "I Love to Sing-a." It would be the same for all the songs written that year: none could be performed on radio, the major outlet for songs in 1936. Without radio exposure the Arlen-Harburg songs had little chance.

There were other obstacles that year. *Strike Me Pink* was released in January 1936 and *Gold Diggers* in December, with the other two films in between. During this same period, not counting lesser programmers, their musical rivals included *Rose Marie*, with Jeannette MacDonald and Nelson Eddy, and two others from MGM, the bountiful *Great Ziegfeld* and Eleanor Powell's *Born to Dance*, with a Cole Porter score. Rogers and Astaire appeared in two hits that year, *Follow the Fleet*, with songs by Irving Berlin, and *Swing Time*, with songs by Jerome Kern and Dorothy Fields. There was even a well-filmed *Show Boat* that retained the romance and quality of the original Broadway production. The audiences lined up for tickets to these, and a couple others, and not the indifferently produced and written minor efforts from Goldwyn and Warner Brothers.

With their Warner contract fulfilled, Arlen and Harburg hoped to find something better to do. In November, Harburg went east to look in on Minnelli's *The Show Is On* and to act as an informal—that is, uncredited and unpaid—show doctor during the show's tryout period in Boston and Philadelphia.

Anya and Harold remained in Beverly Hills, preferring to relax and spend time with the Gershwins. George, Ira, and Ira's wife, Leonore (Lee), had arrived late in August 1936, the brothers to write songs for the next Rogers and Astaire film. They soon settled into a large house on North Roxbury Drive in Beverly

Hills; their immediate neighbor was the composer Sigmund Romberg, and Mr. and Mrs. Eddie Cantor lived across the street.

The Gershwin ménage became, as it had in New York, a bustling social center, especially for musicians and writers. Anya and Arlen were invited in September to "a big party," as Gershwin described it, "for Moss Hart's new teeth." Among the seventy or so guests, besides the guest of honor, were Dashiell Hammett, Lillian Hellman, and the Gershwins' artist cousin, Henry Botkin. George and Ira acted as waiters on the lawn.

Reels of film taken around the Gershwin pool caught the cavortings of Dorothy Fields, Jay Gorney, and his wife, Edelaine (Eddy), who would in a couple of years become Yip Harburg's second wife. Seated around the pool were Ira Gershwin, George Gershwin, and Oscar Levant, definitely not dressed for the occasion, in a dark suit with vest, shirt, and necktie. In one scene he creeps up on the unwary George Gershwin and attempts unsuccessfully to give him a hotfoot.

These were lively, delightful times, and it was the consensus of the Gershwin group, especially the wives, that Anya and Harold made a beautiful couple. Emily Paley, Leonore Gershwin's sister, remembered them as ideal, she so beautifully vibrant and Harold so handsome with his wavy hair, blue eyes, and well-proportioned physique. They were a perfect Hollywood pair, in Emily's view—and they dressed so smartly.

But Lee Gershwin had other views. As the virtual leader of the Hollywood wives, she launched a campaign for the legal union of Anya Taranda and Harold Arlen, a source of uneasiness for both. Still, Arlen thought it was not such a bad idea, though he knew his parents would be upset by an out-of-faith marriage. Earlier that year Anya's mother, Mary, came to visit with her young son, Willie. The films Harold took of them show Mary as relaxed and smiling and Willie as a tall, thin teenager happy to be a Hollywood tourist visiting the Warner Brothers lot. There would be no friction from the Taranda quarter if Harold Arlen could bring himself to take the final step. Considering that he and Anya had been living together for close to three years, it seemed like a natural next move. But it was not easy, and he fretted over it. The talk and gossip around the Gershwin pool or tennis court helped not at all.

There being nothing to do momentarily in Hollywood, Arlen decided to take some time out and see some shows in New York. One was *Vincente Minnelli's The Show Is On* (as the revue was billed when it premiered at the Winter Garden on December 25, 1936). It was the final musical of the year and a major hit. Soon after its enthusiastic critical reception, Anya and Harold boarded a train for New York. The plan was to see *The Show Is On* and the other good musicals still running there, including Rodgers and Hart's *On Your Toes* and Cole Porter's *Red Hot and Blue*, which starred Ethel Merman. By the time they reached Chicago to switch to the *Twentieth Century* for Manhattan, Harold Arlen had made up his mind about his Annie.

8

HOORAY
FOR WHAT!

For propriety's sake, Harold booked separate rooms for himself and Anya in their New York hotel. One night, after returning from the theater—they had seen *The Show Is On* and Harold had filmed Bert Lahr in his wood-chopper routine—Anya found a note slipped under her door:

> Dearest Anya—
> We're getting married tomorrow—
> 'bout time, don't you think?
> All my love.
>
> H.

The following day, January 8, 1937, Anya and Harold took an easy drive up to Harrison, New York. In the car with them were Jerry Arlen and Abe Berman, who had provided transportation. The two men were to serve as witnesses, and Berman would handle the marriage license.

When his brother had gone off to California, Jerry Arlen had remained in New York making a name for himself in the band business. "Julius" had been discarded when he was still a student at Syracuse University and a member of the varsity football team. The quarterback objected to such a "sissy" name and dubbed him Jerry. When he joined the Paul Whiteman band he also dropped the Arluck for the more mellifluous Arlen. Everyone in the music business knew he was Harold Arlen's brother; it was not as if he was exploiting the family connection.

Jerry had done well on his own after wisely abandoning songwriting. In Whiteman's band, besides playing the saxophone, he sang as one of the trio known as the "Rhythm Boys," which had replaced the original group made up of Harry Barris, Al Rinker, and Bing Crosby. This trio had contributed to Whiteman's popularity and record sales as well as to Whiteman's headaches. The new, more reliable, and less alcoholic "boys" consisted of Jack Goodman (no relation to Benny Goodman), Jerry Arlen, and a Georgia boy recently transplanted to Brooklyn, John H. Mercer.

When Whiteman replaced the Rhythm Boys with the King's Men, Jerry Arlen filled in for his brother at the Cotton Club in 1933 during Harold's first brief Hollywood phase, for *Let's Fall in Love*. No memorable song came out of the Jerry Arlen–Jimmy Van Heusen score for that year's *Parade*.

Late in 1934 Jerry Arlen conducted the pit orchestra at Billy Rose's Music Hall (conducting was his first love); Benny Goodman and his band appeared on the same bill. From this job Jerry brought to the Arlen apartment in the Croydon Hotel an offspring of the music hall's dog act, a full-fledged mongrel that, in appearance, was no credit to dogdom.

When Harold saw the mutt for the first time, he fixed his brother with a stern look and said one word: "Out!" The command went unheeded while the puppy won Harold over to become a member of the household. He was appropriately named Schmutts and frequently accompanied one of his roommates in walks through Central Park. Schmutts soon revealed an ear for music and often sang along to the phonographic strains of Ravel and Stravinsky. He was not as aristocratic an example of canininity as Gershwin's highly bred wirehaired terrier, Tony, but he fit into the Arlen bachelor penthouse nicely. When Anya appeared on the scene, Schmutts adored her.

While Jerry listened to his brother and new sister-in-law exchange vows, he was concerned about the match. His parents were absent, of course, but he knew his father especially would be upset. This was a civil, not a religious ceremony. A Russian Orthodox wife? There would be an outcry and lamentation in Syracuse. Neither he nor Berman brought up the subject; Anya and Harold were too happy. As they drove back to New York, Jerry's conclusion was, let it be.

The newly married Arlens had a typical New York honeymoon (some friends joked about whether it was the third or fourth). They saw the shows. Besides the reunion with Ethel Merman in the Cole Porter hit, there was the Noel Coward playlet anthology and minimusicals *Tonight at 8:30*. There were no fewer than two *Hamlet*s, one starring Leslie Howard and the other John Gielgud. One of the skits written by Moss Hart in *The Show Is On* had Beatrice Lillie, as "Mrs. Slemp," causing a disturbance at the Gielgud production. The comedian Reginald Gardner portrayed the harried Gielgud. As Mrs. Slemp noisily made her way to her seat, chattering as she went, anyone attempting to quiet her was imperiously dismissed with "Communist!" When the distraught Gielgud offered Mrs. Slemp (from the stage) a ticket to the Howard *Hamlet*, she sweetly declined, explaining that it had been Howard who had given her the ticket to Gielgud's production.

Broadway limped in the face of the economic pinch; hit shows were rare. Clare Boothe's devastating comedy *The Women* and Kaufman and Hart's gentler comedy *You Can't Take It with You* were amusing and successful, but few musicals survived. The first of the year had been *The Illustrators' Show*, of historic significance because it was Frank Loesser's first Broadway effort; it closed after five performances. A German import, *White Horse Inn*, an operetta starring Kitty Carlisle, enjoyed a good run. But in an otherwise poor year, the Shuberts rounded it out with the most successful musical, *The Show Is On*.

Their Manhattan honeymoon over after a flurry of theatergoing, the Arlens were eager to desert New York's January weather and return to California. On the way they made a brief stopover in Syracuse to face the music. Their reception was reserved but cordial. Arlen recalled that several months before, during a visit with his parents, Samuel broached the subject of marriage. The son admitted that he was seriously in love and that he was considering marriage.

"I hope you know what you are doing," was his father's only comment.

Now that Anya and Harold were legally married according to the laws of the state of New York, the subject was ostensibly closed. But an undercurrent of censure and bitterness remained.

After they returned to California, the Arlens and Harburg moved out of the Tibbett house. Harburg took an unpretentious place (for the locale) near the Gershwins in Beverly Hills. The Arlens found a splendid, white two-story house in Laurel Canyon on Lookout Mountain Road. The yards, front and back, provided plenty of room for them and their dogs, Stormy and Pan. During the afternoons they would meet at the Gershwins' for tennis or a swim. Jerome Kern's home, around the corner from the Gershwins', served as the setting for all-night poker sessions.

The Arlens frequently dined out with Irving Berlin and his wife, Ellin, and it amused Arlen, especially, when they went to a Chinese restaurant, to watch Berlin, unannounced, enter the kitchen and supervise the making of their dinner. "He always ate with chopsticks," Arlen recalled.

It was all very pleasant socially, but there was little work for Harold Arlen or Yip Harburg. To keep in trim, they wrote a few songs, and Arlen recorded several "possibles" that he delivered to Harburg, Ira Gershwin, or Ted Koehler, hoping that one of the tunes might stir up the lyrical juices. Gershwin was by then too busy with his brother working first on *Shall We Dance* and, immediately after, *A Damsel in Distress*. Koehler, too, was tied up. Harburg finally found the solution to their idleness.

While Anya and Harold attended to settling into their new home, Yip Harburg kept a wary eye on a troubled world. The international scene was even more explosive than Depression-afflicted America. Japanese armies had invaded northern China, Mussolini's Italian troops occupied Ethiopia, and Hitler's *Wehrmacht* took over the Rhineland. All of this was, to Harburg, ominous, and he fumed that few in the United States were aware of it. Even the apolitical George Gershwin wrote to a friend in New York that he was shocked by American apathy, influenced by his new friends, the composers Ernst Toch and Arnold Schoenberg, who were both refugees from Hitler's Germany.

Harburg was no admirer of the military, most governments, and all politicians. His concern with "the lords of war" was evident in his lyric to "The New Parade," which had been dropped from *Stage Struck* in favor of the less political "All's Fair in Love and War" the year before. It is an appeal for peace, brotherhood among the nations, a new parade with "banners of peace flying high." Arlen took the theme seriously also, marking the music *maestoso* (majestic, dignified). The march did not inspire Busby Berkeley, however.

Harburg had been mulling over an antiwar idea for some time. As early as 1935 he had been working on an outline for a musical about a bumbling, eccentric horticulturist-chemist. The character was inspired by Victor Moore's portrayal of Throttlebottom, the inept vice president in the Gershwin political operetta *Of Thee I Sing*. Inadvertently, while developing an insecticide for his apple orchard, he produces a gas that is devastating to humans if not insects. Harburg's plot was woven around the attempts by several of the major powers to get their hands on this new weapon of war.

When the scene shifts to Geneva, headquarters of the League of Nations, munitions makers, military men, and spies flock to the Grand Hotel de L'Espionage. One spy, Stephanie Stephanovich, manages to copy the formula for the gas, with the aid of a mirror. Reversed, the gas is no longer deadly and spreads laughter, brotherhood, and peace among the warring powers.

When Harburg outlined his antiwar, antifascist plot for the Shuberts, they found it good but turned it over to the newly formed writing team of Lindsay and Crouse. Howard Lindsay had been an actor and director for several years before joining a former newspaperman and publicist for the Theatre Guild, Russel Crouse, in 1934 to rewrite the libretto for the Cole Porter hit *Anything Goes*. Two years later they followed with another successful Porter musical, *Red Hot and Blue*. The collaboration of Lindsay and Crouse was one of the most celebrated in the American theater, with such highlights as the nonmusical *Life with Father* (1939, which starred Lindsay) and Rodgers and Hammerstein's *The Sound of Music* in 1959.

The program of *Hooray for What!* credits Harburg with the show's conception and Lindsay, Crouse, and Harburg with the book. It can be assumed that a good percentage of Harburg's political views remained, but one other factor would defang the bite of the show.

That was Ed Wynn. Because Victor Moore was not available, the Shuberts decided a good "name" for the part of Chuckles, the befuddled inventor, was the man known as "The Perfect Fool."

Wynn had begun in vaudeville around 1901 and built his career around a giggle, a lisp, peculiar costumes, wild inventions (an eleven-foot pole for people who would not touch anything with a ten-foot pole), and impossible puns. He was not as foolish as his stage personality. In 1919 he participated in an Actors' Equity strike against theatrical management, led by the Shuberts. As a star, Wynn, who did not belong to Actor's Equity, did not need his salary protected by the union. He sided with the underpaid members against the Shuberts and their allies, which did not endear Wynn to the powerful producers.

He then struck out on his own as producer, writer, even songwriter. In 1921 he billed himself as the Perfect Fool in a revue of the same title. In 1937, when *Hooray for What!* was booked to open, Wynn had been away from Broadway for six years, since 1931, when he had starred in *The Laugh Parade* (which closed down every Tuesday evening so he could appear on radio as Texaco's clownish Fire Chief). This national stardom encouraged the Shuberts to forgive Wynn his actions during the Equity strike. His presence in a show would be a major draw. The Shuberts had forgotten, however, that in their production of *The Passing Show* (1916), Wynn had wreaked mayhem with the plot. During one performance he had turned, faced the audience, and said, "I *am* the plot." Neither Harburg, Lindsay, nor Crouse had heard that confession.

While Lindsay and Crouse prepared the book and Harburg polished it and spotted songs, Harold Arlen enjoyed a creative reunion with Ted Koehler, who had been working steadily in films since he had arrived in Hollywood in 1935. Koehler had collaborated with Ray Henderson on Shirly Temple's *Curly Top* and had completed the nondescript *23½ Hours' Leave* with Sammy Stept when the opportunity came to do the songs for a Jack Benny musical, *Artists and Models*. With Burton Lane he wrote "Stop, You're Breaking My Heart" and with Arlen, "Public Melody Number One." The song was a vehicle for Louis Armstrong and Martha Raye, but did little for the Arlen-Koehler catalog. When *Artists and Models* was released in August 1936, Anya, Harold, and Yip were in New York.

Before they left California early that July, they had finished half a chorus of the new musical's title song, expressing Harburg's concept of the show:

> *Come along and shout hooray for what!*
> *Get a drum, get a flag,*
> *For the war to end wars is again in the bag.*
> *Come along and shout hooray for what!*
> *Get a fife, get a horn,*

For a hero is made when a sucker is born.

When the title song was completed, it was watered down to accommodate the sweet, detached zaniness of Ed Wynn. The theme was one of patriotism, though Harburg did manage to evoke the names of Hitler and Mussolini.

Before leaving for Manhattan, the Arlens and Harburg called on an ailing George Gershwin. Because of friction in the Gershwin house, George would move into Harburg's soon-to-be-vacant place. Ira's wife, Leonore, was repelled by her brother-in-law's strange behavior; he dropped his food on the table, dribbled water as he tried to drink, stumbled on the stairs, complained of severe headaches. Sadly mistaken, Leonore believed this repugnant behavior was Gershwin's neurotic reaction to his poor treatment in Hollywood. The true cause, a brain tumor, had not yet been diagnosed. To smooth the situation Harburg gave the keys to his house to Paul Mueller, Gershwin's man of all work; he, a male nurse, and George Gershwin would move in to spare Leonore and a very upset Ira Gershwin. In later years Ira would feel guilty about not having defended his fatally ill brother from his wife.

When he saw Gershwin that July, Arlen was shocked. This listless man with a ghastly complexion was not the George Gershwin he had known. He recalled that the dynamic, tanned, and happy Gershwin had dropped in on him and Anya only the past October. Unannounced, Gershwin had entered the house in Laurel Canyon (doors were not locked then) with a new song he and Ira had just written for Fred Astaire. He had hurried to the piano and played "They Can't Take That Away from Me," which was duly appreciated by his small audience. Following a few encores, he was joined by Anya, who sang a wordless obbligato in what Arlen referred to as "her little voice."

They were both shaken to see Gershwin in July. Arlen knew he was not faking and should have been in a hospital, not Yip's house.

On July 4, 1937, Gershwin was taken to Harburg's house as the Arlen-Harburg trio boarded the train for New York. Except for bits and pieces, they would have to write most of the score in a mere two or three months. Work began initially on Ed Wynn's yacht, then continued in Vincente Minnelli's apartment, which he turned over to the Arlens when he left for a short trip to Hollywood.

With work under way, Arlen and Harburg decided to take a Sunday off and, with Anya, escape to the fresher and cooler air of the country upstate. The east was suffering a heat wave, and the weather in town was miserable. The drive along the Hudson was refreshing and, with the convertible's top down, breezy. On their return to Manhattan, Arlen turned on the radio for the news. The Japanese were approaching Peking in China; the navy's search for Amelia Earhart continued. Then they heard the shocking news from California. On that day, July 11, 1937, George Gershwin died following surgery for a brain tumor.

They drove on in mournful silence. Four days later the funeral took place at

Temple Emanu-El in New York, on a bleak, wet Thursday. Gershwin's death was a deep personal loss to all, but to Harold Arlen it signified the end of an exciting era in American music. He was always grateful for Gershwin's encouragement and appreciation for his work, but Gershwin was more than a champion and a friend.

For the rest of his life, Harold Arlen, when asked who was his favorite composer, invariably answered, "George Gershwin." Like Gershwin, Arlen made no distinction between "serious music" and song. On hearing Leonard Bernstein refer to Aaron Copland as one of "America's great composers" on television, Arlen disagreed. He felt that Copland lacked true individuality, that he was a great musician, a musical architect, but no great composer. Arlen was an admirer of Stravinsky's *Firebird* and found the Russian composer to be a great melodist. Beethoven was "too grand." He enjoyed the romantic modernism of the English composer Ralph Vaughan Williams, but it was Gershwin he admired most.

Work on *Hooray for What!* was interrupted when soon after the Gershwin funeral Arlen began to complain of headaches; even Dr. Elias accused him of overreaction to Gershwin's death. Perhaps, but the headaches were real, and painful, to Arlen. After it became impossible to work, an exhaustive physical uncovered a cyst in the antrum of the upper jaw that pressed on a nerve, causing the headaches. A removal of the cyst ended the crisis, and Arlen returned to work with Harburg.

This marked the true beginning of an education in Shubertiana for all concerned. The Shuberts assigned a man named Harry Kaufman to watch over their interests. He hired, he fired, he offered unsolicited advice and, worse, controlled the Shubert purse for the show. He was not loved.

The Shuberts did not skimp, however. Besides Wynn, Arlen, Harburg, Lindsay, and Crouse, they had signed Vincente Minnelli to stage, direct, and design the settings, brilliant young Raoul Pene Du Bois to create the costumes, and Agnes de Mille to do the choreography. Besides the dances, she would devise a ballet for the eminent modern dancer Paul Haakon.

Although his voice swooped and gurgled, Ed Wynn was not a singer, not even in the comic style of Bert Lahr. The musical portions of *Hooray for What!* were to be handled by Hannah Williams and Roy Roberts (the juvenile leads), and by Kay Thompson as a singing spy. Williams had been one of the two Williams Sisters, who had sung in vaudeville. She was an attractive blonde, best known as the wife of the boxer Jack Dempsey. Roberts was young, had an adequate voice, and was not well known on Broadway. Kay Thompson was a radio personality and, besides her voice and wit, brought her own group of singers with her. In this group were the vocalist-pianist-arranger Hugh Martin and a newcomer named Ralph Blane. Out of this union, in time, would come the singing group called the Martins and the songwriting team of Martin and Blane.

That there would be complications was soon evident in some of Ed Wynn's casting suggestions, which raised eyebrows: Sue Hastings's marionettes and Al Gordon's dogs, for example. Harry Kaufman kindled Agnes de Mille's fiery temperament with his advice on the selection of the women members of her corps de ballet. All were most attractive, but few could dance. De Mille suspected that Harry Kaufman was attending to the art of pleasing backers instead of the art of dance. Kaufman, too, was not above lending a hand in the music division; he believed the score lacked a sure hit "jingle," as he called it. This amused Arlen, who never found that jingle.

Kaufman's schedule called for rehearsals to begin in mid-September, in time for a Boston tryout sometime in October and a New York opening a month or so later. That was not to be. No theatrical project ever comes to life without problems, and those that afflicted *Hooray for What!* began before the show got to Boston, where the final warring erupted.

As Harburg visualized it, his idea was to take a hard, critical look at the arms race then in fatal progress; "peace" conferences and duplicitous diplomacy were all very real in the summer of 1937. But the Shuberts, and Harry Kaufman, were suspicious of a musical with political overtones. Gershwin's antiwar musical *Strike Up the Band*, in its original 1927 version, had closed out of town, although its 1930 rewrite, with a gentler book, had been a hit. *Of Thee I Sing* had succeeded in 1931, but its bitter sequel depicting an American dictatorship, *Let 'Em Eat Cake*, had failed two years later. More recent history also advocated caution: In 1936 Kurt Weill, a recent refugee from Nazi Germany, had collaborated with the American playwright and poet Paul Green on *Johnny Johnson*, a brilliant musical commentary on the waste of war. (Interestingly, as in *Hooray for What!*, a laughing gas turned the tide of war.) That somber "play with music" closed after sixty-eight performances.

By October's end, Arlen and Harburg had finished the score, rehearsals had gone well enough, and the show was deemed ready for Boston. Below the surface there were smolderings; De Mille had begun to wonder during rehearsals, when Kaufman brought in backers to meet the cast, whether she was a choreographer or part-time madame. Kay Thompson and Kaufman had begun hostilities during auditions, innocently initiated by the eager Ralph Blane.

Early one afternoon he had auditioned twice, first as a singer, then a dancer. Kaufman rejected him each time. Desperate, Blane called a friend, who sent him to Thompson, rehearsing her Kay Thompson Singers. She listened while he sang but neither accepted nor rejected him. The singers were summoned to the theater for their Kaufman audition. Blane simply attached himself to the group and went along. Trying to hide in the back, Blane was spotted by Kaufman who, with customary insensitivity asked, "Didn't I throw you out of here twice today?"

Blane admitted it, and Kaufman showed him the door again. Thompson, furious, defended Blane and, at that instant, made him one of her singers. Kaufman was adamant but gave in when Arlen, Harburg, and Minnelli told him how much they liked the voice of the nervy Blane.

Kaufman bided his time. He would also from time to time remind Arlen that he was still waiting for that hit jingle. Shubert shows almost invariably had a jingle to promote the show—the previous year's *The Show Is On* had "Little Old Lady," and the *Follies* produced "I Can't Get Started" (hardly a jingle, but definitely a hit).

When *Hooray for What!* arrived in Boston, it was not, like *Of Thee I Sing*, an integrated, well-plotted, socially conscious satire, but a jumble of international politics, comedy (most of it from Wynn), and vaudeville. That it did not work was evident in the first road casualties, all Kaufman's doing.

Agnes de Mille was the first to go; the show premiered on October 30, and she was fired on October 31. A more Broadwayish dance director, Robert Alton, came in to eliminate most of de Mille's highbrow dances (Alton, in fact, had been waiting in the wings even before the company left for Boston). De Mille was followed soon after by the romantic leads, Hannah Williams and Roy Roberts. There were some exciting moments when Jack Dempsey confronted Kaufman, but the fights were only verbal, to the disappointment of many in the cast.

Kay Thompson was next, but not before she could phone de Mille in New York to tell her some good news. It was about two in the morning when she awakened the choreographer.

"Harry Kaufman fell off the stage and broke his back!"

"You're just telling me that," de Mille replied, "to make me feel good."

Earlier, some time after that night's performance, Kaufman, caught up in a harangue from the Colonial Theatre's stage, took a giant step and fell into the orchestra pit, damaging some instruments and himself. Although he had not broken his back, he was given time off by the Shuberts. In the hospital for several days, he had Kay Thompson fired. She was replaced by Vivian Vance (later of *I Love Lucy* fame), Hannah Williams by June Clyde, and Roy Roberts by Jack Whiting.

And the broken and damaged instruments were replaced by Kaufman's checkbook. The Shuberts were not brothers of mercy.

When Arlen and Harburg visited Kaufman in the hospital, Arlen momentarily felt that the accident had brought about a change in the man. Kaufman waxed philosophical, telling the boys, as he called them, that from that moment on there was nothing more important in one's life than one's health. All else was secondary. Then, without missing a beat, he asked, "Where's the jingle?"

Kaufman's fall and the string of dismissals and changes, as well as the ensuing sense of chaos, forced the postponement of the New York opening. Still, with Kaufman hors de combat, preparation for New York went more smoothly. Harold Arlen, who rarely exhibited personal revulsion, had come to dislike Kaufman and referred to him as "High Collar Harry." Kaufman, for a man of the theater, dressed peculiarly: dark, conservative suits, celluloid collars, and quiet neckties. Vincente Minnelli saw him as an evangelist, though others thought mortician was more appropriate. Minnelli believed that Arlen's "baiting," as he called it, was all in fun, a manifestation of the composer's impudent and contagious sense of humor. But during their extended enforced stay in Boston it had worn thin.

Hooray for What! finally opened at the Winter Garden on December 1, 1937, about a month behind schedule. Ed Wynn received the good press, and some reviewers, including the man from *Time*, suggested ignoring the plot, which, he wrote, "shuffled dully between old-fashioned musicomedy and pretentious satire." Forget the plot and watch Wynn. Forget the songs, too.

There were fine songs in the show, more traditional musical comedy songs than were Gershwin's integrated numbers in his political operettas. Only a few reflected Harburg's original social barbs or views. These were the title song that brought up the curtain, the not quite patriotic "God's Country," "Viva for Geneva," "Embassy Ball," and the anti-Nazi and -fascist "I Click Ze Heel and Kees Ze Hand," which Arlen marked *marciale e giocoso*, and which was abandoned in Boston. So was one of Arlen and Harburg's finest songs, "Buds Won't Bud," written for Hannah Williams. A typical Arlenesque blues, "Moanin' in the Mornin'," was written for Vivian Vance and was probably the replacement for "Buds Won't Bud."

The first-act finale was a typical Arlen rhythm number, the lively and lyrically derisive "Down with Love," which, like "God's Country," was performed long after *Hooray for What!* closed. While the song was being sung, such sentimental items associated with romance (and mentioned in the lyric) as flowers, rice, and shoes were tossed onto a bonfire onstage. (Coincidentally, "Down with Love" was introduced in Boston by the three principals who were cashiered there.)

Three fine songs could have been conceived to fit into any libretto or screenplay; one was the lovely but neglected "I've Gone Romantic on You," in which the composer syncopates the melody with memorable groups of three notes at several points. Another special song is the waltz (with a touch of blues) "Life's a Dance." In the show it was sung by Robert Shafer and segued into a ballet by Paul Haakon, Ruthanna Boris, and the company.

"Life's a Dance" is also structured around three-note groups (two quarter notes and a dotted half): a statement ("Life's a dance"), a variant a fourth higher ("Life's a toy"), then another variant ("Life's a glove"), also a fourth higher, transforming the waltz into a blues in a poignant melodic turn. The unexpected switch from major to minor is an affecting touch in an affecting song.

The third song that could have worked in any plot was the more conventional, but for Arlen and Harburg most influential, "In the Shade of the New Apple Tree," a gentle parody of the popular song of 1905 sentimentalizing an old apple tree. Its single plot concession is the song's setting, an apple orchard near Geneva. The melody is quaintly turn-of-the-century, with such Harburgian twists as

"Your dress is another's, / But your smile is still your mother's" and "Though you bob your hair and show your knee." He even tosses in a "Hey, nonny-oh" for the final eight bars, which surprisingly do not repeat, as is the customary practice, the A section of the song.

"In the Shade of the New Apple Tree," with its gentle melody, swinging rhythm, amiable harmonies, and whimsical A-A-B-C structure, was an unlikely prelude to the music that followed (after a brief scene with dialogue in the orchard). When it is discovered that Wynn's formula does not produce a deadly gas, he is challenged to a duel by four diplomats, infuriated because his invention would bring peace instead of profits for armament dealers. Generals and admirals would have to join the unemployed. War then erupted on the Winter Garden's stage.

The program at this point reads:

"Hero Ballet"
> Danced by PAUL HAAKON
> Philip Gordon and the Corps de Ballet
> Ballet Music Composed by Harold Arlen
> Choreography by Agnes George de Mille

This was de Mille's single program credit; not credited specifically for the orchestration is Don Walker, the show's principal orchestrator, there being three others named in the program. Significantly, perhaps, of the names associated with "Hero Ballet," de Mille's was set in the smallest type.

Arlen's music for the ballet, "very Stravinsky," as he called it, ranges from the poignant to the aggressive. The ballet does not glorify war; it is set on a barbwired battlefield and in the last portion—the battle—the music is spiky, harsh, and dissonant. One reviewer referred to this ballet as "a bayonet dance," as the dancers wore gas masks and brandished guns. The music, the choreography, and the deliberately unglamorous costumes left no latitude for Broadway allure and charm. It was this portion of the show that had initially soured Harry Kaufman on de Mille.

The ballet begins with the opening theme from the neglected "Mood in Six Minutes"—the desolate, deserted city sound, a bleak *andante*, with flutes carrying the sorrowful theme over the sound of a ticking clock (time running out?). The theme is developed to a point that Arlen marks "with tension," as the orchestra, in full cry, states the theme. The ensemble Walker employed was no common pit band but a large, virtually symphonic, orchestra.

Lasting about ten minutes, "Hero Ballet" bristles with shifts in rhythms and dynamics; there are some two dozen tempo changes in the forty-five pages of the orchestral score. The introductory *andante* is succeeded by a *vivace* section, then *energico*, and so on through *barbarico*, *robusto*, *marziale*, and even *strepitoso* ("noisily"). There are also such nontechnical directions as "tenderly," "bravely," and "cannibalistic," adding a touch of Arlen humor. The conductor, Robert Emmett Dolan, had his hands full keeping the orchestra together as the rhythms agitate abruptly through 3/4 to 4/4 to 6/4.

Not since Richard Rodgers's "Slaughter on Tenth Avenue" (from *On Your Toes*, with choreography by George Balanchine), the previous year, had theatergoers seen so complex a ballet in what was described as a musical comedy. The Arlen music is much less romantic (despite the "slaughter" in the Rodgers title). Melody is sacrificed to nervous rhythms and dissonance. "Hero Ballet" is one of Harold Arlen's most original compositions, with turbulent themes and sounds germane to the action. Though innovative, the ballet received little notice (even de Mille disparaged it years later). The music was ignored and the grim mood dissipated upon the return of Ed Wynn and his foolish antics with the Sue Hastings Marionettes. Yip Harburg's message was lost on the audience.

Still, some of his points were made in the most-quoted bits of dialogue in reviews and musical theater histories. The most popular has Wynn telling foreign diplomats, whose countries were heavily in debt to the United States after the war, "Don't you fellows know that if you miss two more payments, America will own the last war outright?" Or Wynn's assessment of a troubled time: "The trouble with the world is that Italy's in Ethiopia, Japan is in China and Germany is in Austria. Nobody stays home." Or this, pure Harburg: "This gas will revive the dead. I've got a big offer from the Republican party."

As delivered by Ed Wynn, such lines were more naïve than caustic. And it was Wynn who carried the show for a good run of six months. Audiences enjoyed the fun and, of all the songs, the one best remembered was the optimistic, patriotic, and pro-Roosevelt ("Thank God for a man called Frankie") "God's Country."

It was a song remembered by an important member of one evening's audience. Arthur Freed, a former songwriter, was in 1937 on the musical production staff of Metro-Goldwyn-Mayer, with dreams of becoming a producer. Part of Freed's job was to see Broadway musicals and to consider them as potential "properties" for MGM.

Freed could not visualize *Hooray for What!* as a film musical; it depended too much on Ed Wynn and was interrupted by nonessential vaudeville acts. But he liked the score, especially "God's Country," which he would acquire for the Judy Garland–Mickey Rooney film *Babes in Arms*, released late in 1939. He was even more impressed with "In the Shade of the New Apple Tree." He had been nurturing a film musical project for some time now and had been wheedling, cajoling, and otherwise pressuring the studio head, Louis B. Mayer, to give him the opportunity to produce a film. He had also been considering a few prospective songwriters. When he heard "Apple Tree," there was something in the song's character, something in the frolicsome, whimsical tune and the lighthearted, witty lyric, that convinced Freed he had found the perfect team to score his film—if it ever got made.

9

A TIME OF
GOLD AND LEAD

*W*ith *Hooray for What!* profitably nestled into the Winter Garden, the Arlens and Harburg realized it was time to return to California. They had
spent close to six months in New York, and Hollywoodians were notorious for
short memories; stars dimmed quickly there.

In the months in Manhattan they saw the shows, some films, visited family
and friends (though most of their professional friends were on the other coast).
The weather was not kind in wintry Manhattan; they missed the outdoor life of
California, the pools, the tennis, and the evenings at poker or word games at the
Gershwins' or Kerns'—and those wonderful evenings playing new songs for their
friends to get their reactions.

But the radio brought a poignant reminder of an exciting era that had come
to a tragic close. While listening to radio's "Hit Parade," they heard one of
George Gershwin's last songs, "Nice Work If You Can Get It." The "Lucky
Strike Hit Parade" during the 1930s was replete with film songs, and listening
to it was practically mandatory. Arlen songs had been conspicuously absent from
the "Hit Parade" for too long.

In February 1938 another "work" song joined the "Parade," "Whistle While
You Work," from Walt Disney's first, and stunningly flourishing, full-length animated fantasy, *Snow White and the Seven Dwarfs*. Arlen and Harburg were impressed with the intelligent handling of the songs, how they meshed with the
plot and characters. Fairy tales, until Disney, had been box-office poison for

Hollywood. Recent attempts at filming fantasy, *Alice in Wonderland* in 1933 and *A Midsummer Night's Dream* two years later, had been dismal failures despite their all-star casts and magnificent productions.

Somehow, without stars and with song, Disney had expanded the animated short subject into a full-length hit movie. Hollywood's golden rule, then as now, was; If a certain type of film fails, forget it; if it succeeds, do it again. Harburg's whimsical juices were stimulated by Disney's pioneering cartoon.

On his own, Arlen had made his contribution to their next assignment. During the period of wrangling in Boston, he had slipped out of town in mid-November to record a couple of songs from the show. They happened to be the two favorites of Arthur Freed, "God's Country" and "In the Shade of the New Apple Tree." To their surprise, Arlen and Harburg were summoned to Freed's new office at Metro-Goldwyn-Mayer when they returned to California.

This was a little puzzling, for they knew Freed only as a staff lyricist at MGM. They wondered what he could have in mind. Freed had been a familiar presence at the studio since 1928, when he was teamed with a former Hollywood real estate broker and part-time composer, Nacio Herb Brown. Brown had studied piano and composition but decided to abandon the artist's life after a brief, unhappy tour in vaudeville as an accompanist. Disenchanted with show business, Brown returned to Hollywood, where he became, literally, haberdasher to the stars, among them Rudolph Valentino and Charlie Chaplin. Later he switched to the lucrative Beverly Hills real estate trade. Nacio Herb Brown soon knew all the right people in a burgeoning Hollywood.

Freed came from a cultured background (though many who knew him later doubted that: Yip Harburg spoke of his "crude, brusque exterior"; his biographer-historian, Hugh Fordin, wrote of his deliberate lack of social polish). His father was an art dealer who traveled a great deal. Arthur was born in Charleston, South Carolina, grew up in Seattle, and attended Phillips Exeter Academy in New Hampshire, where he began writing poems. He was one of eight gifted children; his younger brother, Ralph, was also an established lyricist.

Like his father, Arthur had a fine singing voice (it is his voice that is heard singing for Leon Ames in the film *Meet Me in St. Louis*). He got an early start in vaudeville with the famous "star maker" Gus Edwards, discoverer of juvenile talent, among them Eddie Cantor, Walter Winchell (before he switched to gossip), Ray Bolger, Eleanor Powell, Groucho Marx, and Mervyn Leroy in his popular "School Days" acts. In this setting, Freed began writing songs for vaudevillians and his own act with another Edwards alumnus, Louis Silvers. Freed worked for a time as a song plugger in Chicago, then drifted westward, where he managed a theater in Los Angeles before finding his spot at MGM.

The fresh-faced Irving Thalberg was then hailed as "The Boy Wonder" because, while still in his twenties, he had made MGM an important and profit-making studio. Thalberg brought Brown and Freed together to write the songs for one of the earliest film musicals, *The Broadway Melody*. Released in 1929, it was a sensational success. Though burdened with a creaky backstage plot, it was blessed with such songs as "You Were Meant for Me," "The Wedding of the Painted Doll," and the title song. *The Broadway Melody* was voted Best Picture of the Year by the recently established Academy of Motion Picture Arts and Science initiating a spate of backstage musicals. In the next decade, Freed and Brown turned out several popular songs for MGM musicals—"You Are My Lucky Star," "Singin' in the Rain," "Temptation," "Pagan Love Song."

Despite this success, both dreamed of bigger things: Brown hoped to abandon songwriting for serious music, and Freed wanted to produce films. Songwriting did not fulfill his larger aspirations.

While working on the Metro lot, Freed absorbed filmmaking on the sound stages and sets. He attended conferences and, to his greater advantage, cultivated a close camaraderie with the studio head, Louis B. Mayer. Because of this intimacy, Freed was regarded suspiciously and with envy by his colleagues. He was, they felt, Mayer's toady, one of his "after-hours slaves," always on call and prepared to offer favorable opinions of Mayer's views and judgments. His rivals at the studio regarded Freed as an ambitious and ruthless contender. His open invitation to breakfast at Mayer's home was a certain sign of this abnormal favoritism.

At one of these meetings, Hugh Fordin has recorded, Freed spoke enthusiastically of a young singer who had appeared in his and Brown's MGM swan song, *Broadway Melody of 1938*. She was the former Frances Gumm, of the Gumm Sisters, who had been discovered singing in a local movie theater by the composer Burton Lane, who arranged for her to sing for the MGM front office to his accompaniment. She impressed the right people and at age fifteen signed a contract with MGM. Her lackluster name was quickly Metroed into Judy Garland, but the studio initially found little for her to do. Then, with a small part in *Broadway Melody*, she endeared herself to the nation, and Hollywood, with her rendition of an arrangement Roger Edens created for her of the popular "You Made Me Love You," prefaced by Edens's heart-tugging "Dear Mr. Gable."

Freed was building up to his major point. Audiences as well as critics, he assured Mayer, "love the kid! I'd put my bet on her if I were a producer." He may have been a yes-man, ambitious and quietly ruthless, but no one questioned his eye and ear for talent or his judgment of a song.

"Well, Arthur," Mayer told him, "now is the time. Find a property and make a picture." As with many a Hollywood grand decision, this was not quite the final word; even Mayer did not have that. Still, energized, Freed went into immediate action.

The "property" (a standard Hollywood term that applied to items owned by a studio, from Garbo's shoes to a piano concerto) Freed had in mind was a "picture" (another generic term) to be based on the stories by L. Frank Baum set in the imaginary land of Oz. Since 1934, Freed knew, Samuel Goldwyn had controlled the rights to the Oz stories and had intended to produce a film starring Eddie Cantor as the Scarecrow. When Cantor's box-office intake began to shrink, Goldwyn lost interest in him and the Oz tales.

Freed was aware, too, of a stage musical contrived from pieces of the Oz stories. Entitled *The Wizard of Oz*, it starred the vaudeville duo of David Montgomery and Fred Stone. With an undistinguished score by several songsmiths, it had been a huge success back in 1902. Early attempts to film it in 1910 and 1925, before the advent of sound, failed. The latter had been produced by Baum's own ill-starred film company.

Disney's *Snow White* had rekindled Hollywood's interest in fantasy and its potential for profit. Freed wanted to do this film and believed that in Judy Garland he had the perfect Dorothy, the central character in the Oz stories. Other gears, however, were grinding. Twentieth Century–Fox had also begun searching into Goldwyn's properties for a vehicle for their reigning queen of the box office in 1937, Shirley Temple. But after six months of legal debate Metro won the property race and paid Goldwyn seventy-five thousand dollars for the *Oz* rights. The *Oz* historian Doug McClelland called the transaction "one of the best buys since the sale of Manhattan."

The final document was not signed until early June 1938, but in fact, Freed had already jumped the legal gun as early as February, when he had returned from seeing *Hooray for What!* He had assumed the deal would be consummated, despite the hypercaution of Metro's legal department, and that he would produce the film, which officially, he would not.

Though Freed was an envied after-hours slave with breakfast privileges, this did not mean the crafty, tough Louis B. Mayer would stick out his neck for him. Mayer was the big boss in Hollywood, but he answered to a higher power, Nicholas M. Schenck, "The General," who presided over MGM's parent company, Loew's, Inc., in New York. This was the money source and the place where the final decisions were made. With Schenck hovering, sometimes menacingly, Mayer was not about to risk placing such a high-budget, ambitious property as *The Wizard of Oz* in the hands of an embryonic producer.

Mayer sorely missed the genius of Irving Thalberg, whose death in 1936 at the age of thirty-seven had left a critical void in Metro's production staff. In 1938 Mayer proceeded to fill it by hiring away another "boy wonder," Mervyn LeRoy, from Warner Brothers. To accomplish this Mayer offered a secret, and excessive, weekly salary of six thousand dollars (the "secret" quickly spread all over town).

LeRoy, a small-framed man who took pride in appearing ten years younger than he actually was (thirty-eight), had, in fact, little experience as a producer. He had directed some estimable films at Warner, among them *Little Caesar*, *I Am a Fugitive from a Chain Gang*, and *They Won't Forget*, all in the gritty Warner

Brothers verité style. His one major screen musical, also as director, was *Gold Diggers of 1933*, and he had also turned out a reasonable facsimile on film of Kern's Broadway musical *Sweet Adeline*.

His production experience (combined with direction) included such now forgotten quasi-musicals as *The King and the Chorus Girl*, *Fools for Scandal*, and *Mr. Dodds Takes the Air*, which was released just prior to his signing with MGM. Unlike Freed, he had had some experience as a producer, though minimal and undistinguished. Years later LeRoy would claim that when Mayer had asked what project he would undertake as his first, he asked for *The Wizard of Oz*.

Once LeRoy was assigned the job, Mayer then appointed Freed as LeRoy's "assistant" or "associate." Freed's name does not appear anywhere in the finished film's credits (a point LeRoy made repeatedly—especially after *The Wizard of Oz* had become recognized as a classic). Nevertheless, Freed worked deftly behind the scenes and was crucial to the film's final musical form; without him, *The Wizard of Oz* would have been a very different work.

Even as Metro massed its legal paper clutter for the June 1938 contract closing, Freed was on the move. He began by compiling a listing of his ideal cast for *The Wizard of Oz*, with Judy Garland at the top. Soon after that had circulated, the local trade paper, *Daily Variety*, prematurely published the news that Metro had acquired the screen rights from Goldwyn and that Judy Garland had been assigned the role of Dorothy. LeRoy was disturbed by the leak; he planned to get a real box-office name for the part.

The next day, Freed and LeRoy met with Mayer. The assistant/associate did not come empty-handed. He had prepared another inventory, ranging from other cast members through special-effects technicians. He was clearly no mere assistant.

He had more. He also had prepared a musical roster with the name of his friend Jerome Kern heading the list. Harold Arlen was second, and Freed's former collaborator, Nacio Herb Brown, was third. The top lyricist was Ira Gershwin, who had, after his brother's death, written a few songs with Jerome Kern. Next came E. Y. Harburg, then Dorothy Fields (who had also written with Kern). With Kern and Gershwin at the top of their respective job descriptions, Freed smoothly assuaged the studio anxiety over name recognition (Irving Berlin, the best-known songwriter in town, was tied up at another studio). Freed, in fact, had already decided that he wanted Arlen and Harburg.

While successive writers (over a dozen eventually) prepared "treatments" and early scripts, new leaks appeared in *Daily Variety*. In March the rumor was that Harry Revel and Mack Gordon would write the *Oz* songs; soon after, the rumored songwriters were to be Nacio Herb Brown and Al Dubin. These publicity releases from who-knows-where caused Arlen no anxiety—his money was on Jerome Kern and either Ira Gershwin or Dorothy Fields. Nor was he aware of Freed's list.

While Arlen waited for film work, he and Anya spent time with the Gershwins, the Warrens, and the Koehlers. They frequently dropped in casually on their near neighbors, Eddie Cantor or Sam Jaffe. In 1938 Beverly Hills was in many ways a village and had not yet become a community of fortresses patrolled by a Gestapo-like police force. Doors were not barred in those halcyon open-house days, and strollers were not confronted by police for questioning. In Beverly Hills, as in New York, Arlen was an inveterate walker—a misfit in a motor-obsessed town.

He recalled an amusing incident from the earlier trip to Hollywood. While on a stroll Arlen decided to pop in on a couple of new friends. He admired the splendid house as he traversed the flower-bordered walk curving up to the front door. With a turn of the doorknob and a step, he found himself in an expansive living room—and there on the luxurious rug, rolling merrily, were his friends Carole Lombard and William Powell.

Powell was the first to sense the presence of the gaping, uninvited, though welcome, guest. He and his playful wife stopped whatever they were doing. Powell, with characteristic aplomb, sat up and said, "So, you wrote 'Stormy Weather.'"

Hollywood's social-political stratification, unwritten but understood, rarely brought songwriters and film stars to the same parties. The elite—producers, studio heads, powerful directors—mingled with the big-name actors. The other members of that society of fabricators, technicians, and creators—from lighting experts and cameramen to musicians—congregated in their own groups. Harold Arlen's and George Gershwin's home movies show members of their respective families and their colleagues: songwriters such as Harry Warren, Ted Koehler, Yip Harburg, and Jay Gorney, and musicians such as Oscar Levant and the arranger and orchestrator Edward Powell. Gershwin filmed his friend and tennis opponent Arnold Schoenberg. Among the writers captured on these films are Irwin Shaw, Lillian Hellman, Moss Hart, and Dashiell Hammett. Vincente Minnelli is the lone film director. Harold Arlen's only footage of Samuel Goldwyn was filmed on the Goldwyn lot. Gershwin did capture Fred Astaire, but on the sound stage dancing.

So it was that the songwriters congregated in their own little world. A favorite center for their frolics was the home of the screenwriter Sonya Levien where some of their performances were recorded on acetate home recording discs. At one of these evening parties Arlen was asked to sing Gershwin, which he did, accompanied by the composer Milton Ager. To the delight of the company, he sang "Summertime" in the original key for soprano and followed with "There's a Boat Dat's Leavin' for New York" in its original key for baritone. His vocal range was phenomenal, his voice controlled, pliant, sensual. His vocal shadings came out of the synagogue and Harlem, with all stops between Broadway and Hollywood. A friend told him he had overheard a glamorous young woman exclaim after an Arlen vocal, "He sings as if his fly was open!"

Ira Gershwin treasured the acetate discs of the *Porgy and Bess* songs performed by Arlen and Ager. He and his wife, Leonore, were also regulars at the Levien evenings. At one, joined by Arlen at the piano, Ira recorded one of his brother's last songs, "Hi-Ho! At Last!," written for but not used in *Shall We Dance*. Though he was no Tibbett, or even an Astaire, Ira's singing is, with its attention to phrasing, pronunciation, and emphasis on rhyme placement, an object lesson in the art of song presentation. Arlen's pianism is sure, perfectly attuned to Gershwin's delivery of the intricate tune. His playing is an extraordinary replication of George Gershwin's. (When he heard the recording thirty-five years later, Arlen's comment was, "I never knew I played so well.")

Another disc preserves the sounds of another evening with Arlen at the piano surrounded by Anya, Ira, Yip Harburg, and a chief heckler, the screenwriter Robert "Doc" MacGunigle, a friend of the Gershwins. Other unidentified voices are also heard.

After some talk, Anya suggests that Harold play a little-known song he had written with Ted Koehler, "Sittin' on a Fence." Ira Gershwin unsuccessfully requests "I Can't Get Started," which he had written with Vernon Duke. In case no one recognizes the title, he hums a few bars. But "Sittin' on a Fence" wins. Gershwin then jokingly suggests, "Annie, you do an obbligato." She laughs and chooses to leave the vocals to her husband. (The small joke was Gershwin's reference to her minor contribution as a singer in *Life Begins at 8:40*.)

"Well," Arlen says with mock resignation, "it looks like we're stuck," and launches into the song. His audience listens through one chorus, then, with MacGunigle leading, begins hectoring the composer. Laughing, Arlen continues to sing and play despite them. (The composer Johnny Green said of Harold Arlen that "he was the greatest laugher I ever knew.")

At one point, Ira Gershwin, the purist, questions a line in the lyric. Arlen sings, "Like Humpty Dumpty I'll soon be slippin' off the wall," as Gershwin observes, "First he's talking about a fence, then he's talking about a wall."

Chuckling, Arlen persists, but is running down. He stops and pleads, "Come on, Mr. I.," to Gershwin.

Harburg has his final word, "I think we're running out of beautiful phrases."

"Take it, Harburg," Arlen says to general laughter.

Early in May 1938, the time had come for Harburg to begin writing beautiful phrases to the music of Harold Arlen. It was official: they had been selected by MGM to write the songs for *The Wizard of Oz*. When Jerome Kern read the news in *Variety*, he was surprised, certain that he would be the composer for the film. When he saw Arlen, he was still a little dazed and asked, incredulously, "You got the job?"

Freed had prevailed. Not only had he gotten Arlen and Harburg, but he had also won Judy Garland. His nominal boss, Mervyn LeRoy, had his heart set on Shirley Temple—a vain hope; Twentieth Century–Fox was not about to further the fortunes of the studio that beat them to the Oz stories. (Fox then made the error of casting Temple in their own fantasy, *The Blue Bird*, one of their major flops.)

Contracts were signed on May 19, 1938. Arlen and Harburg were given fourteen weeks to write the *Oz* score and a not particularly generous sum of $25,000. (Irving Berlin, with a widely known name and a reputation as a tough bargainer, had received, three years before, $75,000 for *Top Hat* from a nearly bankrupt RKO Radio Pictures. The next year, RKO hired the Gershwins for $55,000 for sixteen weeks, with the prospect of an additional $70,000 should the studio option a second film—and it did.) Arlen and Harburg did not haggle, acknowledging that theirs were lesser names among Hollywood's songwriting elite and that the film promised to be an important one. Harburg especially was caught up in the idea and during the production would offer script suggestions beyond his lyric contributions.

Further, theirs was the standard "work for hire" contract. Like any other technician on the film, they were paid for the job. They were entitled to the customary song sheet and recording royalties as well as the ASCAP income from radio and other sources. But, alas, MGM's contract gave the studio all rights to the songs from the film in perpetuity. Neither Arlen nor Harburg nor Metro considered the future importance of television, then undergoing a premature birth at the National Broadcasting Company to promote the primitive sets being sold by its sister company, Radio Corporation of America. (In short, when *The Wizard of Oz* became a television staple in the late 1950s, it got the film out of its red ink and made a mint for CBS and NBC, but no additional income for Arlen and Harburg.)

Even before the contract signing, the studio had an early version of the script, primarily the work of Noel Langley, based on several treatments and assorted bits and pieces from others and his own initial screenplay. He had marked that copy, in capitals, "DO NOT MAKE CHANGES." Langley was an Ozian dreamer if he believed his work was inviolate. Several other writers, often simultaneously and unaware of one another, had a crack at it. After Langley quit, or was fired, in early June, additional changes were introduced by Freed, LeRoy, and Harburg. By then, *The Wizard of Oz* was officially on the MGM schedule as "Project No. 1060."

"I loved the idea," Harburg told Max Wilk, "of having the freedom to do what were not just songs, but scenes." The studio's copies of some of the musical numbers are titled "sequences," rather than songs: "The Munchkin Musical Sequence," in which Dorothy is welcomed by the Good Witch and the Munchkins to Munchkinland, is a complete scene, as Harburg hoped for; it runs some seventeen pages (the published "Over the Rainbow," by comparison, is four pages long). Other sequences include "The Jitterbug" and "Renovation," better known as "The Merry Old Land of Oz."

"That was our idea," Harburg informed Wilk, "to take some of the scenes of the book and do some of the scenes in complete verse. All of that had to be thought out by us and then brought in and shown to the director so he could see what we were getting at."

Working from Langley's script and a considerable list of song ideas supplied by Roger Edens, Freed's chief musical overseer of the film, they began working on the score. They practiced a little economy by lifting "I'm Hanging On to You" from the score of *Hooray for What!*, from which it had been dropped, and refashioning it into "If I Only Had a Brain."

Then with Harburg leading the way, they tackled the long "Munchkinland Musical Sequence." For this scene Harburg wrote the dialog as well as lyrics, as he would for other scenes. The major musical section (following the Good Witch's summons to the Munchkins, "Come out, come out, wherever you are") is "Ding Dong! The Witch Is Dead." With this long, truly integrated musical scene in hand, they felt they were ready to demonstrate a little of what they had accomplished in the past month. It was then early July, with about eleven weeks to go.

Arlen drove to the studio as an excited Harburg bounced in his seat and talked about what they had done—no one had ever written such a piece for a musical film before. (Rodgers and Hart had attempted it in Jolson's *Hallelujah, I'm a Bum*, but the film had failed.)

They assembled in Freed's office (neither Arlen nor Harburg mentioned Le-Roy's presence in later interviews, but he was probably there). Before Arlen played, Harburg began expounding, outlining, and otherwise proclaiming their aims, intentions, and philosophies, which would make *The Wizard of Oz* a trail-blazer in musical film.

Arlen listened, as bewildered as anyone else in the office. Harburg, Arlen remembered, was using "such involved language that I had trouble following him. . . . We never did get to demonstrate the song. When we left the office, I jumped Yipper. 'What were you up to, what were you trying to tell them? We didn't even get to play the song.' "

Harburg turned to him, in a daze, his face a blank, to ask, "What did I say?"

The composer's approach to their job was less messianic and intellectual than the lyricist/script doctor's. It was an important assignment at a large studio, and it could be fun. Arlen's first films had been disappointing (though also fun): small, low-budget B pictures, with trite plots and often wasted songs. Working on *The Wizard*, as he told Fordin, was "lovely for me. I went to the studio when I damned well pleased, or when they called me. Got my check every week [often delivered by clamorous motorcycle]. . . .

"It was a great life," Arlen recalled. "Most of us played golf or tennis, or swam and did our writing at the same time. I wrote at home. I could write at midnight, or five in the afternoon, at nine—it made no difference. As long as I came up with something that the so-called producers liked."

One of those "so-called producers" was Mervyn LeRoy, who wisely left the musical decisions to Arthur Freed. But Freed's decisions did not always work. Early in July "The Jitterbug Sequence" was ready for the arrangers (in addition to the overall musical director, Herbert Stothart, there were four staff arrangers). This was to have been a dance number for the principals: Dorothy, the Cowardly Lion, the Tin Man, and the Scarecrow. The title alluded to a current dance craze out of Harlem and a campus jukebox favorite.

The sequence was shot, and then Stothart asked for a change. In the original form, "The Jitterbug" begins with a *mysterioso*, parlando, verselike introduction, combining speech and song. A month later, Arlen and Harburg were asked to eliminate the parlando and write a more standard verse. The chorus remained the same; the verse, now *quasi mysterioso*, has the quality of a spiritual ("Listen all you chillun to that voodoo moan"), employs a reference to another popular dance rhythm of the time, boogie woogie, which altered the point of the sequence. Not that it mattered, since objections were raised: "jitterbug" and "boogie woogie" would date the picture and were out. Unfortunately the footage was lost.

The Wizard of Oz did not lack cooks.

As the number of revised scripts grew, two important writers reworked Langley's "hands off" screenplay—Florence Ryerson and Edgar Allen Woolf. New cooks contributed to the stew, thus revising the song content. Langley's early version had the Wicked Witch plotting to overthrow the Wizard and install her loutish son on the throne. There was a spot then for a song for her, "Death to the Wizard of Oz," a song that Arlen and Harburg were not keen to write. "Ding Dong! The Witch Is Dead" already had a somewhat morbid title, and one song about death in a fantasy, they reasoned, was enough.

Ryerson and Woolf eliminated the need for the song by making Dorothy the main object of the Witch's malevolence; they also dropped the son and two plot-cluttering characters, a Prince and a Princess. Arlen and Harburg were spared writing a song they wished to avoid, and the new writing team clarified and simplified the plot, which made Langley very unhappy.

Freed, Arlen, and Harburg had liked Langley's work. Serving as peacemakers, they succeeded in talking him into returning to the film after he had seen the newly worked-over screenplay. He flew into a rage, confronted LeRoy, whom he considered a mere "straw boss" and "a mediocre non-talent," and stormed off the picture. He left again, officially discharged on October 31, 1938, by which time there was a final shooting script, credited to him, Ryerson, and Woolf. In fact, the filming had begun on October 13.

In the meantime, Arlen and Harburg were approaching their August deadline for the songs. On the second, Metro had their penultimate song, Bert Lahr's "If

I Were King of the Forest," another operatic parody in the style of their wood-man's song.

They had completed all of the "lemon drop songs," as Arlen called the light songs of the Munchkins, Lion, Scarecrow, and Tin Man, but lacked, in the composer's view, a real ballad. He and Harburg talked Freed out of inserting a "Wizard's Song" near the end of the film. Instead, Harburg wrote the scene in which the Wizard presents, in an incisive satirical view of some of society's trite values, the Scarecrow with a brain, the Tin Man with a heart, and the Lion with courage. Harburg rounded things out with an idea he borrowed from a Freed memo (which delighted Freed), Dorothy's declaration in the final scene, "There's no place like home."

But Arlen was not yet comfortable. Their score lacked a real melody, something "with a broad, long line" to balance the lemon drops. His almost religious belief assured him that it was out there somewhere and he only needed to choose the right notes. Yet waiting for inspiration to strike seemed not to work. The "unsought-for phrase," something he frequently spoke of, eluded him.

Arthur Freed, unconsciously, had pointed in the right direction as early as April in a perspicacious memo he had sent to the harried Langley. It defined what Freed (as if he were in fact in LeRoy's shoes) had in mind for *The Wizard of Oz*, how it might be accomplished, and how each song would fit into his scheme.

In conversation, Arthur Freed was not known for being articulate; he spoke in non sequiturs and vague allusions. Often, but not always, you had to know him to understand him. As Harburg said, "Whenever Arthur talked, all you could do was guess at his meaning."

His memo to Langley was not only clear and lengthy but also to the point. He outlined the theme of the film and made suggestions for simplifying the plot and honing the story and characters. Freed indicated that in *Snow White*, obviously his model, "the whole love story . . . is motivated by the song, 'Some Day My Prince Will Come.' . . . Dialogue could not have accomplished this half as well." Music, he continued, would contribute to the "emotional side" of the story and that it needed "a musical sequence on the farm (i.e., before Dorothy lands in Oz). Doing it musically takes all the triteness out of a straight plot scene."

Whether Arlen saw the memo is not certain (John Fricke, an *Oz* historian, suggests he did), but the placement and types of song were undoubtedly discussed in the early conferences. According to Hugh Fordin, Freed suggested a ballad for Dorothy; Arlen agreed, but Harburg did not, preferring the patter songs to coordinate plot and character.

There was a scene in one of the early Langley-Ryerson-Woolf scripts in which a snappish Aunt Em, preoccupied with counting newly hatched chicks, orders the lonely, troubled Dorothy to get out from under foot and find some place "where you won't get into any trouble." This seemed to be a good spot for a Dorothy ballad, a song about her longings and wish for a place without trouble. She is also spurned by the three farmhands, busy with their chores. She turns to her dog, Toto, for comfort in a quiet corner of the barnyard.

An ideal spot for a broad, long-lined melody. But to Arlen's frustration, it would not fall from the sky. One impediment was that a screen ballad had hitherto always been a love song. *The Wizard of Oz*, though overflowing with love, was not a film about romantic love. Dorothy spends the bulk of the film with a Tin Man, a Scarecrow, a Cowardly Lion, and numerous Munchkins. The song for the barnyard spot would have to be a different kind of ballad, and it eluded Arlen.

He gave up one afternoon and suggested that Anya and he take time off for a matinee at Grauman's Chinese Theater in Hollywood, a short drive away.

Too wound up, Harold suggested that Anya take the wheel. They rode in silence to Sunset Boulevard, where she turned east and steered through traffic on Sunset Strip. Suddenly Harold touched her arm and exclaimed, "Stop! Pull over!" Calmly, though startled, she moved into a parking space in front of the fabled Schwab's Drugstore (where, according to legend, many future stars were discovered at the soda fountain). Anya watched her husband without a word as he searched his pockets for pencil and paper (he never could recall whether he found one of his jot books or the legendary crumpled envelope). On the slip of paper he wrote down a theme, the jot, that had suddenly come to him out of the blue.

"It was as if the Lord said, 'Well, here it is, now stop worrying about it.' "

If it was the Lord, He had spoken too soon.

According to Harburg, he was at home when the phone rang.

"Yipper," he heard Arlen say, "can you meet me at my house in ten minutes? I think I got a nugget."

"Great, where are you?"

"In Schwab's Drugstore."

Harburg continues his story:

I ran to meet him at home. He approached the piano with the usual blue-eyes-toward-heaven ritual and played the first eight bars. . . . My heart fell. He played with such symphonic sweep and bravura that my first reaction was: "Oh, no, not for little Dorothy! That's for Nelson Eddy."

Harold, always sensitive, never aggressive or defensive, was shattered. His Hillcrest [country club] suntan suddenly took flight. I was miserable. Respect for Harold's taste troubled my hasty judgment for days. I finally phoned Ira Gershwin to come verify my fears.

Harold played the tune for him, this time much more casually. Ira listened. He loved it. Without much ado, I went to work on the lyrics. Several days later I brought Harold the title [one of several, actually]. He sang it and played so trippingly that I began to sense the flexibility as well as the strength of the tune.

Arlen did not quite recall the writing of the ballad as Harburg did, with embellishments due to the passage of time. Whereas Harburg, during a lecture at the New York Ninety-second Street Y "Lyrics and Lyricists" series in 1970, said that the call from Schwab's came at midnight, Arlen remembered that the phone call didn't come until the next day. Once he had made the jot in the parked car, he and Anya, Grauman's forgotten, hurried home, where he developed the melodic cell that had dropped out of the heavens. The next day he contrived a simple, contrasting bridge, which he based on the idea of a child's piano exercise. There it was—to his wonder, a standard thirty-two-bar song (plus a four-bar tag). His musical signature was there in the first bar, an octave leap, after which the melody moved searchingly, rising and falling. Not only did it have sweep, it soared. He marked the bridge "dreamily," as its childlike quality brings the big theme (which so upset Harburg) down to earth.

Not only was Yip Harburg a gifted lyricist, but he was an equally inventive storyteller. He often revealed a wily leprechaun's way with an anecdote and rarely resisted the temptation to make a story more colorful—more mythical, so to speak. The midnight call from Arlen is one example.

Once Ira Gershwin voted in favor of Arlen, Harburg went to work. Since Dorothy lived in a flat, drab Kansas, he reasoned, "an arid place where not even flowers grow [at that time, Harburg had never been in Kansas], her only familiarity with colors would have been the sight of a rainbow." One of Ryerson and Woolf's early script revisions had employed the device of a magic Rainbow Bridge, which an aroused Langley had eliminated. Obviously, the idea of a rainbow had been hovering around MGM; Harburg took it from there.

"I thought," Harburg told Aljean Harmetz for her study *The Making of the Wizard of Oz*, "that the rainbow could be a bridge from one place to another. A rainbow gave us a visual reason for changing to color" from the monochromatic Kansas farm to the resplendent hues of Oz. But the opening octave jump still bothered him.

"For a while I thought I would just leave those first two notes out"—had he tried that, it would have required more than the intervention of Ira Gershwin to resolve the reaction from the otherwise "never aggressive or defensive" Harold Arlen. "It was a long time before I came to 'Somewhere over the rainbow.' " The score, two weeks after their contract expired, was finished, except for some small requests from a director or two (Victor Fleming, the main director, asked for additional Munchkinland lyrics, and "We're Off to See the Wizard" was revised as late as June 1939). Once off *The Wizard of Oz*, Arlen and Harburg were assigned the next LeRoy production, starring the Marx Brothers.

One of Yip Harburg's most imaginative tales about "Over the Rainbow" concerned the composer's difficulty in finding an appropriate release for the song. Years later, at his Ninety-second Street Y lecture, Harburg told the story of writing "Over the Rainbow." Harold Arlen was seated in the overflow audience.

Harburg, perched on a tall stool and every inch the leprechaun, enthralled the audience with his wispy vocals and his charmingly told anecdotes. The audience was delighted when he confessed to his initial obtuseness and rejection. "More horrifying (I confess with my head bowed low), the song almost suffered extinction by *me* while it was still a-borning."

Warming up to appreciative merriment, Harburg continued, "Next Harold couldn't get a middle. Well, Harold had a little dog, Pan, a silly little dog, who ran away. Harold had a little whistle for him that went like this (whistles). I said, 'Harold,' " and convinced the composer they had their release.

"Not true," rang out a voice from the auditorium. The middle already existed, based on the beginner's piano piece. The group seated around Arlen, including the singer Margaret Whiting, tittered. Harburg recognized the distinctive voice but, unperturbed, continued with his stories.

This thirty-two-bar miniature classic survived worse twists and turns. Harry Link, the representative of the publisher, Leo Fiest, objected to the octave skip on the word "somewhere" because it would be difficult for the average singer. Nor did he care for the "child's piano exercise" in the bridge. Arlen refused to change anything, so the unhappy Fiest was stuck with this ugly duckling of a song.

There was more: while Victor Fleming directed the greater part of the film, there were no fewer than three other directors involved: Richard Thorpe participated for two weeks, George Cukor for three days, Victor Fleming for four months, and King Vidor for ten days. The wonder of the finished film, considering the number of writers and directors and a producer who left many decisions to his more musical assistant, is that it held together at all. Even the cast fluctuated: the original Dorothy was to have been Shirley Temple or Deanna Durbin; the Wizard might have been W. C. Fields, but turned out to be Frank Morgan; even the Wicked Witch switched from Gale Sondergaard (LeRoy's choice) to Margaret Hamilton. The one major constant was the score, give or take several bars here and there.

In February 1939, when the filming was winding down, Fleming exchanged jobs with King Vidor, then directing *Gone with the Wind*. Vidor gratefully abandoned that monster for the comparative simplicities of directing the Kansas scenes of *The Wizard*, including the scene in which Dorothy sings "Over the Rainbow." (An earlier take had to be discarded because it included Buddy Ebsen, who had originally been cast as the Tin Man, but whose severe reaction to the metallic makeup had led to his replacement by Jack Haley.)

In his version of the scene, Vidor dispensed with the farmhands and filmed

Dorothy moving about the farmyard singing to her dog, Toto. Vidor's handling was simple, uncluttered, and affecting. As he admitted to Doug McClelland, "I always wanted to do a musical film." (In 1939 he was known for several silent films and such later dramas as *Street Scene*, *The Champ*, and *Stella Dallas*.)

"I wanted to keep the movement going," he said, "just as we had in silent pictures. . . . I also did some of the cyclone scenes and 'We're Off to See the Wizard.' " Vidor, incidentally, refused to take credit for directing "Over the Rainbow" and the other sequences.

Fleming, even as he worked on *Gone with the Wind*, kept his hand in *The Wizard*. By mid-June he had prepared a rough cut of the film, which he and Freed screened. Freed saw no point to "The Jitterbug," which had nothing to do with the plot except as an excuse for dancing. "Cut it," he ordered. But Fleming suggested, even insisted, they try it out on an audience.

Soon after, a sneak preview was booked into a theater in Santa Barbara, which resulted in two musical casualties. Freed had prevailed and "The Jitterbug" was rejected. There was word that some in the Santa Barbara audience had danced in the aisles, disrupting the screening.

Although studio voices were raised against "Over the Rainbow," Arthur Freed did not agree. There was a consensus on one matter: the film was overlong and needed trimming. The studio chiefs' decision of what to trim became evident at the next screening.

The second sneak was set for the Fox Theater in Pomona on June 16. The Arlens and Harburg drove the short distance from Beverly Hills to Pomona, just east of Los Angeles. Harburg grumbled about the cutting of "The Jitterbug" (he had heard about that), but realized that their contract was concluded and that they had little say in anything. He did have something to say later about the Pomona preview: "Unbearable."

They found seats in a taped-off section for the MGM contingent—and others. No preview is ever truly sneaky. The audience grew quiet as the titles began over Stothart's finely wrought overture, a medley based largely on the lollipop songs from the Munchkinland sequence, enclosing seven bars from "Over the Rainbow." The titles credited LeRoy and Fleming, as well as the twice-deposed Langley, who had not been invited to the screening. (When he saw the film after its Hollywood opening, he wept and "loathed" it.) Ryerson and Woolf were given their credit with a curious addition: "adaptation by Noel Langley." Seeing his name twice apparently staunched no tears.

Anya gripped Harold's hand when the screen read: "Lyrics by E. Y. Harburg; Music by Harold Arlen." After the LeRoy and Fleming credit frames, another appeared to dedicate *The Wizard of Oz* "to the Young in Heart." As the overture wound down, the screen faded out and then into a road and a farmhouse as characters were introduced. A long shot showed Dorothy and Toto, a medium had Dorothy worrying about Toto's injury from an irate neighbor. Another long shot brought in Aunt Em and Uncle Henry, busy at "an old coal-oil five-hundred-chick incubator."

These scenes moved swiftly with bits of business, chickens, hogs, dialogue introducing the three farmhands, Zeke (later the Lion), Hunk (the Scarecrow), and Hickory (the Tin Woodman), all too busy to listen to Dorothy and her story about Toto's run-in with the unpleasant neighbor, Miss Gulch (the Wicked Witch). Dorothy again pleaded with Aunt Em, who then cued in the first song with "Now, you just help us out today and find yourself a place where you won't get into any trouble!"

Then: no song. The next scene, a long shot, showed the approach of Miss Gulch on her bicycle.

Harold stiffened as Anya gripped his hand tightly; Harburg gasped. He turned to glare at Freed, who gestured that he knew nothing about the elimination of "Over the Rainbow."

Any magic in *The Wizard of Oz* that may have been anticipated by the bitterly stunned trio was dissipated on that "unbearable" night. They drove back in glum silence. When they entered their living room, Harold turned to Anya and vowed, "No more previews! From now on I'm going to write 'em the best I can, turn 'em in, and forget 'em!" Brave, angry words. In the future he did turn them in, but rarely forgot them.

According to most accounts, including those of Arlen, Harburg, and Freed himself, Freed rushed to Mayer's office the next day (skipping over LeRoy) and succeeded in having "Over the Rainbow" reinstated for the next preview. Arlen chose, true to his word, not to attend. Then came another preview. To Freed's chagrin, no "Rainbow." He charged into Mayer's office again. And so on ad nauseum—"Over the Rainbow" had been cut three times.

An incensed Freed was determined to have it out with the front office once and for all. He believed in the song and what it meant to the picture. A meeting was held in Mayer's office attended by, among others, Eddie Mannix, the music division's executive producer; Sam Katz; a Mayer assistant; and Jack Robbins, head of MGM's music publishing division. Their assorted objections boiled down to a few: The song slowed down the opening of the picture. Why was the scene set in an unsightly farmyard? The song was too difficult, would not sell sheet music, would get no radio play—and who would record it?

Freed listened, then came to the point with unusual lucidity: " 'Rainbow' stays or I go." The ultimatum was most timely. He was then completing his first (credited) production, *Babes in Arms*, which was stirring up enthusiasm and was the germinal musical of what would become the illustrious Freed unit at Metro.

In again, "Over the Rainbow" was heard at the preview screened at the Westwood Village Theatre on July 18, 1939. There were no Arlens present, but the audience loved it. LeRoy recalled that after the full 101 minutes (the final cut), there was what seemed like a minute of silence followed by cheering. (Years later he also claimed that he had argued "Over the Rainbow" restored to the film, but that is not how Arlen and Harburg recalled the episode.)

Mervyn LeRoy deserves his due, despite the inclination to minimize his work on *The Wizard of Oz* because he had so little to do with the score. When he later stated that the production of the film had been "one gigantic headache," he was not exaggerating. Considering his other problems, he must have been happy to leave the musical portions of the film to Freed. As producer he was confronted with the technical aspects so seamlessly crafted by various anonymous engineers and artists: a cyclone, Oz itself, flying monkeys. He could not have contrived these any more than he could have written words and music. He hired, paid for, and oversaw their work.

From the beginning LeRoy was confronted with medical interferences, ranging from Ebsen's makeup poisoning, which resulted in costly scrapped footage, to Judy Garland's $150,000 cold, which shut down production for a week (of this her own paltry salary—five hundred dollars a week—was a small portion). Then there were the six weeks it took Margaret Hamilton, the Wicked Witch, to recover from burns she suffered when the timing of a special effect went wrong. Instead of flying away from Munchkinland on her broom in a swirl of smoke and flame, she was ignited before her flight and severely burned. (Her physician, who resented the studio's frequent calls demanding to know when she would return, could not fathom Hamilton's refusal to sue. Simple: she wanted to keep working in Hollywood. A troublemaker reputation often led to unemployment.)

The celebrated Munchkins escalated the producer's migraines. Harburg believed that many of the Munchkin tales were inflated. He did recall that one had bitten a Metro policeman in the leg when the guard had barred his way. Stagehands and others on the set were shocked by the female Munchkins and their sexual invitations. "Memories are distorted," Harburg cautioned, "because these few—biting policemen, carrying knives, soliciting business from men they faced at crotch level—were applied to all Munchkins."

He was right, but the anecdotes flourished. Judy Garland, in later years, recalled them as "drunks. They got smashed every night, and the police had to pick them up in butterfly nets." In Noel Langley's opinion, they were "very raunchy people. They raided the lot. The show girls had to be escorted in bunches by armed guards."

Partly true, as LeRoy recalled. "Every night there were fights and orgies and all kinds of carryings-on. Almost every night, the Culver City police had to rush over to the hotel to keep them from killing each other."

"I was very happy," he concluded, "when their part in the picture was over." One MGM staffer summed it up: "Disney can thank Christ his seven dwarfs weren't real!"

The Arlens had no unpleasant incidents with the "little people," as they preferred to be called. Neither was propositioned. (Judy Garland complained about a pinch now and again.) Although Harold and Harburg were finished, Arlen would take time out from their work on the Marx Brothers' *At the Circus* to visit the Metro lot to look in on the filming. Bringing his camera, Harold photographed makeup tests of the principals, "The Jitterbug Sequence" from behind the scenes (the only surviving film of the scrapped number), and a long shot of the Emerald City—which is as close as any Munchkin got to Anya Arlen.

The filming was concluded on March 16, 1939 (except for the extra few minutes of "We're Off to See the Wizard" added in June under King Vidor's anonymous direction). Then, with postproduction editing completed, Metro's promotional guns began booming. As early as February a large billboard erected outside the front office promised: "The Greatest Picture in the History of Entertainment / in Glorious Technicolor."

An early impressive coup occurred two days after a preview at San Luis Obispo on June 27. Practically all of a coast-to-coast broadcast, the popular Maxwell House "Good News Hour," was devoted to the creation, some of it fictional, of *The Wizard of Oz*. Virtually the entire score was performed, including "Over the Rainbow," no fewer than five times. Apparently upper-echelon hostility to the song had evaporated in the wake of the later previews.

With the actor Robert Young as host (and substitute for an absent Haley as the Tin Man), the regulars of the show, Fanny Brice (as "Baby Snooks") and Frank Morgan (as the resident bamboozling fabricator), joined Garland, Lahr, Bolger, and Fred Stone (the Scarecrow of the 1902 stage production) in a massive promotional broadcast. Arlen and Harburg appeared in a contrived scene in which they played the song for Judy Garland for "the first time," after which she sang it note-perfectly with Harold accompanying her. Young promised at the close of the first half that *The Wizard of Oz* would "be released throughout the country on August 25." In fact the "gala" Hollywood premiere filled Grauman's Chinese Theatre on August 15; two days later it opened at New York's Capitol.

Judy Garland had already recorded an album in Decca's Los Angeles studios late in July. She sang "Over the Rainbow" as well as the rejected "Jitterbug." The set was rounded out with the Munchkinland sequence, "The Merry Old Land of Oz," and "If I Only Had a Brain." These were sung with authority by the Ken Darby Singers, Darby having been one of the vocal arrangers for the film.

This recording was a good sign, Arlen and Harburg believed as they finished off the songs for *At the Circus*. An even more propitious sign was the first appearance of "Over the Rainbow" on "Your Hit Parade" on August 19, only two days after the New York premiere. In 1939 the "Hit Parade" was highly regarded as a fine barometer of a song's popularity in the trade. A song's position was supposedly determined by a tally of sheet music sales, radio performances, and record sales. For an additional fourteen weeks, from August to November, "Over the Rainbow" broke the "Hit Parade" record of the time and swept the country. For seven weeks it was in the Number One spot, always closing the program with mounting expectancy and an exciting fanfare. Such popularity reflected warmly on Harold Arlen and Arthur Freed in their belief in the song.

And again there was more. That widespread popularity—its plugging of the film, its financial benefits to studio and publisher—set the scene for the finale of the saga of "Over the Rainbow."

The twelfth awards ceremony of the Academy of Motion Picture Arts and Sciences was held at the Ambassador Hotel in Hollywood on February 29, 1940. Hindsight now designates 1939 as one of Hollywood's vintage years. Though *The Wizard of Oz* was generally relegated to the kiddie category, it was in competition as Best Picture with *Gone with the Wind*, *Stage Coach*, *Wuthering Heights*, *Of Mice and Men*, *Mr. Smith Goes to Washington*, *Goodbye Mr. Chips*, and a couple others.

As usual on such an expectant, glittering evening, there was electricity in the air. Anyone acquiring a copy of that evening's *Los Angeles Times* before entering the Ambassador's lobby, however, would have already known what was not supposed to be known until the final moments of the ceremony—that *Gone with the Wind* had been selected by the academy members as Best Picture of the year. (This jumping the gun led to the introduction the following year of the now traditional sealed envelope and total secrecy.)

The keyed-up Arlens were not encumbered by the *Times* as they took their places in the grand dining room of the hotel. Anya was as gorgeous as any star or starlet in her gown, and Harold, in a tuxedo, sported his customary "bluie," a red carnation, and stood out from the other formal dressers with his slender, minimal black tie.

He was also in a sweat. "Over the Rainbow" had been nominated as one of the year's best songs, along with "Faithful Forever" by Leo Robin and Ralph Rainger, from *Gulliver's Travels* (another animated cartoon musical); "I Poured My Heart into a Song" by Irving Berlin, from *Second Fiddle*; and B. G. DeSylva's "Wishing," from *Love Affair*. From the same film, though not nominated, was a song superior to DeSylva's tedious ditty, "Sing My Heart" by Ted Koehler and Harold Arlen.

As the evening stretched, expectant excitement rose (unless you chanced to bring along the untimely *Times*). The Metro tables turned melancholic when *Gone with the Wind* took the Art Direction Oscar and *The Rains Came* the Special Effects. Spirits rose when Herbert Stothart was awarded an Oscar for the "original score" for *The Wizard of Oz*.

This was a curious and misleading category. Stothart had been the film's musical director, assigning arrangers, conducting, and "adapting" not only Arlen but a bit of Schumann, Mendelssohn, and Moussorgsky here and there in the score. The cyclone music had been written by the arranger George Bassman and the associate conductor George Stoll. Bassman and Stothart also contributed "The March of the Winkies," a close musical relative of the "Song of the Volga Boatmen." Stothart also shared composer credit with Arlen on the charming "Optimistic Voices (You're out of the Woods)." Why this was done is now impossible to know; in an early demonstration recording Arlen and Harburg perform it as published.

The high, though not really expected, moment of the evening came late that Thursday when "Over the Rainbow" was announced as Best Song of the year.

Two happy Arlens drove back to Beverly Hills early Friday morning to be greeted by the joyful Stormy and Pan. Harold was elated. He, Ira Gershwin, and Freed had been right. He was additionally grateful to Ira for suggesting the song's tag, which Harburg graciously accepted:

> *If happy little bluebirds fly*
> *Beyond the rainbow*
> *Why oh why can't I?*

10

YIP, JOHN,
AND TED AGAIN

*T*wo weeks after the release of *The Wizard of Oz*, world events literally exploded when German Luftwaffe Stuka dive bombers attacked Polish cities on September 1, 1939. Within days, Britain, France, and the Soviet Union were embroiled in a conflict that would escalate into the Second World War. To most Americans, and particularly Hollywoodians, such perennial European bloodletting was a continent and an ocean away and not their concern. On September 5, President Franklin D. Roosevelt proclaimed American neutrality and placed an embargo on the shipment of arms, munitions, and war machines to all the countries in which, as he phrased it, "a state of war unhappily exists."

In a swift blitzkrieg, Hitler's armies overran Poland, with the help of his ally, Stalin, who had attacked from the east. Then the Soviets moved against Finland to the north. Hitler, stymied temporarily at the French border, kept a wary eye on his Soviet "ally" and contemplated Scandinavia.

In Hollywood it soon became clear that Hitler and Stalin had cut off a large market for their "product." Of the world's approximately 67,000 movie houses, only the 17,000 in the United States remained, plus those south of the border. But the elimination of the box offices of Europe was a serious reverse embargo. Even in neutral America receipts declined as the public remained at home to listen to the news from Europe. While radio brought dramatic programs and music of all kinds, comedians ruled the airwaves during those parlous days: Fred Allen, Jack Benny, Fibber McGee and Molly, "Duffy's Tavern." And all were free.

Movie theater managers attempted to compensate by showing double features and advertising Bank Nights and Dish Nights. But people stayed away, some to try their hands at the new popular card game, gin rummy. Even Harold Arlen brought home a pad of gin rummy score sheets from the Hillcrest Country Club. Studios curtailed productions in 1940 from the usual sixty annual releases to forty.

Roosevelt, elected to an unprecedented third term to the presidency, continued to expound American neutrality. He tempered that with the introduction of a Lend-Lease bill that enabled the British (France had already fallen to the Nazis) to borrow or lease arms, food, and other essential supplies as a "nation whose defense the President deems vital to the defense of the United States." He also introduced a peacetime draft and called for an expansion of American industry. The economy hummed. The war in Europe accomplished what the New Deal had failed to do: the termination of the Great Depression. Within a year Hollywood, too, bounced back, not only with the release of more features but with a resurgence of the film musical as well.

Even as *The Wizard of Oz* endured its final permutations, virtually all concerned were otherwise employed. Freed made his formal debut as the producer of *Babes in Arms*, purportedly based on the Rodgers and Hart stage success. Judy Garland starred, Florence Ryerson and Edgar Allen Woolf (uncredited) worked on the screenplay, Roger Edens handled the musical adaptation, and George Stoll was the musical director. The score contained a number of early Brown and Freed songs and many by Edens, among others, as well as Arlen and Harburg's "God's Country," which Edens worked into a stirring finale with Sousa's "Stars and Stripes Forever," underscoring aroused Hollywood's patriotism. The film provided a rich musical menu but left room for only two of the stage version's eleven Rodgers and Hart songs. It was also a huge box-office success, having introduced a new song-and-dance team, Judy Garland and Mickey Rooney. Almost immediately, Freed went into his next production with them, *Strike Up the Band*.

Arlen and Harburg were not so lucky. Free of the Munchkins, Mervyn LeRoy took one final fling as a producer with the Marx Brothers' *At the Circus*. Arlen and Harburg were commissioned to write the songs. The screenplay was written by Irving Brecher, one of the several anonymous writers who had worked on *The Wizard*'s numerous scripts.

The transition from Oz to the Marxes was strange. Though their films featured enough music for Chico to do his keyboard tricks and Harpo to wax serious with the harp, the Marx Brothers films were not true musicals. Consequently, Arlen and Harburg had little to do. Since the male star was Kenny Baker, who had come to Hollywood after a long run as resident tenor of the Jack Benny radio show, they had one good voice to write for.

The plot deserves no retelling beyond its circus setting and how the Marxes save it, zanily, from a loan shark. Besides Baker's numbers, there was a song spot for Groucho Marx, a friend of Harburg's. Harburg recalls that he was inspired by an evening at Marx's devoted to Gilbert and Sullivan. "He would gather us there, play complete operas, and sing along with them." Through a song for Groucho, Harburg could fully demonstrate his dexterity with "the rhyming scheme and verbal juggling." The resultant effort, one of Arlen's pet lyrics by Harburg, was "Lydia, the Tattooed Lady."

The description of Lydia's body decorations and their implied positions caused problems with the Breen office, the arbiter of what was good and clean in Hollywood:

> *On her back is the Battle of Waterloo*
> *Beside it the wreck of the Hesperus too*
> *And proudly above waves the red, white and blue*
> *You can learn a lot from Lydia.*

or:

> *When her muscles start relaxin'*
> *Up the hill comes Andrew Jackson.*

"That song," Harburg told one of his Ninety-second Street Y audiences, "was thought to be risqué, and we had a hell of a lot of trouble with it. . . . This was 1939 and censorship was at its full height—no sweaters on the screen, they were too erotic. We were told we would have to cut it out of the picture. Harold and I were mad," arguing with the Breen office to no avail.

"Finally, we got an idea for how to save the song. We put in a final verse to legitimize the song, which went like this:

> *She once swept an admiral clear off his feet*
> *The ships on her hips made his heart skip a beat*
> *And now the old boy's in charge of the fleet*
> *For he went and married Lydia."*

That song, and Marx's leering rendition in *At the Circus*, provided Harburg with a pat answer to the frequent question: Who is your favorite among the vocalists who have sung your songs? How not to ruffle the feathers of Judy Garland, Lena Horne, Al Jolson, Deanna Durbin, as well as numerous pop singers? His reply was "Groucho Marx" (unless it was Bert Lahr; these got a laugh and Harburg off the hook).

The best tune from the film was the ballad "Two Blind Loves," ingeniously based on a borrowed jot—the initial three notes from the traditional nursery song. The four *At the Circus* songs were decidedly minor, excepting the lyric to "Lydia, the Tattooed Lady."

That, temporarily, ended that phase of the Arlen-Harburg collaboration. According to Harburg, who told Max Wilk, Arlen "felt he needed a change and so did I." Harburg then left for New York, where he collaborated on a musical for Jack Haley that, eventually, starred Al Jolson, *Hold On to Your Hats*.

Arlen found himself adrift, there being, despite the kudos for *The Wizard of Oz*, no immediate film or stage project at hand. It was then that the *Oz* broadcast bore additional fruit, a commission from Meredith Willson, the radio hour's musical director. Willson, who years before had been a flutist in the New York Philharmonic, was also the composer of a symphony and the *O. O. McIntyre Suite*, a tribute to the newspaper columnist whose "Thoughts while Strolling" was widely read. Willson, in addition, wrote songs, the most popular of which in the late 1930s was "You and I." He would, in 1956, make his mark in the theater with *The Music Man*.

Willson planned, when his Maxwell House "Good News Hour" returned to the air for its fall series, to feature patriotic orchestral compositions by American songwriters. Among the writers he approached were Duke Ellington, who contributed an "American Lullaby," Ferde Grofé ("March for Americans"), Louis Alter ("American Serenade"), and Peter DeRose ("American Waltz"). With the American economy, and people, gearing up for war, Willson's idea was to provide a little musical patriotism every week. Each piece was to last about three minutes, roughly the length of a popular song, and thus fit on a ten-inch recording that Willson would include in an album for Decca Records, ten American compositions in all.

Harold Arlen, in an unusual choice, proposed to write an "American Minuet" to be based on the classic seventeenth-century dance. His inspiration was Anya, who had studied ballet and frequently danced solo at parties. Willson told Arlen that he hoped to broadcast the minuet during one of the December 1939 programs.

Arlen took the commission seriously, as evidenced by the volumes of minuet collections he acquired. He researched through Lully, Pachelbel, Alessandro Scarlatti, and Haydn. He also listened to many recordings of the traditional minuet. His record collection included the multivolume *Columbia History of Music*, comprehending the musical gamut from Gregorian chant to Stravinsky (an excerpt from *Les Noces*). His library was also well stocked with books on music, ranging from the recent biography of George Gershwin (affectionately signed by the author, Isaac Goldberg) to the formidable seven volumes of the *Oxford History of Music*.

Having done his homework, Arlen sketched out a piano copy, then recorded it, with variations, several times until he was pleased with the results: an elegant work, an old dance with a contemporary, American accent.

The "American Minuet," in proper three-quarter time, begins with a five-bar *energico* introduction before the principal sixteen-bar minuet theme ("with expression and grace"). The sixth bar of the theme injects a touch of Arlen—a jazzy grace note. The second theme, a contrasting, singing *cantabile*, leads to a recapitulation of the minuet theme with small tempo and harmonic variations. The third theme, marked *sentito* ("with expression"), introduces a contrasting, faster tempo (*mosso*), followed by a restatement of the original minuet. The conclusion, an extended twenty-bar *cantabile*, ends with a two-measure *allargando* in a final strong statement.

For the broadcast, Willson had the minuet orchestrated (he may himself have been the orchestrator). Except for the broadcast, Willson's album (now long gone), and the composer's solo piano recording, the "American Minuet" remains unperformed, one of Arlen's unfortunately neglected miniatures.

It was time to return to song. Despite the "noise," as Arlen called it, of *The Wizard of Oz*, no new work came of it. There were no film offers, but he kept in creative trim—when not golfing—by setting future song motifs on paper and recording the most promising, which he called "possibles," to send to potential lyricists, among them Ira Gershwin. Following his brother's death, Gershwin began his professional recovery working on single songs with Jerome Kern. Gershwin liked one "possible" and appended a lyric titled "I'll Supply the Title, You'll Supply the Tune." The song was not published.

Because Ira Gershwin was not yet ready to take on a full-scale job, Arlen turned to the dependable Ted Koehler. Sometime in 1938 Koehler and he had begun work on a spiritual that had grown out of an eight-bar jot. They were in no hurry, there being no great demand for spirituals at that moment. Arlen was busy with *The Wizard of Oz*, though he and Koehler wrote the graceful "Sing My Heart" for Irene Dunn's tearful *Love Affair*. It was unnoticed and overshadowed by the popularity (fourteen weeks on "Your Hit Parade") of B. G. DeSylva's "Wishing." "Sing My Heart" was greatly admired by Jerome Kern, who, according to Arlen, arranged to have it published by one of the subsidiaries of Chappell and Company.

Even as they developed their idea of the spiritual and other songs, Koehler and Arlen finished a few songs, including the bluesy ballad "When the Sun Comes Out." A vintage Arlen invention, it bristles with his musical sleight of hand, unexpected key changes, and ingenious melodic twists. ("Sleight of hand" is borrowed from Alec Wilder, who states unequivocally that no one but Harold Arlen could have written that song.) Though not a popular hit, "When the Sun Comes Out" was taken up by some of the big bands of the period, most notably Tommy Dorsey's.

Upon completing his work on *At the Circus* and the "American Minuet," Arlen reunited with Koehler to continue the composition of their spiritual fantasy. Once the initial eight-bar phrase was completed, beginning with Koehler's suggested "There'll be no more work / There'll be no more worry," the composer had his springboard for the rest of the song. When completed it was entitled "Big Time Comin'," an elaborate piece employing solo voice, chorus, and piano.

They had a song but no place to go with it. There was still no demand for spirituals in 1941. Someone suggested that it might be incorporated into a suite of songs in the Negro idiom as a set of vernacular art songs.

The work went slowly, there being no deadline and Arlen's dedication— almost an addiction, he admitted—to golf. "The game consumed me," he acknowledged. Arlen spent a good deal of time at the Hillcrest Country Club, beginning in the morning, when he studied the game with the pros of the club. He discussed the game with such champions as Ben Hogan and accumulated a library of books on golfing.

Ted Koehler did not share his love of the game, but Arlen played with Ira Gershwin, Harry Warren, the boxer Joe Louis, and the comedian Lou Clayton. Jerome Kern also joined their group of golfing songwriters, who called themselves the "Pitch 'n' Putt Society." Each member aspired not only to defeat the others but also to feature a degree of eccentricity: Kern, whom Arlen drove to the club each morning, fancied outlandish hats, Arlen odd shoes, and Ira Gershwin went through the game smoking cigars.

When not on the links, they joined the boys at the Roundtable. Most members of this group were there not for the golf but to gather around the table for affectionate insults and laughs. Among the regulars at the Roundtable were Jack Benny, George Burns, Groucho and Harpo Marx, George Jessel, and Danny Thomas. Benny rarely contributed anything to the hilarity because Burns, with his laconic comments, kept him in paroxysms of laughter.

With his day at Hillcrest complete—lesson, a bucket of balls to practice his swing, the Roundtable—Arlen would drive to Gershwin's club, the California Country Club, for a game, then go home to see a neglected Anya and to get back to work with Koehler, who may have spent his day less strenuously at woodworking or painting.

Arlen and Koehler worked on the set of songs for a period of about two years, while occupied from time to time with other work, including some incidental songs of their own, such as "Like a Straw in the Wind." They completed their final song, the sixth, some time in September 1940. Entitled "Reverend Johnson's Dream," it is a sermon (of over 140 bars) in which a minister invokes the aid of "de Lawd," lamenting the warring state of the world in 1940. The minister cries out to the Lord that "de devil's down here posin' lak a natchal man an' spreadin' evil all over de lan' ":

> He's got your chillun fightin' an' raisin' san'
>   He's spreadin' evil all over de lan'!
> (Chorus:) You better come down here Lawd, Lawd!

The set of songs, some partly sung, partly spoken, with solos and choral commentaries, they decided to call *Americanegro Suite*, subtitled "four spirituals, a dream, and a lullaby."

As published, the suite begins with "Reverend Johnson's Dream." The first spiritual, "I Got Dat Feelin'," is a lively declaration of faith, marked "with abandon (rhythmically moving)." The second, "I'm Here Lawd," is a more subdued sequel, with its declaration "Oh Lawd! My sins have been washed away."

Contrasting with the sermon and spirituals, the lullaby, "Little Ace o' Spades," despite the unfortunate title, is one of the suite's melodic high points. A mother sings her child to sleep in one of Arlen's most beautiful creations. While Koehler's heartfelt lyric was acceptable, at least in some circles, in 1940, it would be regarded racist fifty years later. The child is the little ace of spades, "kinky head" is rhymed with "inky head," and there is reference to Pappy "rollin' de bones with de men folks." Such expressions, even among blacks at the time, were artistic conventions. Neither Arlen nor Koehler was afflicted with racism in any form and would have been shocked by such an accusation. When in 1986 the soprano Judy Kaye recorded the *Americanegro Suite*, slight changes were made in the lyric with the composer's approval. The title of the lullaby was altered to "Little Angel Child," with no harm to Koehler's poetry. Koehler, unfortunately, had died before the album was recorded.

"Little Ace o' Spades" is asymmetrically composed of a five-bar piano introduction, a sixteen-bar chorus (the main melody), an eight-bar release, an eight-bar variation on the main theme, and a seven-bar closing, partly hummed. The melody, largely based on the interval of a third, with an occasional rise or fall of a fifth and a generous use of grace notes in the vocal and accompaniment, gives the impression of rocking gently. It is an impressive and memorable song.

The third spiritual, another high point of the work, is the richly dramatic sinner's supplication "Where Is Dis Road A-Leadin' Me To?" The demanding sixty-six-bar aria is characterized by shifting tempos. In the initial two bars the vocal line ranges from C to G-flat, an octave and a tritone. When the suite was recorded under the composer's supervision, about 1942, by Decca Records, the song was sung by a Juilliard graduate, Ruby Elzy (who had appeared as Serena in Gershwin's original production of *Porgy and Bess* and the 1942 revival). Other vocalists included William Gillespie, Lois Hudnut, and the Jubilee Singers.

The suite concludes on a more joyous note in the final spiritual, "Big Time Comin'," which had initiated the composition of the *Americanegro Suite*. The suite was almost immediately published by Chappell in an elaborate hardcover folio, with illustrations by the Gershwins' artist cousin Henry Botkin, an essay on the genesis of the collection by Arlen's longtime friend Robert Wachsman, and impressive endorsements from the composer-critic Deems Taylor, Irving Berlin, Ira Gershwin, Hall Johnson, and Jerome Kern.

Kern praised both composer and lyricist "for successfully avoiding the sham of pseudo-Negro spirituals. Here are a half-dozen genre pictures: conceived, it is true, in the Negro narrative idiom, but they are almost without exception genuine musical creations, not experiments in imitation." After the completion of the set, Arlen visited Kern to play and sing the songs. Kern listened attentively and, apparently moved, left the room. He returned with a handsomely carved walking stick and presented it to Arlen. Kern had treasured it for years, a gift from the critic Alexander Woollcott, because it had once belonged to the operetta composer Jacques Offenbach. Although Arlen never used the fancy cane, he, too, treasured it.

The Hall Johnson comment on the suite was particularly commendatory. A composer, arranger, and choir director, Johnson had absorbed the style of the spiritual as a choirboy in a black Methodist church in Athens, Georgia. He played in pit bands on Broadway and eventually formed the celebrated Hall Johnson Choir; at the time he knew Arlen, he led the Festival Chorus in Los Angeles. Besides his many choral arrangements of traditional spirituals, his best-known work is the folk play *Run Little Chillun*. Johnson was most familiar with the idiom:

> Of all the many songs written by white composers and employing what claims to be a Negroid idiom in both words and music, these six songs . . . easily stand far out above the rest. Thoroughly modern in treatment, they are at the same time, full of the simple sincerity which invariably characterizes genuine Negro folk-music and are by no means to be confused with the average "Broadway Spirituals" which depend for their racial flavor upon sundry allusions to the "Amen corner," "judgement day"— "Gabriel's horn" and a frustrated devil—with a few random "Hallelujahs" thrown in for good measure. Here are singable tunes wedded to sensible texts, resulting in six songs which all lovers of real Negro music will enjoy.

After the completion of the *Americanegro Suite*, the Arlen-Koehler association became primarily social. In addition to a few nonproduction songs over the next three or four years, when each collaborated with others, their most important score was the diminutive one written for their final film together, *Up in Arms*. Produced by Samuel Goldwyn, it was Danny Kaye's film debut and also starred Dinah Shore in her first important film role. Kaye, formerly a comic on the Borscht Circuit (New York's summer resort area in the Catskill Mountains), had been catapulted to fame in his first major Broadway musical, *Lady in the Dark*, in 1941. That same year he also appeared in *Let's Face It*, a Cole Porter wartime musical. By 1943, when *Up in Arms* was produced, he was a major star with a well-defined comic personality: rapid patter, mugging, and routines that bordered on ballet. Because he had also become known by means of radio and nightclubs, some of his best-known routines were inevitably worked into the film. Included in the Kaye package, so to speak, were the special songs written for him by his wife, Sylvia Kaye, and Max Liebman (including his famous "Theater Lobby Number" and the timely "Melody in 4F"). Consequently, only three Arlen-Koehler songs are heard in the movie, including Dinah Shore's finely sung "Now I Know" and the intricate, long-lined, bluesy "Tess's Torch Song," both among the writers' best work. Rounding out their part of the score was the mandatory deference to patriotism, "All Out for Freedom," whose dedication (rare in popular song) reads "To Anya."

Anya was frequently welcomed to the Arlen-Koehler work sessions, a practice dating back to the Cotton Club years. Late one afternoon, some time before America's entry into World War II, all three converged in Arlen's study with his piano and recording equipment. The composer had written a brooding melody, almost Slavic in sound—a tribute to the new ally, Russia, but more so to Anya.

Koehler liked the melody and came to the Arlens' to hear it played a few times. With the recorder running, Arlen began with the comment, in an almost devout tone, "If this isn't a hit, so help me." He then launched into the beautiful, long Slavic blues (if such exists), singing wordlessly to give Koehler some idea of where the melodic and rhythmic emphasis fell in the melody.

In a rich, Russian accent, he says, "Introducing Anushka Baronovich Taranda singing Ted Koehlerovich and Harold Arlenovich's new ballade." Koehler is heard applauding from the background.

Anya (no words yet) begins to vocalize charmingly to Harold's accompaniment, though she has some difficulty reaching some of the upper notes. Harold, chuckling, assists her by adding his voice, leading her through to her own (limited) register. She gets lost again and he joins her again.

"Faster, Annie," Koehler coaches.

"I will not stand for dot!" the Slavic Harold exclaims.

Exasperated, Anya gives up, stops singing to say something in Russian.

"What all dot mean?" Harold asks, laughing.

They continue after Anya says, "You follow me." He does as she finishes her solo in a questionable key. Harold joins her in a florid, operatic conclusion, then has the final word, still in his extravagant Russian voice: "I ahm sorree I could not play it for Anushka Baronovich Taranda in the right key—"

"You said it!" she interjects.

"—and she feels like a fool and has purrfect rrright. I ahm verry sorry and *dobra noche* [good night]." If Koehler wrote the lyric, it does not exist in the Arlen collection of papers, nor does the music, except on the worn, poorly recorded, acetate disc. In that imperfect form, the recording captured a fine melody and a happy, playful moment in the summer of 1941, when Anya and Harold Arlen, that "ideal Hollywood couple," were light-hearted and with a happy future ahead. But that was then.

Ted Koehler worked on two musical films after *Up in Arms*: a Dorothy Lamour vehicle, *Rainbow Island* (1944), with Burton Lane, and a film biography of the tenor Chauncey Olcott, *My Wild Irish Rose* (1947), with M. K. Jerome. He then chose to bow out of the Hollywood jungle. Nor did Broadway lure him east again. In 1943, the year before *Up in Arms*, he had collaborated with Frederick Jackson on the screenplay for *Stormy Weather*, a film notable not so much for the story as for its remarkable cast: Lena Horne, Bill Robinson, Cab Calloway, Fats Waller, Katherine Dunham, the Nicholas Brothers, and the notable jazz musicians Zutty Singleton and Benny Carter. Many of its cast had begun at the Cotton Club, although the only song interpolated from the *Parade*s was the title song, with which Lena Horne has been associated ever since.

Once finished with these chores, Koehler, in his early fifties, quietly faded into the serenity of Beverly Hills to tend his garden, make things in his well-appointed woodworking shop, or paint. He did an excellent portrait of Arlen, among other works.

The Arlens, more peripatetic, had moved from one canyon to another: from Laurel Canyon they moved into a roomy house on Lindecrest Drive in Coldwater Canyon. Their good friend, the comedian Fanny Brice, loved interior decorating and was good at it. She had done the same for the Gershwins on Roxbury Drive. While Harold improved his golf game, Anya and Brice scoured the Beverly Hills shops for the proper furnishings for what Harold referred to as the white house.

His den had plenty of shelf space for his growing library and record collection. He placed his Gershwin oil of Jerome Kern in the living room. There was wall space, too, for his paintings, a couple of Botkins, including one he had done for the *Americanegro* folio; there was also a watercolor self-portrait of Gershwin and a Dali.

After the publication of the *Americanegro Suite*, in the spring of 1941, Arlen was brought together with a new collaborator, Johnny Mercer, with whom he had written in 1932. They were perfect choices for a film centered on jazz musicians, originally entitled *New Orleans Blues*, then *Hot Nocturne*.

Mercer, like Arlen, and unlike so many great songwriters of that period, was not a native New Yorker. He was born in Savannah, Georgia, on November 18, 1909. The Mercers were "quality" and could trace their family history to the American Revolution; a Mercer had served under Washington as a brigadier general. The lyricist's father, George, was a successful attorney who also dabbled in real estate.

Although young John Herndon Mercer had had some musical training as a youngster, family legend has him exhibiting a taste for music as well as a strong will at the age of six. One morning he followed the Irish Jasper Greens, a local marching band, to a picnic grounds and spent the day there while his distressed family combed the town for him in vain. In the evening little John returned unescorted.

His mother, Lillian, assigned a maid to keep an eye on the errant music lover to avoid another such incident. One afternoon, however, Lillian Mercer encountered the overseer alone in the street, apparently distraught.

"Where's Johnny," Lillian asked sharply, "and why did you leave him?"

"Nothing else I could do," she was informed.

"Why?"

"He fired me," the maid replied.

As a boy Mercer began to study the piano, then gave it up for the trumpet, which he abandoned by the age of ten. In time he was sent off to the "exclusive" Woodbury Forest School in Orange, Virginia. He became a member of the chapel choir and revealed an interest in dramatics, becoming active in little theater groups in Savannah.

During summer vacations he worked in his father's office; the writer Worth Gatesworth reported, "The firm was months recovering from his services." Mercer's older brother, Walter, elaborated: "We'd give him things to deliver—letters, checks, deeds, and things like that—and learn days later that he'd absent-mindedly stuffed them in his pockets. There they stayed."

This seeming abstraction stayed with Mercer for life, for Harold Arlen often referred to him affectionately as "Cloud Boy." When concentrating on a lyric, Mercer could distance himself from his surroundings to a remarkable degree. Harry Warren, who collaborated with him on several films, recalled one example. They were working in their office on a studio lot when lunchtime came. Warren decided to go out while Mercer worked at a yellow pad. As he left Warren inquired about Mercer's wife. "How's Ginger?"

Mercer said nothing. Warren shrugged and left. When he returned about an hour later, Mercer brightened as he entered and said, "She's fine."

In prep school, too, his mind was frequently on things other than schooling. "He'd be doodling on a lyric," his brother recalled, "when he should have been hitting the books." All plans for his future educational polishing were drastically settled when his father's businesses failed. Then about seventeen, and with no higher learning before him, Mercer polished his thespian talents and joined a local little theater group, which won him a trip to New York to participate in a dramatics competition.

He returned to Georgia with the praise for his performances ringing lyrically in his ears. Encouraged, and now all of twenty, John H. Mercer decided to return to New York for a career in the theater. The decision was not well timed; the year was 1929. The former Georgian spent a year trying to break into the business without success. Despite his father's misfortunes, the family helped to nurture his faltering theatrical career.

During that lean period, his mother came up for a visit and found her son sharing "a terrible one-room apartment, four flights up, in Greenwich Village," with two other aspiring actors. "The place," Lillian Mercer noticed, "had no sink or washbasin, only a bathtub. Johnny insisted on cooking a chicken in my honor—he's always been a good cook—and I'll never forget him cleaning the chicken in the tub."

In the spring of 1930 Mercer heard that the Theatre Guild was hiring for *The Garrick Gaieties*, their musical comedy revue. Besides acting, he could sing, so he appeared at an audition where he was informed by the assistant casting director, Everett Miller, "We only need girls and songs" (most of the songs were written by Vernon Duke, in his first American effort; lyrics were mostly by Yip Harburg, with a little help from Ira Gershwin).

Mercer was never at a loss for words—he had been composing song lyrics since he was fifteen. An inattentive scholar at Woodbury Forest, he had written a song entitled "Sister Susie, Strut Your Stuff." He had also revealed an early affinity for the music of Savannah blacks, including his sweet-voiced "Mammy," who sang to him.

He provided Miller with a lyric, "Out of Breath and Scared to Death of You." Miller was equal to the task and supplied the melody (if he ever wrote another song, there is no record of it). John Mercer, then, made his Broadway debut in June 1930 as a songwriter rather than an actor. He also made two enriching acquaintances: E. Y. Harburg, who became an encouraging mentor, and one of Miller's "girls," Brooklyn-born Elizabeth "Ginger" Meehan, one of the show's dancers.

They married in 1931 and moved into a small apartment near Ebbets Field, home of the Dodgers, in Brooklyn. With few Broadway opportunities, newlywed Mercer took "a regular job," as his brother recalled, "misplacing stocks and bonds in a Wall Street brokerage office."

In between, he kept his hand in music, writing lyrics, singing, and recording his way out of Wall Street with the bands of Frankie Trumbauer, the Dorsey Brothers, and eventually Paul Whiteman. While with Whiteman he met Jerry Arlen for the first time as a member of the new Rhythm Boys.

He met Harold Arlen around the same time when Yip Harburg asked him to join them in collaborating on "Satan's Li'l Lamb" for *New Americana*. Mercer wrote special songs for the Whiteman band, and it was Whiteman who brought Mercer and Hoagy Carmichael together. The latter had abandoned a law career to write songs following the success of "Stardust" in 1929. Both Carmichael and Mercer had a gift for the folksy, and their first collaboration was the popular "Lazybones," the first in a long line of Mercer hits.

Mercer's ingratiating personality, his winning Southern voice, with a touch of vibrato, and his witty songs enabled him to concentrate on a band career. As with Arlen, songwriting was still incidental. He left Wall Street and Whiteman to join the Benny Goodman band, which broadcast regularly on the "Camel Caravan" radio program. The Mercer voice won him an invitation to Hollywood to appear in a film, *To Beat the Band*, with another former Whiteman bandsman, now turned leader, the violinist Matty Malneck. The two also wrote the songs for the film, released by RKO in 1935. That same year Mercer appeared as "the Colonel" (later another favorite Arlen nickname for him) in *Old Man Rhythm* (also RKO). The music was written by Lewis Gensler for this film, and Mercer sang his lyrics in each.

Mercer was elated, sensing that his acting career was being resuscitated. But neither the films nor their songs attracted much attention, and Mercer found that his lyrics were more admired than his screen presence. When an interviewer inquired about his brief screen career, Mercer responded in his characteristic laconic manner: "I was never in another picture; that's a pretty good answer."

"Right after that," he told Max Wilk, "they sent me back to the typewriter, and I've been there ever since." Mercer went on to collaborate with some of the outstanding film composers of that era of the blossoming of the musical film. He wrote with the elite of Hollywood's composers, among them Richard Whiting ("I'm an Old Cowhand," "Too Marvelous for Words," and "Hooray for Hollywood"), Harry Warren ("Jeepers Creepers"), and Jimmy McHugh, briefly. Non-film songs written over the same period that were enormously popular include "Pardon My Southern Accent," "Goody Goody," "Bob White," "Day In, Day Out," and "Fools Rush In."

Buddy Morris, who had signed Harold Arlen to his first contract in 1929, had also moved on to Hollywood and was head of Warner Brothers' music department. It was he who brought Mercer and Whiting together in 1936 for a Bing Crosby musical, *Rhythm on the Range*, and the Dick Powell hit *Hollywood Hotel* a year later. Whiting's early death at the age of thirty-eight of a heart attack ended what began as a most promising collaboration.

Once Arlen had finished with *The Wizard of Oz* and found himself in a Hollywood limbo, and Mercer had completed a couple of scores with McHugh and Arthur Schwartz, Buddy Morris believed that an Arlen-Mercer collaboration could prove most fruitful and profitable.

Both agreed. Arlen had known Mercer in Hollywood from the latter 1930s, when they often met at the Gershwins' or at parties, and each admired the other's work. As Mercer put it, "we [didn't] come from the same neck of the woods or anything, but we really [had] a thing about jazz and blues, and creativity and originality, and structure."

When this new partnership was consummated, jazz and blues were decidedly in the Hollywood air. The big bands were riding high on radio and recordings and cross-country one-night stands. Inevitably they would come to the film capital; in 1940 movies featuring the bands of Bob Crosby, Artie Shaw, Kay Kayser, and Paul Whiteman were released.

This, plus the revived popularity of old jazz recordings, out of print and acquired at great cost, generated articles, discussions, and arguments in the jazz press and even the slicker magazines such as *Mademoiselle*, in which George

Frazier held forth on the definition of True Jazz. Even *Fortune* and the *Saturday Evening Post* published articles on the subject.

The theme of the most serious writers was that true jazz was superior to the fake jazz (often called swing), definitely superior to the commercial products of Artie Shaw, even Benny Goodman, and especially to the "Mickey Mouse" products of such successful bands as those of Kay Kayser, Guy Lombardo, and Wayne King, who in the view of the critics dispensed "corn."

Hollywood cared little for hairsplitting, but the popularity of the bands, of whatever type, was encouraging, as was a recent emergence of a boogie woogie style evidenced by the hit recording of "Beat Me, Daddy, Eight to the Bar" by the Will Bradley Orchestra, followed by other bands.

Hollywood could not be far behind. Paramount arrived first with *Birth of the Blues*, released in September 1941. Starring Bing Crosby, the plot was based on the formation of the first all-white jazz combo, the Original Dixieland Jazz Band, and its struggle for acceptance and recognition (many scholars did not believe a white band was capable of playing jazz). It achieved both, though the film's score was hardly true jazz, running from "Wait till the Sun Shines, Nellie," through producer B. G. DeSylva's (with Henderson and Brown) title song (which is not a blues), to Handy's authentic "St. Louis Blues." Johnny Mercer contributed words and music to the novelty number "The Waiter, the Porter and the Upstairs Maid."

Warner Brothers followed with their more socially conscious Arlen and Mercer treatise, which was released the following December. Since much of *Birth of the Blues* was set in New Orleans, the studio decided to discard the first title, *New Orleans Blues*, in favor of *Hot Nocturne*. Its rather overwrought screenplay was written by Robert Rossen, who had done the same for *The Roaring Twenties* and *The Sea Wolf*. Rossen based his script on the theme that occupied jazz historians: the chasm between the true jazz performed by dedicated musicians and the commercial stuff purveyed by musicians devoted to money.

Rossen's protagonists were the members of a small band and what was known at the time as a "girl singer." Their pianist-leader is so dedicated to his kind of music that he scarcely notices her. The band's struggle to perform true jazz and make a living without going commercial fuels the plot, with help from a troublesome vamp and an escaped convict. The film turns melodramatic when the pianist leaves to join a successful big band, only to suffer a nervous breakdown caused by playing the same arrangements night after night instead of jazz improvisations. The happy ending comes with the elimination of vamp and convict, along with the pianist's recovery and return to jazz and the girl singer.

While it was true that Arlen and Mercer came from different forests, the concordance of their two personalities would raise the overwrought *Hot Nocturne* above its script. They began with a romantic but lightly swinging ballad for the band and vocalist, "This Time the Dream's on Me." The film's vocalist is

Priscilla Lane, who had, as one of the three Lane Sisters, sung with Fred Waring's Pennsylvanians. She and the band also performed a perfect example of an Arlen-Mercer "jive" (rhythm) number, "Hang On to Your Lids, Kids," the uptempo contrast to the ballad. The tune is based on a "riff," a short, repeated phrase:

> So what—if we're busted chum,
> So what—if we're on the thumb,
> Hang on to your hats, cats,
> Here we go again.

This riffing song, written by musicians who knew their bands and singers, was characteristic of the swing era (as was being short of funds, the point of the lyric).

Another rhythm number, and one of their best, "Says Who? Says You, Says I!," was turned over to the commercial band, whose own girl singer renders a "Micky Mouse" ("Woody Woodpecker" may be more appropriate) version of the song. Presented for laughs, and to show the former jazz pianist on the verge of his breakdown, Mercer's poetic imagery was lost: "the skies are full of butterflies" and "that daisy crew is breaking through," for example. An undated period piece, "Says Who?" is a gem if heard properly, with humor but without parody.

One song was not used, the rueful "Wait'll It Happens to You." The manuscript piano-vocal copy is dated June 28, 1941, when the film was still titled *New Orleans Blues*; this was only six months before the film was released. There remained a spot for a song set in a jail cell, after some members of the band end up there for some reason or other. What with "hot" and "blues" regularly bandied about, it seemed logical that the jail would be a fine place to introduce a blues song. (Among Arlen's undated manuscript sketches is one marked "Blues for 'Hot Nocturne.' ")

They had their ballad, their riff tune, their novelty for the commercial band, and their reject. All the score lacked was a blues. In the scene, the pianist, the trumpeter, and an enthusiastic jazz fan and hopeful amateur clarinetist whom they tolerate (portrayed by the future director Elia Kazan) are tossed into jail. In their cell they hear a black prisoner singing the blues, unaccompanied, except for soft choral responses from other inmates. The white musicians are transported by what one calls "a real low-down New Orleans blues." They leave the jail happily with a great new number for the band (in the film it is later played by the Jimmie Lunceford Orchestra). The incarcerated blues singer, incidentally, was William Gillespie, the Reverend Johnson on the Decca recording of the *Americanegro Suite*.

Arlen was determined to write an authentic blues for that spot in the film. Mercer, who preferred working from a tune, left it to the composer to give him something to use. Arlen then applied himself. "So I did a little very minor re-search. I found out that the blues was always written in three stanzas, with twelve bars each. That was the first thing." (His source was the classic W. C. Handy collection *A Treasury of the Blues*.)

The second thing he did was to go into seclusion. He had a small studio, separate from the house, and after telling Anya he was not to be disturbed until he emerged or called, he did not come out of the studio for a day and a half.

Armed with Handy and his recording machine, he began, admitting he "didn't have a handle for this blues thing," no jot, no possibility. Then, as he played and recorded, "I got this little notion." He knew he had it and filled his acetates with variations on the notion until "the fires went up and the whole thing poured out!"

What poured out was an expansive fifty-eight-bar song that blends the twelve-bar blues stanza with the standard A-A'-B-A song form. Each A section is a complete blues stanza of twelve bars; the second A has an entirely new melody. The release is a pair of eight-bar periods. A two-bar transition into the final A and a four-bar tag round out the form.

Arlen knew it was his song, not a Tin Pan Alley blues. It was strong, and he knew Mercer could write the lyric that would give it life. ("I can't tell about melodies until I get the lyric," he told Max Wilk; the wrong lyric, no matter how strong the tune, would vitiate the song.) He sketched out the music, played it through, then shouted, "Annie!"

Although he later claimed that he went casually to see Mercer with no work in mind, in fact he was excited and wanted his collaborator to hear what he had conceived. Mercer was in his workroom at his desk. Arlen had learned over their weeks of collaboration that if Mercer winked it was a sign that he had had "a big night" and that there would be no work for that day. Mercer was not always a wise drinker.

Mercer did not wink, and Arlen sat at the piano and played the blues. Mercer still said nothing, no suggestions, no criticisms. Arlen played the song a couple more times, then left. Later, when he anxiously returned, he found that Mercer had written several lyric ideas. They were fine, but Arlen felt that the first, and crucial, twelve bars of the lyric "didn't hang together."

Disappointed, he shuffled through the four pages of Mercer's sketches and was struck by some lines Mercer had put down but had not included in the song. While Arlen had never suggested lyrics to Mercer before, he placed the sheet before Mercer at the desk and suggested that they use that lyric up front. Mercer agreed, discarded the original stanza, and replaced it with:

> *My mama done tol' me, when I was in kneepants,*
> *My mama done tol' me, son!*
> *A woman'll sweet talk, and give ya the big eye,*

But when the sweet talkin's done,
A woman's a two-face,
A worrisome thing who'll leave ya t' sing
The blues in the night.

According to Mercer, the final shaping of "Blues in the Night" took about a week. Soon after, on a Saturday night, Mercer and Arlen dropped in on the Whitings, mother and daughter, with whom Mercer had kept in close touch since the death of Richard Whiting. Margaret Whiting, then about sixteen, recalled that evening for Max Wilk:

We always had a Saturday-night get-together at our house in those days. People came and went, songwriters dropped by, we were a show-business family and all of us sort of hung together. All of us were Hollywood kids then. Mickey Rooney was there, and Judy Garland, Martha Raye, an old friend, and Mel Tormé. . . . around nine thirty or ten Harold and Johnny came by, they'd just finished the song, and they went to our piano and did "Blues" for the first time.

Well, I want to tell you, it was like a Paramount Pictures finish—socko, boffo, *wham!* At one end of the room, Martha Raye almost passed out; for once she didn't have a funny line. Tormé was so knocked out by the musicianship, he just sat there. Mickey Rooney kept saying, "My God, this is unbelievable!" And Judy and I raced over to the piano to see which of us could learn the song first! You knew right away the song was so *important.* When they put it into the picture, they really murdered it.

A slight exaggeration, perhaps. The jailhouse scene was effective and, in another, "Blues in the Night" was given a fine big-band treatment by Lunceford. The film's murderous plot might have eclipsed any other song, but not "Blues in the Night." Once it was played for the producer, Hal B. Wallis, and the director, Anatole Litvak, *New Orleans Blues* and *Hot Nocturne* went into discard and the movie became *Blues in the Night.*

If the song was not given its deserved full treatment (no song was) in the film, after its release "Blues in the Night" literally swept the country. Following the movie's December premiere, "Blues in the Night" made the "Hit Parade" on January 31, 1942, and remained for thirteen weeks, through April 25, several times in the Number One spot. During this time there was a scramble among the big bands to record the song—Goodman, Woody Herman, Harry James—all except Lunceford, it seems.

"He refused to record it," Arlen told Max Wilk. "Hated it!" Why this was, Lunceford never revealed, but he resisted recording "Blues in the Night" until Jack Kapp of Decca Records, who held Lunceford's recording contract, applied some pressure. Curiously, not only did Lunceford's band record the song around the time of the film's release in December, but it filled both sides of the 78-rpm record, a rare practice in popular music at the time. What amused the composer later was that Lunceford's recording of "Blues in the Night" became one of the band's best-selling discs.

On Saturday, February 14, 1942, when "Blues in the Night" moved up from the Number Three spot to Number Two (it would be in first place the following week), the Number Eight song marked a fateful turn in the nation's history. Its title was "Remember Pearl Harbor."

The Japanese aerial assault on Pearl Harbor's naval and aircraft installations on December 7, 1941, galvanized the film industry into an even greater frenzy of patriotism. Before the Pearl Harbor attack, a number of service-oriented films had been made, inspired by the nation's first peacetime draft. Most were comedies in which inept civilians infuriated, always thwarted, and eventually won over the professional military man, the tough sergeant or the slow-burning chief. The military life was a fun-filled lark in those pre–Pearl Harbor films, which were designed for such unlikely military material as Abbott and Costello and Bob Hope. Even Fred Astaire was cast as a dancer-director who gets drafted in the Cole Porter–scored *You'll Never Get Rich*. Released three months before *Blues in the Night*, the film depicts the delights of basic training. Still, for one reason or another, Astaire spends a great deal of time in the guardhouse, dancing.

Once war came, however, dramatic films turned serious and somewhat propagandistic under the guidance of the Office of War Information and other bureaucracies. During the period of the Nazi onslaught and Pearl Harbor, Harold Arlen not only kept informed of events in Europe by means of the radio but also ordered and saved airchecks of speeches by Winston Churchill, Franklin D. Roosevelt, even Hitler, which were recorded professionally by a Hollywood recording studio. Japanese aggression, when it came, was a shock—for some reason it had seemed so remote.

Concurrently with the making of the more weighty war films, the lighter, entertaining musicals, with a solemn patriotic moment or two, became a studio staple. Most of these fell under the category of the cliché "star-studded." The first of this type, and there were others based on the G.I. or sailor meeting the girl of his dreams while on leave, was *Star Spangled Rhythm*, released a year after *Blues in the Night*.

Virtually plotless, these all-star filmed variety shows were morale builders with a slight suggestion of recruitment stimulus; servicemen got to meet pretty girls and even well-known movie stars. *Star Spangled Rhythm* glittered with Paramount's full roster, from Bing Crosby, Bob Hope, Dorothy Lamour, and even such nonmusical luminaries as Paulette Goddard and Fred MacMurray, on through two directors, Cecil B. DeMille and the comic genius Preston Sturges. Everyone on the Paramount lot, it seemed, appeared in *Star Spangled Rhythm*.

Arlen and Mercer were chosen to provide the film's musical moments. These were to be sandwiched between the comedy skits and whatever plot surfaced from time to time. Working from the star-studded cast rather than the slight plot, Arlen and Mercer supplied such appropriate numbers as "On the Swing Shift," a lively tribute to the women who worked in factories between the early and late shifts, from four in the afternoon to midnight. They also gave Betty Hutton a chance to do one of her energetic renditions (riding in a crowded Jeep) in the mildly suggestive "I'm Doing It for Defense" and turned out a flag-waver, intoned by Bing Crosby—"Old Glory," a song Arlen preferred to forget. Its presentation against a background of the presidential visages carved into Mount Rushmore, with an all-American chorus, speeches, and questions and answers about democracy and the enemy, was fitting, if a bit overdone. An obvious throw-away number, one on which Mercer did more work than Arlen, was "A Sweater, a Sarong, and a Peek-a-Boo Bang," sung by three of Paramount's stars who were celebrated for these attributes, Paulette Goddard, Dorothy Lamour, and Veronica Lake. This was, in a popular phrase of the period, "something for the boys."

"Sharp As a Tack" was sung and danced by Eddie "Rochester" Anderson, joined by the anthropologist-turned-dancer Katherine Dunham. The song extols the wartime male apparel known as the "zoot suit," created in Harlem, taken up by white, particularly Mexican, toughs, and reviled by many. Rochester's long jacket with trousers pulled high above the waist were outrageous, loud, and fashionably overstated. His appearance is improved, however, when he gets into an army uniform. This, too, is primarily a Mercer lyric song, though Arlen's riffy tune was perfect for the dance. Mercer had the vernacular, and the styling, down pat:

> *Jackson, you're sharp as a tack*
> *With a belt in the back*
> *Draped to the bricks* [sidewalk]—
> *Muggin' lightly killin' the chicks.*

None of these songs was particularly memorable, but two were outstanding and one, a classic. Their relationship to the plot is minimal. "Hit the Road to Dreamland" is a swinging good-night song in which Mercer, as in "Sharp As a Tack," draws upon contemporary musician argot: "Dig you in the land of nod," "knocked-out moon . . . a-blowin' his top," and the title phrase. Sung by Dick Powell and Mary Martin, "Hit the Road" featured an infectious rhythmic counterpoint by the Golden Gate Quartet, a black gospel group that also performed secular material. (Unfortunately, this fascinating portion of the song is not in the published version.) The staging, in a train's diner with the Golden Gate Quartet cast, of course, as waiters, it was one of the more exhilarating musical highlights of *Star Spangled Rhythm*.

The score required a dance for a production number in which the ballerina Vera Zorina would dance to the choreography of her then husband, George Balanchine. With that in mind, Arlen played a "possible" for Mercer, an insistent melody over a reiterating bass figure. Mercer liked it but, despite its length, suggested that a few additional bars would enable him to write the ballad in the form of a narrative rather than the usual romantic movie song. Arlen complied, producing an A^1-A^2-B-A^3 song whose sections are double the usual proportions, with an extra extension in the final A. As Arlen put it succinctly, "I played the melody for John. He went away." Mercer took seventy-two bars of music with him, and when he returned, he had a song entitled "That Old Black Magic."

It was Arlen's turn to be pleased. Henceforth, he always insisted that the lyric was essential to the song's popularity. "The words sustain your interest," he claimed, "make sense, contain memorable phrases, and tell a story. Without the lyric the song would be just another long song."

He recalled, too, that initially there was resistance to "That Old Black Magic" from the film's production team. They were overruled by a former songwriter, now Paramount's executive producer, B. G. DeSylva. In the film the song is sung by a former band and radio singer, Johnnie Johnston, playing a soldier who dreams about Zorina, who then comes to life out of her pinup picture on the side of the soldier's tent to dance to Arlen-Balanchine. It was the most "artistic" sequence in the movie ("arty" may be more apt, but it pleased audiences and the sailors in the film's appreciative audience).

"That Old Black Magic" flowered into another Arlen-Mercer standard and was taken up by several bands and popular vocalists, among them Margaret Whiting, who recorded it for Capitol Records one week after her eighteenth birthday. Capitol Records, by coincidence, had recently been established by an astute trio: Glenn Wallichs, who had once managed a music shop in Hollywood; B. G. DeSylva of Paramount; and Capitol's first president, Johnny Mercer. In time, Capitol would become a serious competitor of the current big three, RCA-Victor, Columbia, and Decca. Its roster of popular best-selling vocalists included Nat "King" Cole, Jo Stafford, Peggy Lee, and quite prominently, Margaret Whiting and Johnny Mercer.

Caught up in making people happy in wartime, the studios followed Paramount's luminary-clustered *Star Spangled Rhythm* with Warner's *Thank Your Lucky Stars*, United Artists' *Stage Door Canteen* (in turn succeeded by Warner's *Hollywood Canteen*), and MGM's *Thousands Cheer*. The less light-hearted dramatic films were also ground out steadily. By late 1943 Hollywood was truly at war.

The months after *Star Spangled Rhythm* were a busy time for Harold Arlen: he worked simultaneously with Harburg at MGM, with Koehler on a project for

Sam Goldwyn, and again with Mercer, this time on an RKO musical for Fred Astaire. In between, when his collaborators preferred sleep, he slipped out to the golf course.

His absence left Anya on her own. She, too, slept while he was at Hillcrest or the California Country Club. Anya awakened to an empty house, except for Stormy and Pan. She had little to do. She might, if she felt like it, paint. She was not a great reader. Estranged from the Hollywood wives, especially Leonore Gershwin and her faction, she had no close friends there.

She would call Ann Ronell, the composer of "Willow Weep for Me" and "Who's Afraid of the Big, Bad Wolf?" and underscoring for films. A protégée of George Gershwin, she was married to the producer Lester Cowan (whose fine war film *The Story of G.I. Joe* she scored). She was gentle and understanding and no threat to Anya. They exchanged phone calls, but Anya never accepted invitations to visit while her husband golfed or worked, nor did she ask Ronell to come by.

Harold was unaware of this withdrawal, for the couple went to parties, even at the Gershwins', and to the track and football games. At these times she appeared to be happy, but he did not realize that it was because they were together. At parties he naturally had the spotlight, not Anya. She did not mind, though some of the attention he attained from his performances made her uneasy, if not jealous. To Harold her occasional moodiness was just that, and she would get over it. Nor did she understand what troubled her, and she could not enlighten him except with a temperamental outburst. He would soothe her, she would calm down, and he would be off to the golf green or to the piano.

During the second full year of war, 1943, he and Mercer tossed off a song for a Bob Hope–Dorothy Lamour comedy, after which he and Harburg added songs to the film version of Broadway's *Cabin in the Sky* (of which more later). He followed that with a contribution to war relief called "If That's Propaganda," with a lyric by Ira Gershwin.

After *Cabin in the Sky* was finished, Arlen joined Mercer on the Astaire film at RKO. It began as *Look Out Below*, with Astaire cast as a Flying Tiger fighter pilot on leave. The Flying Tigers were mercenaries, most on leave of absence from the U.S. Navy or Marines, who fought for China before Pearl Harbor. After the Japanese attack, many returned to the United States to rejoin their original units. Thus, when the film opens, after Astaire is seen shooting down a Japanese plane, he appears in the States in civilian clothes. Instead of being recognized as an "ace" with eleven Japanese planes to his credit, he is regarded with suspicion as a draft dodger despite his earlier good press.

The Astaire scholar John Mueller classified the film, retitled *The Sky's the Limit* by a Gallup Poll, as "Fred Astaire's dark comedy." In the film, Astaire and his buddies (one of whom is portrayed by a cynical Robert Ryan), having experienced war, find civilian attitudes naïve, even fatuous. In one scene Astaire lectures a superpatriotic aircraft manufacturer on the inferiority of the planes his factory produces (a tragic, unpublicized truth at the time). He is disgusted by the remarks of a civilian, safely 4F, who tells him, "We gotta give 'em a taste of cold American steel." While the plot echoes the early Astaire-Rogers musicals, with Astaire, in Mueller's view, as a "cocky, charming, highly competent, enigmatic character," preview audiences found *The Sky's the Limit* "different" and "unusual." It was not a typical Fred Astaire song-and-dance gossamer comedy, nor was it a standard wartime flag-waver.

Like *Blues in the Night, The Sky's the Limit* is more drama than musical. Only Astaire's presence and that of three Arlen-Mercer songs (one a classic) place it into the quasi-musical category, or perhaps, borrowing from Mueller, it could be called a noir musical.

Playing opposite Astaire was eighteen-year-old Joan Leslie, whose singing was dubbed by Sally Sweetland; while not in a Ginger Rogers or Rita Hayworth class, she kept up with Astaire on the dance floor remarkably well. In the film Leslie is a magazine photographer whom Astaire pursues while in New York before returning to the war in the Pacific as a navy pilot. This was an unusual but winning pairing. Leslie is believable and lovable as the feisty young woman who holds Astaire at a distance and tries to help him make a meaningful contribution to the war effort. She also was finishing high school during the filming. As Astaire put it, "Gosh, the older I get, the younger they get." He was then forty-four, an advanced age for a fighter pilot.

Arlen and Mercer wrote two songs that were war-related; both were tossed out. At least one, "Harvey, the Victory Garden Man," was filmed. Sung by Ella Mae Morse, with backing by the Freddie Slack orchestra, it praised the efforts of urban agriculturists who planted small plots of vegetables in unlikely settings.

The second reject was a good-humored capitulation to rationing. Arlen's jumpy tune mirrors Mercer's witty lyric:

> *No more stuff 'n' things*
> *Trouser cuff 'n' things*
> *No more aluminum*
> *'Cause Uncle Sam's consumin' "um"*
> *No more tires t' own*
> *Goodyear-Firestone*

And so on through a list of shortages—fuel, milk, silk, metals ("vanadium . . . scarcer now than radium")—and closing with:

> *Take my meals away*
> *Rubber heels away*
> *But if I lose the whole shebang*
> *I'm hangin' on to you.*

Not all Americans shared Mercer's patriotic philosophy, and a small but profitable black market flourished during the war years. Even as the lyricist lamented of "no more beef in sight," it could be got from your local friendly butcher at a price. The beef shortage even brought about a revival of cattle rustling in the west. More sophisticated than their forebears, the new generation of rustlers used trucks as mobile slaughterhouses before making sales to packers. In Beverly Hills high prices were taken for granted. When Harold Arlen, Ira Gershwin, and Harry Warren drove to the golf links they saved on tire wear and fuel by pooling resources. Taking Arlen's car, either Arlen or Warren would drive (Gershwin did not drive), and they alternated with their gas rations.

What remained in *The Sky's the Limit* after the two war songs were eliminated was golden. The first was a ballad, one of Arlen's personal favorites, "My Shining Hour." He often referred to it when raising objections to his typing as a "blues writer."

Imbued with a direct melodic simplicity and a lyric to match of pure, simple poetry, "My Shining Hour" is the film's thematic expression of wartime's uncertain hope. Not only is it "sung" by Leslie in a nightclub (to prove she could return to show business and give up photography to her boss, Robert Benchley, in a fine performance as a hapless suitor), but it is also used throughout as underscoring as the breezy near-romance evolves. It also is the music for a most effective dance as the two now-committed people realize that, in a wartime phrase, "this is it." The musical director, Leigh Harline, makes the melody a leitmotif for the romance as it develops from a lark (Astaire's intentions are obviously not honorable in the beginning) into a bittersweet love by the close of the film, when Astaire leaves for the Pacific and Leslie realizes he was doing his part, after all.

Not only is "My Shining Hour" a fine song; its melody, without Mercer's lyric, works hauntingly as background scoring. Arlen had no special, out-of-the-blue tale about the writing of the song; it simply happened. Its structure was typically Arlen in its assymetry: a six-bar introduction, a fifteen-bar verse, and a thirty-seven-bar chorus, the last two bars of which are purely instrumental over a sustained note.

The other outstanding song in the score is "one of the most startlingly original of popular songs," as Mueller called it in *Astaire Dancing*. Arlen called it "another Arlen tapeworm" (his designation of his customary more-than-thirty-two-bar melodies). It began, "a wandering song," as one of his "possibles," which he set aside for future use. He studied his home recordings of this new idea and, as he told Max Wilk, "I wrote it as if it were natural to me to write that kind of song, but then I started thinking, 'Jesus, how could a lyric-writer dig *this*, or even understand it?' Because I'd started in one key [E-flat]—I didn't even realize it at the time—and I wound up in another key [G]. Unlike anything I'd ever done, or heard."

But Mercer took this tapeworm (fifty-eight bars, plus a three-bar instrumental tag) and produced what the composer regarded as "the best torch lyric of our time." It has become the classic "saloon song" of any time, "One for My Baby (And One More for the Road)."

It is also the music for Astaire's most violent solo dance in any of his films. Drinking after his breakup with Joan Leslie (a noble gesture, since he realizes he is in love but must leave the next day), he is depressed as he moves from bar to bar. Inebriated, he ends up at the bar where he and Leslie had met. It is empty except for the bartender and himself.

The song begins with one of the most original first lines ever written, "It's quarter to three," as he unburdens himself to "Joe," the bartender. He dances off his frustration, anguish, and anger on the floor, then on the bar, and then begins devastating the place, demolishing glasses and finally, with a bar stool, shattering the mirror behind the bar. Leigh Harline's arrangement of the disturbing song matches Astaire's emotions, with its rhythmic tensions, dissonant brass, and sudden transitions from loud to soft.

The astonished bartender, dressed to leave, confronts Astaire. Smiling wanly, Astaire explains, "That's how it goes," tosses a roll of bills on the bar, slips a tip into the man's pocket, deftly kicks his hat up off the floor, and casually leaves to set out on "That long, long road."

This literally smashing sequence was choreographed by Astaire, and if the music was unlike anything Arlen had done before, neither had there been an Astaire dance like that before. It had interesting repercussions. After a preview, the studio received a complaint from a theater manager. He wanted the scene deleted because it served no dramatic purpose and complained that such wholesale destruction of glass was "extremely distasteful if not unpatriotic." (In fact, the studio, to save money, had acquired factory rejects for the scene.)

The film's inconclusive ending, with Astaire flying westward as Joan Leslie, like many women at the time, watched tearfully, was unsettling for audiences. Critics, expecting another *Top Hat*, dismissed it along with the dances and songs.

Astaire recalled that neither of his songs made an impression at the time—although "My Shining Hour" and two other Arlen songs were nominated for Oscars in 1943. In due time, Astaire noted, " 'My Shining Hour' became the number one song of the day and 'One for My Baby' has become a standard classic popular song and one of the best pieces of material written especially for me."

The enduring popularity of the unique "One for My Baby" is curiously difficult to pinpoint. Even the loquacious (especially about Arlen) Alec Wilder is at a loss for words. In fact, he assigns most of the song's power to Mercer's lyric, confessing its personal meaning for him. He finds it "unlike any melody of Arlen's I've ever heard" and that he "must assume that the lyric had greatly to do with its almost old-time piano-player character."

Wilder was unaware of the melody's conception before the words were written. Absent is Arlen's trademark octave leap, or any other large interval. Instead, the melody makes sinuous chromatic turns within a small range—somewhat like the opening of "Stormy Weather," without that song's dramatic octave drop. The accompaniment is typical of Arlen, a characteristic blues ostinato reflecting the still-current eight-to-the-bar boogie-woogie piano style. Arlen was one of the few white musicians who could play these authentic styles; not even Gershwin equaled Arlen in playing the blues.

"One for My Baby" evokes a smoky downtown nightclub with Arlenesque echoes of Harlem and of the synagogue—the piquant cantorial turn, the tiny melisma on the word "baby." Like its near-relative of a different mood, "That Old Black Magic," it is a song that unfolds inexorably with its tale of despondency.

Too complex melodically for the pops market, it has become a staple for so-called saloon singers (who appear only in very expensive supper clubs catering to sophisticated audiences)—Frank Sinatra (among the first), Tony Bennett, Bobby Short, and others. For the published version Mercer deleted the singer's self-reference—"Don't let it be said / Little Fred- / die can't carry his load"—though he retained the reference to Joe the bartender. This is probably the only song in American popular music addressed to someone named Joe.

Although *The Sky's the Limit* and Arlen's other projects of 1943–44 touched on martial themes, he himself remained out of the military. At thirty-eight, with a change in the draft law, he was ineligible for service. His brother, Jerry, then thirty, was eligible, however. When Jerry's number came up and he passed the physical, he was resigned to the military life. Samuel Arluck, not happy with this development, unleashed a torrent of letters from Syracuse demanding that Harold do something for his younger brother. In truth, neither Arlen would have made much of a military man. Their temperaments were not attuned to that way of life and death.

Harold Arlen did pull strings successfully. His good friend David Rose was then a sergeant in the air force and associated with a show Moss Hart had written for the air force, *Winged Victory*. All proceeds were to go to the Air Force Emergency Fund. Rose was drafted, literally, to compose the score and to conduct. More a drama than a musical, *Winged Victory* used music to emphasize the theme of young American men making the transition from civilian to military life. Hart also brought in the families of these men to portray the civilian side of the war, something that the *New York Times* reviewer found "most warming in the theatre."

The show's extraordinarily large cast, all on army salaries, came largely from Hollywood and included Pvt. Red Buttons, Pfc. Edmond O'Brien, Sgt. Ray Middleton (later to star in Berlin's *Annie Get Your Gun*), Pvt. Lee J. Cobb, and a onetime comic, Peter Lind Hayes, a staff sergeant. Rose had also dipped into the air force's rosters and formed a chorus and orchestra.

He arranged to have Pvt. Jerry Arlen transferred from his air force unit into the *Winged Victory* orchestra as a saxophonist. The show premiered in November 1943 for a long Broadway run that kept Jerry Arlen out of harm's way for the duration.

Ironically, it was Jerry's older brother who got nearer to the war. Harold spent some time, as a guest of the navy, aboard a battleship and an aircraft carrier safely at dock in San Diego, in connection with one of his wartime films. But he and Anya had a close brush with death in their own home in Beverly Hills.

He took some time off from work one weekend and used up some of his gas ration to drive down to Palm Springs. After a little golf for him and lounging around a pool for Anya, they returned late on a Sunday night and immediately went to bed. They did not disturb Anya's younger brother, on leave from the air force and asleep in the downstairs den. Though in his early twenties and a member of the crew of the B-29 Superfortress bomber, he was a slender, tow-headed youngster they called Willy. He was also quite wild and had a drinking problem.

Around one that morning Arlen awakened and thought he saw the garden lights on. Sleepily, he got out of bed to turn them off. When his feet touched the floor he was shocked to find it hot. Then he smelled smoke and realized the house was on fire.

He rushed back to Anya, who snapped awake instantly. Ordinarily, she required at least two cups of coffee and some time to counteract the sleeping pills she took at bedtime. More alert than her husband at that moment, she stopped him from opening the door to go downstairs into the flames and smoke.

"Follow me," she snapped and pulled him toward the window. She jumped first, landing on a neighbor who had seen the fire, had come to help, and was standing under the window. Arlen followed and landed, unscratched, in a rose bush.

Willy stood some feet away, dazed it seemed, staring at the flames. Arlen knew that Stormy and Pan were bedded down in the back of the house. He ran to the back and released the dogs into the garden and returned to Anya and Willy. The flames had spread into the living room and had engulfed the den, where he sometimes worked.

Then he remembered something and rushed into the house to Anya's scream, "Where are you going?"

He stumbled into the smoke-filled living room, holding his breath and scarcely able to see. He made it to a wall and snatched a large painting. Coughing now, he staggered out of the inferno into the yard, where he found a distraught Anya. She was relieved when she saw him emerge with George Gershwin's last painting, the portrait of Jerome Kern. It was the one painting hanging in that part of the house that he was able to save. Others went up in flames, including a couple by Henry Botkin. (One of the paintings Botkin had painted for the *Americanegro Suite* survived.) Several books burned, including a prized copy of *Porgy and Bess* bound and signed by the Gershwins, DuBose Heyward, and Botkin, who had done some illustrations for the limited edition. His copy of Goldberg's Gershwin biography was slightly scorched but salvageable.

Part of the damage, which was substantial, could be attributed to a simple matter of political jurisdiction. When he called from their neighbor's phone for the fire department, Arlen learned that though they lived in Beverly Hills, the nearest aid was denied them because the house was not in the right county.

"By the time the firemen came from over the canyon," Arlen recalled, "the main part of the house, the living room, and the little den were gutted." What the flames did not destroy, Arlen maintained, the firefighters did, in a release of "Freudian" energy "to chop up everything there was in order to put out the fire."

All the paintings, except the Kern portrait, in that part of the house were lost, as was the furniture and a piano. Because most of his library was in the larger study, few books were burned. "After this horror was over we decided to redo the house and went all the way and built a pool, which Annie designed. . . . We learned that the fire had been caused by a short in the radio in the den."

Hollywood gossip from that time on intimated another tale. The word spread through Beverly Hills that an angry, jealous Anya had ignited the fire. This story fueled the rumors that the Arlens were having marital problems because he was so preoccupied with work and she felt neglected, brooded, and depended on pills.

Another account, more likely but no more verifiable, was that her brother, Willy, inebriated, had fallen asleep in the den while smoking. This more plausible version of the fire's origin was not as prevailing as the one casting Anya in the role of disturbed, vindictive arsonist. When he told the story to a writer in the 1960s, Arlen did not mention Willy Taranda. Years later, though, he did, suggesting that a cigarette had caused the blaze. Anya chose to forget it.

During the rebuilding of the house, Anya was happily occupied with designing the new swimming pool and two bathhouses. As Arlen worked with Johnny Mercer in the studio (once a garage) or at the lyricist's home, Anya oversaw the redesign of their house—they had also decided to add a small bar. She was radiant and content doing something useful.

Early in 1944 Mercer and Arlen were at work on what was to be their final war film, a glorified recruiting musical initially entitled *Song of the Waves* (WAVES being Women Accepted for Emergency Service in the navy). Starring Bing Crosby and Betty Hutton in a dual role, it was finally released at the end of the year as *Here Come the Waves*.

The plot's concept has Bing Crosby as Johnny, a 4F singer, the reluctant objective of adoring bobby-soxers in satirical treatment of the rampant Frank Sinatra phenomena at the time. As Johnny sings, the bobby-soxers scream and faint in their seats, just as they did when Sinatra sang at the Paramount in New York (some of this frantic reaction was staged by Sinatra's agents). Johnny frets over being mobbed by nubile young women and, even more so, being denied service in the navy, since he has come from a long line of navy men. When the navy lowers its recruitment standards, he immediately enlists but cannot escape his celebrity.

Betty Hutton comprises both halves of a sister act, the red-headed, smart, sensible Rosemary and the scatterbrained blonde Susie, one of Johnny's most ardent fans. Susie has fainted at one of his theater appearances (singing "That Old Black Magic"), to Rosemary's disgust. The sisters, notably, have been popular nightclub singers until Rosemary enlists and Susie follows. Johnny ends up with the sensible twin and his sailor friend Windy (Sonny Tufts, a genuine 4F, owing to a knee injured when he played football at Yale) with the kinetic one, after the usual misunderstandings. The film closes, as expected, with a morale-raising, recruitment-inspiring musical aboard an aircraft carrier (courtesy of the U.S. Navy) before the two happy sailors fly off to combat duty in the South Pacific.

In the four months or so devoted to their work, Arlen and Mercer produced ten songs, four of which were rejected, still leaving a pretty substantial score for a movie. Two of the songs were obvious in intent, "The Navy Song (Join the Navy)" and "Here Come the Waves." They were properly stirring, if routine.

Except for these two martial airs and one other song, the musical numbers were not tied to the plot. Crosby sang in a theater, the Hutton "sisters" in a club, and the ensemble, including Tufts, in the big variety-show finale on the carrier flight deck. The exception, a ballad, was Crosby's solo, "Let's Take the Long Way Home." A lesser "My Shining Hour," it is the turning point in the plot, in an outdoor setting, when the sensible Hutton realizes that she is in love with the man her sister adores. Melodically and lyrically it is middling Arlen-Mercer, attractive but unmemorable.

Here Come the Waves was the first important casting at Paramount for Hutton, who had left the Vincent Lopez band to play feature roles in musicals. She was by then noted for energetic renditions of unrestrained rhythm numbers, such as "Arthur Murray Taught Me Dancing in a Hurry" and "Murder He Says." With that in mind, Arlen and Mercer provided her with two "specialties": "There's a Fella Waitin' in Poughkeepsie" and "My Mamma Thinks I'm a Star." The first was Mercer's witty reversal on the venerable "sweetheart in every port" naval tradition. The song grows out of a skit, "If Waves Acted Like Sailors" (inspired no doubt by *Star Spangled Rhythm*'s variation on the old George S. Kaufman sketch for a 1923 *Music Box Revue*, "If Men Played Cards Like Women"). Mercer's added switch is that all the beaux in Susie's active romantic life live in ports that are situated inland.

"My Mamma Thinks I'm a Star," one of the last completed songs, was not used. It is a long production number in which one of the sisters, probably Susie, the scatterbrain, laments her life under the ambitious drive of a stage mother. It may have been intended for the variety show but was simply dropped, leaving Hutton with only her "Fella in Poughkeepsie" solo number.

As sensible Rosemary, however, she joins Crosby in the film's fine ballad "I Promise You," in a scene in the closing variety show. The song has a slight relationship to the plot in the verse's reference to "these good-byes," as Crosby is about to desert the show to rejoin his ship, an original twist on going AWOL.

In the key of C and in common (4/4) time, "I Promise You" is one of Harold Arlen's most sensitive ballads, graced with Mercer's apposite lyric. Arlen's melody employs what was for him an unusual technique: the repeated tone. The first two bars of the refrain, on the words "I promise you," consist of the same note (G), a sustained line that is not easy to sing. The melody develops in small intervals, seconds and thirds, until in the twentieth bar of the refrain the interval rises to a tenth (on the word "poor") in a climax leading to the release and resolution. The opening bars are not repeated in the resolution, though the phrases "A faithful heart" and "A star or two" from the lyric are. The unusual structure is A-B-C, divided into sixteen, nineteen, and eight measures respectively. "I Promise You" belongs among the Arlen art songs.

The film's one hit, as with other incidents, came out of the blue and served as the number for the film's most tasteless sequence. Arlen and Mercer had spent some time at the Paramount studio one day and learned that they needed a duet for Crosby and Tufts as the opening of the variety show on the carrier, an up-tempo rhythm number to follow the moderate "Let's Take the Long Way Home." They noodled around in the office assigned to them, but nothing came. Giving up, they decided to take a drive into the hills. They were glum, written out, and facing the obstacle of that last "socko" number for the movie. "Let's go home," someone suggested, and Arlen turned the car toward Lindecrest Drive.

As they drove, Mercer had an idea. "How does that little thing go," he inquired, explaining, "I've heard you humming it—the spiritual?"

The composer had unconsciously hummed a snatch of something for days without giving it much thought. It was spiritual-like, perhaps, and syncopated. He hummed the two bars or so. Mercer, expressionless, listened. Arlen repeated the phrase and Mercer brightened.

"You've got to accentuate the positive?" he said.

Arlen sang the words, which fit the rhythm. As they drove, the idea grew, and he sang while Mercer responded with more words. "Before we got home," Arlen remembered, "the song was written [except for some final polishing], and it was the final one we needed for Bing Crosby. . . . It must have pleased John—it was the first time I ever saw him smile." (An exaggeration, as Mercer pointed out on a television production devoted to Arlen years later, saying, "I smile a lot.")

They tested their new song by singing it into Arlen's home recording machine, decorating it with some quite jazzy scat choruses. Crosby and the producer-director Mark Sandrich concurred, and Arlen and Mercer were finished with the picture (Crosby presented Arlen with an electric razor as a parting gift, a gadget he never used, having developed the daily barber habit).

To round out the chorus, they prepared a slow verse ("sermon-like"), to set the mood. The chorus, marked "moderately (with a steady rock)," uses that last word long before it became a pop music commodity. Undoubtedly the opening sermon and the rocking, uplifting spiritual encouraged the unfortunate staging of the production number, now entitled "Ac-cent-tchu-ate the Positive (Mister In-be-tween)." Mercer apparently was not taking any chances, making his rhythmic syllabification clear.

The song is done in blackface, alas. The two sailors have changed uniforms; Crosby is a white-tufted mailman and Tufts wears a resplendent doorman's outfit, plumed hat and all. The skit opens with each admitting he needs some cheer, and with the aid of a choral group they go through the stereotyped routine. A month after *Here Come the Waves* premiered, "Ac-cent-tchu-ate the Positive" began a three-month stay on the "Hit Parade" and, to the credit, and profit, of Arlen and Mercer, was recorded by Crosby as well as Mercer and played extensively on the air. In time, unfettered by racist paternalism, the song has become a standard.

During the filming of *Here Come the Waves* and until the time of its December 1944 release, roughly a year, the fortunes of war in Europe and the Pacific had turned. The Allies were solidly in North Africa, and the army and navy had begun moving toward the Philippine Islands, out of New Guinea, and into the Marshall Islands. From Moscow word would come that the Nazi forces were being driven out of that city and beleagured Stalingrad. In March the U.S. Air Force initiated the daylight bombing of Berlin, joining the Royal Air Force, which bombed under cover of night. On June 4 the Allies liberated Rome after severe fighting in Italy, and two days later, D-Day, Allied troops landed on the beaches of Normandy and by late August were in Paris.

The bitter end was in sight as the Russians savagely pushed the German armies into Poland. In the Pacific, as he had promised, General Douglas MacArthur returned to the Philippines in October. That it was not yet over was jarringly brought home around the time of the release of *Here Come the Waves*. The Battle of the Bulge occurred in mid-December, when the Germans counterattacked in the Ardennes. The German attempt was in vain, but the bloody battle was sobering for the Allies. Even so, Hollywood began losing interest in war pictures—as did the public.

Arlen's final wartime film, *Out of This World*, with Mercer, was neither a war movie nor really a musical. Its obvious raison d'etre was the persisting Sinatra adulation by the adolescent (and older) female. The brainstorm, obviously inspired by *Here Come the Waves*, may be credited to the songwriter Sam Coslow ("Cocktails for Two," "My Old Flame"), who was about to make his debut at Paramount.

Coslow's rationale was simple: to spin out the plot around, as he put it, "the Sinatra legend, swooning bobbysoxers and all." He contributed another element to the legend based on the rumor "that several different people owned a 'piece' of Sinatra, and that he was paying out more than half his salary on various percentage deals."

For his Sinatra stand-in Coslow chose the comedian Eddie Bracken, who had recently scored in an irreverent film written and directed by Preston Sturges, *The Miracle of Morgan's Creek*. Although that film, in the opinion of the historian Richard R. Lingeman, poked "fun at the flag, motherhood, and heroism" in the middle of the war, it became a hit.

Bracken in *Out of This World* is again an antihero, a shy messenger boy who is inadvertently pushed onstage, where he is coaxed to sing at a benefit with an all-girl band. When the hardly imposing Western Unioner opens his mouth to sing, the dulcet tones of Bing Crosby fill the auditorium and the audience of bobby-soxers scream and swoon.

Coslow's contract stipulated that he would write the songs for Bracken/ Crosby to sing, but in a flush of extraordinary modesty, he demurred. He explained to his boss, B. G. DeSylva, that since he would be credited with the "original story" and as producer, somehow flashing "Words and Music by Sam Coslow" on the screen might be excessive. When DeSylva questioned this decision, Coslow told him, "Well, I could use Harold Arlen and Johnny Mercer . . ."

DeSylva wondered why they should hire two more songwriters when they already had one, him, under contract. Coslow countered that he had Bracken, who was now big in films; he had Veronica Lake, she of the peek-a-boo bangs, to portray the manager who hires the screaming bobby-soxers. Arlen and Mercer, he continued, were "the hottest songwriting team in Hollywood." DeSylva told him to go ahead.

To his dismay, Coslow learned that Arlen and Mercer, while temporarily at liberty, had increased their fee, per picture, to sixty thousand dollars. Convincing Paramount's budget watchers required more persuasion, but Coslow succeeded there, too.

DeSylva liked the title *Divided by Five*, that is, a contract with five quarters: five investors each buying what he thinks is a quarter of a contract. But Coslow preferred a current "hipster phrase . . . that has gone into the language," *Out of This World*. Thus, he handed Arlen and Mercer their first song title. According to Coslow, they "earned their $60,000 in something like five days, coming up with a flock of great songs that included their marvelous title song."

This is only partly true. "Out of This World" is, indeed, a marvelous creation, an extraordinary "wedding" (Arlen's favorite word for a song that skillfully fused music and lyric). It is not "hip," though the music is otherworldly. Alec Wilder waxes ecstatic, as he does over so many Arlen songs, in *American Popular Song*:

> This long-lined ballad, without a verse, instantly sets up a *misterioso*, out-of-this-world mood. Its immediate melody point is, in the key of E flat, a long-held *d* flat. It creates a modal feeling, the mixolydian mode [i.e., the ancient Greek major scale with a minor seventh] to be precise. But unlike many other later and much less professionally written modal songs [a swipe at rock 'n' roll], this melody achieves an unearthly effect in its use of this one note.
>
> Its sections are sixteen, twenty, eighteen, and twenty measures long, A-A^1-B-A^1. It is one of Arlen's most direct and deliberately unrhythmic melodies, and unlike any of his other lyric ballads.

Coslow employed only one other Arlen-Mercer song in the film: "June Comes Around Every Year." In conventional thirty-two-bar form, this song's distinguishing feature is a countermelody for women's chorus in the repeated refrain. The film's presentation of both songs is somewhat marred, "Out of This World" by dialogue and "June Comes Around Every Year" by appreciative screams from bobby-soxers.

Overcoming his initial modesty, Coslow contributed four of his own songs to the score; another by Ben Raleigh and Bernie Wayne was also added. *Out of This World* was definitely not an Arlen-Mercer musical film. Both were happy to take their quickly earned capital and move on to other more fulfilling work—Mercer to work with Harry Warren on a Judy Garland film, *The Harvey Girls*, and Arlen to reunite with Yip Harburg.

WHEN THE WIND
BLOWS SOUTH

*O*f the eight wartime Hollywood musicals to which Harold Arlen contributed the music, the most imaginative and richly scored had no link to the war, patriotism, or even boy-meets-girl. During this creative period, roughly from September 1941 through the summer of 1943, Harold Arlen concurrently worked with Johnny Mercer twice and once with Ted Koehler. Harburg, too, collaborated with others, namely Arthur Schwartz and Burton Lane.

Harburg and Lane returned to the West Coast after their misfortunes with Al Jolson and the musical *Hold On to Your Hats.* Jolson, who backed the show, cast his wife, Ruby Keeler, as his co-star. At the beginning of the show's tour in Chicago, Lane and Harburg realized they had a problem. For his curtain call, Jolson ran through his top hits repertory, from "Swanee" to "California, Here I Come," essentially erasing the Lane-Harburg songs from the audience's memory. At one performance Jolson followed Keeler onstage, continuing a spat begun in the wings. To the mystification of the audience, the dialogue seemed to have nothing to do with the plot. Jolson berated his young wife, insisting that the problems in their marriage were the fault of a meddling mother. Keeler walked offstage and never returned. She was replaced by Martha Raye for the New York premiere in September 1940, around the time Arlen and Koehler were writing the *Americanegro Suite.*

Hold On to Your Hats was well received on Broadway, though it was Jolson, straying regularly from the book, who gleaned most of the attention. And despite the objections of Lane and Harburg, he continued to regale his fans with the show-stealing medley of songs of yesteryear. He also got bored and closed the show when he, its backer as well as star, left.

The first Arlen-Harburg collaboration after Harburg's return to California was the first in a trio for MGM. A trifle, *Rio Rita,* was a starring vehicle for the popular comedy team of Bud Abbott and Lou Costello. Because it was vaguely based on a 1927 hit musical of the same title, and employed some of its original songs, the vocal side of the film was assigned to the fine voices of Kathryn Grayson and John Carroll.

The plot spun around a dimwitted Costello, who outwits Nazi spies and saboteurs, interrupted by a favorite Abbott and Costello routine and a song now and then. From the original Harry Tierney–Joseph McCarthy score, Carroll sang the title song to Rita (Grayson), as well as the stalwart "Ranger's Song." Also in the film was a dancer with the memorable name of Eros Volusia, playing herself in a lusty Brazilian dance.

All of which left little footage for Arlen and Harburg to fill; with the Grayson voice in mind, they went to work optimistically. They wrote a duet for her and Carroll, two solos for her, and a novelty comedy duo (not for Abbott and Costello)—four songs, two in the Arlen art song class. The latter were, it hardly needs to be said, the first to go. One of their best, "Unusual Weather," was actually shot for the film's opening scene and then scrapped (the dialogue between Grayson and her maid sets up the cue and remains in the print, but the song doesn't follow).

The boogie-woogie accompaniment represents a joyously expectant young woman awaiting the arrival of her girlhood sweetheart, now a famous singer. The chorus sparkles with Harburgian phrases: "The crickets crickin' off the beat," "There should be frozen up noses / Instead it's coming up roses," and the concluding "All nature's cookin' with clover / It's all so silly and sweet."

The melodic structure is asymmetric (i.e., typically Arlen). The one conventional component in the song's hundred bars is that the chorus is the standard thirty-two measures. In the chorus Arlen uses portions of the verse's underscoring as a ritornello. That this ingenious work was written for a trained voice is evident in the melismas (on the word "day") in the thirty-six-bar coda.

Arlen and Harburg rounded out 1941 with yet another song for an MGM film. Harburg and Lane provided most of the songs to a quite scanty score for a film starring Red Skelton and Eleanor Powell. In it Skelton portrayed a comic sailor; since Bert Lahr was also cast as a sailor, Harburg suggested that he and Arlen write a mock sea chantey for Lahr. The idea was accepted, and they wrote "Heave Ho! Let the Wind Blow" for Lahr and a sailors' chorus. They turned it in a week after the Japanese bombed Pearl Harbor, which led to complications for the production.

A month after Pearl Harbor, the Japanese drove General Douglas MacArthur out of the Philippines. The film's original title when Arlen and Harburg fashioned "Heave Ho!" had been *I'll Take Manila,* which now had indeed been taken. By the time of the film's release in June 1942, Harburg had altered his and Lane's title song to "I'll Take Tallulah," and the Bert Lahr chantey was out. Harburg tried again later in the war, for his own production, *Meet the People,* in which he had cast Lahr, but the song was cut.

Arlen and Harburg's final MGM film was the second of their MGM trio that amounted to virtually nothing. Entitled *Kismet,* it was based on a 1911 play by Edward Knoblock. The hero (originally Otis Skinner) was a roguish poet disguised as a beggar—Ronald Colman in the film. The setting was Baghdad in the distant past under the fist of a wicked vizier. The poet-beggar cleverly cleans up the town, arranges for his daughter's marriage to a handsome caliph, and rides off into the desert with the deposed vizier's captivating wife, portrayed by a diaphanously gowned Marlene Dietrich.

The film was long on derring-do and short on song, another slight MGM score for Arlen and Harburg. They were occupied lightly during the spring and summer of 1943 turning out four songs, three of which were used, one of which was ill-served. This was the crucial "Tell Me, Tell Me, Evening Star," which leads the poet to his long-lost daughter, apparently the only person on earth besides himself, he believes, who knows the song. It is first heard, however, in a tonally ambiguous rendition in Dietrich's quasi-baritone. The song's distinctive Arlenian feature, a dip into the minor that is held for nine beats, is brought out better when sung by the long-lost daughter, Joy Ann Page, in a glowingly rich soprano. Page also sings "Willow in the Wind" with a lovely choral backing. The background music, scored by the *Wizard of Oz* veteran Herbert Stothart, was fittingly orientalized, Hollywood-style, but the songs were merely incidental, wasted, and also vanished into the desert. (The venerable Arabian Nights–like tale fared better on Broadway in 1953 with a score appropriated by Robert Wright and George Forrest from Alexander Borodin.)

Between their unfortunate minimusicals at MGM, Arlen and Harburg, thanks to Arthur Freed, worked on a score worthy of their talents. According to Harburg, once Freed acquired the Broadway succès d'estime *Cabin in the Sky,* a 1940 musical with music by Vernon Duke, he told Harburg, "This show needs some Southern songs and hasn't got any."

Harburg agreed, informing Freed that when Duke approached him initially to do the lyrics for the admirable book by Lynn Root, he refused. Writing music for a show advertised as a "Negro fantasy," Harburg believed, was not Duke's forte. The composer found a more compatible collaborator in the gifted John Latouche, celebrated in 1940 as the lyricist of the pop cantata *Ballad for Americans.* After that rejection, it was years before Duke spoke to Harburg again.

Some of the Duke-Latouche songs had become popular during the show's run, especially the title song, "Honey in the Honeycomb," and "Taking a

Chance on Love" (with the co-lyricist Ted Fetter). These were retained for Freed's production and, indeed, they were typically Duke, well formed, cosmopolitan, but not particularly at home in a "Negro fantasy." Freed and Harburg agreed that if anyone could infuse the score with an authentic southern flavor, it was Harold Arlen. Duke was unavailable, having enlisted in the U.S. Coast Guard, which made things easier for Freed. Duke often proved to be a combative employee. While he admired the musicianship of Harold Arlen, Duke would have protested ejecting eleven of his songs.

The plot of *Cabin in the Sky* centers on a likeable but shiftless gambler-philanderer, Little Joe, who is married to good, hardworking, deeply religious Petunia. When Joe is shot in a card game dispute, his soul becomes a battleground between the Lord's General and the devil's son, Lucifer Jr. Only Petunia's heartfelt prayer gains Little Joe a six-month reprieve, during which he is given a chance to redeem himself. But he strays with Lucifer Jr.'s ally, the beautiful Georgia Brown (Lena Horne in the film, the dancer Katherine Dunham in the theater). At the climax in a dance hall, Petunia is fatally shot; despite Joe's backsliding, her prayers again move the Lord, and she and Joe, in white robes, move into heaven and their cabin in the sky.

That was the stage show's ending. A film concluding with its main protagonists dead and heading heavenward would not fit into the Arthur Freed musical formula. The happy ending in the film reveals that the fatalities happen in Joe's fevered dream, and he awakens in his own bed, a reformed sinner. The appropriation of this cinematic cliché (already old hat when it was similarly tacked on to the film version of L. Frank Baum's *Wizard of Oz*) was the sole major change in the plot from that of the Broadway show.

Inevitably there were musical alterations as well. Duke Ellington and His Orchestra were brought in to provide the dance hall music; thus an Ellington song was interpolated into the film's score. Louis Armstrong appeared as the Devil's Trumpeter, so he was given his musical moments. The superb dancer John W. Sublette (better known as Bubbles and for his classic portrayal of Sportin' Life in Gershwin's *Porgy and Bess*) was given his special spot, singing one of his specialty songs, written by Ford Dabney and Cecil Mack, "Shine." A traditional spiritual, "Old Ship of Zion," was also used. This left little musical space for Arlen and Harburg.

Cabin in the Sky, for its time, was venturesome, even risky. Its entire cast was black. Although from the inception of the motion picture such movies had been made, they were never intended for general distribution. Categorized as "race movies," they were shown only in the black sections of large cities or the southern towns with a predominantly African American population.

At MGM Freed encountered resistance from some executives, and when the film was announced, he was attacked in the African American press. Precedent for this criticism dated back to 1929, when a drama, with music by Irving Berlin and directed by King Vidor, was released. Entitled *Hallelujah,* it was a serious but flawed attempt at depicting black life in the south. There were objections to its stereotyping and patronizing sentimentality. Warner Brothers fared worse with their 1936 release *The Green Pastures,* with its depiction of heaven as one big happy fish fry. Its simplistic view of African American religion was still fresh in 1942, when work on *Cabin in the Sky* was scheduled to begin.

Freed managed to defuse some of the criticisms by issuing statements to the black press praising the contribution of African Americans to the theater, the originality and talent that "rendered a great service to the world of entertainment and the culture of the nation." And he reassured African American readers that "the motion picture industry in its basic forms will never discriminate" and that "more than ever before we are aware of the Negro problem and are daily moving toward a better understanding."

To assure peaceful filmmaking, MGM brought in Hall Johnson as a script adviser and to conduct the Hall Johnson Choir. Johnson found the plot inoffensive, though he felt that "the dialect in your script is a weird but priceless conglomeration of pre–Civil War constructions mixed with up-to-the-minute Harlem slang and heavily sprinkled with a type of verb which Amos and Andy purloined from Miller and Lyle, the Negro comedians; all of which has never been heard or spoken on land and sea by any human being." (Some of the language was subsequently changed.) Johnson closed with an astute observation. "If your director," he wrote, "is as sympathetic and intelligent as your script writer you will turn out a picture which will delight everybody and offend no one without an inferiority complex—an affliction, by the way, which has almost completely died out among modern Negroes."

Freed, reassured, began to move. He took one other risk, luring Arlen's friend Vincente Minnelli away from Broadway to give him his first film assignment (the Broadway directors were George Balanchine and a co-producer, Albert Lewis). After some argument with the front office, whose members questioned the wisdom of employing a director with no film experience, Freed was able to put Minnelli under contract. As a safety measure, Lewis, who had experience in filmmaking as well as on Broadway, was signed as associate producer. His job was to advise Minnelli on technical matters; the film's uncredited associate producer was another Arlen friend and a respected member of the Freed unit, Roger Edens.

Filming was set to begin at the end of August 1942 with a cast headed by Ethel Waters, repeating her role as Petunia from the Broadway version; Little Joe would be Jack Benny's "Rochester," Eddie Anderson; Georgia, Lena Horne; Lucifer Jr., Rex Ingram, who had appeared as De Lawd in the despised *Green Pastures.* The concert baritone Kenneth Spencer would play the Reverend Green and, in Joe's dream, the Lord's General. Bubbles appeared as the gambler and killer Domino Johnson.

The wisdom of the choice of Minnelli was demonstrated early during the production. Ethel Waters, who had turned to religion, "objected violently," as she phrased it, "to the way religion was being treated in the screenplay." She also detested Lena Horne and clearly resented sharing the film with her. As Horne learned from others, Waters was "not notably gentle toward women and she was particularly tough on other singers." What Horne neglected to say was that Waters was extremely tough on younger, more beautiful singers. A diplomatic admirer of both Waters and Horne, Minnelli kept the two stars apart, and the filming moved smoothly enough. All filming was concluded by October 28, 1942.

Arlen and Harburg were not confronted with the film's racial problems, nor were they aware of the Waters-Horne friction. They had a solid, if at times excessively folkish, screenplay. They had three well-defined characters and, not least, the Hall Johnson Choir. One of the first of the eight songs they wrote for the film was the spiritual "Li'l Black Sheep," sung in a backwater church somewhere in Georgia. It is a rhythmically lively but sincerely devotional song of the south. As do all the songs Arlen and Harburg conceived for the film, it employs dialect. For Harburg this was a first; he had never written for rural black characters before. For Arlen, it was a return to a less-sophisticated Cotton Club, especially in the reunion with Waters, Horne, and Ellington.

Beginning late in May, Arlen and Harburg turned in their final song, "Jezebel Jones," by mid-August. Written for Lena Horne, it was not used, possibly because Ethel Waters, the film's major star, objected. Another Horne solo, "Ain' It de Truth?," was shot during a bubble bath sequence, only to be eliminated not because of Waters but because of the Breen Office, whose censors found it too provocative. When the film was released, Lena Horne was left with one solo number, the Duke-Latouche "Honey in the Honeycomb," which was reprised later by Ethel Waters.

Horne and Anderson shared one of the film's wittiest songs, "Life's Full of Consequence," in which she extols a life of pleasure and he, while agreeing, tries to retreat from her charms and remain faithful to Petunia. Arlen's rhythm is slow and steady, deliberate as each character presents the case of pro and con:

JOE: *Life's full of consequence,*
           Dat ole debbil consequence,
           He takes all the frivol out of fun,
           When you got the candle lit at both ends,
           The scandal it creates always keeps you on the run.
GEORGIA: *Life's full of consequence,*
           But who's scared o' consequence?
           Let's sip the honey while it's sweet.

We could be messin' 'round
But you is digressin' round
While I'm tossin' nature at your feet.

The outstanding song of the film was Ethel Waters's moving "Happiness Is a Thing Called Joe," more in her character and the tone of the film than the Duke-Latouche-Fetter "Taking a Chance on Love." The genesis of this song is curious, depending on the teller. During one of his evenings at New York's Ninety-second Street Y, Harburg told the audience, "Harold had a tune. He had it for a long time and he was not proud of it. . . . Here he had a tune that he never wanted written out. He thought it was too ordinary, and I'd always loved that tune. I'd always begged him to write it, and when we got to *Cabin in the Sky* I said, 'Will you dig that tune out of the trunk?' And he did. And when I said, 'Happiness is a thing called Joe,' for the tune, he began liking [it] and he let me use it." Harburg intimated also that Arlen had considered throwing the melody into the wastebasket.

That is a likely, if romantic, tale.

Arlen's version, revealed to a friend long after, was different: Harburg arrived one day for work, excited over a poem he had clipped from a popular women's magazine (he forgot which). A contributor had written a verse about happiness being a thing called . . . Arlen forgot that name, too. A slight change in name would result in "Happiness Is a Thing Called Joe." Arlen liked it, but he had qualms. They could not lift an idea from a large-circulation publication and not expect some sort of repercussion and legal retaliation. Harburg was persuasive, assuring the uneasy Arlen that their song would not be an arrant plagiarism, but a variation on the theme. Besides, Harburg further assured Arlen, if the original author raised an issue, they would share the royalties (which would have been considerable).

There was no clamor after the film's release and the subsequent popularity of "Happiness Is a Thing Called Joe." While he may have borrowed the idea from *Woman's Home Companion* or *Ladies' Home Journal,* the poetry of the lyric is pure Harburg. In the verse are the lines "Caught a bluebird by the toe, / A rainbow by the tail." He evokes images of lilacs and angels in the chorus and, in the resolution, the reality of southern black poverty: "Sometime the cabin's gloomy and the table bare / Then he'll kiss me an' it's Christmas everywhere."

Despite the Harburg flair for a good story, it is more likely that the melody was crafted to Harburg's final lyric—this was not a trunk tune. A distinctive Arlen touch in the verse is the unexpected triplet grace notes on the words "shine" and "mine."

The Arlen trademark in the chorus is piquantly evident at the song's close ("Does he love me good, / That's all I need to know"), preceding a twelve-bar tag, mostly hummed. Although the song is in the key of C, the final note, on the word "know," is a D, the second degree of the scale, and is preceded by a blue note (E-flat), imbuing the song's final moments with a tone of irresolution, uncertainty, and melancholy.

Despite the infelicitous fate of the bulk of their score, *Cabin in the Sky* was superior to *Rio Rita* and *Kismet*. It was a major success and established Vincente Minnelli as one of the finest directors of musical films. Once their work on the film was finished, Arlen and Harburg moved on to other collaborators. They placed "Ain' It de Truth" in their trunk, along with another unused song they had written for Bubbles, entitled "I Got a Song." Both, in time, would resurface in two of their most notable musicals, not in Hollywood but on Broadway.

12

THE CIVIL WAR
BALLET

*E*arly in 1944, when the Academy of Motion Picture Arts and Sciences held its annual Oscar fest, Harold and Anya Arlen attended the celebration with high expectations. Three Arlen songs had been nominated that year: "That Old Black Magic," "My Shining Hour" and "Happiness Is a Thing Called Joe." This was a unique and enviable distinction. Among the other composer nominees were Jule Styne, Jimmy McHugh, Arthur Schwartz, Cole Porter, and Harry Warren, each with a single song to Arlen's three.

Warren, with the lyricist Mack Gordon, took home the Oscar that year for their sentimental, geared to the war, and hugely successful "You'll Never Know." The Arlens were disappointed but happy for their good, often acerbic friend, who stoically accepted the weighty effigy representing the respect of his peers. This, his second Oscar, would be beneficial when the next contract was negotiated.

Warren's multiple Oscar wins, Arlen recalled, gave birth to a characteristic Warren one-liner. A couple of years later, on deciding to skip the awards ceremony, the Arlens and Warrens drove down to Palm Springs to visit Carolyn and Buddy Morris. Morris was then Arlen's publisher and would later be his partner in the Harwin Music Company. Like so many in music publishing, he had moved westward with the business.

As they drove south that night, the quartet listened to the presentations on the car radio. There was no Arlen nomination that year, but Warren's "On the Atchison, Topeka, and the Santa Fe," written with Johnny Mercer, was one of the songs of the year. Arlen was impressed with Warren's demeanor; he seemed indifferent, not even excited when his song was awarded the Oscar. The Arlens were more demonstrative as Warren drove on tranquilly. When they arrived at the Morrises', still low-key, he led the group to the door, then turned to Arlen and quipped, "Walk three Oscars behind."

The Oscar Arlen did not receive in February 1944 had only a fleeting effect on him. When the Oscars were distributed, he was immersed in what he regarded as more substantial than any motion picture he had worked on during his war years—a Broadway musical about war.

He had finished *Here Come the Waves* when his agent, Nat Goldstone, sent him a script of a play written by a little-known writing team, Lilith and Dan James. They were having no luck with placing their play, set in the spring of 1861. The plot was based on the crusade for women's rights, the abolition of slavery, and other causes advocated by the contentious Amelia Jenks Bloomer, better known to history as Dolly Bloomer. On reading the play, Goldstone sensed that it could make a fine period musical, with emphasis on Dolly Bloomer's campaign to free women from the cumbersome hoopskirt.

Her weapon was readily at hand. Another fashion dissenter, Mrs. Elizabeth Smith, had designed a knee-length skirt to be worn with pantaloons, gathered at the ankle. This comfortable outfit scrapped the impractical hoopskirt but scandalized and outraged a large proportion of the populace. Not Dolly Bloomer, however. She set up shop in Seneca Falls, New York, where she published a paper called *The Lily,* disseminating her views on temperance, women's suffrage, and slavery. From Seneca Falls she regularly embarked on fiery lecture tours, during which she wore Mrs. Smith's despised garment. In time this fashion statement became known as the "bloomer," and the women who flaunted it, "bloomer girls." For this daring innovation, Smith was given the credit and Bloomer the immortality.

Since at the time of the play's setting Dolly was married and of a certain age, the Jameses created a rebellious niece, Evelina, who shares her aunt's political and social beliefs. By chance, Horace, the father of the niece and the brother-in-law of Dolly, is a wealthy manufacturer of hoopskirts.

Evelina is his youngest and only unmarried daughter, and Horace plans to arrange a marriage for her with a young southern business associate, Jeff Calhoun. An aristocratic slave owner, Jeff is as impecunious as he is charming. In the beginning, Evelina is suspicious and distant, but by the play's curtain she has won over Jeff to the cause of emancipation, and he has won her, with a little help from Dolly and President Lincoln.

The play's action unfolds on the eve of the Civil War, and its themes, touching on the plight of women and blacks in the United States, were enlightened even in 1944. On finishing his reading of the play, Arlen could visualize it as a musical and, considering its political themes, saw it as a natural for Yip Harburg.

But Harburg resisted for six months, according to Arlen's recollection. Initially, the lyricist was occupied with the production and lyrics of the movie *Meet the People* and, soon after, a collaboration with Jerome Kern on Deanna Durbin's *Can't Help Singing*. Arlen refused to give up and enlisted Eddie Harburg (Edelaine, the former Mrs. Jay Gorney who had married Yip about 1942) as his confederate. Bright, witty, and politically enlightened, she began working on her husband. With its period Americana plot, Harburg sensed echoes of *Oklahoma!* and, as a "costumer," too much like operetta, which he refused to do. He also did not like the book. The conception was fine, but its working out did not please him.

Harold and Eddie prevailed, and Yip agreed to do the show. But as he often did, he had the final word. He brought in the screenwriters who had written *Meet the People* for him, the veteran Sig Herzig and newcomer Fred Saidy. Harburg joined them in converting the Jameses' play into a musical they called *Bloomer Girl*. Herzig had Broadway experience writing for revues and worked regularly in Hollywood. Saidy, when he and Harburg met at a Hollywood party, was known only as a witty versifier and newspaper writer; although he had some film experience, he had never worked on Broadway. The nearest he came to that street was as drama critic for the New York University *Daily News* during his student days. For a brief time he edited a periodical, *Broadway,* before leaving for the West Coast and his meeting with Harburg. They realized that they were compatible in many ways, including politically. Both belonged to what was known as Hollywood's radical circle at the time—a group that exercised its First Amendment rights and frequently spoke out in favor of the Soviet Union. The subject matter of *Bloomer Girl* neatly fit their political perspectives.

Once Goldstone knew the project was under way and Arlen and Harburg began work on the songs, his next move was to consider the realities of production, beginning with the crucial financing. He approached the producer-director John C. Wilson, then in New York, where he had recently directed a revival of the Rodgers and Hart 1927 musical *A Connecticut Yankee*. Wilson had been in the theater since the mid-1930s, when he was associated with Noel Coward as a financial advisor as well as the producer of *Tonight at 8:30.* From a banking family, Wilson was an astute businessman and knew where the money was.

In mid-April 1944 Wilson traveled to California to meet with Goldstone, who would be his "associate" on the production, and with the team working on the show. By this time Arlen and Harburg had nine complete songs, and a tenth almost complete. In a matter of a month or so they had written the bulk of the score for *Bloomer Girl*.

Wilson approved of the play's treatment, liked the songs, and made his agreement with Goldstone. Before Wilson returned to Manhattan, Arlen and Harburg drove to the Radio Recorders studios, on Santa Monica Boulevard in Hollywood, to provide their producer-fundraiser with materials for his part of the effort.

At the piano, Arlen sang, with a little vocal aid from Harburg, the ten songs they had for the show. The recordings were cut onto glass-based discs, since the conventional, less fragile, acetates were no longer available: the source of the materials, including shellac, which was also used for commercial records, had been cut off by the war in the Pacific.

On the set's first side, Arlen can be heard saying, "Jack, this [the song "Right As the Rain"] is incomplete, but we thought you'd like to know where we're heading." Midway through the second chorus he runs out of lyric and hums through the rest of the melody. Later, when he completed the lyric, Harburg decided to eliminate the line "The breeze that dares to kiss your cheek" as a bit precious. Also somewhere between Hollywood and New York "The Handsome Young Man with the Whiskers" was transformed into a rakish young man.

When Wilson took the five discs to New York, Arlen and Harburg had but a half dozen songs to go to complete their score, and the writers were spared the ordeal of backers' auditions. Wilson, gingerly, placed the records on a turntable and applied the needle. Arlen was an extraordinary song salesman, and Wilson had little trouble raising the money, about half of which was contributed by MGM with the promise of the picture rights should the show be a hit. By July the production was ready to go and rehearsals were scheduled for the end of the month.

Before leaving, the Arlens had a musical evening at which Arlen and Harburg treated their guests to a preview of their *Bloomer Girl* songs. Among the guests, Arlen recalled, was Abe Burrows, a radio scriptwriter (for the comedy show *Duffy's Tavern*) who also wrote witty song parodies and, years later, would be the librettist of *Guys and Dolls*. Walter Huston had come to the celebration and sang his wistful signature, "September Song."

The next day, the Arlens and Harburgs left for New York. On the way, Anya and Harold made a stopover in Syracuse for a few days. He was anxious to see his mother, who had been ill, and was reassured when he learned she was clearly recovering. He was interviewed by a reporter from the *Syracuse Herald-American* at his parents' home on University Avenue. According to the newsman, "Mr. Arlen disclaims any clairvoyance, either natural or acquired, concerning the public taste in popular music."

"I have to please myself," Arlen told the reporter, "and then hope the songs will please other people." He spoke of *Here Come the Waves,* which had gone into production at Paramount, but kept returning to the subject of *Bloomer Girl.* "If it gets across," he said, "that will really be something. I'm even willing to make one little prophecy—even if the show turns out to be a dud— the song 'The Eagle and Me' will be a hit." In this Arlen proved his lack of clairvoyance.

Leaving Syracuse, Harold and Anya reunited with Yip in New York, where

Wilson had succeeded in finding a suite for them in the Dorset Hotel. Arlen recalled that he and Harburg wrote one of their last songs, "Sunday in Cicero Falls," on a very humid July Sunday afternoon in the hotel.

New York had changed since their last stay, during the production of *Hooray for What!* at the close of 1937. Broadway's glitter was back after the furious Battle of the Atlantic ended the threat of German submarines' preying on Allied ships, which the city's lights had made easy targets. The "dimouts," as well as the blackouts (a precaution against air raids, which never came) were over. That there was a war on was evident by the men and women in uniform in the streets and theaters.

New York resonated with their laughter and high spirits. By July 1944 the war news was promising. In June, Arlen and Harburg had stopped work to hear radio reports of Eisenhower's D-Day invasion, when, on the sixth, Allied forces landed on the beaches of Normandy. By the twentieth, the Allies were solidly established in France, initiating its liberation and driving the Nazi armies back to Germany. Late in August, during the *Bloomer Girl* rehearsals, the company was cheered by the news of the Allied entry into Paris. In the Pacific, General MacArthur, with the aid of Admiral Nimitz's naval forces, began driving the Japanese out of New Guinea and little islands few Americans had ever heard of, Saipan and Tinian.

The mood of the *Bloomer Girl* cast was cheerful and hopeful as rehearsals started. Internecine warfare inevitably followed.

Arlen and Harburg had completed their score, which included elaborate solo and ensemble openings for the two acts, and a miniature operetta: an abolitionist tract based on *Uncle Tom's Cabin* in act 2, scene 3. Scene 4, a ballet, would generate the musical's one major feud, which would pit the peace-loving Harold Arlen against a combative Yip Harburg.

At the center of the battle was Agnes de Mille, who could be as belligerently defensive as Harburg. But that battle would occur when the pieces of the show began to fuse.

Inevitable, too, was *Bloomer Girl*'s association in many Broadway minds with *Oklahoma!,* which had opened in March 1943. Both shared the period Americana classification, and as producer, Wilson chose most of his creative staff from the *Oklahoma!* roster: de Mille, Lemuel Ayers (sets and lighting), Miles White (costumes), and Robert Russell Bennett (orchestrations). Like *Oklahoma!,* *Bloomer Girl* did not feature big-name stars, but Wilson's Evelina was to be Celeste Holm, who had scored a major success in the Rodgers and Hammerstein musical as Ado Annie. Also from *Oklahoma!* came the dancer-comic Joan McCracken. Though untrue, Broadway hearsay stereotyped *Bloomer Girl* an exploitation of *Oklahoma!*

Oklahoma!, it is true, initiated the Broadway plot ballet. De Mille followed that triumph with her choreography for the Kurt Weill musical *One Touch of*

Venus before moving on to *Bloomer Girl*. Others followed her, including Jerome Robbins with Leonard Bernstein's *On the Town* and Helen Tamaris with Sigmund Romberg's *Up in Central Park*. If *Bloomer Girl*'s choreography was indebted to that of *Oklahoma!*, so was the dancing in many another Broadway musical of those years.

There was an additional parallelism: *Bloomer Girl*, like *Oklahoma!*, was an "integrated" musical. This much-overworked, not always semantically precise term signified, to a greater or lesser degree, that the songs and (especially in the wake of *Oklahoma!*) the dances delineated character and advanced the plot. But before 1943 there had been such integrated musicals as *On Your Toes* (1936), *I'd Rather Be Right* (1937), *Knickerbocker Holiday* (1938), *Louisiana Purchase* (1940), and *Lady in the Dark* (1941). Salient features of the integrated musical may even be found in *Show Boat* (1927). What made *Oklahoma!* so significant, probably, was the show's youthful and hardly known cast, its unabashed Americana, the lovely and sprightly songs, and, of course, de Mille's charming ballets.

One noted theater historian stated that *Bloomer Girl* "had little of *Oklahoma!*'s seriousness" and that its book was "superficial and somewhat silly, if entertaining." Yet, as another historian noted, "The simple tale [of *Oklahoma!*] is mostly concerned with whether the decent Curly . . . or the menacing Jud Fry . . . will take Laurey Williams . . . to the box social," while *Bloomer Girl* addresses civil rights, abolition, and the impact of war.

In short, there is little of *Oklahoma!* in *Bloomer Girl* except the felicitous availability of two bright young stars, set and costume designers, and choreographer.

De Mille's presence undoubtedly inspired the colorful, incisively satirical "Sunday in Cicero Falls," which opens the second act. Harburg does to the pious gentlefolk of Cicero Falls what Sherwood Anderson did to the people of *Winesburg, Ohio* and Sinclair Lewis to the hypocritical citizens of Gopher Prairie in *Main Street*.

The long scene lasts a full fifteen minutes as the townspeople stroll, men in stovepipe hats and women in hoopskirts, on the village green. In their Sunday best, the choruses extol their dress, as solo voices stand out from the groups to make satirical comments. The caroling of pieties is interspersed with Harburg's critical sarcasms. Arlen's music is melodically true to the period, but his rhythmic, almost monotonous underscoring suggests a dull day, smugness, and spiritual sham:

CHORUS: *In this lovely merry land*
            Main Street looks like a fairyland
            When the Angelus calls
            Ginghams are bright

SOLO VOICE: *Collars are white*
Sunday in Cicero Falls
Hearts never blunder where
Girls wear such underwear
Sunday in Cicero Falls

To carry Harburg's message Arlen composed, over his pedestrian walking accompaniment, a tune for the women's chorus and a contrasting tune for the men, fusing them contrapuntally for the finish. The provincial quiet is shattered by the parading suffragists, wearing bloomers and carrying signs announcing a production of *Uncle Tom's Cabin* on Monday. This disturbance interrupts the strolling, but once Evelina and her aunt Dolly are hauled off to jail, dull serenity returns:

> *The sinners join up with the virtuous fringe*
> *They pass the saloon with that righteousness cringe*
> *And bartender Murphy remarks with a twinge*
> *"Virtue is its own revinge [sic]."*

And

> *Even the rabbits inhibit their habits*
> *On Sunday in Cicero Falls*
> *Sunday in Cicero Falls.*

The extended expository song that opens act 1 of *Bloomer Girl,* "When the Boys Come Home," takes on a subtle and, for 1944, timely poignancy when it is reprised at the close of act 2. In the opening, the musical's feminist theme is introduced on an almost frivolous note with an undercurrent of impending defiance of women's place in "the sorry scheme of things" as they "Stitch, stitch, pray and sleep / Men must work and women must weep / 'Twas ever thus since time began / Woman, oh woman, must wait for man." The singers are Evelina's married, contented (to a point) sisters, under their husbands' thumbs. The "boys" who are expected home are their husbands, traveling salesmen on the road selling the Applegate hoopskirt. With the song's reprise, closing the show, "the boys" are now, all hope, returning from war.

The "boys" offer their waggish exposition of what would come to be called male chauvinism in "The Farmer's Daughter," which is countered by the feminists' "It Was Good Enough for Grandma":

> *When granny was a lassie*
> *That tyrant known as man*

HAROLD ARLEN

Thought that women's place
Was just the space
Around a frying pan.

The theme of emancipation, or civil rights, is eloquently expressed in two numbers, "The Eagle and Me" (act 1, scene 3) and the brief but powerful "Man for Sale," which ends the *Uncle Tom's Cabin* performance at the close of act 2, scene 3. While *Bloomer Girl*'s period was patently the 1860s, the message of the songs was pertinent in the United States in 1944. Around the time Arlen and Harburg began serious consideration of writing their musical, a savage race riot erupted in Detroit in June 1943. And Detroit was only the first; there were others in Mobile, Alabama, and one of the worst in August 1943 in New York's Harlem, leaving six dead and over five hundred injured. Blacks in the armed services, purportedly fighting for democracy and freedom, were segregated. Harburg's lyric was unquestionably inspired by such injustices and misunderstandings. The final stanza of "The Eagle and Me" summarizes the emotions of a runaway slave:

Free as the sun is free
That's how it's gotta be
Whatever is right for bumble bee
And river and eagle is right for me
We gotta be free
The eagle and me.

"Man for Sale" is a slave auctioneer's chant, the most operatic song in the show. The auctioneer exclaims over the slave's "strong cotton pickin', rock bustin'," and "log-rollin' steamboat-loadin' hands" and that

He good as forty mules
Look at them shoulders
Good shoulders
They can hold up the sky
He's yours for the price of a rabbit's foot
And he don't eat much and he don't dream much.

The song ends abruptly because the man portraying the slave in *Uncle Tom's Cabin* is arrested as a runaway in Cicero Falls on his way to Canada by means of Dolly Bloomer's underground railway. The scene that follows, a de Mille ballet that precedes the reprises of "The Eagle and Me" and "When the Boys Come Home," would be the cause of the show's most serious ego clash.

If in staging "Sunday in Cicero Falls" de Mille had encroached upon Harburg's territory, he invaded hers in the last scene of act 2. Harburg had staged all of the musical scenes of the show except "Cicero Falls" (William Schorr directed the book), and de Mille was the one and only official choreographer. When Harburg interfered with her work, a behind-the-scenes conflict ensued. With the Civil War raging onstage, another smouldered off.

De Mille had been inspired to do a "serious" ballet before she agreed to work on *Bloomer Girl*. As she recalled:

The score contained one rhapsodic outburst, a colloquial Hymn to Freedom, "The Eagle and Me," and eight or ten of the loveliest songs I'd ever heard. When Arlen first sang "Eagle" for me, I found I could not speak for some seconds. (It is a remarkable song and he is a movingly fine singer.) I quickly agreed to do the show. . . .

I thought I saw an opportunity to do a ballet which would embody the almost universal feeling of sacrifice of those at home.

But, she asked herself, "would they accept a serious play about women's emotions in war? About why people were willing to go out and die? About why we were willing to let them?"

The consensus was, at first, yes. "They hoped this would be a show with significance, seriousness, and poignancy." In four days, with a fine group of young dancers she admired, she worked as if inspired. "The dancers," she wrote, "fired by my frenzy, began to feel they were engaged in something important." The music, running to twelve minutes and based on several Arlen themes from the score plus a quote from "The Battle Cry of Freedom," was arranged by her rehearsal pianist, Trude Rittman, as Arlen remembered it. The piano score credits the musical director, Leon Leonardi, and Rittman received no program recognition. Beginning with her next show, *Carousel,* de Mille made certain that Rittman received her proper program credit as dance arranger, a special skill in itself. Rittman's handling of the half dozen Arlen themes is no mere arrangement but a genuine composition.

On the fifth day after working on her ballet's plot, de Mille, filled with pride and self-satisfaction ("I was never so smug in my life"), was ready to show off her work and her troupe to her bosses, as she called them: John Wilson, Saidy and Herzig, Harburg and Arlen.

Trude Rittman, at the piano, began the music, and the dancers entered. About twelve minutes later the final *fortissimo* chord was succeeded by total silence. No one spoke.

"Harburg found voice first," de Mille later wrote, "and, stepping over the bodies of three prone, sweating girls, addressed me."

"No, no, no," Harburg snapped. "This is all wrong. Where is the wit? Where is the humor?"

"Humor?" de Mille snapped back. "In war?"

Arlen watched, saying nothing. He had been touched by the ballet and liked Rittman's arrangement of the music—that, too, was moving and affecting. Ego clashes made him uneasy, and he listened with embarrassment as Harburg objected because he had found the work tragic. "Where is the courage?" he demanded. "This isn't real de Mille. This isn't what we bought."

"How the hell do you know what the real de Mille is?" she asked him. "If you wished to buy *Oklahoma!* you're a little late."

The silence broken, the suggestions began pouring onto the stage. Arlen could offer only the idea of closing with a peace celebration with all the troops returning alive. Still believing in her work, as did the company and some of her friends, de Mille compromised, using Arlen's suggestion, and provided a happy ending that pleased "the bosses"—but not the dancers, not herself, not Rittman. When she asked them which version they liked best, the collective reply was, "Are you kidding?"

Arlen agreed, and as the dancers watched them, he and de Mille held a whispered conference, the beginning of a conspiracy.

Her dancers were puzzled. One asked, "Is he all right? Is he on our side? Or is he on theirs?"

De Mille didn't answer, but one night in a moment of despair, as she and Rittman sought and failed to rework the now offensive and falsely sweetened dance—not everyone returns alive from a war—she burst into tears. She thought of her husband, the serviceman Walter Prude, away at war, and she wept even more. Then, unconsciously, she reached out for him. Rittman saw that gesture as one that could be used in the ballet, and then they were determined to salvage it, Harburg or no Harburg.

"Oh, my God!" was his response when he saw the ballet soon after. "Can't we get rid of this somber, dreadful ballet?" Harburg was now appealing to the higher authority of the producer, Wilson. Women would faint, he railed. They would weep, they would walk out on the show. Agnes de Mille disagreed, and so did Harold Arlen.

Wilson had now become nervous and agreed that the morose version must go. He sympathized with de Mille but thought Harburg was right. With Arlen in on the intrigue, the company rehearsed the approved version for the bosses and then worked on a final, fourth version as the time for the Philadelphia tryout approached. Whenever she yielded to a suggestion for a change from the management, de Mille felt that her bone-tired company of dancers despised her. So the ballet was rehearsed in their version while one of the dancers remained on post; at the approach of a boss, they would rehearse the approved version.

Arlen's view was, as he told de Mille, "I hope to God it stops the show opening night and shuts their clamoring mouths. It's close to great. Let's fix what's wrong."

The clandestine rehearsals continued and, early in September, the company left for Philadelphia; the opening was scheduled for Monday, September 11, at the Forrest Theatre, for a two-week tryout. After a rehearsal, at two in the morning, Wilson gave de Mille her terminal jolt. The "Civil War Ballet" had to go. "Yes, darling," he told her, "it's beautiful, but it's going to ruin our show."

She could not do anything "cheap" to replace it, she told him, and he agreed. But something had to fill out ten minutes of show time. She suggested they perform the ballet on Monday night, then cut it for subsequent performances. Wilson agreed and promised that the time would be filled with a choral number for which she would not be held responsible.

That *Bloomer Girl* was destined to be a hit was obvious as early as the first act's third scene, in which Joan McCracken's solo in "It Was Good Enough for Grandma" filled the opening-night house with laughter and applause. In the next scene, her genteel striptease to "T'morra', t'morra'" (she sheds her hoopskirt to model her bloomers) further endeared her to the audience, which was fully prepared for the rest of the show.

"Sunday in Cicero Falls" literally stopped the show at the beginning of the second act. "I Got a Song" (which Arlen and Harburg retrieved from their *Cabin in the Sky* trunk) was sung by Richard Huey. The song's syncopations, sung in counterpoint with two other voices in its closing trio, was a problem for Huey, who was coached by Arlen to get it right. During the dress rehearsal the day before the premiere, a disgusted Huey left the stage before finishing the song. There was some talk about replacing "I Got a Song," but Harburg refused, and it was back to the keyboard for Arlen and Huey.

On Monday night it stopped the show. Unlike others in the score, the song has nothing to do with the plot. It is just a happy song about songs.

The show moved from one highlight to another, through the *Uncle Tom's Cabin* scene, which ends abruptly with the announcement of the outbreak of war. At this point Harold turned to Anya and said, "Here we go, Annie."

What the audience and the appalled bosses saw was de Mille's secret fourth version of the "Civil War Ballet." The curtain rose on a deserted stage, framed on either side by trees; the sky is overcast, the setting grim. Center stage, a wracked tree, one limb cracked and hanging, stands tilting against the sky. The upper branches, with windblown leaves, are starkly silhouetted against the lowering sky. The auditorium was hushed as Leonardi raised the baton and gave the downbeat. Arlen and de Mille exchanged wan but hopeful smiles.

"White-faced," de Mille recalled of that first public performance,

the dancers performed with a tension that tightened the exchange between stage and audience to the point of agony. Their gestures that night were absolute, their faces like lamps, and in the hush when Lidija Franklin faced [James] Mitchell, looked into her returned soldier's eyes and then covered her own because of what she saw, no one breathed. In the stillness around me several women bowed their heads.

I stood at the back holding Trude's hand. At the end, there was no sound, but as Mitchell and Franklin returned for the hallelujah parade ["The Eagle and Me"], there was cheering.

As the people filed out past me, one woman, recognizing me, stood for a moment with her eyes covered and then quietly handed me her son's Navy wings.

Once the dancing had begun, Harburg realized what was happening and fumed. Wilson stiffened and sat up in his seat. Arlen took Anya's hand and watched, hoping.

The first-nighters, transfixed, watched what *Variety* called a "grimly serious" ballet unfold: a carillon, a square dance, and two *pas de basques* (the choreographer's variation on the traditional French-Spanish kick step, a de Mille trademark). The ballet ended with the women onstage alone, with those whose men had not returned in mourning. The underscoring is measured, progressively slower (*allargando*), repeating the same doleful chord through four measures and closing on a triple *forte.*

Harburg remembered the silence that de Mille had sensed, and was certain he heard what sounded like a muffled sob. After the final orchestral chord, the applause and cheers filled the theater. The final two song reprises were practically superflous, dramatically anticlimactic, although closing with the heartening "When the Boys Come Home" brought down the curtain on a buoyant note.

Harburg was stunned by the audience's standing ovation. Wilson, too, was shocked into the realization that he had been wrong, and he told de Mille at the party that followed, "Darling, it gives me great pleasure to state we were quite, quite wrong."

Harburg was more forceful, if less contrite, when he exclaimed, "Goddammit! I've begun to like the dreary thing. To think that a lousy bit of movement can make people weep, and me among them. A lousy bit of movement!"

Harold Arlen simply said, "Hurrah!" and kissed de Mille.

Reading Wednesday's *Variety* was gratifying. The knowledgeable "Waters" had praise for all, but the paragraphs devoted to the songwriters were especially exciting. "Hard to figure who rates the biggest laurel wreath after Wilson," he wrote, "but the score by Harold Arlen and E. Y. Harburg stands high on the list. Word had drifted in about Arlen's score, and there was no exaggeration." He then named five, beginning with the ballad "Evelina," and believed there are "two or three others. *Bloomer Girl*," he went on,

has the best score since *Oklahoma*, with which, for many obvious reasons, this musical will be compared.

When a chorus number, generally figured as just an act-opener, like "Cicero Falls," stops a show, it's a pretty good indication of the caliber of the tunes.

With all due credit to Arlen, however, Harburg should not be overlooked. His lyrics—easily the best he has ever done—are exceptional, comparable to the late Larry Hart's and often Gilbertian.

The word was decidedly out. Before the New York premiere, Harold and Anya stopped at the Shubert's stage door to revel in the sight of a box-office queue stretching along Forty-fourth Street from Shubert Alley westward to Eighth Avenue. Such preopening success prompted a churlish tone from the *New York Post*'s Wilella Waldorf, who began her review blaming *Bloomer Girl* on *Oklahoma!*, predicting that it was "the first of what is sure to be a long series of elaborately cute period pieces. . . . It was a box-office success before it moved in [to the Sam S. Shubert Theatre, on October 5], ecstatic tidings of its greatness having drifted in from the out-of-town tryout. Tickets are already being booked for the Christmas matinee of 1946" (an exaggeration, but close—*Bloomer Girl* would have a run of 654 performances).

Waldorf's scathing review—she obviously could not stand Celeste Holm—was one of only two unfavorable appraisals. Four, according to the historian Steven Suskin, were "raves," and two "favorable."

The other negative review was that of Burton Rascoe of the *New York World-Telegram*; he had a problem with Joan McCracken. He also objected to some of the show's political overtones, finding in the phrase "that man in the White House" a veiled parallel between Lincoln and Franklin D. Roosevelt, who was so referred to by his affluent detractors who could not bear to use his name. The *World-Telegram*, significantly, was a conservative paper and anti-Roosevelt. Rascoe dismissed *Bloomer Girl* as "probably the least entertaining musical in town."

His confreres disagreed:

Bloomer Girl is a show of magical delight. In the loose framework of a musical, it blends songs, dancing, drama and spectacle in an enchanting and prodigal entertainment. . . . The Harold Arlen score, the choreography of Agnes de Mille, the costumes of Miles White and the infinitely modulated performing of the company headed by Celeste Holm and Joan McCracken make for what might well be termed an event. (Howard Barnes, *New York Herald Tribune*)

Preceded by approximately as much fanfare as the elections, *Bloomer Girl* moved into the Shubert last evening. Let the elections be as satisfactory. . . . It probably will be resident on Forty-fourth Street until the hoop skirts, in the usual cycle of women's fashions, come back again. (Lewis Nichols, *New York Times*)

Ward Morehouse, of the *New York Sun*, praised music and lyrics and found the "Civil War Ballet" "exciting and imaginative." Not John Chapman of the *New York News*, however, who lauded "Sunday in Cicero Falls" but confessed, "When Miss de Mille's otherwise delightful dancers chose to fight the whole Civil War in ten minutes I got downright restless."

The critical and box-office votes were in, and the next Wednesday's *Variety* had the final word in a headline: "Bloomer Latest Broadway Smash."

On the Sunday before, three days after the premiere and the cast's day of rest, everyone assembled at the studios of Decca Records to record the bulk of the score (unfortunately excluding the ballet music). The mood was good, spirits were high, and, not least, rehearsal and out-of-town acrimony was forgotten in the wake of the show's reception. Harold and Anya Arlen arrived at the studio to find the orchestra in place and microphones set up, two in front for the vocalists and others to pick up the chorus and orchestra; the floor was a gnarled network of cables and wire. Concerned nonparticipants, Wilson, Harburg, and Saidy, were positioned in chairs out of harm's way.

Arlen added his voice to those of the cast; he sang a couple of lines from "Sunday in Cicero Falls." He was eliminated from the album, however, when it was released on 78-rpm records. Including the complete song would have required an additional odd side. When reissued on compact disc, the missing portion of the song, with Arlen's brief stint, would be restored.

His most important contribution to the cast album was his singing of "Man for Sale," in place of Alan Gilbert, whose song it was in the show. Arlen was in good and vibrant voice that Sunday, and the recording is a strong and sweeping rendition of one of his most striking creations. In their study of Harburg's lyrics, Harold Meyerson and Ernie Harburg make a fine point when they note that "Man for Sale" was, "by the standards of the 1944 musical stage, virtually avant-garde" and that it is "not a conventional song, but a melodic, bluesy chant, set against harsh, shifting harmonies, now black, now Jewish. . . . It is the kind of a number that began to appear in the musical theater in the sixties and thereafter: more operatic, less dependent on conventional melody and rhyme—although it is underpinned by the composer's and lyricist's craft in greater measure than most of its latter-day counterparts."

Another notable divergence from the convention of the time was that there are only two ballads in the *Bloomer Girl* score, and only one is the traditional Broadway love song. The first is the slightly comic but seductive "Evelina," introduced by Evelina's southern suitor, Jeff. Arlen fashioned it, deliberately, as a quasi-folkish period song. It is also typically Arlen, with no verse, piquant grace notes in the accompaniment for southern flavoring, and witty, sophisticated variations on barbershop harmonies. Evelina's reply is caustic when they join in the duet. Commenting on his view that theirs would be a perfect hitch, " 'Cause you're so handsome, / I'm so rich" and to his declaration he'd "be content with only you" she replies:

> And just a chambermaid or two
> Tell me, tell me how long
> You're gonna keep delayin' the day
> Don't ya reckon it's wrong
> Triflin' with finance this way?

Her change of heart is evident in their more traditional duet, "Right As the Rain," the other ballad. Though it has the conventional thirty-two-bar length, it divides, not into the usual A-A-B-A sections, but into even halves, each spinning variations on the initial (or "front") phrase that gives the song its title. The second half introduces a rising sequence that reaches an emotional climax (measure 25) with the return of the initial phrase an octave higher. The chorus is followed by an eight-bar tag in which Evelina and Jeff blend their voices in a lovely closing statement that "This love, this love must go on."

With the Decca sessions finished, the Arlens were ready to head home. They packed their luggage and prepared to leave, but before departing they visited Sgt. Jerry Arlen with the *Winged Victory* company in Atlantic City, then made another detour in the journey west to visit with Harold's family in Syracuse. It was a happy time, for Celia Arluck was well and Samuel was delighted with his son's hit Broadway show. The Arlucks and the Arlens were joined by Harold's cousin Earl Crane and his wife for a celebration. Samuel and Celia were cordial, if slightly reserved, with Anya. She was more comfortable with the Cranes. Still it was a pleasant, uncomplicated, brief visit.

The highlight, just before they entrained for Los Angeles, was a Sunday evening broadcast of Andre Kostelanetz's "Coca-Cola Hour." The broadcast was to feature songs from *Bloomer Girl*, and Arlen had been asked to say a few words. A radio line was brought into the house on University Avenue—further cause for excitement on the block and in the Arluck household. The "Coca-Cola Hour" was broadcast nationally—from coast to coast!

Arlen was to speak before the *Bloomer Girl* medley was aired. After a few bars of "When the Boys Come Home," he told the listeners that the song expressed his and Mr. Harburg's hopes (he was formal for the occasion), as well as those of many whose sons, husbands, and daughters were away engaged in a war. "Music," he concluded, "doesn't argue, discuss, or quarrel" (the "Civil War Ballet" skirmish notwithstanding); "it just breathes the air of freedom."

Kostelanetz then led his lush orchestra in the *Bloomer Girl* medley, employing a choral group out of which came the pre–Metropolitan Opera Eileen Farrell in a fine rendition of "Right As the Rain." This was a good ending to the nearly four-month *Bloomer Girl* experience, most of it excitingly rewarding, even pleasant except for the ballet commotion. Nearly two decades later, Agnes de Mille remembered Harold Arlen with affectionate warmth and discernment.

"He has much better taste," she told an interviewer in 1960, "than anyone else around him. But he must stand up for his rights."

Arlen was, unfortunately, more capable of fighting for the rights of others. He avoided personal confrontation; he preferred skirting the often ego-generated bickering that seemed to afflict every show. In Hollywood he worked at home, not at the studio, knowing his suggestions would be ignored. Why fight the inevitable and the unwinnable?

His relationship with the kinetic Harburg was curious. They did not agree on political matters, and Arlen at times admonished Harburg over the "propaganda" in some of his lyrics. Yet he never refused to set them to music. Though Harburg during most of their collaboration was a "progressive" (in the 1940s meaning on the left wing of politics), and a very vocal one, he was not a Communist party member. Nor did Arlen belong to any party, though he frequently voted Republican.

As for his marriage, in this, too, Arlen shunned confrontation. Anya often had temper tantrums, especially in the Hollywood compound she felt trapped in. Harold was gregarious, she was not. To avoid her outbursts, he would leave the house before Anya had awakened for some rounds of golf and laughs with the boys in the clubhouse.

But their best moments were when they were together, with Stormy and Pan, or with those friends Anya felt at ease with—Irving Berlin, Harry Warren, Buddy Morris, and their wives. This was not a large circle of friends, and Arlen was required by his work to associate with many people, even some he did not like. De Mille thought some of his associates took Harold Arlen for granted.

But in November 1944, back in Hollywood and with a hit Broadway show, he found there was nothing to do but golf and spend more time with Anya and the dogs. *Here Come the Waves* was released in December. Late in January 1945 "Ac-cent-tchu-ate the Positive" began a thirteen-week stay on "Your Hit Parade," including four as the Number One song in the nation. It was joined briefly by "Evelina" in February. This was good for Arlen's ego, but did not generate commissions for new scores.

Hollywood was nervous. The war was bloodily grinding to an end. With peace approaching, there would soon be no market for the patriotic all-star variety musical without a plot, or for the flag-waver to perk up morale on the home front (by 1944–45 these films were a source of merriment to GIs viewing them on military bases). In planning for the postwar future, the front office floundered in search for new, or different, themes for the musical film. "Different" rarely worked, and "new" generally meant looking backward to those tried-and-true properties that had worked in the past, biographical musicals that were long on music and short on biography (Gershwin, Kern, Porter, Rodgers and Hart, et al.—even Al Jolson, in one of the most profitable film musicals of all time). There was the borrowed-from-Broadway staple in Hollywood's future—*Oklahoma!*, *Carousel*—and originals deploying wholesome Americana, such as *Meet Me in St. Louis, State Fair, The Harvey Girls*, and *Centennial Summer*.

In this transition period after his return from New York, the only work Harold Arlen accomplished was the trifling *Out of This World*, one of the last of the war films, with Johnny Mercer. Arlen then devoted his time to setting down "possibles" on his recording machine, playing golf and gin rummy, and reading. As he awaited reactions to his possibles from Gershwin, Mercer, and Harburg, he was restive.

Early in the spring of 1945 he got a call from Arthur Freed, not for a film but another Broadway musical. Was he interested? Maybe with Johnny Mercer? Harold Arlen was very interested.

Samuel and Celia Arluck with their son Hyman, Buffalo, ca. 1912. Hyman was then about seven; in two years he would begin to study music. Arlen Archive photo.

Harold Arluck in New York, at the beginning of his career as a songwriter, 1929. Arlen Archive photo.

On the Croydon roof with Shmutts, the music-loving mongrel that Jerry Arlen brought home. Arlen Archive photo.

Flyer announcing the 21st Edition of the Cotton Club Parade, 1932. Arlen Archive.

Front cover of the Cotton Club's menu. Inside, a filet mignon is listed at $2.25 and an illegal bottle of beer is a dollar. There is no hard liquor on the menu, but a "Canadian Dry split" sold for a dollar. The "stuff" was readily available. Arlen Archive.

Lyricist Ted Koehler, vocalist Ruth Etting, and Harold Arlen on the Columbia Pictures soundstage, 1933. The writers were then working on the songs for their first film, Let's Fall in Love. *Ruth Etting had introduced their first song hit, "Get Happy," three years before. Arlen Archive photo.*

Songwriting, Hollywood-style. With a sheaf of "jots" on the piano, Koehler and Arlen work on their Let's Fall in Love *film score. Arlen Archive photo.*

George Gershwin and Harold Arlen reading over the script for "Music by Gershwin," a Sunday radio show on which Arlen was a guest in September 1934. Arlen Archive photo.

Anya and Harold Arlen, at home, Beverly Hills, 1937. With them are Stormy (left) and Pan. Arlen Archive photo.

Arlen, with Stormy, and E. Y. "Yip" Harburg around the time they were writing songs for Warner Brothers musicals in the late 1930s. Arlen Archive photo.

Arlen with lyricist and aspiring film actor Johnny Mercer at the Gershwin house on Roxbury Drive, Beverly Hills, late 1936. Photo by George Gershwin. Courtesy of the Ira and Leonore Gershwin Trusts. Used by permission.

Harold Arlen and Ira Gershwin on the popular Gershwin tennis court, which was set aside for the weekly visit of composer Arnold Schoenberg, also a tennis fan. Gershwin Archive photo.

George Gershwin, Arlen, and baritone Lawrence Tibbett at another favorite spot on Roxbury Drive, the Gershwin pool. Gershwin Archive photo.

*The Wicked Witch (Margaret Hamilton) gives instructions to a Winged Monkey on how to
capture Dorothy (Judy Garland, in the crystal ball), in* The Wizard of Oz, *1939. Arlen
Archive photo.*

An onstage conference during rehearsals of Bloomer Girl. *Seated, Harold Arlen and orchestrator Robert Russell Bennett; standing, stars Celeste Holm and David Brooks. With lyrics by E. Y. Harburg,* Bloomer Girl *was Harold Arlen's longest-running Broadway show. Arlen Archive photo, courtesy of Rita Arlen.*

Bing Crosby in "The Land Around Us" number in The Country Girl, *1954. This was Arlen's last collaboration with Ira Gershwin. Paramount Pictures photo.*

The creative team for House of Flowers. *From the top: Jerry Arlen, conductor; Peter Brook, director; Oliver Messel, designer of sets and costumes; and from bottom right: Truman Capote, librettist and co-lyricist; Harold Arlen; Arnold Saint Subber, producer. Arlen Archive photo. Photo by Zinn Arthur. Courtesy of Rita Arlen.*

A House of Flowers *dance number. Friedman-Abeles photo from the Arlen Archive, courtesy of Rita Arlen.*

Jerry and Harold Arlen conferring during the recording of the House of Flowers *cast album, January 1955. Arlen participated in the recording, singing in the chorus and providing one high note to "I Never Has Seen Snow" (which Diahanne Carroll could not reach because of a cold). Arlen Archive photo.*

Celebration of Marlene Dietrich and her Las Vegas debut. The third celebrant is British songwriter-playwright Noël Coward. Arlen Archive photo.

Arlen recording for Walden Records in March 1955 with Louise Carlyle. Arlen Archive photo.

Harold Arlen juggling at the reception after the premiere of Porgy and Bess, *Moscow, January 10, 1956. Wilva Breen, wife of the producer of the opera, Robert Breen, stands to Arlen's right. Columnist Leonard Lyons observes. Photo by Leonore Gershwin. Courtesy of the Ira and Leonore Gershwin Trusts. Used by permission.*

Wilva and Robert Breen, with Arlen, celebrate the triumph of Gershwin in Moscow. Arlen had arrived only a few hours before, just in time for the opera's curtain, after his visa complications in Helsinki. Photo by Leonore Gershwin. Courtesy of the Ira and Leonore Gershwin Trusts. Used by permission.

Leaving Moscow, January 1956. Ira Gershwin barters with caviar; his amused customer is Horace Sutton, who covered the Porgy and Bess *event for the* Saturday Review of Literature. *Arlen Archive photo, courtesy of Horace Sutton.*

Arlen in the summer of 1959, during rehearsals of Saratoga; *in the background, the stage doors of the* Winter Garden Theater. *Arlen Archive photo.*

Saratoga *leads Howard Keel and Carol Lawrence. This was the composer's last Broadway musical. Arlen Archive photo, courtesy of Rita Arlen.*

A scene from Blues Opera/Free and Easy, *Paris, January 1960. Irene Williams, as Della, makes her entrance. Arlen Archive photo.*

Rehearsal with Lena Horne at Carnegie Hall. The song is "It's a New World" from A Star Is Born. *For a concert, "March on Washington for Jobs and Freedom," which took place in September 1963, Ira Gershwin revised the lyric to fit the themes of the concert. Arlen Archive photo.*

Besides a couple of campaign songs, with lyrics by Martin Charnin, Arlen also contributed his portrait of John Lindsay in his campaign for mayor of New York in 1965. The painting was auctioned to raise funds for Lindsay's effort. Arlen Archive photo, courtesy of Rita Arlen.

Bobby Short and Arlen at a Gershwin film festival, New York Cultural Center, September 1973. Arlen credited Short with bringing him back to songwriting after he had abandoned it following Anya's death. Arlen Archive photo.

Speaking at Gracie Mansion, the mayoral home of Mary and John Lindsay, February 25, 1973. Arlen received the Handel Medal on this occasion. Directly to Arlen's left are Gloria Vanderbilt and Arlen's attorney and friend, A. L. Berman. In the foreground are Wilva Breen and Mayor Lindsay. Arlen Archive photo.

One of the last photographs of Arlen, taken at the Songwriters Hall of Fame dinner at which he was presented by Dinah Shore with the Johnny Mercer Award, March 15, 1982. Arlen Archive photo. Photo by Samuel Teicher. Courtesy of ASCAP.

Rita Arlen, the composer's sister-in-law, who began organizing the Arlen Archive in the last months of his life. She holds the Oscar she found in one of the crates that had been in storage for several years (and had been thought lost). The charcoal drawing of Arlen's hands is by an artist named Torman. Arlen Archive photo, courtesy of Leon Smatt.

13

*H*arold Arlen's curiosity was piqued by Freed's call. Why would the head of MGM's most prestigious musical production unit phone him about a Broadway show? The answer lay in a convoluted sequence of events that began with Edward Gross.

Gross had been a film producer until the late 1930s (Joe E. Brown's *The Gladiator,* 1938) before moving to Broadway. His comedy of the previous season, *Chicken Every Sunday,* was well into a satisfying run. Looking for something else to do, Gross came across a little-known play, *God Sends Sunday,* originally produced in the early 1930s and revived, with little success, as a Federal Theater Project in 1938. The play was based on Arna Bontemps's 1931 novel of the same title, considered the valedictory work of the Harlem Renaissance, the great flowering of African American writing in the 1920s. Bontemps converted the novel into a play with the help of another Harlem Renaissance figure, the poet Countee Cullen.

The play was set in turn-of-the-century St. Louis and told the story of a black jockey, Little Augie, who falls in love with a woman of questionable fidelity, Della Green, who is regarded the property of a saloonkeeper named Biglow Brown. In the aftermath of an argument between Augie and Brown, the saloonkeeper is shot by a discarded mistress. Brown, believing that it was Augie who shot him, places a dying curse on the superstitious jockey. Augie's winning streak ends, and Della leaves him. In time, after the mistress confesses to the shooting, Augie's luck, and Della, return for a happy ending.

Possibly the recent success of a revival of *Porgy and Bess* gave birth to the idea. *God Sends Sunday* required an all-black cast. Why not convert it into a musical? The play abounded in colorful characters and settings (stables, Biglow's bar, a funeral parlor, a ballroom), as well as flashy period costumes. Gross took the idea to Lemuel Ayers, then celebrated along Broadway as the set designer for *Oklahoma!* and *Bloomer Girl*. In Hollywood he had worked for Freed on *Ziegfeld Follies* and *Meet Me in St. Louis*. For a musical version of *God Sends Sunday* Gross hoped to get Harold Arlen to write the music and Johnny Mercer the lyrics. As he explained to Ayers, what was first required was backing. Ayers, remembering that MGM had put money into the production of *Bloomer Girl*, immediately thought of Arthur Freed.

They met soon after in Freed's office, where Gross outlined his plan. Once the money was in the bank, he would produce the musical, Ayers would direct, and Arlen and Mercer would provide the songs. Freed recognized the potential: Lena Horne would be perfect for the part of Della Green. She had been beautifully provocative in *Cabin in the Sky* and proved she could act in *Stormy Weather*—and, further, she was under contract to MGM.

Freed's mind moved quickly. Once the show scored on Broadway—how could it miss?—MGM could acquire it for a Freed production. He then turned crafty. He called in his friend Sam Katz from Metro's music department. He explained the possibilities to Katz, suggesting that he and Katz, not MGM, form their own company, back the musical, and *then* sell it to MGM.

Katz saw the beauty of this proposition. He and Freed formed Alliance Productions (the allies being Freed and Katz). Thus covertly they provided Gross with the funding for the show with an eye on a profitable, if anonymous, future. In the musical's program Gross is credited as producer; the names of Freed and Katz appear nowhere in the publication. Deep inside, on page 23, a special notice appears stating that the musical was "owned by Alliance Productions, Inc."

Once the backing was assured, Bontemps and Cullen reworked their play into the form of a musical they entitled *St. Louis Woman*.

When they received an early copy of the script, neither Arlen nor Mercer was especially happy with it. The authors indicated spots for songs, even suggested titles, but the songwriters felt that, as the script stood, the first act was dramatically overloaded, with its stable, saloon, shooting, and wake. The second act simply petered out, despite the happy ending, with few moments for songs.

With the promise of revision, some pressure from Arlen, and the fact that he was currently unemployed, Mercer agreed to do *St. Louis Woman*. By the summer of 1945 he had completed his work with Harry Warren on *The Harvey Girls* and, like Arlen, preferred work to inactivity. Working from the early script, into which Arlen had added notations, jots, and tentative titles, the collaborators began in their customary offhand, relaxed manner; by the fall they had begun shaping their score.

Mercer recalled one October evening he had casually stopped by the Arlens'. Deciding to do some work, they went into Arlen's study, where he had his small upright Martha Washington piano. He left Mercer, saying he would go into the living room, where he had a Steinway, "to toy around with an idea." Mercer said nothing, simply nodded.

Arlen returned soon after with the idea, a melody with only two pitches, the first repeated rhythmically for two bars, dropping to the second note in the third bar. Mercer listened but said nothing. Arlen played it again, only three bars. The warm harmony and the melody's conversational quality gave him an idea, and he said, "I'm gonna love you like nobody's loved you . . ."

He stopped there and Arlen, chuckling, added, "Come hell or high water."

"Of course," Mercer said, "why didn't I think of that? Come rain or come shine." Before he left the Arlens' house that evening, the song was completed.

Their work flowed smoothly as usual, but Edward Gross had reached a point in the planning when he was quite certain his show was a sure thing. His announcement of the pending musical erupted into a rain of slings and arrows. The first came from Walter White, secretary of the National Association for the Advancement of Colored People, who claimed that the characters in *St. Louis Woman* "detracted from the dignity of our race." While it was unlikely that he had seen the show's libretto, he could have read the novel or seen the 1938 production of the play.

Whether he had done either, however, he was not far off the mark. Despite the authors' race, their descriptions of their characters suggested an almost insensitive stereotyping: "heavily jeweled . . . young brown girls dressed in the finery of the period"; the "Macks" [men], "as in all primitive society, are even more brilliantly attired than the women." Those words would be helpful to Ayers in his costume design, and although the audience would be unaware of what was in the script, such language did offend White and others.

Among them, after White's statement circulated in the press, was Lena Horne. *St. Louis Woman,* whose script she had seen, "sets the Negro back a hundred years [and is] full of gamblers, no-goods, etc., and I'll never play a part like that." She thereupon withdrew from the production. As a consequence, her career at MGM rapidly withered.

Arlen and Mercer avoided the controversy and tended to their songs, avoiding stereotyping, vaudeville minstrelsy, and parody. Mercer's lyrics drew on honest dialect used in Missouri by both races; Arlen composed a lullaby, cakewalks, a powerful spiritual, street cries, even arias, balanced by typical Broadway tunes. By the first of the year they were prepared for New York, the casting, and rehearsals.

Gross had been attending to the casting, and the objections of White and

Horne apparently had little effect on his search. Without Lena Horne, he had no true name star for the leading role of Della. According to the show's playbill, he and his staff scoured drama schools and conservatories seeking "a glamourous actress who could also sing"; Gross discovered a high school student from Richmond, Virginia, named Ruby Hill who had the qualifications, he thought. She was then in New York studying voice with the vocal coach Al Siegal, who had been Ethel Merman's mentor. Gross sent Ruby Hill to Hollywood to audition for Arlen, Mercer, Bontemps, and Cullen; she passed the test, returned to New York, and signed a contract to appear in her first Broadway show as Della Green, the St. Louis woman.

The other principal cast members were more experienced and known primarily for their nightclub, and some film, work. Rex Ingram, cast as the saloonkeeper and villain Biglow Brown, had had a long career, beginning in 1928, when he quit the medical profession for the theater. On the stage and in film he had acquired the stature of one of the finest African American actors. His most notable appearances had been as "De Lawd" in the maligned film *The Green Pastures* and as Lucifer Jr. in *Cabin in the Sky*.

The role of Augie, the jockey, was filled by Harold Nicholas, best known as half of the superlative dancing team the Nicholas Brothers. The other was Fayard, who was cast in *St. Louis Woman* as Barney, the consistently losing jockey. Both had a great deal of experience, beginning in vaudeville, as well as in clubs, stage (in a recent *Ziegfeld Follies*), and several films. They were also stars at the post-Arlen Cotton Club in the late 1930s, after it moved to Broadway.

Pearl Bailey, cast opposite Fayard Nicholas as the sharp-tongued employee in Biglow's saloon, was also a veteran of vaudeville and clubs and once was a singer with the Count Basie band. *St. Louis Woman* was to be her Broadway debut. In the trade she had a reputation for her wit and timing, particularly in comedy songs.

June Hawkins would portray the discarded mistress, Lila, who murders Biglow. She was a trained singer who had appeared as Bess in a revival of *Porgy and Bess* and, more recently, in Oscar Hammerstein's *Carmen Jones,* an Americanization of Bizet's opera. Juanita Hall had made her debut in the folklorish *Sing Out, Sweet Land* in 1944, and had left the chorus of the *Show Boat* revival to try for the part of Leah, Augie's religious sister. Three years later she would make a more memorable Broadway appearance as Bloody Mary in *South Pacific*.

Although Gross had not mustered a ticket-selling cast, he had one consisting of fine voices and, in Harold Nicholas, Rex Ingram, and Pearl Bailey, winning, strong personalities.

Arlen and Mercer were happy with the company, though they continued to have qualms about the sprawling libretto. Then came another jolt: two days before the start of rehearsals, Countee Cullen, aged forty-three, died. That left Bontemps alone to struggle with a clumsy book. The suddenness of Cullen's death cast a shadow of gloom over the company, but as was the custom, the show continued. Arlen was pleased with the handling of the songs and the rich, apposite orchestrations by a team consisting of Ted Royal, Allan Small, Menotti Salta, and Walter Paul; the choral arrangements were by the conductor Leon Leonardi—all under the composer's supervision. The orchestrations for *St. Louis Woman* are among the most distinguished created for a Broadway musical. Unfortunately, the orchestra parts have been missing since the show closed.

Arlen's major criticism, as he sat through a dress rehearsal in preparation for the Boston tryout, was the structure. Most of the music was stuffed into act 1. The second act seemed cluttered with plot as if in a haphazard search for a conclusion. It was small compensation, he felt, that in each act Pearl Bailey's dry, knowing delivery of her song brought a bright touch of humor to a disorganized show.

He was proved right: at the opening in Boston on February 19, 1946, Bailey stole the show with her two songs, "Legalize My Name" and "A Woman's Prerogative." The audience response and the reviews also confirmed his anxieties; as he said to Anya, "We're in trouble." Mercer was noncommittal and his face expressionless. He knew they had more work to do.

Gross, in near panic (the show had suffered a similar reception earlier in New Haven), called Arthur Freed. Freed called Rouben Mamoulian, then in New York, where he had directed the new hit *Carousel* and the still-running *Oklahoma!* (Mamoulian had also directed the original production of Gershwin's *Porgy and Bess* in 1935.) Freed arranged to meet with Mamoulian in Boston to see *St. Louis Woman,* and following some discussion, Freed appointed Mamoulian the designated fixer.

This put Lemuel Ayers out of a job. He remained as the designer of the sets and costumes, but by the time the show arrived in Philadelphia in early March, Mamoulian was the official director. The classically trained choreographer Antony Tudor was replaced by a more Broadway-wise former dancer and vocalist, Charles Walters, who was called in from Hollywood, where he had directed, most notably, the dances for *Meet Me in St. Louis.* Before *St. Louis Woman* departed Philadelphia, one of Mamoulian's major changes was to replace Ruby Hill with the more experienced Muriel Rahn, who had sung one of the alternating Carmens in *Carmen Jones.*

The alteration that most affected Arlen and Mercer, however, was Mamoulian's revision of the libretto. He discarded the original two-act form and divided the show into three acts, ending each with a typical Mamoulian flourish. The lively, colorful, and show-stopping "Cakewalk Your Lady," an exciting, high-stepping cakewalk competition featuring eight couples in dance variations, had been buried in the middle of act 1; he made it the first-act finale. The break at this point left the audience with a more cheerful sense of expectation than had the original ending of act 1, Lila's embittered apostrophe to the corpse of Biglow,

"Sleep Peaceful, Mr. Used-to-be." Likewise the opening of the new second act: instead of a funeral and spiritual, Mamoulian opened it with the duet "Come Rain or Come Shine" and moved the funeral scene to the end of the act, where his handling of the chorus reminded some critics of his religious scenes—the patterning of groups and use of shadows—in *Porgy and Bess.* Mamoulian's modifications thus closed the first two acts with striking, memorable dramatic and musical panache.

Act 3 began with a reprise of "Come Rain or Come Shine," which in the show's early form was heard immediately after the spiritual; the contrast between the full mixed chorus and the duet had weakened the effect of the musical's major ballad. With an intermission between the funeral and the reprise, the audience made the transition from death to love more readily. Mamoulian offered further suggestions to Bontemps, such as revising the close of the new act 3, which was still plot-heavy and short on songs.

In the early version from which Arlen began spotting the songs and dances, the final scene had switched from St. Louis to a restaurant in Saratoga, New York. There Augie and Della are reunited and, after she has sung the haunting aria "I Wonder What Became of Me," they leave the restaurant together. End of show—in a fizzle. Mamoulian moved the action back to St. Louis and staged an imaginative onstage horse race (the horses are not seen), in which Augie wins to the cries of "Come On, Li'l Augie." Upon winning, Augie makes a high leap over the fence through which others in the cast had been watching the race. He and Della unite in the finale to sing, with the entire cast joining them. The new ending endowed *St. Louis Woman* with a requisite happy ending that made more dramatic sense than petering out in Saratoga.

Mamoulian's cutting and pasting in Philadelphia necessitated some switching around of the songs, as well as some unfortunate cuts and the need to engage in writing under pressure. One of the sad cuts was that of "I Wonder What Became of Me." The consensus was that its mood and tempo were similar to Lila's lament in the first act, "I Had Myself a True Love." That, along with the introduction to the spiritual "Talkin' Glory," was out, along with three other numbers that were eliminated in Philadelphia. Arlen and Mercer labored to fill the musical voids: in place of Augie's declaration, "A Man's Gotta Fight," they wrote the amusing "We Shall Meet to Part, No Never," delivered by a boy singer, Herbert Coleman.

They did most of the out-of-town work on the revised third act, enlivening it with the spirited "Ridin' on the Moon," the philosophical "Least That's My Opinion," and the rousing choral number "Come On, Li'l Augie." This done, all concerned, including Mamoulian, felt they were ready for New York.

There, on the morning of Saturday, March 30, 1946, with *St. Louis Woman* set to premiere that evening, another crisis erupted. Led by a confident Pearl Bailey (hadn't she stopped the show twice in every performance in three cities?), the company confronted Gross and Mamoulian with a nonnegotiable ultimatum. Bailey and the rest of the company had been chafing over the dismissal of Ruby Hill in Philadelphia. Bailey had been chosen to present their demand to Gross: No Ruby Hill, no opening.

The preopening rumors about the show were bad enough; a rebellious cast would be too much. Gross conceded, even though he had placed newspaper ads touting Hill's replacement, Muriel Rahn. Anya and Harold were spared this uprising, for they had settled into their hotel and were resting for that night's premiere. Harold was uneasy. Mamoulian felt he still needed more time to put the show into shape. That Gross had chosen to open on a Saturday night indicated his lack of certainty in the show's future: a Saturday night premiere meant that the opening-night reviews would be shunted from the Sunday papers to the little-noticed Monday editions.

Monday was the proverbial morning after for *St. Louis Woman*. It began promisingly with John Chapman in the *New York Daily News:*

The best Negro musical in many seasons, and the best new musical of this season up to this late date. Mr. Arlen is one of the dwindling number of songsmiths who still believe that a man should turn out a tune, even if he has to steal it from himself, and Mr. Mercer is a lyricist who can work up a mess of words which is neither arty or smarty, but just right. In the main *St. Louis Woman* is a pleasure . . . I think, because every number is a number. Each scene, each song, has been presented as though it was designed to be the best of the evening. I suppose much of the credit for this must go to Rouben Mamoulian. . . . Mr. Mamoulian is at his best when handling the movement of groups, and in *St. Louis Woman* he has three chances for spacious effects. The first is the first act finale—a cakewalk contest in a ballroom, in which various Negro couples compete by dancing for the huge prize cake. Here, of course, the dance direction of Charles Walters and the Arlen-Mercer song, "Cakewalk Your Lady," are of no little help to Mr. Mamoulian. (Here, incidentally, I believe Mr. Arlen picked his own pocket. "Cakewalk Your Lady" sounds much like his "The Eagle and Me" from *Bloomer Girl*.)

Mr. Mamoulian's second chance comes with the second-act curtain, a funeral scene, in which some of the old *Porgy and Bess* technique is useful. And the third is the third-act curtain, an exciting and intricate spectacle of a crowd watching a race from outside a fence.

The players . . . are amiable and able. The Nicholas brothers, familiar as hoofers for at least 15 years, are cast as rival jockeys, and the smaller of them, Harold, nicely reveals his ability to carry a plot and sing some songs. . . . Ruby Hill, playing the jockey's girl, is remarkably handsome and can sing a song in a small but torchy voice. Twice during the proceedings a big, funny girl, Pearl Bailey, stops the show with lighter numbers, and June Hawkins sings a couple of laments from an aching heart.

Burton Rascoe (*New York World-Telegram*) was the only other critic to agree with Chapman, writing that he "enjoyed [it] so much that, when the final curtain descended I felt I should have liked to see the whole thing all over again." After these heartening appraisals, further reading became daunting. Lewis Nichols in the *New York Times* dismissed the plot as " a curse" and assailed the score. "No one expects Mr. Arlen to write a 'Stormy Weather' every time he goes to the piano, but in truth his score is not his best. An occasional air is catchy, but there are no great novelties. The blending of composer, lyricist, and singer is reached completely only twice, when Miss Bailey cries down 'Legalize My Name' and 'A Woman's Prerogative.'"

Another critical sentence that tightened the Arlen solar plexus was written by Louis Kronenberger, a professor of English and drama critic for both *Time* magazine and the very independent (it accepted no advertising) tabloid *PM.* In the latter, a favorite of liberal intellectuals, Kronenberger objected to the book's "triteness and long-windedness," reprimanded the "work of two very reputable Negro authors," and questioned "whether the kind of glib characterization [the book] falls back on, the kind of stock humor and melodrama, is in the Negro's best interest."

Then he got to Harold Arlen. "First-rate music," he wrote, "might yet have turned the tide, but Harold Arlen's songs and orchestral tags and tid-bits are second-rate even for him. They are most of them romantic or atmospheric enough, but they lack distinction, they lack melodic urgency, they lack the excitement and cohesive power that folk drama demands. It is an agreeable score, but nothing more than that."

Though not a faithful reader of *PM,* Arlen was unsettled by Kronenberger's opinion of the score, especially when added to the other negative views. Even *Variety* found the show's chances limited.

Despite the unfortunate critical reception, the recording of an original cast album for Mercer's Capitol Records began on Sunday, April 7, 1946. The bulk of the score was preserved, and the omissions, dictated by the inherent limitations of recording in the pre-long-playing era (only two years in the future), were slight. Mercer later made a single 78-rpm recording of the cut "Least That's My Opinion"; even later, in 1954, Arlen recorded "Come Rain or Come Shine," also for Capitol Records.

Minus the cumbersome plot, the songs and exceptional orchestrations were beautifully recorded; even the voices that did not project well in the theater were sensitively picked up by the microphones. When the sessions ended on the ninth, Arlen was pleased with the results and believed that, in time, his and Johnny Mercer's work would be appreciated.

That critical revaluation came soon after the album was released (on 78-rpm shellac discs), and even more when it went out of print and became a costly collector's item. Through the recording, *St. Louis Woman* achieved the recognition, appreciation, and circulation it had not gotten in the theater, as collectors made copies to pass around among devotees of show songs. The variety and richness of the score was evident; individual songs were taken up by radio and, especially, nightclub singers, not only "Come Rain or Come Shine" but the show's art songs, "I Had Myself a True Love" and "I Wonder What Became of Me." Pearl Bailey had acquired two more songs for her spicy repertoire in "Legalize My Name" and "A Woman's Prerogative." She had also won the Donaldson Award for her performance in the show.

St. Louis Woman was eventually released in the long-playing format, first as a ten-inch disc, than as a twelve-inch recording (the latter sometime in the 1960s); they too went out of print and into the expensive collector's bin. Finally, in 1993, the intact album was reissued on compact disc. The recorded sound is remarkably vibrant and unconstricted. By then the score had come to be acclaimed as one of the finest written for the American theater.

The sessions over and the show limping along, the Arlens, tired and discouraged, decided it was time to return to Lindecrest Drive. They made the usual stopover in Syracuse to see his parents and, in a surge of nostalgia, decided also to make a stop at Buffalo. Arlen wanted to see something of his hometown, as much of it as remained after two decades.

The Pine Street Synagogue, where his father and he had sung, was still there. Accompanied by the Cranes, they were about to enter the building when Arlen saw a face he recognized. He was certain the elderly, bearded man seated in the sun on the steps was the shammes (sexton) from the days when he was a boy singer in the choir.

As the Cranes and Anya continued into the shul, Arlen stopped and greeted the shammes. "Shalom."

The bearded man remained seated, studied the composer for a moment, then asked (in Yiddish), "You Cantor Arluck's son?"

Surprised to be recognized after so many years, Arlen nodded.

The sexton had another question. "And the girl," he said, "your wife?"

Arlen agreed again.

Momentarily silent, the shammes reached into a pocket, took out a snuffbox, sniffed, then asked his third question, "Got any children?"

"No," Arlen admitted.

"What good are you?" was the final question.

At the time, as he ascended the steps into the old shul, Arlen was amused. But the traditional, Old World, Talmudic even, judgment by the older man coincided with that of Cantor Arluck and his wife. It was deeply ingrained in his father's heritage. Harold, his eldest son, should perpetuate the family name, which he had had the temerity to change. He was now forty and there were no children. Anya was a barren woman, of another faith. The bearded shammes on the steps merely expressed Samuel Arluck's attitude. This was concealed readily during the occasional visits and would remain so as long as the Arlucks lived in Syracuse and the Arlens in Beverly Hills. That situation would soon change, however. When Samuel Arluck retired, he and Celia would leave Syracuse for California. The inflexible ideology of centuries, and of one autocratic, obstinate man, would have a lamentable effect on "the girl" and the marriage of Anya and Harold Arlen.

WASTELAND:
BEVERLY HILLS

In the time between the apex of *Bloomer Girl* and the nadir of *St. Louis Woman*, World War II ended with a rubble-strewn Germany and a burned-out Japan. History's most pervasive, most devastating war reeled to a stop; by the spring of 1946 the boys were really coming home, among them Sgt. Jerry Arlen.

Out of the air force as well as out of work, he soon found a position with the aid of his father, with some pressure from Celia (for Jerry was her favorite). Samuel wrote to Chaim enjoining him to do something for his younger brother. Harold complied by arranging for Jerry to get the job of conductor with the *Bloomer Girl* touring company after the show closed in New York. Jerry unquestionably was an accomplished musician with plenty of recent experience in the theater orchestra of *Winged Victory*. He had had earlier experience as a band leader in the 1930s. After leaving Paul Whiteman's orchestra, he had formed his own band to appear at Billy Rose's Music Hall. In 1938 he disbanded his group to replace Robert Emmett Dolan as conductor of *Hooray for What!*

Harold, certain his brother could handle the job, called Jack Wilson and arranged for Jerry's immediate transition from military to civilian life. By May 1946 *Bloomer Girl* returned to the Shubert in Boston, with Nanette Fabray as Evelina and Jerry Arlen conducting.

This did not work out well. To Harold's dismay and Wilson's chagrin, the cast eventually complained about problem cues and erratic tempos from performance to performance. Wilson's letter to Harold was typically considerate, but in view of the cast's unhappiness, he felt that Jerry Arlen had to be replaced. Harold unhappily agreed. Jerry's temper flared under criticism and pressure, but he was eased out. He blamed the ouster on his brother's unwillingness to stand up for him (which he did as long as he could); Samuel Arluck did not take kindly to the incident either. Jerry returned to New York for some band work, then a couple of years later had much better luck as conductor of a successful Broadway revue, *Make Mine Manhattan.*

Harold Arlen, after his return to Beverly Hills, chose to rest a while. *St. Louis Woman* had proved to be an exhausting grind—they had been on the road for six weeks even before the Broadway opening. However, after a few months, and several wordless "possibles," he grew restless. Mercer was busy at other things, Harburg was in New York working on a musical that would become *Finian's Rainbow,* and Ira Gershwin, too, went east to complete his final Broadway effort, *Park Avenue,* with Arthur Schwartz. None of the old standbys was available.

Bob Wachsman, who had moved west, as always, had an idea. He had guided Arlen's vaudeville career with some success in the 1930s; now he felt it was the moment for a venture into radio. The program could be beamed from Hollywood, with Harold as the master of ceremonies and performer (as George Gershwin had been in the 1930s). Wachsman added a further bright idea; Sidney Skolsky, the Hollywood-based columnist for the *New York Daily News* and a former Earl Carroll press agent, would appear with a segment of Hollywood inside stories, closing with his column tag, "But don't get me wrong, I love Hollywood."

Wachsman took the idea to the Columbia Broadcasting System with the title "Songs by Arlen, Stories by Skolsky." A script was worked up, probably by Wachsman, Skolsky, and Arlen, although no credits were given. Though not broadcast, a test program before a studio audience was tried and recorded. The show's theme was "I Got a Song," presented by a chorus with orchestra. Harold was then introduced to sing Irving Berlin's "I Got the Sun in the Morning" from Broadway's current hit, *Annie Get Your Gun.* He then presented his own "It's Only a Paper Moon," after which he introduced Sidney Skolsky, with his Hollywood tales of little moment. Skolsky then called Harold back to sing "his latest hit," "Come Rain or Come Shine."

CBS did not buy it. Though only fifteen minutes long, it was short on musical content, and Skolsky's trivialities were tepid and virtually pointless.

Another attempt was made in January 1947, sans Skolsky. Retitled "Songs by Arlen," the new show put more emphasis on song, with a more generous programming of Arlen. The theme of the program was switched to "It's Only a Paper Moon," followed immediately by "Come Rain or Come Shine." His friend Irving Berlin's "Sun in the Morning" remained, and that of another, the late Jerome Kern, was added, "They Didn't Believe Me." Arlen's singing of the song was sensitively expressive. The audition concluded with a medley of Arlen successes, from "Stormy Weather" through "Blues in the Night," ending with Arlen and chorus in "I Got a Song." The reception by the studio audience was encouraging, but not enough for a final good word from Columbia, not even for a local broadcast.

Wachsman persuaded the studio to give them another chance, with yet another revision in format. The new signature was "Hooray for Love" when "Songs by Arlen" was tried again on June 1, 1948. The song was one Arlen had written with a new (for him) lyricist, Leo Robin, for a film, *Casbah,* released only a month before. Arlen then went into "I Got the Sun in the Morning," accompanied by the pianist Walter Gross and his quintet. Arlen then introduced another plug for *Casbah* by singing "For Every Man There's a Woman." Gross and his quintet performed a jazzy (and composer-approved) version of "Over the Rainbow." The program went into a more traditional presentation, sung by Harold, of "my dad's favorite song," Victor Herbert's "I'm Falling in Love with Someone." The finale was a reprise of "Hooray for Love" sung by the composer and backed by the Gross quintet.

When the efforts of CBS and Bob Wachsman found no sponsorship for the show, the idea was abandoned. By 1948 "cool winds were blowing in Hollywood," observed the *Variety* historians Abel Green and Joe Laurie Jr. "Profits slid 45% . . . a wave of economy hit pictures with heavy layoffs of studio personnel and East Coast office staffs. Producers were jittery, wondering whether this was the first impact of TV, the high cost of living, poor stories or an unhappy combination of all three. . . . The situation in Hollywood during 1948 rapidly fouled up."

As had radio in the 1930s, television was beginning to affect the studios and, worse, the box offices. It was more than the novelty of a new gadget, it was the free entertainment. The public attitude was simple: why go through all the motions of driving into town to see Bob Hope at the Regent, when you could stay home, without the need of a babysitter, and watch him at home? By the late 1940s the studios tightened their purse strings, and the making of musicals dwindled.

This new disturbance was compounded by the tremors that began shaking Hollywood in 1947 with the arrival of members of the House Un-American Activities Committee in a witless, headline-seeking investigation of Hollywood's "Reds." Harold Arlen, who rarely expressed a political opinion and who, like his father, generally voted Republican, escaped this attention. But Yip Harburg's "progressive" views led to his blacklisting, and he left for New York. Even the gentle Ira Gershwin was called before the committee, but was dismissed untainted by the red brush when he laughed in the faces of members on being asked if he was now or ever had been a member of the Communist party. Most of the victims of the later-discredited Tenney Committee (the California division of the House Un-American Activities Committee led by J. Parnell Thomas) were writers or actors (among them Gershwin's friends Humphrey Bogart and Lauren Bacall) and a handful of songwriters. Since the West Coast branch of the committee was chaired by a former Communist and failed songwriter, Jack B. Tenney, the joke in Beverly Hills was that he was merely hoping to weaken his competition.

At the time, however, there was little laughter. Under the pressures of economy and politics, film producers were cautious in selecting their subject matter and the people to bring it to the screen. At MGM, for example, Arthur Freed was in a delicate position. One of Hollywood's most zealous Communist hunters was his boss, Louis B. Mayer. In the past, Freed, who thoroughly disagreed with Yip Harburg on all things political, hired him because he respected his work. In 1948 it was no longer possible.

After nearly two years of inactivity, except for the accumulation of recorded "possibles," reading, golfing, and a meager social life, Harold felt he should get back to work. Anya preferred staying at home to going to parties. Even these had dried up in the aftermath of Tenney and company. Only the Gershwins continued with their weekend open house, but Anya was uncomfortable there. She did not like golf, nor was she a reader, except for the fashion magazines. One friend recalled once hearing her express a single literary opinion—a fondness for the poetry of Rod McKuen.

She painted when the creative urge came, but that was infrequent. She was a late riser and spent a good deal of time in bed. She eluded social engagements, often claiming illness. The composer Ann Ronell, who saw her rarely, would call to invite Anya to lunch, or would even attempt to invite herself to the Arlens', but Anya always managed to invent an excuse. Ronell, a kind and most sensitive woman, was worried.

So was Harold, but he attributed Anya's diffidence and occasional emotional outbursts to her isolation in Hollywood and to boredom. No one then considered the possibility of an organic cause for her unhappiness. Arlen himself frequently escaped to Hillcrest to meet with his golfing friends and drink too much.

A break in this distressing routine came late in 1947, when Nat Goldstone, who had brought Harold into *Bloomer Girl,* came to Universal with the idea of producing a musical version of the popular 1938 film *Algiers.* That in turn had been a remake of the grittier French movie *Pépé Le Moko,* which starred Jean Gabin as the romantic criminal who sacrifices himself for the love of a woman. The American remake was notable for the Hollywood debut of Hedy Lamarr, as the fatal love, and for a phrase never uttered by Charles Boyer (as Pépé), "Come with me to the Casbah." *Algiers* had also made money; yet another remake, this time with songs, could very well do the same. Goldstone believed that a new title, *Casbah,* would benefit from years of radio comics imitating the famous line never spoken by Charles Boyer.

Goldstone had dreamed up a peculiar cast. As Pépé Le Moko he had selected a former band singer with his own popular radio show, Tony Martin. He had some film experience in small parts, as a sailor in Irving Berlin's *Follow the Fleet* (his first film) and as a heart-throbbing vocalist in MGM musicals such as the Jerome Kern tribute *Till the Clouds Roll By*. And in another tribute in 1941, Martin sang "You Stepped Out of a Dream," in a scene in which Anya Arlen appeared with Lana Turner, Hedy Lamarr, and Judy Garland. The film was *Ziegfeld Girl,* Anya's last appearance as an extra. For Martin, *Casbah* was the one major film in which he actually starred.

Marta Toren, a Swedish beauty fresh out of drama school, was cast in the Hedy Lamarr part; *Casbah* was to be her film debut. Goldstone rounded out his cast with Peter Lorre, Yvonne DeCarlo, and the Katherine Dunham dancers. It was a decidedly international cast.

Although Martin did not make a convincing French criminal in exile in Algiers, safe as long as he remained sequestered in the exotic Casbah quarter, he had a fine, romantic voice and came to the film with plenty of radio exposure and a solid list of popular records. Goldstone knew Harold Arlen could write for that voice and for the film's exotic setting. Harold was happy to take the assignment after two years of living off his ASCAP income and other royalties.

The question of his collaborator arose, since Koehler was in retirement and Harburg, Mercer, and Ira Gershwin were otherwise occupied. When the name of Leo Robin was mentioned, Harold unhesitatingly agreed. Highly regarded but little known outside Hollywood musical circles, Robin already had over forty film scores to his credit and five Broadway shows, including the Vincent Youmans success *Hit the Deck,* dating from 1927.

Leo Robin was born in Pittsburgh in 1900, studied law, then worked as a news reporter. He had a flair for writing, and after two years in journalism he tried his hand at public relations. In college he had revealed an interest in dramatics and a talent for writing verse (his parents were literary, according to Robin). Deciding to break into the theater, he bought a one-way ticket to New York, withdrew all his savings (six hundred dollars) from the bank, and managed to acquire a few letters of introduction to important theatrical figures. Among them was George S. Kaufman, also a former journalist turned playwright who had left Pittsburgh for New York.

Kaufman listened to Robin's story and his plans, read his plays, and on learning about the savings withdrawal, suggested that the young man use half of the money on "a hell of a good time, and go back to Pittsburgh." In 1925 New York was indeed a lively place, but Robin decided not to take Kaufman's advice. He did, however, talk Kaufman into introducing him to Lewis E. Gensler, an active man-about-the-theater who was a songwriter as well as a producer.

Gensler suggested that, since Robin had songwriting aspirations, he try his hand at writing lyrics, which Gensler would study, criticize, and perhaps even set to music. This continued for a couple of months as Robin's supply of cash shrank. Somewhat impressed, Gensler promised an introduction to B. G. DeSylva, by that time already an important lyricist and publisher.

"Robin sat in his hotel room," the historian Jack Burton records,

> writing lyrics, waiting for the DeSylva telephone call that never came, and watching his cash reserves dwindle down to $25.
>
> Finally, in desperation, Robin wrote a parody lyric to DeSylva's "Look for the Silver Lining" and sent it to Buddy, who was so impressed with the appeal that he arranged for Leo to write a song for the Greenwich Village Follies for which he received $200.

The door to Tin Pan Alley opened. Robin teamed up with the composer Richard Myers for a couple of musicals, which met with some success. In 1927 he contributed lyrics to four musicals, two with Myers, one with Charles Rosoff, and an important one with music by the difficult Vincent Youmans, *Hit the Deck.* Robin was one of the three suffering lyricists who worked with the driven Youmans; he wrote the words to "Hallelujah!" and collaborated with Clifford Grey on "Why, Oh Why?" Irving Caesar contributed the lyric for the show's other major hit, "Sometimes I'm Happy."

But it was in Hollywood, with the advent of sound, that Leo Robin truly came into his own. In the late 1920s he moved to Hollywood, where he collaborated initially with Richard Whiting before forming a long and most productive partnership with Ralph Rainger. He also wrote film scores with Harry Warren, Arthur Schwartz, and Jerome Kern.

Arlen was familiar with Leo Robin's substantial catalog (to use a trade term). With Whiting he had written "Beyond the Blue Horizon," "My Ideal," and "One Hour with You," with Rainger he created several of Bing Crosby's most popular songs, among them "Blue Hawaii," "Please," "June in January," and "Love in Bloom." Their Academy Award–winning song, written for *The Big Broadcast of 1938,* "Thanks for the Memory," was introduced by Bob Hope and Shirley Ross. The film marked the comedian's film debut, and the song soon after became his radio theme music. Robin's credentials were impressive, and Arlen relished the opportunity to work with a man he called "a great craftsman." Robin, in turn, found his new collaborator to be "a very conscientious craftsman" as well. Theirs was a working arrangement based on deep mutual respect.

Although they had known one another for several years, having met at parties, ASCAP functions, or at the Gershwins', Arlen and Robin had never collaborated before. The discrepancies in their work habits would require a style of partnership new for each of them. Leo Robin admitted, "I don't make much sense till after midnight," while Arlen preferred the earlier portion of the day or night for work.

"I never sat with him while he was 'digging' for a tune, as I have with other composers," Robin said of Arlen. They generally met during the afternoon to discuss each song and what the general point might be, where it fit into the film. With Martin's the only voice in the film, there was no problem for Arlen with keys or range. Once their discussions were finished, Arlen would begin his "digging." They would meet again as soon as the composer thought he had found a suitable melody and he would play it for Robin.

Robin was an inveterate pipe smoker and pacer who deliberated long before producing a completed lyric. "Ordinarily," he told an interviewer, "when a composer submits a tune to me, I take a lot of time—sometimes a month or more—before I hit on a title that I like. But in the case of *Casbah* I hit upon a title within minutes after Harold played the melody for me. (And then took a lot of time, as usual, to complete the lyric.)"

Robin's modesty amused Arlen. The lyricist would bring him a lyric claiming that it was a mere suggestion, a "dummy lyric," not yet the finished, polished song. But, as Arlen recalled, chuckling, "it always turned out to be the right one." To Robin's surprise, too, he was never asked to revise any lyric, including "Hooray for Love," in which, to his later dismay, he found that he had unconsciously ended every line in the chorus with the word "love." He had repeated the word eight times and was certain that Arlen would object to the verbal monotony. But it worked, and despite its being lost in the film under dialogue, "Hooray for Love" was the hit of a not very successful movie.

The gem of the score is "What's Good about Goodbye?," a surging ballad in whose dummy lyric Robin wrote two logical, almost obvious lines, that no one had ever written before: "What's good about goodbye? / What's fair about farewell?" The opening sixteen-bar musical statement is equally simple, but then, in a characteristic turn, Arlen's melody soars. The next statement begins with an ascending octave (C to C), then rises a minor third to E-flat. The octave repeats, now followed by a climactic E-natural, then subsides to a quiet close. At sixty bars, including the ten-bar tag, it is another Arlen "tapeworm."

"What's Good about Goodbye?" is also typically Arlen in its hopeful melancholy. Robin was aware of this, noting that he hadn't known anyone who enjoyed joking so much, accompanied by "his hearty laughter. . . . In fact, he gives the impression of being a very lighthearted person, but some of his music, of course, belies this."

During their brief collaboration Robin was not aware of any problems in the Arlen house. Anya was unobtrusive and, of course, Robin did most of his work at his home. He rarely had more than a glimpse of her, passing through or in the garden with the dogs. And, too, as president of the Hollywood Sweet Fellows Society (Ira Gershwin was vice president), Robin would have made a point of not noticing strife or unusual behavior. The Sweet Fellows was the creation of Harry Warren, possessor of one of the sharpest tongues in the west. The Robin and Gershwin aversion to gossip and backbiting, even criticism of their peers (all favorite pursuits in the Hollywood desert), earned them top membership in Warren's mythical society. Harold Arlen could have readily been appointed secretary.

Once the *Casbah* score was finished, Arlen suffered through another dry period of almost two years. Unfortunately, he and Robin never worked together again.

During that slump, the senior Arlucks moved into Beverly Hills, and Jerry Arlen followed, hoping (without luck, as it turned out) to find work in films. The proximity of her husband's family added to Anya's emotional distress and isolation.

Early in 1950 Harold was relieved from some of the close-to-the-surface strife in his home when he was reunited with Johnny Mercer to work on a minor film, *The Petty Girl.* A fluffy concoction, it celebrated the pinup airbrush paintings of the *Esquire* illustrator and advertising artist George Petty. (The film's main character, played by Robert Cummings, was actually named "George Petty," though the movie hardly qualified as biography.)

An unmemorable production, *The Petty Girl* could be credited with a charming sequence set in the streets of New York. Cummings's co-star, Joan Caulfield, cast as an independent, unattached career woman, expresses her cheerful philosophy in "Fancy Free," a sweeping, spirited waltz that the composer noted should be sung "with great spirit." The song is one of the least characteristic Arlen-Mercer collaborations—no blues and no folksy words.

Another atypical number preceded the Harry Belafonte era by a couple of years; this was "Calypso Song," which capitalized on a West Indies folk form then coming into vogue. Mercer provided, calypso style, several clever verses on subjects suggested by an on-screen audience: television, coconuts, scotch. Mercer's final word on the subject:

> Soon Calypso de people say
> Is de big thing in de U.S.A.
> Will it become de national song?
> Man, you should Calyp-so-long!

The title song is an extended production number as the film's predictable finale. Arlen's melody is subservient to Mercer's lyric celebrating the Petty girl, commercially, over the period of a year, with appropriate costumes for each month (the Petty girl was never overdressed).

The Petty Girl was released in August 1950, a year not notable for its original film musicals. The big film of the year was an adaptation of Irving Berlin's Broadway success *Annie Get Your Gun.* MGM's *Three Little Words,* another success, was yet another attempt at songwriter biography, this time Harry Ruby and Bert

Kalmar, with the obvious device of filling out the plot with musical numbers. Another quasi-original was *Summer Stock,* still another variant on the let's-put-on-a-show-in-the-barn musical. As was the practice, the film starred Judy Garland and, in the place of Mickey Rooney, Gene Kelly. With songs mostly by Harry Warren and Mack Gordon, its most exhilarating musical sequence was one filmed two months after the shooting had officially ended. Judy Garland's absenteeisms, because of emotional and health problems, had prolonged the making of the movie over a period of eight months (and ended her career at MGM). When she recovered, twenty pounds lighter, she performed one of her finest musical routines ever filmed, singing "Get Happy," the Arlen-Koehler song interpolated into the film. Unfortunately, another Arlen song was eliminated after the filming, an exquisite rendition of "Last Night When We Were Young."

In September of that same lean year, a month after the release of *The Petty Girl,* Twentieth Century–Fox premiered one more now-forgotten film musical, *My Blue Heaven.* The title number was the old (1927) Walter Donaldson and Richard Whiting hit. The rest of the score was by Harold Arlen with yet another new collaborator, Ralph Blane. Like so many films of that year, *My Blue Heaven* did not make history. It did mark Harold Arlen's debut as a lyricist, however. Over the years, privately, he had tried his hand at setting his music to words, but *My Blue Heaven* would be his first public attempt.

TOIL AND
TROUBLE

The earliest extant example of the work of Harold Arlen, wordsmith, dates from 1940 and was inspired by an annoying incident in the life of Ira Gershwin. He and Kurt Weill had worked long on a special production number, "Song of the Zodiac," for the Broadway musical play *Lady in the Dark*. This was Ira Gershwin's first major effort after the death of his brother, George, in 1937.

In the show, the number is one of several in a dream sequence. Gershwin was especially pleased with himself; he had worked up a couple of dozen witty couplets (some a bit outrageous: "To be born under Leo / Is no panaceo," "Life is sour and lemon-y / Under Gemini"). The song, considered "too dour and oppressive" by the show's producer, Sam H. Harris, and the librettist and co-director, Moss Hart, was eliminated from the show in the first week of rehearsals. Gershwin, who had returned to California that week, was forced to return to New York to concoct "something lighter and perhaps gayer [Hart's suggestion] about a woman who could not make up her mind." Grudgingly, Gershwin and Weill went back to work and produced the showstopping "Saga of Jenny." Gershwin returned again to Beverly Hills, where he poured out his tale of woe to a sympathetic but amused Harold Arlen. This was unusual for Gershwin. From the beginning of his professional career, if he and his brother found that a producer, or even a singer, objected to a song, the Gershwins simply wrote a new one. But "The Zodiac Song" meant a lot to him, and he felt like grousing.

Arlen listened, went home, and contrived his own ballad, "The Ira Song," commemorating the event. With Anya's help (she contributed an obbligato), Harold made a recording of his song, with a little shameless borrowing from Gilbert and Sullivan and with mock seriousness, in a three-part effort of some complexity:

Through the night, The dismal night—
My zest for rhyme keeps waning.
And soon a voice within me cries,
"Ira, my boy, the public needs entertaining."
Then I question the man who isn't there
For one good reason for my despair.

One good reason why the likes of me
Should be burdened with ennui,
Should not be able to sleep a wink
Even with the aid of a capsule pink.
To turn and toss and nightly grapple
For a phrase to be OK'd by Sam or Chappell.

Alas, alack, I broke my back
On the Zodiac.
'Las, 'lack, Zodiac
Ah, they're driving me to ruin and rack,
Why did I have to break my back
On the goddamn signs of the Zodiac?

There's be no reason for this tirade
If it weren't for the mess of a mish Moss made.
If it weren't for the mess of a mish Moss made
There'd be no reason for this tirade.
    [Repeated; this is the Gilbert and Sullivan section]

Through the night, the dismal night—
My zest for rhyme keeps waning,
And soon a voice within me cries,
"Ira, my boy, the public needs entertaining."
Ah, little man who isn't there
Why this burden do I bear?

With a tear in his eye and resignation
He said, "Ira, my boy
It's for Art, ASCAP and the Gershwin Plantation."

Gershwin rewarded Harold with one of his diffident smiles and a quiet chuckle, then complimented him on his debut, at least to Gershwin, as a lyricist.

(The term Arlen preferred was *lyric writer*.) It had been fun and he would try again.

A decade later, he got his chance to be a "lyric writer" with Sol Siegel's offer for him to write the music for a Betty Grable picture. Arlen was happy to do the film; he was tired of doing nothing, and Betty Grable was still an important presence at Fox, where she had reigned during the war as the nation's queen of the pinup girls. She had had some recent film misfortunes in the poorly received *Shocking Miss Pilgrim, That Lady in Ermine*, and *The Beautiful Blonde from Bashful Bend*. Siegel planned to star her opposite Dan Dailey, with whom she had worked so well when they were first teamed in the successful *Mother Wore Tights* (though Grable had expected, and had hoped for, James Cagney or Fred Astaire). *My Blue Heaven* was to be their third Fox musical.

Dailey was a lanky song-and-dance man with experience in vaudeville and cabaret and several films, beginning in 1940. He exuded an air of self-confident charm, was a skilled dancer, and sang well. Though he never achieved the renown of Astaire or Gene Kelly, Dailey was a dependable trouper who could act.

Arlen found that Siegel had no lyricist in mind at the start of the planning. Did Harold have a preference or suggestion? He did, but momentarily no one was free. Harold mentioned this to Harry Warren, who unhesitatingly brought up the name of Ralph Blane, with whom he had recently completed the songs for a Doris Day musical film, *My Dream Is Yours*. Its hit was "Someone Like You." Earlier, in 1948, Warren and Blane had written the score for the MGM musical version of Eugene O'Neill's *Ah, Wilderness!* Starring Mickey Rooney and titled *Summer Holiday*, the film was graced with the popular "Stanley Steamer."

Warren, always honest and frank, assured Harold that he would find Ralph Blane "very musical and great to work with," primarily because he was, as Warren saw him, a collaborator rather than a lyricist who went away and came back with the words. Much of the quality of the unfortunately neglected *Summer Holiday*, Warren also believed, could be attributed to Blane's working from the O'Neill story for the placement of the songs.

Blane's agent, Irving Lazar, called to tell him that Harold Arlen wanted him to write the lyrics for the new Grable musical. Blane's response was, "Harold Arlen! My God!" Lazar then tended to his business of the contracts.

Ralph Blane had come a long distance since he bluffed his way into the chorus of *Hooray for What!* in order to appear in a Harold Arlen musical. After the show closed, he formed a musical partnership with another member of the chorus, Hugh Martin. As the Martins, they sang in clubs and on the radio. They also wrote vocal arrangements for musicals by Rodgers and Hart, Cole Porter, Irving Berlin, and Jerome Kern.

In 1941 they collaborated on the vivacious college musical *Best Foot Forward*, out of which came such exceptional songs as "Ev'ry Time" and "Buckle Down, Winsocki." The show was taken up by Hollywood, and the team of Martin and

Blane moved west. In 1944 they wrote an outstanding score for Judy Garland's *Meet Me in St. Louis*: "The Trolley Song," "The Boy Next Door," and "Have Yourself a Merry Little Christmas." Their published sheet music invariably read "Words and Music by Hugh Martin and Ralph Blane," though Blane was considered the lyricist and Martin the composer. Actually, they worked so closely that only they knew who contributed what to any specific song.

When Martin went into the army during World War II, Blane worked with others or alone. Working with Harold Arlen was, to him, an even greater opportunity than collaborating with Harry Warren, another giant. But there would be a problem.

Arlen studied the script and found a spot where it called for a spoof of the long-running Rodgers and Hammerstein musical *South Pacific*. He soon had an idea for the music for what was to be a production number; he based the first two notes—his trademark octave leap—on the first two tones of Rodgers's "Bali Ha'i." He invited Blane to his home to play the song, and a nervous lyricist arrived clutching a crisp, newly purchased notebook.

Arlen played what he had a few times as they discussed the music and how the lyric might go. They did not get further than to decide on a title, "The Friendly Islands," which Blane wrote across the top of the first page of his notebook. He then drove home.

For three days Blane could not think of one word to write under that title; he could not sleep and confessed to his wife that he was so in awe of his collaborator that he could not find words good enough for the music. In desperation, drained with worry and insomnia, he called Lazar and demanded that he be taken off the job, ending the call with, "I am going to die!"

Moments after Blane dropped the phone into its cradle, it rang. It was Arlen. Lazar had explained Blane's problem—Arlen remembered a time when he had been intimidated by Jack Yellen and sympathized.

"Come over," he suggested, "and we'll work on it." Together Arlen and Blane conceived the lyric to "The Friendly Islands." The creative ice broken, Blane was able to work closely with the composer on the film. As for Arlen, he found great pleasure in finding the words. "I was hell-bent," he told a friend, "and we had a great time doing it. It wasn't labored, and we didn't have any trouble [with the studio] when we turned in the songs." Arlen was so taken with his newfound talent that he covered reams of paper with lyric ideas. "Annie thought I was crazy," he recalled. He became as obsessed with lyric writing as he had been with golf—he even borrowed Ira Gershwin's rarely used rhyming dictionary.

Grable and Dailey were cast as a married song-and-dance team with a small family of adopted children. To the surprise of all, the wife becomes pregnant (which generates a song for the husband, "What a Man!"). During the late stages of the pregnancy the wife must stop dancing, and a new partner for the husband introduces the problem of the other woman. A subtheme is a satirical view of television and Madison Avenue advertising (in an amusingly vapid commercial, "Cosmo Cosmetics"). The television background was the ideal setting for the Grable-Dailey song-and-dance routines.

Ira Gershwin enjoyed the enthusiastic productions of the neophyte lyricist who dropped by frequently to perform his and Blane's latest song. Gershwin's favorite was "It's Deductible," a song extolling the financial gain achieved by failure and hoodwinking the Treasury Department:

> *A Texan drills an oil well,*
> *The oil well don't produce,*
> *The Texan doesn't worry 'cause he's got a good excuse*
> *It's deductible,*
> *It's deductible.*

And in the same spirit:

> *Producer gets an angel, producer gets a flop,*
> *The angel doesn't worry, 'cause the flop comes off the top.*

The song could easily have been written for a Gershwin political operetta. A "Special Interlude" consisted of a list of the numerous exemptions possible, closing with the sardonic "It's irrational, but it's national, / So throw a ball and charge up all the folderol to Sam. (*Spoken*: Uncle Sam?) What a lamb."

"The Friendly Islands" became the most ambitious production number of the film, scored for soloists, chorus, and orchestra and cast in six sections—one, a dance, makes extensive use of percussion. In another, Dailey does a heavily accented impersonation of Ezio Pinza, the male star of *South Pacific*. Lest the point be missed, there are references to "happy talk" and meeting "some enchanted stranger" in the lyric.

The most truly Arlenesque melody is marked "slow, steady, lazy blues tempo," and in fact is the one true plot song, "Live Hard, Work Hard, Love Hard." It is the wife's warning to her husband's new (and temporary) partner, Mitzi Gaynor, and the suggestion that she find a new job.

Arlen's favorites from *My Blue Heaven* were the sprightly, quasi–Cole Porterish "I Love a New Yorker" and the jesting "Halloween." Having gently tweaked Richard Rodgers, they thought they could have a little fun with Irving Berlin. The verse explains why they chose to write about that particular holiday. It was the only unsung holiday because "along came a man by the name of Berlin / Who took every holiday that ever has been" and used them in his wartime film *Holiday Inn*.

Mischievously pleased with himself, Arlen played it for Berlin, who, with a twinkle in his eye, said, "You son of a bitch."

The busy and big "Friendly Islands" number made an impression on the front office at Fox, as did their happy songwriting, for with *My Blue Heaven* finished, Arlen and Blane began on the songs for their next musical film, with the working title *The Friendly Islands*.

As soon as their schedules were clear, they began writing in September 1950, completed eight songs by October, and when they were asked to produce a comic number, wrote the final song, "The Opposite Sex," in December. Again the ghost of *South Pacific* hovered over the script. The setting is an island in the Pacific after the war, occupied by United Nations–like troops commanded by an American officer. His petty fiefdom (described in "I'm the Ruler of a South Sea Island") is disrupted by an American newswoman. The troops are restless and homesick, as expressed in "Back Where I Come From" and the excellent "Twenty-seven Elm Street," which gets lost under some dialogue of the contentious officer and reporter, William Lundigan and Jane Greer.

Another topic touched on in the film is fraternization with the islanders and the implied miscegenation (another *South Pacific*-ism). The "native girl" love interest was a deeply tanned Mitzi Gaynor in a sarong. (She and David Wayne had also moved directly from *My Blue Heaven* into *The Friendly Islands*.) Theirs were the biggest box-office names in the cast. Jack Paar, in an early movie part, was virtually unknown.

In brief, *The Friendly Islands* had no stars, a familiar plot, and a director, Edmund Goulding, with minimal experience with musicals. The producer, Sol Siegel, was occupied with another musical, so Fred Kohlmar, who also had little experience with musicals, took his place. The final result was dismal in many respects. The title was changed to *Down among the Sheltering Palms*. The film was kept canned for two years and, following some injudicious editing (and excising of songs), was released in June 1953, not a good year—or month. Sol Siegel's *Gentlemen Prefer Blondes*, with Marilyn Monroe, was also released in June, shortly after Ethel Merman in Berlin's *Call Me Madam* and before *The Band Wagon*, with Fred Astaire, and the film version (in 3D!) of *Kiss Me Kate*. *Down among the Sheltering Palms* was eclipsed by this overflow of musical films, all with Broadway echoes.

The songs went down with the sinking film, which excited little attention and slipped in and out of movie houses leaving nothing behind. Only one of its songs was published, an affecting ballad, "Who Will It Be When the Time Comes?" Another, a charmingly simple folklike ballad, "What Make de Diff'rence?" should have been published as well. In each the theme is that of the thoughts of a young woman longing for love. The more sophisticated of the two, sung by the reporter, "Who Will It Be?," is distinguished by Arlen's frequent use of a triplet on the words "Will it be John, will it be Jim, will it be Joe"; on the last "be" he uses a surprising blue note. On their demonstration record of the song, Arlen and Blane hold that tone before dropping the melody a tritone. The effect is at once poignant and whimsical. The worldly, traveled newswoman is in a position to pick among a number of suitors, but will wait until "the time comes I'll know my boy." This last is probably the one infelicitous line in the lyric. She was not looking for a "boy" so much as Arlen and Blane were looking for a word that rhymes with "joy" in the previous line.

The related, though contrastingly ingenuous, song expressing the puzzled longing of the naïve Mitzi Gaynor character is "What Make de Diff'rence?" She cannot understand the military policy of nonnfraternization with the "natives." What difference, she sings, does it make if the man is tall and the girl is small?

> He look at big moon
> So high above,
> I look at same moon
> And fall in love.

The melody rises, with sad sweetness, on her plaintive, "All alone am I / Lookin' at same big sky." Her final question is "What it all about?"

The songs from *My Blue Heaven* and *Down among the Sheltering Palms* were published by the recently formed (1948) Harwin Music Corporation, a company whose chief proprietors were *Har*old Arlen and Ed*win* H. Morris. Buddy Morris's already established company, Edwin H. Morris Co., would handle the business end of Harwin as the "sole selling agent." With the formation of Harwin, Harold Arlen, like Berlin, the Gershwins, and Rodgers and Hammerstein, would have complete control of his own work.

The Harwin-Morris imprint had first appeared on the sheet music of *My Blue Heaven*—six songs, practically the entire score. That "Who Will It Be When the Time Comes?" was the sole publication from *Down among the Sheltering Palms* is significant. There were other good songs in that score in addition to the overlooked "What Make de Diff'rence?": a swinging ballad, "When You're in Love," and, one of the composer's favorites, "Twenty-seven Elm Street." When decisions about the publications from the film were made, Harold Arlen was preoccupied with disruptions in his personal life.

This emotionally charged period coincided, partly, with the entrance of yet another new collaborator, Dorothy Fields.

When *Down among the Sheltering Palms* was belatedly released, in June 1953, so was *The Farmer Takes a Wife*, with music by Harold Arlen and lyrics by Dorothy Fields. Their work initiated between Arlen's two collaborations with Blane, with still another *South Pacific*–afflicted film, *Mr. Imperium*, which starred the operatic basso Ezio Pinza, billed as "The Famed Former Star of 'South Pacific.' " His co-star was Lana Turner. At the time it seemed like an excellent idea. Arlen was finished with *My Blue Heaven*, and Blane began working on his next Broadway effort, *Three Wishes for Jamie*, for which he would write music and lyrics.

Dorothy Fields, in from Broadway, where she had recently done a period musical with the composer Morton Gould, *Arms and the Girl*, was in Hollywood looking in on the film production of the musical she had written with the late Sigmund Romberg, *Up in Central Park*. Working with his old friend Dotty was an exciting prospect for Arlen. Fields was unique in popular music, the most successful and highly honored woman songwriter. She was among the best in a small company—Anne Caldwell (who had written with Kern), Kay Swift, Ann Ronell, Betty Comden (of Comden and Green).

Dorothy Fields, in addition to being one of the most distinguished songwriters of either sex of her time, was a librettist who collaborated on musicals with her brother Herbert. (Another brother, Joseph, was also a librettist.) Like Harold Arlen, she got her start at the Cotton Club, collaborating with the composer Jimmy McHugh in the 1927 production. Unhappy at the club because she objected to the risqué "special material" lyrics, which the customers mistakenly attributed to her, Fields moved with McHugh to Broadway and then, like Arlen, to Hollywood.

After a couple of films, she hit her stride in a collaboration with Jerome Kern when, in 1935, his Broadway show *Roberta* was filmed. Fields contributed lyrics to some of the added songs. One of them was the elegant "Lovely to Look At," for which she shared the credit for lyrics with a disgruntled Jimmy McHugh.

That same year, she worked with Kern on a full score for *I Dream Too Much*, starring the coloratura soprano Lily Pons. The title song was an exceptional (and typically Kern) ballad. Then, too, there was the extraordinary novelty number "The Jockey on the Carousel." Once again McHugh was appeased, sharing credit for this song. He and Dorothy Fields did not work together again. Among their Hollywood songs, however, were such successes as "Cuban Love Song," "I'm in the Mood for Love," and "I Feel a Song Comin' On."

The crowning Fields and Kern film, starring Astaire and Rogers, was *Swing Time* (1936). Highlights of that memorable score were the rhythmic "Pick Yourself Up," a surging orchestral "Waltz in Swing Time," a big production number tribute to the dancer Bill Robinson (with Astaire in blackface), "Bojangles of Harlem," the amusing "A Fine Romance," and the Academy Award–winning "The Way You Look Tonight."

Harold Arlen and Dorothy Fields had known each other for years, first in New York as members of the songwriting fraternity and then in California, when both were members of the Gershwin poolside and tennis court set. Fields was intelligent, often funny (she was the daughter of the comedian Lew Fields), and very businesslike when it came to work. In Hollywood she had learned to play golf from George Gershwin and was filmed by him and Harold Arlen swimming in their respective pools. The composer and collaborator Arthur Schwartz described her as "elegant," and, as the films confirm, a fine and graceful swimmer.

At that time, the late 1930s, she was never asked to work with Arlen but did write with such disparate composers as Fritz Kreisler (*The King Steps Out,* 1936) and another member of the Gershwin circle, Oscar Levant, who frequented the Gershwin pool area fully clothed—dark suit, shirt, and tie. For a Ginger Rogers film (without Astaire), *In Person,* Fields wrote the lyric to one of Levant's best melodies, "Don't Mention Love to Me." But she was happy working with Kern, for she was one of the few of his collaborators he did not intimidate.

Fields left Hollywood in 1939 to work in the musical theater. With Arthur Schwartz she did the songs for the Ethel Merman–Jimmy Durante Hollywood satire *Stars in Your Eyes* (1939) and then, with her brother Herbert, worked on the librettos for a string of successful shows with scores by Cole Porter: *Let's Face It, Something for the Boys,* and *Mexican Hayride.* That was followed, in 1945, by a gorgeously scored addition to the Americana musical of the time, *Up In Central Park,* with music by Sigmund Romberg, her lyrics, and a book by herself and brother Herbert.

Brother and sister then came up with an idea for a musical, starring her good friend Ethel Merman, based on the life of the Wild West sharpshooter Annie Oakley. With Herbert she worked up a book with that title. Dorothy's plan was to lure Jerome Kern away from Hollywood to write the music to her words. She and Herbert then approached Rodgers and Hammerstein, who had branched out recently into production, to produce *Annie Oakley.* They agreed and Kern agreed.

Tragically, in November 1945, while in New York engaged in a *Show Boat* revival, Kern suffered a fatal cerebral hemorrhage while antique shopping on East Fifty-seventh Street. Determined to go on with the production, Rodgers and Hammerstein, then occupied with their own *Carousel,* talked a reluctant Irving Berlin into doing the show (Berlin had recently returned from a touring production of *This Is the Army* and was exhausted from appearances in the South Pacific). His decision to get involved put Dorothy Fields, lyricist, out of a job. However, she graciously stepped aside and still had the gratification of co-writing one of the most honored musicals of the American theater.

She followed that with another excursion into Americana, *Arms and the Girl,* with Morton Gould. Set in the time of the American Revolution, the musical was unsuccessful. When the offer came for her to work with Harold Arlen on the Pinza-Turner film, Fields felt it was time to return to the West Coast. She left New York and settled into a bungalow at the Beverly Hills Hotel.

Harold remembered years later that "Dotty was easy to get along with—there never was any strain." She was also a well-organized, methodical worker. She was an early riser who typed up her lyrics written the previous day and was ready when he arrived in the morning, usually by eleven. After discussing the idea for a song, Arlen would play a tune he believed might do, then sketched out a lead sheet. He and Dorothy would have lunch on her patio, after which he would leave. Thus, easily, they wrote their skimpy score for Pinza's *Mr. Imperium*. That he preferred to work with Fields at her bungalow was a sign of problems at home. Anya's temperamental and, to Harold, unreasonable outbursts led to the decision. Her emotional displays in the company of others mortified him. He was reluctant to discuss Anya's difficulties even among close friends, but they affected him drastically.

This turmoil was not evident during the brief *Mr. Imperium* collaboration. The film was a waste of effort and was poorly received. Pinza, then pushing sixty, was cast as an exiled king who meets a young American woman (in real life Turner was twenty-eight years younger). While this age gap had succeeded on Broadway (Pinza opposite Mary Martin's American nurse), filmgoers, preferring a more romantic match and probably a less operatically weighty voice, avoided the film. The negative votes of the critics didn't help, either.

Considering its star, the music for *Mr. Imperium* was decidedly slight. Only three songs were required from Arlen and Fields, and there was, inexplicably, an interpolation, "You Belong to My Heart." Written by the Mexican songwriter Agustín Lara, it was originally sung in Disney's *The Three Caballeros* (1944) to Donald Duck. With an English lyric by Ray Gilbert it was popular in the mid-1940s, though its presence in the score of *Mr. Imperium* is now impossible to rationalize.

Pinza's ethnic and operatic background was established in the Italianate, folk-like "Andiamo," with lyrical references to pizza, antipasto, and "a very bad wine" and music marked *presto, allegro,* and *vivace,* as well as the vocal flourish in

> Do you love mi fa sol la si
> La-ha-ha-si do.

There is also a duet, "My Love an' My Mule," introduced by Lana Turner (with the dubbed voice of Trudi Irwin), joined by Pinza. Its playful melody is in keeping with the comparison of man and animal: those "crazy critters so dog-gone arbitrary" who manage "to make a monkey out of one pig-headed fool." It is a minor song that would have been served better as an instrumental. In some repeated passages of eighth and sixteenth notes, Pinza, a great performer then past his prime, had trouble with articulation.

One song was worth the effort: "Let Me Look at You." It is Pinza's most operatic moment in the film and contains some perceptive Fieldsian lines underscoring the May-September romance. He describes her as "young and strong and sure of your heart" and emanating "such beauty and life" that he asks her to "Just stand alone, please do and let me look at you." The melody's compass stretches a ninth, no problem for Pinza. "Let Me Look at You" remains another little-known Arlen art song.

The tunes he wrote for Fields, she believed, exemplified Arlen's versatility. "This man," she told an interviewer, "can write anything." His songs, she found, were lyrically pure and in good taste, reflecting the man himself, "a man full of love." Only a year older than Arlen, Dorothy Fields recalled him with warmth and affection, almost maternally, calling him "Schnitta," a term of her own invention. Arlen, when not calling her Dotty, addressed her as "The Red Arrow," a tribute to her speedy way with a lyric.

This was not to be the case in their final collaboration, *The Farmer Takes a Wife,* which began almost immediately after the composer and Ralph Blane completed *Down among the Sheltering Palms.* Twentieth Century–Fox was interested in another Arlen score, and Dorothy Fields seemed to be the ideal collaborator. The "property" was promising, a film musical adapted from the popular Henry Fonda–Janet Gaynor 1935 film of the same title. That, in turn, had been based on the play, which had also starred Fonda, by Frank B. Elser and Marc Connelly. The original source, *Rome Haul,* had been a best-selling novel by Walter D. Edmonds back in 1929.

Edmonds's novel was set in the 1850s in New York State, when the busy Erie Canal was used to carry assorted cargoes, from pigs to apples, between Rome and Buffalo. The sprawling book was filled with colorful characters, including strong-minded women, and culminated in a race on the canal. Scattered throughout the book were several period folk songs. The new screenplay was written by Walter Bullock, Sally Benson (whose Americana-flavored *New Yorker* stories had inspired the film *Meet Me in St. Louis*), and Joseph Fields, Dorothy's brother. With its setting, characters, and romantic depiction of an earlier time in American history, it appeared to be a natural for a big, splashy musical film.

Betty Grable was starred as a canal cook, on the boat owned by John Carroll, a brawling, hard-drinking keelboat man. Because of his temper he has a difficult time getting help and keeping it. Enter Dan (Dale Robertson in the Fonda role), an innocent young farmer who wants to work on the canal only long enough to buy a farm and marry. Molly (Grable), who grew up on a barge, resents farmers. The farmer, a gentle soul nevertheless capable of physically handling their captain, does take the wife in the final reel.

Work on the score of *The Farmer Takes a Wife* was neither speedy nor happy, however. It began well enough around October 1951, after *Mr. Imperium* was out of the way. The songs were readily spotted into the script. Taking a cue from the novel, Fields and Arlen conceived a grand opening number for chorus and orchestra, "On the Erie Canal." Among Arlen's papers are piano copies of the songs prepared by a studio copyist. One, entitled "I Could Cook," is dated November 1, 1950. Two, "Somethin' Real Special" and "Yes!," are dated October 24, 1951. "I Was Wearin' Horse Shoes!," which was not used, is dated

January 8, 1952. Another, "Look Who's Been Dreaming," written for Grable and not used, is not dated, and the manuscript is not in Arlen's hand.

Obviously, in the period between the specific dates of November 1, 1950, and January 8, 1952, something had happened. Although "I Was Wearin' Horse Shoes!" may have been a last-minute addition to an already ample film score, there are inordinate gaps between the preparation of songs.

Whether it was because Arlen was so occupied, even preoccupied, with work during that time with Blane and Fields, or because of the proximity of the senior Arlens since Samuel Arluck's retirement, Anya Arlen exploded emotionally. She resented her husband's absences; she screamed accusations (even about his completely professional association with Dorothy Fields), and she broke things during her outbursts. She was thoroughly isolated and estranged (certainly from her husband's family), a Beverly Hills housewife with nothing to do. Her outbursts were attributed to a neurotic reaction to her empty life—and to pills. Because of her deep-seated fear of doctors, it is unlikely that she had consulted one. Unlike Lee Gershwin, she was not an avid shopper who terrified sales clerks along Rodeo Drive or gossiped at Nate and Al's, the Manhattan-style delicatessen. Anya was unhappy at parties. Harold's response was to flee, to go to the club for drinks and more drinks. There were times, his old friend and business associate Buddy Morris recalled, when he was found sleeping on someone's lawn in Beverly Hills.

This had an effect on Arlen's work on *The Farmer Takes a Wife.* The work routine they had established during *Mr. Imperium,* in deference to Dorothy Field's love of order, was upset. When it was time for their first *Farmer* meeting at her bungalow, Harold arrived, to Dorothy's surprise, accompanied by Jerry Arlen, who had aroused his brother and then delivered him to her door. She would be less surprised when this mode of travel became the new routine. Harold was puffy, red-eyed, and slow to focus on their work. That he managed to work at all is one of the wonders of that period of stress, which persisted for several years.

When the time came to take Anya to an institution—her doctor felt she had become a danger to herself and to Arlen—Harold could not bring himself to do it and recruited Jerry for the unpleasant task. The job had to be done more than once, and a pattern soon developed, to Jerry's annoyance. A few days after Jerry had chauffeured Anya, Harold would drive to the hospital in Malibu, sign her out, and take her home, until the next flare-up. Jerry would again deliver her into temporary exile. For the rest of Anya's life, from those unhappy days in the spring and summer of 1951, she resented Jerry.

One day the Beverly Hills police came to the Arluck home inquiring whether Samuel Arluck was related to Harold Arluck—the name they had found on a document in an automobile that had been parked at the Los Angeles airport for the past two days. This visit set off a distressing alarm. Jerry Arlen set out in search of his brother. He was not at home, nor was Anya. Jerry then returned to his home in Malibu. He phoned several friends without luck. Harold was not at Hillcrest and hadn't been there for days. Jerry was worried, but as usual, also furious; his parents, especially Celia, were distraught. There was simply no word; had something happened in the vicinity of the heavily policed Beverly Hills, they would have heard about it.

A day and a night passed: Harold Arlen had been missing for over three days, though his absence was not reported in the press. Then word came from a wildly unexpected locale: Honolulu. As he told the story later with mortification, Arlen had left a bar and driven to the Los Angeles airport for a flight to New York (though there was no reason to go to New York). Instead, he managed to board a flight to Hawaii. During the flight his alcoholic intake caught up with him and he became violently ill; as soon as the plane landed he was conveyed to the hospital. After detoxification, he was returned to the mainland, contrite and temporarily temperate.

Despite intermittent crises, time out for pacifying the critical Arlucks, and bouts of stomach pain that intimated serious illness, Harold Arlen and Dorothy Fields continued with their film score, which was ostensibly completed before the end of 1951. Generally, it is not regarded as one of Harold Arlen's major efforts. This might be attributed to his personal traumas at the time. Or it could be that his rich, gentle score was not enough to energize what the screen historian James Robert Parish dismisses as a "lumbering musical."

Lumbering it was, although the opening sequence holds promise with shots from several angles of the bustling canal springing into activity with the melting of the ice after the winter freeze. The event is announced by the chorus in "On the Erie Canal." The music is stirring as overhead visuals show the waterfront, barges, and shops filled with people hailing the coming of spring. This scene begins the film with the splashy impetus of a Broadway show. That mood continues with the introduction of Betty Grable in the lively "Today I Love Ev'rybody," joined by a children's chorus. It is a perky song, which Alec Wilder finds "fairly conventional, but not cliché," although an unconventional deceleration leads to a slower "ad lib. strain," a sixteen-bar verse that leads back into the chorus. This, too, added a touch of Broadway.

The Farmer Takes a Wife was a box-office failure not because of its quasi-Broadway musical content but because, despite its colorful outdoors sets, it is a dull film. The lively dance episodes, choreographed by Broadway's Jack Cole, include a kind of water ballet, with dancers cavorting in the canal, "We're in Business" (in which Cole employed his student-assistant, Gwen Verdon). The sparkle of these scenes dims in the dramatic segments (except for the final brawl across the decks of adjacent barges) and in the less energetic ballads, the bucolic "With the Sun Warm upon Me" and the period waltz "When I Close My Door." These songs alone are proof of Arlen's ability to leave his problems at Fields's bungalow door and produce fine, if not his best, songs. The quality of their songs transcended the quality of the film, however. It had taken more time than anyone had hoped, but when finished the score was more than adequate, and several songs are stamped with the Arlen trademark—little melodic, bluesy curlicues in the instrumental passages between sung phrases in "Somethin' Real Special," the unexpected interlude of "Today I Love Ev'rybody," the rhythmic pulse of "We're in Business," whose melody is based on repeated three-note phrases.

Another handicap, despite the presence of Thelma Ritter and Eddie Foy Jr., is that the film lacks humor. The latter contributes a vaudeville turn in a saloon with "Can You Spell Schenectady?" but has little else to do except dodge Ritter, bent on a sixth marriage. She does get one good line. Since her five marriages have been profitable (leaving her with the saloon, among other properties), she is ready to take up the penniless gambler Foy "on the house."

Dale Robertson, who had appeared primarily in westerns, brings a reasonably pleasing voice to his part, is convincingly the country boy, and delivers, with a straight face, the film's other funny line. He is explaining to Grable (by then drawn to him) why he did not marry the girl back home: her well-to-do father did not approve of him and forbade the marriage. Grable asks what the old man might do if country boy and city girl were to elope. Robertson replies, "He'd horsewhip me if he liked me better."

When the film opened, Bosley Crowther, in the *New York Times,* dismissed it but thought that its one redeeming feature was the "nice"—faint praise— Harold Arlen–Dorothy Fields score.

Early in 1952, with the final *Farmer* song finished, Arlen felt he had earned some time off after a full year of work and harrowing disruptions in his personal life. He had written about forty songs for five films, none of which appeared to amount to anything. Musical Hollywood was shrinking again. Maybe it was a good time to get away.

Harry Warren agreed. He, too, was tired of Hollywood and suggested a European vacation, with a good deal of time spent in the country of his ancestors, Italy. Buddy Morris was brought in on the plan, and it was decided that, with their wives, they would touch down in London, fly on to Rome, and then visit Naples and Pompeii. At the last stop, according to Morris, "Harold must have taken a photo of every statue." Anya, happily, was able to accompany them and, like Harold, relaxed and had a delightful time. She was comfortable in the company of Josephine Warren and Carolyn Morris.

They rounded off the trip by stopping off in Paris, where they attended a performance at the Folies-Bergère (an inveterate souvenir collector, Arlen brought home a program). While in Paris, he was taken with the paintings of a young Spanish artist named Montañes. Arlen acquired one of his signature pieces, an oil of a waif with large, melancholy eyes. When Arlen, who obviously saw something of himself in that lonely figure, wished to commission a portrait,

Montañes refused. Arlen persisted and the artist resisted, until he learned that his patron was the composer of "Stormy Weather."

The several weeks of touring Europe, including the beauties of Pompeii and the carefree, sybaritic moods of Paris nightlife, were healing. Anya was not threatened by Josephine and Carolyn, atypical Beverly Hills consorts. Harry Warren was a source of acerbic, funny, and often profane commentary. Anya delightedly participated in their tourism and laughter. To Harold it was like a return to an easier time at Earl Carroll's, the Cotton Club, or, best of all, the Croydon Hotel. Away from the pressures of Beverly Hills, and with him almost constantly, Anya Arlen was herself again.

Harold reveled in this second honeymoon. They were far from Hollywood and the studios that junked your work. It was a joyous time of renewal and buoyancy, simple joy.

But it would not last.

16

JUDY

*T*heir European idyll over, the travelers returned to California, the Arlens with renewed hope. For Harold, happy with Anya's return to herself, there was no professional prospect in his immediate future as far as he knew, no Broadway show, no film. Late in 1952 Hollywood was suffering through a musical film slump and investing in adaptations of Broadway hits rather than "originals." The next year, 1953, would be the year of *Call Me Madam, Gentlemen Prefer Blondes, The Band Wagon, The Beggar's Opera* (a top hit of 1758), *Kiss Me Kate,* and lesser efforts, but not one outstanding conceived-in-Hollywood musical.

Work now, as their plane approached Los Angeles, was essential. That year, 1952, had not seen one Arlen song published, and now that it was closing, happily he thought, he would get back to work.

"I always went back to Hollywood," Arlen told Max Wilk, more or less explaining his rare excursions to Broadway, "to the comforts of Beverly Hills. Kept on writing pictures. Some good, some bad. Kept on wandering from one lyricist to another. I don't know what the reason for that was. I suppose I didn't want to be pinned down." Later in the interview, however, he observed, "Maybe I should have written more for the theatre."

Soon after he and Anya had settled into their Beverly Hills home, Harold was invited to the Gershwin Plantation. Present at this meeting on a Sunday in January were Ira Gershwin and Moss Hart. Their subject: a film for Judy—Garland of course.

While the Arlens were in Europe, they had read about her third marriage to someone none of the party knew, Sidney Luft. The Arlens had been close to both of her preceding husbands—the composer and conductor David Rose and Vincente Minnelli, a friend since all had met during the production of *Hooray for What!* It was a small, warm circle. Anya had provided the title for one of Rose's most popular instrumental compositions, *Holiday for Strings,* and Minnelli had served as a permissive chaperon during Harold and Anya's courting days at the Croydon. A further coincidence: Ira Gershwin had been best man at the marriage of Judy Garland and Minnelli.

But Sidney Luft was an unknown quantity. He was, Hart informed them, to be the producer of the film. Though it was reputed that his Hollywood experience had been limited to the production of B pictures, his résumé emphasized his early career in the Royal Canadian Air Force and as a test pilot, as well as that he had "an extensive background in the entertainment world as a producer of Aquacades, stage musicals and motion pictures."

There was some skepticism, since neither Harold nor Ira had heard of any of these efforts. In addition, Gershwin harbored an innate aversion to amateurs, a mildly pejorative term in his lexicon. He was also cautious about unknown quantities. But Luft had succeeded in talking Jack Warner into investing in Luft's and Garland's production company, Transcona Enterprises, one of whose projects was to be a musical version of *A Star Is Born* in which she would have the lead part. This would be her first Hollywood film since *Summer Stock* in 1950.

With Warner Brothers, Judy Garland, Harold Arlen, and Moss Hart involved, Ira Gershwin sensed that enough professionals would be contributing to the film, and he, too, joined the effort. Writing with Arlen for Judy was enough to excite him.

As for Sidney Luft, Lauren Bacall best defined him when she said, "Sid was a wheeler-dealer, but not a bad guy. He and Judy were crazy about each other. He was very good for her. . . . She had lots of fears—she was terrified of going on stage, she was ruthless sometimes in dealing with people. But she needed constant reassurance; whatever quirks Sid may have had, he was the one who helped her get through."

It was Luft who reignited Garland's career after her divorce from Vincente Minnelli, a suicide attempt, a mental breakdown, and a final dismissal from MGM's *Annie Get Your Gun* for "unreliability." Luft, then (1950) associated with the William Morris Agency, booked her into the London Palladium, where she scored a triumphal comeback in a one-woman show. After further British success, Luft felt Garland was ready for a return to the States. On October 17, 1951, Judy Garland literally brought vaudeville back to New York's Palace Theatre after an eighteen-year hiatus. This marked the inception of the Judy cult that would in time take its toll, but that October, and beyond, she was adored and cheered, and she sold tickets. Her four-week booking was extended to nineteen. Such public demonstration of Judy Garland's "reliability" and of her control of audiences on both sides of the Atlantic assured Luft that it was time to think Hollywood.

When the record-breaking run at the Palace ended, they moved the show to the Los Angeles Philharmonic Auditorium in April 1952. The effect of Garland on her audiences was the same as in London and New York. She had returned to Hollywood with a decided bang, and certain wheels began turning. As a happy conclusion to all their accomplishment, Judy Garland married Sid Luft in June and settled in a new house on Mapleton Drive in Beverly Hills.

From there Luft initiated his wheeling and dealing. He had the idea that his new bride could star in a musical remake of the Janet Gaynor–Fredric March classic released in 1937. The plot, in a screenplay by Dorothy Parker, Alan Campbell, and Robert Carson, was a jaundiced view of Hollywood in which an aging, heavy-drinking actor discovers an unknown, ambitious actress and makes her a star. As her career flowers, his shrivels, and realizing he is a handicap to her, he commits suicide. All the plot required was a skillful rewrite and a change of the lead from an actress to a singer-actress.

When Luft revealed his idea to Garland, she laughed. She had wanted to do a film version of A Star Is Born since 1942, when she had appeared in a radio presentation on the Lux Radio Theatre. When she brought her idea to MGM it was rejected. L. B. Mayer saw its merit, but it was turned down by Nicholas Schenck, who could not visualize such a "sad and tragic story" as a "musical for our precious Judy."

Now, with Luft as producer, they would do it. As producer, Luft had to acquire the rights to the film (a tricky process that took time), raise the money, which he was able to do once Jack Warner came his way, and hire the people to make their dream a reality.

Once the final agreement with Warner was signed in December, the project was truly on its way. But that it was to be a troubled enterprise was ominously foreshadowed in November. On the twenty-first, Lorna Luft, their first child, was born. Four days later Judy Garland slashed her throat, and Sid Luft's quick actions were credited with saving his wife's life.

Such behavior did not go down well in Hollywood, and this could have had a disastrous effect on any contracts between Transcona and Warner. To quash the rumors that sped through Beverly Hills, the Lufts gave a party at their home early in December. Judy was as radiant and funny as ever, apparently recovered from childbirth, and except for a high-collared dress, revealed no signs of any suicide attempt. A few days later Jack Warner signed the contract.

Judy Garland contributed to the solution of Luft's search for a composer, script writer, and director. The first two were longtime friends, Harold Arlen and Moss Hart. For director she wanted George Cukor, with whom she had never worked, but admired.

The choice of lyricist was solved by Irving Lazar, who represented Arlen and Hart—and Ira Gershwin. Meanwhile, Luft was occupied with the search for a leading man; he began with Laurence Olivier and Richard Burton, both of whom rejected the offer. By early January Luft had begun to negotiate, in an informal way, with Cary Grant at the Hollywood Park racetrack. While Grant was his guest, Luft would broach casually the possibility of a part in *A Star Is Born.* He was not successful: Grant, though friendly, was businesslike, and his asking fee was impossible.

Moss Hart had already been working on the screenplay down in Palm Springs when, on that Sunday in early January 1953, he met with Ira Gershwin and Harold Arlen at the Gershwin home on North Roxbury Drive to discuss the songs. Hart was no novice to musicals. He had collaborated with Irving Berlin on the Broadway successes *Face the Music* and *As Thousands Cheer,* with Cole Porter on *Jubilee,* and with Ira Gershwin and Kurt Weill on *Lady in the Dark.* His most recent Hollywood musical had been *Hans Christian Anderson,* with songs by Frank Loesser and starring Danny Kaye; it was one of the major box-office attractions of 1953 (and Hart's script was the twenty-second; producer Sam Goldwyn had rejected the previous twenty-one).

Moss Hart clearly knew his way around the fabrication of a musical. He outlined the plot of his film, presented a list of seven song spots, and described what their function would be. As he read from his list, Ira Gershwin made his own.

Hart's list began, "1. Benefit show—Esther (Garland) and orchestra." In this opening scene, Hart satirizes a typical Hollywood benefit in the Shrine Auditorium in Los Angeles, with klieg lights, limousines, important persons in furs and evening dress. Backstage are cowboys on horseback, dancers, and a band, not to mention confusion. The scene, Hart told them, introduces a band singer, Esther Blodgett, and an inebriated backstage troublemaker, Norman Maine (not yet cast). Maine belligerently shoves his way onstage in the middle of Esther's song, which she is performing with a vocal-dancing quartet and the band. Maine dodges the attempts to get him off the stage, and the quick-witted Esther, arms around him to steady him, makes him a part of their routine. The boozy star completes the act, saved from making a fool of himself before most of Hollywood, and goes off to tumultuous applause. Sobered somewhat, Maine graciously takes Esther out for a bow. As Hart described the scene, Arlen and Gershwin saw its point; the two major characters meet, their characters and talent are defined, and the audience is prepared for the birth of a new star.

What he wanted here, Hart said, was a rhythm number, "the kind of song you can never hear the lyrics to." Arlen chuckled to see Ira Gershwin's eyebrows rise quizzically. Ira then made a note: "Shrine Auditorium—Judy and band."

Next on Hart's breakdown was "2. 'Dive' song—Esther and Small Group." This song, as Hart sensed it, was the film's most significant. The dive he visualized was the nightclub in which Esther and the band regularly appeared. It is after hours and dark, but the band and Esther, keyed up after their auditorium appearance, relax with an early-morning jam session. It is during this song that a now completely sober Norman Maine finds them. As he quietly sits in the shadows of the club, he realizes that Esther is wasted singing with a little band in an obscure club. She is not only a great singer but an extraordinary talent as well. Hart's description of the scene and the song gave Gershwin an idea.

And so the afternoon continued as noted by Ira:

3. Preparation in rehearsal (gay song) (Then at preview complete #)
4. Song on sound stage (proposal with interruptions)
5. Motel song (probably one to reprise later)
6. Prop # Tour de force (in Malibu sings all parts & imitations) [Hart's note was a little more explicit: "Malibu beach house song (funny song; she tries to cheer Norman up)." To Ira it was a "Prop #" because in the performance Garland uses several household items at hand to improvise costumes.]
7. Reprise of 5 probably

Hart left, and composer and lyricist agreed that they would begin at the beginning, with the "Shrine song." Harold was aware of Ira's preference for up-tempo numbers, as Hart had suggested. Three days later, he returned to the Gershwin house with a tune he liked and, once played, Ira liked. In a couple of weeks—with some time out for Gershwin's bout with a case of Spanish flu he brought back from Las Vegas—they had a lively musical "opener" for the film, "Gotta Have Me Go with You."

Gershwin's affliction had been successfully treated with a new antibiotic, Ilotycin, but Arlen's symptoms at the end of January 1953 were not readily treated. He suffered from stomach discomfort, chronic but not severe, which he chose to live with. In part, he attributed this upset to his concern for his father, Samuel, who had become ill and was bedridden and weak. Possibly worse, Anya, once back in hostile Beverly Hills, retrogressed. In one especially upsetting incident, she slapped Celia Arluck's face. Harold realized that he could not contend with Anya's outbursts and that she required treatment and medication. Jerry Arlen, not reluctantly, returned her to the care of Dr. Morris Steinman, and again she was placed in the sanitarium at Malibu. She would remain there for the next six years.

Such was the state of Arlen's personal life at the time he presented Gershwin with the happy-go-lucky "Gotta Have Me Go with You." The two collaborators then decided to try Hart's "Dive Song." Harold came fully prepared. But first he had to captivate Gershwin.

"I know how Ira's ear works," he recalled years later, "and I was sure he would like the theme . . . one that I'd had for some time—an eight-bar phrase." This was, in fact, the opening phrase of a song he had written years before with Johnny Mercer. In relating the story behind the song to Max Wilk, Arlen did not name names. In explaining to Wilk how the fate of a song often depended on a memorable title or, even more, a phrase in the lyric that matches melody, he recalled this particular song.

"I wrote a song," he said, "with a pretty goddam wonderful lyric-writer. He brought me a lyric that didn't have any strength. Sometimes a lyric depletes a melody, just as a poor melody can deplete a good lyric. The lyric he brought in didn't really weaken it, it just made nothing out of the song.

"Fortunately, it came out of the show I was doing [*St. Louis Woman,* possibly, though he did not identify it], and then later I got another assignment and I knew this other lyricist might like it."

Gershwin's ears perked up when he heard Arlen play the eight bars, an insistent melody over an equally urgent harmony. Short phrases obsessively repeat a few chromatic notes, then the narrow range opens up to an expansive minor seventh. Gershwin was mesmerized.

"Play it again, Harold," Ira suggested. Gershwin listened intently, pencil and pad in hand. When Arlen stopped he said, "The man that got away?"—words that fit the close of the eight bars, at the climax.

"I like" was Arlen's response, and they began to work on their Dive Song, in the phrase of the historian James R. Morris, "the quintessential torch song, and completely American in thought and musical form."

After a couple of rejected beginnings—"The song is played out" and "There's just no sleeping"—Gershwin found the words for the song's assertive opening (there is no verse):

> *The night is bitter,*
> *The stars have lost their glitter,*
> *The winds grow colder*
> *And suddenly you're older*
> *And all because of the man that got away.*

Both were pleased with what they had wrought. They now had two songs, with four or five to go. The day's work done, they would take time out for a snack or move downstairs into what might be called the recreation room. Its major furnishing was a pool table and to one side, a desk and assorted file cabinets for the growing Gershwin archive, the province of a former UCLA professor, Lawrence D. Stewart. He had resigned from the Department of English to assist Gershwin in assembling and annotating Gershwin's papers for the Library of Congress. An Arlen devotee, Stewart observed the composition of *A Star Is Born* with warm concern and made notes of each day's progress.

While Arlen was not a skilled billiards player, he and Gershwin shot a few balls and often spent the afternoons watching television—the news, sports. Both were football fans and frequently wagered on the games. Ira was devoted to UCLA, to whose home games he had been awarded a lifetime season pass since 1936, after he and his brother reworked "Strike Up the Band" to be the university's official song.

The studio's piano-vocal copy of "The Man That Got Away" is dated February 19, 1953, suggesting that possibly the song had been completed a week or more before (another song, "It's a New World," number 5 on Hart's list as "Honeymoon song in motel," is dated the twentieth). Between the completion of "Gotta Have Me Go with You" and "The Man That Got Away," or soon after, Harold Arlen suffered a heavy bereavement, the death of his father. Early in February Samuel had weakened severely and soon after died in the hospital of liver cancer. Harold and Jerry Arlen tried to console their distraught mother as well as attend to the funeral arrangements.

Once through this trying time, Harold took up his work with Gershwin, who wrote to a friend, "Our work has been somewhat delayed because of Arlen's father's illness and subsequent death—but Harold is taking it exceptionally well." He also praised Arlen's "wonderful spirit."

That spirit was evident in an incident that occurred after they had finished "The Man That Got Away." After two weeks of solid work, Arlen begged off for a weekend, announcing to Gershwin, "Ira, I want to go to Palm Springs."

"Don't," was Gershwin's response.

"Why not?"

"Well," Gershwin explained, "Moss is there, and Judy is there, and you'll be playing the songs for them and it's much too early. You'll spoil things."

Harold assured him. "Ira, I promise you. I'm not going there to see Moss and Judy. I just want a break."

Palm Springs, less than a hundred miles east of Los Angeles, was a small affluent community, a resort situated in a virtual oasis. Palm Springs to Hollywoodians was much like the Hamptons, in far eastern Long Island, are to Manhattanites: a place for expensive relaxation.

Arlen continues his story (as told to Lawrence D. Stewart): "I went out that Saturday morning. Because I wasn't feeling too well, I wasn't supposed to play. But I saw Judy and Sid, large as life, just teeing off [at the Tamarisk golf course]. I said: 'I'll walk around with you.' Nobody said anything about the picture."

As he followed the Lufts, he unconsciously began whistling, very softly, "The Man That Got Away." "I don't know what tempted me," he told Stewart, "it was a kind of tease. . . . I love Ira and I love Judy, and, well, I just whistled."

A few whistles later, Garland turned to him and asked, "Harold, what are you whistling?"

"Nothing, I don't know," he told her, but went on with his tease. Unlike the cautious Gershwin, he had no doubts about the strength of that song, whose lyric he pronounced "glorious."

Garland stopped in her tracks and demanded, "Harold, what *are* you whistling? Don't tell me it's something from the picture."

"No," he fibbed.

"Harold," Garland said, "I've got an idea it *must* be from the picture—don't hold out on me."

At this point in the confrontation, Luft hit his ball into a sand trap and, while he dug himself out, Judy Garland led Arlen into the clubhouse, sat him at the piano, and ordered him to play.

"It's just something we've been working on," he cautioned her. "I don't know how well you'll like it." He played both "Gotta Have Me Go with You" and "The Man That Got Away." When Luft came into the room, Arlen played the songs for him. "They went wild with joy," Arlen told Stewart. "Ira, Schmira," he thought. "He'll be happy about it."

The Lufts took Arlen to the Harts'; Mrs. Hart was the former opera, theater, and film vocalist Kitty Carlisle. They, too, were excited by what they heard and even insisted that they call Gershwin to tell him how much they liked both songs.

"Don't," Arlen pleaded. "I promised him not to play them."

That request went unheeded, and all four took turns on the phone to tell Gershwin how wonderful they thought the songs were. He was delighted. "And when I came back he was beaming and never said a word about my broken promise."

Back at work, Arlen and Gershwin moved more speedily than Luft in his search for Norman Maine, after Cary Grant could not come to terms that satisfied Jack Warner. After going through nearly a dozen possible co-stars, including Humphrey Bogart and Frank Sinatra, Luft, working through an agent, Charles Feldman, signed James Mason for the part. As it turned out, this was an excellent choice. Mason became a member of the *A Star Is Born* company in May 1953.

In mid-April Arlen and Gershwin had completed, they thought, the score; in addition to the first two songs, they had written a throwaway television commercial ("Coconut Oil Shampoo," a calypso) and four more songs: "Lose That Long Face," "Here's What I'm Here For," "It's a New World," and "Someone at Last."

Hart was revising his screenplay, and plans were under way to begin production as soon as possible. But even sooner the Judy Garland of old began reemerging: she postponed or skipped costume and makeup tests. Her weight fluctuated. These delays disturbed Jack Warner, who sent a memo to Luft saying, "I am worried about all the delays and nervous tension, and we want to get this picture going."

On August 9 Warner sent another memo to Luft confirming the start date of the production: September 1, when shooting would begin. Four days later, on

August 13, Warner production number 386 officially got under way. On the twenty-first Judy Garland arrived at Sound Stage 9 to begin recording the songs under the conductor Ray Heindorf. Garland, who had been taking Dexedrine to lose weight, was in a foul mood. She and her old friend and vocal coach Hugh Martin disagreed about her interpretation of "Here's What I'm Here For." On the twenty-third she recorded "Gotta Have Me Go with You." The next day gossip columns spread the word that Judy Garland and Hugh Martin had exchanged salty comments, at times at high volume, about her vocalizing.

Martin, who knew Garland's voice, its capabilities and limits, felt she was straining. He had written for her (*Meet Me in St. Louis*) and had frequently served as her accompanist; he felt she was not doing justice to Arlen's music. A devotee of Arlen's works, Martin was fond of the man and believed the songs could be better served. He may not have been aware of the effect of Garland's "diet pills" on her performance and temperament.

The big blowup came on September 4 (three days after the first announced start date, which was postponed to the sixteenth). Neither Arlen nor Gershwin was invited to the recording sessions, but the lyricist, concerned about the rumors and gossip circulating about the film, sent Lawrence Stewart to Sound Stage 9 to look in on the recording of "The Man That Got Away."

What he witnessed did not bode well for the picture. The song's orchestral arrangement, by Skip Martin (no relation to Hugh), existed in two keys. Ray Heindorf found when he ran through each with Garland that one was too high and the other too low. He transposed the orchestration to a middle key, C major. But Garland preferred the higher version (in D-flat), which afforded her the opportunity for a bravura performance. Hugh Martin found that interpretation, Stewart heard him say, "too loud and brassy"; he wanted the song to be "sweet and in a lower key."

Garland disagreed, and as reported in the next day's *Variety*, "a heated verbal hassle" ensued. That puts it gently. The argument was blazing and profane. During a pause for breath, Martin stood, stalked off the stage, and that evening was aboard an airliner for New York.

While the personal tensions, delays, and technical and financial problems that would afflict the making of *A Star Is Born* were beyond the ken of Arlen and Gershwin, they, too, would be drawn into the production maelstrom as time passed. After yet another missed start date, the production finally began shooting on October 12.

Following the completion of their *Star* songs, Arlen and Gershwin rested and turned to other things. Harold Arlen, temporarily adrift, spent a good deal of time with his grieving mother and would regularly drive to Malibu to visit a rehospitalized, sedated Anya. He began considering a move back to New York but had not made up his mind. He was faced with closing the house and arranging for the storage of his papers, books, recordings, and art. Depressed, he chose to ignore the mail; even small bills went unpaid (followed by dunning reminders), fan mail went unanswered, royalty checks were not deposited.

When Ira Gershwin called in October, Harold was happy to take on a new picture, if only to be working; work released him from his day-to-day sorrows.

Two of Gershwin's friends, the producer William Perlberg and the director George Seaton, were planning an adaptation of a Clifford Odets play, *The Country Girl*, for Paramount. It would star Bing Crosby as an alcoholic singer on the way down. Seaton would write the screenplay as well as direct. Gershwin was assured that it would not require a great deal of work, just a few songs for Crosby to underscore his failure. As Gershwin visualized the film, it "was a strong psychological study," and "the result won't be a musical."

He was right; the script called for four musical numbers, which Arlen and he wrote in the period of several weeks beginning in November 1953 and finishing in January 1954. As they had with *A Star Is Born*, Arlen and Gershwin worked at an easy pace with time out for talk and television. They discussed the film version of Cole Porter's *Kiss Me, Kate*, which had been released in October. On New Year's Day 1954 they made their traditional bet on the Rose Bowl game. Arlen took Michigan State and Gershwin, as ever, was faithful to UCLA. As usual, Arlen had picked the winning team.

Soon after, the *Country Girl* score was completed. Gershwin reported to a friend that the songs were "well liked," and that "one number ('The Land around Us') is given a stage setting." In this scene Crosby, having conquered his alcoholism with the help of his faithful wife (Grace Kelly), makes his triumphant comeback to the musical stage. This number, in fact, was a long, vapid sequence and hardly a credit to Arlen and Gershwin. In the film it appears to be an *Oklahoma!* reject.

Arlen's judgment was succinct: "We didn't give it our best." The two published songs, however, were quite good, especially a characteristic Arlen blues, "Dissertation on the State of Bliss," whose title, thankfully, appears nowhere in the lyric. It was originally entitled "Love and Learn"; as Gershwin later explained. "I subsequently learned that there had been at least three songs so named, and when one of the creators of one of them objected, it was a simple matter to make the phrase the subtitle and to decorate the number with the rather impressive 'Dissertation on the State of Bliss.' " Gershwin kindly omitted the name of the objecting creator and refrained from pointing out that song titles (like those of books and movies) cannot be copyrighted.

A month later, in February, Gershwin could report that the filming of *A Star Is Born* "should be finished . . . by the end of the month. Almost like the Von Stroheim days—twenty or so weeks." But he and Arlen were not finished, as he would learn.

On March 25, with Arlen in New York, Gershwin saw a rough cut of the film and enthusiastically found it "great in looks and sound." But, he added,

"There's only one problem: what to do about a production number that's to wind up the first half (the showing is to have an intermission—the picture runs about three hours so far). Have no idea what's going to happen to this spot. Arlen and I wrote two songs for it ('Green Light Ahead' and 'I'm Off the Downbeat'), both good by anyone's standards." A third, "Dancing Partner," exists in Arlen's holograph, as an unharmonized single-line melody; it was probably not considered for the spot.

Ira continued with their problem: "It seems the choreographer couldn't get any production ideas. Could be they may even interpolate an outside number, which would be a shame. However, there's still a chance that Arlen may be able to leave N.Y. for a week or so and we'll try to give them what they think they want." That Gershwin was unhappy with the turn of events is clear in the touch of sarcasm in the last sentence, for he was skeptical. He doubted that "they"—an anxious Jack Warner and a harried Sid Luft—had any real idea of what they thought they wanted. Also, at the time, late March 1954, Harold Arlen was unable to leave New York.

In contemplating the musical number to precede the intermission, Jack Warner said, "We need a big musical number here," and Luft's opinion of the two new Arlen-Gershwin songs was that they were "bad songs."

Luft contacted Roger Edens at Metro, invited him to his home, and asked him to concoct a big, exciting number to close the first half of the picture. Edens had helped stage and arrange Garland's Palace show; Luft hoped he could work the same magic for *A Star Is Born*. There was a legal technicality: because Edens was under contract to Metro, he could not do any credited work for Warner Brothers. From behind the scenes, he worked out a musical quasi-biography of the Judy Garland character with the aid of a young songwriter, Leonard Gershe.

They called it "Born in a Trunk." The original portion of their piece, into which they wove a half dozen songs by others, related the saga of Esther's long struggle to "overnight" stardom. Garland and Luft loved the idea, and Garland suggested the interpolated songs. The length of the film and added costs bloated into what Stanley Green perspicaciously characterized as a "rousing but superfluous 25-minute mini-musical." On its own it was an exciting Garland tour de force; in the film it was stultifying.

When he learned of this newest tack in the twisted tale of making *A Star Is Born*, Ira Gershwin was unhappy but resigned. In April he philosophically said, "they [Warner and Luft] decided that any one new number wouldn't be socky enough . . . they feel it's some kind of insurance and with 4½ mill. invested so far, I hope they will find these additional costs worthwhile." He was more critical in a note he had prepared for his *Lyrics on Several Occasions* some years later. In his annotation for "I'm Off the Downbeat" Ira wrote, "It added fifteen minutes to a three-hour film, held up the show, and cost $300,000. Big mistake (but all none of my business)." On thinking it over, Gershwin decided to delete this observation from the book. But once the film was released, the addition of "Born in a Trunk" *would* become his business, two songs' worth.

Late in 1954, by ironic coincidence, *A Star Is Born* and *The Country Girl* were released within a month of each other. Both films were thus eligible for the next year's Academy Awards, leading to a concatenation of frustration and bitter disappointment. Judy Garland and Grace Kelly were nominated for the Best Actress Oscar, "The Man That Got Away" for Best Song. *The Country Girl* also had a Best Picture nomination; a strange absence in that catagory was *A Star Is Born*, undoubtedly one of the best pictures of 1954. James Mason and Bing Crosby received nominations for Best Actor. The coming awards ceremony generated tensions, excitement, and expectations.

Oscar night, March 30, 1955, was more bizarre than normal. In anticipation of a Judy Garland Oscar, a television crew arrived at the hospital where she had given birth to Joey Luft the night before. Forbidden to set up their cameras inside the hospital, the crew erected a four-story construction outside her window and set up their cameras. A nurse was drafted to open the venetian blinds, on cue, when Judy Garland would exchange quips with Bob Hope and make her acceptance speech from her bed, "in a new bed jacket . . . flat on my back trying to look cute." Lauren Bacall was to serve as her proxy at the ceremonies to receive her Oscar.

Grace Kelly won Best Actress for *The Country Girl*.

Marlon Brando, not Mason, won Best Actor, for *On the Waterfront*.

The lugubrious but widely popular "Three Coins in the Fountain" (Jule Styne and Sammy Cahn) was selected as Best Song. *A Star Is Born* was eliminated in its other categories, six in all, and received no award. Despite mostly fine reviews, especially for Garland and Mason, *A Star Is Born* was the big loser of 1954.

The indignities had begun even before the premiere, when Jack Warner, concerned about the film's length, began cutting it. This, in turn, dismayed George Cukor, who had had nothing to do with the "Born in a Trunk" portion and who found Warner's snippings "inept and insensitive . . . muddying things up, making scenes pointless and incomprehensible." Warner was so daunted by Cukor's fury that he permitted him to put most of the pieces back and to do his own editing. Cukor eliminated a portion of "Born in a Trunk" (a death scene and "When My Sugar Walks Down the Street") and a reprise of "It's a New World." Before the official premiere, however, further cuts were made by an anonymous film editor. When Cukor saw the film, he believed that the studio had mutilated his work and boycotted it for the rest of his life (even the restored version released in 1983).

There was worse for Arlen and Gershwin in the near future. After the film's New York opening in two Times Square movie houses, complaints about the length came in. Furthermore, theater managers were losing money on the two-a-day showings and clamored for a film of more or less standard length, without an intermission. When the reedited, abbreviated *A Star Is Born* was released, it was missing several dramatic snippets and two complete musical numbers, "Lose That Long Face" and "Here's What I'm Here For."

Arlen's attitude was "What can you do?" and Gershwin's, "None of my business." He was busy on his lyrics collection. Arlen did not attend the Academy Awards in March 1955. He was then busy in recording studios in New York. He also had a beautiful but sick show on his hands.

YEAR OF
TRANSFUSIONS

*E*arly in November 1953, while Ira Gershwin and Harold Arlen were working on *The Country Girl*, Arlen received an early draft of a play entitled *House of Flowers*. It was the work of a bright young (then twenty-nine) man of American letters, Truman Capote.

The sender of the packet was himself a young (about thirty-five) man of the theater, Arnold Saint Subber (he eventually dropped the Arnold). Born to the theater (a grandfather made costumes and his parents ran a theater ticket agency), he began as a teenage office boy in the Lee Shubert organization. After less menial experiences as production assistant for assorted shows, he made his first major contribution to the Broadway musical with Cole Porter's *Kiss Me, Kate* in 1948. Two years later, his production of Porter's *Out of This World* failed. But while in London for the production of *Kiss Me, Kate*, he read the galleys of a Capote novel, *The Grass Harp*, which convinced Saint Subber that the story and Capote belonged in the theater. The dramatic version of the novel failed also, but he continued to have faith in Capote the playwright.

Nor had Capote lost faith in himself. In 1950 his short story "House of Flowers" won an O. Henry Award. Three years later, while involved in the writing of John Huston's *Beat the Devil* (starring Humphrey Bogart and Jennifer Jones), he adapted his story into a play, which he sent to Saint Subber. The producer was enthralled with what he read, sent a copy off to Arlen, then traveled to Italy to get Capote to transform his play into a musical with music by Harold Arlen. Capote's response was, "Who's Harold Arlen?"

Saint Subber easily enlightened him with a list of some of Capote's favorite songs, especially "Stormy Weather," "Blues in the Night," and "Over the Rainbow." Capote agreed to convert *House of Flowers* into a musical.

Arlen was familiar with Capote's work. Like Ira Gershwin, he kept up with the current literary scene, had read the celebrated *Other Voices, Other Rooms,* with its infamous photoportrait by Harold Talma of a boyish Capote languidly peering from a sofa in a checkered vest, bow tie, and bangs. Arlen was impressed with Capote's writing and was attracted to the new play. But, to Saint Subber's disappointment, Arlen did not believe he was the composer for the job. *House of Flowers,* Arlen told Saint Subber, seemed more suitable to the talents of such a pop-serious composer as Gian Carlo Menotti, then noted for his well-received score for the 1951 television opera *Amahl and the Night Visitors.*

Though disappointed, Saint Subber persisted, phoning frequently from New York. In Beverly Hills, his work on *The Country Girl* finished, Arlen reread Capote's play. The original story had been inspired by Capote's sojourn in Port-au-Prince, Haiti, in 1948. Bored with drinking in his elegant hotel's bar, Capote wandered into the city's suburbs and, along a country road, found a small settlement of houses near the edge of town. Upon being invited onto a porch by an attractive young woman, he learned that he had discovered a cluster of bordellos.

He became a regular visitor, and rocking in a chair on the porches (there were about four "houses"), he drank, exchanged gossip, and joked; he was not in the least bored. The young women found him amusing and adorable—and they loved the American beer he brought from town.

Capote's House of Flowers is run by Madame Fleur, who names her charges horticulturally: Tulip, Gladiola, Pansy, and her newest intern, a young innocent named Ottilie, who will be called Violet once she has passed the test. An interloper, also a young innocent, a country boy named Royal, complicates the madame's plan for Ottilie. He hopes to take her to live in his tree house, which is, in fact, made of flowers. The young lovers face two obstacles, Monsieur Jamison, to whom Madame Fleur has promised Ottilie, and Royal's evil, voodoo-practicing grandmother, Old Bonaparte. The story's comic subplot concerns the professional rivalry between the madames of adjacent houses, Madame Fleur and Madame Tango. The latter's staff also bears fanciful names, such as Mamselle Honolulu and Mamselle Cigarette.

As he reread the play, Arlen was captivated by the possibilities: the colorful, exotic sets, bright costumes, poetic songs, and vivid percussion, characteristic of West Indian music. He changed his mind and, as he recalled later, "I jumped at it because I really liked the story and, especially, because I admire Capote's work. I said yes, and don't regret it. I had a good time writing it." Writing with the talented, mischievous Capote may have been fun, but the *House of Flowers* experience proved to be like a trip through purgatory.

The beginning of the Arlen-Capote collaboration was unique. "We worked together the first three months without personal contact," Capote told the writer William K. Zinsser.

> During this time I was living in Rome, while his base was California. I would send him scenes and scraps of lyrics, and back came homemade phonograph records: Arlen playing melodies that the tentative lyrics had tentatively suggested, singing and talking to me.
>
> We had never met, I knew very little about him. It was quite odd, listening to this disembodied voice and trying to derive from it some notion of what sort of man he might be, my collaborator. Obviously he was a gentle man, a modest one, but someone capable of immense intensity; and, had I not known differently, I would have thought he was a Negro. His voice, especially his singing voice, had a warm, plaintive, muddy-colored tone, and the diction also had a certain very pleasant Negro quality.

Their first long-distance song was suggested to Arlen by a Haitian folk belief from Capote's story: if you catch a bee and hold it in your closed hand, thinking of your love, and the bee does not sting, then you have found your true love.

In December Capote received an acetate disc from Arlen that opened with, "Dear Truman: Introducing little ol' me, Harold." He tells Capote that he feels "flip about a particular tune," then goes on to demonstrate it. The recording continues: "In the [phone] discussion the other night, I thought that this might set quite a charming key for Miss Ottilie in the first scene with the Houngan [the voodoo doctor], and I will give you what I *think* may be workable. I'm sure the tune has enough quality and captures the mood. I hope the dummy few lines—and I call them that because they *are* that—mean something to you to clarify what I'm stumbling about." (A "dummy lyric" is a provisional text that helps clarify the meter and scansion required of the final lyric.) Arlen plays the melody after reading from the dialogue between Ottilie and the Houngan, then sings:

> *When a bee lies sleepin'*
> *In the palm of your hand,*
> *And true love comes a-creepin'*
> *And your heart understand . . .*

To emphasize the melody, Arlen plays it three times, adding, "More lyric here, we hope," and hums along with the piano. After a couple more suggestions for the scene, Arlen assures Capote that his dummy lyric could be "corrected later."

The final lyric would indeed be expanded and "corrected" (the melody would also be slightly changed), although Arlen's initial two lines would be retained for the final version of the exquisite song, "A Sleepin' Bee."

As Capote admitted to Zinsser, "I had no true understanding of songwriting (and Lord knows, still do not). But Arlen, who I suppose had never worked with an amateur before, was tolerant and infinitely encouraging and, well, just a gent about the whole thing." Thus, they corresponded through the rest of December and into early 1954. By January Capote had moved to Paris and put in a call to Arlen, who was still in Beverly Hills but preparing to move to New York. Arlen was excited about an idea he had for the title song and, for what seemed to Capote hours, played the melody that became Royal's "House of Flowers." In the same costly, unorthodox manner they produced one of Arlen's classic songs, "I Never Has Seen Snow." By January both writers were on their way to Manhattan.

Abe Berman's staff had found the expansive Park Avenue apartment of the British vocalist Constance Carpenter, who had replaced the fatally ill Gertrude Lawrence in *The King and I* and was then on tour. Although he was certain that the move away from Hollywood was permanent, Arlen traveled light. Except for a few books and paintings, virtually everything in the Beverly Hills house was boxed and placed in storage. Sadly, he realized that it was better for all if Anya remained in Malibu. The former Carpenter apartment was furnished, and it was an easy transition to settle in with Celia Arluck and Jerry. It had already been decided that Jerry would be the conductor of the show.

When Capote and Arlen met in February, "I found all my long-distance impressions confirmed," Capote told Zinsser. "The sadness, the echo of loneliness that wails through much of Arlen's music, seemed to me the foundation of his sensibility, for he is obsessed by the tragic view of life." Capote was not aware of Anya in California, for Arlen rarely shared his troubles even with friends. "At the same time, amid the sighs, the long sad looks, laughter was always ready to run rampant. He had one of the most distinctive laughs I've ever heard—a wild high-pitched chuckling that reddens his face and fills his eyes with tears."

The work on *House of Flowers* continued at 375 Park Avenue, with Capote— "Tru" to Harold—a regular habitué. In Arlen's relaxed presence, he made himself readily at home. Before Arlen's mother realized who Capote was—in informal slacks and sweater Tru seemed to her to be a high school senior playing hookey—she slapped his hand when she caught him with it in the refrigerator.

They worked in Arlen's bedroom, where a piano had been placed. Still relaxed, Capote stretched, or curled up, on the couch, as the composer remembered, "thinking and making his little notes [Capote's handwriting was near microscopic], and I would be making my large ones on a big drawing tablet." When they agreed, more or less, on a lyric, Arlen's eternal question was, "Does it sing?"

Soon after their initial meeting, Arlen was brought into Capote's circle; Capote was already, in the phrase of John Malcolm Brinnin, "the mascot of café society" and cultivated the wealthy, the celebrated, and the notorious. On Arlen's forty-ninth birthday, Truman Capote had been booked into the Ninety-second Street Y's Poetry Center to read from his works, a performance that Brinnin, the center's director, described as a tour de force "that began in a low key and ended in clamor." The Arlen birthday celebration could not be so readily described; it was neither low key nor clamorous.

Brinnin, after finishing up at the Y, arrived at the Arlen apartment around midnight. A "bushy-haired man" told him to deposit his coat on a bed, in which he found the playwright William Inge fast asleep. The bushy-haired man was himself a playwright, George S. Kaufman. Capote appeared, offering to introduce Brinnin around. He saw Joan McCracken, who since *Bloomer Girl* had appeared in *Billion Dollar Baby* and was currently dancing in Rodgers and Hammerstein's *Me and Juliet.* She was the ex-wife of a former dancer turned writer, Jack Dunphy, who had left her for Capote. Brinnin noticed that she was frightfully thin and smoking a black cigarette with a gold tip.

More spectacular was Marlene Dietrich, "wearing something less like fabric than molten silver" and standing near a sofa with the actor Montgomery Clift, in a too-large suit. They were locked in close embrace and exchanging what Brinnin believed were monosyllables and fervent kisses.

As Brinnin attempted to cross the room to speak with the *New Yorker* writer Janet Flanner, he was interrupted when the host sat at the piano to play and sing what he had written for "Judy's next picture"—"The Man That Got Away." Brinnin was unimpressed and recalled that Arlen's voice "scratched at every phrase."

Brinnin's traverse was interrupted again when, at Dietrich's suggestion, Abe Burrows relieved Arlen at the keyboard. Dietrich requested that Burrows sing his "Holland Song," a party song that would have entertained the audiences at the old Cotton Club and to which Arlen would not have signed his name. He politely and dubiously applauded.

The party ended around four in the morning: tired and not feeling well, Arlen went to bed hoping that the festivities had not disturbed his mother.

A day or two after, as he and Capote began the mildly suggestive "Two Ladies in de Shade of de Banana Tree," Arlen collapsed with severe abdominal pains.

Taken to Doctors Hospital, he was relieved to see his friend and former resident at the Croydon Hotel during the Cotton Club period, Dr. Miguel Elias. There were signs of internal hemorrhaging, and Elias urgently suggested that immediate exploratory surgery be done to determine the cause. As the doctor explained the situation to Jerry Arlen and Abe Berman, Harold Arlen realized that his was a serious predicament.

"Harold," Elias said, "I think we should operate. Do you agree?"

Arlen assented, and as he drifted into the pleasant haze of sedation and was wheeled into the operating theater, the last thing he remembered was Berman's exclamation, "We don't even have a will!"

Assisted by a half dozen physicians, Elias proceeded carefully and was appalled by what he found: a profusely bleeding, ulcerated liver. This condition was almost always fatal and inoperable. Feeling helpless, he staunched the bleeding and closed the incision. Elias's one consolation was that the liver is an organ capable of regeneration—although he had doubts about Arlen's. The hospital staff could only give him transfusions and wait.

In his two decades as a practicing physician, Elias had never seen anyone who could take so much blood (or lose such quantities) over so short a period of time. The Year of the Transfusions, as Arlen laughingly referred to it later, had begun. Miraculously, within a few days he was still alive and anxious to return to work.

Capote recalled how this "brave gent," "against all doctors' orders, against all laws of human fortitude as well, . . . continued composing. It was one rainy winter afternoon, while he was hospitalized, that we made up [in fact, completed] 'Two Ladies in De Shade of De Banana Tree'—Arlen, weak and ghost-pale, rapping out the rhythm with a pencil and humming at, very literally, death's door." At another work session, Arlen remembered, his performance was impeded by an intravenous tube. He tapped out the beat with a spoon on a dinner tray until the head nurse arrived to stop the noise.

Capote was a regular visitor, and his presence brightened Arlen's afternoons. His collaborator would sweep into the hospital room, trailing a long scarf and bubbling over with gossip—from the upper reaches of society, usually—picked up in his haunts, the Plaza Oak Room, the Colony, or the Blue Angel. Arlen's circle—the theater, music, Hollywood—also fascinated Capote. Usually his first action was to riffle through the composer's messages and mail, in search of show-business grist for his gossip mill. Amused, Arlen one day hid the day's collection of communications. After a quick search, a frustrated Capote exclaimed, "Dads, where are they?"

As he improved, to the surprise of many, Arlen became more sportive. Capote arrived on another afternoon, made his search, and triumphantly held up the day's cache. One envelope was addressed to him, and upon tearing it open, he read:

T——
Aren't you ashamed of yourself,
you little bastard?
H——

Not in the least.

As soon as Arlen was released, they took up work again at 375 Park Avenue.

Arlen was shaky, medicated, and on a rigorous diet—no alcohol, no greasy foods, even the crust of bread was stricken from his intake. But he could sit at the piano for a time as he and Capote created their songs for a beautifully burgeoning score.

Their sessions continued until April, as they worked toward the summer rehearsals, when Arlen suffered severe esophageal bleeding. Elias realized this was a most serious aftermath of the initial emergency, that it was more life-threatening, and that surgery would be futile if not fatal. He impeded the bleeding with an infusion of the drug vasopressin, then inserted a tube, to which were attached stomach and esophageal balloons. Inflated, these stopped the hemorrhaging, after which he stabilized his patient's condition with an injection of a sclerosing agent.

Once again, contrary to every medical expectation, Arlen survived, and the year of the transfusions continued. To the annoyance of Dr. Elias, there were complications. This was nationally announced in print by John O'Hara in his column in *Collier's*. He referred to Arlen as his "favorite meteorologist" thanks to "Stormy Weather" and "Ill Wind." "Harold is an old friend of mine," he began, explaining that they had met at the home of Ira Gershwin, "and when I heard he was in the hospital I wanted to go to see him, but then I read that a frequent visitor to his bedside was Marlene Dietrich."

Dietrich was only half of the complications, though she was the most troublesome. Notorious as a show-business angel of mercy, she attended to her ill friends with a vengeance that was no doubt appreciated, though not by medical personnel. Elias found her particularly meddlesome when she insisted on participation in medical consultations. One afternoon when he looked in on Arlen, he found Dietrich in his bed with her blouse unbuttoned and Arlen's hand on her breast.

The other complication was the vocalist Lisa Kirk. She had made her Broadway debut in Rodgers and Hammerstein's *Allegro* (1947), which was followed by a highly regarded performance the next year in Porter's *Kiss Me, Kate*. She followed that with a career in clubs, from which she had originally sprung. She was striking, the *Kate* program's description read, in part because she added up to "123 pounds of curves topped with auburn hair." In her club act she exploited her attributes with songs to match. Kirk had met Arlen through Saint Subber and managed to get him to write a song for her, with a lyric by Howard Dietz, entitled "There's No Substitute for a Man."

Like Dietrich, Lisa Kirk was a constant visitor to Doctors Hospital. Dr. Elias believed that she and Arlen planned to marry once they had divorced their current spouses. This may have been the impression she gave, but Arlen did not discuss any such plan with friends then or later. And once he had left the hospital and the rehearsals of *House of Flowers* had begun, Kirk was conspicuously missing while Dietrich was not.

The consensus among the medical staff was that they needed to keep these two formidable women from meeting; both were strong willed, and Dietrich especially came armed with a sharp tongue. Elias recalled a day when Arlen was "particularly low" and Kirk was at his bedside. Suddenly the nurses were alerted to the approach of Dietrich and scurried to get Kirk out, proffering some medical reason or other. How did they know that Marlene Dietrich was on her way? They heard the siren of a New York City police car. It had become a practice of the star to hail the official vehicle as if it were a taxicab.

For several reasons, Dr. Elias and his beleaguered staff were elated and relieved when Harold Arlen had improved enough to leave the hospital. Fortunately, there were no further medical crises as he and Capote proceeded with *House of Flowers*. There were daily interruptions, however, during late May and June of that year. Capote, who refused to own a television set, insisted on watching, on the Arlen set, the hearings of Senator Joseph McCarthy's charges of subversion in the U.S. Army hearings. That a brilliant, pixieish, Boston attorney, Joseph N. Welsh, revealed to millions that the senator was a cynical, lying bully was worth watching.

Soon after, with their score virtually complete, Arlen and Capote, with Saint Subber, flew to London, where the producer, with the aid of the writers, hoped to sign two Britons for the show. They were the director Peter Brook and the designer Oliver Messel. Neither had worked on a musical before, although Brook had recently directed Laurence Olivier in a film adaptation of *The Beggar's Opera*. He had also directed a production of Gounod's *Faust* at the Metropolitan Opera. Messel had designed sets and costumes for Hollywood films as well as various stage productions in London, notably an opulent *La Belle Hélène* for the eminent English producer C. B. Cochrane. Saint Subber was determined to have Brook and Messel for *House of Flowers*. Their names were soon added to an impressive roster that included that of choreographer George Balanchine, the highly regarded director of the New York City Ballet Company and choreographer of the famous "Slaughter on Tenth Avenue" ballet from Rodgers and Hart's *On Your Toes* (1936).

Brook, in fact, was Saint Subber's second choice as director and would prove to be a problem. Initially Robert Lewis, an actor turned director, had been approached. He had directed Lerner and Loewe's *Brigadoon* and Marc Blitzstein's opera *Regina*. He had also directed the ill-fated Saint Subber production of Capote's *The Grass Harp*, an assignment he had accepted after reading only the first act; he had come to regret that hasty decision. When Capote came to him again, Lewis was wary.

"When Truman offered me just the first act of his next script," he told the writer Terry Driscoll, "and even sang me the 'Bee Song' himself with the composer Harold Arlen at the piano, I was not going to be sucked in, even by such juicy bait, without clapping my eyes on the second part of the show. I demurred."

Once Brook and Messel agreed to do the show, Arlen and Capote recorded several of the songs for them. Apparently Mrs. Brook, the actress Natasha Parry, had impressed them. At the conclusion of one of the recordings, "Bamboo Cage," they exclaimed, in unison, "We have a pash-a for Natasha." On these London studio recordings Arlen's voice is strong and rich; his playing is sure and sensitive. He does not sound like a man who only weeks before had been seriously ill. As for Capote, it took courage to sing along with Harold Arlen, though his vocals do have a peculiar charm.

In the summer of 1954 everyone gathered in a Manhattan theater to put the show together, which is when it began to fall apart. Capote had retitled the musical *Ottilie's Song*, since the plot's focus was on the young girl. She was to be played by nineteen-year-old Diahann Carroll, a recent sociology graduate from New York University and winner of a Metropolitan Opera School scholarship with some experience in television. *Ottilie's Song* was to be her first Broadway show. During rehearsals Carroll was shy, quiet, even timid.

She was overwhelmed by the intimidating Pearl Bailey, who was cast as Madame Fleur. Her dominance would become more evident as the rehearsals went into the summer. She, too, had been second choice for the part. Saint Subber had been hoping for Eartha Kitt, then noted for her slinky nightclub act in which she purveyed what at the time were regarded as sophisticated erotic songs. She turned him down, and Bailey entered the scene.

By late August, the columnist John O'Hara was referring to the musical by its final, and original, name, *House of Flowers*. The simple tale of young lovers had diminished as the part of Madame Fleur grew and the feud between her and her competitive neighbor, Madame Tango (portrayed by Juanita Hall) expanded and became more central to the plot. Before his eyes, Capote watched his original conception mutating as Brook and Saint Subber made subtle alterations, adding here and subtracting there. The extent of their changes was not immediately apparent during the early rehearsals, however, since the dramatic portions were read in one part of the theater, the songs and musical sequences in another, while Balanchine conceived his ballet on the stage. Nor did Arlen notice much awry when he looked in on the song rehearsals with his brother, Jerry, and discussed tempos and phrasings with the rehearsal pianist, Harry Sitz. Not until all the pieces were assembled would the revisions be obvious.

Nevertheless, at least some of the show's afflictions became evident early, when Peter Brook met the cast for the first time and proceeded to commit his first gaffe. Peering over the assemblage, a sea of sepia in variegated shadings, he saw only two white faces, that of the Italian actor Dino DiLuca (as Monsieur Jamison, the older rich man who hopes to win Ottilie) and Jacques Aubuchon, as Captain Raven, the villain and accomplice of Madame Fleur in a plot to rid the threat of Royal (Rawn Spearman) to her house if he succeeds in winning Ottilie himself.

Introducing himself, Brook announced, "I should like all of you to know, first off, that I am not prejudiced."

Except for exchanging knowing glances, the cast let that one go by. But they had been alerted. Then the work began in the various parts of the theater. Arlen was present daily in his dapper suit and the traditional "bluie" (usually a tiny red rose). Capote was his sartorial opposite, in a long bulky sweater and slacks. No longer the boyish figure of the Talma photo, his rotundity was accentuated by his mode of dress. Pearl Bailey, relaxed on the surface as usual, shuffled around in old carpet slippers, a friend to all, but with a vigilant eye on Peter Brook. Diahann Carroll, like Capote, was unobtrusive until called, as was her youthful co-star, Rawn Spearman. It was all cacaphonous, confusing, and exciting—and about to turn sour. Almost daily, too, Marlene Dietrich would appear, stunningly dressed, but willing to make coffee and tea and, in the words of Terry Driscoll, to act "as charlady, chauffeur and general dogsbody."

But it was Bailey who dominated the scene. As Capote soon came to believe, "We hired Pearl Bailey for the lead, which is the one thing we shouldn't have done. Pearl began kicking up almost right away, as soon as we went into rehearsal. She overpowered poor little Diahann Carroll, who'd not done anything on the stage before, taking away most of her songs."

Jerry Arlen soon realized that Bailey was appropriating some of Ottilie's songs (Capote's "most" exaggerates somewhat) and objected. The songs had been fashioned for Carroll and were not appropriate to Bailey's singing style. Most were returned, but Bailey retained Ottilie's "Don't Like Goodbyes," which, in her rendition, lacked Ottilie's sincerity, making the gentle farewell song somewhat cynical. Jerry Arlen's defense of Carroll did not endear him to Pearl Bailey. As for Capote, he told Driscoll, "I was rewriting and rewriting and getting further and further away from what we'd had in mind." His original conception, he maintained, was "altered to death."

Among the first to leave during rehearsals was Jacques Aubuchon, whose part was altered to near-extinction, as were his vocals (he was a bass baritone). He was replaced as the conniving Captain Raven by Ray Walston (later to be television's favorite Martian), now renamed, for some reason, Captain Jonas. He did not sing.

Around this time Capote also threatened to leave when he heard the rumor that Johnny Mercer was about to be summoned to fix the lyrics. Arlen had his own complaint—again with Pearl Bailey somewhere in the background. Saint Subber took one of Arlen's tunes and gave it to the lyricist Michael Brown, whose forte was "special material" for revues (*New Faces of 1952*), to write a special song for the Bailey character. The result was "Indoor Girl," whose too obviously suggestive lyric offended the composer. It may have been tailored for Bailey—complete with artificial ad libs written into the song—but Arlen did not believe it belonged in *House of Flowers*. Nevertheless, he deferred to Saint Subber and let it go. His opinion of the song is evident in the piano-conductor's score, however: one word, underlined twice, "shit." Saint Subber rationalized his decisions about the revisions as necessary responses to "the realities of the theater." Too much art does not sell tickets.

House of Flowers, which had begun as a labor of love for Saint Subber, was, with his sanction, changing into an extended nightclub act for Pearl Bailey. The larger her part in the show became, the greater a problem she became for Diahann Carroll, Jerry Arlen, and especially Peter Brook.

The grim realities of the theater coalesced with a vengeance in Philadelphia, where the show was to open for a three-and-a-half-week run on November 25, 1954. *House of Flowers* was by then a near-shambles with a smoldering cast, which bridled under Brook's condescension. He and Bailey were soon battling in public, to the elation of New York's gossip brigade.

Diahann Carroll found Brook the major problem. She believed that he

had relatively little experience with black actors and seemed to think that we were all charming and cute rather than fully-fledged professionals. He became patronizing.

If he couldn't make the scene work, if he couldn't make us understand what he wanted, he let his confusion about how to give direction to these "naïve children" lead him to reduce his requirements so as not to put "too much pressure" on the poor little things. In his head he wasn't dealing with actors, he was dealing with "Black People." And the result was that the show suffered badly. . . . When we realized that he didn't believe in us, our spirits were totally deflated.

These were her reflections some years later; at the time she was more an observer than participant. She could not have overlooked the effect that Pearl Bailey was also having on their show.

Bailey's slouchy, casual performance—at times speaking her lines with a knowing look to the audience rather than to the actor onstage—was disconcerting to the classically trained Brook. Her style was astutely defined by *Variety*'s Hobe Morrison when he wrote that hers was a "distinctive personality" and that her "style [is] quite limited, and she reveals only a dim idea of how to read lines. Under the circumstances, unless she's singing her special brand of songs, she becomes monotonous." He liked a couple of her renditions, but criticized her "Don't Like Goodbyes," which she had appropriated from Diahann Carroll. The song, he observed, "isn't well-suited to her special throw-away café-floor delivery."

In all this, Arlen and Capote were rendered almost incidental, Capote particularly. "Tru," Arlen remembered, "just went to his room and stayed there," while his creation was recreated almost daily. Arlen remained but said little. The professional angel of mercy, Marlene Dietrich, looked after him, seeing to it that he ate his several light meals a day. She also made things easier for the cast, running their errands, cheering and consoling them. An old hand, she realized that her good friend's show was in trouble.

Before the opening of *House of Flowers* at the Erlanger Theatre, Saint Subber arranged for Peter Brook to allay some of the negative press they were garnering. Brook admitted to a group of reporters that "there were problems during rehearsal. . . . They've been solved settled and reconciled. . . .

"Rumors in the papers," he went on with a perfectly straight face, "are out of date and put us in the situation of people who were divorced and remarried and are now reading about their divorce. . . . I never did say anything against Pearl Bailey, for whom I have great respect and affection."

When she was questioned about the statement, Bailey replied, "No comment," which was more than sufficient.

But the show opened as scheduled on November 25, to quite favorable reviews, although the general consensus was that it needed work before the New York premiere. Pearl Bailey received high praise, as did the gorgeous sets by Oliver Messel. The Bailey accolades did not bode well for Peter Brook.

The good reviews were encouraging, but to the creative crew it was not enough. After the curtain descended on that first night, a glum group met in Harold Arlen's suite. Dietrich studied them with disdain. As Saint Subber described the gathering, what she saw was Capote "with his boyfriend," as were Messel and Noël Coward with theirs.

"I'll tell you what's wrong with this show," Dietrich proclaimed. "I'm the only one here with balls!"

She had not taken Pearl Bailey into account. Once she had the good reviews and the delighted audience reactions to her credit, she began to move and shake even more. Josephine Premice, a polished club singer and comedian, had been cast as one of the flowers, Tulip. Her reception had been too warm, and her comic antics garnered too many laughs. Bailey wanted her out, and she went. Her replacement was a former Katherine Dunham dancer, Dolores Harper, whose part was rewritten—that is, diminished.

George Balanchine, unhappy with the press reaction to his work, and to its revisions, resigned. The musical's showstopping dance was not Balanchine's, but Geoffrey Holder's. A Trinidadian, Holder based his choreography on a voodoo dance, the banda, and he himself danced the role of the Baron of the Cemetery. It was a wild, furious dance that secured for him instant notice.

Balanchine was readily replaced by a less arty, more Broadwayish Herbert Ross, who had been lurking in the wings at the request of a nervous Saint Subber. Ross had experience as a dancer in revues; his one Broadway credit as choreographer was *A Tree Grows in Brooklyn* in 1951. Balanchine's imaginative choreography was jettisoned (besides Holder, he had such other fine dancers as

Carmen de Lavallade and Alvin Ailey in his troupe), and Ross proceeded to liven up the show. Within days he would don yet another *House of Flowers* hat.

Ten days before the Philadelphia closing, the Brook-Bailey feud spewed violently. Brook thereupon packed his bags and left town. Herbert Ross was handed his other hat: director as well as choreographer (he was uncredited for the direction, however, in Philadelphia and New York). This new jolt ushered in more Sturm und Drang. Capote remained in his self-imposed exile. Harold Arlen was at a loss—though, in the disarray, Saint Subber did not expect new songs to add to the confusion.

As the end approached, Arlen received another jolt. On their last Friday night in Philadelphia, as everyone felt the show was as tidy as it would ever be, Pearl Bailey collapsed in midperformance, claiming "overwork and exhaustion." The show went on with all her scenes eliminated, leading one columnist to write that "the audience observed that Miss Bailey's absence destroyed [the show's] continuity"—a reasonable observation, since the script had been rewritten around her.

The Saturday matinee performance was canceled because Bailey was still in a state of exhaustion and refused to appear. At the evening performance Madame Tango—Juanita Hall—took over for Madame Fleur. His heart sinking, Arlen, with a bemused Marlene Dietrich at his side, watched Hall pinch-hitting for Bailey, reading onstage from the most recent version of the script.

Madame Bailey was sufficiently rested and recovered to appear on the opening night, December 30, 1954, at the Alvin in New York. It was an evening of expectant glitter. Arlen's friend John O'Hara covered the event with mordant bite: "There was Gloria Vanderbilt Di Cicco Stokowski sitting with Frank Sinatra, first row on the aisle. In the same row a couple of seats away, Mrs. Alfred Gwynne Vanderbilt without Mr. Vanderbilt watching a troupe of native dancers. Out in the lobby there was a little man who was being taken for Truman Capote, but wasn't. Oh, the place was full of celebrities and that curious category of people who are not celebrities but whom celebrities know, and who pretend not to be impressed by celebrities (boy, couldn't I give you a bunch of names of *those*)."

He objected to the dress of members of the self-consciously arty crowd "in their '54–'55 uniform, which is the black suit with the narrow pants: too, too Edwardian. There was the English actress—a good one, too—giving a performance in the aisle, much more professional, I must say, than the walk-through given on stage by Pearl Bailey." He neglected to mention that Harold Arlen was present with a stunningly gowned Marlene Dietrich and Grace Kelly was accompanied by the designer Valentino.

Most critics, except *Variety*'s Morrison, did not agree with O'Hara on the magnitude of Pearl Bailey. In the *New York Times* Brooks Atkinson declared her "the star performer. Throwing away songs with smart hauteur and strutting imposingly, she has an amusing style but feeble material." He was repelled by the show's bordello setting and opined that even "the music is commonplace."

Other critics had good words about the songs. Robert Coleman, in the *New York Daily Mirror*, wrote that "Arlen has composed a score that makes the pulses race." Walter Kerr (*New York Herald Tribune*) wished that the overture could have been played twice, then proceeded to find fault with the book. John Chapman (*New York Daily News*) agreed, pronounced the music "grand," but felt that Capote had "conceived the first scene of *House of Flowers* out of a dirty little mind." And so it went in a series of what is called "mixed reviews," with Capote taking most of the lumps.

There was a decided division in critical opinions. The theater historian Steven Suskin notes that the show received two "rave" reviews, two "favorable," no "mixed," three "unfavorable," and no out-and-out pans. His list was compiled from the newspapers—the magazines were generally unfavorable. In the *New Yorker* Wolcott Gibbs, writing about the music, doubted that "any of it is particularly distinguished," and all the weekly critics agreed that the major problem was the book. The message to the playgoer was simply Don't Go.

Of the two raves, one appeared in the *Post* in which the musically astute Richard Watts Jr. hailed *House of Flowers* as "the town's newest hit." After reading the opinions of his colleagues, he felt compelled to defend Capote in his Sunday column. He suggested that, as anyone who was familiar with the rumors that had filtered up from Philadelphia should know, Capote's libretto "had dwindled to virtually nothing by the time the show had reached New York" and that "it does seem to me that some of my colleagues were unnecessarily upset by the libretto's choice of subject matter. . . .

"Nevertheless," Watts concluded, "I agree that the book is the weak feature of 'House of Flowers,' whatever it may have been when rehearsals started. But the show has so many pleasant virtues that this doesn't hurt much. Those lovely sets by Mr. Messel, the warm, charming and atmospheric score of Mr. Arlen. . . . I doubt if enough has been written concerning Mr. Arlen's music. . . . one of the best song writers in America, he is too frequently omitted when the names of the great popular composers are being listed."

Another defender was the dean of American theater critics, the erudite and often acerbic George Jean Nathan. Like Watts, he found the music to be "richly atmospheric, but all the more appropriate because of its lack of the kind of tunes that convert their hearers into counterparts of whistling roast peanut machines." As for the disparaged book, Nathan dismissed the views of his fellow critics with a snappish observation that "perfectly regulated plots in musical shows are for ploughboys and are best forgotten."

Despite the critical discord, Goddard Lieberson supervised the recording of the cast album for Columbia Records early in January 1955. Arlen, his face reflecting the weeks of strain, appeared to be wan and tired. During the session he sat near Jerry Arlen, with whom he frequently conferred. Arlen was happy, for that Sunday Jerry and the no longer rebellious cast preserved the extraordinary score. Arlen himself participated in the recording, contributing a little scat singing to the big dance number "Mardi Gras." And when Diahann Carroll, suffering from a cold, could not reach a high note in "I Never Has Seen Snow," Arlen sang it for her. In the penultimate bar a skip of a seventh to a high G eluded Carroll. After a few attempts revealed she could not make it, Arlen sang the one note, which was edited into the master tape. Only a careful listening to the recording reveals this minor deception; on the word "like" there is a slightly noticeable difference in the texture of the voice.

Despite Diahann Carroll's constricted vocal range, her singing throughout the album is excellent, sensitive, and true. Pearl Bailey was true to herself, as was her practice; she even interjected a couple of alleged "ad libs." In "One Man Ain't Quite Enough" she jokingly confesses that she could not clean up the lyric. Missing from the cast album, significantly, is her "Indoor Girl." In a second ad lib she confesses that she had no ad lib for that spot because she and the company have been so busy at the Alvin that there was no time to come up with one.

A likely story. There were still backstage frictions and uneasiness over the criticisms. The consensus was that the second act did not measure up to the first. When Peter Brook materialized offering to restage the act, Pearl Bailey dismissed that with "Hogwash!" She continued to refuse to work with Brook, even as the show's box office began slipping.

By late April, with the advance ticket sales expended and box-office sales minimal, Saint Subber announced that he would close the show early in June, before the summer slump set in. He hoped that this ploy would bring on a box-office rush. It did not. Ticket sales continued to founder, and Saint Subber reluctantly decided to close on May 21, 1955, after the final Saturday night performance.

That last night was a belated love fest, "a ripsnorter of a wake," the *News* reported, "that kept the capacity audience in its seats until the early hours."

Pearl Bailey spoke after the curtain descended, and the expectant audience settled in their seats. She told the full house that all the troubles, "family quarrels" she called them, had been solved and happiness now reigned. She called Arlen to the stage, and as he stood there uneasily, Bailey led the audience through a medley of his best-known songs. Her stage rival, Juanita Hall, then joined Bailey onstage and together they tossed roses into the audience. In tears, Juanita Hall gazed into the crowded Alvin Theatre and asked, "Where were you last week?"

There was a sequel to the bedeviled history of *House of Flowers*. In March 1960, five years after the show's closing, a still optimistic Saint Subber revealed plans to revive it in June in its original form. Other projects intervened until January 1968, when Saint-Subber (now with a hyphen) tried again at the off-

Broadway Theatre de Lys in Greenwich Village. Capote finally had the opportunity to see the show he had originally conceived. The revisions made room for several new songs and the ejection of others, including one of Arlen's least favorite, "The Turtle Song." Also ejected was the salacious "Slide, Boy, Slide" sung in the original by Madame Tango. It was ejected when someone pointed out the double entendre in the lyric to the composer.

The plot once again focused on the young lovers and Ottilie's confrontation with her aged, superstitious grandmother, Old Bonaparte. She was portrayed by a heavily madeup Josephine Premice, who also appeared as Madame Fleur, Pearl Bailey's role. It was Bailey who had had Premice ejected from the original *House of Flowers.* The rivalry between the two madames was secondary and that of Ottilie and Old Bonaparte primary. Its climax, and a jarring one, was the death of the grandmother from Ottilie's voodoo. Capote, and perhaps Saint-Subber, got his wish, but miniaturized (sets, orchestra, cast, and stage), the musical failed again, with Capote again taking the worst of the criticisms.

Arlen took small comfort in his accolades. "The score, however," the *Variety* reviewer noted after dealing with the book, "is rewarding." In the *Times* Clive Barnes wrote, "Harold Arlen's score remains one of his greatest achievements." Barnes recalled the original cast album as a "legend" and how the music and cast had enchanted him. The production at the Theatre de Lys had disenchanted him. The revised *House of Flowers* remained there for only a month and a half.

Random House, Capote's publisher, printed the new libretto, for which Arlen and Capote conceived a fitting dedication: "For Saint—Poor Soul."

In the period between the original production of *House of Flowers* and its hapless revised revival, its score had indeed become legendary. Although it has been called a cult musical, the revival canceled that out; it is the score that has kept the title alive. Alec Wilder attributed the show's failure to the fact that it "was simply too elegant, too subtle, too far beyond the deteriorating taste of an expense-account clientele." That clientele has sustained many a poor musical, as witness the long-running musicals of the 1980s rooted in spectacle and technology but with flimsy plots and flimsier scores.

Such songs as "A Sleepin' Bee," "I Never Has Seen Snow," and the title song have continued to be sung and recorded by vocalists since 1954. Richard Rodgers recalled that for some time after, he rarely attended an audition at which "A Sleepin' Bee" was not sung and that hearing it "was always a pleasure." Rodgers believed too that the score was "gravely misunderstood and underrated."

Harold Arlen had remained out of the frenzy that had dogged *House of Flowers.* He preferred the sidelines, was noncritical and nonconfrontational. The feuding and the egos lay in the realm of others: Capote on the book, Saint Subber on the managerial aspects. Except for his unhappiness over "Indoor Girl," he had loved being back on Broadway. The year he had devoted to the show, and its clamor, had left little time to worry about Anya, still in California unchanged, according to Dr. Steinman. But now that the turmoil was over, Arlen fretted; something would have to be done about his wife, too many miles away.

Arlen was still, as he phrased it, "on protein and prayer," eating gingerly, drinking nothing more potent than water. He felt well enough, though he tired easily and rested a good deal. Despite these inconveniences, he soon became involved in three projects simultaneously.

PEREGRINATIONS

"The only important thing is work," Arlen said frequently during interviews following his "escape" from Hollywood in 1954. "And work," he stressed, "is experiment, searching." He spoke, mystically, of the "unsought-for phrase," as exemplified by "Get Happy," "Over the Rainbow," and "Blues in the Night." "The ideas are there, disorganized maybe—it's up to the creator to organize them."

Work temporarily took his mind off Anya, an anodyne provided by writing, rehearsals, conferences, interviews, radio appearances, and an exciting evening on the Ed Sullivan Show during which a medley of his songs was featured and he introduced "The Man That Got Away." But when these activities ended, after *House of Flowers* opened, Arlen needed work, even diversion, to keep busy. He did not talk about Anya, particularly with close friends, some of whom were hostile toward her and intimated that she had always hindered his career.

He kept family matters within the family. Celia Arluck chided him about being seen with Marlene Dietrich and linked with her in gossip columns (Lisa Kirk, by early 1955, had faded from the scene). He shrugged off this reprimand; he and Dietrich may have been a column item, but privately were just friends. Others with whom he was seen or photographed were Margaret Truman, photographed at the premiere of a film, and Gloria Vanderbilt Lumet (she was then married to the film director Sidney Lumet). Vanderbilt was at the time writing poetry and painting. Arlen acquired several of her paintings and said of her,

"This is no society girl doing something very chichi. She is disciplined, dedicated, mature about her work."

Another "date" was Marilyn Monroe. One evening while she and Arlen were dancing, he said, "People are staring at us."

"They must know who you are," she told him.

The press attention initiated by the production of *House of Flowers* continued even after the show opened. Earlier, during the final week in Philadelphia, in his article in the *New York Herald Tribune* entitled "Harold Arlen, Unsung Hit Composer," William K. Zinsser referred to a work in progress, *Blues Opera.* Some weeks later, in his Sunday column in the *New York News,* Robert Coleman, after prematurely declaring *House of Flowers* a hit, reported:

> While composing the "House of Flowers" score, Arlen started work on what he considers to be his most ambitious and distinguished project, "Blues Opera." This will have a book by Mr. and Mrs. Robert Breen, based on "St. Louis Woman."
>
> "Blues Opera" is to be included on the agenda of Blevins Davis and Breen's American Musical Repertory Theatre. It will have a cast recruited from "Porgy and Bess," when that U.S. ambassador of good-will to Europe returns in triumph to our country. [On the day the article appeared, February 27, 1955, *Porgy and Bess* had concluded an acclaimed run at La Scala in Milan, Italy.] Arlen's favorite composer is George Gershwin, so it is fitting that "Blues Opera" should command the attention of Breen and Davis.

Brave new words. It would be five years before this grand venture would come to an unhappy fruition. But in Wilva and Robert Breen he found two devoted friends, as well as knowledgeable colleagues with a great deal of theatrical experience. They had been brought together by Ira Gershwin and would remain lifelong friends.

The post–*House of Flowers* Arlen was neatly delineated by "our man Stanley" in the "Talk of the Town" section of the *New Yorker.* He found the composer to be "a worried-looking, friendly man with thick black hair and sparkling eyes, [who] will be turning fifty in a week or so."

"Stanley" attributed Arlen's obscurity to his

> past seventeen years in Hollywood, where actors get famous and songwriters don't. Arlen is now on parole in New York and determined to go straight. . . . Though reformed, he makes no effort to repudiate his past.
>
> "Hollywood did well by me and I did my bit for Hollywood," he told us. "I'm a day-to-dayer, rather than a planner, but I'm convinced that New York and the theatre are where I belong. There's something unhealthy

about writing songs for a movie, which you can never really be a part of. Luckily, though, a song has a life of its own. If a movie happens to be weak, and a song in it is strong, the song's remembered. I guess I shouldn't mention my own songs, but I will. If the song is Blues in the Night, it's remembered."

He did not mention his recent unhealthy experiences with *House of Flowers*. And in this *New Yorker* encounter, the only reference to Anya Arlen is parenthetical: "(Arlen's wife, a former showgirl in the 'Vanities,' is out on the Coast at the moment.)" Anya is not mentioned by name.

During this period Arlen frequently used the phrase "day-to-dayer" in the course of interviews, a guarded reference to his still precarious health. A new threat came as a result of the transfusions, and he was then undergoing treatment for serum hepatitis. Despite his need for more rest than usual, he maintained a social as well as professional life. Capote pretty much faded from Arlen's circle, preoccupied with the café society scene, though they occasionally met at the apartment of John Barry Ryan (of the Long Island Ryans and a grandson of the financier Otto Kahn). The youthful Ryan, destined for a career in stocks and bonds, preferred show business and especially the musical theater. He and Arlen had met when Ryan was one of the stage managers for *House of Flowers;* his wife, D. D. Ryan, who was prominent in the fashion world, was credited in the show's program as a production assistant. The Ryans were close friends with Gloria Vanderbilt and Capote.

One Sunday afternoon, at the Ryan's East Side apartment (a building celebrated because it also housed Greta Garbo), Arlen was introduced to a young television scriptwriter (for the "Topper" series) and aspiring songwriter named Stephen Sondheim. Arlen had been accompanied by the fashion writer and editor Edith Garson, her husband, and the pianist, composer, and musical theater authority Alfred Simon. Arlen played and sang several songs, which Ryan recorded on tape. Sondheim then performed songs from his early musical *Saturday Night,* probably written in his teens (he was about twenty-five when he and Arlen met).

As they left the Ryans, Arlen admitted that he was not impressed by Sondheim's juvenilia. Years later, he would change his mind.

His musical friends in New York included Irving Berlin and Yip Harburg. Both were represented by A. L. Berman. Arlen and Berlin spent a good deal of time on the phone together, discussing the current state of popular music and exchanging usually off-color jokes. Arlen had a great professional respect for the older man, and Berlin reciprocated. Harburg was frequently around, generally with a plethora of ideas for shows, films, and songs—and politics. Like Arlen, he was an enthusiastic walker, and they often engaged in ambulatory discussions. During one such walk the subject of the atom bomb arose. Harburg maintained that the root of the problem behind the stockpiling of atomic bombs was the American capitalistic economy that thrived on it. Arlen contended that a solution might be a better understanding between the peoples of the Soviet Union and the United States. Harburg disagreed, apparently laying most of the blame on the American economy and its dependence on continuing the Cold War. Arlen returned home in an agitated state, swearing that he would never discuss politics with Harburg again—only art and songs. Yet before too long they would collaborate on a song entitled "Leave de Atom Alone." Arlen did not disagree with Harburg's views in that song.

Of his newly made friends, Wilva and Robert Breen were the closest and most enduring. Late in 1953, Breen wished to form a touring company with a new musical work to follow in the successful worldwide travels of *Porgy and Bess,* possibly with the same cast. He made a list of songs that he considered models of the indigenous American sound he wanted. He took the list to Cab Calloway, then portraying Sportin' Life in the Gershwin opera. Breen was certain that since Calloway had been a bandleader for years he might be able to name the composers of the eight songs he had chosen.

"Harold Arlen," Calloway informed him, "wrote all these songs." This was Breen's story, and he was not above coloring a tale for dramatic effect, but it is probably true.

Breen had heard the name of Arlen, but like so many did not associate it with the songs, which included "Stormy Weather" and "Blues in the Night." This "Did he write that too?" reaction was typical at the time.

Arlen, though registered as a Republican, was not a political activist. He rarely discussed political issues, though events concerned him. He read several daily papers, the news magazines, and, of course, the trades, *Variety* and *Billboard.* He was well informed on the wars in the Middle East, the Cold War, and sports. He and Irving Berlin closely watched an emerging Israel. Later on, it disturbed him that members of the Chicago Seven, tried after the riots during the Democratic National Convention of 1968, were Jewish. The Richard Nixon of the Watergate period revolted him; he did not support the war in Vietnam. These were issues on which he could agree with Harburg, however dogmatic. Arlen approached political and military injustice with his heart, not his mind.

His politics were more instinctive and personal than defined by party. During the period Arlen lived in the East Side's affluent "silk stocking" district, his representative was the liberal Republican John Lindsay. Arlen supported him regularly and in time they became friends. After he moved to the West Side, out of Lindsay's district, Arlen crossed town to vote for him, since he was still registered at his East Side address. Later, when Lindsay ran for mayor of New York, Arlen, with the lyricist Martin Charnin, wrote campaign songs for him. Even when Lindsay switched from the Republican party to the Democratic, Arlen faithfully continued to support him. His loyalty was as much personal as political.

Bob Breen, like so many in the theater, was a liberal, though he rarely spoke out, as Harburg frequently did. Harburg and Arlen avoided the subject of Fidel Castro, whom Harburg admired for a time. Breen and Arlen stuck to the subject of song. Breen, however, was not particularly interested in music or opera. He once confessed, "I'm the sort who got more genuine rest and sleep at English and Continental opera performances than I got in bed." Traditional opera was boring, he believed, dull, dated. When he staged *Porgy and Bess* after a long career in the theater as actor and director, Breen accelerated the movement onstage and moved some of the songs around. His was a kinetic production, and one that not all Gershwin admirers found laudable—but its animated stagecraft captivated audiences in twenty-nine countries from New York to Moscow, with stops in the Middle East and South America. Breen's dream was to add a Harold Arlen work to his repertory.

When he learned about Arlen from Cab Calloway, Breen reached Ira Gershwin, hoping to learn the whereabouts of the composer. At the moment, it happened, Gershwin and Arlen were at work on *A Star Is Born.* Since Arlen was planning to move to New York, he arranged to meet Breen there early in 1954. Breen, a persuasive, often dramatic advocate of his ideas, outlined his plan. Though occupied with *House of Flowers* and incapacitated by his illness, Arlen listened and liked Breen's idea, although he did not quite agree with attempting to place himself in Gershwin's operatic sphere.

Breen suggested several possibilities: an operatic treatment of the John Henry legend, about a black "steel-drivin' man" who, with his hammer, is victorious over a steam drill but dies in the attempt. His feat was celebrated in folk tales and song and seemed a natural for Breen's company and Arlen. That was rejected, and Breen suggested a musical based on Jean Giradoux's *The Madwoman of Chaillot,* even the whimsical *Mrs. McThing,* neither of which would have been germane to the Americana concept that Breen hoped to continue with his opera company.

Frustrated, but not discouraged, Breen discussed his idea of an Arlen opera with the lyricist Betty Comden, who suggested that he listen to the *St. Louis Woman* cast album. At the time the musical had opened and closed, Breen had been president of the American National Theater Academy and too involved with his ANTA Experimental Theater and other production enterprises to see musicals. He was completely unfamiliar with *St. Louis Woman* except for "Come Rain or Come Shine." Upon hearing the recording, Breen knew he had his complement to *Porgy and Bess.* He began discussions with Arlen about transforming the musical into a popular opera. Arlen believed that the second act needed drastic revision. That was no obstacle, Breen assured him: he and Wilva would rework the book. Arlen's contribution would be to enrich the original score with new songs as well as instrumental bridges, dances, and underscoring—in short, to create a true opera. While Arlen found the plan to salvage his and Johnny

Mercer's score exciting, he was dubious about operatic pretensions. But he was impressed with Breen's propulsive enthusiasm, his dedication, and his belief in such a work. And, it might be added, for Breen, money was the least of it; the play was the thing.

Discussions of the *St. Louis Woman* restaging were intermittent, interrupted by Arlen's work with Capote and his hospital stays. Breen was also occupied with the touring *Porgy and Bess* company, then moving around Europe.

Even as he worked with Capote and talked with Breen, Arlen returned to the recording studios to set down his own interpretations of his songs. These would be his first real sessions—his *House of Flowers* contributions hardly counted—since he had sung on the *Bloomer Girl* cast album a decade before. Ira Gershwin was responsible for that reappearance. He had whimsically become associated with a small independent label, Walden Records, that had been founded by a friend. Walden specialized in the recording of American music with emphasis on the unjustly neglected songs of the great American songwriters. By the time Arlen had returned to New York, Walden had released several critically praised albums of songs by Cole Porter, Rodgers and Hart, and Arthur Schwartz, as well as two sets of "Gershwin Rarities" and "Lyrics by Ira Gershwin." Gershwin was pleased with the aims of the underfunded little company and frequently served as an unpaid consultant and advisor.

During the early Walden sessions, which began in 1952, musicians and vocalists often inquired about an Arlen album. Many maintained that he was America's most gifted songwriter, even greater than Gershwin. Arlen would have disagreed, but the devotion to his work by these professionals was gratifying to him.

Production of the Walden album began during the writing of *House of Flowers* and continued off and on into early 1955. By March the recording began in the Robert E. Blake Studio in Carnegie Hall. Arlen, like Gershwin (as well as the two proprietors of Walden), worked without compensation. The subject of payment was simply never mentioned—possibly because Gershwin may have informed Arlen of the company's limited funding. Arlen, like Gershwin, Arthur Schwartz, and Cole Porter, whose songs Walden also recorded, liked the company's policy of issuing lesser-known songs in authentic interpretations. Another distinctive feature was the Al Hirschfeld caricatures for the album jacket covers; the great *New York Times* illustrator had also taken a liking to the Walden way with popular songwriters; he joined its staff (now numbering three) and produced his striking work for the same salary—nil.

Shortly after the Walden project had gotten under way, Arlen was asked to do a long-playing collection of his songs for Capitol Records. His singing on several television and radio shows had impressed the producer Dick Jones, who convinced Arlen that another set, highlighting his best-known songs, was worth doing.

Common to both albums was the arranger-pianist-conductor Peter Matz. In his twenties, Matz was already a veteran, having accompanied, among others, Mae West and Kay Thompson. Matz and Arlen first met during the *House of Flowers* chaos, when he was summoned to spice up the dance music and some of the songs, for which he received no program credit. Arlen found young Matz to be an extraordinary musician, an imaginative arranger, witty and dependably businesslike (a unique quality in the world of music).

Matz had been suggested to Walden by the Ryans. Arlen readily and happily agreed. When the Capitol contract came up, Arlen suggested that Matz arrange and conduct that set also. Arlen worked closely with Matz on the arrangements and orchestrations for both albums. Capitol could afford a large studio band, while Walden's largest group was an octet, which Matz somehow made to sound like a fuller orchestra. Matz also joined Arlen for two-piano accompaniments, and, luckily, Arlen was cajoled into accompanying himself and playing two solo pieces.

The sessions were relaxed and informal. Arlen, though held in awe by the vocalists and the members of the band, contributed to the ambiance with quips, easy conversation with the crew, and warm friendliness. He and Matz, particularly, were compatible. Nevertheless, Miriam Burton, who had appeared in *House of Flowers* and was gifted with a lovely soprano voice, became so flustered during a session when Arlen looked in on it that she could not continue. She had been assigned two of the finest songs from *St. Louis Woman*, "I Wonder What Became of Me?" and "I Had Myself a True Love." She had done the first beautifully before the composer's arrival. An unintimidated June Ericson recorded "True Love" splendidly.

The telephone was an important device during the sessions. No matter where he was, Arlen could almost always be reached by phone. Between takes he spent time on the phone in Blake's control room. By coincidence, on the afternoon that he had finished recording "It's a New World," its lyricist, Ira Gershwin, checked in from Beverly Hills. The sessions went smoothly for a while until the engineer, Robert Blake, began to irritate Arlen. A classically trained pianist, he made a point of the fact that his mother had known George Gershwin. He was also opinionated and frequently made acerbic comments about the music and musicians that annoyed Arlen. During one delay, Arlen turned to one of the producers and said, "It's a Walden and Bailey world."

When he had had enough of Blake, he spoke with Leon Seidel, the colorful Walden troubleshooter (an almost Runyonesque character, Seidel had raised the money for the recording sessions by working as a part-time waiter in Catskill resorts or gambling in the stock market). Seidel stopped the session in midsong, changed engineers, and moved the enterprise across Fifty-seventh Street into Carl Fischer Hall. Blake's replacement was David Hancock, also a former pianist and Juilliard graduate. He had learned the science and art of recording from

Peter Bartók, son of the composer Béla Bartók, and the most respected and innovative recording engineer in New York. He had recorded some of Walden's first releases. As a Bartók protégé, Hancock was a credit to his mentor.

He was also an eccentric, given over to lecturing on the subject of music, conversing with the more attractive vocalists, or arguing with the managers of Fischer Hall. All of this took up studio time, prolonged the sessions, and diminished Walden's always modest bank account. But Hancock was a superb technician with a fine ear for balancing voices and instruments, a characteristic that gratified Ira Gershwin. Every word of a lyric could be heard. Like Blake, Hancock was opinionated. When his participation in the recordings began, he was not familiar with much of Arlen's music. After hearing Arlen speak, Hancock observed, "He's not just another dumb musician."

After a take in which Peter Matz had accompanied Louise Carlyle in "One for My Baby," Hancock said, "You play good piano for a clarinetist." Matz had begun his career as a clarinetist in a West Coast band. He had also studied with the eminent French composer Arthur Honegger. The rapport among musicians, vocalists, and eccentric engineer contributed to the making of a greatly admired album of songs.

Hancock's first step was to complete the recording of "Moanin' in the Mornin'," which Arlen had begun in the Blake studio. He had completed the verse and one chorus of the song to his own accompaniment when Seidel decided to leave Blake. Fischer Hall would have a different sound acoustically and even a different piano. Hancock and Matz conferred and solved the problem. The final chorus would have an orchestral accompaniment, with Matz at the piano and Arlen singing. It worked perfectly after Hancock spliced Blake's take with his own. It is one of the few recordings made in two different halls. Although the complete song could have been done in Fischer, the producers wanted to retain Arlen's piano accompaniment.

A final crisis occurred during the last session, late one evening in May 1955. Walden had run out of funds, a situation that could be attributed not to the garrulous Hancock but to the ambitious plan of the album. It was to be a two-record long-playing set, a rarity in the field of popular music; it employed five vocalists, besides Arlen, who were paid (albeit minimal fees); two pianists (Arlen or Matz, who also performed as a team); trios; quintets; and an octet. Though Matz contributed more time than he was paid for, all musicians, because of the musicians' union, were paid. Walden's "staff" worked without salary.

Walden on that May night had the masters for an elaborate album, marvelous photographs taken during the sessions and from Harold Arlen's family album, an Al Hirschfeld cover drawing (the first in his Walden series that had his daughter Nina's name drawn into Arlen's hair. It was not a flattering drawing and Arlen was not happy with it, but it remained).

Still without money, there would be no album jacket for the drawing, no

pressings to go into the sleeves, no annotations to accompany the set document-
ing Arlen's career with details about each song. The album's producer, in speaking with Ira Gershwin the next day, revealed Walden's inability to produce and
release the Arlen album. A day or two later a letter from Beverly Hills, marked
"Special Delivery," arrived in New York. In it were an encouraging note and an
even more encouraging check. Arlen never learned that Gershwin had financed
the release of *The Music of Harold Arlen,* nor was Gershwin repaid for his investment. Sadly, the release of the album coincided with the closing of *House of
Flowers.*

With both recordings finished, Arlen continued to ponder the reworking of
St. Louis Woman into a quasi-opera whenever he could meet with the Breens
between their *Porgy and Bess* presentations in Switzerland and Belgium. Meanwhile, A. L. Berman was researching the rights to the libretto. Arlen, with nothing
in the way of a contract hovering over him, took time out to fly to Europe to see
Marlene Dietrich in London and Paris with her new and extremely successful
cabaret act. While she toured, he sublet her apartment for a brief time.

He now needed his own apartment and left the spacious rooms on Park
Avenue. Around this time Jerry Arlen had married and, with his wife and infant
son, Samuel, also secured new living quarters. They found a comfortable apartment for Celia Arluck nearby, and Arlen himself eventually moved into a small
duplex on East Fifty-fifth Street above an antique furniture and decorator shop.

An uneventful summer slipped away, and bored, he flew to Las Vegas to see
his friend Dietrich again. Also there at the time was Noël Coward, an old friend,
with his witty song-and-patter show. His accompanist was Peter Matz, who had
gotten the job on Arlen's recommendation. It was a warm reunion for all, and
Dietrich, particularly, was doing extremely well. It was rumored that she commanded a fee of thirty thousand dollars a week in Las Vegas. While that was
undoubtedly close to the truth, during her stay in Las Vegas she nevertheless
wrote to Arlen after his return to New York asking for a loan, "for one week,"
of two thousand dollars. Slightly mystified but unquestioning, he sent the check
off posthaste.

Meanwhile, after the Latin American tour, Breen took *Porgy and Bess* back to
Europe. The opera and its vivacious cast had indeed proved to be a goodwill
ambassador, generating accolades wherever it played. This reception gave Breen
an idea: with the aid of the State Department he managed to break through the
Iron Curtain. He had some cooperation also from the Soviets, and arrangements
were made for a production of the opera in Leningrad (which as St. Petersburg
had been the birthplace of the Gershwins' parents) late in December, with a
booking into Moscow's Stanislavsky Theater in mid-January 1956.

Breen's fertile imagination went further. Why not make the Moscow premiere
a gala international event? He promised the Soviets that he would convince Ira
Gershwin to attend—an event in itself. Gershwin rarely left his home, let alone

California. Leonore Gershwin had already joined the troupe and may have had something to do with getting her husband out of Beverly Hills. Breen's little plot widened. He knew of Gershwin's aversion to travel, but also knew that he was fond of Arlen and might make the trip if Arlen traveled with him. Arlen's presence would initiate interest in the company's next production, the Arlen "opera."

Arlen, amused by Breen's audacity, promised nothing but agreed to attempt to talk Gershwin into flying over the top of the globe to see yet another production of *Porgy and Bess*. At Christmas he joined Gershwin in Beverly Hills, and after some pressure, the lyricist reluctantly agreed.

Arlen then made a mistake. While discussing the expedition with Breen, he suggested that Everyman Opera (as the company was called) also bring over Truman Capote as the official scribe of the Moscow Gala. Another friend, the benign gossip columnist Leonard Lyons (a friend, too, of the Gershwins') might come along as a daily chronicler for the *New York Post*. Breen thought the suggestions were capital and managed to raise the money (Everyman was more an artistic success than a financial one) for the fares of Gershwin, Capote, and Lyons. But as he explained in a letter to Arlen, that was all he could afford. Arlen paid his own way.

That was merely the beginning of an episode that Arlen remembered as a "Warner 'B' picture." It would employ a rather large cast before the climax in Moscow. Gershwin's assistant-secretary, Lawrence D. Stewart, played a major role in the hectic preparations. Another secretary, Peggy Martin, had a supporting part.

The decision to make the flight had been so precipitate that too little thought had been expended on some necessities—passports, for instance. For reasons never explained, Arlen's was in Washington, D.C. Anticipating miles of red tape at the State Department, Arlen called his friend Richard Coe, the theater critic for the *Washington Post,* to look into the problem. Somehow, no doubt because he was a well-known Washingtonian, Coe managed to retrieve the Arlen passport. By wild coincidence, Coe also was the friend of a pilot who happened to be flying to Los Angeles that night. At six in the morning, Peggy Martin was at the airport to meet the plane.

Time was rapidly running out; Arlen and Gershwin were scheduled to leave for Stockholm that same evening. These arrangements had been taken care of by Stewart, a genius at attending to bothersome details. In checking Arlen's passport, he noted that it lacked an official stamp; it was, in fact, invalid. Alerted, he examined Gershwin's and found the same oversight. He soon learned, too, that the required stamp for the two passports could be obtained only in the Customs Office in San Francisco. Peggy Martin raced Stewart back to the airport, where he boarded the next flight for San Francisco. He obtained the proper stampings and was back in Beverly Hills, with papers in order, in time for a pair of nervous travelers to make their plane for Sweden.

In Stockholm, Arlen learned that he had also neglected, in the blur of events, to get a Russian visa. Frantic international phonings ensued, with the unflappable Stewart arranging to have the visa waiting for him at their next stop, Helsinki, Finland. While in Stockholm they enjoyed a serene dinner listening to the resident orchestra of the Grande Hotel performing a medley of Cole Porter songs from *Can-Can*. At Arlen's suggestion, they wired the news to Porter in New York. Later, when they were in Moscow, Porter sent a message to them: "Have fun, boys."

Alighting in Helsinki, Arlen faced his next snag: the Russian visa had not arrived. He readily understood Gershwin's preference for his chair in the living room of the Plantation, or his box at Hollywood Park, when the urge to travel came upon him. Arlen now contemplated the actions of Bob Breen with some hostility. In Helsinki—it was now January 6, 1956—their paths converged with those of Jenifer Heyward, the daughter of DuBose and Dorothy Heyward. Heyward was representing her mother, then in a hospital, at the grand celebration of the Gershwin-Heyward opera in Moscow. She was accompanied by Ella Gerber, the opera's dramatic coach and assistant to Breen. The presence of a Gershwin and a Heyward contributed to the historic event in Breen's mind; Harold Arlen, he believed, would add a fine touch as one of America's greatest living composers.

As the plane was announced for Leningrad, the next stop on their itinerary, a discouraged, tired, and visaless Arlen said, "You go on, Ira," and to his consternation, Gershwin left him alone at the airport and took off in the company of the two young women.

On his own, without the visa and unable to speak the language, Arlen found himself in a traveler's limbo. "I went to the Russian Embassy, ended up in the Intourist section. No one seemed to know anything about my visa. I tried to get into their favor by telling them my wife was of Russian descent, but that meant nothing. I began to panic.

"I'd get on the phone and talk to Bob Breen or Lenny Lyons or Truman in Moscow, and they'd all tell me everything would be fine. I'd make the trip from my hotel to the Russian Embassy, tired, troubled, and all alone in the reception room—except for very large photographs of Lenin and Stalin."

After hours of waiting and wondering if the trip was worth the trouble, Arlen saw a Russian Embassy bureaucrat bustle into the reception room. Beaming with official bonhomie and a magisterial manner, he came to Arlen and handed him a visa, saying, "You see—no problem." Arlen boarded the next plane for Moscow, a craft he regarded with some doubt, noting that it was of uncertain vintage and unproven reliability. It was an adventurous flight, with a stopover in Leningrad for lunch. It made him nervous to see passengers casually walking about during the takeoff and the landing. Moreover, there were no seat belts, nor was smoking restricted during the critical moments of takeoff and landing.

He was pleasantly diverted from doubts about Soviet aviation when he recognized the violinist David Oistrakh as one of his fellow passengers. He lurched over to the great performer to tell him how much he had enjoyed a recent recital of his at Carnegie Hall. But the Russian's English vocabulary was as slight as was Arlen's Russian. "Carnegie Hall, Russian Tea Room, Essex House" appeared to be the only English Oistrakh knew. Arlen was delighted with his pronunciation of "Carr-neigh-gee Hull." Their mutually limited vocabularies and the noise of the engines made further conversation futile.

The aircraft bounced into Leningrad; it was around noon on January 10; *Porgy and Bess* was to make its Moscow premiere at the Stanislavsky Theater that evening. It was close to curtain time when the plane touched down at the Moscow airport. Warner Watson, a Breen assistant, was waiting for Arlen with a limousine. There was time only for Arlen to leave his luggage at the Metropole Hotel before racing to the Stanislavsky, which had been virtually sold out for the opera's entire run even while the company was still in Leningrad.

Watson led Arlen into the packed lobby, filled with Russian actors, dancers, musicians, diplomats, and high government officials. All mingled with the common workers who had been presented with seats to the historic performance "for excellence and productivity." Arlen, near exhaustion, happily slipped into his seat. Truman Capote, in a seat behind Arlen, greeted him with a smile and a wave of his hand. Breen was onstage, made an introductory speech, then brought Leonore and Ira Gershwin onto the stage to thunderous applause from more than fourteen hundred people.

Arlen, relaxing in the warm auditorium, began to drift into sleep. He was alerted by Capote pounding him on the back and gesturing for him to stand. Breen had presented him to the Russian audience as "Harold Arlen, that great American composer." Arlen stood, and the mystified audience dutifully applauded. Few, however, had any idea as to the identity of the man in a rumpled suit with a two-day beard. He appeared to be one of the production workers, not one of the tuxedoed and gowned Americans on the stage.

Once the seemingly interminable speeches were over, the conductor, Alexander Smallens, began the overture. Portions of the opera were a mystery to the Russian audience—such as the significance of a buzzard to the people of Catfish Row (to the superstitious, the bird was a sign of bad luck), and a quite graphic seduction scene shocked many in the audience. Yet the powerful music, Breen's dynamic staging, and a marvelous cast moved the audience to an eight-minute ovation when the final curtain descended.

Arlen stood applauding with the rest and was amused to see the diffident Ira Gershwin dragged onstage again. Arlen then hurried back to the hotel, where he shaved and changed before being driven to Spasso House, the residence of the American ambassador Charles Bohlen, for the traditional opening-night celebration. The embassy resonated with the sounds of the voices of the exhilarated cast, press (Russian and American), "people's artists" (mostly singers), and Soviet officialdom.

Arlen recognized the former ambassador to the United Nations, now a member of the Central Committee of the Communist Party, Andrei Gromyko. Arlen was more interested in the Armenian composer Aram Khachaturian, whose "Saber Dance" he had heard Oscar Levant play frequently. The composer was friendly; though Khachaturian seemed to know the name of Levant, associating it with Gershwin, Arlen was not certain he had made his point about "Saber Dance."

There were drinks, but not for Arlen, who was happy with water and genuine Coca-Cola, a rarity in Moscow. There was plenty of food, including fresh fruit, also scarce in Moscow, which several guests slipped into their pockets before leaving. Members of the *Porgy* company provided an impromptu song-and-dance fest and then, when a young Russian with a rich, bass voice sang "Ol' Man River," they joined him in an improvised choral backing. It was dawn on a cold Tuesday when a weary Harold Arlen finally fell into bed.

The week that followed was an exciting blur. Under the watchful eyes of their hosts, guides, an interpreter, and security police, they were steered to selected sites: the Kremlin, the Ministry of Culture, the tombs of Lenin and Stalin, and the celebrated subway. Their overseers were often agitated by the more adventurous members of the cast, who slipped away from the group to do their own, unsupervised, touring. The black members of the party were a curiosity to Muscovites who had been indoctrinated to believe that in America all black people lived in poverty. Before their eyes they saw them wearing furs and decked in jewels.

Truman Capote was even more of an enigma. The smallest member of the group, he attracted public attention with his flamboyant posturing and dress accentuated by a long yellow cashmere scarf, loosely wrapped around his neck and trailing down his back, almost brushing the street. Capote left the party before the end of the opera's run to assemble his notes for his story of the premiere of *Porgy and Bess* in Leningrad. The wicked aftermath was *The Muses Are Heard,* published serially in the *New Yorker* and in book form by Random House in 1956. It contains devastating, at times fanciful, portraits of Leonore Gershwin, the Breens, and Leonard Lyons. Capote made it obvious that he detested *Porgy and Bess* as a poor representation of American culture—a black slum, of all places, and such depressed people. His comments about the opera earned him the nickname of "Little Eva."

The Muses Are Heard is an entertaining tale, but its theme and point were keenly discerned by the critic Meyer Levin, who observed that "Mr. Capote has long, sharp fingernails. Anyone who wants to learn to be a cultural snob in one lesson need only read this report and follow the Capote line of attack." Capote, Levin noted, made "everyone but himself look vulgar and sound stupid. Virtually every remark he quotes is inane. And the reader's pleasure comes, of course, in feeling that like Capote, he, too, is smarter than all those supposedly bright and clever here impaled."

Harold Arlen was not among them because he was not in Leningrad at the time. He spent most of his time in Moscow with the Gershwins and the Breens and spoke only occasionally with Capote about the possibility of another production of *House of Flowers.* When Capote flew out of Moscow, Robert Breen had no idea that when he financed Capote's tour with the *Porgy* company, he had bought himself a great deal of grief; he was shocked when the first installment of *The Muses Are Heard* appeared in the *New Yorker* in October.

Arlen missed out on a role in that book, but interestingly, years later, in November 1975, Capote's *Answered Prayers* was published in *Esquire,* to the dismay and alienation of virtually everyone Capote knew, but not Arlen. This was evidence of Capote's genuine affection for his onetime collaborator. Although *Answered Prayers* was never completed, more was published, and again, Arlen was spared.

Two final highlights rounded out the festive week; on Monday, January 17, the company's Serena, Helen Thigpen, and Sportin' Life, Earl Jackson, were married in the Moscow Baptist Church. The church was packed, and a curious crowd of Muscovites gathered outside. The groom was more resplendent than the bride in his brown tails, with lapels of champagne-colored satin. It was a front-page event, as the flamboyant Jackson had predicted when the idea of a Moscow wedding was proposed. They were to be the first black couple married in Moscow.

Arlen was formally dressed (in black tie), as was Leonard Lyons, who stood on a stairway near the altar. Breen wore a white tie. The Gershwins were somewhere in the mob around the bridal pair. But Capote was absent, already having left to begin his mischief making. Also in attendance was a small army of members of the press, including a Soviet newsreel crew.

The sumptuous finale was the Ministry of Culture's farewell party in the Metropole's vast restaurant. There were the usual speeches, with toasts to "peace and friendship"; Gromyko represented the Soviets. Even Gershwin rose to thank the Russians for a whirlwind visit marked by "efficiency, thoughtfulness, and kindness." Breen expatiated on the value of cultural and artistic exchange. Entertainment was provided by Russian vocalists, but as Ambassador Charles Bohlen observed, "The *Porgy and Bess* cast again surprised the Russians by singing difficult classical arias in five languages, including Russian. [They] had no idea that the black artists had been so solidly grounded in classical music."

Arlen, who had chosen not to speak, was so carried away by the warmth and excitement of the evening that he hurried to his room and placed a call to Anya in Santa Monica. The staff of the sanitarium did not particularly appreciate the early-morning call (it was six A.M.), even if it came from Moscow. Still, Anya was awakened to speak with her husband, which the staff was certain would prove salutary. Hearing a rational, composed, and laughing Anya was more thrilling than all the talk in the Metropole restaurant. On hanging up the phone, Arlen was determined that he would be reunited with her as soon as Dr. Steinman believed it possible.

The festivities and the run of *Porgy and Bess* concluded, Gershwin and Arlen returned to Beverly Hills—Lee Gershwin chose to remain with the company—by Friday, January 20, 1956. Gershwin returned to annotating his brother's papers for deposit in the Library of Congress.

Instead of returning to New York, Arlen registered at the Beverly Hills Hotel to work on a musical film. The short-lived experience would be unexpectedly peculiar. Arthur Freed had a script created about the adventures of a nineteenth-century woman journalist, Elizabeth Seaman, who wrote under the name of "Nellie Bly." One of the early muckrakers, she achieved a degree of notoriety by getting herself committed to New York's infamous Blackwell's Island by feigning insanity and then publishing an exposé of conditions there entitled *Ten Days in a Mad House*. Her most glamorous exploit, inspired by Jules Verne's *Around the World in Eighty Days,* was to attempt the same trip for her paper, Pulitzer's *New York World.* She made it in seventy-two. This 1889 feat was to provide the major portion of the film's plot. The various settings afforded plenty of opportunities for a colorful score.

Freed, who had assigned the production to Roger Edens, then approached Yip Harburg about the words. Harburg found it an exceptional idea, what with its feminist statement and a chance for him to work with Harold Arlen, who Freed thought would be right for the music. Freed was serious, for he arranged, at MGM's expense, for Harburg to fly to California around the time that Gershwin and Arlen had returned from Russia.

Though he had been back since late January, Arlen informed a friend in New York on February 6, "Picture work slow in getting started." This was an understatement.

Although both Joseph McCarthy and the Thomas Committee had been discredited, Hollywood remained under the cloud of the blacklist. When Freed submitted the names of the creative staff for *Nellie Bly* to Roy Brewer of the International Alliance of Theatrical Stage Employees (Brewer was also head of the American Legion) Brewer told Freed, upon seeing Harburg's name, "Nothing doing. This picture will be boycotted."

Though he disapproved of Harburg's politics, Freed wanted his lyrics for the film. Intimidated, he thought Harburg himself could "just clear things up if you just go there [the IATSE office]." Harburg went and underwent a bizarre interrogation. Brewer summoned in a confessed former Communist (Harburg recalled his name as Cardigan). He entered with a file folder—"thicker than all my works"—marked E. Y. HARBURG. Although his interrogator admitted that they had no documentation of Harburg's membership in the Communist party (because he had never been a member), Cardigan asserted, "We know all the tricks."

Harburg asked, "The tricks?"

Cardigan countered, "But you did things."

Harburg replied, "Like what?"

The interrogator went on shuffling through the file: Harburg had contributed money to the Chinese relief (during the war, when China was an ally of the United States) and to the Spanish Loyalists fighting Franco, an ally of Adolf Hitler and Benito Mussolini. Harburg admitted this, saying he had invariably been an enemy of fascism, abroad and at home (he had been a founder of the Hollywood Democratic Committee).

Now Cardigan was certain he finally had Harburg. "Well," he said again, "did you write a song called 'Happiness Is a Thing Called Joe'?"

"Yes, for *Cabin in the Sky*. A big hit."

"Which Joe were you talking about?" Cardigan asked. "Was it Joe Stalin?"

Harburg laughed in his face, and after insulting the American Legion's periodical, *The Legionnaire* (for which his friend Edward G. Robinson had written "I Was a Dupe for the Communists"), calling it a fourth-rate magazine, Harburg stormed out of the office. *Nellie Bly* was finished—although he and Arlen had completed one song, "Stay Out of My Dreams." Arlen chose to remain with Harburg in the fiasco and left the film also. So, because of contractual technicalities, did Roger Edens. Paramount Pictures reminded him that he owed them a film. Edens was temporarily released by MGM to produce what turned out to be the outstanding *Funny Face,* with Gershwin songs and starring Audrey Hepburn and Fred Astaire.

An angry and exasperated Harburg returned to New York, where such brainless blacklisting was no longer in force. Harold Arlen, after a brief and pleasant reunion with Anya and a discussion with her doctor about her release in the future, followed Harburg to Manhattan the first week in March. He was tired of travel, and of Hollywood, a place in the doldrums again and still fearful. For Arlen, Hollywood had too many sad memories. New York was now home.

YANKEE
DOLLARS

hen Arlen returned to New York, he found Harburg waiting for him. For the past couple of years Harburg and Fred Saidy had been working on a musical that renounced the duplicitous values of contemporary society, the cold war mentality, and the alleged advantages of "civilization." His experience in Roy Brewer's office incited him to do something about it. Their play was entitled *Pigeon Island*, a mythical fishing village and simple community somewhere in the Caribbean. He approached Arlen with a star in mind, Harry Belafonte, who was then extremely popular in clubs and on recordings as the leading exponent of the calypso, a West Indian folk import.

This folk form was Harburg's kind of song, with its steady African beat, short melodic phrases, and lyrics reflecting on society, politics, and personal matters. Arlen, however, resisted. His last Broadway venture in the Caribbean had failed, and he had calypso trouble. Because the rhythm was the major element to highlight the words, the form, Arlen believed, "lacked a strong melodic nature. I think [the calypso] is boring and repetitious, if done authentically." And while he admired Belafonte and found him delightful and interesting on recordings, calypsos, he told Harburg, would prove to be "theatrically uninteresting. You couldn't build a whole show on them."

Harburg was prepared with a counterargument (with Saidy joining in): theirs would be a Broadway musical, not a musicological treatise. (Arlen, he noticed, had acquired several Belafonte albums and folios of published calypso collections). They would write a characteristic Arlen-Harburg score with plenty of romantic ballads for Belafonte and a few calypsos commenting on human foibles "for laughs."

Arlen was not convinced, not wishing to remine the musical materials he had drawn upon for *House of Flowers*. He was, however, also bored with inactivity. In April 1956 he reluctantly capitulated. Belafonte needed no convincing; he remembered when, as a boy, he loved the song "Over the Rainbow." To appear in a Broadway musical with songs by its composers was enough for him. It took little persuasion, what with the names of Arlen, Harburg, Saidy, and especially Belafonte involved, to get backing for the show. In May the producer David Merrick announced that his next production would be *Pigeon Island*, starring Harry Belafonte. The word was that it would prove to be an enormous hit, as had been Merrick's previous successes, *The Matchmaker* (Thornton Wilder's comedy, later to be the musical *Hello, Dolly!*, also a Merrick production) and the musical *Fanny*. A former attorney, Merrick, by his own admission, was renowned for his "aggressive promotional methods." Arlen, Harburg, and Saidy would, in time, learn a great deal about promotion as well as aggression.

The Harburg-Saidy plot was straightforward. Koli (Belafonte) is a young, happy fisherman in love with the beautiful Savannah. He also loves Pigeon Island, but she longs for the island of Manhattan, with all its "civilized" conveniences. Their wedding depends on Koli's taking her to New York and demonstrating commercial acumen beyond fishing in the waters around Pigeon Island. But New York comes to them in the form of an entrepreneur from Harlem, Joe, who spoils the island paradise by coaxing the fishermen to abandon their nets and to take up the more lucrative and dangerous occupation of pearl diving. The contented Koli is the one holdout. Savannah, impressed with Joe's enterprise, even considers leaving Pigeon Island for New York with Joe.

All is resolved by the timely onset of a hurricane (in the original version, it was an enormous atomic mushroom cloud that ended act 1). Cut off from the outside world, the islanders, and Savannah, realize that Koli's fish are more precious than Joe's pearls. Joe returns to Manhattan, and Savannah remains on the island with Koli: happy ending.

One of the first songs written for Belafonte was the exquisitely complex "There's a Sweet Wind Blowin' My Way," sixty-eight bars of pure melody. Melodically asymmetrical, the song's structure is intricate even for Arlen. While it is in the same key (C) throughout and in common time, its form is A-A'-B-C-D, divided into 16, 12, 16, 16, and 8 bars. None of the sections conform to the popular song formula, and the divisions are not crystal clear: the release (B) begins as if it were a continuation of the A^1, which in fact is truncated in comparison with the surrounding sixteen-bar sections. It is a difficult song to get right, and it goes without saying that it was not used in the show. When asked about this cut, Arlen replied, without elaborating, "We couldn't find anyone who could sing it."

Once work was under way, Arlen and Harburg met either at the lyricist's large apartment on Central Park West or Arlen's small duplex on East Fifty-fifth Street. Arlen's Steinway grand was placed near a window facing the street. Behind the piano bench, flush to the wall, a small table held a tape recorder and a sheaf of jots. (Of all the initial melodic fragments, only one was developed for the score.) On the wall above the table was the Montañes portrait of Arlen. The bedrooms were on the floor above, reached by a circular staircase. The apartment was definitely "cozy," comfortable and temporary.

Arlen looked forward to the day Anya would be well enough to join him, when they would need larger quarters, but the duplex would serve for a while. He knew, too, that he would settle in New York and began discussing Anya's transfer, in time, to a treatment center near Boston. The doctor agreed but advised waiting longer—even a year.

Collaborating with the mercurial Harburg kept him occupied. "We'd jump around a lot," he told an interviewer. "We'd begin a song, leave it, begin another. This is how we worked for a year and a half without getting too bored with any one number. Once we'd set the mood and point of the song, we knew what we still had to do with it when the time came." When they had completed about a quarter of the score, Arlen and Harburg were certain they were home free. Later, he told another radio interviewer that writing the songs was "a devilish job."

Though he and Harburg avoided boredom by skipping around, one day, when playing some of the score for a friend, Arlen half-jokingly said, "God, how I hate calypsos!"

But they were a greater distance from home than Arlen had imagined even with much of the score complete by the summer of 1956. In June Belafonte's engaging husky baritone turned raspy, and it was found that there was a problem with his vocal cords. He temporarily stopped singing as Arlen and Harburg went on with the work. Around the same time, Arlen took a day off to drive out to Idlewild (now Kennedy) airport to greet Robert Breen and the *Porgy and Bess* cast, which had flown in from Amsterdam. (By November all rights for *St. Louis Woman* were cleared and the Breens and Arlen would be free to continue work on Everyman Opera's next production.)

In mid-September Arlen received an encouraging note from Dr. Steinman informing him that he had talked with Anya and that she "sounded fine at the time." The final phrase, however, took some edge off the good report.

So it was back to work. The new year, 1957, brought a severe jolt to *Pigeon Island*. Harry Belafonte required surgery on his vocal cords and would be out of action for a long period of recovery. Show-business rumors attributed this inaction to Belafonte's fear of starring in a Broadway show and implied that he was not ill at all. These rumors were stifled by the reality of his successful operation.

Still, the Merrick camp was thrown into dismay. Of all connected with the production that February of 1957, Belafonte recalled, only Harold Arlen was willing to wait for his recovery and return to singing.

Merrick could not wait. In desperation, he offered the part of Koli to the popular Sidney Poitier (who had made a deep impression with his role in the film *The Blackboard Jungle* a year or so before). That Poitier did not sing seemed not to concern anyone except Arlen and Harburg; Merrick and company wanted a name. But Poitier did not want the part.

During one of their desperate meetings, out of the blue, Harold Arlen suggested a name: Lena Horne. That rang a bell and warmed many hearts. She had recently returned from a successful European tour, then reigned for eight equally successful weeks that spring in the New York Waldorf-Astoria's Empire Room. Her recent record album, *Lena Horne at the Waldorf-Astoria*, was a current bestseller. The consensus was that getting her could save the show. Inadvertently, innocently, Harold Arlen had tossed the proverbial monkey wrench into the works. If they got Lena Horne, the focus of the plot would shift from the contented Koli to the determined Savannah.

Lena Horne had never starred in a Broadway show. She had been featured in *Blackbirds of 1939* for all of its nine performances. She had not made a film since 1950, and that in yet another one of her specialty bits in a Van Johnson–Esther Williams water epic, *The Duchess of Idaho*, produced by MGM. That she had been welcomed back at the studio, after her refusal to appear in *St. Louis Woman*, indicated forgiveness. Considering the quality of the film, it was more like revenge. Since that filmic mishap, she had done much better in London (the Palladium), Paris (the Olympia Music Hall), New York, and Las Vegas.

Lena Horne, David Merrick was happy to hear, would love to appear in a musical with a Harold Arlen score. She told an interviewer that his music was "difficult but soul-rewarding," that he wrote as he did because of his honesty and love, that "he writes from the inside." She admired Arlen because he avoided "cheap commercial tripe." They had been good, if not close, friends since meeting at the Cotton Club twenty-two years before. The Arlens, she recalled, had come to see her when she appeared in Hollywood clubs. She had recorded several of his songs over the years and was more closely associated with "Stormy Weather" than Ethel Waters.

Soon after Merrick had signed her for the part of Savannah, Lena Horne appeared on the Ed Sullivan television show. When her host inquired about her future plans, she told Sullivan, and a nationwide audience, that she would appear in a Broadway show, now called *Jamaica*, with songs by Harold Arlen and Yip Harburg. To Merrick's joy, advance ticket sales for the show shot to a million dollars within weeks. This, in itself, was a revelation. Her representative, Ralph Harris, said that at this time he was unable to get Horne her own television show (thus the cameos on such variety shows as Ed Sullivan's), nor until *Jamaica* could he find the producer to star her on Broadway. Also, she detested working in clubs. But because of the "color line," Lena Horne had found work difficult to get in Hollywood and on Broadway. *Jamaica* was to be a landmark effort for her and Broadway.

As the Sullivan show had proved, getting Lena Horne as a star was an emphatic asset for the box office. But for Harburg and Saidy, especially, and to a lesser degree Arlen, it meant more work and some shifting of creative gears. The basic plot was retained, with the happy-go-lucky, humble fisherman in love with the ambitious, restless dressmaker who longs to leave simple Pigeon Island for exciting Manhattan. The musical's spotlight would concentrate on Savannah, and Koli would become a subordinate character. One of the first musical modifications was the elimination of "There's a Sweet Wind Blowin' My Way," which was not regarded as a "Lena song." Since the fisherman (whoever that might be) would not be required to sing as Belafonte would have, there would be more room for Lena Horne to vocalize, solo and in concert with others. "Special material" needed to be fashioned for her. This was music to Merrick's ears, accompanied by the ringing of the box-office till.

Revising the role of Savannah would not be a particular strain on the songwriters; in fact, it gave them the opportunity to salvage Horne's bathtub song, "Ain' It de Truth," which had been cut from the film *Cabin in the Sky*. Writing for Horne's distinctive voice and delivery was easy. But the show's authors, Harburg and Saidy, were destined for anguish.

While they reworked the book, Merrick's efficient publicity machine, headed by the astute Harvey B. Sabinson, began to whir. Among the first releases was the announcement that Robert Lewis would direct. Fresh from Hollywood, where he had directed Bing Crosby in *Anything Goes*, Lewis took the job without doubts, unlike *House of Flowers* with its missing act 2. *Jamaica* was complete, but as fate would have it, the book he read initially was not the one that would finally arrive in New York.

A fine casting choice placed Ricardo Montalban in the role of Koli. A versatile actor, Montalban had recently returned from Japan, where he had appeared in the film *Sayonara* as a Kabuki actor; he had portrayed a Frenchman in the previous season's musical miss, *Seventh Heaven*. He was best known for his appearances opposite Esther Williams (*Neptune's Daughter*, in which he sang "Baby, It's Cold Outside") and Cyd Charisse (*Sombrero*, in which they danced). His acting abilities were evident in such nonmusicals as *Battleground* and *Border Incident*. Mexican-born, a good dancer with a pleasant baritone voice, Montalban was a perfect choice to portray the Jamaican fisherman.

Rounding out the cast of leading roles, Adelaide Hall returned from two decades in Europe to appear as Grandma Obeah, who predicted the future by reading messages in the clouds. Like many African American performers in the 1930s, Hall had found working conditions more congenial in London and Paris, where she had her own clubs. She appeared in the London productions of Porter's *Kiss Me, Kate* and Hugh Martin's *Love from Judy*. She had been the star of the Cotton Club *Parade of 1934,* in which Horne appeared as a secondary singer and dancer. Arlen and Koehler had written "Ill Wind" for her.

There was another reunion. Josephine Premice, one of Pearl Bailey's *House of Flowers* castoffs, was signed to appear as Savannah's romantic rival. Merrick's publicity proclaimed her "the first American to sing Calypso in this country" (she was born in Brooklyn, though she had spent her early childhood in Haiti). Her dry, sardonic style inspired Harburg and Arlen to write two politically trenchant calypsos, "Yankee Dollar" and "Leave the Atom Alone." Joe Adams, a popular West Coast radio personality—"the West's first Negro disc jockey"—who had appeared in the film *Carmen Jones,* would make his Broadway debut as Joe, the Harlem city slicker. With the casting set, the rehearsals and the troubles began.

The *Jamaica* score had been ready for the orchestrator, Philip J. Lang, in April; Peter Matz worked from the score in preparing the dance arrangements. This gave Arlen time to continue transforming *St. Louis Woman* with the Breens and with the opera's orchestrator, Samuel Matlowsky. They also extracted a suite from the score for Andre Kostelantz for its premiere in Minneapolis late in August and a Carnegie Hall performance in November. Thus, the shaping of the two works proceeded concurrently; the heightened pace would take its toll on a not yet fully recovered Arlen.

Rehearsals were held in the Winter Garden in the summer. Arlen looked in on the proceedings and, so far as the songs went, things looked fine. But there were changes. The lovely "Cocoanut Sweet," intended for Montalban, was given to Adelaide Hall and Lena Horne in the first act and was sung solo by Horne in the second, at Robert Lewis's suggestion. To Arlen this did not seem a calamity, but a certain process was under way. Horne was being moved into the foreground and the rest of the cast, the amiable Montalban included, to the back.

But as Harburg noticed, when looking in on the libretto rehearsals, Horne's part was being magnified to the detriment of the plot as well. As he said to Arlen, upon Arlen's return from Minneapolis for the Philadelphia premiere in mid-September, "They're changing the goddamn thing." "They," according to Harburg, were Merrick and Lewis. Out-of-town revisions were nothing new to Harburg; he'd suffered them before, but not to this extent. *Jamaica* was becoming a one-woman show, and the plot was being swept out the stage door.

In Philadelphia the *Variety* reviewer verified Harburg's qualms. In the opening paragraph the pseudonymous "Waters" wrote, "This big musical has a couple of positive tangibles in its corner and a couple that certainly don't hurt any. But producer Merrick, who worked wonders with 'Fanny' several seasons back after its ragged tryout here, is going to have to do as well this time."

The positive assets, he averred, were Lena Horne and "Harold Arlen's luminous score." But "the book by E. Y. Harburg and Fred Saidy only occasionally bursts into flame. More often it is only pedestrian." There is no reference to the Harburg lyrics. Waters also complained about the noncooled theater on a sweltering night but praised Horne for managing "a galvanic and almost breathtaking tour-de-force" with "unflagging energy and verve" despite it. "The show ran," he concluded, "just short of three hours at the opening and was well received by the audience that was evidently waiting for the love passages between Miss Horne and Montalban; they were quite torrid." He then added a word of caution: "The whole thing is likely to present problems for filming."

The reception of Lena Horne by the audience and adoring reviewers confirmed Merrick's dedication to making *Jamaica* a Lena Horne show. He placed an order for two additional songs for her—she already, as *Variety* had noted, participated in no fewer than a dozen of the show's twenty musical scenes. But that proved impossible, for soon after the premiere, Arlen's work with Breen as well as Harburg, plus the travels between New York and Minneapolis and now Philadelphia, overtook him. He collapsed and entered the hospital in Philadelphia. The fate of what had once been *Pigeon Island* remained in the contentious hands of Yip Harburg.

After recuperating to a degree, Arlen returned to New York for more rest, while Harburg and Saidy stayed with the show. Harburg reported to Arlen about the progress, if any. "The show," he wrote, philosophically, "like every creation in rehearsal, is a hodge-podge of whirly-gig and raw nerve tissue. Out of it somehow will come discipline and tempo, light and color, words and music, harmony and laughter. The ego will be nourished, the scars healed, and I will be off on my white charger toward greener fields and sweeter challenges."

When *Jamaica* reached Boston early in October, its three-week run sold out, Harburg's dispute with Merrick detonated. The diluted book made him and Saidy appear to be virtual amateurs. He became a clamorous dissenter during the preopening rehearsals, and consequently he and Saidy were locked out of the theater.

Arlen, though not fully recovered from his collapse in Philadelphia, traveled up to Boston in time for the opening on October 8. He chose to side with Harburg and Saidy, though he contributed nothing to the fracas. He sympathized with Harburg (while admiring Horne's handling of several songs; his favorite was the sultry "Take It Slow, Joe"). But he also realized that, as producer in full command of the show, Merrick had an unfortunate free hand, even to the banishment of the show's creators. Finance, not art, was the object.

As before, the critics singled out Lena Horne for special consideration. Eliot Norton, of the *Boston Daily Record,* praised Arlen's "highly inventive score" but found the libretto "silly." He felt that Lewis had not learned to "harness" the "remarkable talents of Lena Horne." "What's to harness?" was Harburg's reaction; most of the evening she was onstage doing a nightclub act as the plot grew sillier and even superfluous.

Harburg gave up after Boston. He refused to attend the opening night on October 31, 1957, "because I did not feel spiritually attached to it. It ended up as good sock entertainment completely overhauled and commercialized for Lena Horne with the soul of creative intention raped and debauched. However, this is what the American critics and the major part of the audience evidently want and it is off to a smash hit. I will therefore follow Omar Khayyam's advice and take the cash and let the credit go."

This, from a letter to his friend Maurice Essex, was written about two weeks after *Jamaica* was initiated into a run of more than five hundred performances. Heeding Omar Khayyam was wiser than battling with an icon and the keepers of Merrick's ledgers. Harburg, like Arlen, took his money and most of the blame.

Lena Horne harvested most of the credit that Harburg was resigned to forge. "To begin with," wrote Richard Watts Jr. in the *New York Post.* "Miss Horne is probably the most beautiful woman in the world, and it is sheer critical cowardice to stick in the weasling word 'probably.'" Watts found *Jamaica* burdened by an "epically feeble book" but blessed with "a striking Harold Arlen score" whose "most notable virtue . . . is that it captures and holds the mood and spirit of West Indian music without losing its personal style, or becoming either trite or monotonous. I suppose it contains its share of hit numbers, although Miss Horne has a way of making all her songs seem in that category. . . . Despite my fairly dim view of the book concocted by E. Y. Harburg and Fred Saidy, it has the virtue of not getting seriously in the way."

Brooks Atkinson (*New York Times*) agreed, saying that Harburg and Saidy were "primarily interested in getting the performers on and off the stage, and they have succeeded admirably." He did manage a couple of favorable sentences about the lyricist Harburg, who "has not tried to dazzle anyone in particular. His rhyming style is relaxed and genial." Atkinson, obviously, was not aware of Merrick's gratuitous contribution to the pacing of the show.

Variety's "Hobe" credited Harburg with "neat lyrics" for a "pulsating . . . strong . . . rich score." He echoed his Philadelphia colleague's concern about "various reactions to the racial aspect of the show." (At one performance, when the stars kissed fervently, a woman in the audience gasped; during the long run of *Jamaica* there were a few, not serious, disturbances over race. Hobe, in his review, pointed out that Montalban appeared to have been "sun-lamped considerably.")

The astute Walter Kerr (*New York Herald Tribune*), himself a veteran of morning-after judgments, put his finger on the show's heartbeat. (Kerr initially moved to Broadway as the writer of the books for two flop musicals, *Sing Out, Sweet Land* in 1944 and *Touch and Go,* in collaboration with his wife, Jean, in 1949, before switching to criticism.) Once Kerr got past singing the glories of Lena Horne, he stated that *Jamaica* had evidently been produced simply because all concerned had such high, happy hopes for the original cast album.

Harold Arlen is of considerable assistance in keeping this marathon going. He has hummed out a low, rolling, altogether affecting lullaby in "Little Biscuit" [*sic;* he confused this racy number with the truly affecting "Cocoanut Sweet"], a bittersweet ballad in "Pity the Sunset," and a couple of antically, light-footed didoes in "What Good Does It Do?" and "Napoleon." . . . And that's about it: two solid sides of LP. Librettists E. Y. Harburg and Fred Saidy haven't even begun to think about supplying their fishermen, pearl-divers and writhing young ladies with so much as the ghost of a plot. . . . The question is: can you make a whole show out of sheet music?

The anonymous critic for *Life* (which ran a splendid picture story about the musical) was as perceptive as Kerr when he pointed out that *Jamaica* gave "its customers the satisfaction of seeing a glorified nightclub show without the bother of dealing with headwaiters."

Kerr took an additional slap at Harburg by pointing out that

no fewer than four E. Y. Harburg lyrics [are] dedicated to preserving the social significance that was so stimulating in the thirties and is so uncomfortable now. Mr. Harburg is, as everyone knows, an absolutely dandy lyricist when he is being lyrical: the "crickets doin' nip-ups around the columbine" is in his vein. But there are an enormous number of rhymes involving barbiturates, cyclotrones, Anna Lucasta, and the fact that we may all soon be "fissionable material," and I suspect that the title of one of these forays—"Leave the Atom Alone"—might well have been taken more seriously by the authors.

It had, of course, but not in the sense meant by Kerr. The social commentary, definitely in the original libretto and in the lyrics, was timely. There was threat of atomic war, colonialism was a paternal, if benign, evil, and greed, then as now, corrupted. And what passed for "civilization" was a glittering sham.

The Harburg and Saidy message was lost in what the *Time* critic perceived as a book of "an idiot simplicity and an almost insolent lack of purpose." With Lena Horne front and center, no one, including the critics, cared. Needless to say, Harburg, Saidy, and Arlen never did another show for David Merrick.

Despite the rough treatment Harburg suffered (primarily as co-librettist), the songs written for *Jamaica* were generously admired. The "smash song hits" that *Variety*'s Waters had predicted from Philadelphia did not materialize. Arlen's work was highly praised by Atkinson, Kerr, the *New Yorker*'s Wolcott Gibbs—

who, like *Variety*'s Hobe, objected to Harburg's political and social commentary. Still, not any of the songs made, in the Arlen phrase, "noise."

Lena Horne, during an interview a couple of years later, admitted that she had been disappointed that she had not been given a song of the stature of "Come Rain or Come Shine" or "A Sleepin' Bee," though she loved "Cocoanut Sweet," "Napoleon" and "Push de Button." Her smoldering showstopper, "Take It Slow, Joe," she felt was more a parody of the type of song suggested by the cautionary title. Partly, she felt this was because the character of Joe was not believable.

Alec Wilder, in his survey of Arlen's output in *American Popular Song,* does not analyze the *Jamaica* songs; possibly, he had exhausted his stock of superlatives. He alludes to "some complex experimental songs" from the show but does not mention them.

He may have had three of the most characteristic Arlen songs in mind: "Napoleon," "Take It Slow, Joe," and "Cocoanut Sweet." The first Arlen called a "moderate strong blues—with humour," an eight-to-the-bar dissertation on the capriciousness of fame. The song is an adaptation of a number he and Harburg had written for *Hooray for What!* They retained the point of the lyric, though both music and lyric are different from the original.

"Napoleon" was designed by the composer to enable Harburg's "lyric fun" to shine. The melody moves over a boogie-woogie ostinato: the vocalist makes a point, then rests for a bar as the accompaniment continues, punctuated with bluesy grace notes (Arlen called them "hickeys"). This gives the listener a chance to absorb the song line by line:

> *Napoleon's a pastry.*
>   (Instrumental interlude)
> *Bismarck is a herring.*
>   (Instrumental)
> *Alexander's a creme de cocoa mixed with rum.*
>   (Instrumental)
> *And Herbie Hoover is a vac-u-um.*

The lyric glows with Harburgian commentary on the greats of history (and their eventual fate): Swift ("just a ham"), Lincoln ("a tunnel"), and Coolidge ("a dam"). A couple of lines were omitted from the cast album, a concession to radio's Victorianism at the time: "Homer is just a swat / King John a you know what." The song ends with the advice, "Better get your jug of wine and loaf of love before that final bow," as the accompaniment fades into three bars of emphatic ostinato.

"Take It Slow, Joe" Arlen subtitled "Blue Mood" and indicated that the vocal should be "slow and sultry." As usual for Arlen, the song does not fit into the standard thirty-two-bar form. The sultriness flows from the slow, restless, beguinelike tempo characteristic of the blues songs by W. C. Handy, whose compositions evidence a kind of tango beat, and from the blues-inflected flatted third. Rarely does the melody stray more than a fourth from the opening C, accentuating the bluesiness of the song. Only at the climactic close, when the word "Joe" is held for six bars, does the melody line reach an octave and a third. "Take It Slow, Joe" is Arlen at his most inventive and experimental.

"Cocoanut Sweet," the show's single ballad, is graced with one of Harburg's most poetic lyrics, in which he draws upon Pigeon Island's flora:

> *Cocoanut sweet*
> *Honeydew new*
> *Jasmine an' cherry an' juniper berry,*
> *That's you.*

Also: "Buttercup true," "spice and sugar plum," and "the peach is ripe, the lime is green, the air is touched with tangerine." To underscore the lyricism of the words, Arlen punctuates the accompaniment with a high G preceded by a chromatic slide. As originally conceived, "Cocoanut Sweet" was to have been a love song, sung by Koli to Savannah, but it was later transformed into a lullaby sung to a young boy, first by Adelaide Hall and then by Lena Horne. In the second act Horne reprised it as a solo. The change did not affect the song's quality. The experimental touch appears in the release, where the lullabylike or balladlike mood switches to a near-violent mood ("The wind may blow / the hurricane whip up the sky") before gently returning to the original mood.

An interesting by-product of the *Jamaica* excursion was an album of its songs (without the lyrics) arranged and recorded by Arlen's friend David Rose and his orchestra. The percussion, as in the show's original orchestrations, is prominent, but Rose's orchestra is also rich in strings. In addition to the three major songs mentioned, Rose also performs several "lyric fun" selections that stand on their own as sprightly, witty, endearing melodies. Lena Horne's "Push de Button," a calypso, is a rhythmic tour de force, and her "Pretty to Walk With" light-heartedly ironic. The comic numbers, "Little Biscuit" and "What Good Does It Do?," amuse even without the lyrics. At the same time, they exemplify that blend, or wedding, as Arlen called it, of words with music that makes a song.

With *Jamaica* established at the Imperial (where it would remain until April 1959), Harold Arlen, two nights after that premiere, found himself in a box in Carnegie Hall for another New York first performance. On November 2, 1957, Andre Kostelanetz conducted the orchestral suite from *Blues Opera*. The composer joked about "Arlen in Carnegie Hall," but he was excited and rather proud. For the occasion he had invited the Cranes and their daughter in from Syracuse; also attending the concert were A. L. Berman and other friends.

The world premiere had taken place in Minneapolis on August 28, during the inception of the *Jamaica* contretemps. Robert Breen had accompanied him to the "Music under the Stars" concert, in which Kostelanetz had conducted the Minneapolis Symphony. The premiere of the suite had been scheduled for the previous evening but postponed because of rain. Breen had jokingly blamed the stormy weather on Arlen's presence. Arlen preferred a more positive view: "We'll get another day in the press," he told Breen. "A plug's a plug."

The suite had been arranged by Arlen and Kostelanetz from the *Blues Opera* score and orchestrated by the conductor-arranger Samuel Matlowsky, who had been the musical director of the long-running revival of Kurt Weill's *Threepenny Opera* at the Theatre de Lys in Greenwich Village. Matlowsky also worked with Arlen as a musical secretary, assisting in setting down all the new music Arlen conceived for the opera and then weaving it into the *St. Louis Woman* score. While he collaborated with Harburg on *Jamaica,* Arlen set aside an hour each day to work with Breen and Matlowsky on *Blues Opera.*

The suite, lasting about twenty-five minutes, is a musical précis of *Blues Opera;* its seventeen sections follow the same sequence as in the opera. It is divided into two parts, played without pause. The first begins with the opening of act 1 and the second with the opening of act 2. Each section consists of familiar as well as unfamiliar music, the bulk from *St. Louis Woman,* plus newly composed songs and instrumentals. In the act 1 section the best-known melodies are "Any Place I Hang My Hat Is Home" and "It's a Woman's Prerogative." Interwoven are atmospheric interludes, passages that Arlen later felt needed vocals. The section concludes with several cakewalks leading into a dance hall brawl ("Pandemonium") that abruptly becomes a stately, tranquil minuet (the "American Minuet" Arlen had composed for the Maxwell House Hour in 1939).

The act 2 segment begins with a flourish: the traditional trumpet call announcing the beginning of the race. On hearing this, one of Arlen's guests turned to the composer and asked, "You wrote *that,* too?" Featured in this section are two of Arlen's finest melodies, "I Had Myself a True Love" and the poignant (but discarded from *St. Louis Woman*) "I Wonder What Became of Me." The last was preceded by one of the new pieces, "Dis Little While." In an interview with Dorothy Kilgallen, Arlen had said, "I feel that the theme of . . . 'Dis Little While,' although not having hit potential, moves me more than anything I've ever written." The suite closes with a big, flashy ending: "One for My Baby" (from 1943's *The Sky's the Limit*); a powerful spiritual, "Leavin' Time"; and a pulsating "Come Rain or Come Shine." A final brief reference to the spiritual brings the suite to a vibrant conclusion.

The final chord echoed throughout Carnegie Hall as the capacity audience responded with enthusiastic applause, which accompanied a round of gesticulation. From the podium Kostelanetz pointed to Arlen in his box, awash in ovation and surrounded by beaming cousins and friends. Arlen stood, then signaled to

Matlowsky to rise and share the acclamation with him and the conductor. He pointed to Kostelanetz and joined in the applause himself. The audience loved the gesture and the decibel level rose. Arlen, his face flushed with pleasure, sat down to continued applause. The *Blues Opera Suite* had closed the program. It had been preceded by Berlioz's *Roman Carnival Overture,* Prokofiev's "Classical" Symphony, Villa-Lobos's *Memories of Youth,* and Rachmaninoff's "Vocalise." The *Blues Opera Suite* ended the concert on a highly charged note and was that evening's hit. Arlen was particularly amused by the appearance of his name in the program: "Arlen," just like Bach or Beethoven.

As Arlen and his friends left the hall, they were stopped by several people waving their programs at Arlen. He graciously signed them as more gathered for autographs. While he signed the programs, he turned to a friend and said, "I pay them to do this."

The party then moved on to Gracie Square, on the East Side near the United Nations building, where Gloria Vanderbilt Lumet gave a party to celebrate the *Blues Opera Suite.* (She herself was celebrating the publication of a volume of poetry.) She and the brilliant young film director Sidney Lumet lived in a spacious duplex; Kostelanetz lived in the same building.

Among the other celebrants were Abe Berman, Fred Saidy (but, inexplicably, no Harburg), the writer John Gunther, the Arlen devotee William Sweigert, Wilva and Bob Breen, the columnist Leonard Lyons—and, explicably, no Truman Capote. Sweigert, a civilian typist for the army during the day who devoted most of his time to collecting Arleniana—recordings, sheet music, programs, and clippings—was drafted by Gloria Vanderbilt to select the recordings (some he knew were Arlen favorites) for the evening's music.

Vanderbilt also presented, with pride, a copy of her new book to Arlen. Writing is but one of her many talents; she has designed jewelry, fabrics, and jeans and simultaneously turned to painting. Arlen admired her work and acquired several of her canvases, including a stark study in Americana, *Lizzie Borden.*

Lumet arrived from another part of the duplex, noisily escorting a party of film people, among them Henry Fonda (who had starred in Lumet's recent *Twelve Angry Men*). The din annoyed Sweigert, also an authority on film, who commented about the clamorous Lumet, whose conversation encroached on the music, "I think he just discovered the f-word and uses it for punctuation."

Kostelanetz arrived late also, bringing good news: he would record the *Blues Opera Suite* for Columbia Records. With the talk, the promise of a recording, and his songs ringing in his ears, a grateful Harold Arlen, accompanied by the Breens, returned to his own, lonely duplex. Something, he believed, would have to be done about Anya; he missed her terribly.

20

FREE AND
EASY BLUES

❧

*W*ith *Jamaica* solidly established on Broadway, Harold Arlen had the time to relax and to reject offers for films and shows. He put the unpleasantness of *Jamaica* behind him—the treatment of Yipper and the consensus that the show's success could be attributed to Lena Horne, not his work and Yip's—and returned to the Breens and *Blues Opera*.

Work on the opera was as much social as professional. The Breens lived above the Hudson Theatre, on West Forty-fourth Street near Times Square. Theirs was a baronial duplex, filled with massive furniture and resembling a set from a Shakespearean play. The stairway up two flights (there was no elevator) was a colorful climb, its walls decorated with *Porgy and Bess* posters from all over the world. Inside, the living room and office quarters were postered with mementos of Breen's years with ANTA and other theatrical artifacts.

Bookcases were crammed with volumes on a variety of subjects, but not one was in its original jacket. Breen loved books, even their physical form. When presented with a book, he removed the jacket, virtually caressed the volume, then tossed the jacket into the wastebasket. Arlen regularly presented the Breens with recordings and books he fancied, among them such weighty items as Morgenstern's *Composers on Music: An Anthology of Composers' Writings from Palestrina to Copland* or Harvey Breit's *The Writer Observed*. The thoughts and observations of creators fascinated Arlen; he was an avid reader of the *Paris*

Review and its author interviews. He also presented the Breens and other friends with lavish art books, especially those devoted to contemporary artists.

His source for these gifts was the Doubleday Book Shop, on Fifth Avenue near Fifty-seventh Street, a frequent stop on his way home from either Abe Berman's office, a few blocks down on Fifth, or the barber nearby. He was a favored customer among the sales staff, particularly in the record department. If a clerk felt a recording would interest Arlen, the clerk would call him (on his hypothetically unlisted number) to let him know. These recordings, usually featuring his own work, would then be shipped by the book shop staff, sparing Arlen a trip to the post office.

Arlen's free-spending generosity disconcerted Berman, who attended to his finances. Finally, in a plea for prudence, Berman ordered a rubber stamp with a message he impressed on the accumulating statements: HAROLD—HOW ABOUT THE BILLS?

Arlen and the Breens worked out a system to prepare *Blues Opera* for a premiere in the spring of 1958 at the Brussels World's Fair. The full score was complete before the extraction of the suite, but after its presentation, Arlen recorded the first of what he called "work tapes" for Breen. The first, marked "Revisions," was made about a month after the Carnegie Hall premiere and is dated December 6, 1957. Through August and September 1958 three additional tapes were recorded by Arlen, often with other vocalists, friends of the Breens. The last of these was dated September 25, after which there were three interruptions, one sadly crushing to Arlen.

Early in October he received a letter from the dramatist Paddy Chayefsky telling him that his play *Middle of the Night,* which Arlen had seen a couple of years before, was about to be filmed. Would Arlen write the music for the film's theme song? Enclosed with the letter was a lyric.

Arlen's initial instinctive reaction was to dictate a polite note and return the lyric. Ever since the heyday of Tin Pan Alley, composers, lyricists, and publishers had learned to beware of over-the-transom, unsolicited songs. They could be troublesome if not costly. Irving Berlin, the Gershwins, and other major songwriters were often sued by aspiring unknown songwriters who had mailed in a song suggestion, later charging plagiarism. Few, if any, won these litigations, but the publicity and the time wasted were vexing. In time, if such obviously manuscript-laden packets arrived in the publisher's mail room, they were returned, unopened, to the unknown sender.

Chayefsky, Arlen realized, was not one of those, and after reading through the lyric a few times, he was satisfied that "it sings," as he told a friend.

The play, and film, tells the star-crossed story of an older man (Edward G. Robinson on the stage) in love with a young woman (younger than his daughter) and the impact of this infatuation on their families. Chayefsky's lyric was the lament of a lonely man, which Arlen marked "brooding and hesitant":

Just lie awake, man—
And let the ache grow numb—
She can keep, man
Get to sleep, man
Before those silent hours come 'cause
Oh, you know, those proud defenses go—
In the middle of the night, in the middle of the night . . .

Arlen's melody is plaintive, reflecting the resignation of the lyric (which suffers from the repetition of the word "man," something a Gershwin, Harburg, or Mercer would not have done). Still, Arlen found it affecting and set the lyric in a characteristic Arlenian manner: thirteen-bar verse and thirty-three-bar chorus. Short rests break up the melody to create an air of hesitancy, and the heartbreak of the lyric is underscored by holding the final "night" for two bars. There is no resolution as "In the Middle of the Night" ends, fading into midair.

This remarkably touching creation was not heard in the filmed *Middle of the Night,* which starred Frederic March. The producers would not meet A. L. Berman's asking fee for the use of Arlen's music. Consequently it went unused and was never published.

Arlen was unconcerned, always leaving business matters to Berman; moreover, at the time, there was a more serious crisis confronting him. In her midseventies, Celia Arluck had been ill for a distressing period. Frail for the past year, she died at the end of November 1958. Arlen bore his mother's death more stoically than that of his father. It was a private sorrow to be shared only with his brother. As he wrote a friend after the funeral, "I'll not go into the emotional end of this mysterious and final curtain."

It was probably sheer coincidence, but quite soon after the death of Celia Arluck, Anya joined her husband in the little duplex on East Fifty-fifth Street, sometime early in 1959. Now in her early forties, she was still strikingly beautiful, svelte, and charming. Anyone not knowing her recent history would not have imagined that this quiet, often subdued but frequently effervescent and amusing woman had been institutionalized for several years. She and Arlen, as before, were seen at the first nights at the theater, preview screenings, and parties. Anya had no difficulty taking up her life, and theirs, again. There was one source of friction, for Arlen rarely saw Jerry Arlen once Anya returned. There was still an undercurrent of the hostility she had harbored toward Jerry since her early breakdowns in Beverly Hills when he was burdened with her hospitalizations because Harold could not face it.

Anya had barely settled into the apartment, after a little readjustment of furnishings and a tour of the better shops, when in April 1959 the Arlens returned to Beverly Hills and registered at the Beverly Hills Hotel. "Believe it or not," Arlen wrote that day to a friend in New York, "when we checked into our room the bell boy put on the television set & Oscar Levant was introducing [Lawrence] Stewart & of course we just froze & listened to both of them gooing charmingly about [Stewart's recent book]. It was a love feast for both of them for the excellence of the book." Delighted, he called Stewart, who was working with Ira Gershwin, to tell him that even before their bags were unpacked they found two friendly faces in California.

Arlen had come to work. Earlier in the year a film assignment of great promise had fallen through, and he was most disappointed; the project would have reunited him with Ira Gershwin. A couple of youthful producers had flown in from London with an idea for a musical film—an animated version of Dickens's *A Christmas Carol* with drawings by Ronald Searle and adaptation and lyrics by Christopher Fry. Except for one detail, Arlen found their plan irresistible. Fry was best known in the United States as the author of the successful plays *The Lady's Not for Burning* and *Venus Observed*. Searle was celebrated in Britain for his freely drawn, sardonic cartoons for *Punch* and, in the States, for the *New Yorker*. His witty series of cartoons depicting life in St. Trinians, a girls' school, had inspired two successful comic films.

His visitors, Arlen sensed, were substantial dreamers, aiming high. His sole objection was to the choice of lyricist. Fry was acclaimed for his style and hailed by critics as the playwright who would revive poetic drama, but Arlen impressed on the two future producers that writing a song lyric was its own special art form.

They were open to suggestions. "Who would you suggest, Harold?" one asked.

"Ira Gershwin," he replied. That sounded like a winning marshaling of talent, and they agreed. The obstacle they now faced was, Arlen knew, would Ira be interested? Arlen immediately called Gershwin, who listened and agreed to listen further. The producers soon after flew to California to outline their project in full for Gershwin, who then said no. His rejection was disappointing to Arlen as well as the Londoners. Gershwin was notorious for avoiding work to an exaggerated degree, and at the time, was engaged in preparing his *Lyrics on Several Occasions* for publication. But one rumor was that he actually backed out of the project because one of the producers had addressed him as "Ira" too soon after their initial meeting. He used "Mister" in speaking to them and believed that such familiarity was inappropriate. Gershwin was not a snob, but he expected a degree of propriety.

With *A Christmas Carol* canceled, an even better proposition had come Arlen's way and had taken him and Anya to Beverly Hills, not for a film but for a Broadway musical. The late 1950s was a poor time for musical films. Only Lerner and Loewe's *Gigi* qualified for an original film musical in 1958. The other outstanding releases that year were adaptations of Broadway successes, *South Pacific* and *Damn Yankees*. The following year offered only an unfortunate Samuel Goldwyn–produced *Porgy and Bess*.

Hollywood was a desert in 1959 for the songwriter.

Arlen had come to Hollywood to work with Johnny Mercer on a musical based on the popular 1945 film *Saratoga Trunk* (based, in turn, on the Edna Ferber novel) starring Gary Cooper and Ingrid Bergman. Ferber's best-seller, a sprawling tale set in the late nineteenth century, followed the adventures of a professional gambler and a beautiful fortune hunter from New Orleans to Saratoga Springs, New York, during the racing season. As with *Show Boat,* the book was a natural for film—colorful costumes, exotic sets in New Orleans, and expensive social settings in the health resorts of Saratoga.

When Mercer was asked by the producer Robert Fryer to write the words to Arlen's music, the lyricist declined. How could such an ambitious story be confined to a stage? "If you're going to do a *Show Boat* sequel," he said, "you're thirty years too late."

Harold Arlen then convinced Mercer they could do the job and that it could work. The ingredient that would accomplish that was Morton DaCosta.

In 1959 DaCosta was renowned up and down Broadway as a hit maker. In a period of less than five years he had staged four hit shows in a row: *Plain and Fancy, No Time for Sergeants, Auntie Mame* (whose film adaptation he also directed), and *The Music Man;* the first and last were extraordinarily successful musicals and the others hit comedies. Arlen's belief was that, since DaCosta had adapted Ferber's novel and would also direct, a hit musical was inevitable. Mercer was not completely convinced but reluctantly signed on the show. (Even a half year later, when the musical was in rehearsal, he was not happy with the effort. When asked why he had taken it on, since he had so little faith in *Saratoga,* he replied, in characteristic offhand Mercer manner, "I'm always doing jobs I don't want.")

Though regarded as a suddenly arrived fair-haired boy on Broadway, DaCosta had served years of apprenticeship in regional theaters as well as New York. An ex-Philadelphian, the last of ten children of an antiques dealer, he went to New York hoping to be an actor but was unsuccessful. After touring with a children's theater, he returned to New York, where he worked with the actor Maurice Evans (and had a part in Evans's GI *Hamlet*) as the great actor's assistant. During this period DaCosta became familiar with every aspect of the theater, from lighting to "the front of the house" (the business of the box office). At Evans's urging and encouragement, DaCosta directed a series of classics—*The Alchemist, She Stoops to Conquer, Captain Brassbound's Conversion*—at the New York City Center in 1950. Other directorial assignments followed, enhancing his reputation as a director. He worked the "folk musical" *Plain and Fancy* in 1955, followed two years later by the overwhelmingly popular *The Music Man,* a show that initially few thought had a chance. Its score was by Meredith Willson, little known on Broadway, who based the story on reminiscences of his boyhood in Mason City, Iowa. It became the hit of the year, even greater than Bernstein's

West Side Story, and ran for 1,375 performances. A good deal of the show's success was attributed to DaCosta's direction and "doctoring" out of town.

If anyone could make *Saratoga Trunk* work, Arlen was certain that Morton DaCosta was that person. Once Mercer agreed to do the lyrics, Robert Fryer announced the future production on Broadway of a musical, *Saratoga,* to be written and directed by Morton DaCosta, with a score by Arlen and Mercer, and, as its star, Hollywood's Rock Hudson. This last point was, in fact, wishful thinking, though it was also announced that Hudson was working with a vocal coach. The "news" alarmed Hudson's studio bosses, who reminded him of his contract for a series of films teaming him with Doris Day, and he bowed out. He was then replaced by another popular film hero, Howard Keel, a baritone who did not need a vocal coach.

For the Arlens, the five months that year in California were idyllic. They rented a house in Beverly Hills and became neighbors of the Warrens, Koehlers, and Gershwins. Mercer, however, had moved his family to Lido Isle at Newport Beach, a couple hours' drive south of Beverly Hills.

Their collaboration, nevertheless, went smoothly and remarkably fast. The distance and time hindrances were easily overcome, thanks to Arlen's tape recorder. Mercer would drive up from Newport Beach, spend some time with Arlen, and then return home with tapes to work on over the weekend. By early May they had completed about half the score.

On the fifth, Robert Breen and Stanley Chase, the latter now co-producer of *Blues Opera,* arrived in Beverly Hills for final discussions. Before they returned to New York, Arlen prepared yet another work tape for them. Breen felt that he should introduce his new associate to Arlen and Mercer. Both knew Chase had been co-producer of the exceptionally successful revival of Kurt Weill's *Threepenny Opera,* which ran for 2,611 performances at the Theatre de Lys in Greenwich Village. Chase's affiliation, like that of DaCosta, boded well for their developing musical—or so Arlen believed.

That he was happy with what he and Mercer had accomplished was evident in a page of thematic jots he had prepared for a friend—"musical chicken scratch" he called them—fifteen songs completed in less than a month. While working hard, he had sent a jesting telegram to the same friend: "Can't understand why you haven't heard from me. Please clarify." On June 16 he clarified:

> If you don't believe my pen is to paper—neither do I—it's bad enough feeling guilty about not working when you're in the pool, let alone having wakeful hours with your [unanswered letter] staring me in the face—Now as to an evening with Arlen—Jule Styne seems to have cornered the present market [at the time composer Styne was touring the club circuit performing his own songs], so may I gracefully say I'd be G-D-pleased [this never came off].

As you know from the lead jots I sent you, John & I did an enormous amount of work up to that point but we've pulled in our reins and have been trotting slowly but surely down the back stretch—

I can't determine its worth or dare guess what it will have out of the theatre but I'm fairly certain it will work *in* the theatre—That is if our principles are cast well—The girl must be an exciting wench—

What does amaze me about the work is the difference in style from Jamaica—Blues—Flowers etc—When I ponder about it & rest assured I do—often—it makes me stop in my tracks & wonder how long this can go on—I don't think an audience nor the critics realize (alas why should they) how much is taken from a writer every time he goes to bat—

That is why I have always been a true lover of & might add slightly in awe of de Goishwins—Porter—Rodgers—Berlin—Hammerstein—Kern—The very few others with a smidgeon of exceptions borrow well—at least well enough to blind the critics ear—I think we've had enough of the above—

As to my work with John—I have a hunch we might come down the finish line by the middle of July or thereabouts—Am taking Dr. [Ralph] Bunche [of the United Nations and recipient of the Nobel Peace Prize] & his wife & daughter to Ira's to-nite—perhaps you will hear from me soon—

Anya sends her love to you both & the children—

Mine too—

The middle of July came and went and Arlen and Mercer were not quite finished, but they were close. Arlen, elated, buoyant, and playful—for the time in California had been a delightful personal experience with Anya and a productive one with Mercer—acknowledged the birth of a friend's daughter with a telegram: "Hooray for Emily the new addition to the femily."

By this time, the end of August, the casting of *Saratoga* had begun, and rehearsals were scheduled for September and the out-of-town (Philadelphia) opening for the last week in October. Arlen looked in briefly on the "cattle calls" (casting), which he preferred to avoid. Long lines of hopeful dancers and singers, from which few were chosen, disturbed him.

Fryer released the names of the leads, Keel as Clint Maroon and Carol Lawrence (who had scored a great personal success in Leonard Bernstein's *West Side Story*) as Clio Dulaine, the illegitimate Creole thorn in the side of a prominant New Orleans family. The advance ticket sales, most to theater parties, by rehearsal time had soared to a million dollars.

The secondary roles were engagingly cast. Clio, despite the fact of her illicit birth, was well provided for if, in turn, she stayed away from her wealthy family. Her subsidy enabled her to travel in style with a colorful entourage: a kind but bossy Aunt Belle; a black, also kind, maid, Kakou; and Cupide, a dwarf, to carry Clio's bags. Clint, who eventually teams up with the trio, was a loner.

Aunt Belle was portrayed by the seasoned Odette Myrtil, who left her job as manager of the Playhouse Inn in nearby New Hope, Pennsylvania. In the early 1930s she had appeared in two Jerome Kern musicals on Broadway, *The Cat and the Fiddle* and *Roberta*. Her most recent Broadway appearance had been in 1952, as Bloody Mary in *South Pacific*. Following a brief Hollywood career and appearances in stock, Myrtil abandoned the theater and film for innkeeping. According to the *Saratoga* souvenir program, she was "lured into taking the role of Aunt Belle" by DaCosta. In fact, after reading in one of the trade papers that the production was searching for a matronly, musical woman with a French accent, Myrtil auditioned like any other aspirant. Arlen found this fact of theatrical life unpleasant.

Carol Brice, a contralto and Juilliard graduate, was cast as the proud Kakou. Although she was a veteran of the concert and recital stage, *Saratoga* was to be her first Broadway musical. The dwarf Cupide was portrayed by Tun Tun, a popular Mexican-born dancer-singer. He was best known in the Spanish-speaking world for his appearances in over forty motion pictures. He was introduced to this country on the Milton Berle show; *Saratoga* would be his Broadway debut.

Also making her musical debut was Jane Darwell, best known for her work in films, especially for her Academy Award–winning Ma Joad in *The Grapes of Wrath*. She appeared on Broadway for the first time in Sidney Howard's first play, *Swords* (1921). She was cast as Mrs. Bellop, who ruled the social scene in Saratoga Springs during the racing and mineral water season, when the affluent flocked to the spa and track. It was here that the hero, Clint, hoped to fleece the wealthy robber barons, and Clio would trap one of their members into marriage. Darwell, then in her late seventies, was to be one of the first casualties of the *Saratoga* maelstrom.

There were more than thirty speaking roles in *Saratoga* in addition to the principals. Added to these were singing and dancing chorus parts as market vendors, townspeople, waiters, hotel guests, and children. These were employed in colorful ensemble scenes in the streets of New Orleans, the wide verandas of Saratoga hotels, even a railroad station and a moving flatcar. In following Ferber's plot, DaCosta's settings moved from Paris to New Orleans to Saratoga, in cathedrals, hotel rooms, a waterfront market, a ballroom, and other venues. This provided DaCosta, as librettist, a wealth of material with which to work, but is also presented DaCosta, as director, with much material to control.

Arlen was certain that "Tec" (pronounced "Teek," from the director's original surname, Tecosky) could bring it off, elephantine as it had become. Mercer, however, continued to sense that the elephant would be rendered whiter as time went by. The book was too unwieldy.

In September Mercer went to New York with Anya and Arlen for final touches and rehearsals. These were held in the Central Plaza on the Lower East Side, a large, many-roomed building, once a popular social center. Because of its spaciousness, it was perfect for rehearsals. In a hot September of 1959, the non-airconditioned building was uncomfortable, especially for the dancers. The several small fans helped but slightly.

The first sign of things to come involved Jane Darwell; she could not remember her lines and rehearsed with a script in hand. Almost eighty, she had depended on cue cards in her recent films and television appearances.

Another serious problem surfaced when the several parts of the show that had been distributed throughout the Central Plaza were assembled in a theater for a run-through. Tec had not stinted on his book, and Arlen and Mercer had followed his lead: a great deal of song had been poured into a show that ran for over three hours. Mercer, resigned to problems, took it all lightly, but Arlen began to worry. When he and Anya, with a joking Mercer, left an afternoon's rehearsal, Arlen laughed at Mercer's impression of their director, but not heartily. He hoped Tec would be able to bring all those disparate pieces together in Philadelphia.

Saratoga opened at the Shubert there on October 26, 1959. The *Variety* review was guardedly optimistic but signaled the need for change. "Robert Fryer's presentation of Morton DaCosta's production of Edna Ferber's novel, 'Saratoga Trunk,' looks destined for a happy future, but it's a good thing the show has five weeks here for revision." Especially disconcerting about the review was that the head—credits, cast, dates, ticket prices, the names of dancers, and titles of musical numbers—required almost as much print as the critique itself. Tersely, "Waters" had praise for the Cecil Beaton sets and costumes (and a reminder that he had done the same for *My Fair Lady,* an unfortunate allusion invoking the theatrical cliché of leaving a musical humming the scenery). Waters granted Arlen three or four agreeable tunes, though the score was not "as noteworthy as some he has done." He said nothing about Mercer's lyrics but credited Jerry Arlen, as conductor, with keeping things moving. He found the stars, Keel and Lawrence, "agreeable performers" and "reasonably effective," phrases hardly suitable for quotation in a *New York Times* advertisement.

Waters found that the "veteran pros, Jane Darwell and Odette Myrtil, score emphatically and a midget programmed as Tun Tun and who looks like Pierre Lautrec [*sic*] is a standout." But his major point was that DaCosta, "who made the dramatization and has also directed, will likely have his hands full with revisions in both classifications"

Waters reported in the review's final sentence that the show was virtually sold out for its five-week Philadelphia residence and urged that during this time DaCosta do "vital re-vamping."

Such an opinion in business-wise *Variety* induced panic and immediate action.

H A R O L D   A R L E N

DaCosta's friend Arthur Laurents (librettist of *West Side Story,* then in its second year) was summoned to assist in the vital revamping.

The desperation was evident in the program changes during the final weeks in Philadelphia. DaCosta realized that, because of the running time, cuts were essential. Within five days of the premiere he excised the prologue, set in Paris, which established the motivation for Clio's return to New Orleans—to "pay back" her relatives who had rejected her mother. Part of the exposition was sung by Aunt Belle as she read from a New Orleans newspaper. That was cut, along with two songs, "I'll Be Respectable" and "You for Me." A couple of weeks later they had been restored, and a new Arlen-Mercer song, "Countin' Our Chickens" was added. Some songs were shifted around, to no great advantage.

Eliminating the prologue left DaCosta with a plot hole, which he filled with dialogue. As the decision-making director, he was obviously looking out for the librettist. It was frustrating to Arlen, who never knew which DaCosta he was confronting, the director or the writer of the book, when songs were eliminated and new ones called for. It was wearing him out; he was tired of the freneticism and worried about Anya, suffering from a cold. Mercer was the picture of imperturbability, serenely ready for whatever came from day to day. Besides, he had never cared for the show anyway.

By the third week, Jane Darwell withdrew from the cast because memorizing new dialogue was too much for her; she was replaced by her understudy, Edith King, whose name was not as celebrated as Darwell's but who was also a seasoned, dependable trouper with experience on stage, screen, and television.

The Arlens followed. Harold was too exhausted to keep up with the demands and, believing that he had contributed more than enough, he left, claiming illness. Anya took to her bed in their apartment, and Harold entered Mount Sinai Hospital to rest, recover, and avoid interviews.

This flight left DaCosta without a composer, so Mercer filled in for his friend. Before the New York premiere, he would write both the words and music for three additional songs without claiming credit for the music. If he suffered from strain or pressure, it is not evident in the lyrics. In the usual witty Mercer style are "Gettin' a Man" ("and gettin' a husband is two different things") and the politically wry robber baron's "The Men Who Run the Country." The ballad for Keel, "Why Fight This?," while serviceable, is obviously not a Harold Arlen melody.

Only one Arlen, Jerry, was present at the New York premiere of *Saratoga* at the Winter Garden the night of December 7, 1959. As the show's conductor, he had watched its convolutions and permutations since the exciting beginnings at the Central Plaza. He was also sadly preoccupied; his wife, Sherry Altman Arlen, was terminally ill with cancer. Perhaps this haunting circumstance affected his conducting; possibly, the show's last stressful weeks in Philadelphia had taken their toll; or maybe it was a simple matter of ego. At any rate, Jerry Arlen and

Howard Keel were frequently at loggerheads. There was dissension over tempos, miscues, and a too-loud orchestra. At one performance in New York, after the unhappy reviews were in and tempers had risen, Keel showed his anger publicly when, upon finishing a vocal—not quite in time with the orchestra—he made his exit, stage right, stopped midway, turned and glared at the pit, then left the stage. Keel, too, was under pressure. During the New York previews and before opening night one of his all-Mercer numbers, "Why Fight This?" was replaced by the melodically superior Arlen-Mercer "You or No One."

Tuesday's reviews contributed further to the company's low morale. The *New York World-Telegram,* in addition to its critic's views, published a boxed compilation of brief quotes from other papers and two news services. Headed "What the Critics Say," the message was largely negative. According to the summary, the critics "awarded six nays, two qualified yeas, and a definite yea to 'Saratoga.' " Had *Saratoga* been a ship, it was destined for the bottom. While DaCosta suffered the most, Arlen and Mercer, too, were surprisingly, and none too fairly, mauled.

Variety's reviewer found the score "shockingly lackluster" (so did Brooks Atkinson in the *New York Times;* in the *New Yorker* Kenneth Tynan, too, applied "shockingly" to the songs and coupled that with "undistinguished"). These views were offset slightly by those of John McClain *(New York Journal-American),* who found *Saratoga* "simply wonderful. It [the score] is singable, whistleable and delightfully in the mood . . . of the novel. Johnny Mercer's lyrics are similarly sympathetic." Walter Kerr began his *New York Tribune* column with "I'm sure all hearts lifted at the sound of the Harold Arlen overture at the Winter Garden last evening. I know mine did. While I don't remember now just which tunes were threaded through it to give it that jubilant air, I solemnly swear to you that they were one and all good."

After which Kerr joined in chorus with his colleagues by pointing out that the "really distressing thing about 'Saratoga' was the quality of the DaCosta book." John Chapman *(New York Daily News),* though he admired "the fine singing songs," condemned *Saratoga* as "the most complicated music-show plot since Richard Wagner wrote 'Siegfried.' " Richard Watts Jr. *(New York Post)* made his point about the book in his column's headline: "A Handsome Musical Play Suffers from Book Trouble." As had virtually all the other critics, he admired the Beaton costumes and sets. And so on, from paper to paper to weekly periodical. " 'Saratoga,' " Tynan observed in the *New Yorker,* "is a musical that has all the pace and vivacity of a three-volume Victorian novel. . . . Mr. DaCosta has directed his own script, and I cannot think of a better seven-word argument for division of labor."

Of the seven daily reviews only one (McClain's) was favorable (there was no "rave") and six were unfavorable. It remained for *Variety*'s "Hobe" to write the show's obituary. The so-called bible of show business, while not widely read by the public, was carefully read by everyone in the music business, the theater, and films. In his opening paragraph Hobe establishes the theme of his review by stating that since DaCosta was both the "author and stager, he must take a double rap for the overpowering dullness of this mammoth, lavishly handsome musical." In the final paragraph he sent a deadly message to the West Coast: *Saratoga,* he concluded, was "understood to have cost somewhere around $480,000 [a grand sum in 1959] to bring in, however, and probably can't break even for much under $40,000 a week. On that basis, it stacks up as a major financial loss [despite the large advance ticket sales]. There's little likelihood of a film sale."

That judgment was the kiss of death, and *Saratoga*'s melancholy cast, troupers all, managed to persevere for an additional ten weeks. The musical would close in February 1960, in time for Harold Arlen's fifty-fifth birthday; it would be his last Broadway show.

Despite his father's advice years ago, Arlen could not ignore the reviews. As he read them in his room in Mount Sinai Hospital, Arlen realized the show could not last long and was resigned to that. DaCosta, in the early weeks after the opening, attempted to salvage the show, but with no success; he then abruptly left for Europe.

After the premiere and the votes were in, a friend visited Arlen in the hospital.

"I've got to get out of here," Arlen told him.

"Then leave."

"I can't, they took my clothes. Go home, get me something to wear, and I'll get out of this damn place."

"I'm not so sure that's a good idea. You haven't been discharged yet."

"But I'm not sick, and I'm through with the *Saratoga* mess. Annie's home, she'll give you something."

Luckily, when the friend arrived, he found Arlen's doctor and friend from Buffalo, Maurice Schachtel, looking in on Anya and her cold. She was in her nightgown.

"Doc, Harold wants to get sprung. I'm supposed to get him some clothes."

"Let him stay there!" Schachtel said, sharply.

"He's miserable and anxious to come home."

Schachtel finally acquiesced. He knew Arlen was not seriously ill, physically. He was fatigued and distressed after Philadelphia.

Various items of clothing, down to the underwear, were stuffed into a small overnight bag, which was then carried nonchalantly past the Mount Sinai reception desk into Arlen's room on the second floor. In a few minutes, unobtrusively, the two men slipped out of the hospital into a cab on Fifth Avenue and sped off, unpursued, downtown to East Fifty-fifth Street and a relieved, welcoming Anya.

But the year of the crisis—1959—was not over.

Blues Opera, the enterprise that had been initiated in 1953 by Robert Breen's letter to Ira Gershwin inquiring about the whereabouts of Harold Arlen, was, even as Arlen fretted in his white-walled room in Mount Sinai, coming to fruition. He was fated, by December 1959, to suffer his next debacle from a distance.

Following their hasty trip to Beverly Hills in May, Breen and Chase returned to New York to prepare for their announced world premiere in Amsterdam on December 7 (coinciding with the New York opening of *Saratoga*), following the "out-of-town" tryout in Brussels. After that would come Paris and other stops in Europe and beyond. By the time the company arrived in Brussels in November the title had been changed to *Free and Easy* at Chase's suggestion. He felt that the "opera" in the original title would be bad for business, though it had not tainted his *Threepenny Opera*. "Free and easy" are the initial words to "Anyplace I Hang My Hat Is Home."

Because of his worsening involvement in *Saratoga*, Arlen had little idea of what was happening with *Free and Easy*. He was mired in Philadelphia when the opera opened in Brussels and not long out of the hospital when it finally had its premiere at the Carré Theater in Amsterdam, ten days later than its announced opening.

In a letter reproduced in the program, Karel Wunnink, the theater's manager, optimistically and unwittingly revealed the incendiary situation: "The curtain rises for a new musical drama: Harold Arlen's 'Free and Easy.' . . . May this baptism on the border of the river Amstel be a good omen, so that the coming tour of Stanley Chase and his Company shall have an equal and triumphant career as the tour of 'Porgy and Bess.' " (The Gershwin opera had had its final European performance at the Carré in June 1956.)

Nowhere in his long letter does Wunnink mention the name of Robert Breen. When *Variety* published a review from its Amsterdam critic on December 30, Breen's name is also significantly missing. The direction is credited to Donald McKayle, Breen's assistant. Then Walter H. Waggoner of the *New York Times* filed an article from Amsterdam with the head "Curtain Rises on a Producer-Director Feud." Harold Arlen, reading in New York, had become an innocent bystander and victim of a deadly, irreconcilable confrontation.

While the battle raged in Amsterdam, Arlen found himself in the center as Breen or Chase phoned, each with his own side of the story. "Each is the heavy," Arlen commented to a friend in a weary voice, "depending on who's talking."

Another participant, Johnny Mercer, rang from California. When he gave his blessing to Breen and Chase, he had assumed that he would be the lyricist. But the *Variety* review from Amsterdam informed Mercer that additional lyrics were the work of Ted Koehler (such songs as "Ill Wind," "I Gotta Right to Sing the Blues," and two songs from the *Americanegro Suite*; nothing new). A new song, "Won't Dat Be de Blessed Day," was attributed to Mercer and was probably done in California while he and Arlen worked on *Saratoga*.

Other songs, among them "Dis Little While," "Many Kinds of Love," and "Blow de Whistle," all specially written for *Blues Opera*, have no lyrics attribution. While the authorship is questionable, the words to these songs may have been written by Arlen or the Breens. Such interpolations infuriated Mercer, who dispatched a blistering letter to Arlen objecting to the Koehler songs. He was unaware of "Live Hard, Work Hard, Love Hard" borrowed from *My Blue Heaven*, with the Arlen-Blane lyric.

The letter upset Arlen, but there was little he could do from a distance, and the word was that *Free and Easy* would not survive, not only because of the acrimonious feud, but also because it was a dramatic and musical mess.

In Manhattan, Arlen followed the destruction of his work by transatlantic, and contradictory, calls from the warring parties, *Variety*, and the *New York Times*. The week after the Amsterdam premiere, Chase announced that Breen was "disassociated" from the production, that his assistant had taken over the direction, and that a play doctor, Meade Roberts, had been called in to rework the book.

This was ironic, for when the first reviews were published, it was Breen who was most praised. Jan Spierdjik, writing in the Amsterdam *De Telegraf*, lauded the set, by the Philippine-born American designer Ballou, and the costumes, by Jed Mace, which he declared were "magnificent," but wrote that the "most striking factor . . . was the staging of Robert Breen." *Het Parool*'s Les Van Deiden believed that "not much could be made out of such a meager story and Breen could only show his great talent as director of the mass scenes."

Another critic found what he had seen to be "neither a dress rehearsal nor yet an opening. The charming and touching qualities of the show, which are already obvious, will undoubtedly be further developed."

But not by Robert Breen, whose idea it was originally to "develop" *St. Louis Woman* into a *Blues Opera*, and who nurtured it for half a decade. He had steered it into the triumphant path he had blazed with *Porgy and Bess*, only to find himself out in the streets of Amsterdam.

One of his impediments was the orchestra, eighteen musicians conducted by the jazz arranger Quincy Jones—"a lot of free spirits unaccustomed to the firm hand of a director," in the opinion of the *New York Times*'s Waggoner.

As Breen explained it, "This was the first time . . . that there had ever been a complete jazz orchestration for an entire musical. It was the first time that a jazz band had appeared on stage not only as musicians doing their work in their own way, but also as characters in a play." Though this idea probably originated with Breen, it was a serious blunder. Jones's orchestration was wrong for Arlen's music, despite Jones's reputation as a brilliant trumpeter and arranger. The apposite and beautiful orchestrations for *St. Louis Woman* were ignored (and, it was later learned, lost), and then-current "modern jazz" orchestrations were inflicted on Arlen's songs and dances. As great as he was, Quincy Jones was not the musician to orchestrate an Arlen musical. Their musical incompatibility was evident in Arlen's comment when he heard a Jones recording of "I Never Has Seen Snow."

"To enjoy it," he said, "you've got to be on the weed."

The free spirits who wandered around the stage, "doing their work in their own way," added little to the staging, and Breen had to persuade these musical thespians not to drown out the singers with their improvisations. Dramatically, even musically, *Free and Easy* was a shambles. Chase, however, intimated that after Breen was "disassociated" and about fifteen minutes cut (still leaving a long three-hour jumble), the show was improved.

On his part, the unrealistically optimistic Breen told the press that he looked forward to joining the company in Paris to put the opera in shape for the premiere at the Alhambra in mid-January. Chase countered that with a statement about the cast and its anti-Breen views and refusal to work with him. Chase also intimated that Breen was mentally unbalanced and on drugs.

Breen remained out in the cold when *Free and Easy* opened on January 15, 1960. The *New York Times* coverage from Paris reported that on a freezing night the performance had "received a warm reception." An audience peppered with "government officials, members of the diplomatic corps and a considerable number of artistic personalities showed their appreciation. If it is shared by the Paris critics, the case should be able to file away some more compliments. . . .

"The musical will play in Paris through Feb. 14 before moving on to Lausanne, Switzerland." It was also reported that *Free and Easy* would return to "the United States after a tour of several more European countries."

Free and Easy shut down nine days later and never got beyond Paris. There had been, as predicted in the *Times*, compliments for the cast, especially for the leads, a stunning Irene Williams as Della Green and Harold Nicholas as Augie, repeating his role from the original *St. Louis Woman*. But word had leaked out during *Free and Easy*'s troubled progress from Brussels to Paris that Chase would bring in Sammy Davis Jr. to replace Nicholas. That "didn't rest well" with Nicholas, *Variety* reported, or with others; "more likely this was ballyhoo that backfired on the general morale." It was also most unlikely; Davis was a good friend of Breen's and would not have taken the part in any case. Sammy Davis had been Breen's original choice for the Augie part, but had been unavailable at the time.

The cast's morale was indeed low. Quincy Jones took his band on a successful tour of Europe, but the rest of the company was, in fact, stranded. One member wrote an anonymous letter to *Variety* contradicting an article that had appeared in the paper proclaiming *Free and Easy* "a great success. . . . Not a word of truth in it. We were a miserable flop.

"On the very day in which this article appeared we were broke, stranded, in Paris and the producer did not have the fare to ship us home. We only managed to get home because of the kindness of two Americans in Paris, a certain Mr. Kaufman and a certain Mr. Reed. But your article stated that business is great and that we are prolonging the run." By this time *Free and Easy* had closed, at a loss of three hundred thousand dollars. The "certain" people mentioned were Wolfe Kaufman, who was associated with impresario Sol Hurok's Paris office, and Joseph Verner Reed of the American Embassy.

The sudden closing of *Free and Easy* came as a stunning surprise to Arlen, after the stream of encouraging reviews and audience receptions. Once the Breen-Chase contretemps became public and Arlen began to hear a confusion of explanations, he chose to remain above the battle. Despite his personal bias favoring Breen, he left all legal matters to A. L. Berman. *Blues Opera/Free and Easy* was shelved, despite Chase's announcement of an autumn 1960 production on Broadway, which never materialized.

Years later there were plans for a revival of *Free and Easy*, or even the less elaborate *St. Louis Woman*, but Arlen was lukewarm about it. He believed that in either version, the second act needed revision. There were additional obstacles. Matlowsky had never completed an orchestration for *Free and Easy*, and only the infelicitous "jazz band" version by Quincy Jones remains. With the loss of the orchestral parts for *St. Louis Woman*, any company with plans to revive that earlier version (the form whose book exists) would be confronted with the expense of orchestrations.

Recognized as one of Arlen's, and Broadway's, finest scores, *St. Louis Woman* has been considered for revival by off-Broadway companies; one by the Opera Ensemble of New York was to have been staged with Arlen's blessing. This had been the idea of an Arlen devotee, Berthe Schuchat, then associated with the Opera Ensemble. Arlen agreed, provided something was done about the second act. The production director, John J. D. Sheehan, a young veteran who had staged operas ranging from Purcell's *Dido and Aeneas* to Vaughan Williams's *Riders to the Sea*, offered to rework the book.

The plan was checked by a projected Broadway production under the aegis of Ginger Mercer, which over time ended up in limbo. Another production was planned by Rosetta LeNoire for her company in Harlem. Since hers was a not-for-profit organization that performed in hospitals and retirement homes, her offer was rejected by the legal firms representing the several estates. There was no money in it. The heirs of Countee Cullen were especially unreasonable, and the project, like that of Schuchat and Sheehan's, died aborning.

More affluent companies, among them the Houston and St. Louis Operas and Washington's Arena Stage, have announced productions, but none have been staged. Complete recordings of all of *St. Louis Woman*, plus the additions written for *Blues Opera*, were also planned. One was stopped by the Ginger Mercer production that never came off, since her company planned to do a new original cast album. Another was simply mired in talk and negotiations.

Arlen took the two failures of 1959 with philosophical resignation. He could look back, a rare thing for him, with equanimity.

"Today," he told John S. Wilson, "it's terribly hard to get a song through unless you have a show on Broadway and a long run. It's fortunate for some of us that we've got standards that can take a beating and still be listenable."

Despite the recent Sturm und Drang, at home and abroad, he decided to take a holiday from theatricals early in 1960. He continued to accumulate jots, but began composing a piece for solo piano. Still untitled, he referred to it as "a rich wail."

21

ODE FOR
ANYA

◢

For more than a year after the *Saratoga* and *Free and Easy* fiascos, Harold Arlen did little creative work except for the piano "wail" and a rhythmic counterpart.

Saratoga closed late in February 1960. Before he left for Europe, DaCosta had the cast assembled onstage to wish them farewell and to admit that everything wrong with the show was his fault. Arlen did not agree. "We were all to blame," he said. "We were all professionals, we should have recognized what was wrong early. But that's in the past . . . we will have to take it in our stride."

Successful or not, his return to New York in the 1950s for *House of Flowers* and the shows that followed had led to his rediscovery; he was no longer "Harold who?" He was sought out for newspaper and radio interviews, patiently and cheerfully enduring the same questions: Which came first, the words or the music? His favorite among his own songs? (The stock answer was generally "Last Night When We Were Young," which few interviewers knew.) He was asked for anecdotes about his work, two favorites being the fate of "Over the Rainbow" and its several preview rejections and the tossing off of "Stormy Weather." He consistently remembered to credit his lyricists with the popularity of their efforts. He was never fully at ease; in some interviews his voice took on a serious, weighty tone, and he spoke with some degree of formality, referring to Yipper or Johnny as "Mr. Harburg" or "Mr. Mercer."

Frequently Anya or a friend accompanied him to the studios, after which he would chuckle and say, "A plug's a plug." It was a rare interviewer who was not impressed with the variety of Arlen's output and the many songs of great popularity that few associated with him.

By late March he completed his piano piece, which he entitled "Ode." Lasting about three minutes, it is a rather "serious" composition, bluesy, improvisational. When he sent his manuscript to Harwin for a clear copy, he jokingly wrote at the top of the first page, "Tennessee Arlen's Ode to the Deeper Side of All of Us." The copyist, not in on the joke, returned the piano copy with that as the title of the piece. When Arlen signed a copy for a friend, he assured the recipient that, despite the pensive title, he was really "a highly spirited boytchik."

He was busy in May. On the twelfth he sat for a series of portraits by the critic-author-photographer Carl Van Vechten. In his eighties, Van Vechten had been a cultural gadfly since the 1920s, when he had encouraged young singers, dancers, writers, and composers, among them George Gershwin. He participated in the Harlem Renaissance and contributed to its excitement with the controversial novel *Nigger Heaven*.

After retiring from writing, Van Vechten took up photography, choosing his subjects from among his gifted friends: Gershwin, Gertrude Stein, Scott Fitzgerald, Virgil Thomson, Marian Anderson, Billie Holiday, Eugene O'Neill, Joe Louis—literally hundreds of literary, musical, theatrical, dance, even sports personalities who fascinated Van Vechten. He had admired Arlen since the Cotton Club years, but the composer somehow had eluded Van Vechten's Leica. With Arlen back in New York, Van Vechten told a friend, "Now I'm going after Harold Arlen."

Arlen, characteristically punctual, arrived at 2:30 P.M. at Van Vechten's apartment on Central Park West at Seventy-fifth Street and was ushered into the small studio where, assisted by his associate Saul Mauriber, Van Vechten took several black-and-white and color portraits of the composer. Now fifty-five, Arlen appeared rather stiff and solemn, with a full head of black hair and a slightly grayish mustache against a colorful floral fabric background, a Van Vechten trademark. In truth these were not among Van Vechten's better photographs, and Arlen was not happy with the results—though he permitted the publication of one and never expressed his opinion of the photographs.

After the session, Van Vechten, Arlen, and Mauriber gathered in the living room to reminisce and to talk about the Cotton Club, Lena Horne, and especially Ethel Waters and her great "natural singing," a rare gift, they agreed. Waters in her early years was very beautiful, they also agreed. Van Vechten told tales of Ethel Waters's violent temper, about a time when she heard that her current husband was involved with a member of the Cotton Club chorus. Waters took the husband's automobile and rammed it into a tree, virtually demolishing the vehicle but escaping injury herself. Also, upon meeting the younger rival, Waters closed the incident with a couple of solid slaps to the face.

Especially gratifying to Arlen was Van Vechten's recollection of a conversation he had had with George Gershwin in the early 1930s when "Stormy Weather" had become a "noisy song." "George said to me," Van Vechten recounted, " 'Harold is the most original of all of us.' "

A couple of days later Arlen was an early-morning guest on the Galen Drake Show. He fielded the same standard questions intelligently and with wit and was pleased with Drake's choice of recorded Arlen songs.

The next day, a Saturday, he agreed to appear at the Metropolitan Opera House in a songwriters' tribute to an ailing Cole Porter. Sponsored by ASCAP, the "Salute to Cole Porter" was a benefit for the Asthma Research Institute, in Denver.

About noon on Sunday, May 15, 1960, a most impressive group of songwriters assembled at the stage door of the Metropolitan on Fortieth Street, near Broadway, for a rehearsal.

Arlen had a happy reunion with his California-based friend Harry Warren. Others present were Lou Alter, Leroy Anderson, Vernon Duke, Ray Henderson, Burton Lane, Frederick Loewe, Jimmy McHugh, Harold Rome, Arthur Schwartz, and Noble Sissle. All would introduce themselves with one of their best-known songs and then join in on a multipiano rendition of Porter's "Begin the Beguine." Richard Rodgers would conduct the chorus and orchestra.

Arlen's comment to Warren was, "Well, Harry, you've finally made it to the Met." Warren was a devoted lover of opera, especially by the great Italians. Warren couldn't think of a snappy comeback and all entered the theater. It was a shambles.

Mike Gross, who covered the event for *Variety,* realized that, as he observed, "Under the strain of little rehearsal time and working on a stage that was much too large for their nonoperatic voices [among the vocalists were Beatrice Lillie, Celeste Holm, and Lisa Kirk], they all delivered handsomely." Then, too, there were other inconveniences: "Despite faulty light cues, mike displacement and emcee memory lapses, the Porter music shone through with an unusual glow. The composer, who has been virtually confined to his Waldorf Towers apartment in N.Y. since his right leg was amputated two years ago, couldn't make the shindig, but he was ably represented by a flock of performers and an extraordinary lineup of his cleffing colleagues in the American Society of Composers, Authors & Publishers."

The "cleffers" were not pleased with the disorder, and the vocalists and chorus found that the arrangements and orchestrations for the Porter songs were often in the wrong keys.

When the time came for the songwriters to join in the tribute, to Arlen's annoyance, he was introduced with a bar or two from "Over the Rainbow." He had expected at least to play, and perhaps sing, a full chorus. Once he appeared onstage and the orchestra managed a couple of ragged measures of the song, he left the stage, turned, and led his colleagues onstage to play "Begin the Beguine" for the concert finale.

Arlen wondered who, if anyone, was in charge (there were actually three producers). He believed that Rodgers also should have been onstage to play, and that the conducting should have been left to Milton Rosenstock, who had conducted the rest of the musical numbers. Several composers, including Arlen, Henderson, and Schwartz, were critical of the performances of their songs.

Rodgers, who arrived at noon, was forced to wait until two before his contribution to the evening's performance could be rehearsed. Both orchestra and chorus were off pitch, as Arlen told a friend the following day. Rodgers stopped the music and asked, "Chorus, can you see me?"

"Yes," they sang out in unison.

"Then," he laughingly observed, "it's your fault." The rehearsal continued in fairly good humor. At the second run-through, later in the afternoon, Arlen was greatly amused to see Rodgers, conducting with gusto, send his baton soaring into the orchestra (there were no injuries).

After the evening's performance, Arlen gleefully related the incident to the erstwhile conductor's wife, Dorothy, and physician brother, Mortimer. On Monday, he had regrets; maybe Rodgers would not think it was funny. "He'll demote me," he said with a laugh. At the time Arlen regarded Richard Rodgers as the most successful American songwriter. (His and Hammerstein's *The Sound of Music,* which had opened the previous year, was well on the way to a long run.)

As the year slipped into summer Arlen became conscious of his creative inactivity, despite the interviews, first nights, screenings, and the Cole Porter event, which had not taken much time or effort.

He was disappointed that a planned *Pickwick Papers* animated cartoon never came off. But he had not been doing much except doodling with the piano miniatures. In July he was occupied with the presidential conventions, but felt guilty about not working.

"The clock," he ruminated in a letter that summer, "with its cold and an' inescapable foreverness keeps slugging its steady course while I keep dipping into books—newspapers—scripts and a smidgeon of work now that the [1960] conventions are over. . . . dreams are what I am made of and procrastination follows as in day so in night. . . . perhaps the world would be saner if we all went back to 'Alice in Wonderland' and 'Wizard of Oz' (forgive plug) and dumped Castro—Krush—and Mao. Make good use of your time (there is that clock again)."

He and Anya were continuing to cram their apartment with shipments out of storage from Beverly Hills. Early in August his own painting, "Clown with Bicycle," arrived. "While not professional," he commented, "it is amusing."

A week later he wrote a friend to tell him he was "Delighted about Ella's recording." Norman Grantz, of Verve Records, was planning to add a "Harold

Arlen song book" to Fitzgerald's growing, and acclaimed, two-LP sets devoted to the Gershwins, Rodgers and Hart, Porter—all the masters of American popular song. Arlen was a longtime admirer of Ella Fitzgerald, but even more exciting to him was that he had prized the stylish arrangements and orchestrations on the earlier recordings by Nelson Riddle.

Still more importantly, he could write, "Have finished my skidding piano piece (at the moment called 'Bon Bon') and am working on piano copy—also finished a song—no lyrics yet—with Belafonte in mind." The song, which he titled "A-1," was never lyricized or published.

At the end of August he sent a telegram to a friend: "Feel Sterile about Fitzgeral'—Harol'." He had just heard that the big-band arranger Billy May had been assigned to the project; there would be no Nelson Riddle. Arlen's renown as a blues-jazz writer continued to haunt him.

His unproductive routine—regular sittings at his barber, a visit with Doc Schachtel to talk baseball and to get a vitamin B12 shot, reading scripts for musicals and occasional films, seeing the shows—took a turn for the better early in 1961. He was summoned to Hollywood to work on a film musical—a rarity at the time—and in television. Once Berman had worked over the contracts, Anya and Harold Arlen, late in May 1961, rented a house on North Crescent Drive in Beverly Hills for a stay of five months.

The Hollywood blacklist having evaporated, Yip Harburg was there also. Arlen and he had been signed to write songs for an animated film whose protagonists were cats and which was preciously entitled *Gay Purr-ee.* That the female cat, Mewsette, would speak and sing with the voice of Judy Garland made the difference. Also, despite the cute title, the feature-length cartoon would be produced by UPA (United Productions of America), which had won acclaim for imaginative, sophisticated, revolutionary cartoons. Economy of line, artful handling of color, and stories for intelligent children (and, often, adults) were evident in such praised cartoons as *Gerald McBoing-Boing,* who spoke in television-inspired sound effects) and the popular series featuring a bumbling, myopic Mister Magoo.

The Hollywood word was that UPA was a serious rival to Disney because, as the film encyclopedist Leslie Halliwell put it, its "spareness of line and sharpness of wit contrasted happily with Disney's chocolate box period." The score for *Gay Purr-ee* would not call for the despised "Mickey Mouse music" used to underscore to a fault each movement, from an eyebrow lift to a pratfall.

The plot for the film was written by Dorothy and Chuck Jones (he was one of UPA's best cartoonists) and told the story of a restless country feline, Mewsette, who slips onto a Paris-bound train in search of big-city adventure; she is followed by her admirer, Juane-Tom (the voice of Robert Goulet) and the accident-prone kitten Robespierre (Red Buttons). Mewsette falls into the hands of Mme. Rubens-chatte (Hermione Gingold), who operates a beauty salon for cats.

The beautified Mewsette poses for celebrated artists (in a gorgeous sequence depicting Mewsette in the styles of Cezanne, Rousseau, Degas, and Picasso). Such beauty does not go unnoticed, and the villian, Meowrice (the voice of Paul Frees, known as the busiest voice in Hollywood) plans to kidnap her and sell her to "a rich, old, Pittsburgh coal cat." Juane-Tom and Robespierre foil the plot, and the three country bumpkins return to the quiet life on their farm.

By July, Arlen and Harburg had the bulk of the score, with two major Garland songs, the sweetly simple "Little Drops of Rain" and the complex, moody "Paris Is a Lonely Town." For Goulet they wrote a spirited "Mewsette," though Arlen was a bit doubtful. After seeing and hearing Goulet in Lerner and Loewe's *Camelot,* he felt the big baritone voice was more suitable to *The Student Prince,* Romberg rather than Arlen. In fact, Goulet comes off well in the film. He and Buttons have a tipsy un-Rombergian drinking song in "Bubbles." Frees was given two plot songs, "The Money Cat," with characteristic Harburg barbs aimed at the affluent, and "The Horse Won't Talk," an amusing seduction number and musically quite Gallic, as is Garland's "Take My Hand, Paree."

By August the score was complete and Arlen began preparing for his television stint. His reappearance in Hollywood after nearly a decade attracted the press. The *New York Times*'s Murray Schumach filed a column early in the month headed "Composer Tells of Movie Abuses," with a subhead, "Arlen Says Industry Spurns Quality Song Writers."

Schumach based his interview on the theme of the "quality song writer" as the "almost undesireable alien in Hollywood" and that Arlen's return had dramatized the question: "What function is there in films for a song writer who refuses to write down to the juke box that has conquered Hollywood and is making enormous inroads on Broadway?"

"At the moment," Arlen replied, "there is nothing to be done for the song writer here. And as for records, they're turned out like waffles." He was referring to the changes in popular music initiated by the rise of a young Mississippi-born singer, Elvis Presley, who introduced a style of performance that was called rock and roll. Presley's first musical film, *Love Me Tender,* a movie of scant distinction except for his presence, had been released in 1956 and was followed by an enormous series of equally undistinguished sequels. In 1962, the year *Gay Purree* would be released, there were no fewer than three features starring Presley. The Beach Boys' singles and albums inspired the later "surf operas" such as *Beach Party* and *Bikini Beach*, aimed at the youth market, as was the "waffle" pressing of their recordings. Arlen and his colleagues found the music primitive, simple to a fault, and repetitious—and the lyrics illiterate.

He harked back to a better time for music, though not for the songwriter, when Hollywood scores were written by the Gershwins, Kern, Berlin, Rodgers, and Porter. "But even in those days," he said, "when we made a lot of money, we still had no prestige. We were considered just song writers. George Gershwin, too. He would be invited to a party and be expected to sit down and play like some hired entertainer. George loved to play. But he resented playing for the guests."

Arlen reiterated his major Hollywood gripe: losing control of his work once he had turned his songs in to the studio. "They would do anything they pleased with your song. They would change the tempo or throw it out if they felt like." He illustrated the point with the saga of "Over the Rainbow." His final conclusion was that the songwriter who believes he has something to say should write for Broadway.

At the same time, he told Herb Stein, who wrote the "Inside Hollywood" column for *Racing Form* ("America's Turf Authority") that even Broadway had its disagreeable side. Especially galling was the "degrading" experience of the backers' auditions, in which the songwriters had to demonstrate their wares.

"I don't believe," Arlen said, "any writer, producer or director of proven worth should be put through the rigor of such trials. If an individual is interested in backing a show, he should have enough confidence in the people who create it and produce it to offer backing on the basis of the past performances of these theatre people."

The opening line he found most irritating was the familiar one, "I don't know anything about music . . ." (one Arlen had heard frequently, too, during his Hollywood years). As for such "experts," Arlen concluded, "if most of these backers knew as much about money as they claim to be sounding boards for the general public on music, they'd be financial bankrupts."

He was, in fact, treated respectfully in the musical handling of *Gay Purr-ee*. The orchestrations and conducting by Mort Lindsay were superb and right for each song. Arlen's mood lightened that summer when he received a telegram from Judy Garland: "Recording 'Gay Purr-ee' is the most pleasure I've had since 'The Wizard of Oz.' The songs are magnificent."

Upon receiving an advance copy of the soundtrack, Arlen described it in a letter as "my special pleasure at the moment. . . . Judy is a treasure and one's musical creation cannot be in better hands. She does a superb job and while the rest of the cast and numbers come off excellently, she alone shines." He was especially moved by her "Little Drops of Rain," "as simple a song as can be written, but these are the hardest to write."

A more typical Arlen melody is another of his "tapeworms" (i.e., in extended form), "Paris Is a Lonely Town," clearly fashioned to the Garland voice (it is marked "sensitively"). Harburg's lyric was one of his favorites, in which "Utrillo" rhymes with "willow" and "Bizet" with "Elysées."

Melodically the structure of "Paris" is unconventional. A four-bar instrumental introduction is followed by an A section of twelve bars—bluesy, but not a standard blues progression. The B section introduces a new theme for eight bars, then repeats the last four bars of A. The C section is also new and takes eight bars; it is the song's emotional climax:

> *Where's that shining flower*
> *'neath the Eiffel Tower?*
> *Where's that fairy land of gold?*
> *Isn't it a pity*
> *That this magic city turned suddenly cold?*

The final section is a thirteen-bar variant of the A section that could be designated the D section after the first two bars, with the introduction of yet another theme:

> *The chimneys moan,*
> *the river cries,*
> *Each glamorous bridge is a bridge of sighs;*
> *River, river, won't you be my lover?*
> *Don't turn me down*
> *For Paris is such a lonely, lonely town.*

Arlen's return to the introduction in the last line is an extraordinary touch. It comes between the final "lonely" and "town," three bars of instrumental interlude, and closes with an arpeggiated sigh on the last word, rounding out the wandering melody with the echoing resolution.

When the film was finally released (a year after Arlen and Harburg had completed their part of the job), it received little attention. It was the most original film musical of a year notable otherwise only for filmed Broadway fare, *The Music Man*, *Gypsy*, and *Jumbo*. Broadway that year—1962—did little better with Richard Rodgers's first solo venture, writing both words and music for *No Strings*; likewise Stephen Sondheim with *A Funny Thing Happened on the Way to the Forum*. Also that year came the opening shot of the British invasion of Broadway, *Stop the World—I Want to Get Off*.

Simultaneously, in popular music, the rock and roll craze dominated, and a dance called the twist was riding high. In the cacaphony, the inventive, gentle, and witty songs of *Gay Purr-ee* were lost.

Arlen, for reasons of his own and despite his love for the soundtrack, did not care much for the finished film. He found it arch, and the sequence in which Mewsette is painted by several French artists smacked too much of a similar long ballet in the film *An American in Paris*. Despite his reservations, *Gay Purr-ee* is a charming film, beautifully executed and scored. But it was to be his and Harburg's Hollywood swan song (except for the title song for *I Could Go on Singing*, in which Judy Garland made her last film appearance).

The End.

Not quite. Immediately after completing *Gay Purr-ee*, he became involved in a television production sponsored by DuPont, an NBC "Show of the Week" entitled "Happy with the Blues." It was projected as an hour-long show starring Peggy Lee, Vic Damone, LaVern Baker, and Joanie Sommers, accompanied by Paul Weston's Orchestra. It was an exciting prospect, considering the stellar quality of the vocalists, all of whom were riding a wave of popularity at the time.

Arlen was accustomed to television production: the confusion, the waits, the tangle of cables, the perspiration-inducing lights, even the noise and sudden hush before the cameras rolled and moved about the set. This was, however, a new and strange experience for Anya, who sat quietly on the sidelines. When not on camera, Arlen kept her company, for she appeared to be withdrawn, strained, nervous. She smiled, and he attributed her uneasiness to the chaos of piecing together a complex television show.

As she watched anxiously from her corner, Anya saw Harold, script in hand, taking directions from the producer-director Bill Colleran. The script had been written by George Foster and used as the evening's springboard a gimmick (as it was damned by Arlen's old friend, the columnist Sidney Skolsky) based on a story Arlen often told about himself.

The show began with a shot of a cab driver (portrayed by the comic Robert Strauss) at the wheel whistling "Stormy Weather." His unseen passenger, his interest roused by the musical cabby, speaks (in the voice of Harold Arlen), asking the driver if he knows the name of the song's composer.

"Irving Berlin," is the answer.

"You're wrong," the voice says. "I'll give you two more guesses." Richard Rodgers and Cole Porter came next.

"Wrong again," says the voice from the back seat. "I wrote that song."

"Who are you?"

"Harold Arlen."

Whereupon the cabby turns in his seat, stares at his passenger, and blurts, "Who?"

The theme was carried through the show to the finale, a ten-minute segment narrated by Bing Crosby, who began by asking, "Who is Harold Arlen?," following that with, as reported in *Variety*, "a sequence capsulizing the Arlen career, with accompanying stills, augmented by some brief Crosby–Judy Garland–Ethel Waters vocals." The reviewer praised the singers, but so far as the gimmick went, "A flimsy thematic continuity (apparently designed to give the whole some story value) could have been dispensed with."

Skolsky was more critical in his "Hollywood Is My Beat" column. "I believed with Arlen's music and such artists as Peggy Lee, Vic Damone, Joanie Sommers and LaVern Baker singing it would be great. It wasn't!

"If those people connected with the show," he concluded, "didn't believe

Harold Arlen and his music were important, they never should have done the show."

Despite such drastic opinions, "Happy with the Blues" was on the whole an entertaining and musically rich evening, though the "Who's Harold Arlen?" theme wore thin. Arlen was pleased, not only with the interpretations of his songs by the soloists as well as a chorus, but also with the generous compilation of his work—more than twenty songs, from "Get Happy" to his own presentation of "Little Drops of Rain" from the still-in-production *Gay Purr-ee*. If Skolsky was not happy with "Happy with the Blues," Harold Arlen was.

But he was more concerned about Anya. Even before they had left for California in May, she had shown symptoms of what might have been a nervous affliction. At times her face contorted, her smile was a grimace. The fingers of her left hand appeared to be arthritic. Anya also refused to see a physician. Although she saw Dr. Schachtel, a general practitioner, often, she refused to see a specialist. Harold could not bring himself to force her to undergo another experience with the medical profession and hoped the problem would go away.

With the DuPont show attended to—it was televised on the evening of September 24, 1961—the Arlens closed their house in Beverly Hills and by mid-October were back in Manhattan, where they began house hunting. Their little duplex on East Fifty-fifth had become too cramped, with too little room for Arlen's books, recordings, "possibles" tapes, and the paintings they were taking out of storage.

After a few weeks of searching, late in November they settled on a ten-room apartment in the San Remo, on Central Park West at Seventy-fifth Street. It was a spacious setting with ample wall space and several closets for storage. The living room, overlooking Central Park, was large enough to hold the Steinway grand, two sofas, several chairs, and a small table adjacent to the piano, on which he had placed warmly inscribed photographs of Judy Garland and Audrey Hepburn, and a Zinn Arthur photo of Diahann Carroll and Pearl Bailey embracing in a scene from *House of Flowers*. His own contribution was a still from a film he had shot of the Gershwins in their workroom; another was a copy of a photo taken in Ciro's in Hollywood of Anya, Irving Berlin, and himself. These last two were reminders of a happier, musically richer time in their lives.

Carefully placed on the stark white walls were paintings by Henry Botkin and Gloria Vanderbilt and the Montañes portrait of Arlen. In pride of place, with a wall to itself, was George Gershwin's portrait of Jerome Kern.

In the foyer, immediately to the right of the door, was an almost life-sized, elegant painting of Anya (at about age seventeen) by Abram Poole. It was a striking oil and impossible to miss either entering or leaving the apartment. This was their first permanent home in almost a decade, and it delighted Arlen, who, in the beginning, spent an inordinate amount of time removing scuff marks from the white linoleum in the foyer and stray bits of fluff in the living room.

The most important room in the apartment was his den, off the foyer, where he spent most of his time. Smaller than the living room, it was the repository for professional and family memorabilia and the small upright piano at which he worked. In the den also were a sophisticated tape recorder, a phonograph, and, along one wall, a bookcase containing in one section a large television screen. His radio was invariably tuned to station WPAT, which played the music of the 1930s and 1940s.

Above the piano was a large watercolor by Botkin of Gershwin at his piano in Beverly Hills, done in the last year of his life. Also on that wall were several framed award citations, including the Academy Award for "Over the Rainbow." The nomination for "The Man That Got Away" was, significantly, relegated to the other side of the wall, in the bathroom.

On another wall Arlen had placed one of his own paintings, a quasi-abstract, though recognizable, portrait of Truman Capote. His model was the famous photograph by Harold Talma of a sloe-eyed Capote with bangs recumbent on a love seat. Arlen was proud of the painting, one of his least primitive. In a surge of generosity, he decided to present it to the subject and invited Capote over. They sat in the den and, to Arlen's chagrin, the writer ignored the new work of art. Finally, Capote gestured and said with what Arlen sensed was a touch of contempt, "Is that supposed to be me?"

Arlen kept the painting.

Like Irving Berlin, who inspired Arlen's return to sketching and painting, Arlen distributed his work among his friends. (In his later years Berlin had taken up painting and turned out dozens of canvases, which he presented to friends, among them Arlen, A. L. Berman, Bing Crosby, and Barbra Streisand.)

Pleased with himself as the busy artist, now neglecting songwriting, Arlen sent one of his efforts to Ira Gershwin, himself an artist of considerable skill and, like his brother, a serious collector of art. In his letter of thanks, Gershwin began with the salutation, "Dear Composer, Lyricist, Painter (in that order) Chaim." Above each of the designated professions, Gershwin placed a circled letter, A over composer, B over lyricist and a C over painter. These were clarified in a footnote:

> A = 4 stars (no question)
> B = 2 stars (pretty good) (not bad)
> C = ½ star (slow starter, but potentially another Van Gogh, as indi-
> cated by his sketch of G.G.)

When he was not preoccupied with his new hobby, and with no musical offerings coming his way, Arlen and Anya devoted their time to their new home. With the help of their former landlord, Joseph Lombardi (who owned the building on East Fifty-fifth Street and was proprietor of the furniture shop on the ground floor), they furnished the new apartment. Anya attended to the greater part of the premises, under Lombardi's eye, and with the additional aid of their new housekeeper, Mrs. Geraldine Owens, a feisty (as they would learn), genial, and tough middle-aged Georgia-born black woman with minimal education but with a quick wit and shrewd intelligence.

Arlen devoted his time to settling into the den, moving books around, and retrieving family portraits from storage, framing them, and placing them on a wide table near a window facing the courtyard. He even found, and framed, his grammar school graduation class photo in Buffalo. He pointed out to anyone interested a little girl in the photograph, Lily Levine, his first boyhood crush.

In the bathroom nearest the den he nearly covered one wall with mock self-pitying letters from Ira Gershwin. It had been their practice over a period of several years to make modest wagers on the annual New Year's Rose Bowl games. The one rule was that Gershwin, who was faithful to California, chose California to win, and Arlen took the other team. Almost invariably, Arlen won.

Gershwin then would send his check (usually twenty-five or fifty dollars, never any large amount) enclosed in a letter lamenting the Arlen luck. Arlen then framed both letter and check and placed them on the bathroom wall. Over the years this played havoc with the complex Gershwin accounting system. There was one year, however, when Gershwin won a twenty-five dollar wager and Arlen, with usual dispatch, sent off the check. Gershwin returned it, marked "Insufficient funds."

The first year in their new apartment, the Arlens initiated an annual event that continued for nearly a decade, the Chanukah-Christmas celebration. This took place on December 25 and was attended by friends (of a mixed religious marriage, like that of the Arlens) with their three children. The first year Jerry Arlen also brought Sammy, his son, then three. Abe Berman, the attorney, came disguised as Santa Claus and distributed to the children gifts from the Arlens that had been awaiting them under a small silver tree near the fireplace in the living room.

The children told stories, or sang into a microphone in the den, and Gerri Owens served delicacies, including cookies and candies, into the late afternoon. In later years, following Jerry's marriage to Rita, she, too, would attend these ecumenical celebrations (as they came to be called; Rita Arlen had been born into a Catholic family). Wilva and Robert Breen also attended a few of the gatherings. Arlen enjoyed having the children around, chuckling at their antics and comments, cigar in hand and operating his tape recorder. Anya, however, was ill at ease, and as her nervous tic grew more perceptible, the children, their ages ranging from about three to ten, exhibited innocent fascination, to Harold's discomfort. Every effort was made to curb the children's interest, though Anya was apparently unaware of her facial twists.

Despite Anya's still-undiagnosed affliction, the Arlens continued their theater-going, and there were periods when the tics ebbed, which was interpreted as a good sign.

Arlen's sole musical activity during the initial months in the Central Park West cooperative was seeing the musicals of others: Frank Loesser's *How to Succeed in Business without Really Trying,* Richard Rodgers's *No Strings,* Stephen Sond-heim's *A Funny Thing Happened on the Way to the Forum.* He preserved the programs, often making notes and comments in the margins. He had some reservations about Rodgers's first major attempt at writing lyrics. And both he and Anya enjoyed the caperings of their rambunctious friend Zero Mostel in the Sondheim musical.

Early in 1962, with nothing professional to do, Arlen agreed to an interview with Jack O'Brian for the *New York Journal-American.* The columnist was eager to get Arlen's views on the current musical scene. He called Arlen an

introspective fellow, known to muse about the intellectual problems of his trade, meaning those beyond getting songs plugged or ingratiating himself with bandleaders.

Harold has remained one of the most respected craftsmen whose output is slow but impeccably high in quality, and he oddly doesn't bemoan the current rock-roll and Twist crazes.

> They're good for the kids [Arlen told him]. They have a good beat. If this makes the kids happy that's great. All that counts for them right now when they're kids.

> It won't educate them but they'll grow right through such crazes and then reach up for the standards. The Twist can be a delight and often it's awful. But as far as hurting the music business—no. The public somehow selects some good music right in the eye of the hurricane of every passing tornado of a fad. Don't worry about it. Music somehow grows on people who can improve their taste. The ones without taste never would have any, Twist or not.

Arlen thinks the movies and TV are asleep to the opportunities of good original musical scores. . . . He feels there is a lack of originality in TV and films which should be corrected. . . . There is, he feels, a trend available and recognizable right now for such musical commodities. As evidence, he points to Broadway.

> The public is paying big money for big, gay, bright musicals.
> Naturally they should be good, not trash. Why, about half the shows on Broadway are musicals. The public loves them. It's a troubled time, and maybe people pour into the musical theatres to forget their troubles. . . .

O'Brian turned to the subject of musical films, and Arlen told him:

What's wrong with Hollywood? They're asleep out there. That goes for TV, too. They simply refuse to tap the talents of the creative people they have at their fingertips. If they won't gamble with a brand new subject, why not the classics? What's wrong with "Alice in Wonderland"? There are so many fine books for adults as well as children suitable for musical handling, they'd never get finished with them.

At the time of the interview, February 1962, *Gay Purr-ee*'s premiere was eight months in the future and *Hair*, "The American Tribal Love-Rock Musical," and all it portended, six years from off-Broadway and later Broadway itself. And *Grease* was not far behind. The troubles he believed would be assuaged by the musical theater were in fact the motivation for a new musical trend—*Hair*'s Vietnam War, drugs, sex, and flower children and *Grease*'s celebration of the disturbing "generation gap" with a rock and roll score.

When Arlen had spoken to O'Brian, it was a time of troubling events, which he followed in the press and the substantial television news broadcasts. Preoccupied with the state of the world that summer of 1962, he philosophically wrote,

The air is full as you know with launching rockets, lunar ferry, orbit space ship, NASA, Van Allen Belt, African Veldt.

> *Gone—the sane season*
> *Gone—the age of reliance*
> *Gone—man's reason*
> *We're up to our ass in science.*

As for work, "Nothing new as far as material for the theatre or movies, but ever hopeful, we go on."

22

A MAN
OF SORROWS

‍‌or the next year Arlen produced little original work, and the clock with its cold inescapable foreverness made him uneasy. So did the news, especially in late 1962 and early 1963; he fretted over the Cuban missile crisis and "Krush" until it was settled in February, when the Soviets pulled their weaponry out. In discussing the crisis with friends, he brooded over the possibility of a third and absolutely final world war.

With no work offers from Broadway or Hollywood, he found some creative relief in writing single songs. Yip Harburg, too, was shaken by the Cuban confrontation (he no longer regarded Fidel Castro as the savior of the Cuban people) and wrote a lyric, whose title was inspired by the title (not the content) of a book by Rachel Carson. *Silent Spring* was a marine biologist's warning against the uncontrolled proliferation of insecticides and their effect on the environment.

Harburg's opening lines allude to Carson's theme: "Not a leaf is heard to murmur, / Not a bird is there to sing," but clearly the lyric as it is developed, is political, not ecological. Its subject is a land in which children hide and "doors are dark and shades are down." It was not acid rain that distressed Harburg but the "rains of hate." Over the past several months he had read, with a sense of dread, of the launching in Florida of the first Minuteman, an intercontinental ballistic missile (February 1961); of the Bay of Pigs fiasco in Cuba (April 1961); of the savage beating of Freedom Riders protesting segregation in Alabama (May 1961). In November the young president, John Kennedy, increased the number of U.S. military advisors in Vietnam to sixteen thousand; in June of the next year two of those advisors would be killed in an ambush. And then, in October 1962, the Cuban missile crisis had taken the world to the brink of a third world war. Fear and hate, Harburg believed, stalked his nation:

> *Is this the land where flags were flown,*
> *To bring this hopeful world a dream of spring unknown?*
> *Is this the dream?*
> *Is this the spring?*

"The Silent Spring" is not an Arlen song that evolved from a jot. It was tailored to the Harburg lyric and in its simplicity (key of C) makes an affecting musical statement. Structurally, it is symmetrical—to a point. Arlen's form consists of three sixteen-bar stanzas: A-A^1-B-C. The C section, a kind of coda, is nine measures long. Despite the song's disturbing topic, Arlen wants it performed "with gentleness," adding to the mood of what Thoreau called "quiet desperation." In the A section he contributes his own sense of anxiety in the line "Why this strange and silent spring?" Arlen indicates a pause between the words "Why" and "this," before descending to a blue note—E-flat, the song's single chromatically altered note—on the word "spring."

The song was briefly taken up by Lena Horne, who recorded it (along with "The Eagle and Me") in an album of songs of "political significance." A single was issued from the LP coupling "The Silent Spring" with Comden, Green, and Styne's "Now!" The latter had in its verse a reference to Walter Cronkite and Channel 2 (CBS) and in the chorus a demand for racial tolerance ("No one's going to grab your sister"). This proved to be too incendiary for CBS, which banned the record; neither song was broadcast, and consequently neither was heard (nor was the album a success). The proscribing of "Now!" inadvertently took "The Silent Spring" with it in a time when radio and television were nervous about political topics.

While Arlen waited for a worthwhile project, he moved into the world of literature; he became, as he put it, "a preface-er." For a children's biography of Gershwin he supplied an affectionate introduction, and another for John Mehegan's *Jazz Improvisation.* Late in May 1963 he not only wrote but also spoke at a Lincoln Center tribute to George Gershwin.

In the afternoon before the evening's concert, he and Anya attended a press preview that featured an exhibition of Gershwin's paintings and drawings as well as photographs. Leonore and Ira Gershwin—who rarely left the Gershwin Plantation—flew in for the event. They were joined by other Gershwins in a lower lobby where the artworks were displayed. Frances Gershwin Godowsky, herself a painter of talent, attended with her husband, Leopold, son of the celebrated pianist. Arthur Gershwin, the youngest Gershwin brother, was there. He had tried to follow his older brothers as a songwriter but wisely turned to stock-broking.

Along with the Arlens were several longtime Gershwin friends, including Kay Swift, Burton Lane, and E. Y. Harburg. The literary community was represented by the Gershwin biographer David Ewen, the novelist John O'Hara, and the poet Carl Sandburg, who provided the Arlens with the big laugh of the day.

Upon being introduced to Sandburg, Gershwin offered him a rarity, a genuine Cuban cigar that Gershwin had had smuggled in via Canada (there was by this time a boycott of all Cuban imports by the United States). As Arlen watched, and to Gershwin's consternation, the folksy, white-thatched poet drew a pen-knife from his pocket and cut the precious Havana in half, presumably for later puffing. This was practically desecration in the eyes of Gershwin, a connoisseur of fine cigars and a gentle law breaker. "Ira's face was something to see," Arlen recalled with a chuckle.

After the Gershwin gala, Arlen was approached by Isaac Kleinerman, who was associated with CBS News as producer of the popular and respected program "The Twentieth Century." This television show was highly regarded for its intelligent coverage of political, historical, and cultural subjects, narrated by CBS's star commentator, Walter Cronkite. "The Twentieth Century" was a half-hour Sunday show, but Kleinerman convinced CBS and the sponsor, the Prudential Insurance Company, that a full hour should be devoted to Arlen.

Kleinerman got his way, and the enterprise snowballed; by October he could assure Arlen of the willing presence of E. Y. Harburg. In quick order he also enlisted the appearance of Ira Gershwin (not as willing, for interviews made him squirm), as well as those of Ted Koehler and Johnny Mercer, who would sit for the television cameras in California. Also included would be one of Arlen's recent collaborators, young Dory Langdon, then married to the conductor, pianist, and composer André Previn.

Meanwhile, Kleinerman's assistant, Burton Benjamin, screened Arlen's home movie collection, concentrating on the latter 1930s period in Hollywood for glimpses of the younger Ted Koehler, Yip Harburg, and Ira and George Gershwin. There were also the on-the-set films of the *Wizard of Oz* cast, which included the lost "Jitterbug" sequence. Portions from the ten reels would be edited into the final program, entitled "The Songs of Harold Arlen."

To round out the participants, Lena Horne and Tony Bennett were selected for two of the best sequences. Horne, with Arlen at the piano, sings "It's a New World" to a revised civil rights lyric by Gershwin. In the Bennett sequence, Arlen conducts the orchestra and Bennett sings a recent Arlen-Langdon song, "So Long, Big Time!"

The camera and sound crews moved into the Arlen apartment, where over a period of several days he was interviewed by Walter Cronkite, for a total of ninety minutes of conversation. Anya was conspicuously absent during those crowded hours; her sole mention occurred in the story Arlen told about "Over the Rainbow" as she drove along Sunset Boulevard. During the shooting she spent time with her mother downtown. She did not wish to be filmed.

Arlen himself, he admitted, became so nervous that he could not bear to watch Cronkite on his daily news program. And when the final film had been edited and was ready for a preview, he turned down an invitation to see it. As he explained to an interviewer, Margaret McManus, "I don't want to see it beforehand because I'm bound to be overly sensitive and too critical. You can't help but be, and then you get unhappy and childish and you become a nuisance and a bore. These people are experienced in television. I'm presuming they know what they're doing."

He was happy when all the components coalesced for the broadcast on Sunday, February 9, 1964, advertised in the *New York Times* as a "profile of one of the most inventive and versatile composers of popular music." Above Arlen's head in a photograph of him at the piano was a list of seventeen song titles followed by "Etc., Etc., Etc." Also promised in the text was the appearance of "fellow composers" who would "pay tribute to him."

In short, this was to be an hour unlike the run-of-the-mill composer "specials" of that time, top heavy with current big-name stars engaged in an "and then he wrote" marathon, much of which often appeared to be a filmed radio broadcast (not unlike "Happy with the Blues" three years earlier). This novel approach to an already hackneyed format displeased (or possibly, caught unawares) Paul Gardner, who wrote in Monday's *New York Times* that the program "could not have been duller." He explained:

> Mr. Arlen and his lyricists were interviewed on how they worked, on why they worked, on where they worked, on how fast they worked, on how songs came to be written. An artist's working habits are unimportant. No one should care whether he uses blue pencils or red crayons. His art is enough.
>
> It must take considerable daring to produce a profile of a composer and then only include brief snatches of five songs. Mr. Arlen deserves a big red satin valentine—for his music and what happened.

Gardner missed the point of the profile: the songwriter, not the song. Many are interested in the how, why, even where, of the creation of classic songs. They are fascinated by their elusive, often unknown and unrecognized creators. That Kleinerman's cameras had caught four of the greatest American lyricists eluded the critic. That they and Arlen spoke about that arcane subject, popular songwriting, bored him, if not countless others. Most of the songs mentioned—"I Love a Parade," "Let's Fall in Love," "One for My Baby," "Ac-cent-tchu-ate the Positive"—were so well known that they required no introduction. And the songs used, not merely as brief snatches but complete, served to define the art of Harold Arlen, his inventiveness and versatility, as promised.

This objective of the "profile" was apparent from the very beginning of the hour, in a sequence during which Arlen and Tony Bennett discuss, rehearse, and then record "So Long, Big Time!" through film clips of Lena Horne ("Stormy Weather") and Judy Garland ("Over the Rainbow," "The Man That Got Away"). The final musical segment presented Lena Horne in a heartfelt rendition of the revised "It's a New World," which she had introduced the previous September at a Carnegie Hall "March on Washington for Jobs and Freedom."

Arlen's wide stylistic range led Cronkite to ask for some definitions, and Arlen offered a couple. A blues, he said, was a song of "melancholy longing, a certain kind of wail" (a term he had applied to his piano "Ode"), "a lament for a lost love," while a torch song was "a popular or sentimental ballad of unrequited love." Despite his now tiresome standing as a blues composer, he made it evident that the only deliberate blues he had ever written was "Blues in the Night." "Stormy Weather" and "The Man That Got Away" were torches; "So Long, Big Time!" was neither. It was a rhythm ballad of resignation tinctured by optimism. The Langdon lyric was of the time, especially in the interlude that Arlen had added to their original, which included such words as "chicks," "fair weather phonies" and, in the conclusion, "cookies," "babes," even "bookies." It is a song with a hard-edged contemporary sound and lyric.

"So Long, Big Time!" is another in the long line of Arlen tapeworms (over seventy measures with repeats of a half chorus and the release). Dory Langdon touched on that aspect of Arlen's writing. "Harold goes on," she said, "until he feels that he has nothing more to say in the song. And the result of this kind of deliberate experimentation results in some marvelous [*pause*] are they accidents?—marvelous accidents. Or do you think—"

Her husband interrupted with, "Harold is more of a composer, in the accepted sense of the word, than a songwriter. Harold does not simply go on and on with song; it never becomes filler. In other words, even if [the song is] twenty bars longer than the norm, you can't take one bar out."

Throughout the hour Arlen emphasized "the happy wedding" of music and lyrics that made the song, not the music alone. Koehler and Gershwin leaned toward the anecdote behind a song rather than analysis. Mercer pointed out that Arlen had "always been original. He's always tried to get away from the usual, the drab. And I think that's why he writes longer forms and different forms— breaks 'em up into different phrases, hardly ever repeats. It's difficult to put your finger on his style—you just know it's there."

Yip Harburg, always history-conscious, began by declaring that Arlen's songs were graced with "a particularly wonderful creative quality—imaginative, new, fresh, and having identification. His songs live! His songs seep into the heart of a people, of a nation, a world, and stay there." He then invoked a subject that irked him throughout his professional life. "This is," Harburg concluded, "what's wrong with our whole age right now . . . we are writing for how many copies will it sell rather than for how many years will it last." The "we" in Harburg's quasi-lecture emphatically did not include Arlen, Harburg, Gershwin, Mercer, Koehler, or Langdon.

All the commentary during that hour, except for Cronkite's, was spontaneous; there were no scripts. Cronkite, hoping to inject a dash of humor into what was becoming a rather solemn discussion of popular song, broached the subject of the poker-faced Johnny Mercer. "You," he addressed Arlen, "made Johnny Mercer laugh—"

"No," Arlen replied, "I made him smile," and he told the story of the writing of "Ac-cent-tchu-ate the Positive" in the car in the drive from Paramount Studios to the Brown Derby (Arlen's phrase was "the Derb' "). By the time they drove into the parking space, the song was finished. Arlen took credit for the line "Jonah in the whale," "which was fine with him. [Then] he looked at me and actually smiled. I knew he liked it."

The scene cut immediately to an unsmiling Mercer, who said, "I don't know. That's his story. I smile a lot."

After hearing so many anecdotes about how easily songs came to the writers, Cronkite asked the composer, "How often do you get a song just walking down the street?" (as he and Koehler had in writing "I Love a Parade").

Rarely, Arlen explained. Earlier in the program he had told Cronkite that in the beginning "I wasn't one songwritin' fella." He wanted to sing, to play in a band. When the fortuitous "Get Happy" came out of nowhere (like "Over the Rainbow," which he maintained was of empyrean origin), transforming him into a songwriter, he took no chances and constantly carried his "jotter" in the event that the unsought-for phrase mysteriously materialized.

"You never write *a* song," he continued. "You might get an idea. It's not easy—always. It's easy to write songs—I mean, if you're a craftsman, and I believe we all are, those I've mentioned [he had referred to Gershwin, Rodgers, Berlin], those I know about certainly can get songs. I could sit down, and I imagine I'm going to put myself to the test now, I should imagine I could get one every five minutes. An actual theme. But that doesn't mean that it's good."

When Cronkite asked Arlen on the chances of producing a hit, Arlen simply replied, "Now? None."

He was expressing a view commonly shared by the songwriters of his generation. The musical world that "The Songs of Harold Arlen" delineated was all but gone. In a prebroadcast interview, he recalled his early career in Hollywood as gone, never to return. As for Broadway, also in flux, he told Margaret McManus that at that moment he was not working on anything specific.

"I haven't had an assignment for two years. I talk with a lot of producers and talent and I read scripts but I'm past the age where I'll take on any script, however dubious, just to be working. I can't invest that kind of energy to close in Philadelphia. Philadelphia, where the sun never shines."

Three days after the broadcast of "The Songs of Harold Arlen," a British airliner touched down at Kennedy Airport. Despite a sizable cordon of police, the aircraft was soon surrounded by a shrieking mob of thousands, mostly teenagers. The Beatles had arrived in the United States. The American musical scene would change drastically in the wake of their frenetic arrival.

In the early Tin Pan Alley era, single songs such as Arlen was now turning out might be interpolated into a revue or show. Now, in the mid-1960s, songs were interpolated into long-playing record albums. With luck, a traditionalist like Sinatra, Bennett, Lena Horne, or Bobby Short would include such a song in a collection—but their records were not the chart busters. Presley, the Supremes, the Beach Boys, and with a vengeance, the Beatles were producing the gold records.

Because he was a partner with Buddy Morris in the Harwin Music Corporation, Arlen was not denied an outlet for his incidental work. During this slack period he teamed with three young lyricists, Dory Langdon Previn, Carolyn Leigh, and Martin Charnin. Arlen then was in his midfifties, the women in their midthirties, and Charnin just thirty. While the lyricists were not of the Presley or Beatles generation, they fell somewhere in between. Though familiar with the traditions of American popular song and the musical theater (Charnin came out of that background), they were open to new expressions and experiment and, of course, in tune with the time.

Arlen and Dory Langdon met late in 1962 when her chief collaborator and husband, André Previn, recorded an album for Columbia Records entitled "Sittin' on a Rainbow." A labor of love, it was a collection of Arlen songs that Previn lushly orchestrated, with his own jazzlike piano embellishment throughout. In a well-balanced compilation of both familiar and little known instrumentals, Previn included "The Morning After" and his own "Anya." That he also chose to do a song, "Life's Full of Consequence," whose effect depended a great deal on Harburg's lyric, was indicative of Previn's admiration for Arlen's music—and "Anya" is a beautiful tone portrait. ("The Morning After" was later recorded, music as well as lyric, by Eileen Farrell, whom Arlen admired.)

Previn and Langdon had met in Hollywood, where he was active in scoring films and she contributed lyrics to films at MGM and UPA in addition to writing television scripts. Among the Previn-Langdon songs were "Where I Wonder," "You're Married," "The Runaround," "Change of Heart," and "Lose Me Now." Previn recorded several of their songs, though none achieved any wide popularity.

Arlen wrote a handful of good songs to Langdon's lyrics, among them Tony Bennett's "So Long, Big Time!" and a setting of the slow theme from "Mood in Six Minutes" entitled "Night after Night." Dory Langdon's words suited the Arlen melancholy and her subject matter reflected, to a degree, her personal life and the dissolution of her marriage. One of the last songs she did with Arlen was "That Was the Love That Was." When her husband took up with a film actress, Langdon was devastated and stopped writing for several months.

Simultaneously, during the early period of Arlen's work with Dory Langdon, he also wrote a single song with Carolyn Leigh. Talented but prickly, Leigh had an impressive catalog. She had begun in advertising and writing for radio; then, in collaboration with Johnny Richards, she wrote "Young at Heart." Frank Sinatra's recording became an enormous hit. The Broadway star Mary Martin heard the recording on her automobile radio and hoped to get the lyricist to write the words to songs for her forthcoming production of *Peter Pan*. The composer of the music was to be Mark, better known as "Moose," Charlap. While *Peter Pan*, with additional songs by Jule Styne and Comden and Green, was no smash, it was Leigh's Broadway debut, and two of the songs by her and Charlap, "I've Gotta Crow" and "I'm Flying," became popular.

Leigh then teamed up with Cy Coleman in a stormy collaboration that produced *Wildcat*, starring Lucille Ball (with one good song, "Hey, Look Me Over!") and *Little Me*, starring Sid Caesar, with a book by Neil Simon. A greater success than *Wildcat*, *Little Me* was brilliantly written and boasted two fine songs, "I've Got Your Number" and "Real Live Girl."

Coleman and Leigh ended their often contentious collaboration with *Little Me*. Arlen, who admired her work, found her personality less than admirable. Drinking was a problem, also. The single song they wrote was fittingly titled "Bad for Each Other."

In this same period Yip Harburg wanted Arlen to work with him on a musical telling the tragic story of the Children's Crusade of the thirteenth century. Harburg and an old friend, the novelist Henry Myers, had adapted the latter's *Our Lives Have Just Begun*, published in 1939, into a timely parable of the generation gap, the abuse of children, and the futility of war. Arlen could not warm up to this project about the most brutal of the crusades, during which children were sold into slavery or died of starvation or disease. Even though Harburg and Myers could inject the necessary romance into the "message" that children could change the world, the reality of that crusade made Arlen decline. (Harburg also attempted to interest Burton Lane in the musical, but he, too, rejected it. Infuriated, Harburg vowed never to work with "neurotic composers" again and sought out younger musicians for the work. Years later, *What a Day for a Miracle*, with music by Myers, Larry Orenstein, and Jeff Alexander, was produced at the University of Vermont, in Burlington. That was its only presentation.)

Of his three youthful collaborations of the early 1960s, the most productive began fortuitously and with a touch of whimsy. The meeting of Arlen and Charnin occurred sometime in 1964; the latter had just turned thirty and was a veteran of the musical theater with many hats—performer, director, and lyricist.

Martin Charnin had been twenty-three when he appeared as Big Deal, one of the Jets in Bernstein's *West Side Story.* His real ambition was to write—songs, sketches. After leaving *West Side Story* and appearing in a revue, *The Boys against the Girls,* he began submitting his songs to off-Broadway revues with some success. He teamed with Mary Rodgers (daughter of Richard) to write a score for a Judy Holliday musical about the Peace Corps, *Hot Spot,* in 1963; it lasted a mere forty-three performances. A few months later, in August, he moved to San Francisco to work with the great but rarely successful Vernon Duke on a musical based on *The Prisoner of Zenda* starring Alfred Drake and Chita Rivera. *Zenda* was supposed to be Charnin's big Broadway breakthrough, once the musical left the Curran Theatre in San Francisco. But that was where it remained, the hapless Duke's final failure.

A dispirited young lyricist returned to Manhattan and then, at a meeting of songwriters, spotted Harold Arlen. They were introduced, and before parting, Charnin slipped something into Arlen's jacket pocket. Puzzled, Arlen waited a while, then withdrew a slip of paper on which Charnin had written, "I could be good for you." Arlen admired his audacity (young songwriters too often approached him with veneration, even awe, which made Arlen uneasy). He arranged to meet with Charnin and soon agreed to collaborate; their first song was entitled "I Could Be Good for You." They were now a team, and other songs followed, with no special vehicle in mind—except for a couple for the successful John Lindsay mayoral campaign.

Early in 1965 Arlen "happily" informed Emory Lewis, the editor of *Cue* magazine (which was celebrating its thirtieth anniversary with a salute to Arlen in Lincoln Center's Philharmonic Hall), "I have a new lyricist, Martin Charnin. Martin is in his thirties, and lives in New York. We meet regularly. We are amassing a little cache of music, getting a head start. We have been working for a few months, and we may surprise you with a musical one of these days."

The musical would be the ill-fated *Softly.*

Before that came about, Arlen and Charnin continued to write. One song, "Summer in Brooklyn," was done for a Barbra Streisand television special that was not produced, nor did the vocalist find a place for it on her several albums. The lyric is folksy and the melody "slow," in Arlen's marking, with the added indication of a fitting "sultry mood."

Arlen was more fortunate in his relationship with Eileen Farrell, who had promised to participate in the *Cue* tribute to Arlen on March 21, 1965. He took time off from his Charnin collaboration to assist the producer, Sid Bernstein, with the behind-the-scenes aid of Robert Breen.

Eileen Farrell, then with the Metropolitan Opera, had touched him with a recording of "Where Is Dis Road A-leadin' Me To?" from the *Americanegro Suite,* and which she planned to sing at Philharmonic Hall. She had also recorded several Arlen songs in her recent Columbia Records albums, beginning with one entitled *I Gotta Right to Sing the Blues,* on which she sang the title song and "Blues in the Night."

Before the evening of the tribute, Farrell asked to visit Arlen to get his ideas about the handling of the songs. Her humility, as well as artistry, deeply impressed Arlen. He was equally awed by her honest, straightforward, often blunt nonoperatic vocabulary, laced with profanity. Farrell was an imposing Alcestis on the stage of the Metropolitan; she was startlingly undivalike off. That day in the Arlen living room, she was a Staten Islander, married to a policeman and completely without affectation. When she left, she borrowed a copy of an album, *Composers at Play,* featuring Arlen singing his own songs (and Cole Porter singing his on the reverse side). She would study Arlen's way with his songs for her portion of the "salute."

In his article published in *Cue* the day before the concert, Emory Lewis referred to the composer, inevitably by then, as "America's unknown celebrity" and described him deftly as "a quiet, urbane gentleman with a dapper mustache and heavy-lidded blue eyes that perpetually look as though they were about to fall asleep." He dispelled for his readers the "unknown" Arlen with a long list of songs and a long biographical sketch on Arlen's accomplishments in Hollywood and on Broadway.

In a more personal vein, Lewis, who had interviewed Arlen in the San Remo apartment, mentioned Arlen's love of walking and his new avocation, painting. He saw a "still-wet portrait of Sammy Davis" and "a near-finished portrait of his wife, Anya," and found her own "sensitive, delicate floral study" to be "one of the apartment's most striking oils." This painting and Arlen's portrait of her (with an anguished face) were the only evidences of her existence, for as usual during an interview, she remained out of sight.

In his note for the program insert, prepared over a couple of days of toil and conferences with a writer friend, Arlen thanked Lewis for "being so patient, observant, and for writing so many complimentary paragraphs which became delightfully embarrassing." He thanked everyone associated with the production and the performers—Sammy Davis; Eileen Farrell; Stan Freeman and Cy Walter, a two-piano team; Luther Henderson, who conducted the orchestra and chorus; and the two "special guests," Lisa Kirk and Bert Lahr—"everyone who gave of their precious time and effort to make this evening come about." He closed the letter, "Most sincerely and with deepest affection, Genuflectingly yours, Harold Arlen."

Happily, the evening came off well, "an evening warm with sentiment, nostalgia and some of the most deeply memorable songs in the contemporary popular repertory," according to John S. Wilson, writing in the next day's *New York Times.* The evening closed with Arlen onstage with the cast for the finale, an Arlen song medley. Elated, he was happy until he and Anya finally went home after the celebration.

Though he preferred not to discuss it, Harold was uneasy about Anya. At times her nervous spasms were too severe to go unnoticed. When an attack flared up, Anya, embarrassed, preferred staying home to accepting all but a few invitations. Often Harold went alone or with the Breens. Many of their friends presumed this conduct was merely a reversion to the neurotic behavior of their Hollywood years. Many considered Anya a burden to Harold, a detriment to his career whose demands for his attention annoyed and angered him.

What was worse, Anya refused to see a physician, despite the urging of Dr. Schachtel and her husband. This unreasoning aversion was excessive, Harold felt. He was incensed when she refused to see an oculist merely to have her glasses repaired, preferring to use tape. Especially annoying were those times when, Rita and Jerry Arlen having invited them to a Friday night Sabbath dinner, they would no sooner arrive than Anya would ask, "When can we go?"

Resigned, Arlen chose to lose himself in his daily walks through the park, with stopovers at Harwin Music and A. L. Berman's offices, his regular visit to his barber, and his work with Martin Charnin. Ideas came to him, at times, during his walks. Around the time of the *Cue* concert preparations, on January 12, 1965, while en route, he stopped, leaned on a mailbox, and sketched a couple of bars above the logo of that day's *Herald Tribune,* a jot he labeled "Kick the Habit."

In May he took time away from Charnin to compose the music and words to his annual birthday greeting to Irving Berlin. That year he celebrated with a recording that he sent on May 11, 1965. Despite his concerns at home, Arlen managed a humorous borrowing from their friend Jerome Kern's usage of the term "burthen" instead of the traditional "chorus." This was a practice Kern brought back from Britain, where as a young composer he worked on English operettas. His colleagues, especially Ira Gershwin, found this usage a bit pretentious. The Pablo in Arlen's lyric is of course, Picasso.

A Sunny Seventy-Seven
(Pablo B.)

Burthen—Brightly—With Proud Reverence

A sunny seventy-seven
No more nights of ennui
A heap of heavenly-heaven
Is due to thee, Pablo B.

The boys can w[h]ine,
They can pine—
'Svet gornisht helfin [It's no use]
The music "box" you are in
You got yourself in

The starlit songs that will stay on

Thumb their nose at reviewers
With your paint and crayon
Immortality's yours

Second Chorus
There's no curtailin'
The F sharp scalein'
Of Izzy Baline
The mighty B.
[Piano—"God Bless America" segue to]
So to sum it up
Hum it up
Fee-fi-fo-fum it up
Music'lly
Happy days
Full of joie d'esprit
A sunny seventy-seven
Pablo B.

Chaim

The rest of the year was quiet, not particularly productive except during October, when John Lindsay ran for mayor on the Republican-Liberal ticket. Arlen, with Charnin, became involved in the campaign by contributing their two songs. Arlen was engrossed and followed the contest closely. Running against Lindsay were Abraham Beame, representing the Democratic machine, and William F. Buckley, as a wild-card Goldwater conservative Republican who frowned upon the association of the word *liberal* with *Republican.* Arlen followed the campaign and clipped, saved, and even dated (rare for him) an essay on the principles involved by the pundit Walter Lippmann in the *New York Tribune.* He too was pro-Lindsay and especially hard on Buckley. Lindsay, much to Arlen's satisfaction, became mayor of New York.

The Arlen-Charnin collaboration also took a positive turn early in 1966, when the *New York Times* published an article by Samuel Zolotow in which he reported that the distinguished actor Jason Robards "may star in an Arlen musical with a book by Hugh Wheeler and lyrics by Martin Charnin." Robards, he explained, would appear as an American civilian in occupied Japan, circa 1948, who falls in love with a Japanese woman from a good family. When Zolotow attempted to confirm this with Arlen, all he received was a rather cautious statement. It was, he said, "a high possibility."

The news stirred up a musically deprived Broadway in a season notable primarily for revivals, a few nearly instant flops, and only two musicals with superior scores: Lerner and Lane's *On a Clear Day You Can See Forever,* which ran for a discouraging 280 performances, and Mitch Lee and Joe Darian's *Man of La Mancha,* which remained in place for over 2,000.

The effort to put Harold Arlen back to work was initiated by the indefatigable "poor Saint," Arnold Saint Subber, the perennially optimistic producer of *House of Flowers, Out of This World,* and other failures. From time to time he tried his hand at nonmusical dramas, also with disappointing aftermaths, as in the case of Truman Capote's *The Grass Harp* and a more recent and poorly received *Look, We've Come Through Safely* (1962) by Hugh Wheeler.

According to publicity releases that began to flow in January 1965, Saint Subber was determined to produce a musical set in Japan during the American occupation, and he had spent six months there searching for a book. He finally found what he was seeking closer to home in 1963, when he read a novella in the *Saturday Evening Post* written by the Indian-born writer Santha Rama Rau. Her story was based on her experiences in postwar Japan when her husband, an American diplomat, was based there in 1947. A sensitive observer of the convergence of alien cultures (one a victor in a devastating war), she conceived a story about an American civilian serving in the occupation forces who falls in love with a young Japanese, whose "good family's only concern," according to one release, was "the getting of food."

This information appeared in a *New York Tribune* article in March reporting Saint Subber's most recent return from Japan and intimating that his cast would employ five bona fide Japanese actors and twenty Americans. About a month later the *Tribune* revealed that Saint Subber had returned to the States again, this time accompanied by the choreographer Hanya Holm. He admitted that he had failed to find the young woman for the lead but had signed two actors in Tokyo who, he cheerfully noted, had learned some English between his visits and "gave promise that they will be able to learn more." Poor Saint meant business.

Once he acquired the rights to the Santha Rama Rau story, Saint Subber turned it over to Hugh Wheeler, whose *Look, We've Come Through Safely* had faded from memory. Wheeler, who had been born in London, had come to the United States in 1934; he was best known as a successful writer of mysteries under the name of Patrick Quentin or Q. Patrick. Several of these were bought by Hollywood. Wheeler was regarded as a reliable writer for stage and screen as well as television. He was also a skilled adaptor of the work of others. While Saint Subber shuttled between the United States and Japan, Wheeler began providing Arlen and Charnin pieces of his adaptation, entitled *Softly.*

After close to a year of writing for the sake of writing, they finally had a story, a draft libretto, a fascinating cast, and Saint Subber out on the money trail. The song "I Could Be Good for You" was readily worked into the plot, as was the smouldering "Midnight," written earlier in the year. There was a richness of source material, beginning with the setting of a stunned, broken Japan that had suffered not only the ignominy of defeat in a war that their emperor and military leaders assured them they could not lose, but also occupation by foreigners, mostly American. Under the command of a benevolent General MacArthur, the occupation troops behaved more like tourists than conquerers. With the aid of civilians, the occupation forces worked with a new parliamentary government to restore Japan's shattered cities and demolished economy.

Within this framework the songwriters had a wide range of characters—the American, the young Japanese woman, her family, the American officers and enlisted men—and an intriguing situation, the meeting of two extremely different cultures. The latter presented Arlen the opportunity to work with Eastern as well as Western musical themes—his customary "authentic ring." In a few weeks Arlen and Charnin completed an extraordinary number of songs based on an incomplete book.

Early in the year Saint Subber announced that rehearsals for *Softly* would begin late in July for an October 1966 opening in New York. To assist the producer in his search for backing, Arlen and Charnin prepared a demonstration recording and participated in the inevitable, and to Arlen detestable, backers' auditions. Arlen's attitude was evident during one of the waits at the recording session, when he said, "Cocktails-for-two time. Don't you hate these goddamn auditions?"

By this time, in April, they were ready with a dozen songs, virtually an entire score. A set of the recordings was sent to Goddard Lieberson of Columbia Records, but the score did not stir up any interest there, which was dispiriting. Columbia had invested in Lerner and Loewe's *My Fair Lady* ten years before, to its profit.

In May the company made up for the rejection with the release of an LP, *Harold Arlen Sings (With Friend);* the friend was Barbra Streisand, at the time of the recording a major Broadway star in the long-running *Funny Girl.* The sessions were held in mid-1965, around the time Arlen and Charnin began their collaboration. Among the dozen songs in the album was their "That's a Fine Kind of Freedom." The "friend" joined Arlen in a duet, "Ding Dong! The Witch Is Dead," and she sang—beautifully—"House of Flowers." She was scheduled for her two songs on an evening when the Winter Garden was dark; Arlen worked two evenings with Anya present. Thomas Z. Shepard, a Lieberson protégé in the production of original cast albums, was the producer. The dependable Peter Matz was arranger and conductor. He was also known as a man who could gracefully and diplomatically work with Streisand, who was by then most impressed with her own near-instant stardom.

That was evident on her evening at the Columbia studio, Matz had assembled a large orchestra for the session, along with Shepard and several technicians, all of which was expensive. All were there, including Arlen, but the "friend" was not.

While Shepard fumed and Arlen joked, the clock ticked and the orchestra was paid for not playing. After about a quarter of an hour an exasperated Shepard decided to begin the session without Streisand. Then, close to a half hour late, Barbra Streisand entered the studio in style, trailing a luxurious new fur on the floor. Tempers cooled, and the recording session proceeded. The star more than redeemed herself in her contributions to the album. But that was all Columbia offered Arlen and Charnin in the middle of May 1966.

Though the *Softly* demos were sent to other recording companies, there was no encouragement from that quarter. Record sales centered on the youth market; original cast albums were not popular with that generation, and sales were down. Meanwhile, Saint Subber continued to approach backers, and Arlen and Charnin suffered through auditions.

Arlen and Charnin worked hard on their *Softly* score, producing enough songs for two musicals. Arlen was not always happy with the lyrics and goaded Charnin into revisions or rewrites, which was unusual for him (during this period he kept a diary, also unusual for him, tracking their work as they progressed). There are good songs among this generous output, some with a pentatonic coloring for the Japanese performers. "Suddenly the Sunrise," for the female lead, is a beautiful ballad; the folkish "Fish Go Higher Than Tigers," is about kite flying; and "Baby-San" fuses Yankee familiarity with Japanese courtesy. Charnin obviously did his homework on the words, as did Arlen on the music.

Charnin's wordplay shines in the satirical comparison of American and Japanese "temples," a view that would have delighted Yip Harburg:

> *There are temples of gold,*
> *Where god never fails,*
> *But are always in bloom—*
> *Bloomin' how?*
> *Bloomin'dale's.*

And so on through Macy's, Bonwit Tell', Saks, and such gods as Chanel and Dior. There is a rousing drinking song, "Been a Hell of an Evening," an American appraisal of time spent in a geisha establishment. There is also a joint minstrel show, in which the Japanese attempt English ("Hello" becomes "Herro" and "My lady fair," "My rady fair," who will arrive on the "Robert E. Ree," etc.), that would not have played well even at the time, let alone in the 1990s. Despite this slip, the songs written for *Softly* deserve a hearing.

The major unforseen problem was Hugh Wheeler's book, which was technically not completed. Although he wrote several endings, Wheeler could not come up with one he could live with. Ultimately he gave up, leaving Arlen and Charnin with a bulging cache of musical orphans. (Curiously, in September 1966, a month before *Softly* had been scheduled for its Broadway premiere, Wheeler's new play opened, an adaptation of Shirley Jackson's macabre *We Have Always Lived in the Castle.*)

Thus, without a whimper, *Softly* expired. Wheeler went on to do better with the books to Stephen Sondheim's *A Little Night Music* and *Sweeney Todd.* Charnin, after collaborating with Richard Rodgers on the unfortunate *Two by Two,* scored mightily in 1977 when he and Charles Strouse carried off the unlikely feat of setting a comic strip to music with *Annie.*

Undaunted, and with Harold Arlen again at liberty, Saint Subber turned from the abandoned *Softly* to the off-Broadway revival of *House of Flowers* in its original form. Capote, too, was free and riding the crest of a wave of success that followed the publication of his best-selling and chilling account of multiple murder in Kansas, *In Cold Blood.* With his book for *Flowers* now as he had originally planned it, Capote was happy to collaborate on lyrics for the additional songs. Within a few weeks at the close of 1967 and the start of the New Year, Arlen, Capote, and Saint Subber were ready for an opening on January 28, 1968. *House of Flowers* was coolly received and closed in March.

Adrift again, Harold spent too much time, in Anya's opinion, away from home during the day. He made his rounds to the Berman office and the newly situated offices of ASCAP, in Lincoln Plaza, a short walk from his apartment. There he talked with "the boys" about the deplorable condition of popular music. At Berman's he went through the scripts that had been sent for his consideration. He often stopped by the Harwin Music office to oversee the publication of a folio of *House of Flowers* songs from both productions.

Anya often resented these absences, despite the comforting presence of Geri Owens, the housekeeper. Anya's mother, Mary, was a frequent visitor, though she could not fathom her daughter's peculiar behavior. The visits often ended stormily with Mary's indignant exit. Anya would sometimes call on a trusted neighbor to keep her company while Harold was absent. One woman arrived with two children in tow. Their noisy presence led to a screaming outburst, and the young mother and little girls fled the apartment.

On another day, with Mrs. Owens out marketing, Anya called another friend. It was a bright summer day, but when he arrived he found Anya sitting in the den with the shades drawn. After an affectionate greeting, Anya and her friend sat on a sofa opposite the bookcase and television set. There was no conversation as the two sat side by side and Anya clutched his hand. She started at the sound of the freight elevator, staring in the direction of the sound as if she had never heard it before.

The man and the speechless woman sat. Her involuntary movements, a contorted neck, a sudden facial spasm were disturbing. A shaken friend left the apartment when Harold returned. Neither said anything of consequence and nothing about Anya, still in the darkened den.

Harold chose not to speak about Anya; he bottled up their problems as well as his own. A couple of years before, during an interview, Margaret McManus asked him how long he had been married. She noted that he

hesitates visibly before he says 26 years. But then he will add:
  "Now why did I hesitate? I don't really mind telling you how long I've been married. One of my eccentricities. I've always been this way. . . . I'm not an easy man to get to, I know that. I don't like to talk about myself. I close up. I don't have the talent for talking that some of my contemporaries have. Everything I feel, everything I want to say, I pour out in my manuscripts. It's all there."

This closing up, even to the point of not confiding in friends, was a characteristic he shared with Judy Garland, who, as George Cukor noted, kept her problems to herself or comically exaggerated them. Harold Arlen kept them to himself silently. And he spared Anya. When the Museum of the City of New York opened a comprehensive exhibition, "Gershwin: George the Music/Ira the Words," on May 6, 1968, Arlen attended the preview alone. He had lent his two Gershwin paintings, a portrait of Kern and a self-portrait, *Me,* to the museum. If he was troubled, it was not evident in his demeanor. He traded quips with the Gershwins' painter cousin, Harry Botkin, with Ira Gershwin, and with Frankie Gershwin Godowsky's beautiful young daughter, Nadia, a Columbia student. He lost himself in the vast collection of memorabilia, manuscripts, photographs, drawings, and sheet music, then slipped out to return to his disintegrating home.

The Gershwin exhibition was generously covered in the *New York Times,* including a photograph of Arlen and Botkin studying a collection of sheet music. It gave Anya, during a period when she was feeling well, an idea. She called the Arlen archivist, collector, and aficionado William Sweigert, asking if it was possible to seek out all possible copies of Harold's published songs. Once collected, the songs could be bound and presented to him on his birthday in February 1969. Her husband, Anya explained, did not have a complete set of his published works, many of which, especially the early songs, were out of print. (She was unaware of what remained in storage in California.)

With selfless dedication, Sweigert began making the rounds of the several publishers. Amazed at their generosity, he soon accumulated a large collection of Arleniana, including most of the long out-of-print, lesser-known songs from the Cotton Club. He even found a mint copy of Harold Arluck's piano piece *Rhythmic Moments.*

While the search continued sub rosa, Arlen himself remained inactive and fretful, partly because he had nothing to do but record "possibles," when he felt up to it, and worry about Anya's fluctuating condition. He and Schachtel agreed that something must be done—her problem was physical, not emotional. They initiated a plan to have her seek a neurospecialist, but it would take time and gentle persuasion.

The sheet music collection was not quite ready in February 1969 for binding because of Anya's worsening health. Maybe it would be completed in time for that year's Christmas-Chanukah celebration.

Arlen found some respite from his professional inertia by being persuaded to run for a position on ASCAP's board of directors. Ira Gershwin, when he learned of Arlen's candidacy, was surprised. Writing to Arlen, he said, "I don't know if you really want to be on the ASCAP board but I did see your name on my ballot and the ballot of the Estate—so—like it or not, I voted for you on both ballots. Did I do right?"

On April 1, 1969, Harold Arlen joined the ASCAP board, which included, along with ASCAP president Stanley Adams, his old friend Buddy Morris, Samuel Barber, Cy Coleman, Morton Gould, Arthur Schwartz, and Richard Rodgers. Arlen took the position seriously and attended the regular meetings, made notes, and listened patiently to frequent lengthy and often disgruntled speeches by members.

One, delivered in May by the veteran lyricist Irving Caesar, required almost two dozen pages in its transcript form; to Arlen's bafflement, Caesar's major subject was money, once he got through his usual nostalgic anecdotes—how he and Gershwin wrote "Swanee" in just a few minutes (with each retelling, the time span seemed to decrease), or how Vincent Youmans had liked a dummy lyric Caesar had written and that was how "Tea for Two" was born. Arlen had heard these tales before. Coming around to the subject, Caesar went so far as to claim that President Adams was overpaid, and that the top writers in ASCAP, Caesar included, who had written the "standards" over the years, contributed to the support of the younger, less talented, new members. Caesar referred to the "philanthropic group of a hundred-odd composers and authors" whose income was diminished—he neglected to say that a few, Irving Berlin, Cole Porter, Richard Rodgers, were millionaires—by ASCAP's system of distributing the money it collected from the various sources it licensed.

To Arlen, this discontent and in-fighting was a new experience. He had never questioned the ASCAP system. As the writer of several long-lived standards, he belonged to the upper echelon of ASCAP songwriters and was happy with his income. He, like the Gershwins, Porter, Berlin, and Rodgers, was in what at the time was the AA category and received a generous income. (The system has since been changed.) Other old-timers, who subsisted on royalties of a song or two, felt that they were entitled to a more sizable income based on seniority. Although she did not register any complaints, Kay Swift lived comfortably on the income from her two songs "Can't We Be Friends?" (1929) and "Fine and Dandy" (1930). Though intermittently busy since the 1930s, she could always count on her ASCAP earnings from these two songs because they were consistently performed, recorded, or used in films.

Arlen had been aware of some of the internal strife, envy, and petty distinctions in the ASCAP pecking order and managed to avoid it. But now, behind the closed doors of the boardroom, he found himself in a mine field. Maybe Ira Gershwin had been right to ask, "Did I do right?"

Still, it was a challenge, and to a degree, it distracted him from his concern for Anya. Frequently he discussed the meetings and other ASCAP matters with Irving Berlin, who chose to remain aloof from the society's internal politics. He refused to authorize even birthday tributes, preferring to have his catalog work for him and for ASCAP.

As a member of the board, Arlen also served on the public relations committee, headed by Cy Coleman. Other members included Arthur Schwartz and the delightful anecdotalist Gerald Marks ("All of Me," "Is It True What They Say about Dixie?"). The committee oversaw the publication of *ASCAP Today,* edited by the novelist Walter Wager. The handsome periodical was replete with articles of concern to members—biographies, news from the world of music, legal matters, performers. Each issue was also filled with photographs of the president, who appeared to be everywhere.

ASCAP Today at this time began to reflect the changes in popular music that disconcerted several members. Pages were devoted to the music coming out of Nashville; photographs displayed new members, often with Stanley Adams at their sides, with long, unkempt hair and beards, from groups with such names as Blood, Sweat, and Tears and Chase. There was a photograph of a heavily madeup Frank Zappa (eye shadow, painted mustache, and goatee). The caption identified him as the "Father of the Mothers."

In discussing the state of their art with "Mr. B.," Arlen agreed the times were indeed a-changing. ASCAP, moving with the times, embraced country and western and rock music.

In the late summer of 1969, Anya's condition worsened. She was lethargic and weak and began complaining for the first time of headaches. She could not stand light and became nauseated. Even she realized she was ill and finally agreed to submit to tests. These revealed that she was suffering from a cerebral tumor and required immediate surgery. The tumor proved to be malignant and was excised, although because of the tumor's location, total removal was impossible. But there was no other possible action. Harold was jolted back to 1937, when Anya, Yip Harburg, and he visited George Gershwin as they prepared to leave for New York and could not help noticing how frightful Gershwin looked, how listless, and within days of his death following a brain tumor operation.

On August 26, 1969, Arlen expressed his anguish on a small slip of paper:

Dear Dear Annie
So little time
and such sorrow

To his joy, Anya survived the surgery, a guarded success. By December she was strong enough to leave her bed for long periods. On the twenty-sixth Anya and Harold celebrated their annual Christmas-Chanukah gathering with Rita, Jerry, and Sammy Arlen and a trio of close friends. Anya greeted them as they came into the living room with its miniature silver tree, under which were presents for the children.

Rising from the armchair, Anya moved among the guests in a long gown; her head was encased in a large bandage about the size of a football helmet. Her gait was unsteady, her left arm dangled uselessly at her side. She moved slowly, gently, smiling. There was something ethereal about her.

Her survival, her apparent recovery, her demeanor, were heartening. Harold was uncharacteristically open in informing friends about Anya's daily progress. In January 1970 he told one friend that they were living happily together as they had, as he put it, "at the beginning," when they were happy young lovers at the Croydon Hotel in the years when he was the musical prince of the Cotton Club.

"It's a miracle!" he exclaimed. There were no more personality shifts, no loud accusations, only tranquil affection.

In February, however, there was an abrupt change. When friends called on the fifteenth to wish him a happy birthday—his sixty-fifth—Arlen sounded subdued, even sad. He had no interest in the significance of the day. He put Anya on the phone; her voice was weak, and the two or three words she managed were unintelligible.

A few weeks later, according to Geri Owens, Mary Taranda visited her daughter on the afternoon of Sunday, March 8. Harold had decided on a stroll, and Mrs. Owens hovered in the kitchen. Suddenly she heard screaming from another part of the apartment. Anya, in an agitated and angry voice, ordered her mother out of her house. In tears, Mary left.

Early the next morning Arlen called a friend, who was instantly apprehensive, for out of consideration for his compatriots (most, especially show people, were late risers), Arlen never called before ten.

His voice was grim, hoarse, as he said, "This morning—about six-thirty—Annie's gone."

"We've run out of miracles."

"Yes," he sighed; the phone clicked.

23

SLOW
CURTAIN

*T*he seemingly interminable Russian Orthodox service was harrowing— more so because of Mary Taranda's clamorous, disturbing eruptions of grief. Anya's father and his wife were quietly present, as was Anya's brother, Willy. Harold Arlen stoically endured the outbursts. He was encircled by Rita and Jerry Arlen and a handful of friends. The funeral was followed by a long, numbing drive to the cemetery in Hartsdale, a few miles north of New York. Arlen appared to be dazed, sedated (he was taking Valium at the time), almost unaware of the others, the personification of Isaiah's "man of sorrows, and acquainted with grief." He did not speak during the drive to Hartsdale.

Nor did he speak on the return to Central Park West and the gathering of people in the apartment—too many people and too much confusion.

The aftermath was devastating. Depressed and in despair, Harold shunned the loss of Anya with Valium (not yet recognized as addictive) and other unidentified pills and tablets. Some weeks after the funeral, concerned because they were unable to reach him during a period when Mrs. Owens was away, Rita and Jerry Arlen entered the apartment and found Arlen in a stupor on the bed. Turning him over, they found several tablets of different colors under his pillow, obviously drugs (the suspicion was that Mrs. Owens may have been the source, but this was never proved). The bedroom was freezing cold; the air conditioner was on high and was crusted with ice. They finally brought Arlen around, to his confused embarrassment, but he explained nothing.

Near the end of March he began to come out of his isolation and reassured his friends. It would take time: "Wait—wait—for more hopefully a clearer future," he pleaded.

He was ready in April to see people—Jerry, Rita, and a few of his closest friends. Work did not interest him. It was as if the death of Anya had ended his professional career. One friend shocked him when he said, "Now that you're rid of her, you can go on with your work."

As Arlen confided to another friend, "They don't understand. It's harder than losing your mom or dad, as you know, they are there from the beginning. But when someone comes out of nowhere and you choose each other, that's different. It's one in a million, once in a lifetime. When it ends, it's hard."

Several friends tried to keep him occupied, inviting him to dinners (where he would be strategically seated next to an eligible woman), a party, or a show. Most of these invitations were rejected. His good friend Dorothy Fields was especially persistent in her pursuit of a suitable companion for Arlen. He complained about her matchmaking efforts to Irving Berlin, his almost daily phone confidant. Berlin suggested that he dismiss Dotty with the suggestion that she do something unprintable to herself. Arlen chose to ignore the advice—that language was not an active part of his vocabulary.

Even Berlin, however, implied that Arlen should remarry after some passage of time, or get a "girl." Arlen recoiled from the last and rejected the first. Except for his monthly appearances at the ASCAP board meetings, Arlen was virtually a recluse. He would see his brother and sister-in-law, as well as a very few friends, and talk to Berlin about the condition of current American popular music or such political topics as the Kent State shootings or the flaring Middle East and its consequences for Israel.

Robert Breen was a regular caller, bubbling with ideas. He was especially eager for Arlen to get back to the keyboard and was prolific in his suggestions.

Early in November, with the Breens, Arlen attended an evening celebrating the lyrics of Dorothy Fields at the Ninety-second Street Y. There were warm reunions with colleagues he had not seen since Anya's death: Richard Rodgers, Burton Lane, Ann Ronell, Kay Swift. Among the vocalists that evening were Ethel Merman and Bobby Short. It was Short who brought him out of his creative isolation.

Referring to Short as "that *good* singer," who had been singing "the right songs for twenty-five years," Arlen realized that despite the drastic change in popular music, there were those (he also sought out Mabel Mercer) who sang the songs of Kern, Jimmy McHugh, Schwartz, and Coleman, as Merman and Short did that night. After that experience, which reminded him that the musical scene wasn't as grim as he believed, he said, "I started to come out of it. I started to work again."

Bob Breen would be the next catalyst.

After the Fields evening, Arlen began leaving his apartment, visiting friends and accepting invitations. December 1970 was quite social. Early in the month he dropped in on a neighbor and friend whose mother was visiting from Michigan. He presented her with a lavish bouquet. A few days later he attended an afternoon of Arlen songs with friends at the Lincoln Center Library Auditorium. The young, fervent vocalist, often drowned out by his accompanying trio, appeared onstage in a flowing blouse, unbuttoned to the waist, and with a heavy medallion dangling from his neck in the crevice. His interpretation, obviously influenced by such current pop icons as Otis Redding and Aretha Franklin, prompted Arlen to comment, with a smile, "He found a new kind of soul?" Bobby Short looked better than ever.

Around this time, too, Arlen began sporting a beard along with the mustache. Also, he wore prescription tinted glasses, even indoors, his eyes having become sensitive to light. As a result, he could have been mistaken for a rabbinical scholar.

Two evenings later, he attended an evening of Yip Harburg's anecdotes and songs at the Y. On December 25, the annual Chanukah-Christmas party was held at the San Remo apartment. The small silver tree had remained in the living room after Anya's death. In the den, Arlen played tapes of earlier celebrations for the children present, singing Chanukah songs as well as Christmas carols.

Jerry Arlen was present, but without Sammy Arlen, who remained home with a cold. Rita Arlen stayed with him. The Breens were there, too, and one friend was conscious of hostility between Jerry and Breen, evident mostly in stern looks and curious silences. (Breen once told an Arlen biographer that he resented Jerry Arlen's intimation that Breen was living off his brother. Breen once threatened to punch Jerry in the nose over some statement.)

Harold Arlen always sensed such tensions and tried to keep Jerry less agitated. But Jerry did not need Robert Breen to set off his temper. He was often at odds with his brother, uneasy, perhaps, in the knowledge that he himself was in fact, living off his older and more successful brother.

Breen was, unquestionably, a devoted friend, constantly seeking out new theatrical adventures and projects, especially with his friend Harold Arlen in mind. He earned a precarious living working as a location authority for film companies planning to shoot in New York. He was au courant with all things concerning the theater. And like so many innovators in 1970, Breen found Broadway a dead end and empty in the hands of accountants. There was more to be found off- or off-off-Broadway, which is where Breen discovered Harold Arlen's next collaborator.

He was the youthful Leonard Melfi (b. 1935), whose work the Breens first encountered in the downtown haven for avant-garde writers in defiance of a profit-driven Broadway, Café La Mama. He was an honored member of the new generation of writers who followed Paddy Chayefsky and Israel Horovitz, a group that included Lanford Wilson, Sam Shepard, and Rochelle Owens.

While he held even off-Broadway in mild contempt, Melfi confessed that he would not object to seeing his name in lights in Greenwich Village. A resident of the East Village, Melfi was known for such celebrated one-act plays (ideal for the basement setting of La Mama's stage) as *Birdbath, Stars and Stars,* and *Night.* Possibly his most commercial effort was a sketch he had written for the notorious *Oh! Calcutta!* His youth (a generation younger than Arlen), his iconoclastic view of the contemporary theater, bawdy humor, and a deep respect (possibly awe) for Arlen convinced Breen that the two should write a contemporary musical.

Arlen, recently inspired by Bobby Short, and with no promising script at hand, agreed. He would not set an existing Melfi play; they would start from scratch with an original.

They made a peculiar pair. Like Arlen, Melfi was an out-of-town New Yorker; he had come from Binghamton, New York, in the late 1960s, near the end of the hippie era. Stocky, he sported a wild hairstyle that appeared to have been created by electricity. Arlen dubbed him "Curley." Their dress was a generation apart, Arlen's Saville Row and Melfi's East Village—boots (scuffed), unmatched slacks and jacket, no tie. Arlen, the Breens, and Melfi formed a group to attend the theater, concerts, and parties. Melfi's wit, irreverent, caustic, slightly wild, made him their court jester.

He had Harold Arlen laughing again.

After a period of light-hearted familiarization and discussion, Arlen and Melfi decided to work in a different medium, particularly for Arlen: television. Melfi's best efforts were in smaller forms, and his two-person play *Birdbath* had been well received as a television production. Its grim plot, about a young woman working in a restaurant who befriends a male customer and informs him that she has murdered her mother before coming to work, was not suitable for an Arlen musical. Melfi suggested something contemporary, the alienation of youth from society, the desire to be free from the demands of that society and its pursuit of money.

His contribution was "a musical play for television," *Clippety Clop and Clementine.* Melfi would write the play and Arlen the music and lyrics. (Clop is the surname of the male lead, a disgruntled black Columbia student on the verge of dropping out.) Naturally, he would be nicknamed "Clippety," but by a Melfian dramatic twist, he also drives a Central Park hansom cab; he names his horse "Psychedelic."

His girlfriend, Clementine, is a fellow student and white. Robert Breen's influence was obvious in the casting of Clippety—Sammy Davis Jr. How a forty-seven-year-old Davis could pass for a Columbia sophomore, or even a senior, did not concern anyone at the time.

Melfi's script was in two sections and subdivided into more than twenty scenes. Between the two sections there is a gap of some ten years. Clippety Clop has become a celebrity cab driver and, in scene 20, discovers a lovely Clementine, now in her late twenties, selling organic food in the Hotel Plaza square. They reunite lovingly, but argue about his diet and hers. They are both as strong-minded and as opinionated (and in disagreement) as they had been as students.

The script and songs were completed by mid-1972; not even Robert Breen, who knew television and film people, and Arlen's name could sell the idea to a network or an independent producer. Melfi and Arlen abandoned *Clippety Clop and Clementine*. Melfi's East Village conception of television drama, despite its general sweet tone, was not welcome on Madison Avenue: "A nine-to-five job is not my idea of freedom. . . . A diploma from a college is a nine-to-five symbol of the future." No more congenial was Clippety Clop's speech to a nasty traffic-jammed driver: "You mean to tell me we pay taxes so that you can waste your time in a steel cage that can't move, along with a million other steel cages that can't seem to move either?" He concludes by calling the trapped driver a human robot and mechanical fool. Such sentiments would not have encouraged sponsorship from General Motors.

Whatever the reasons for the rejection of their television musical, there seemed no reason to go on with it. Arlen could afford the time off, but Leonard Melfi would feel the pinch. He had a problem controlling the plot and the characters; only the lead characters are developed to any degree. But the plot strays, and a reading of the script would cause one to wonder where the songs belong. Five of the eight songs are spotted in one version of the script, omitting the most important ballad of the score, "I Had a Love Once." The mélange of hard fact (garbage, pollution, graffiti) and fancy (dancing animals) did not blend. The sardonic attempts at social commentary were more bitter than satirical.

Had there been any interest from a television producer, more work on the script by both Melfi and Arlen might have salvaged *Clippety Clop and Clementine*. But none surfaced, Arlen lost interest, and worse, the death of Melfi's mother upset the playwright; their creation died on the vine, leaving a not quite polished libretto and eight songs—all Arlen rarities.

Arlen had no illusions. As a lyricist, he would never belong in the company of Gershwin, Harburg, Mercer, or Koehler. But his words for the songs are felicitous, sprightly, and amusing. "A Happy Recipe" (subtitled "A Nonsense Song") is sung by Clippety Clop to the children in the zoo during the scene in which the animals are released from their cages:

> *One by one*
> *Two by two*
> *Three by three*
> *Four by four*

A crocus, a chickadee, a dove
Can't help but rhyme with love.

Arlen's marking reads, "obviously a march, crisply." (In the release he slipped in a twinkling musical reference over the words, "We love a parade.") "Organic Food," his satiric view of a current fad, is to be sung in a "sprightly" manner:

Taste buds reverb
While chewing organic herb,
*   Organic herb.*
Virility will flower
While chewing organic by the hour
*   By the hour.*
It's manhood, it's womanhood,
It's that which we seek,
These itty, bitty veg'tables
Bring color to your cheek.

The score's most significant song is "I Had a Love Once." In the Arlen art song genre, it is one of his most personal creations, a resigned lament, a plaintive song for Anya. It is a fine example of the Previns' definition of an Arlen song: it stops after thirty-five measures, after Arlen had expressed what he wished to say.

The special Arlen touch occurs in the accompaniment, underlining the composer's marking, "in a pensive mood." The song opens, without words, with two bars of a richly undulating chord, which continues under "I had a love once . . ." The chord weaves in and out of the thirty-five bars and closes the song, as it began, without words. These oddly affecting measures of static harmony, in twos and singly, unify the form, one of Arlen's most original. It was his last song.

This fact is contradicted by his works chronology. The *Clippity Clop* score dates from 1972; four years later two additional numbers, with lyrics by Harburg, appear. These songs, in fact, had been virtually finished in the late 1940s or early 1950s. Under the pressure of Harburg's ineluctable prodding, Arlen agreed to polish them for publication. In 1981 the Goodspeed Opera, of East Haddam, Connecticut, probably the finest musical revival theater in the nation, announced a revival of *Bloomer Girl*. The excited, galvanic Harburg promised the company a new song for their production. In the recent past Harburg had had an unhappy experience at Twentieth Century–Fox. On reading Arthur Laurents's screenplay of the book, Harburg, who "loathed" it, refused to permit the filming.

Harburg was certain that Goodspeed would do justice to *Bloomer Girl* (he was correct) and felt he and Arlen should write a new song to stir up interest and a little press. Arlen refused, feeling he was not up to it. Instead, one of the recently refurbished songs, "Promise Me Not to Love Me," was interpolated into the score. When *Bloomer Girl* premiered in East Haddam on September 27, 1981, Arlen, by then virtually house-bound, was not there.

Something had happened to him in the four years between "I Had a Love Once" and "Promise Me Not to Love Me." The abandonment of *Clippety Clop and Clementine* left him in limbo again, except for his ASCAP activities. These included the regular monthly board meetings as well as various functions that as a board member he was expected to attend: the celebration of the issuance of the George Gershwin stamp at Lincoln Center's Music Division, Eubie Blake's ninetieth birthday at the Hampshire House, a party for the cast of Alan Jay Lerner's *Music! Music!* at the ASCAP offices. The *New York Times* writer John Corry, covering the event, noted that Stanley Adams stood up to introduce "the eminent composers and lyricists" present and "another man from ASCAP got up, pointed to a piano, and said he hoped some of them might be prevailed on to play their songs."

Whereupon, he also noticed, Harold Arlen "slipped out of the room."

The Lerner party occurred in April 1974. In his article Corry observed that although Arlen had a grayish beard, he did not look old enough to have played the piano in *Great Day!* fifty years before. But he felt old; the walk to ASCAP left him tired; his gait was uncertain, a shuffle at times. In the den, as he watched sports on television, his hands trembled. These aberrations came and went. He attributed them to age; in fact, they were the early indications of the onset of Parkinson's disease.

The disease is slow in developing and its symptoms are similar to those of a stroke, a head injury, even an adverse reaction to medication. By the spring of 1975 it was obvious to his doctor that Arlen had Parkinson's disease. He and Jerry Arlen decided not to inform Harold Arlen of his condition because of the emotional impact it might have. He was still in depression over the death of Anya and the bleak musical scene, even the state of world politics. As the doctor explained to Mrs. Owens, because Arlen had been taking tranquilizers for years, another form of medication would not make him suspicious.

While it would not stop the progress of Parkinson's, Dr. Schachtel prescribed levodopa (L-dopa). Its function was to increase the amount of dopamine to the brain, thereby improving his balance, his ability to move, and other symptoms. While the L-dopa helped, to a degree, there were side effects, and the administration of the drug had to be carefully handled, timed, and increased as the disease progressed.

That he was unaware of the nature of his illness befuddled Arlen. He could not understand why it was difficult at times to rise from his chair, why his shuffling walk would come and go, his speech slur. There were times too when he was reasonably normal, but he also realized something was frightfully wrong.

He curtailed his movements, preferring to remain at home, most of the time in the den watching television. He turned down invitations or, if he accepted, changed his mind at the last minute. He was self-conscious about needing a constant handkerchief or tissue for his eyes and nose. He avoided seeing people and being seen. Late in October 1975 he resigned from the ASCAP board and brooded. He saw only a few friends and Jerry and Rita Arlen, who had him over for their Sabbath dinners. Often, even these visits were unpleasant, for he had difficulty getting in and out of cabs. When he arrived at his own address, the doorman assisted him out of the cab and up to his apartment.

His fluctuating physical disabilities annoyed, confused, and depressed him. Not knowing was half the problem. Yip Harburg, early in 1976, was the catalyst who would solve it.

Initially Harburg believed that his friend avoided him because he did not wish to work, was in his usual blue mood and wallowing in self-pity. When he discussed Arlen's plight with a friend he learned that Arlen was not faking but had Parkinson's disease.

"He never told me," Harburg said.

"He doesn't know."

"Why don't they tell him?"

"I don't know. When I asked Jerry that a couple of days ago he damn near chewed my ear off."

"He should know," said a determined Harburg.

Harburg, who had friends and relatives in medicine, managed to get Arlen to a neurologist. When he learned the nature and seriousness of his illness, Arlen retreated to his den, sat in his recliner, and spoke to no one. After two days Mrs. Owens summoned a nearby friend, one of the few Arlen would see, to attempt to end the disturbing silence.

He finally spoke. "I know what I got."

"I know."

"They can't cure it," he said morosely.

"You don't die from it and you can control it. And we know what's really going on. Your trouble walking and those strangers you see here"—Arlen often said he saw strangers in the apartment—"they're not here and are probably something to do with the medication. And it's not painful"—not in fact true, since a change in medication as the illness progressed could be excruciating—"and except that you've slowed down some, you're as sharp as ever."

Arlen chuckled, then said, "I should get back to work." He never did, however. The next decade of his life was, in essence, a vacuity brightened only by the almost daily calls from Irving Berlin and an occasional excursion (which became more hazardous month by month). Berlin amused him with his racy jokes, engaged him in political discussions or commiseration on the state of music. An insomniac, Berlin too spent his time at the television set and would report to Arlen how many Arlen songs he had heard the night before. If something came up at a reasonable time, he would get on the phone and order Arlen to turn to the proper channel and be reminded that the music of Harold Arlen was not forgotten.

Berlin one day, at the end of February 1977 (probably inspired by a musical birthday salute to Arlen on the radio), suggested that Arlen "consider doing a one-man 'and-then-I-wrote' show with your wonderful catalogue." Arlen's answer: "I've shot my wad."

Soon after, Arlen received a poem from Berlin entitled "I've Shot My Wad":

> *A nightingale looked up to God*
> *And said, "Dear God, I've shot my wad,*
> *No longer can I do my thing,*
> *Dear God, no longer can I sing."*
> *And He replied, "Don't be a schmuck,*
> *No nightingale has had such luck,*
> *Your songs have built a golden nest*
> *For Stanley Adams and the rest.*
> *They're praying for the moment when*
> *You get off your ass and sing again."*

During the final decade of his life, though inactive, Arlen was the recipient of honors and recognition that brought some joy and life into this vacuum. But he had become conscious of mortality, his and that of others. This was evident after a Players Club "Pipe Night" honoring him with an excellent Arlen songfest entitled *A Sense of Style: The Music of Harold Arlen* on the evening of November 23, 1975. The revue had been conceived several months before by the pianist Robert Tartaglia and the dancer and singer Richard Benneville. Arlen was pleased with their work, having watched over them since the beginning and frequently looked in on their rehearsals. The Pipe Night was their first New York performance. The Players Club is an exclusive show-business fraternity for writers, performers, producers, and others associated with show business and entertainment. Founded in 1888 by Edwin Booth—the "great American Hamlet of his time" and brother of the infamous John Wilkes Booth—the Players was housed in a gracious building in the also "exclusive" Gramercy Park.

At the time the club's president was the Broadway vocalist Alfred Drake (*Oklahoma!, Kiss Me, Kate,* etc.), who began the black tie evening by speaking eloquently about Arlen's contribution to American song. Tartaglia, at the piano, then swept into the introduction of an evening that highlighted close to forty songs. After long applause, Drake rose to exclaim that Harold Arlen's work "is not only of my generation but all generations!"

Although there had been a stipulation that Arlen would appear at the Players but would not speak (he found it difficult to rise and his speech slurred), Drake, in his enthusiasm, asked for a few words, and Arlen, touched by the Tartaglia-Benneville tribute, rose slowly from his seat. The large room became silent.

"I want to thank my collaborators," he said softly. "Three of them are ill, two of them are deceased. I must do something to them. Ira Gershwin is ill. Yip Harburg is ill. Johnny Mercer is ill. Dorothy Fields is deceased. Ted Koehler is deceased." He also named Leo Robin, who was alive. Then he switched from that morbid theme and closed on a happy note with, "And I want to thank this group for this marvelous night." This melancholy, brief, spontaneous utterance encapsulated Harold Arlen's view of the future.

Despite his melancholy and the arid years he foresaw ahead, Arlen prevailed; he did not give up. He endured, and at times suffered, the medication, a walker and a wheelchair (which he hated), a cheerful therapist, and a succession of practical nurses, some of whom clashed with Mrs. Owens, who ran the household her way. Arlen, too, at times found the young women annoying, particulary one who, on learning who he was, sang Arlen songs as she worked. She lasted only a day or two.

There were other reminders during those years with the recordings of his songs, Arlen revues, awards, and other accolades. Synchronously, the theme of his Pipe Night talk haunted him. In June of the next year, 1976, Johnny Mercer succumbed to a brain tumor in Bel Air, California. After a brief hiatus, the inexorable necrology continued with the death, from a heart attack while driving in Hollywood, of Yip Harburg on March 5, 1981.

For the ASCAP tribute to Harburg, Arlen prepared this statement: "We all lost a great contributor to our popular song, one of the rare poets of our profession. I personally lost a good and faithful friend in Yipper. His wit, his playfulness with words, his brilliance, produced a torrent of lyrics. We truly collaborated in every sense of the word. I miss him, we will all miss him. There was only one Yipper."

In September of the same year, one of his oldest friends, Harry Warren, died. That June, Arlen and a guest had seen *42nd Street,* then in its second year. Because of its Warren score, he had been anxious to see it, even though an evening at the theater was physically taxing; Arlen had difficulty walking and standing. He made a single comment about the slick, mechanized David Merrick production. When the curtain lowered at the end of the first act he said, "This doesn't move me." Unfortunately that night, when his guest turned away from him to signal for a taxi, Arlen's legs gave way and he fell to the sidewalk. That was one of his last trips to the theater. Now Harry was gone.

In August 1983, after a stroke and a lingering illness, Ira Gershwin died. ASCAP requested from Arlen "some brief words (not more than 30 seconds) about Ira or the songs to be performed" at the Ira Gershwin tribute that took place at the Gershwin Theater at noon on August 27. Arlen was not able to attend, but again prepared a few words that were read by ASCAP's new president, Hal David:

> *Poetry and wit,*
> *Twinkle-in-the-eye satire,*
> *Unsentimental love songs,*
> *Erudite and gentle—*
> *That was Ira.*
> *His delicious creations, like George's, are forever.*

While working over the piece, Arlen remembered an exchange between Ira Gershwin and Oscar Levant. The topic was sex, prompting Gershwin to observe, "Sex is a gentle thing." Levant disagreed, arguing that "friendship is gentle, not sex." That exchange, recalled years later, led Arlen to begin an early draft of his eulogy with, "As a friend and collaborator Ira was unique," but in the final draft settled for "gentle." Interestingly, the two tributes reflect the art of the two lyricists: Gershwin's is spare and Harburg's more florid.

This unhappy time was leavened periodically by a growing appreciation for his songs, which pleased and, now and then, seemed to surprise him. This renewed recognition began as early as 1973, barely three years after the death of Anya (and a month after the death of Ted Koehler). On February 25, at the invitation of Mayor Lindsay, Arlen and a group of friends and colleagues gathered at Gracie Mansion for cocktails and a buffet dinner "in honour," the invitation read, "of Harold Arlen and the NBC show featuring his music."

The evening's high point was a presentation by Lindsay of the city's Handel Medallion to Arlen, a high honor indeed. The show that followed was less festive. The assembly, which included Mary Lindsay, Wilva Breen (whose husband was absent), Gloria Vanderbilt, A. L. Berman, and others, watched an hour-long television show entitled "Jack Lemmon: Get Happy." It was not a happy show, despite the presence of Dinah Shore, Diahann Carroll, and Johnny Mathis. The show dangled from a wispy thread of a story—Lemmon's search for Harold Arlen on a yellow brick road.

Kay Gardella, writing in the next day's *New York News*, headed her column "A Lemmon of an Hour," which Arlen marked with arrows in the copy he clipped. She believed, and rightly, that "the great Arlen music was lost in this precocious hour that devoted more time to props, gimmicks and format than to a proper musical production of a number." One of the gimmicks was beginning and closing the show in black and white, as had been done in *The Wizard of Oz*. Color was used after Lemmon stumbles on a television stage, is knocked unconscious, and begins his search for Harold Arlen.

Another gimmick, Gardella pointed out (though she approved), was "the oversized Miss [Cass] Elliot—a good tongue-in-cheek touch." Elliot appeared as a fairy princess to assist Lemmon in his journey over the rainbow (of course), where he finds the composer. Others found the exploitation of Cass Elliot's corpulence more tasteless than amusing.

The criticism closed with a final swipe at Arlen: "Like so many of his musical peers, he sings lousy." In his copy Arlen underlined the last word and added in the margin the word "nu!" (The Yiddish expression roughly means "so," but depending on the delivery can mean anything from "so what" to "oh, yeah?" Leo Rosten described *nu* as a "huffy/whimsical emphasizer.") Arlen intended it as an amused sigh of resignation, for he agreed with the tenor of her review.

During the drive home, he did not mention the show or the absence of Robert Breen, who was in fact boycotting the production. The most conspicuous absence was that of Rita and Jerry Arlen. Obviously there was another period of estrangement. Arlen was happy to settle for the Handel Medallion, New York's highest award to one of its citizens for his or her contribution to the arts.

That evening at Gracie Mansion was the beginning of a steady series of events celebrating Arlen's contributions, ranging from small revues to radio programs in the United States and Canada. Following the Players Pipe Night, the most important was his Johnny Mercer Award.

This was an honor bestowed by his peers who belonged to the National Academy of Popular Music, which had been founded in 1977 by a group of songwriters, among them Johnny Mercer and Sammy Cahn. After Mercer's death a special award was instituted in his name to outstanding members of the Academy's Songwriters Hall of Fame. Arlen was selected as the recipient in 1982 at the suggestion of a trustee, and devoted friend, Burton Lane.

There was uneasiness about the nomination. The question was, Could Arlen make the dinner and awards ceremony, which was to be held at the New York Hilton on March 15? Two years before, when he had attended an event honoring Frank Sinatra at the exhortations of then President Cahn, he left at mid-dinner, before he was to have been introduced by Cahn. The spotlight fell on an empty place at Arlen's table.

Against the advice of friends that day in 1980, Arlen, feeling he owed it to the academy, decided to attend the dinner. Robert Breen offered to serve as an escort. By late afternoon—cocktails were scheduled for 6:30 and dinner for 7:30 at the Hilton—he was not in good form; he had trouble walking, even standing. Nevertheless, he was dressed in a blazer and flowing tie and would not hear about canceling. That night Ginger Mercer was to present the first Mercer Award to Sinatra; he had to go.

Over Breen's and another friend's protests they set out in a cab (with difficulty) and stopped off at Arlen's barber, luckily across the street from the Hilton. Possibly, the two friends agreed, by spending some time in the chair as he had a trim, his nails polished, and a sun lamp treatment, Arlen might relax and either be up to the event or realize it was best to skip it.

But that did not work. When he reached the sidewalk, one of his legs locked and he was forced to hang on to his companions on either side of him, carrying him across the street.

"Everybody thinks I'm drunk," he muttered.

"Harold, I think we should go home."

"No."

Across the street the odd trio, attracting curious glances from passersby, reached a bar adjacent to the hotel lobby and sat at a table. Nearby, on a raised platform, a young pianist was playing a current popular song. She obviously recognized Arlen and instantly began a long, well-played Arlen song medley. The three friends ordered drinks (Arlen was then permitted a glass or two of white wine, nothing stronger) and relaxed to the unexpected flow of music. Arlen managed a smile.

When she finished her set, the pianist came to the table to tell the composer how much she loved his music and what a joy it was to play. He smiled again and thanked her. He was now in shape for the walk to the elevator, a short distance from the bar. They skipped the cocktails in the foyer of the Grand Ballroom and went inside to sit at their table. It was an enormous room with a sea of about seventy tables, a large stage, and a bandstand. Among those at Arlen's table were Jo Sullivan, Mr. and Mrs. Joshua Logan, and the composer Marvin Hamlisch. All were acquainted with him, and their expressions made it obvious that his appearance was upsetting.

When it became known that Harold Arlen was in the ballroom, many guests stopped by the table to greet him. Arlen felt obligated to rise as each individual came by, or remain standing if they arrived in groups. Both actions were difficult for him, and he was virtually commanded by Breen to remain seated. The dinner came and went, and just as the lights dimmed for the speeches, performances, and awards, Arlen said, "Let's get out of here."

He was helped up by his two escorts, who, holding him, threaded their way through the tables in the darkened room toward a still-open door and the light in the foyer. A man stopped them halfway there, saying, "I'm a doctor. Is he all right?"

He was assured that Arlen was, but that he was not feeling well enough to stay.

In the foyer, as the three staggered toward the elevator, they were blocked by a quartet: Leonard Bernstein, Lauren Bacall, Betty Comden, and Adolph Green, who had been seated at an adjacent table. All were concerned about Arlen, and questioned him. Green insisted on telling him several times, "But Harold, your color is good."

Arlen, his head lowered, shuffling, appeared unaware of their blocking his path to the elevator. He then muttered, "She [Bacall] didn't send me her book."

(Arlen and Bacall had been good friends in Hollywood and frequently met at the Gershwins'.) She promised to send a copy of a recent best-seller, *By Myself*.

With the aid of his friends they managed to elbow past the group and continued to the elevator. Arlen said something again.

"What?"

"I think Lenny looks terrible." (Bernstein was suffering from emphysema and that night his color was not so good.)

Now, in 1982, the year of his Johnny Mercer Award, Arlen arrived with a phalanx: Rita and Jerry Arlen, the Breens, and his secretary, Jeanne Matalon. Also at their table were Mr. and Mrs. Tony Randall; the actor was to be the evening's master of ceremonies. Over seven hundred people crowded into the ballroom on the night of March 15.

In the two years since the encounter with Bernstein and the others, Arlen's condition had remained about the same, though on that evening he was not only supported by family and friends but also proved capable of staying through the long evening.

After the dinner, during which Rita Arlen assisted him with the utensils, Randall introduced the several inductees into the Songwriters Hall of Fame, among them Harold Rome, Jerry Herman, Meredith Willson, Paul Simon, and Bob Dylan. In time, Dinah Shore received a Lifetime Achievement Award, after which she sang a medley of Arlen songs, as reported in the academy's newsletter, "as a prelude to presenting Arlen—already in the Hall of Fame—with the Johnny Mercer Award. The audience thundered affection and admiration as all the performers [Shore, Barbara Cook, Larry Kert, Carol Channing] came towards Arlen to salute his genius in chorus with his standard 'Over the Rainbow.' "

Arlen stood, using the cane, as Dinah Shore presented him with the handsome plaque, surrounded by the vocalists Lynn and Burton Lane, the composer Charles Strouse, Marvin Hamlisch, and many others. With Rita Arlen in the vanguard, the Arlen party attempted to leave the ballroom through a crowd of admirers and autograph seekers. Harold Arlen, head lowered, moved through the crush as friends explained that he was not able to please the disappointed throng who carried programs and pens.

Arlen seemed dazed as he followed Rita, but brightened when Meredith Willson broke through the mob, embraced him, and then burst into tears. Finally the elevator deposited them on the ground floor, and a cab whisked them home.

Once in his den, Arlen studied his award, with its profile of Mercer embossed in gold, and remarked, "That's a poor likeness of John."

There is a line from a *House of Flowers* song that goes: "And that's the way the days go by / The livin' of the life goes by." Its fitting title is "Waitin'." Two years went by after the Mercer Award, and each day was the same. Arlen spent his waking hours in the den with an unwatched television set on. He dozed, talked on the phone, mostly with Berlin. He called a few friends, though he had a problem dialing, which Mrs. Owens managed. His sleeping was so erratic that he had little conception of time, often waking at three or four in the morning, ready for the day.

Between March 1982 and April 1984 a handful of days were memorable. February 15, 1984, Arlen's seventy-ninth birthday, was proclaimed "Harold Arlen Day" by Mayor Tom Bradley of Los Angeles. This coincided with the production of a revue, *Get Happy: The Music of Harold Arlen*, at the Westwood Playhouse. When the official proclamation arrived it came with a birthday card signed by the cast of *Get Happy* and his producer friends Dick DeBenedictis and Bill Dyer. Arlen treasured the card even more than the elaborately lettered (and worded) proclamation.

The show was well into its sold-out run when, on April 19, 1984, Harold Arlen managed to leave his apartment in the afternoon to accept the high honor of the "ASCAP–Richard Rodgers Award." Dorothy Rodgers had initiated the award as a memorial to her husband. The ceremony was to take place in the office of the president, Hal David, in the presence of a few guests, among them Mrs. Rodgers, Mrs. Arthur Schwartz (whose husband was also a recipient but not well), and the TV producer William Harbach (son of the lyricist Otto Harbach).

Though he was deeply honored, the event was not a happy one for Arlen. He was now dependent on a wheelchair (or, at home, a walker). He hated the chair and hated to be seen in it. With some misgivings, he agreed to attend the ceremony. With the help of ASCAP's Michael Kerker, an Arlen favorite and himself devoted to the composer, and Mrs. Owens, Arlen was taken by cab to the ASCAP offices. A freight elevator took them to David's office. Arlen was dismayed to see a large crowd and, in an adjoining room, a long table set for an impressive lunch.

The ceremony was mercifully brief as Mrs. Schwartz and he received checks for five thousand dollars for "outstanding contributions" to the musical theater. Arlen managed a few words of gratitude, then got into the chair and left; he knew he could not endure the luncheon. Kerker got him into a cab, and as he headed home, Arlen quipped, "We took the money and ran." (He contributed the sum to a charity.)

The Westwood Playhouse *Get Happy* was the climax of a series of tributes using Arlen's songs that had begun with the Players Club's Pipe Night almost a decade before. These unpretentious revues defined the quality and versatility of his songs—and, more importantly, served to remind Arlen who he was and what he had accomplished. He was reminded of songs he had forgotten. As much as he was able, Arlen contributed to these lovefests for the music and the man. The producers knew Arlen personally and saw him during the creation of their entertainments; all were amazed by his gentle appreciation, modest poise, and flashes of humor. Because of his illness and its progress over the period between the Players Club tribute and *Get Happy*, the composer was not always in condition for discussions or rehearsals but was always a warm presence.

When his new attorney, who had replaced A. L. Berman after his death, attempted to block one of the productions and demanded an excessive fee for the rights to the songs, Arlen reassured the anxious young producer, Julianne Boyd. He told her to proceed and checked the attorney with, "He's too greedy."

Arlen, for some reason of his own, relished the name of the co-producer of *Get Happy*, Dick DeBenedictis. He was even more amused when DeBenedictis and his partner, Bill Dyer, spent an afternoon with him. While he and Dyer talked in the den, DeBenedictis spent the time in the living room. As a composer himself, he felt compelled to play Arlen on Harold Arlen's Steinway.

These diversions, provided by the artists involved, intermittently eased some days as they went by and made Arlen's life less bleak.

The first of the revues, *Sweet and Hot*, began in Washington, D.C., at the New Playwrights' Theatre in June 1977; it ran through mid-September and then was booked into the Museum of the City of New York for the evening of November 7. The "cabaret revue" was conceived by Berthe Schuchat and Ken Bloom, who also directed, and featured no fewer than forty songs, including several rarities. Arlen, though a bit shaky, attended the evening with Yip Harburg and Robert Breen.

This was followed the next year, in May, with Julianne Boyd's *Happy with the Blues* at the Manhattan Theatre Club. As reported in the *New York Times*, "Current preview performances . . . happen to be sold out, but fans of the composer are encouraged to submit their names for a stand-by ticket list." Arlen, with Harburg and a few friends, attended the opening night's performance, to the delight of the producer and cast.

Because of distance, as well as his now frail health, Arlen was unable to attend the next two tributes, but he was aware of them and heard recordings of the performances.

Kevin Cole, who as a teenager had charmed Arlen by performing, authentically, popular theater and film songs written before he was born, presented "An Evening of Gershwin and Arlen" in his birthplace, Bay City, Michigan, in November 1981. (Cole is regarded as one of the most impressive interpreters of Gershwin in the country, beginning with the Gershwin family. Arlen, too, admired his way with an Arlen song or piano piece.)

Though his program contained many of the expected standards, Cole also worked in several lesser-known works by both Gershwin and Arlen. He spoke between the selections to acquaint the audience in the packed auditorium with some of his esoteric selections. The audience was remarkably responsive, considering the state of popular song in 1981.

Soon after the evening Cole sent a tape of it to Arlen, who spent a pleasant afternoon listening—he was pleased, even surprised, that the audience apparently caught on to some of Harburg's sophisticated lyrics. Arlen was also pleased to have been coupled with his admired friend Gershwin. Although he did not draw parallels, Cole juxtaposed two miniature suites for piano. In the Gershwin half, he played Gershwin's early ragtime study, "Rialto Ripples" (1917), and the Three Preludes. In the Arlen portion, he played Arlen's ragtime composition "Rhythmic Moments" (1928) and the "Minuet" and "Ode."

The decade gap between the ragtime pieces underscored the Gershwin of the 1920s and the Arlen of the 1930s, the snappy Jazz Age and the troubled Depression. Arlen enjoyed Cole's Gershwin, as he did Cole's Arlen. He was especially charmed by baritone Thomas Scholten's moving rendition of "Promise Me Not to Love Me," in its first public hearing, and the delicate presentation of "Now I Know" and the dramatic "I Had Myself a True Love" as sung by soprano Katherine Wells-Paauw.

As he had years before, Arlen was taken with Cole's accompaniment as well as his solo work. Cole's arrangement for piano solo of "The Man That Got Away" intrigued the composer. Cole played the song more slowly than sung by Judy Garland but magically held the composition together with his hypnotic beat and melodic and rhythmic nuance. When the final chord faded, Arlen said, "Now, *that's* interesting!" Though he was visibly tiring, he asked to hear the performance again.

The Dyer-DeBenedictis *Get Happy* came next. Before it opened on Arlen's birthday in 1984, its tryout took place at the small Pilot Playhouse in Hollywood in November of the previous year. "The boys," as Arlen called them, kept him abreast of their progress, brightening his otherwise dark days. The *Los Angeles Times* headed Sylvie Drake's review "Happiness Is a Thing Called Harold Arlen":

> Prophetically titled "Get Happy," the show's subtitle—"The Music of Harold Arlen"—tells you what you need to know and probably don't.
> Wonderful music.
> Wonderful Arlen, who composed the deathless score for "The Wizard of Oz," but has proved a greater and far more prolific wizard than most people imagine. In the reams of popular songs turned out by him in 78 years (and counting), few are ever given proper attribution. Why the songwriter and the song have become so distanced remains a mystery, but it fills "Get Happy" with repeated happy shocks of recognition.

Soon after the opening, Dyer wrote:

> Get Happy is a big, big hit. . . . We plan to extend at the Pilot for two/three weeks, close the show and reopen at a major house out here. Both

the Westwood Playhouse and the Huntington Hartford want us. The phones continue to ring and everyone is turning out including Bob Hope, Lew Wasserman and all of Los Angeles. . . . Dick and I are bursting with pride. After so long! Everyone who comes is overwhelmed by Arlen's music.

Now, no one will ever say, Harold who?

The show was as enthusiastically received when it reopened at the Westwood. When the show's program arrived during its preview stage, Arlen was asked, "How does it hit you to have fifty songs in a show?"

"It hits me," he said softly, "that I even wrote fifty songs."

He prepared a telegram to send for the show's premiere. As usual, he struggled over it. Initially, he came up with, "All my love to all of you and a very happy birthday to me." He discarded that for: "Forget your troubles and just get happy. Best wishes and love to all."

Later that same year young Ken Bloom, who had been associated with *Sweet and Hot,* reentered Arlen's lonely world. He had founded an independent record company with Bill Rudman, a musical theater authority and, like Bloom, an Arlen devotee. In Cleveland, where he made his home, Rudman broadcast a weekly radio program devoted to show music and the great popular songs; he was also associated with the Great Lakes Theater Festival. Bloom had moved to New York from Washington and was researching his forthcoming encyclopedic survey of American popular song.

Bloom and Rudman, in concert with the pianist and arranger Keith Ingham, planned to produce an album starring the seventy-three-year-old Maxine Sullivan singing over a dozen Arlen Cotton Club songs. The album, *The Great Songs from the Cotton Club,* was recorded in November and released in time for Arlen's eightieth birthday, in February 1985. Sullivan was in fine vocal fettle, with an appropriate jazz-hued accompaniment by the Keith Ingham Quintet.

When the album was ready, Rudman flew in from Cleveland. He and Bloom called on Arlen to present him with the first set. Rudman, who unabashedly regarded Arlen as the greatest of all American songwriters, was thrilled to meet the gray-bearded, shrunken man whose music he loved. As for Arlen, he loved the album. He had known Maxine Sullivan for years, although they had not worked at the Cotton Club at the same time.

Arlen was touched by the veneration for his work evidenced by the new record production team. He was impressed with their knowledge of his work. That they dared include several of the lesser known songs—" 'Neath the Pale Cuban Moon," "In the Silence of the Night," "Primitive Prima Donna"—was especially gratifying. After the elated Bloom and Rudman left, Arlen, with the album in hand, chuckled and called them "monsters," his affectionate term for talented young people. (Some years later Bloom, Rudman, and Ingham produced an album of rare Arlen songs by Peggy Lee.)

Later that year, in September, Arlen's health suffered another setback. His physician realized that Arlen evidenced the discomfort and pain associated with an enlarged prostate and that he would require hospitalization, probably surgery. By this time Arlen had lost so much weight and was so frail that it seemed unlikely he could endure the traumas of an operation. But there was no choice; in Mount Sinai hospital he underwent transurethral resection—and survived.

When his surgeon—another "monster"—learned that the disheveled little man in the bed had written "Over the Rainbow," he became excited and questioned Jerry Arlen about his brother. The attractive and, yes, young nurse, upon discovering that her patient was Harold Arlen, began trying to cheer him up with a string of jokes. The composer turned to a visitor at his bedside and said, "I'm fighting for my life and she's telling funnies."

He left the hospital on October 9, 1985. Despite the ordeal, there was some improvement. Sporting a trim by a barber, Arlen looked neater, managed to walk better, and was even perky. Soon after he arrived home, another "monster," David Bickman, surprised him with yet another verification of his stature, *The Harold Arlen Songbook*. The seventy-six songs in the lavishly printed collection, carefully edited by Bickman, proved again that Arlen had indeed written more than fifty songs.

The publication, under the direction of Joseph Weiss, of Paul McCartney's MPL Communications, which had taken over a large proportion of the Arlen catalog, was a major milestone in Arlen's life. There had been Gershwin, Rodgers, Kern, and Porter songbooks, and now Arlen had his own. The compilation is a significant addition to the library of popular song, not only because of Bickman's correction of printing errors in the early publications but also because of the restoration of out-of-print songs and the first publication of others. To Arlen, Bickman's delivery of the *Songbook* was almost a miracle: although the practice of publishing songbooks had faded by the 1970s because they did not sell, the first edition of the Arlen songbook quickly sold out, and a second was printed.

After the brief *Songbook* interlude the Arlen household shifted back into the usual daily routine. About midmorning Rita Arlen would arrive to sift through the California crates. With the aid of an archivist, the contents were spread over the bed, the floor, and any available surface in what had been Anya's bedroom. Arlen no longer entered the room. There were boxes of letters, recordings, papers, photographs, books, and other memorabilia in virtually every part of the room, with a path leading in and out.

One day they came across a long-lost item, Arlen's "Over the Rainbow" Oscar, which Mrs. Arlen excitedly took to the composer in the den, where he now spent virtually all his waking hours. He was happy, thanked her, and held the award the rest of the morning. Although he had been aware of the search going on in Anya's room, as time went on he was disturbed by the noise of the crates being opened and the hammering until he drifted to sleep.

The arrival and departure of several nurses became part of the routine, until a dramatic incident. Geri Owens often had differences, shouting matches, and other outbursts with individual "norses." One she accused of beating Arlen and threatened her with serious violence. The Arlens and Jeanne Matalon believed that both the nurse and Mrs. Owens must go. Accordingly, after several years in Arlen's employ, Mrs. Owens left for Atlanta and the apartment became more pacific. Arlen reluctantly agreed, for she had been more than a housekeeper and a good, often fiercely protective friend.

Jeanne Matalon, too, arrived several days a week. The small dining room had been converted into her office, from which she attended to the household expenses, oversaw Arlen's investments, and otherwise handled all business matters. She had moved out of the Berman office when Arlen could no longer get around. She also helped him prepare a will. Arlen wanted his Steinway grand in the living room to go to ASCAP; his little Martha Washington upright in the den would belong to Rita and Jerry Arlen. In a curious twist, he adopted Jerry's son, Samuel, as his son and named him his primary heir. Other sums of money were divided among several charities.

He was ready, and he waited.

The improvement in his condition after the prostate procedure was temporary. At the time it was found that his prostate was cancerous. By November his decline was obvious, even to those who saw him daily; then late that month another cheering diversion occurred.

Stuart Triff, an authority on show music who had worked in radio and recordings, produced an album featuring the *Americanegro Suite.* The vocalist was a remarkable soprano, Judy Kaye, then notable for her Broadway appearance in *On the Twentieth Century* (and later, *Phantom of the Opera*). Her arranger and accompanist was another Broadway veteran, the pianist Peter Howard. Besides the suite, several songs from shows and films were included; in the former, Kaye was backed by the Premiere Gospel Quartet.

The recording sessions were held in a large complex in Queens across the East River from Manhattan. On the first day Arlen listened in by telephone and liked what he heard. The release of the recording was postponed by "various problems and vicissitudes" until 1990, according to Premiere Records' founder, Robert W. Stern.

Thanks to Triff, however, an unedited tape of the sessions was prepared for Arlen, who heard it on January 15, 1986, one month before his eighty-first birthday. Alert, attentive, and charmed by the often soaring operatic voice of Judy Kaye, Arlen kept time by tapping on the arm of his chair—he often closed his eyes and sang along with her. On hearing Kaye's rendition of "Little Angel

Child" (formerly "Little Ace of Spades") Arlen's response was a resounding "Bravo!"

At another point, between bands, he gazed at the engineer and said, "Thank you." When the tape ended, he applauded.

In the morning of April 23, 1986, Rita Arlen arrived at the Arlen apartment for her daily stint at the crates and classification of the contents. She brought a portion of her own matzo ball soup from the night before. She knew Arlen loved it and could have it, warmed, for lunch. He could not wait and insisted on a sample, even cold, laced with horseradish, in the den.

Early in the afternoon he asked the nurse to help him to his bedroom, an unusual request that early in the day. Quietly, peacefully, around four o'clock Harold Arlen died. Present at the moment were Rita and Jerry Arlen, a sobbing nurse, and a close friend. A decade-long ordeal for him and those close to him was over.

Not quite. When Jerry attended to the arrangements for his brother's interment beside Anya at Ferncliff Cemetery in Hartsdale, he found that at the time of Anya's burial sixteen years before, Harold had acquired only a single plot. There was no space next to, or even near, Anya. This caused dismay among the funeral directors and further distress to a weary, anguished Jerry after his experiences with paramedics, a blue nightmare of police (because Harold Arlen had not died in a hospital in the presence of a doctor), and the newspapers.

The solution was the single touch of poetry on that somber, bewildering day. Anya and Harold would be buried in the same grave.

On April 25, Burton Lane, representing ASCAP as well as himself, and his wife, Lynn, close friends of Arlen for years, spoke at the funeral services. The eulogy was cogent, eloquent, and honest. In part, Lane said:

It is always sad when one loses a friend. And all of us are sad today. But somehow, deep inside me, I feel a certain sense of relief knowing that Harold has finally found peace.

Harold's private life was not an easy one. He had come from an orthodox Jewish family and had fallen in love and married outside his religion. He suffered great pangs of guilt because of this; he adored and never stopped adoring his beautiful wife, Anya. It was a great blow to him when she died, and, I believe, he never recovered from it.

But looking back on Harold's life, it seems to me there was much to celebrate. There were many good years, and he enjoyed them. He knew his own value as a composer. He liked a good joke and he liked to laugh. He liked a good cigar, a good wine, a well-cut suit, and a flower in his lapel. He was much loved and respected by his peers and everyone who knew him, as well as by millions of music lovers all over the world who never even met him. I feel especially privileged to have had him as a friend.

Harold was a giant and he worked with giants. Just think of it: Ted Koehler, Johnny Mercer, Yip Harburg, Ira Gershwin, Dorothy Fields, Leo Robin, Lew Brown, Truman Capote. They were all blessed to have his music fit their words. . . .

All human beings long to leave something of themselves behind when they die, something that will give meaning and continuity to the life they have lived. Many of us leave children and that seems to satisfy that need. But people who create, songwriters, poets, authors, painters, hope that what they have created will have a life of its own, long after theirs has ended.

Well, Harold Arlen has left such a legacy. He was a musical genius. Like Mozart, like Schubert, like Gershwin, like Kern, his gorgeous melodies are timeless and will go on and on.

An hour later Harold and Anya were united for eternity.

On that day, the *New York Times* reported, a strange phenomenon was sighted by several people: spectacular rainbows in the sky. "All the rainbow reporters mentioned two facts: that they hadn't seen a rainbow in a long, long time and that April 25th was also the day that Harold Arlen was buried."

APPENDIX A: THE WORKS OF HAROLD ARLEN

Lyricists' names follow song titles in parentheses.

1924 My Gal, Won't You Come Back to Me? (My Gal, My Pal) (Hyman Cheiffetz)
I Never Knew What Love Could Do (Hyman Cheiffetz)

1925 Easy Strain (Phil Shapiro)
I Want Your Kisses If You Want My Kisses (Phil Shapiro)

1926 Minor Gaff (Blues Fantasy), for piano, by Harold Arluck and Dick George

1927 Buffalo Rhythm, for piano, by Harold Arluck, Ivan Beaty, and Marvin Smolev

1928 Rhythmic Moments, for piano
Jungaleena (Herb Magidson and James Cavanaugh)

1929 The Album of My Dreams (Lou Davis)
Bring Him Back Here (Lou Davis)
Can't Be Bothered with No One But You (Charles Tobias)
Rising Moon (Jack Ellis)
That's What I Call Love (Jack Ellis)
Does This Go On Forever? (Jack Ellis)
Don't You See What Troubles Me (Jack Ellis)
Who Could Say No? (Ted Koehler)
Heap o' Misery (Ted Koehler)
Gladly (Ted Koehler)

1930 Gee, It's So Good, It's Too Bad (Ted Koehler)
You Wanted Me, I Wanted You (Ted Koehler)
Get Happy (Ted Koehler)
    These three songs were interpolated into the *Nine-Fifteen Revue,* produced by Ruth Selwyn at the George M. Cohan Theatre, February 11, 1930; seven performances. With Ruth Etting, Harry McNaughton, Nan Blackstone, Oscar Ragland, others. Sketches by Ring Lardner, Paul Gerard Smith, Eddie Cantor, Anita Loos, others. Songs also by Kay Swift and Paul James (James P. Warburg), George and Ira Gershwin, Victor Herbert and Edward Eliscu, Vincent Youmans and Paul James, others.

Earl Carroll's Vanities of 1930
Lyrics by Ted Koehler. Sketches by Eddie Welch and Eugene Conrad. Produced by Earl Carroll at the New Amsterdam Theatre, July 1, 1930; 215 performances. With Jack Benny, Jimmy Savo, Patsy Kelly, Faith Bacon, the Collette Sisters, others. Additional songs by Jay Gorney and E. Y. Harburg.
    Contagious Rhythm

Hittin' the Bottle
The March of Time
One Love
Out of a Clear Blue Sky

Biff-Boom-Bang
Lyrics by Ted Koehler. Presented at the Silver Slipper; cast and dates unknown. Probably produced and directed by Dan Healy.
Opening
Steps
Shakin' the African
Old Fashioned
On the Beat
I'll Call It Love
I Was Born with the Blues in My Heart

Brown Sugar (Black Berries of 1931)
Lyrics by Ted Koehler. Produced and directed by Dan Healy, fall 1930, with Duke Ellington's Orchestra, Leitha Hill, Maud Russell, Cora La Redd. (There were two revues each year, with dates and runs hard to come by. Songs from an earlier revue were often retained for the later one. This was the first Cotton Club score by Arlen and Koehler.)
Linda
Song of the Gigolo
Harlem's Hot as Hades
Chase the Cat
La Rhumba
My Man Must Dance
Misbehavin' Hips
Heap o' Misery
Toothache Blues

1931 *You Said It*
Lyrics by Jack Yellen. Book by Yellen and Sid Silvers. Produced by Yellen and Lou Holtz at the Forty-sixth Street Theatre, January 19, 1931; 192 performances. With Holtz, May Lawler, Stanley Smith, Lyda Roberti, Benny Baker, Peggy Bernier, Hughie Clark, others.
If He Really Loves Me
It's Different with Me
Learn to Croon
Sweet and Hot
They Learn about Women from Me
What Do We Care?
What'd We Come to College For?
While You Are Young
You'll Do
You Said It

Alma Mater
Beatin' the Blues
Bright and Early
Best Part College Days
Harlem's Gone Collegiate
Where, Oh Where?

Rhyth-Mania
Lyrics by Ted Koehler. Staged by Dan Healy at the Cotton Club, March 1931, with Cab Calloway's Orchestra, Aida Ward, others.
  Between the Devil and the Deep Blue Sea
  Breakfast Dance
  I Love a Parade
  Kickin' the Gong Around
  'Neath the Pale Cuban Moon
  Trickeration
  Without Rhythm
  Get Under the Sun
  Satan Leads the Band

Ha-Ha-Ha (Gang Song) (Ted Koehler)
Tell Me with a Love Song (Ted Koehler)

1932   The Song That Makes Me Blue (Jack Yellen)
I Forgive You (Jack Yellen)
Y' Got Me, Baby (Jack Yellen)
Stepping into Love (Ted Koehler)
Music, Music, Everywhere, But Not a Song in My Heart (Ted Koehler)
Another Night Alone (Ted Koehler)

Earl Carroll's Vanities of 1932
Lyrics by Ted Koehler. Sketches by Jack McGowan. Produced by Earl Carroll at the Broadway Theatre, September 27, 1932; 87 performances. With Will Fyffe, Milton Berle, Helen Broderick, Lillian Shade, John Hale, Harriet Hoctor, others. Additional songs by Haven Gillespie and Charles and Henry Tobias, Edward Heyman and Richard Myers.
  The Most Beautiful Girls in the World
  Swingin' Along
  Rockin' in Rhythm
  I Gotta Right to Sing the Blues

Satan's Li'l Lamb (E. Y. Harburg and John Mercer)
  Interpolated into *New Americana,* sketches by J. P. McEvoy. Produced by Lee Shubert at the Shubert Theatre, October 5, 1932: 77 performances. With George Givot, Francetta Malloy, Doris Humphrey, Jose Limon, Charles Weidman, Albert Carroll, Georgie Tapps, Lloyd Nolan, others. Additional songs by Harburg and Vernon Duke; Harburg and Jay Gorney; Harburg and Burton Lane; Harburg, Mercer, and Richard Myers; Mercer and Henry Souvaine.

Cotton Club Parade (21st edition)
Lyrics by Ted Koehler. Dances staged by Elida Webb. Produced by Dan Healy at the Cotton Club, October 23, 1932. With Aida Ward, Leitha Hill, the Nicholas Brothers, and Cab Calloway's Orchestra.

    Harlem Holiday
    In the Silence of the Night
    I've Got the World on a String
    Minnie the Moocher's Wedding Day
    That's What I Hate about Love
    The Wail of the Reefer Man
    You Gave Me Ev'rything but Love
    Let's Put On the Ritz
    A la Lenox Avenue
    All Aboard
    Deep Sea Divin' Papa
    New Kind o' Rhythm

Cabin in the Cotton (Irving Caesar and George White)
Two Feet in Two-Four Time (Irving Caesar)
These two songs, with "I Love a Parade," were interpolated into *George White's Music Hall Varieties.* Produced by George White at the Casino Theatre, November 22, 1932; 72 performances. With Harry Richman, Lily Damita, Bert Lahr, Eleanor Powell, Betty Kean, Vivian Fay, others. Additional songs by Herb Magidson and Sammy Stept, Herman Hupfeld and Carmen Lombardo.

If You Believed in Me (E. Y. Harburg and Billy Rose)
Interpolated into the play *The Great Magoo* by Ben Hecht and Gene Fowler. Produced by Billy Rose at the Selwyn Theatre, December 2, 1932; eleven performances. With Paul Kelly. The song was published as "It's Only a Paper Moon."

1933   *Cotton Club Parade* (22nd edition)
Lyrics by Ted Koehler. Staged and produced by Dan Healy at the Cotton Club, April 6, 1933. With Ethel Waters, George Dewey Washington, the Nicholas Brothers, Cora La Redd, Duke Ellington and His Orchestra.

    Get Yourself a New Broom
    Happy As the Day Is Long
    Raisin' the Rent
    Stormy Weather
    Calico Days
    I'm Lookin' for Another Handy Man
    Muggin' Lightly

Shame on You (Edward Heyman)

Let's Fall in Love
Lyrics by Ted Koehler. Screenplay by Herbert Fields. Directed by David Bur-

ton. Produced by Felix Young for Columbia Pictures. Released January 1934. With Ann Sothern, Edmund Lowe, Tala Birell, Gregory Ratoff, Miriam Jordan, Betty Furness, Arthur Jarrett.

Let's Fall in Love
Love Is Love Anywhere
This Is Only the Beginning
Breakfast Ball (not used)
She's Not the Type (not used)
The Swede Is Not a Swede (not used)

1934   *Cotton Club Parade* (24th edition)
Lyrics by Ted Koehler. "Entire production conceived and supervised by Ted Koehler," Cotton Club, March 23, 1934. With Adelaide Hall, Juano Hernandez, Lena Horne, Avon Long, Leitha Hill, Pops and Louie, Dynamite Hooker, Jimmy Lunceford and His Orchestra.

Twice a Year
Primitive Prima Donna
Those Who Dance
You Sure Don't Know How to Shake That Thing
As Long As I Live
Ill Wind
Here Goes
Breakfast Ball (from *Let's Fall in Love*)

Life Begins at 8:40
Lyrics by Ira Gershwin and E. Y. Harburg. Sketches by David Freedman, H. I. Phillips, Alan Baxter, Henry C. Smith, Frank Gabrielson, Ira Gershwin, and E. Y. Harburg. Directed by John Murray Anderson. Produced by the Shuberts at the Winter Garden, August 27, 1934; 237 performances. With Bert Lahr, Ray Bolger, Luella Gear, Frances Williams, Brian Donlevy, Earl Oxford, Dixie Dunbar, Josephine Houston, Adrienne Matzenauer, the Weidman Dancers, others.

Life Begins (At Exactly 8:40 or Thereabouts)
Spring Fever
You're a Builder Upper
My Paramount-Publix-Roxy Rose
Shoein' the Mare
Quartet Erotica
Fun to Be Fooled
C'est la Vie
What Can You Say in a Love Song?
Let's Take a Walk around the Block
Things
All the Elks and Masons
I Couldn't Hold My Man
A Weekend Cruise

It Was Long Ago
I'm Not Myself
Life Begins at City Hall (Beautifying the City)
I Knew Him When (cut)
I'm a Collector of Moonbeams
Album Song
It Was Never Like This

1935   Mood in Six Minutes
Orchestration by Robert Russell Bennett. Commissioned for the "General Motors Symphony Hour"; broadcast April 14, 1935.

Last Night When We Were Young (E. Y. Harburg)

1936   *Strike Me Pink*
Lyrics by Lew Brown. Screenplay by Frank Butler, Francis Martin, and Walter DeLeon. Directed by Norman Taurog. Produced by Samuel Goldwyn for United Artists. Released January 1936. With Eddie Cantor, Sally Eilers, Ethel Merman, Parkyakarkus (Harry Parks), William Frawley.
    The Lady Dances
    Calabash Pipe
    Shake It Off (With Rhythm)
    First You Have Me High (Then You Have Me Low)
    If I Feel This Way Tomorrow

The Singing Kid
Lyrics by E. Y. Harburg. Screenplay by Warren Duff and Pat C. Flick. Directed by William Keighly. Released by Warner Brothers, April 1936. With Al Jolson, Sybil Jason, Edward Everett Horton, Allen Jenkins, Claire Dodd, Lyle Talbot, the Yacht Club Boys, Cab Calloway and His Orchestra.
    Here's Looking at You
    I Love to Sing-a
    My How This Country Has Changed (cut)
    Who's the Swingingest Man in Town?
    Save Me, Sister
    You're the Cure for What Ails Me

Stage Struck
Lyrics by E. Y. Harburg. Screenplay by Tom Buckingham and Pat C. Flick. Directed by Busby Berkeley. Produced by Hal Wallis for Warner Brothers. Released September 1936. With Dick Powell, Joan Blondell, Warren William, Frank McHugh, Jeanne Madden.
    Fancy Meeting You
    In Your Own Quiet Way
    The New Parade
    Why Can't I Remember Your Name?
    You'd Be Kinda Grandish
    Four Fugitives from a Bolero Chain Gang
    Love Theme (instrumental)

Gold Diggers of 1937
Lyrics by E. Y. Harburg. Screenplay by Howard Duff. Directed by Lloyd Bacon. Musical sequences directed by Busby Berkeley. Produced by Hal B. Wallis for Warner Brothers. Released December 1936. With Dick Powell, Joan Blondell, Victor Moore, Glenda Farrell, Osgood Perkins, Lee Dixon, Jane Wyman. Additional songs by Harry Warren and Al Dubin.

    Hush Ma Mouth
    Let's Put Our Heads Together
    Life Insurance Song
    Speaking of the Weather
    The Whippoorwill in the Weeping Willow Tree
    ²/₄ "Girl Number" (instrumental)

Song of the Woodman (E. Y. Harburg)
    Written for Bert Lahr and interpolated into the revue *The Show Is On,* produced by the Shuberts at the Winter Garden, December 25, 1936; 237 performances. Additional songs by the Gershwins, Arthur Schwartz and Howard Dietz, Hoagy Carmichael and Stanley Adams, Vernon Duke and Ted Fetter, Rodgers and Hart.

How's By You? (E. Y. Harburg)
I'll Thank You to Stay Out of My Dreams (E. Y. Harburg)
It's a Long, Long Way to Broadway (E. Y. Harburg)

1937   The Peter Pan of Tin Pan Alley (E. Y. Harburg)
      When the Wind Blows South (E. Y. Harburg)

Hooray for What!
Lyrics by E. Y. Harburg. Book by Howard Lindsay and Russel Crouse, based on an idea by Harburg. Production staged by Vincente Minnelli; book staged by Lindsay. Produced by the Shuberts at the Winter Garden, December 1, 1937: 200 performances. With Ed Wynn, Paul Haakon, June Clyde, Vivian Vance, Hugh Martin, Ralph Blane, the Sue Hastings Marionettes, Al Gordon's Dogs, others.

    Hooray for What!
    God's Country
    Long Ago, Far Away, Once upon a Time
    I've Gone Romantic on You
    Moanin' in the Mornin'
    Life's a Dance
    Viva for Geneva
    Napoleon's a Pastry
    Down with Love
    A Fashion Girl
    The Night of the Embassy Ball
    In the Shade of the New Apple Tree

Hero Ballet (orchestrated by Don Walker; choreography by Agnes de Mille)
Buds Won't Bud
I Click ze Heel and Keez ze Hand (cut)
I'm Hanging On to You (cut)

Public Melody Number One (Ted Koehler)
Interpolated into the film *Artists And Models,* starring Jack Benny; the song was sung by Louis Armstrong. Additional songs by Burton Lane and Ted Koehler, Leo Robin and Frederick Hollander, others.

1938   Love's a Necessary Thing (Ted Koehler)

1939   Let's Hit the Nail on the Head (Ted Koehler)
You've Got Me Sitting on a Fence (Ted Koehler)
Sing My Heart (Ted Koehler)
Interpolated into the film *Love Affair,* starring Irene Dunne and Charles Boyer; released by RKO Radio Pictures, March 1939.

The Wizard of Oz
Lyrics by E. Y. Harburg. Screenplay by Noel Langley, Florence Ryerson, Edgar Allen Woolf, and Lee Mahin (uncredited). Directed by Victor Fleming and King Vidor (uncredited). Produced by Mervyn LeRoy for MGM. Released August 1939. With Judy Garland, Frank Morgan, Ray Bolger, Bert Lahr, Jack Haley, Billie Burke (vocals by Lorraine Bridges), Margaret Hamilton, Charley Grapewin, Clara Blandick.
Over the Rainbow
Munchkinland: Come Out, Come Out
Ding Dong! The Witch Is Dead!
Follow the Yellow Brick Road
We're Off to See the Wizard
If I Only Had a Brain/a Heart/the Nerve
The Jitterbug (not used)
Optimistic Voices (You're Out of the Woods)
The Merry Old Land of Oz (Renovation Sequence)
If I Were King of the Forest

At the Circus
Lyrics by E. Y. Harburg. Screenplay by Irving Brecher. Directed by Edward Buzzell. Produced by Mervyn LeRoy for MGM. Released November 1939. With the Marx Brothers, Kenny Baker, Florence Rice, Margaret Dumont, others.
Two Blind Loves
Lydia, the Tattooed Lady
Swingali
Step Up and Take a Bow

American Minuet, for orchestra.

Commissioned and conducted by Meredith Willson on the Maxwell House "Good News Hour," broadcast December 1939.

1940   I'll Supply the Title, You'll Supply the Tune (Ira Gershwin)

1941   Lonesome and Low (Ted Koehler)
       Like a Straw in the Wind (Ted Koehler)

Americanegro Suite (Ted Koehler)
    Big Time Comin'
    I Got Dat Feelin'
    I'm Here Lawd
    Little Ace o' Spades
    Reverend Johnson's Dream
    Where Is Dis Road A-leadin' Me To?

When the Sun Comes Out (Ted Koehler)
The Bug, for piano

Blues in the Night
Lyrics by Johnny Mercer. Screenplay by Robert Rossen. Directed by Anatole Litvak. Produced by Hal B. Wallis for Warner Brothers. Released December 1941. With Priscilla Lane, Richard Whorf, Jack Carson, Wallace Ford, Betty Field, Elia Kazan, William Gillespie (uncredited), and the orchestras of Jimmy Lunceford and Will Osborne.
    Blues in the Night
    Hang On to Your Lids, Kids
    Says Who, Says You, Says I!
    This Time the Dream's on Me
    Wait'll It Happens to You (cut)

Heave Ho! Let the Wind Blow! (E. Y. Harburg)
    Written for film *Ship Ahoy,* 1941; not used.

1942   The Moment I Laid Eyes on You (Ted Koehler)
       Life Could be a Cakewalk with You (Ted Koehler)
       Captains of the Clouds (Johnny Mercer)
    Title song for film about the Royal Canadian Air Force.

Rio Rita
Lyrics by E. Y. Harburg. Screenplay by Richard Conell and Gladys Lehman. Directed by S. Sylvan Simon. Produced by Pandro S. Berman for MGM. Released May 1942. With Bud Abbott and Lou Costello, Kathryn Grayson, John Carroll, Tom Conway, Peter Whitney, Eros Volusia. Additional songs by Joseph McCarthy and Harry Tierney from original stage production; others.
    Long before You Came Along
    Poor Whippoorwill (cut)
    A Couple of Caballeros (not used)
    Such Unusual Weather (cut)

Star Spangled Rhythm
Lyrics by Johnny Mercer. Screenplay by Harry Tugend. Directed by George
Marshall. Produced by Joseph Sistrom for Paramount. Released December
1942. With Eddie Bracken, Victor Moore, Betty Hutton, Bing Crosby, Bob
Hope, Dick Powell, Mary Martin, Veronica Lake, Dorothy Lamour, Paulette
Goddard, the Golden Gate Quartet, Johnnie Johnston, Cass Daley, Vera Zor-
ina, many others.

> He Loved Me till the All Clear Came (cut)
> Hit the Road to Dreamland
> I'm Doing It for Defense
> Let's Go Sailor (Shore Leave)
> Old Glory
> On the Swing Shift
> Sharp As a Tack
> A Sweater, a Sarong, and a Peek-a-Boo Bang
> That Old Black Magic

1943   If That's Propaganda (Ira Gershwin)
Palsy Walsy (Johnny Mercer)
> Interpolated into the film *They Got Me Covered.*

Cabin in the Sky
Lyrics by E. Y. Harburg. Screenplay by Joseph Schrank, Marc Connelly, and
Eustace Cocrell, based on the book by Lynn Root. Directed by Vincente Min-
nelli. Produced by Arthur Freed for MGM. Released May 1943. With Ethel
Waters, Eddie "Rochester" Anderson, Lena Horne, Rex Ingram, Kenneth
Spencer, Louis Armstrong, John Bubbles, Ford Buck, the Duke Ellington Or-
chestra, the Hall Johnson Choir, others. Additional songs by Vernon Duke,
John Latouche, and Ted Fetter (from original stage production); Roger Edens;
Duke Ellington; others.

> Li'l Black Sheep
> Happiness Is a Thing Called Joe
> Life's Full of Consequence
> Ain' It de Truth (not used)
> Some Folks Work (Is You Man or Mule?) (not used)
> Petunia's Prayer (not used)
> Jezebel Jones (not used)
> I Got a Song (not used)

The Sky's the Limit
Lyrics by Johnny Mercer. Screenplay by Frank Fenton and Lynn Root. Di-
rected by Edward H. Griffith. Produced by David Hempstead for RKO Radio
Pictures. Released September 1943. With Fred Astaire, Joan Leslie (vocals
by Sally Sweetland), Robert Benchley, Robert Ryan, Freddie Slack and His
Orchestra.

> A Lot in Common with You
> My Shining Hour

One for My Baby (And One More for the Road)
Harvey, the Victory Garden Man (not used)
Hangin' On to You (not used)

1944   *Up in Arms*
Lyrics by Ted Koehler. Screenplay by Don Hartman, Allen Boretz, and Robert Pirosh. Directed by Elliot Nugent. Produced by Samuel Goldwyn for RKO Radio Pictures. Released February 1944. With Danny Kaye, Dinah Shore, Dana Andrews, Constance Dowling, Lyle Talbot, others. Additional songs for Kaye by Sylvia Fine and Max Liebman.
   All Out for Freedom (dedicated to Anya)
   Now I Know
   Tess's Torch Song

Kismet
Lyrics by E. Y. Harburg. Screenplay by John Meehan. Directed by William Dieterle. Produced by Everett Riskin for MGM. Released August 1944. With Marlene Dietrich, Ronald Colman, Edward Arnold, James Craig, Joy Ann Page.
   Willow in the Wind
   Tell Me, Tell Me, Evening Star
   I See a Morning Star (not used)

Here Come the Waves
Lyrics by Johnny Mercer. Screenplay by Allan Scott, Ken Englund, and Zion Myers. Directed by Mark Sandrich. Produced by Sandrich for Paramount Pictures. Released December 1944. With Bing Crosby, Betty Hutton, Sonny Tufts, Ann Doran, Gwen Crawford, Noel Neill, Catherine Craig, Marjorie Henshaw.
   Ac-cent-tchu-ate the Positive
   Here Come the Waves
   I Promise You
   Let's Take the Long Way Home
   My Mamma Thinks I'm a Star
   The Navy Song
   There's a Fella Waitin' in Poughkeepsie
   A Woman's Work Is Never Done
   Got to Wear You Off My Weary Mind (not used)
   I Owe It All to You (not used)

Bloomer Girl
Lyrics by E. Y. Harburg. Book by Sig Herzig and Fred Saidy, based on a play by Lilith James and Dan James. Dances by Agnes de Mille. Production staged by Harburg; book directed by William Schorr. Produced by John C. Wilson in association with Nat Goldstone at the Shubert Theatre, October 5, 1944; 654 performances. With Celeste Holm, Margaret Douglas, Joan McCracken, David Brooks, Dooley Wilson, Mabel Taliaferro, Matt Briggs, Toni Hart, Joe E. Marks, Richard Huey, Hubert Dilworth.

When the Boys Come Home
Evelina
Welcome Hinges
The Farmer's Daughter
It Was Good Enough for Grandma
The Eagle and Me
Right as the Rain
T'morra', T'morra'
The Rakish Young Man with the Whiskers
Pretty As a Picture
Style Show Ballet
Sunday in Cicero Falls
I Got a Song
Lullaby (Satin Gown and Silver Shoe)
Simon Legree
Liza Crossing the Ice
I Never Was Born
Man for Sale
Civil War Ballet

1945   *Out of This World*
Lyrics by Johnny Mercer. Screenplay by Walter DeLeon and Arthur Phillips. Directed by Hal Walker. Produced by Sam Coslow for Paramount Pictures. Released June 1945. With Eddie Bracken (vocals by Bing Crosby), Diana Lynn, Veronica Lake, Cass Daley, others. Additional songs by Coslow, Eddie Cherkose, Felix Bernard, Ben Raleigh, and Bernie Wayne.
June Comes Around Every Year
Out of This World

1946   *St. Louis Woman*
Lyrics by Johnny Mercer. Book by Arna Bontemps and Countee Cullen (based on Bontemps's novel *God Sends Sunday*). Directed by Rouben Mamoulian. Dances by Charles Walters. Produced by Edward Gross at the Martin Beck Theatre, March 30, 1946; 113 performances. With Harold and Fayard Nicholas, Pearl Bailey, Rex Ingram, Ruby Hill, June Hawkins, Juanita Hall.
Li'l Augie Is a Natural Man
Any Place I Hang My Hat Is Home
I Feel My Luck Comin' Down
I Had Myself a True Love
Legalize My Name
Cakewalk Your Lady
Come Rain or Come Shine
Chinquapin Bush (Lullaby)
We Shall Meet to Part, No Never
Sleep Peaceful, Mr. Used-to-be
Leavin' Time

A Woman's Prerogative
Ridin' on the Moon
Least That's My Opinion
Racin' Form
Come On, Li'l Augie
I Wonder What Became of Me (cut)
High, Low, Jack and the Game (not used)
A Man's Gotta Fight (not used)
Somethin' You Gotta Find Out Yourself (not used)
Sow the Seed and Reap the Harvest (not used)
Lim'ricks (not used)
Talkin' Glory (not used)

1947   After All (Ted Koehler)

1948   *Casbah*
Lyrics by Leo Robin. Screenplay by L. Bush-Fekete and Arnold Manoff. Directed by John Berry. Produced by Nat C. Goldstone for Universal International Pictures. Released May 1948. With Tony Martin, Yvonne DeCarlo, Marta Toren, Peter Lorre, Katherine Dunham and Her Dancers.
It Was Written in the Stars
What's Good about Goodbye?
For Every Man There's a Woman
Hooray for Love
Hotel Oasis (instrumental)
The Monkey Sat in the Cocoanut Tree

1949   Tell Me in Your Own Sweet Way (Bob Hilliard)

1950   *The Petty Girl*
Lyrics by Johnny Mercer. Screenplay by Nat Perrin. Directed by Henry Levine. Produced by Perrin for Columbia Pictures. Released August 1950. With Robert Cummings, Joan Caulfield, Elsa Lanchester, Melville Cooper, Audrey Long.
Ah Loves Ya!
Calypso Song
Fancy Free
The Petty Girl
Try Your Luck

My Blue Heaven
Lyrics by Ralph Blane and Harold Arlen. Screenplay by Lamar Trotti and Claude Binyon. Directed by Henry Koster. Produced by Sol C. Siegel for Twentieth Century–Fox. Released September 1950. With Betty Grable, Dan Dailey, David Wayne, Jane Wyatt, Mitzi Gaynor, Una Merkle.
Cosmo Cosmetics
Don't Rock the Boat, Dear
The Friendly Islands

Halloween
I Love a New Yorker
It's Deductible
Live Hard, Work Hard, Love Hard
What a Man!

1951   *Mr. Imperium*
Lyrics by Dorothy Fields. Screenplay by Don Hartman and Edwin H. Knopf. Directed by Hartman. Produced by Knopf for MGM. Released October 1951. With Ezio Pinza, Lana Turner (vocals by Trudi Irwin), Marjorie Main, Cedric Hardwick. Additional song by Lara, English lyric by Ray Gilbert.
   Andiamo
   My Love an' My Mule
   Let Me Look at You

1953   *Down among The Sheltering Palms*
Lyrics by Ralph Blane and Harold Arlen. Screenplay by Claude Binyon, Albert Lewin, and Burt Styler. Directed by Edmund Goulding. Produced by Fred Kohler for Twentieth Century–Fox. Released June 1953. With William Lundigan, Jane Greer, Mitzi Gaynor, David Wayne, Gloria DeHaven, Jack Paar, Lyle Talbot, Billy Gilbert.
   The Friendly Islands
   I'm a Ruler of a South Sea Island
   Who Will It Be When the Time Comes?
   What Make de Diff'rence?
   Twenty-seven Elm Street
   When You're in Love
   Inspection
   The Opposite Sex
   Back Where I Come From
   From Island to Island

The Farmer Takes a Wife
Lyrics by Dorothy Fields. Screenplay by Walter Bullock, Sally Benson, and Joseph Fields. Directed by Henry Levin. Produced by Frank P. Rosenberg for Twentieth Century–Fox. Released June 1953. With Betty Grable, Dale Robertson, Thelma Ritter, John Carroll, Eddie Foy Jr., Charlotte Austin.
   Can You Spell Schenectady?
   The Erie Canal
   I Could Cook
   Look Who's Been Dreaming
   Somethin' Real Special
   Today I Love Ev'rybody
   We're Doin' It for the Natives in Jamaica
   We're in Business
   When I Close My Door
   With the Sun Warm upon Me

Yes! (not used)

I Was Wearin' Horse Shoes! (not used)

1954   *A Star Is Born*

Lyrics by Ira Gershwin. Screenplay by Moss Hart. Directed by George Cukor. Produced by Sidney Luft for Warner Brothers. Released September 1954. With Judy Garland, James Mason, Charles Bickford, Jack Carson, Tommy Noonan, Grady Sutton, Laurindo Almeida, Lucy Marlow, Chick Chandler, Mae Marsh. Additional songs woven into the "Born in a Trunk" medley, arranged by Roger Edens (uncredited) and Leonard Gersh, by George Gershwin and Irving Caesar; Roy Turk and Fred Ahlert; Irving Mills, Jimmy McHugh, and Gene Austin; DeSylva, Brown, and Henderson; Rodgers and Hart; others.

Gotta Have Me Go with You

The Man That Got Away

TV Commercial (Trinidad Coconut Oil Shampoo) (cut after premiere)

Here's What I'm Here For (cut after premiere)

It's a New World

Someone At Last

Lose That Long Face (cut after premiere)

I'm Off the Downbeat (not used)

Green Light Ahead (not used)

Dancing Partner (not used)

The Country Girl

Lyrics by Ira Gershwin. Screenplay by George Seaton, based on the play by Clifford Odets. Directed by Seaton. Produced by William Perlberg for Paramount. Released November 1954. With Bing Crosby, Grace Kelly, William Holden, Anthony Ross, Gene Reynolds, Jacqueline Fontaine.

The Pitchman/It's Mine It's Yours

Commercials: Liebermeyer Beer, Jamaica Chewing Gum, Honey-Sweet Peanut Brittle, Ups-a-Daisy Shaving Cream, Boston Ballpoint, Dr. Brett Dog and Cat Food

The Search Is Through

The Land around Us

Dissertation on the State of Bliss (Love and Learn)

There's No Substitute for a Man (Howard Dietz)

House of Flowers

Lyrics by Truman Capote and Harold Arlen. Book by Capote. Directed by Peter Brook. Dances and musical numbers by Herbert Ross. Produced by Arnold Saint Subber at the Alvin Theatre, December 30, 1954; 165 performances. With Pearl Bailey, Diahann Carroll, Juanita Hall, Ray Walston, Dino DiLuca, Rawn Spearman, Geoffrey Holder, Ada Moore, Enid Mosier, Dolores Harper, Frederick O'Neal.

Waitin'

One Man (Ain' Quite Enough)

Madame Tango's Tango
A Sleepin' Bee
Smellin' of Vanilla (Bamboo Cage)
House of Flowers
Two Ladies in de Shade of de Banana Tree
What Is a Friend For?
Mardi Gras
I Never Has Seen Snow
Husband Cage
Can I Leave Off Wearin' My Shoes?
Has I Let You Down?
Slide, Boy, Slide
Don't Like Goodbyes
Turtle Song
House of Flowers Waltz (instrumental)
Indoor Girl (lyric by Michael Brown)
Love's No Stranger to Me (not used)
What a Man Won't Do for a Woman (not used)
Un Garçon Cette (not used)
Can You Explain? (not used)
These Moments (not used)
Monday through Sunday (not used)

1956   Stay Out of My Dreams (E. Y. Harburg)
        Written for unproduced film, *Nellie Bly*.

1957   *Blues Opera Suite*
        Orchestration by Samuel Matlowsky.
        Premiere by the Minneapolis Symphony, Andre Kostelanetz conducting,
        August 28, 1957.

        Jamaica
        Lyrics by E. Y. Harburg. Book by Harburg and Fred Saidy. Choreography by
        Jack Cole. Directed by Robert Lewis. Produced by David Merrick at the Impe-
        rial Theatre, October 31, 1957; 557 performances. With Lena Horne, Ricardo
        Montalban, Josephine Premice, Joe Adams, Alan Shayne, Ossie Davis, Ade-
        laide Hall, Alvin Ailey, Christine Lawson, Ethel Ayler, others.
        Savannah
        Savannah's Wedding Day
        Pretty to Walk With
        Push de Button
        Incompatibility
        Little Biscuit
        Cocoanut Sweet
        Pity de Sunset
        Hooray for de Yankee Dollar
        What Good Does It Do?

Monkey in the Mango Tree
Take It Slow, Joe
Ain' It de Truth
Leave de Atom Alone
For Every Fish
I Don't Think I'll End It All Today
Napoleon
There's a Sweet Wind Blowin' My Way (not used)
What Did Noah Do? (not used)
Whippoorwill (not used)

1958 In the Middle of the Night (Paddy Chayefsky)

1959 *Saratoga*
Lyrics by Johnny Mercer. Book and direction by Morton DaCosta. Choreography by Ralph Beaumont. Produced by Robert Fryer at the Winter Garden, December 7, 1959; 80 performances. With Howard Keel, Carol Lawrence, Odette Myrtil, Warde Donovan, Carol Brice, Tun Tun, James Milhollin, Richard Graham, Truman Gaige, Isabella Hoopes, Edith King, Jeannine Masterson, Gerrianne Raphael, Ina Kurland, others.
Reading the News
Al Fresco (not used)
Bon Appetit (not used)
Countin' Our Chickens
The Cure
Dog Eat Dog
Love Held Lightly
A Game of Poker
Goose Never Be a Peacock
Have You Heard? (Gossip Song)
You or No One (earlier title: Here Goes Nothing)
I'll Be Respectable
I'm Headed for Big Things (cut)
Lessons in Love (not used)
The Man in My Life
One Step, Two Step
The Parks of Paris (not used)
Petticoat High
Promenade: Market Cries (not used)
Saratoga
Workman's Song (not used)
You for Me
Gettin' a Man (music by Mercer)
Why Fight This? (music by Mercer)
The Gamblers
The Men Who Run the Country (music by Mercer)

Blues Opera/Free And Easy

Lyrics mostly by Johnny Mercer. Book, based on Bontemps and Cullen's *St. Louis Woman,* edited by Robert Breen and Wilva Breen; additional dialogue by Robert Armstrong and Justus Shiffers. Directed by Robert Breen. Produced by Stanley Chase at the Carré Theatre, Amsterdam, December 17, 1959; at the Alhambra, Paris, January 15, 1960, where it closed. With Irene Williams, Harold Nicholas, Moses LaMarr, Martha Flowers, Irving Barnes, Paul Harris, Ruby Green, Elija Hodges, Quincy Jones and His Orchestra.

The songs and musical sequences of *Blues Opera* flow from one to the next. There are no set "numbers" as in a standard musical; most of the dialogue is sung (recitative). Many of the songs borrowed (for want of a better term) are only heard fragmentarily. The following list is taken from the score.

Act 1

Overture
Conjure Man
Cake Song
Live Hard, Work Hard, Love Hard (lyric by Ralph Blane and Harold Arlen)
Blind Man
Natchul Man (Li'l Augie Is a Natural Man)
I Ain't Afraid
Della's Entrance (Whatcha Sayin', Della?)
Wheel 'Em and Deal 'Em
Sweetnin' Water
Least That's My Opinion
Ladies 'n' Gentlemen
Bees 'n' Flowers
Second Wind
Free and Easy (Anyplace I Hang My Hat Is Home)
I Gotta Right to Sing the Blues (lyric by Ted Koehler)
Blues in the Night
Streak o' Lightnin' (from Natchul Man)
Like Clouds up in the Sky
Dressing Up Sequence (instrumental: Ridin' on the Moon)
Lookin' for Somebody?
Rainbow
(That Old) Black Magic
Toastin' Sequence
Lumpin'
A Woman's Prerogative
First March, Second March, Third March (instrumental)
Cakewalk Your Lady
Cakewalk Turns: Soft Shoe, Sword Dance, Tambourine, Genteel Bastard,
    Boogie, Tangissimo, Blues, Waltz, Dixieland
Pandemonium (instrumental)
(American) Minuet (instrumental)

Act 2

Overture
Ya Pushin' Ya Luck
Whatcha Sayin', Biglow?
Higher den de Moon (On Top of the World)
Dis Is de Day (theme from Leavin' Time)
Legalize My Name
Lullaby/Chinquapin Bush
Killing Sequence (instrumental)
Curse
Sleep Peaceful, Mr. Used-to-be
Elegy (instrumental)
Fix Yo'self Up
Dissolves (instrumental)
I Had Myself a True Love
Reap the Harvest
Ill Wind (lyric by Ted Koehler)
Racin' Form
Bettin' Calls
Look What a Hole You're In
Easy Street
Race
Champagne for de Lady
High, Low, Jack and the Game
Dis Little While
I Wonder What Became of Me?
Somethin' You Gotta Find Out fo' Yo'self
One for the Road
Leavin' Time
A Baby's Born
Come Rain or Come Shine
Riding on the Moon
Additional songs: Many Kinds of Love, Then Suddenly, Flower Song, De Right Answer, Won't Dat Be de Blessed Day?, News Chant, Blow de Whistle, Snake Eyes.

1960   Ode, for piano
Bon-Bon, for piano

1961   Happy with the Blues (Peggy Lee)

1962   *Gay Purr-ee*
Lyrics by E. Y. Harburg. Screenplay by Dorothy Jones and Chuck Jones. Directed by Abe Levitow. Produced by Henry G. Saperstein for UPA Productions. Released by Warner Brothers, December 1962. With the voices of Judy Garland, Robert Goulet, Red Buttons, Hermione Gingold, Paul Frees, Morey Amsterdam, Mel Blanc, Julie Bennett, Joan Gardner.

Mewsette
Little Drops of Rain
The Money Cat
Take My Hand, Paree
Paris Is a Lonely Town
Bubbles
Roses Red, Violets Blue
The Horse Won't Talk
Free At Last (not used)

Abstractions, or The Flight of the Sleeping Pill, for piano

I Could Go On Singing (E. Y. Harburg)
    Title song for film starring Judy Garland.
The Morning After (Dory Langdon)

1963   So Long, Big Time! (Dory Langdon)
        You're Impossible (Dory Langdon)
        Bad for Each Other (Carolyn Leigh)
        The Silent Spring (E. Y. Harburg)

1964   Hurt but Happy (Dory Langdon)
        I Could Be Good for You (Martin Charnin)
        Night after Night (Dory Langdon)
            Based on the slow theme from "Mood in Six Minutes."
        That Was the Love That Was (Dory Langdon)

1965   That's a Fine Kind o' Freedom (Martin Charnin)
        A Girl's Entitled (Martin Charnin)
        John-John-John (Martin Charnin)
        Let's Give the Job to Lindsay (Martin Charnin)
        Little Travelbug (Martin Charnin)
        Shoulda Stood in Bed (Martin Charnin)
        Summer in Brooklyn (Martin Charnin)
        This Ol' World (Martin Charnin)

1966   Come On, Midnight (Martin Charnin)
        Spring Has Me out on a Limb (Martin Charnin)

        Softly
        Lyrics by Martin Charnin. Book by Hugh Wheeler, based on a story by Santha
        Rama Rau. Unproduced.
            Once I Wore Ribbons Here
            Been a Hell of an Evening
            Temples
            The More You See of It
            Baby-San
            Pacific

Momma Knows Best
Minstrel Show:
    Hello
    My Lady Fair
    You're Never Fully Dressed
Yellow Rain
Happy Any Day
The Brush Off
Suddenly the Sunrise
You Are Tomorrow
Don't Say "Love"—I've Been There and Back
I Will
We Were Always to Be Married
Why Don't You Make Me Like You?
Fish Go Higher Than Tigers
Earlier songs—I Could Be Good for You; Come On, Midnight; Little
    Travelbug—were in the score also.

1968   *House of Flowers* (Revised version)

Lyrics by Truman Capote and Harold Arlen. Book by Capote. Directed by Joseph Hardy. Choreography by Talley Beaty. Produced by Saint-Subber at the Theatre De Lys, January 28, 1968; closed in March. With Yolande Bavan, Josephine Premice, Robert Jackson, Thelma Oliver, Hope Clarke, Novella Nelson, Charles Moore, others. New songs:
    Albertina's Beautiful Hair
    Dark Song
    Do Not Be Afraid of Love
    Jump de Broom
    Madame Tango's Particular Tango
    Somethin' Cold to Drink
    Walk to de Grave
    Wife Never Understan'
    The Wonders of a Barrel

1973   *Clippety Clop and Clementine*

Lyrics by Harold Arlen. Teleplay by Leonard Melfi. Unproduced.
    Clippety Clop and Clementine
    Dreamin' Suits Me Just Fine
    A Happy Recipe
    I Had a Love Once
    Is What It's All About
    Organic Food
    Ridin' Through the Park in a Hansom Cab
    This Way or No Way at All

1976   Looks Like the End of a Beautiful Friendship (E. Y. Harburg)

Promise Me Not to Love Me (E. Y. Harburg)

Undated and unsourced songs
> I See a Rainbow (Ted Koehler)
> Little Lady on the Cameo (Ted Koehler)
> Memories of Long Ago (Ted Koehler)
> Out of My Dreams into My Heart (Ted Koehler)
> Is the Curtain Up? (Harold Arlen)
> Refrain (music only)
> Daniel the Social Lion (probably E. Y. Harburg)
> Love Alone Lives On (probably Ted Koehler)

APPENDIX B: SELECTED RECORDINGS OF MUSIC BY HAROLD ARLEN

Because Harold Arlen is one of the most recorded of American songwriters, a truly complete discography would be as unwieldy as it would be impractical. The recordings in this compilation are (a) either primarily devoted to his songs or otherwise valuable, and (b) readily available on compact disc. Not included are collections devoted to such vocalists as Judy Garland, Frank Sinatra, Tony Bennett, Lena Horne, Bobby Short, and Barbra Streisand, as well as various jazz groups and soloists, many of which feature fine renditions of Arlen songs.

Song Collections

Harold Sings Arlen (With Friend)
Harold Arlen; Barbra Streisand; Peter Matz, arranger and conductor
Columbia CK 52722
Blues in the Night; Little Biscuit; Ding Dong! The Witch Is Dead (Arlen and Streisand); A Sleepin' Bee; In the Shade of the New Apple Tree; Hit the Road to Dreamland; Ac-cent-tchu-ate the Positive; My Shining Hour; Today I Love Ev'rybody; House of Flowers (Streisand); For Every Man There's a Woman; That's a Fine Kind of Freedom.

This is currently the only album featuring Arlen as vocalist. Prepared with his cooperation, it is a fine survey of, mostly, the better-known songs. The "friend's" rendition of "House of Flowers" is a classic.

Harold Arlen: American Songbook Series
The Smithsonian Collection of Recordings RD 048-5/A 22407
Over the Rainbow (Judy Garland); I Gotta Right to Sing the Blues (Jack Teagarden, Benny Goodman Orch.); You're a Builder Upper (Ethel Merman); Stormy Weather (Lena Horne); It's Only a Paper Moon (Nat Cole); That Old Black Magic (Margaret Whiting); Ac-cent-tchu-ate the Positive (Bing Crosby, the Andrews Sisters); Happiness Is a Thing Called Joe (Frances Wayne); Get Happy (Judy Garland); The Man That Got Away (Judy Garland); Don't Like Goodbyes (Pearl Bailey); A Sleepin' Bee (Diahann Carroll); Lydia, the Tattooed Lady (Bobby Short); Come Rain or Come Shine (Joe Williams); My Shining Hour (Mabel Mercer); One for My Baby (Fred Astaire); Blues in the Night (Ella Fitzgerald); I've Got the World on a String (Tony Bennett); Last Night When We Were Young (Tony Bennett); Between the Devil and the Deep Blue Sea (Oscar Peterson Trio); Right As the Rain (Maureen McGovern); When the Sun Comes Out (Mel Tormé).

Not only a fine compilation of Arlen's work, but a wonderful assemblage of some great performers.

The Song Is . . . Harold Arlen
Harold Arlen, Judy Garland, Bing Crosby, Cab Calloway, Duke Ellington, Artie Shaw, Benny Goodman, Dinah Shore, Billie Holiday, Dick Powell, Lawrence Tibbett, others. ASV Living Era CD AJA 5159

This is one of the best collections of Arleniana on record, intermingling the best-known songs with several rarities—twenty-five songs in all. Among the highlights: Arlen's renditions of "Stormy Weather" (with the Leo Reisman band) and "Ill Wind" (with Eddie Duchin and orchestra), Lawrence Tibbett's 1935 recording of "Last Night When We Were Young," Judy Garland's "Buds Won't Bud" and, inevitably, "Over the Rainbow." Dinah Shore contributes "Blues in the Night" and Bing Crosby the neglected "I Promise You." Discerning producer Peter Demsey includes Artie Shaw's "That Old Black Magic" as well as a delightful "Two Blind Loves." An album of musical riches.

Ella Fitzgerald Sings the Harold Arlen Songbook
Ella Fitzgerald; Billy May, arranger and conductor
Vol 1. Verve 817-527-2
Blues in the Night; Let's Fall in Love; Stormy Weather; Between the Devil and the Deep Blue Sea; My Shining Hour; Horray for Love; This Time the Dream's on Me; That Old Black Magic; I've Got the World on a String; Let's Take a Walk around the Block; Ill Wind; Ac-cent-tchu-ate the Positive.
Vol. 2. Verve 817-528-2
When the Sun Comes Out; Come Rain or Come Shine; As Long As I Live; Happiness Is a Thing Called Joe; It's Only a Paper Moon; The Man That Got Away; One for My Baby; Get Happy; I Gotta Right to Sing the Blues; Out of This World; Over the Rainbow.

Arlen prized the singing of Ella Fitzgerald, and while he did not disown these albums, he had hoped for rich, romantic arrangements by Nelson Riddle, who had worked on previous Fitzgerald songbooks, rather than May's big-band jazz approach. Still, these are worth having.

Lee Wiley Sings the Songs of Rodgers and Hart and Harold Arlen
Lee Wiley, with the Eddie Condon Quintet, Sextet, and Orchestra (Ernie Caceres, Dave Bowman, Bob Haggart, Billy Butterfield, Bobby Hackett, Lou McGarity, Buddy Morrow, Condon, George Wettling)
Audiophile ACD-10
Let's Fall in Love; Moanin' in the Mornin'; Between the Devil and the Deep Blue Sea; Stormy Weather; Down with Love; I've Got the World on a String; Fun to Be Fooled; You Said It.

Legendary, difficult to classify, Lee Wiley was an especial favorite of jazz musicians; she was also a popular band singer (Leo Reisman, Paul Whiteman) and a radio personality. She was a pioneer in the songbook album devoted to great popular composers (other such albums include the Gershwins and Cole Porter), accompanied by musicians associated with Eddie Condon. She was unique too in that she frequently recorded little-known, even unpublished songs. Among her admirers were George Gershwin and Harold Arlen. This album was recorded in 1940.

Harold Arlen and Vernon Duke Revisited, Vol. 2
Blossom Dearie, Sandy Duncan, Helen Gallagher, Dolores Grey, Tammy Grimes, Arthur Siegel; arrangements, accompaniment by Dennis Deal and Albert Evans
Painted Smiles PSCD 127
Life Begins at 8:40; Will You Love Me Monday Morning?; Such Unusual Weather; When the Wind Blows South; Things; Sweet Wind Blowin' My Way; Promise Me Not to Love Me; The Elks and the Masons; C'est la Vie.

Ben Bagley's "Revisited" albums are a mixed bag, high camp combined with wonderful (and not so) songs by an eccentric band of vocalists selected by the producer. Still, ragged as some of the presentations may be, there are treasures. Recommended, with reservations.

Harold Arlen: "Americanegro Suite"
Judy Kaye, the Premier Gospel Quartet, and Peter Howard, piano
Premier Recordings PRCD-1004
Americanegro Suite (I Got Dat Feelin'; Reverend Johnson's Dream; I'm Here Lawd; Little Angel Child; Where Is Dis Road A-leadin' Me To?; Big Time Comin'); The Man in My Life; Goose Never Be a Peacock; For Every Man There's a Woman; Come On, Midnight; This Time the Dream's on Me; First You Have Me High (Then You Have Me Low); Fancy Free; Green Light Ahead; Sing, My Heart; God's Country.

The rich, beautiful soprano of Judy Kaye does full justice to the songs; Howard's accompaniment is ingenious and apposite—in tune with the period of some of the songs. The composer loved this collection.

Eileen Farrell Sings Harold Arlen
Eileen Farrell, Loonis McGlohon Octet
Reference Recordings RR-30CD
Let's Fall in Love; Out of This World; I Wonder What Became of Me; I've Got the World on a String; Like a Straw in the Wind; Down with Love; Happiness Is a Thing Called Joe; A Woman's Prerogative; Come Rain or Come Shine; Little Drops of Rain/ Over the Rainbow; When the Sun Comes Out; As Long As I Live; My Shining Hour; Last Night When We Were Young.

Eileen Farrell came out of retirement in 1987 after a career in opera and teaching and began recording the songs of our master songwriters, among them this excellent album devoted to Harold Arlen, one of her most admired composers. In turn, she was one of his most admired interpreters. The jazz-inflected accompaniment, in arrangements by the pianist, McGlohon, features Joe Wilder on trumpet and flugelhorn. The album notably ranges through the composer's output, highlighting his versatility—he would have loved that.

Peggy Lee: Love Held Lightly
Peggy Lee, the Keith Ingham Octet
Angel CDC 54798
Look Who's Been Dreaming; Love Held Lightly; Buds Won't Bud; Can You Explain?; Wait'll It Happens to You; Come On, Midnight; Happy with the Blues; Bad for Each

Other; Love's No Stranger to Me; I Could Be Good for You; Got to Wear You Off My Weary Mind; I Had a Love Once; Love's a Necessary Thing; My Shining Hour.

A gem that includes eight songs never recorded before, a couple of which were neither published nor written down (these were transcribed from Harold Arlen's performances from recordings by the arranger-pianist, Ingham). A word about courage, too. Now in her seventies, Peggy Lee is in precarious health, yet somehow she perseveres (on these record dates she sang from a wheelchair). She took on the project, when approached by producers Bill Rudman, Ken Bloom, and Keith Ingham, because she liked the idea of doing several unknown Arlen songs. She was touched by "I Had a Love Once," finding it "especially powerful." So is this remarkable album.

Harold Arlen's Songs
Richard Rodney Bennett, vocals, piano
Audiophile ACD-168
Anyplace I Hang My Hat Is Home; It's Only a Paper Moon; Moanin' in the Mornin'; Promise Me Not to Love Me; Fun to Be Fooled; A Sleepin' Bee; Come Rain or Come Shine; In Your Own Quiet Way; As Long As I Live; When the Sun Comes Out; A Woman's Prerogative; Goose Never Be a Peacock; Ain' It de Truth?; I Wonder What Became of Me" Buds Won't Bud; It Was Written in the Stars; So Long, Big Time!; My Shining Hour.

An eminent British composer of concert works and brilliant film scores, Bennett is a great admirer of American popular song, two of his favorite composers being Gershwin and Arlen. While his voice has a fitting informal saloon quality, his choice of songs and performance at the keyboard gives the album a touch of New York's Rainbow Room.

Rosemary Clooney Sings the Music of Harold Arlen
Rosemary Clooney with sextet accompaniment
Concord CCD 4210
Hooray for Love; Happiness Is a Thing Called Joe; One for My Baby; Get Happy; Out of This World; My Shining Hour; Let's Take the Long Way Home; Stormy Weather.

This jazz-inflected presentation has no surprises but good Clooney performances.

KT Sullivan: Sing, My Heart—The Songs of Harold Arlen
KT Sullivan, vocals; Mike Renzi, arranger, conductor, piano
DRG Records 91437
Two Ladies in de Shade of de Banana Tree; Ill Wind; I Gotta Right to Sing the Blues; The Silent Spring/It's a New World; This Time the Dream's on Me/Hit the Road to Dreamland; Fun to Be Fooled; If I Only Had a Brain; Sing, My Heart; Let's Take a Walk around the Block; A Sleepin' Bee; Don't Like Goodbyes; Little Drops of Rain/ Right As the Rain; Out of This World; I Wonder What Became of Me.

A fine encapsulation, exquisitely and warmly sung, of the range of Harold Arlen's artistry, from the simple, folklike "Little Drops of Rain," to the complex, arialike "I Wonder What Became of Me," with excursions into jazz, the blues, swing, and comedy—the variety of his output that Arlen hoped people would recognize. Without gimmickry, KT Sullivan's beautiful soprano voice does each song justice. She also, as Arlen would have liked, gives the lyricist his due. Her melodies are true and her words clear. Mike Renzi's accompaniments are exemplary, even in his jazzier excursions. The Arlen music is always there.

Over the Rainbow: The Music of Harold Arlen
Numerous performers, including Betty Garrett, Patrick Cassidy, Celeste Holm, Joely Fisher, Joanna Gleason, Brock Peters, Charlotte Rae, Heather MacRae; musical director, Larry Blank; guest conductor, Don Pippin
DRG Records 12612 (If not available in local record shops, the address of DRG Records is 130 West 57th Street, New York, NY, 10019)
Gotta Have Me Go with You; Get Happy; Right As the Rain; Evelina; Fancy Meeting You; Ding Dong! The Witch Is Dead; With the Sun Warm upon Me; A Sleepin' Bee; House of Flowers; Last Night When We Were Young; Happiness Is a Thing Called Joe; The Eagle and Me; Out of This World; Anyplace I Hang My Hat Is Home; I've Got the World on a String; This Time the Dream's on Me; I Wonder What Became of Me; A Woman's Prerogative; I Had Myself a True Love; Stormy Weather; One for My Baby; Don't Like Goodbyes; Let's Fall in Love; I Gotta Right to Sing the Blues; The Gal That Got Away; Come Rain or Come Shine; Blues in the Night; Over the Rainbow; Over the Rainbow Finale.
A location recording of a salute to Arlen at the Wilshire Theatre, Beverly Hills, California, in February 1995, a benefit for the AIDS Healthcare Foundation; proceeds from the two-CD set go to the foundation. Arlen scholars and lovers, as well as the press, found the evening exciting and a fitting tribute to the composer.

Film Soundtracks

The Wizard of Oz (1939)
Judy Garland, Ray Bolger, Bert Lahr, Jack Haley, Frank Morgan, Billie Burke (vocals by Lorraine Bridges), Margaret Hamilton, the Munchkins
CBS Records AK 45356
Overture; Over the Rainbow; Twister; Munchkinland; Ding Dong! The Witch Is Dead; Follow the Yellow Brick Road; If I Only Had a Brain; If I Only Had a Heart; Lions and Tigers and Bears; If I Only Had the Nerve; Optimistic Voices; The Merry Old Land of Oz; Courage; Audience With the Wizard; The Witch Captures Dorothy; The Castle of the Wicked Witch; Return to the Wizard; Dorothy's Farewell to Oz; There's No Place Like Home/Finale; The Jitterbug.
There is little that can be added to what has already been said or written about this classic score and its inspired performances. As can be noted from the listing, both musical and dramatic portions of the film are included. In "The Jitterbug," not used in the film, the voice of Buddy Ebsen, the original Tin Man, is heard.

The Wizard of Oz (1939)
Original cast, as above
Turner Classic Movies Music/Rhino Movie Music R2 71964
Truth in advertising applies here: "The Deluxe Edition." This two-compact-disc set is

accompanied by a copiously illustrated booklet of forty-eight pages in which the *Wizard* authority John Fricke covers all aspects of the film, from historical to technical to musical. The film's complete score is included, not only the Arlen-Harburg songs but also the additional scoring by Herbert Stothart and others. Especially appealing to the Arlen enthusiast or *Wizard of Oz* devotee is the supplemental material on the second disc—alternate takes of songs, including discards. Particularly valuable are the demonstration recordings made by Arlen and Harburg performing the "Munchkinland Sequence" and "Optimistic Voices." Another treasure is an alternate version of Judy Garland singing "Over the Rainbow" with Roger Edens at the piano. The sound throughout is fine.

Star Spangled Rhythm (1942)
Dick Powell, Mary Martin, the Golden Gate Quartet, Betty Hutton, Dorothy Lamour, Paulette Goddard, Veronica Lake, Johnnie Johnston, Eddie "Rochester" Anderson, Marjorie Reynolds, Donna Drake, Betty Rhodes, Bing Crosby
Sandy Hook Records 2045
Overture (opening credits); Hit the Road to Dreamland; On the Swing Shift; I'm Doing It for Defense; A Sweater, a Sarong and a Peek-a-boo Bang; That Old Black Magic; Sharp As a Tack; Old Glory.

This transfer from the film's soundtrack is included for the sake of completeness; it may be difficult to find. All the songs from the film are included, as are a couple of comedy sketches with such Paramount worthies as Ray Milland, Fred MacMurray, Franchot Tone, and Bob Hope, doubling as master of ceremonies. An interesting period piece with two outstanding Arlen-Mercer songs, "That Old Black Magic" and "Hit the Road to Dreamland."

A Star Is Born (1954)
Judy Garland, chorus and orchestra under Ray Heindorf
Columbia CK 44389
Overture; Gotta Have Me Go with You; The Man That Got Away; Born in a Trunk (Swanee, I'll Get By, Black Bottom, The Peanut Vendor, My Melancholy Baby); Here's What I'm Here For; It's a New World; Someone at Last; Lose That Long Face.

The complete film score, including the cut "Here's What I'm Here For" and "Lose That Long Face," as well as the non-Arlen "Born in a Trunk" sequence. The recording preserves Judy Garland at her peak and a superior score by Arlen and Ira Gershwin.

Broadway Original Cast Albums

Bloomer Girl (1944)
Celeste Holm, David Brooks, Joan McCracken, Dooley Wilson, Matt Briggs, Toni Hart, Mabel Taliaferro, Richard Huey, Hubert Dilworth, Harold Arlen, orchestra and chorus under Leon Leonardi
MCA Classics MCAD 10522
When the Boys Come Home; Evelina; Welcome Hinges; The Farmer's Daughter; It Was Good Enough for Grandma; The Eagle and Me; Right As the Rain; T'morra', T'morra'; The Rakish Young Man with the Whiskahs [*sic*]; Sunday in Cicero Falls; I

Got a Song; Lullaby (Satin Gown and Silver Shoe); Liza Crossing the Ice; Never Was Born; Man for Sale; Finale.

Virtually the complete score minus "Pretty As a Picture" and the ballet music. One of Decca's better efforts in their original cast album series, initiated in the early 1940s with Gershwin's *Porgy and Bess* and striking it rich with Rodgers and Hammerstein's *Oklahoma!* The sound has been well reproduced, and happily without fake stereo. The singing is charming, and Arlen's presence is a special bonus.

St. Louis Woman (1946)
Harold Nicholas, Ruby Hill, June Hawkins, Robert Pope, Pearl Bailey, chorus and orchestra under Leon Leonardi
Angel ZDM 7 64662 2 4
L'il Augie Is a Natural Man; Any Place I Hang My Hat Is Home; Legalize My Name; Cakewalk Your Lady; Come Rain or Come Shine; Lullaby; Sleep Peaceful, Mr. Used-to-be; Leavin' Time; It's a Woman's Prerogative; Ridin' on the Moon.

Originally a 78-rpm album (and later ten-inch, then twelve-inch, long-playing discs, which like the original became costly collectors' acquisitions). The sound is exceptional for the time, capturing the voices (the choral passages are outstanding) and the bountiful orchestrations (now either lost or misplaced). The cast boasts no big names (Harold Nicholas was the most prominent, as one of the Nicholas Brothers; Pearl Bailey made her first indelible impression in the show). The voices of June Hawkins and Ruby Hill do full justice to the Arlen-Mercer creations.

House of Flowers (1954)
Pearl Bailey, Diahann Carroll, Rawn Spearman, Juanita Hall, Dolores Harper, Ada Moore, Enid Mosier, Miriam Burton, orchestra and chorus conducted by Jerry Arlen
CBS Special Products A 2320
Overture; Waitin'; One Man Ain' Quite Enough; A Sleepin' Bee; Bamboo Cage; Two Ladies in de Shade of de Banana Tree; What Is a Friend For?; Slide, Boy, Slide; I'm Gonna Leave Off Wearin' My Shoes; Has I Let You Down?; I Never Has Seen Snow; Turtle Song; Don't Like Goodbyes; Mardi Gras.

Though the show failed (twice), the cast album has become a kind of legend with a cult following, especially after its long-playing version went out of print. Restored to compact disc, the score remains one of Arlen's greatest, with superior performances by the entire cast, particularly the young Diahann Carroll; Bailey is her usual casual, or so it seems, comic self. The composer's brother infuses the orchestra with the proper languid romanticism. One of the great show albums.

Jamaica (1957)
Lena Horne, Ricardo Montalban, Adelaide Hall, Josephine Premice, Ossie Davis, Hugh Dilworth, Augustine Rios, Joe Adams, chorus and orchestra conducted by Lehman Engle
RCA 09026-68041-2
Overture; Savannah; Push de Button; Savannah's Wedding Day; Pretty to Walk With; Incompatibility; Little Biscuit; Cocoanut Sweet; Pity de Sunset; Hooray for de Yankee

Dollar; What Good Does It Do?; Monkey in the Mango Tree; Take It Slow, Joe; Ain' It de Truth?; Leave de Atom Alone; I Don't Think I'll End It All Today; Napoleon; Savannah (reprise).

A good, if not highly rated by some, score. Because the show centered around Horne, the cast album flavor is obscure. But the cheerful, mischievous, and witty performances by others—Montalban, Premice, and Davis—retain some of the Broadway feel of the show. The Harburg lyrics come through sharply, and the music is well treated by Engle. And Lena Horne is superb.

Revues
The Great Songs from the Cotton Club (1931–34)
Maxine Sullivan and the Keith Ingham Quintet
Mobile Fidelity Sound Lab 836
Happy As the Day Is Long; You Gave Me Ev'rything but Love; As Long As I Live; Raisin' the Rent; 'Neath the Pale Cuban Moon; Ill Wind; Between the Devil and the Deep Blue Sea; I Love a Parade; Harlem Holiday; Get Yourself a New Broom; Stormy Weather; In the Silence of the Night; That's What I Hate about Love; Primitive Prima Donna; I've Got the World on a String.

A legend in the 1930s, Maxine Sullivan came out of retirement to make three CDs for the production team of Rudman, Bloom, and Ingham (the others: songs by Burton Lane and Jule Styne); appropriately, the Cotton Club album was first. It is a unique and distinguished tribute to Arlen and Koehler and a peerless memorial to one of our greatest vocalists.

Other Recordings
Rhythmic Moments (American Piano, Vol. 4)
Joseph Smith, piano
Premiere Recordings PRCD 1028
Rhythmic Moments, Ode, Bon-Bon, plus piano pieces by Stephen Foster, Victor Herbert, Scott Joplin, George Gershwin, James P. Johnson, Leon "Bix" Beiderbecke, Oscar Levant, and Duke Ellington.

Joseph Smith manages to interpret these delightful pieces without the stiffness that many classically trained musicians bring to their performances of jazz- or pop-inflected compositions. (I have heard a pianist attempt the Ode and could not recognize it; I did hear the composer's performance; Joseph Smith's stands up beautifully.) This disc is worth acquiring not only for the Arlen pieces; the Levant is a revelation.

Special Occasions
Richard Rodney Bennett, arranger and keyboards
DRG Records 6102
Civil War Ballet (from *Bloomer Girl*); Hero Ballet (from *Hooray for What!*); also Cole Porter's *Within the Quota* (1924) and Richard Rodgers's *Ghost Town* (1939).

For this album of rare ballets by composers generally associated with songs, Bennett reduced their orchestrations to arrangements for two pianos, both of which, through electronic legerdemain, he plays. These are the only recordings of the Arlen ballets, and the playing is idiomatic and intelligent. As with the Joseph Smith album, you don't have to be an Arlen fan to treasure this set.

APPENDIX C: SELECTED FILMS WITH SONGS BY HAROLD ARLEN

The following list consists of films available on videocassette at the time of writing.

The Wizard of Oz (1939)   *MGM/UA Home Video M301656*
Judy Garland, Frank Morgan, Ray Bolger, Bert Lahr, Jack Haley, Billie Burke, Margaret Hamilton, Charlie Grapwin, the Munchkins
   What *My Fair Lady* was to the stage musical, *The Wizard of Oz* is to the film musical: sheer perfection in every aspect. The video presents a fine, clear copy of the complete original film, plus added attractions: promotional trailers, an excerpt from the Academy Awards ceremony in 1940, some of Harold Arlen's film taken on the set during the filming, etc. A very deluxe version is also available, complete with book and other collectibles. The number of the video applies only to the VHS print; *The Wizard of Oz* exists also on laser disc.

At the Circus (1939)   *MGM/UA Home Video M500121*
The Marx Brothers, Kenny Baker, Florence Rice, Eve Arden, Margaret Dumont, Nat Pendleton
   Not one of the Marxes' best, with a skimpy, though well-sung, score. "Two Blind Loves" is a charming if not exceptional ballad, and Groucho's "Lydia, the Tattooed Lady" is definitive. Best for hopeless Marx Brothers fans.

Rio Rita (1942)   *MGM/UA Home Video M202434*
Bud Abbott, Lou Costello, Kathryn Grayson, John Carroll, Patricia Dane, Tom Conway, Peter Whitney, Eros Volusia
   A very dated period piece (Nazi spies, etc.), with even less Arlen-Harburg than remained in *At the Circus*. Grayson and Carroll are in fine vocal fettle, although their operatic voices are better suited to the McCarthy-Tierney songs from the original stage productions. Typical Abbott and Costello routines punctuate the film, to no great comic advantage.

Star Spangled Rhythm (1942)   *MCA Universal 81939*
Eddie Bracken, Betty Hutton, Victor Moore, Bing Crosby, Bob Hope, Dorothy Lamour, Dick Powell, many others
   One of Paramount's early wartime revues, using most of its stellar roster in various comic skits, songs, and dances and little plot. Best sequences: Mary Martin, Dick Powell, and the Golden Gate Quartet in "Hit the Road to Dreamland" (complete) and Vera Zorina's dream dance to "That Old Black Magic." "Sharp As a Tack" is sung by Eddie "Rochester" Anderson and danced by Katherine Dunham in an unfortunate stereotyped scene. There are also nonmusical appearances by the directors Cecil B. DeMille and Preston Sturges.

Cabin in the Sky (1943)   *MGM/UA Home Video MV300558*
Ethel Waters, Eddie "Rochester" Anderson, Lena Horne, Rex Ingram, Kenneth Spencer, Louis Armstrong, John Bubbles, Ford Buck, the Duke Ellington Orchestra, Hall Johnson Choir

This historic classic, based on the Broadway original by Lynn Root, was the first all-black film since 1929's *Hallelujah* (and followed the next month with the release of *Stormy Weather,* starring Lena Horne and Bill Robinson). The folkish story, retaining only three of the Vernon Duke–John Latouche–Ted Fetter songs from Broadway, was enriched by the Arlen-Harburg contributions (not enough of which, alas, were used, though, happily, two were salvaged, "Ain' it de Truth" and "I Got a Song"). Waters's performance is touching; the entire film is blessed—undoubtedly the touch of the director, Vincente Minnelli, on his first film assignment—with intelligence, no stereotyping, no condescension. The songs are sensitively handled. Despite the paucity of Arlen, it is a fine film with good musical performances.

The Sky's the Limit (1943)   *Republic Pictures 7737*
Fred Astaire, Joan Leslie, Robert Benchley, Robert Ryna, Freddie Slack and His Orchestra

Another wartime relic, but with two outstanding songs: one of Arlen's personal favorites, "My Shining Hour," and Astaire's stunning "One for My Baby." This was one of Astaire's more serious films (and his last at RKO, home of the more characteristic Astaire and Rogers musicals). Some of the interpolated music, such as Slack's specialty of the time, "Cuban Sugar Mill," is not Arlen's. Benchley's after-dinner speech is also a (nonmusical) highlight.

Up in Arms (1944)   *Embassy Home Entertainment VHS 3072*
Danny Kaye, Dinah Shore, Dana Andrews, Constance Dowling, Lyle Talbot, the Goldwyn Girls

This film was designed as a Danny Kaye vehicle (his film debut) rather than a musical, and though the Arlen-Koehler songs are not wasted—Shore's "Now I Know" is especially memorable—the film spins around Kaye and his routines, including the celebrated "Lobby Number," written by his wife, Sylvia Fine, and Max Liebman. A product of wartime Hollywood, *Up in Arms* is replete with required patriotism, which, thanks to Kaye, is treated with less solemnity than might be expected. This one is good for the songs and for Kaye and Shore.

Here Come the Waves (1944)   *MCA Universal 81883*
Bing Crosby, Betty Hutton, Sonny Tufts

A wartime flagwaver in which Crosby portrays a crooner with a Frank Sinatra–like following of female fans, among them one of two Betty Hutton characters (the zany one); the serious Hutton wants to do her bit by joining the Waves. So does Crosby, who joins the navy also. Since he is a singer and the two Huttons a sister singing team, they unite to produce an elaborate show. The Arlen-Mercer score is noted for two ballads, "I Promise You" and "Let's Take the Long Way Home." The film's big hit was "Ac-cent-tchu-ate the Positive," in an unfortunate blackface sequence. The film is good for the songs, Crosby and Hutton, and even Tufts. The navy's cooperation is evident in the Waves training footage.

The Farmer Takes a Wife (1953)   *Key Video VHS 1724*
Betty Grable, Dale Robertson, Thelma Ritter, John Carroll, Eddie Foy Jr., Charlotte Austin

This video's major raison d'être is Betty Grable, but the Arlen-Fields score may be an even better reason. Written during one of the composer's most difficult periods, the charmingly "authentic ring" period score is more than adequate, and "With Sun Warm upon Me," "When I Close My Door," and "Somethin' Real Special" are more than that. A beautifully filmed musical of life on and along the Erie Canal in the nineteenth century, *The Farmer Takes a Wife* simply did not sparkle, despite its rich Technicolor. Still, the video is worth viewing for several reasons besides the songs: Thelma Ritter and Eddie Foy Jr., for example. Its quasi-Broadway score includes two eye-catching production numbers, "Today I Love Ev'rybody" and "The Erie Canal."

A Star Is Born (1954)   *Warner Home Video 1133A/B* (2 cassettes)
Judy Garland, James Mason, Charles Bickford, Jack Carson, Tommy Noonan

This set is labeled "restored version," the dedicated, assiduous work of the film historian Ronald Haver. The songs deleted after the premiere are restored, as are several dramatic scenes whose omission so upset the director, George Cukor (where actual film was not found, stills were worked in over the soundtrack dialogue). The result is a masterpiece.

The Country Girl (1954)   *Paramount 5905*
Bing Crosby, Grace Kelly, William Holden, Anthony Ross, Gene Reynolds, Jacqueline Fontaine

The songs are incidental to Odets's drama about a fading musical comedy star (Crosby) and his redemption through an understanding, faithful, stoic wife (Kelly, who earned the Academy Award for her performance). The three leads are superb, and if the Arlen-Gershwin songs are not among their best, they are better than most that were coming out of Hollywood at the time.

Gay Purr-ee (1961)   *Warner Home Video 11500*
Animated film with the voices of Judy Garland, Robert Goulet, Red Buttons, Hermione Gingold, Paul Frees, Morey Amsterdam, Mel Blanc, Julie Bennett, Joan Gardner

Despite the composer's reservations, this is a delightful, charming, and exquisitely executed film—and the score is lovely, witty, and altogether one of the best by Arlen and Harburg. It is difficult to place the film in any specific age category; some of the humor in the screenplay as well as the lyrics is sophisticated enough to go over some young heads. Still, the movement, the color, and the cuddlesome cats make up for such subleties.

NOTES ON SOURCES

*

INTRODUCTION

Ira Gershwin's comments about Arlen appear in his *Lyrics on Several Occasions*, p. 109. Zinsser's Capote interview appeared in *Harper's Magazine*, May 1960, as did his story about Robert Breen on "H. Arlene."

1 · THE CANTOR'S SON

Prohibition and its effect on the United States in the 1920s and 1930s has been the subject of several popular and scholarly histories, among them Stanley Walker's *The Night Club Era* and Paul Sann's illustrated volumes *The Lawless Decade* and *The Desperate Years*. The Dan Healy story comes from Walker, whose tales of the gangster years were also drawn upon for subsequent chapters. Thomas M. Coffey's *The Long Thirst* was also a valuable source. The early history of the Arluck family I learned from Arlen; his brother, Jerry; and several relatives, particularly his cousins Earl Crane and Samuel Hyman, all of whom were interviewed for my earlier book *Harold Arlen: Happy with the Blues*, though not all of their views and comments appeared in that book. The interview with Harold Sandler appeared in the *Buffalo News* Sunday magazine, May 10, 1987. Jack Yellen was the source of the story about Arlen's break with his father. I interviewed Yellen on April 19, 1960, for *Happy with the Blues*; his saltier recollections are used here for the first time. Sandler provided details of the evolution of the Snappy Trio in 1960 (a letter) and, in more detail, in 1987.

2 · THE BUFFALODIANS AND THE BIG TIME

The early history of jazz is well covered in Frederic Ramsey Jr. and Charles Edward Smith's *Jazzmen* and Rudi Blesh's more sober *Shining Trumpets*. Leonard Feather's *Encyclopedia of Jazz* provides precise dates and capsule biographies. My own *Encyclopedia of American Music* came in handy, too. James T. Maher supplied me with the names and instruments of the Buffalodians published in the November 1927 *Orchestra World*. The band's history was gleaned from my meetings with Arlen in 1960, Sandler's recollections in 1987, and Harold Arlen's Buffalodian scrapbook, found after his death. The early history of radio, with dates, may be found in Green and Laurie's *Show Biz*. Cantor Arluck's reaction to Louis Armstrong's "riffs" appears in Wilk's *They're Playing Our Song* (p. 153), as does Jake Shubert's treatment of Arlen (p. 163). E. Y. Harburg's comments on the Shuberts were made at one of his 92nd Street Y "Lyrics and Lyricists" appearances in December 1970. Ray Bolger's recollections of Arlen come from an interview at the Waldorf Hotel on May 4, 1960. Harold Arlen and his attorney, A. L. Berman, recalled Vincent Youmans in 1960 and later; Youmans's biography and work are covered fully in Gerald Bordman's *Days to Be Happy, Years to Be Sad*.

3 · PICKUP AND JOTS

The story of the evolution from pickup to "Get Happy" has been frequently told by Arlen in countless interviews with me, Max Wilk, and others; he was consistent.

Biographical materials about Ted Koehler appear in ASCAP's *Biographical Dictionary* and an article based on an interview with R. A. Wachsman published in 1939. Earl Carroll's doings have been documented in the press, including especially *Variety*. See also Walker, *The Night Club Era*, and Sann, "The Big Bath," in *The Lawless Decade*, p. 153. Durante on the "stick-up man" is from Jimmy Durante and Jack Kofoed, *Nightclubs*.

4 · COTTON CLUB

The effects of the 1929 market crash are succinctly treated in Allen's *Only Yesterday*, pp. 320–23. Harris, Levitt, Furman, and Smith's *The Black Book*, Hughes and Meltzer's *Black Magic*, and particularly Haskins's *The Cotton Club* chronicle the personalities and history of Harlem during Prohibition and the Depression as well as before and after. Walker's *The Night Club Era* concentrates on the Prohibition period from a downtown point of view. Arlen, Koehler, and Healy recalled their experiences at the club—Arlen in several interviews, Koehler in a long letter, and Healy in interviews at the Lamb's Club in March 1960. Roger Edens on Arlen in the Cotton Club is from a letter to me, May 1960; quoted in *Happy with the Blues*, p. 68. The Lena Horne interview, at the Waldorf, occurred on May 4, 1960. Additional gangster material was gleaned from Giles's *1927* and Ethel Waters's *His Eye Is on the Sparrow*. The borrowings by jazz performers from Gershwin are found in an essay by Martin Williams in the booklet that accompanies *The Smithsonian Collection of Classic Jazz*, pp. 9–10. Alec Wilder's and George Gershwin's observations on "Stormy Weather" are in Wilder's *American Popular Song*, p. 262. E. Y. Harburg's initial impression of Arlen was told to Deena Rosenberg during interviews in February 1977 and is quoted in Meyerson and Harburg's *Who Put the Rainbow in "The Wizard of Oz"?*, p. 65.

5 · EXCURSIONS AND ANYA

Much of this material is drawn from interviews with the Arlens beginning in March 1960 until the death of both; some, of course, appeared in *Happy with the Blues*, with many omissions. During some of this time—from March to about September 1960—I interviewed Buddy Morris, Jack Yellen, Dr. Miguel Elias, Harry Warren (the last two on the same day, March 29, 1960), and Leo Reisman at Lindy's in July. Roger Edens on Ethel Merman is contained in his letter of March 1960. Jerry Arlen's recollections about this period were also helpful, as were A. L. "Abe" Berman's. Robert Wachsman was a rich source of stories about the early and later career of Harold Arlen. The state of the musical film in 1930–31 is neatly surveyed by Stanley Green in *Hollywood Musicals, Year by Year*, p. 15; also on this subject, Jack Burton's *The Blue Book of Hollywood Musicals* is invaluable.

6 · LIFE BEGINS . . .

Yip Harburg and I were friends from the time we first met in 1960 until his death in 1981. He was an outspoken, often rather inventive tale teller and devoted to Harold Arlen. Long after *Happy with the Blues* we frequently discussed his work with Arlen and songwriting in general; I attended at least two of his Ninety-second Street Y lectures with song. Other sources: Max Wilk's *They're Playing Our Song* for Arlen's comments on collaborating with Harburg and Gershwin (p. 155, Harburg on the Gershwins p. 219), Harburg on John Murray Anderson (p. 154), Harburg on the opening scene of *Life Begins at 8:40* (p. 154). Harburg on Arlen's versatility appears in *Who Put the Rainbow?*, p. 78, based on an interview with Deena Rosenberg; also Gershwin's reaction to "Last Night When We Were Young," p. 95 (Arlen told me the same story). Ira Gershwin's comments on Arlen's personality and work practices appear, in part, in *Happy with the Blues* (p. 89) and in a letter to me, augmented by conversations (not formal interviews) over several years. The George Gershwin quote on inspiration is from his introduction to Goldberg's *Tin Pan Alley*, p. viii. The coverage of the Boston premiere of *Life Begins at 8:40* appeared in the *New York Post*, August 7, 1934. Goldberg's interview with Arlen appeared in the *Boston Evening Transcript*. The description of Bert Lahr's rendition of "Things" appears in John Lahr's *Notes on a Cowardly Lion*, p. 39; the transcription of the lyric was made from an acetate home recording, circa 1938, in a performance by Ira Gershwin and Harold Arlen.

7 · HOORAY FOR HOLLYWOOD?

A. L. Berman, in conversation, told me the story about Lew Brown's association with Waxey Gordon; the gangster's money-losing venture on the production of *Strike Me Pink* is chronicled in Stanley Green's *Ring Bells! Sing Songs!*, p. 80. Judy Garland's fondness for "Last Night When We Were Young" comes from a letter to me of April 14, 1960; Harburg on the song is from Meyerson and Harburg's *Who Put the Rainbow?*, p. 96, and the Wilder opinion is from *American Popular Song*, p. 266. Harburg on Hollywood is quoted from Bernard Rosenberg and Ernest Goldstein's *Creators and Disturbers: Reminiscences by Jewish Intellectuals in New York* (New York: Columbia University Press, 1982), p. 149. Harry Warren on interpolating songs into *Gold Diggers of 1937* is from Tony Thomas's *Harry Warren and the Hollywood Musical*, p. 88. Harburg as show doctor appears on page 103 in *Who Put the Rainbow?*

8 · HOORAY FOR WHAT!

Harold Arlen and A. L. Berman were the sources of Arlen's proposal and marriage. Harry Kaufman and his association with *Hooray for What!* were told to me by Arlen, Ralph Blane, Hugh Martin, and Agnes de Mille (in 1960 interviews); de Mille also wrote of her experiences with the show in *Dance to the Piper* (1952) from which came her "You're just telling me that to make me feel good," on hearing about Kaufman's accident in Boston. Arlen's dubbing Kaufman as "High Collar Harry" is from Minnelli's *I Remember It Well*, p. 87.

9 · A TIME OF GOLD AND LEAD

Harburg on Arthur Freed is quoted from Harmetz, *The Making of "The Wizard of Oz,"* p. 73. Hugh Fordin on Freed appears on p. x, and throughout, in *The World of Entertainment*. The Gus Edwards roster may be found in Green and Laurie's *Show Biz*, p. 45. The Freed–L. B. Mayer relationship and meeting is from Fordin, p. 7. The home recordings mentioned in this chapter made by Arlen and others are in my collection of Arleniana. The date of the signing of *The Wizard of Oz* contract appears in *Who Put the Rainbow?*, p. 123. Arthur Freed's memo to Noel Langley is reproduced in Fricke,

Scarfone, and Stillman's *The Wizard of Oz: The Official 50th Anniversary Pictorial History*, p. 30. Freed on writing a ballad for *Wizard* appears in Fordin, p. 15. Harburg's "Harold Arlen, 'Over the Rainbow' and Me" appeared in *TV Guide*, February 24, 1973, pp. 28–29. Harburg's recollections about *The Wizard of Oz* and the writing of "Over the Rainbow" were made at his "Lyrics and Lyricists" talks (December 20, 1970) and quoted in *Who Put the Rainbow?*. The succession of *Wizard* directors is covered thoroughly in *The Making of "The Wizard of Oz,"* pp. 136–65. King Vidor's contribution to *Wizard* is noted in McClelland's *Down The Yellow Brick Road*, p. 117. Harburg on the Munchkins is from the Harmetz book, p. 192, and LeRoy on the Munchkins is from McClelland, p. 104. Garland's and Langley's views of the Munchkins are from Harmetz, p. 188. Langley's opinion of the finished *Wizard* is also from Harmetz, p. 59. The "Hit Parade" appearances of "Over the Rainbow" are from John R. Williams's *This Was Your Hit Parade*, p. 98 ff.

10 · YIP, JOHN, AND TED AGAIN

The history of the effect of World War II on Hollywood is fully documented in Green and Laurie's *Show Biz*. Harburg's comments on "Lydia, the Tattooed Lady" were gleaned from Meyerson and Harburg's *Who Put the Rainbow?*, p. 163, and from Harburg's Ninety-second Street Y talk, December 20, 1970. His belief that Arlen "needed a change" appears in Wilk's *They're Playing Our Song*, p. 226. Wilder on "When the Sun Comes Out" is from his *American Popular Song*, p. 269. Arlen on golf ("The game consumed me") was lifted from *Happy with the Blues*, p. 158; he also mentioned this in radio and print interviews. Harry Warren told me the Johnny Mercer ("How's Ginger?") story in March 1960. Lillian Mercer's anecdote about her New York visit appears in *Happy with the Blues* and was based on a long article I no longer have. The various quotations by Arlen, Mercer, and Margaret Whiting are from Wilk's *They're Playing Our Song*, pp. 140, 157, 158, 160. The revival of cattle rustling during World War II is reported in Richard R. Lingeman's *Don't You Know There's a War On?* (New York: Putnam, 1970), p. 276. John Mueller on *The Sky's the Limit* and Fred Astaire come from his *Astaire Dancing*, (pp. 225–26, 236). Alec Wilder on "One for My Baby" and "Out of This World" comes from his *American Popular Song*, pp. 277, 280. Astaire on the songs in *The Sky's the Limit* is from his letter to me, ca. April 1960; see *Happy with the Blues*, p. 144. The review of *Winged Victory* by Lewis Nichols appeared in the *New York Times* on November 22, 1943. The story of the Arlen fire, with significant omissions, was told to me by Arlen during interviews for *Happy with the Blues*; later, Willie Taranda's part in it became known. This was recently corroborated by Rita Arlen, widow of Jerry, from whom she got the story. The writing of "Ac-cent-tchu-ate the Positive" is described in *Happy with the Blues*; Arlen repeated it in his television interview with Walter Cronkite on *The Songs of Harold Arlen*, February 9, 1964. Sam Coslow on the production of *Out of This World* is from his autobiographical *Cocktails for Two*, pp. 238–41. Lingeman's opinion of *The Miracle of Morgan's Creek* appears on page 185 of *Don't You Know There's a War On?*

11 · WHEN THE WIND BLOWS SOUTH

Hugh Fordin's *The World of Entertainment*, pp. 72–76, is one source of the problems Arthur Freed encountered in the production of *Cabin in the Sky*; other incidents were related to me over several years in conversations with Arlen and Harburg. The latter's story behind the writing of "Happiness Is a Thing Called Joe" was told at Harburg's Ninety-second Street Y night (December 20, 1970); Arlen, some years later, told me his version of the story, involving a poem from a magazine. Hall Johnson's letter to Freed's associate director, Albert Lewis, appears in Fordin, pp. 74–75.

12 · THE CIVIL WAR BALLET

The *Syracuse Herald-American* interview with Arlen appeared in the issue of July 16, 1944. The opposing views on the "seriousness" of the plot of *Oklahoma!* appear in Bordman's *American Musical Theatre*, p. 542, and Green's *Broadway Musicals*, p. 119; I happen to agree with Stanley. The statistics on the civil disorders in 1943 are chronicled in Lingeman's *Don't You Know There's a War On?*, pp. 323–29, as well as other histories and newspapers of the time. Agnes de Mille's story about the conception and conflict over the *Civil War Ballet* is told in her *And Promenade Home*, pp. 192–200; Arlen and Harburg told me their sides of the story in the interviews of 1960. The *Variety* review of *Bloomer Girl* appeared in the issue of September 13, 1944, p. 46. The other reviews are quoted in Suskin's *Opening Night on Broadway*, p. 92. Harburg on "Man for Sale" appears in Meyerson and Harburg's *Who Put the Rainbow?*, p. 210.

13 · THE BLUES

Arlen and Mercer on the writing of "Come Rain or Come Shine" appears in *Happy with the Blues*, pp. 148–49, and in Wilk's *They're Playing Our Song*, p. 141. Ruby Hill's biography is taken from the playbill of *St. Louis Woman*, p. 24. Chapman's review appeared in the *New York Daily News*, April 1, 1946; Rascoe's in the *New York World-Telegram* and Nichols's in the *New York Times*, same date.

14 · WASTELAND: BEVERLY HILLS

The economic situation in Hollywood during the late 1940s is covered in Green and Laurie's *Show Biz*, p. 541. Ann Ronell told me about her attempts to see Anya Arlen during the period of this chapter. Before her death in 1993 we became good friends, and over the phone she told me many stories about Hollywood and the music business she knew so well. Biographical material on Leo Robin appears in his entry in the ASCAP *Biographical Dictionary* and Jack Burton's *The Blue Book of Tin Pan Alley* (Watkins Glen, N.Y.: Century House, 1950), p. 464. Robin expressed his views on writing with Arlen in a letter to me (ca. the spring of 1960) printed, in part, in *Happy with the Blues*. The source of the anecdote about Judy Garland's belated filming of "Get Happy" for *Summer Stock* is Stanley Green's *Hollywood Musicals Year by Year*, p. 161.

15 · TOIL AND TROUBLE

Ira Gershwin's story of the fate of the Zodiac song appears in his *Lyrics on Several Occasions*, p. 208; the complete lyric to "Song of the Zodiac" is reproduced in the Kimball collection of Gershwin's works, pp. 300–301. Harold Arlen's "Ira Song" is transcribed from a home recording disc made by Arlen ca. September 1940. Harry Warren's endorsement of Ralph Blane appears in Thomas's *Harry Warren*, p. 245, and in *Happy with the Blues,* p. 166, based on an interview with Warren on March 29, 1960. Ralph Blane talked about his anxiety over working with Arlen on March 24, 1960. Arlen told me about Berlin's reaction to "Halloween." I interviewed Dorothy Fields some time in the late spring of 1960; she told me the story of adding Jimmy McHugh's name as co-lyricist of "Lovely to Look At" a few years later. Jerry Arlen and Buddy Morris told me about Arlen's drinking, the former ca. May 1968 and the latter on March 10, 1960.

16 · JUDY

The bulk of the *A Star Is Born* material on the production of the film is from Haver, *A Star Is Born,* p. 24. Ira Gershwin's list of the songs suggested by Hart appears in *Happy with the Blues,* p. 174, and Hart's in Haver, *Star,* p. 52. Gershwin's letters to me (January 1953–April 1954) are the source of his travails with *A Star Is Born.* Arlen on the golf course appears in Gershwin's *Lyrics on Several Occasions,* pp. 243–44. Arlen's story of "The Man That Got Away" (without mentioning names) is from Wilk's *They're Playing Our Song,* p. 159. That there is also a Johnny Mercer lyric to the same melody is known among popular music historians. The Judy Garland–Hugh Martin argument appears, as recalled by Lawrence Stewart, in Haver, *Star,* p. 94; the incident was corroborated by Martin in a discussion with Kevin Cole in August 1994. Ira Gershwin's unpublished note on the unused *A Star Is Born* songs appears in *The Complete Lyrics of Ira Gershwin,* ed. Kimball, p. 376. The antics of the television crew on Oscar night 1955 are reprinted in Haver, *Star,* pp. 219–20, based on an interview from *Photoplay* as recalled by Judy Garland for Joe Hyams. Other sources: the souvenir program from *A Star Is Born,* current newspapers, and various Arlen interviews on radio and television.

17 · YEAR OF TRANSFUSIONS

Biographies of Arnold Saint Subber appeared in the 1954 *House of Flowers* souvenir program and his obituary in the *New York Times,* April 19, 1994. His comments on the show were made during an interview in May 1960. William Zinsser's article "Harold Arlen, Secret Music Maker" appeared in *Harper's,* May 1960, pp. 42–47. Thanks to Michael Feinstein, I have a copy of Harold Arlen's recorded letter to Capote about "A Sleepin' Bee." The description of Arlen's birthday party after Capote's readings at the Ninety-second Street Y comes from John Malcolm Brinnin's *Truman Capote: Dear Heart, Old Buddy,* pp. 201–2. The details of Arlen's medical crisis in the spring of 1954 are based on an interview with Dr. Miguel G. Elias, March 29, 1960. The John O'Hara quote comes from his *Collier's* column, August 20, 1954. Terry Driscoll's *House of Flowers* postmortem, "Forgotten Musicals," was published in *TheaterWeek,* January 18–24, 1988, pp. 36–40. Brook's opening remarks to the *House of Flowers* cast I heard from Jacques Aubuchon. Capote on Bailey and Dietrich's part in keeping the cast happy comes from Driscoll; likewise Diahann Carroll's feelings toward Brook. Morrison's criticism of Pearl Bailey appeared in his review of *House of Flowers* in *Variety,* January 12, 1955. Steven Suskin's opening-night *House of Flowers* "Scorecard" appears in his *Opening Night on Broadway,* p. 323. Peter Brook's offer to restage the show and Bailey's "Hogwash" come from Driscoll, "Forgotten Musicals," p. 39. Richard Rodgers on "A Sleepin' Bee" and the score of *House of Flowers* is from an interview, May 16, 1960.

18 · PEREGRINATIONS
Arlen's Gloria Vanderbilt comment appeared in a magazine caption; I have a copy, but the publication is not identified. Arlen told me the Marilyn Monroe dancing quip. Zinsser's Arlen article appeared in the *New York Herald Tribune,* December 19, 1954; Coleman's in the *New York Daily News,* February 27, 1955. The *New Yorker* "Talk of the Town" piece appeared in the January 29, 1955, issue. Robert Breen on sleeping at the opera is quoted in Hollis Alpert's *The Life and Times of Porgy and Bess,* p. 152. The Arlen-Gershwin Moscow trip comes from several sources: Arlen, Lawrence D. Stewart, Horace Sutton, the late Jenifer Heyward, and Alpert, *The Life and Times,* pp. 240–41, 248. Meyer Levin on the motives of Truman Capote appeared initially in the *Newark Star-Ledger* and are reprinted in Alpert. Harburg on the *Nellie Bly* blacklisting incident was broadcast during a WBAI radio interview in 1976 and reprinted in Meyerson and Harburg, *Who Put the Rainbow?,* pp. 290–91. I was present at the Walden Records sessions.

19 · YANKEE DOLLARS
Arlen's "We'd jump around a lot . . ." is from my "Unsung Songsmith of Jamaica," *Theatre Arts,* October 1957, p. 88. His reference to the writing of *Jamaica* as "a devilish job" was made during an interview with Ed Herlihy on NBC's Monitor broadcast, December 13, 1957. The Lena Horne interview occurred at the Waldorf, May 4, 1960. Harburg's letter to Arlen regarding *Jamaica* is printed in Meyerson and Harburg, *Who Put the Rainbow?,* p. 311. The Kilgallen interview appeared in the *Journal-American,* February 18, 1960. I was present at the *Blues Opera Suite* premiere at Carnegie Hall and the Vanderbilt party.

20 · FREE AND EASY BLUES
The quotations from Harold Arlen's letters are from my collection. Arlen's comments, as well of those by Johnny Mercer and Stanley Chase, were made to me: Arlen's on Quincy Jones's orchestration of "I Never Has Seen Snow" on March 31, 1960, and Chase's about Breen's sanity on March 17, 1960. Walter H. Waggoner's article from Amsterdam appeared in the *New York Sunday Times,* probably in mid-December; I have the article but no date. The report from Paris appeared in the January 16, 1960, *New York Times. Variety* published the letter from a *Free and Easy* cast member in the issue of March 30, 1960, as did *Variety's* clarification of what occurred after the Paris premiere and the Sammy Davis announcement. The Chase plan for an autumn production in the States, starring Davis, appeared in Leonard Lyons's *New York Post* column, March 14, 1960.

21 · ODE FOR ANYA
The bulk of the material for this chapter and the remainder of the book is taken from a diary I kept during the writing of my first Arlen biography; the diary was a gift from Anya and Harold Arlen on my birthday in March 1960. Though I had never kept a

diary before, I was reasonably faithful for several years, up to the death of Anya in 1970. About a decade later, when Arlen became ill, and following the death of my wife, I took it up again after I began spending a great deal of time with Harold. It was not a happy time, and as that time went on until the composer's death, it became more necrology than diary and I stopped.

Mike Gross's coverage of the Cole Porter tribute appeared in *Variety,* May 18, 1960. Arlen's impressions were gleaned during the first rehearsal the day of the concert, and Richard Rodgers's in an interview, May 16, 1960. "The clock . . . keeps slugging" is from a letter from Arlen to me, August 8, 1960. The Halliwell quote comparing UPA to Disney appears in his *The Filmgoer's Companion* (New York: Hill & Wang, 1965), p. 291. Murray Schumach's Hollywood interview appeared in the *New York Times,* August 10, 1961; Herb Stein's in the *Racing Form,* July 2, 1961. Jack O'Brian's "Are Movies and TV Asleep at the Switch?" in which Judy Garland's telegram to Arlen on *Gay Purr-ee* was published, as were some of Arlen's views, appeared in the *New York Journal-American,* February 18, 1962. Arlen on the Judy Garland *Gay Purr-ee* soundtrack is from a letter, Harold Arlen to EJ, August 14, 1962. *Variety* on the DuPont "Show of the Week," September 27, 1961; Skolsky's "Hollywood Is My Beat," *New York Post,* September 28, 1961. Arlen on "The air is full . . . with rockets" is taken from a letter, Harold Arlen to EJ, August 14, 1962.

22 · A MAN OF SORROWS
Leonard Lyons ran an item on "The Silent Spring" in his column in the *New York Post,* October 29, 1963. Kleinerman's letter to Arlen on the proposed "profile" on CBS television is dated October 24, 1963; Paul Garner's unfavorable opinion of "The Songs of Harold Arlen" appeared in the *New York Times,* February 10, 1964. "A Composer Shatters His Privacy" by Margaret McManus is dated February 8, 1964. Arlen's file contains a copy, but no source identification. The piece is quoted throughout, as indicated, and is valuable because of its revelations by Arlen—Hollywood, his "closing up," "Philadelphia, where the sun never shines," etc. Emory Lewis's "A Salute to Harold Arlen" appeared in *Cue,* March 20, 1965. Ira Gershwin's letter to Arlen about the ASCAP board membership is dated March 3, 1963.

23 · SLOW CURTAIN
Rita Arlen told me about the "several tablets of different colors." The comment about Anya Arlen—"Now that you are rid of her"—was revealed to me by the man who said it to Harold Arlen. The Dorothy Fields tribute attended by Arlen took place on November 1, 1970. Bobby Short's effect on him was told in an interview by John Corry, *New York Times,* April 1974. Leonard Melfi's views on the American theater appear in *Playwrights, Lyricists, Composers on Theater,* ed. Otis L. Guernsey Jr. (New York: Dodd, Mead, 1974). Harburg's opinion of Laurents's screenplay of *Bloomer Girl* appears in Meyerson and Harburg, *Who Put the Rainbow?,* p. 331. Irving Berlin's "I Shot My Wad" is dated February 28, 1977. Kay Gardella's criticism of the Jack Lemmon television show was published in the *New York Daily News,* February 26, 1973. The *Newsletter* of the National Academy of Popular Music reported Arlen's Mercer Award in the issue of December 1982. Howard Thompson's comments on Julianne Boyd's Arlen

revue were printed in the *New York Times,* "Going Out Guide," May 8, 1978. Sylvie Drake's review of *Get Happy: The Music of Harold Arlen* appeared in the *Los Angeles Times,* November 2, 1983. Excerpts from Burton Lane's eulogy for Harold Arlen, April 25, 1986, are from Lane. The rainbow reports appeared in Rod Alexander's "Metropolitan Diary," the *New York Times,* May 7, 1986.

BIBLIOGRAPHY

Besides the clippings quoted from various sources, I was able to refer to the original playbills that had been collected by the late Bill Sweigert, who saw every Arlen musical from *Bloomer Girl* on. He not only preserved the programs but, most helpful to me, also clipped and pasted in magazine and newspaper reviews and pictures. Published sources of value follow.

Allen, Frederick. *Only Yesterday.* New York: Harper, 1931.

Alpert, Hollis. *The Life and Times of Porgy and Bess.* New York: Knopf, 1990.

Bergman, Andrew. *We're in the Money: Depression America and Its Films.* New York: New York University Press, 1971.

Bickman, David, ed. *The Harold Arlen Songbook.* New York: MPL, 1985.

Bordman, Gerald. *American Musical Theatre.* New York: Oxford University Press, 1978.

Brinnen, John Malcolm. *Truman Capote: Dear Heart, Old Buddy.* New York: Delacorte Press, 1986.

Burton, Jack. *The Blue Book of Hollywood Musicals.* Watkins Glen, N.Y.: Century House, 1953.

Capote, Truman. "House of Flowers." In *Breakfast at Tiffany's.* New York: Random House, 1958.

Capote, Truman, and Harold Arlen, *House of Flowers.* New York: Random House, 1968.

Coffey, Thomas M. *The Long Thirst.* New York: Norton, 1975.

Coslow, Sam. *Cocktails for Two.* New Rochelle, N.Y.: Arlington House, 1977.

de Mille, Agnes. *And Promenade Home.* London: W. H. Allen, 1989.

Durante, Jimmy, and Jack Kofoed. *Nightclubs.* New York: Knopf, 1931.

Engel, Lehman. *Their Words Are Music.* New York: Crown, 1975.

Fricke, John, with Jay Scarfone and William Stillman. *The Wizard of Oz: The Official 50th Anniversary Pictorial History.* New York: Warner Books, 1989.

Gershwin, Ira. *The Complete Lyrics of Ira Gershwin.* Edited by Robert Kimball. New York: Knopf, 1993.

Giles, Carl H. *1927: The Picture Story of a Wonderful Year.* New Rochelle, N.Y.: Arlington House, 1971.

Green, Abel, and Joe Laurie Jr. *Show Biz: From Vaude to Video.* New York: Holt, 1951.

Green, Stanley. *Ring Bells! Sing Songs! Broadway Musicals of the 1930's.* New Rochelle, N.Y.: Arlington House, 1971.

———. *Encyclopedia of the Musical Theatre* New York: Dodd, Mead, 1976.

———. *The World of Musical Comedy.* 4th ed. San Diego: A. S. Barnes, 1980.

———. *Encyclopedia of the Musical Film.* New York: Oxford University Press, 1981.

———. *The Great Clowns of Broadway.* New York: Oxford University Press, 1984.

————. *Broadway Musicals Show by Show*. Milwaukee: Hal Leonard Books, 1985.

————. *Hollywood Musicals Year by Year*. Milwaukee: Hal Leonard Books, 1990.

Harmetz, Aljean. *The Making of "The Wizard of Oz."* New York: Delta Books, 1977.

Harris, Middleton, Morris Levitt, Roger Furman, and Ernest Smith, eds. *The Black Book*. New York: Random House, 1974.

Haskins, Jim. *The Cotton Club*. New York: Random House, 1977.

Haver, Ronald. *A Star Is Born*. New York: Knopf, 1988.

Holbrook, Stewart H. *Dreamers of the American Dream*. Garden City, N.Y.: Doubleday, 1957.

Hughes, Langston, and Milton Meltzer. *Black Magic: A Pictorial History of Black Entertainers in America*. New York: Bonanza Books, 1967.

Jablonski, Edward. *Harold Arlen: Happy with the Blues*. Garden City, N.Y.: Doubleday, 1961; repr. New York: Da Capo, 1986.

Kisseloff, Jeff. *You Must Remember This*. New York: Harcourt Brace Jovanovich, 1989.

Langley, Noel, Florence Ryerson, and Edgar Allen Woolf. *The Wizard of Oz*. Screenplay edited by Michael Patrick Hearn. New York: Delta Books, 1989.

McClelland, Doug. *Down the Yellow Brick Road: The Making of "The Wizard of Oz."* New York: Pyramid Books, 1976.

Marquis, Alice M. *Hopes and Ashes*. New York: Free Press, 1986.

Merman, Ethel, with George Eells. *Merman: An Autobiography*. New York: Simon & Schuster, 1978.

Meyerson, Harold, and Ernie Harburg. *Who Put the Rainbow in "The Wizard of Oz"? Yip Harburg, Lyricist*. Ann Arbor: University of Michigan Press, 1993.

Minnelli, Vincente. *I Remember It Well*. Garden City, N.Y.: Doubleday, 1974.

Mueller, John. *Astaire Dancing*. New York: Knopf, 1985.

Sann, Paul. *The Lawless Decade*. New York: Bonanza Books, 1957.

————. *The Desperate Years*. New York: Bonanza Books, 1962.

Schoener, Allon. *Harlem on My Mind, 1900–1968*. New York: Random House, 1968.

Sennett, Ted. *Warner Brothers Presents*. New Rochelle, N.Y.: Arlington House, 1971.

Suskin, Steven. *Opening Night on Broadway*. New York: Schirmer Books, 1990.

Taylor, William R., ed. *Inventing Times Square*. New York: Russell Sage Foundation, 1991.

Thomas, Tony. *Harry Warren and the Hollywood Musical*. Secaucus, N.J.: Citadel Press, 1975.

Thomas, Tony, and Jim Terry Smith. *The Busby Berkeley Book*. Greenwich, Conn.: New York Graphic Society, 1973.

Walker, Stanley. *The Night Club Era*. New York: Stokes, 1933.

Waters, Ethel, and Charles Samuels. *His Eye Is on the Sparrow*. Garden City, N.Y.: Doubleday, 1951.

Wilder, Alec, with James T. Maher. *American Popular Song*. New York: Oxford University Press, 1972.

INDEX

Parades. *See* Cotton Club Parades

Pardon My English (Gershwin), 65

Parish, James Robert, 228

"Paris Is a Lonely Town" (Arlen-Harburg), 312, 313–14

Patricola, Tom, 20

Pennington, Ann, 20, 21

Perlberg, William, 240

Petty, George, 214

Petty Girl, The, 214–15

Phoenix Cereal Beverage Company, 36, 38–39

Piantadosi publishers, 28, 30

Pickford, Mary, 77

Pigeon Island, 277–80. *See also* Jamaica

Pinza, Ezio, 220, 222, 225–26

Pitkin, Walter B., 84

Players Club, The, 349

Poitier, Sidney, 280

Pons, Lily, 223

Porgy and Bess (Gershwin), 80, 88, 94, 175; revivals of, 198, 265, 269–73

Porter, Cole, 224, 234, 271, 309–10

Powell, Dick, 96, 102–3, 105, 152, 158

Powell, Eleanor, 173

Premice, Josephine, 255, 259, 282

Presley, Elvis, 312

"Pretty to Walk With" (Arlen-Harburg), 286, 287

Previn, André, 327

Previn, Dory Langdon, 96, 323, 325, 327–28

"Primitive Prima Donna" (Arlen-Koehler), 358

Prinz, LeRoy, 34

Prohibition, 3, 7, 8, 9, 33, 37–38, 54–55

"Promise Me Not to Love Me" (Arlen-Harburg), 346–47, 357

"Public Melody Number One" (Arlen-Koehler), 112

"Push de Button" (Arlen-Harburg), 286, 287

"Quartet Erotica" (Arlen-Gershwin-Harburg), 86

Racism, 41–42, 146, 175–76, 177, 187, 199

Radio, 21, 75, 143, 208; "Coca-Cola Hour," 194–95; "Hit Parade," 120, 137, 156, 169, 195; and licensing, 106; "Majestic Hour," 21; and World War II, 140

Rahn, Muriel, 201, 203

Rainbow (Youmans), 23

Rainer, Luise, xvi

Rainger, Ralph, 212

Ratoff, Gregory, 77

Raye, Martha, 172

Recordings, xvii, 52, 99, 159, 204–5, 266–67, 312–13, 358; race records, 18

Red Nichols and His Five Pennies, 47, 66

Reisman, Leo, 52, 90, 91

Remick Music Corporation, 27, 28, 32–33

"Renovation" (Arlen-Harburg), 127

"Reverend Johnson's Dream" (Arlen-Koehler), 145–46

Revues, xvi, 47; all-black, 40; of Arlen's songs, 356–59; creation of, 49; on film, 75

Rhapsody in Blue (Gershwin), 17, 75

Rhyth-Mania, 48, 49, 68

"Rhythmic Moments" (Arlen), 30, 337, 357

"Rialto Ripples" (Gershwin), 6, 357

Richman, Harry, 20, 21

Riddle, Nelson, 311

"Ridin' on the Moon" (Arlen-Mercer), 202

"Right As the Rain" (Arlen-Harburg), 194, 195

Rio Rita, 173–74

"Rising Moon" (Arlen-Ellis), 30

Ritter, Thelma, 229

Rittman, Trude, 188–89

Roadhouses, 14

Robbins, Jack, 135

Roberta (Kern), 65

Roberti, Lyda, 63–65, 67–68

Roberts, Meade, 303

Robertson, Dale, 229

Robin, Leo, 209, 211–14

Rodgers, Dorothy, 355

Rodgers, Richard, 119, 141, 259, 309, 310, 314, 338

Rogers, Buddy, 58

Rogers, Ginger, 76, 106, 224

Ronell, Ann, 71, 160, 210, 223

Rooney, Mickey, 141